Selfless Self

Talks with

Shri Ramakant Maharaj

Shri Ramakant Maharaj

Selfless Self

Talks with

Shri Ramakant Maharaj

Edited by
Ann Shaw

www.ramakantmaharaj.net

admin@ramakantmaharaj.net

www.selfless-self.com

admin@selfless-self.com

Comments

Alan Jacobs
President Ramana Maharshi Foundation UK

"Ann Shaw has done truly remarkable work in editing this great spiritually encyclopaedic work recording the Teachings of the Self Realised Sage and Jnani, Sri Ramakant Maharaj, successor to the esteemed Jnani Nisargadatta Maharaj. In over 400 pages Sri Ramakant explores every aspect of the necessary Spiritual Practices or Sadhanas, which are needed for the ardent aspirant to achieve Self Realisation. In this important book questions are put to the Sage and then lucid answers are given which are precisely appropriate to the question. In this book the earnest aspirant will surely find the question and answer appropriate to his or her need. In reading the whole book he or she will find all that is essential for him or her to form their own synthesis, and proceed on their great journey towards Enlightenment. This is truly a great book and a worthy successor to the much celebrated 'I AM THAT', Talks given by Sri Nisargadatta Maharaj, Sri Ramakant's own Master."

John Wheeler
Author and Teacher of Non-Duality, California

"The content is pure gold."

Ricky James
Manager, Watkins Books, London

"'Selfless Self' will – without doubt – become a 'Direct Way' classic. If you have a copy of 'I Am That' by Nisargadatta Maharaj on your shelf then this more than deserves a place next to it. The author (Shri Ramakant Maharaj), spent 19 years in 'physical proximity' with his Guru and these talks have not been filtered through a translator as they were spoken in English. Written by Selfless Self for Selfless Self. Page after page, this book hits you straight between the eyes."

"The seeker is he who is in search of himself."

Shri Nisargadatta Maharaj

"I am One with the Devotee. There is no other Self except Me in any being. This is Oneness without a second."

Shri Siddharameshwar Maharaj

"To say I is illusion, to say you is illusion, to say God is illusion. Everything is illusion."

Shankaracharya

"When no happiness is required, you have reached the destination."

*"Be a Master of Reality,
and not just a Master of Philosophy and Spirituality.
A Professor may teach by talking about Truth,
whereas a Master lives it."*

*"Be clear! There is no 'I am', there is no 'you are'.
These are just words.
Reality has nothing to do with words."*

Shri Ramakant Maharaj

CONTENTS

PART ONE: *SELF-ENQUIRY*

PART THREE: *SELF-REALIZATION*

PREFACE

We are very fortunate to have Shri Ramakant Maharaj, a rare Self-Realized Master, in our midst. This English-speaking Master is a direct disciple of Shri Nisargadatta Maharaj. The book, *I Am That*, (1973, Ed. Maurice Frydman), containing the teachings of Nisargadatta Maharaj, greatly helped to bring the ancient Advaitin Teachings of Nonduality, to the attention of the rest of the world. It is now widely considered to be one of the greatest spiritual classics of the 20th century.

This book *Selfless Self*, follows in the footsteps of *I Am That*. These are the undiluted words of the Master, delivered verbatim, in English, without the need of a translator or interpreter. What a boon! This reduces the likelihood of possible misinterpretation, of these most precious and rare teachings. The talks have been recorded and transcribed, as far as possible, in Maharaj's original words. The objective of the book is to convey the meanings in a clear and simple fashion. These teachings are ground-breaking, radical and absolute: "In our Lineage, we give 'Direct Knowledge' to your 'Invisible Presence', and not to the body-form. The body-form is not your Identity", says the Master.

This is not just another book on the subject of awakening or realization to feed the intellect. The knowledge in this book is not intellectual knowledge, but 'Spontaneous Knowledge', Direct Knowledge, which goes beyond the vocabulary of *Brahman, maya* etc. "Our Lineage Masters played down the polished words in their teachings to facilitate Direct Knowledge", he reveals. Ramakant Maharaj goes a step further, eschewing these 'sweet' words as far as possible, and focussing on 'Reality' which has no language whatsoever, ie the state 'prior to language'.

Selfless Self is not filled with concepts, offering the spiritual seeker more pointers. It is beyond pointers, beyond knowledge, "beyond words and worlds". The book vibrates with the Master's Presence. He is very much there, guiding the reader back to himself. He is as near, and as present, as if you were sitting beside him.

"It is my duty to share this Knowledge, the same Knowledge that my Master shared with me". With this intention, he authorized the editor to carry out the task of presenting the teachings, in simple down-to-earth language. It is 'user-friendly' for both beginners, and the more advanced, as well as for complete 'newbies' to Advaita, Oneness, Nonduality. The book title, *Selfless Self*, was chosen by the Master, as well as the current format of the book, to encourage and allow easy reflection, contemplation, and absorption of 'Reality'.

The 'Invisible Speaker' in the Master, and the 'Invisible Listener' in you, are one and the same. He addresses the Invisible Listener in you. The Invisible Listener's recorder is always switched on, fully present and receptive. When he speaks, it is from the 'Bottomless bottom of Reality', 'Thoughtless Reality'.

"This book narrates Your story, the 'Story of Selfless Self'", says the Master. "It is a book that conveys your Reality simply and directly, boosted by the strength, power and energy of my Master, Shri Nisargadatta Maharaj. We are dealing with an energy that comes from 'Oneness'. This means that the Reader, the Listener, and the Writer are One. There is no difference, no separation. It is all One. And that is why the book lives. You become One with that energy. That matter, that energy, is incorporated within this book".

He explains further: "It is as if someone wrote your story, your biography, and then you exclaim: 'Ah! It's my biography!' When you are reading this book, you 'Know' that it is speaking about you: 'Ah! This is my Knowledge!' This rare state of Knowledge, understanding and Oneness is built into the very fabric of the book. In fact, it is the fabric of this book which makes it unique. As you read it, you are one with the material. There is recognition".

Shri Ramakant Maharaj's words are not up for debate. He is a 'Knower', a *Jnani,* whose words have the potential to reawaken your Inner Master. To make this happen, a method of hammering and repetition is used to penetrate the layers of illusion, along with Self-enquiry and Meditation.

The body is a material body and all knowledge is material knowledge. No knowledge is Knowledge. "You are unborn. You are not the body, you were not the body, you will not remain the body", states the Master. When this Reality, of what you are not, is fully accepted, this is called 'Spontaneous Conviction'.

"Everything is within you. You are the Source". What follows is your story, the story of *Selfless Self.* Somehow, until now, this all-important Source book, 'You', had been missed, bypassed, or not even noticed at all. In a world populated by 'Selfies' and such like, it is perhaps no surprise that 'Your Story', the story of *Selfless Self* has been completely overlooked!

How did this happen? The Master quotes Nisargadatta Maharaj: "You forgot your Selfless Self. Except for your Selfless Self, there is no God, no Brahman, no Atman, no Paramatman, no Master". All the right 'spiritual' books were read, with their stories about Reality, Masters, God, *Brahman,* but, asks the Master: "You have read the books, but have you read the reader?"

You gained knowledge, but it was dry knowledge from all these body-knowledge concepts, not True Knowledge, not Self-Knowledge, not Your Knowledge. 'Prior to Beingness', You were formless. There was no knowledge, no books. Nisargadatta Maharaj says, "Stay as you were, Prior to Beingness, and you will have no problem!"

"All these books, all this reading, who is it for?" challenges the Master. "And what is your conclusion?" The conclusion is, that while reading all these spiritual books, you forgot to read your own book! You forgot your Source Book, that fundamental Manual, that essential Foundation Text Book, which is You without form, Formless You!

This book, the Final Edition, *Selfless Self,* slipped your attention. It was not to be found in any library or bookshop. You had forgotten about *Selfless Self.* You forgot to add your own, and all-important, one-off autobiography to your list of 'must-read' books. Better late than never! It has, at last been found with the grace of the Master.

This book was written by *Selfless Self,* for *Selfless Self.* The speaker, Ramakant Maharaj, and the Invisible Reader, are One and the same. This is Your story, the Only True Story. The Master opens the book of *Selfless Self* and begins to narrate Your story without beginning, without end.

These pages remind you of your forgotten Identity, your Ultimate Reality. *Selfless Self* is your very own portable Master, Guru, your 'Spiritography', which will guide You Home, slowly, silently, permanently.

EDITOR'S NOTE

Selfless Self: Talks with Shri Ramakant Maharaj is divided into three parts: Self-Enquiry, Self-Knowledge, Self-Realization, this with the understanding that there is no process, and no set order. The book shines with an unprecedented simplicity. This clarity is complimented by a methodical presentation of these high teachings.

Reading and Listening: The talks are arranged systematically as a cohesive whole, to be read as a manual or guide book that takes the reader from the very foundations to the summit and beyond. Best read and absorbed slowly, from beginning to end.

The Master is not addressing you, but the 'Invisible Listener' in you. Listen to the music of these teachings with the internal ear, and absorb them without question. Let the words dissolve you. The Master is expounding the highest knowledge in a clear and direct manner. He is hammering you with Reality, trying to convince you! Be open, accepting and grow in self-conviction!

To get the most out of this book, Self-enquiry is essential. Meditation is encouraged as a tool for concentration. Use any mantra of your choice. This can be, "I am *Brahman, Brahman* I am", "*Aham Brahmasmi*", or whatever works best for you. Sing devotional songs if you feel like it, as this lifts the Spirit, or maybe listen to the *bhajans* on Maharaj's website. Don't feel pressured! Do what suits you!

Teaching Method: Hammering is used as a method to shift ingrained illusion and concepts to convince the reader/listener. This repetition may appear a little tedious at times, but is, in fact, essential to the process of clearing out body-knowledge. A lifetime of impressions are to be erased, therefore perseverance is absolutely crucial.

Not Pointers: The teachings in this book are NOT meant to be read as concepts, or taken to be mere pointers or ideas. There is no question of debate. Master says: "Reality is not up for discussion or debate". Look for the meaning behind the words. This book is replete with Spontaneous Knowledge that directly conveys Reality. The Master speaks from the "Bottomless bottom of Reality". Spontaneous Knowledge has nothing to do with intellectual knowledge. This kind of Knowledge, coming from the Realized Master, is very rare.

Spontaneous Knowledge is inseparable from Reality and the Realized Master. It is Oneness beyond knowledge, and is therefore not to be grasped, or understood with the intellect. Be like a blank page, and try to read this book, as if it is the first book you have ever read. "Everything you have ever read or heard up until now, forget it, and just listen!"

Trust the Master: His words are Truth, again - not up for debate. These words have immense potential to penetrate and awaken your Inner Master. Don't get caught up by the words and take them too literally. Maharaj is trying to convince you. Accept what you hear, convince yourself, and let the Conviction deepen.

If you read these discourses regularly and ponder over them, your Spiritual Power will surely be regenerated. The Master's Presence pulsates in every line of this book which sparkles with Spiritual Truth. Concentrated rays of Light from the Master come through his words, to ignite your Masterly Essence. This Knowledge is your Knowledge. It is your rightful inheritance. Help yourself! Take it all!

Nisargadatta Maharaj's Master, Siddharameshwar Maharaj, said: "The Realized Ones truly speak from the fountain of their own experience and there is great conviction in their speech. Their speech has the capacity to discard the ignorance of the ego. Every line spoken has the power to eradicate the reader's ignorance about his True Self and bring forth the True Nature of his Being".

At Maharaj's request, this book contains few Sanskrit terms. The aim of these teachings is to eradicate all concepts, all body-knowledge and return to 'Prior to Beingness': without language and words, without knowledge, nothing.

It is a great honour and a very humbling privilege, to present these Direct Teachings, this Spontaneous Knowledge. The sole intention has been to follow the Master's instructions, and be trusting and open to Selfless Self guiding the pen. Sincere apologies for any omissions and errors.

Ann Shaw   *10 March 2015*
Editor   London

~~~~~~~

"I am not making you a disciple, I am making you a Master."

WHO IS SHRI RAMAKANT MARARAJ?

Shri Ramakant Maharaj (b. 08 July 1941), is a direct disciple of the late Shri Nisargadatta Maharaj (d. 08 September 1981), and spent 19 years with him. He is an Indian spiritual teacher of Advaita, Nonduality, and a Guru, belonging to the Inchegiri branch of the Navnath Sampradaya. He offers initiation to this Sampradaya.

Ramakant Sawant was brought up in rural Phondaghat, Gadgesakhal Wadi. In 1965, he attended the prestigious establishment of Elphinstone College, Bombay, at the behest of Nisargadatta Maharaj. Following this, he graduated from Bombay University in 1972, (M.A in History and Politics). In 1976, he obtained his LLB qualification, from Siddhartha Law College, Bombay. He worked in banking, in the Legal Department, from 1970 until his retirement as Manager in 2000.

He is married to Anvita Sawant, also a long-standing disciple of Shri Nisargadatta Maharaj. They have two sons.

In 1962, Ramakant Maharaj was introduced by relatives to his future Guru, Shri Nisargadatta Maharaj. After spending a few months with the Master, he took the *Naam Mantra*, the Guru Mantra on 2nd October, 1962. From then on he attended faithfully, and listened to Nisargadatta Maharaj's discourses regularly. He was present at his Master's *Mahasamadhi* on 8th September 1981.

During the last decade or so, at Ranjit Ashram in Nashik Road, (Nashik, Maharashtra), Shri Ramakant Maharaj has been introducing students, disciples and devotees from around the world to these teachings and, on occasion, initiating them into the Inchegiri Navnath Sampradaya Lineage.

About his life, Maharaj says, "I know my past and where I have come from. I am a miracle. All thanks to my Master, Shri Nisaragadatta Maharaj".

1977 with his Master Shri Nisargadatta Maharaj

2015

INTRODUCTION

Shri Ramakant Maharaj is like a physician. A new person presents himself. This seeker's case is no different to any that have come before him in search of a cure. The diagnosis is one of 'Mistaken Identity'. The patient's condition is a universal one. He is suffering from 'Chronic Illusion'. He does not know that he is unborn.

As the embodiment of Ultimate Truth, the Master, is also a debunker who knows what must be done. Wasting no time, he gets to work. With the skill and precision of a top surgeon, the Master commences the operation. Every day, he operates on these 'patients'. A few of them are minor ops, but what is required for most, is intensive treatment, a major overhaul. He makes a couple of incisions, cutting into the 'body' placed before him, then, without further hesitation, he penetrates the numerous layers of body-knowledge, until reaching the heart of the matter, the source of the disease.

Deep-rooted values and attachments are thrown out, whether they be intellectual, egoistic, personal, social, familial, ethical, experiential, spiritual, etc. Theoretical knowledge, and knowledge from books, including the different philosophies and religions of the world, etc, are all chucked into the dumpster, and made ready for the dissolution process.

Orthodox rituals and expressed codes of conduct, along with widely-held conformist/non-conformist, alternative, and unconventional belief systems are blown sky high. Spirituality in all its myriad forms is brought under the spotlight.

The Master's Knowledge is Living Knowledge, Spontaneous Knowledge, pragmatic Knowledge. He challenges the validity of all the ideas, preconceptions, and everything that has been learned from childhood till today.

In its totality, all that is 'known', is 'body-knowledge', and 'body-related knowledge'. 'Prior to beingnesss', there was no 'body' and no 'body-knowledge', therefore everything to date, all the knowledge that has been amassed, is second-hand knowledge sourced from outside, useless illusion.

"Your foundations were built on illusion, not Reality". This is the diagnosis given by the physician, to the latest patient. "Prior to beingness, you had no need of language, no need of knowledge and no need of spirituality." The only treatment available for this condition, therefore, is the dissolution of all illusion, all body-knowledge including concepts, memories, experiences, etc. "Forget everything!"

"And what about spirituality?" enquires the newbie. He answers: "The purpose of spirituality is to know yourself in a real sense, to erase illusion, and dissolve all body-knowledge. At present, you know yourself only in the body-form. This is not your Identity. Your Spontaneous Presence is Silent, Invisible, Anonymous, Unidentified Identity."

The physician knocks the bottom out of the falseness and hollowness of everything that apparently underpins the individual's reality, and indeed underpins the very fabric of society. All that is perceivable and conceivable, those things that are usually accepted and considered as the accepted norms, are brought under scrutiny and dissected. He thus explodes the myth of body-identity, sense of self, and perception of the world. In fact, he systematically challenges and quashes the constructs of reality and self-image to their very core.

One by one, he shoots down the illusory concepts that have become indicative of 'reality' so-called.

He bursts these hot air balloons, the *raisons d'être*, that carry people adrift throughout this long dream of life. He cuts through the many layers of illusion with masterly accuracy, and finally reveals the patient's 'Reality', 'Ultimate Truth', 'Ultimate Reality'.

The Master shakes the so-called individual's fragile foundations, his self-perception and self-identifications, and demolishes his once comfortable house. In time, the foundations that were built on illusion begin to crumble, preparing the way for Reality to be established on firm and very solid foundations.

What is the physician's assessment and advice? "This body is a material body", he states. "Everything this material body knows is material knowledge and therefore illusion". He advises the patient, "Erase everything from childhood till today. Be like a blank screen and then you will find real Knowledge from within". Real Knowledge is Self-Knowledge. It is what remains, "after waking up from the dream".

"Firstly, you must co-operate. Discover for yourself that you are 'Ultimate Reality'. Secondly, this Knowledge must be pragmatic. To eradicate your disease from your system, I am prescribing a highly potent spiritual tablet, namely, the *Naam Mantra*. Take and use it in your daily life".

If these instructions are followed and accepted seriously, then the outcome of the treatment will be very favourable indeed. Excellent, in fact!

What is the prognosis? The physician presents a very rosy picture. The patient will be cured. He determines that there will be an abundance of happiness, without any material cause, and a peaceful end for the body, without any feeling of attachment, loss or fear.

When it's time for the dream to end, knowledge will be engraved: There was never a beginning, and there is no end because you are unborn. Next patient, please!

As more people are inexorably drawn to these eternal teachings, the surgery is going to busy-up. During the 1970's, Shri Nisargadatta Maharaj visited a disciple, Babusav Jagtap, at his home in Nashik. There, he made an auspicious announcement:

"Treat this day, 25ᵗʰ January, as a Festival Day. In the future, some great and wonderful things are going to happen in this corner of Nashik. Build an ashram here! One day, it will become a very busy ashram with visitors from across the globe".

The present ashram in Nashik Road was built in 2002. An annual Programme is held on 25th January, following the wishes of Nisargadatta Maharaj. The area is now called 'Jagtap Mala', in honour of this disciple, and his Master.

~~~~~~~

DIRECT LINEAGE
To Ramakant Maharaj.
Origins in DATTATREYA

NINE MASTERS

The origin of the Navanath Sampradaya Lineage goes back over a thousand years, to Dattatreya. One branch of the Navnath Lineage, (Nine Masters), eventually became the Inchegiri Navnath Sampradaya, founded by Shri Bhausaheb Maharaj. This is the direct line that leads to Shri Ramakant Maharaj.

This Lineage is relatively unknown as the Masters were all very humble. They did not give themselves importance, but were dedicated to spreading the Knowledge, and teaching. Shri Bhausaheb Maharaj, Shri Siddharameshwar Maharaj and Shri Nisargadatta Maharaj were all ordinary people.

Oneness of knowledge and devotion, (*jnana* and *bhakti*), is key in the Lineage teachings. Devotion is the Mother of Knowledge. Only by intense devotion to the Guru, and worshipping Him with full faith, will the knowledge of Self-Realization be revealed. In the end, there is total unity between knowledge and devotion.

The Lineage is a Guru-centred one where the Master makes Masters out of disciples. The Guru initiates the disciple with the Guru Mantra *(Naam Mantra)*, the Master Key. The Mantra, the Guru and the Initiation are inseparable. Faith in, and complete acceptance of the Guru, and Guru Mantra are essential. The Masters of this Lineage have all recited the same Mantra. By taking the Sacred *Naam*, one is receiving the help and power from the Masters of this Lineage. Ultimately, one becomes One with the Master, *Sadguru*. Ramakant Maharaj says, "Reciting the Guru Mantra leads to true Self-Knowledge, and is the only truly effective way to return to the Original State".

Siddharameshwar Maharaj, himself, gave all credit to Bhausaheb Maharaj. Nisargadatta Maharaj did the same with Siddharameshwar Maharaj. Similarly, Ramakant Maharaj gives all credit to his Master, Nisargadatta Maharaj. There is a very strong connection right through the whole Lineage: "I am just a skeleton, a puppet of my Master", says Ramakant Maharaj.

"In our Lineage, we give 'Direct Knowledge' to your 'Invisible Presence', not to the body-form", says the Master. "This Knowledge is Spontaneous Knowledge, it is not bookish knowledge, it is Spontaneous Knowledge. The words are different, the style of speaking may be different, but the principle is the same: There is nothing except Selfless Self". The Knowledge is Rare Knowledge, as the Masters do not simply talk about Reality, but will show the Reality in oneself, in the disciple. This Direct Knowledge coming as it does, from this long line of sparkling Masters, is further empowered by the sacred *Naam Mantra*.

The teachings are solid and strong, with the whole Lineage behind them. They are pure and extremely powerful. The Masters share all the secrets. Nothing is kept hidden. It is Open Truth that has always been shared freely, without any expectations. There is to be no commercial abuse of the Knowledge that is one's inherent property - Truth. Bhausaheb Maharaj said, "In our Lineage, you are not to take any monies from devotees. Any association with money will spoil the *Naam Mantra*. The *Sampradaya* does not demand anything"

Bhausaheb Maharaj (1843-1914), was initiated by Shri Raghunathpriya Maharaj. His Sadguru was Shri Gurulingajangam Maharaj whom he loved deeply. He was known as the saint of Umadi, and was a householder. Bhausaheb Maharaj had many disciples, including Shri Siddharameshwar Maharaj, Shri Gurudev Ranade, and Shri Amburao Maharaj, to mention but a few.

Gurulingajangam Maharaj

Bhausaheb Maharaj

Nisargadatta Maharaj

Siddharameshwar Maharaj

His way is known as the 'Ant's Way', using meditation, dispassion and renunciation. His main emphasis was through the medium of meditation, rather than knowledge. This was because many of the disciples, came from rural communities and were illiterate. Bhausaheb Maharaj endured great hardships, as he strove to find Reality. He stood in the forest for eighteen years without rest, meditating for twelve hours at a time. Stressing the importance of remembering the Divine Name, he would say, "Take it to your bones. Always do fierce repetition of the Divine Name in the mind with meditation".

Siddharameshwar Maharaj (1888-1936), was born in Pathri, Sholapur. When Bhausaheb Maharaj saw Siddharameshwar Maharaj for the first time, he announced, "This man is greatly blessed", and gave him Initiation on that very same day.

He was in the company of his Master for seven years. After his passing, he was so determined to attain Self-Realization, he was prepared to sacrifice his life for it. He started intense meditation, coupled with penance. It is said that he reached such extraordinary heights while meditating, that he emitted a beautiful nectar-like fragrance, which perfumed the air all around him.

Siddharameshwar Maharaj, like many other Masters of this lineage, worked, and had a family. Being a householder was not to be seen as an obstacle, but instead, as an opportunity for selflessness and detachment.

Through his practice, it was becoming clear to him, that meditation was only the beginning stage in the process of reaching Final Reality. And so, he advanced the teachings, moving from the 'Ant's Way', to the 'Bird's Way'. Reality can be reached through discrimination and dispassion: "'Illusory' means that one does not have to throw it away. One just has to realize its deceptive form, and then bring it into action in every day life. Otherwise, even if the knowledge of the Self is understood intellectually, it will never be totally imprinted on one's heart and mind. It would not become active". His spirituality, like his Master's before him, was a pragmatic spirituality.

Two years later, his beloved Master, Bhausaheb Maharaj, blessed him with a vision and communicated: "Now you have reached the Final Reality. There is nothing left for you to do".

He started teaching, using simple language to communicate knowledge and devotion. It is said that he initiated many people from all walks of life. The figure is not known exactly, but it is believed that dozens were realized through this extraordinary Master! These include Ganapatrao Maharaj, Bainath Maharaj, Nisargadatta Maharaj, Ranjit Maharaj, Muppin Kaadsiddheshwar Maharaj, Balkrishna Maharaj.

He kept his teachings practical, using examples from daily life. The method of Self-enquiry, discrimination and dispassion were encouraged.

To prevent knowledge from staying dry and hollow, Siddharameshwar Maharaj stressed the importance of devotion, and honouring one's Master. The book, *Master of Self-Realization,* containing his teachings, is a spiritual classic.

Nisargadatta Maharaj (1897-1981), was devoted to his Master, Shri Siddharameshwar Maharaj. He was very fortunate to have met him, only about three years before his Master's passing, at aged forty-eight.

Remarkably, a few years later, he, himself, attained Self-Realization. Maharaj advanced the teachings yet again, with his sometimes snappy, yet always piercing, Direct Knowledge. His remarkable teachings awakened many seekers. The famous book, *I Am That,* published in 1973, with the clarion call of, "The seeker is he who is in search of himself", brought a flurry of Western visitors.

Speaking on the *Naam Mantra*, Nisargadatta Maharaj said: "The Mantra is very powerful and effective. My Guru gave me this Mantra and the result is all these visitors from all over the world. That shows you its power".

Ramakant Maharaj (born 1941), was initiated in 1962 by his Master, Nisargadatta Maharaj, and has evolved the teachings of the Lineage once more. His approach is ground-breaking, radical and absolute. He does not entertain concepts, quickly cutting through everything, including the 'I Am' concept. He offers a short-cut to Self-Realization, presenting the Highest Teachings, in down-to-earth language.

These Lineage Masters are passing on the highest knowledge, selflessly and openly. Dependency on the Master, and the Master's form, is strongly discouraged. Their sincere and noble wish is to transform the disciple into a Master. Therein lies the uniqueness of the Inchegiri Navnath Sampradaya.

~~~~~~~

"The Guru is not a person.
He is the Impersonal Unmanifest Absolute
in manifest form."

Shri Ramakant Maharaj

"It is by the Grace of my Master
Shri Nisargadatta Maharaj,
that I am sharing this Knowledge with you,
the same knowledge that He shared with me."
Shri Ramakant Maharaj

PART ONE: *SELF-ENQUIRY*

1. *You Are Already Realized*

Ramakant Maharaj: My Master, Nisargadatta Maharaj, said: "I am not making you disciples, I am making you Masters". That Masterly essence is already within you. Everything is within you.

YOU ARE ALREADY REALIZED,
YOU JUST DO NOT KNOW IT.

You are not the body, you were not the body, you are not going to remain the body.

THE BODY IS NOT YOUR IDENTITY.
THIS IS A LONG DREAM.
REALIZATION MEANS, 'AFTER THE DREAM'.

Listen and Contemplate! Know what you are not! I am pointing to your original place, to how you were prior to beingness. I am talking about 'prior to', before the Spirit clicked with the body, before your Spontaneous Presence was covered by layers of illusion.

THE WAY YOU WERE PRIOR TO BEINGNESS
IS REALIZATION.

There is no difference between you and me, except that I know I'm not the body, whereas you do not. You have forgotten your Identity.

THE INVISIBLE SPEAKER IN ME,
AND THE INVISIBLE LISTENER IN YOU,
ARE ONE AND THE SAME.

You are covered with the ash of illusory concepts. The Master removes the ash. He reawakens and regenerates your Inner Master.

Here, we are sharing Direct Knowledge. I am addressing the Invisible Questioner. Prior to beingness, you had no questions. You did not even know the word 'knowledge'.

YOU ARE UNBORN! NOTHING HAS HAPPENED,
NOTHING IS HAPPENING,
NOTHING IS GOING TO HAPPEN.
ALL YOUR QUESTIONS ARE BODY-BASED QUESTIONS.

There is no birth or death for you. Your Presence was there prior to beingness. It will be there after beingness dissolves. It is here now, as the holder of the body.

Knowledge is not intellectual knowledge, experiential knowledge, book knowledge, literal knowledge, dry knowledge or second-hand knowledge. Everything you know, all the knowledge that you have gathered from childhood till today, is body-based knowledge which has come out of impressions, illusory concepts, conditioning and pressures. It has kept you trapped in the circle of body-knowledge. Come out of the circle of body-knowledge and know yourself in a real sense!

EVERYTHING HAS TO BE ERASED, INCLUDING ALL THE MEMORIES AND EXPERIENCES, FROM CHILDHOOD TILL TODAY.

You need a Realized Master to take you out of illusion. The Master knows all the details first-hand, therefore, he can guide you. To erase illusion and regenerate your power, you will need to undergo a process of Self-Enquiry, Meditation, Knowledge and Bhajan.

This is your time. You have a golden opportunity to know Reality.

BUT UNLESS ALL BODY-KNOWLEDGE DISSOLVES, REALITY WILL NOT EMERGE.

You are to forget about everything you have ever read, and ever learned. Be like a blank screen, and then listen, and absorb. It is open fact that the body is not your Identity at all. Prior to beingness, there was nothing. There is nothing apart from you, or separate from you, or outside of you. Everything is within you. There is nothing except for your Selfless Self. My *Sadguru*, Nisargadatta Maharaj, summarized Reality in one sentence:

EXCEPT FOR YOUR SELFLESS SELF, THERE IS NO GOD, NO *BRAHMAN*, NO *ATMAN*, NO *PARAMATMAN*, NO MASTER.

2.   What is the Purpose of Spirituality?

Maharaj: The purpose of spirituality is to know oneself in a real sense, erase illusion and dissolve all body-knowledge. Listen again:

THE PURPOSE OF SPIRITUALITY IS TO KNOW ONESELF IN A REAL SENSE, ERASE ILLUSION, AND DISSOLVE ALL BODY-KNOWLEDGE.

We must know what the purpose of human life is, and what exactly, it is that we want. We must know! Human beings are endowed with intellect so we can find out. You are interested in spirituality, you are searching, seeking, so you come here looking. What are you looking for? What do you want?

"I want happiness", is often the reply. Everybody wants happiness. We need peace, a fearless life, a tension-free life.

YOU WILL NOT FIND WHAT YOU ARE LOOKING FOR FROM EXTERNAL SOURCES.

Here, you will listen to, and rediscover your own Knowledge, your own Spontaneous Knowledge. Your Invisible Spontaneous Presence is the Source of your Happiness. Everything is within you, but you are unaware of that. Your Presence is an Open Secret.

YOUR PRESENCE DOES NOT NEED ANYTHING, THEREFORE, WHO WANTS PEACE? WHO WANTS HAPPINESS?

YOUR SPONTANEOUS PRESENCE IS UNKNOWN TO ITSELF.
YOUR SPONTANEOUS PRESENCE IS SILENT, ANONYMOUS,
INVISIBLE, UNIDENTIFIED IDENTITY.

After years of spirituality, have you reached a conclusion? Book reading alone is not enough. It is dry knowledge, material knowledge.

FOR WHOM ARE YOU READING ALL THESE BOOKS?
YOU ARE FORMLESS,
YOU ARE ULTIMATE TRUTH.

You are not the body, you were not the body, you are not going to remain the body. This is to be your Conviction. The only way of establishing this Conviction, is through meditation and Self-enquiry. Forget about spirituality for a moment. The body is not your Identity because it undergoes change. The body has a time limit. Open fact! One day, it will be buried or burned.

THE UNKNOWN CAME INTO EXISTENCE
AND BECAME KNOWN THROUGH THE BODY.
THE UNKNOWN CAME TO BE KNOWN.
THE KNOWN WILL BE ABSORBED IN THE UNKNOWN.
SIMPLE TEACHINGS!

When the Spontaneous Presence came into existence in body-form, pain started: physical pain and mental pain. Spirituality gives you the courage to face pain. Attachment and loss are causes of pain. Psychological problems, emotional problems, all of these bodily disturbances will dissolve with the help of meditation.

Nisargadatta Maharaj says: "Though you may have good knowledge, good spiritual knowledge, the only way this knowledge can be absorbed, is with the help of meditation".

Prior to beingness, there was no body, no problems and no needs. No language, no words, no concepts. You had no need of food, no need of knowledge, no need of spirituality. There was no Master, no disciple and no need of Realization. You had no name, no wife, no husband, no mother, no father, no brother, no sister, no friend. All relations are body-related. The world is the Spontaneous Projection of your Spontaneous Presence.

THIS IS DIRECT KNOWLEDGE.
IT IS NOT AN INTELLECTUAL APPROACH,
NOT A LOGICAL APPROACH,
NOT AN EGOISTIC APPROACH,
AS ALL THESE THINGS CAME AFTER YOUR PRESENCE.

You are here to know yourself in a real sense, to know Reality. For this to happen spontaneously, you have to erase everything that you are not, with the help of Self-enquiry, meditation, and Knowledge from the Master.

YOU WERE NEVER IN BONDAGE.
YOU ARE FREE AS A BIRD.
YOU HAVE JUST FORGOTTEN YOUR IDENTITY.
THE MASTER IS HERE TO REMIND YOU.

You are Ultimate Truth, Ultimate Reality, Final Truth. You are Almighty God!
**YOU ARE EVERYTHING,
AND EVERYTHING IS WITHIN YOU.**

3. *Selfless Self*

Q: What do you mean by Selfless Self?

Maharaj: 'Self', is related to body-knowledge: This means everything that has come along with the body. When all this body-knowledge is dissolved, we call that which remains, 'Selfless Self': Self without any content, Self without Illusion.

Selfless Self is one's Spontaneous, Invisible, Anonymous Presence which is beyond identification. All these words indicating this Unknown Identity, are supposed to be dissolved totally, once the address has been reached. When their work is done, throw them away. Remember! Selfless Self is beyond words.

Self is related to body-knowledge and all body-related illusion: "I am somebody, I am somebody else, I am an individual". There is no 'somebody'. This is body-knowledge. Self refers to the identification with the body: 'myself', 'himself', 'herself'. Selfless Self refers to 'nothing'. It means that there is nothing there: no witness, no experiencer. Nothing!

Q: Yes! And you also say that our Presence is an 'Open Secret'. What do you mean by that?

Maharaj: Yes, your Presence is an Open Secret. Your Spontaneous Presence is covered with the body. You may be unaware of it, but your Presence is there. You are not giving yourself attention, and neglecting yourself. You are looking outside of yourself all the time, instead of looking within. Everything is inside you; nothing is outside.

Q: So it's an open secret to Selfless Self?

Maharaj: Yes, to Selfless Self, not to self. Everything comes out of nothing, and everything dissolves back into nothing. And in the nothing, there appears to be something. When you don't know any better, when you are not aware of your Presence prior to beingness, you accept this nothing as something.
**PRIOR TO BEINGNESS YOU WERE UNAWARE OF EVERYTHING AND ANYTHING.
YOU DID NOT KNOW ANYTHING,
NOT EVEN THE WORD 'KNOWLEDGE'.**
After leaving the body, you will not know what is going on in the world. After leaving the body, you will remain unknown. Therefore, everything comes out of nothing, and everything dissolves back into nothing.
**EVERYTHING COMES OUT OF NOTHING,
AND DISSOLVES BACK INTO NOTHING.**
Now, in between, we are considering ourselves as 'something'. We believe ourselves to be something. However, this 'something' is only related to body-based knowledge. As a matter of fact, this body is not going to stay constant; therefore although it appears as something, it is, in fact, nothing. Prior to the body, there was no name, no shape, no form, no experience, no experiencer, no witness, no witnesser.

This open fact will become clearer through meditation. This world has fooled you into accepting that you are a man or a woman, that you're born and are going to die.

THE BODY HAS THE APPEARANCE OF SOMETHING,
BUT IT IS NOTHING.
IT IS ILLUSION.

Listen carefully! Prior to beingness, you were unknown to you. After leaving the body, you will be unknown to yourself. At present, you know yourself in the body-form. This body-form is not going to endure. This body is not your permanent Identity, and is not going to last. This something, whatever this something is, that you consider yourself to be, must have come out of nothing. Therefore, that which you consider to be something, is, in fact, illusion.

REALITY IS PRIOR TO BEINGNESS.
REALITY IS AFTER BEINGNESS.
THIS SPAN OF LIFE IN THE BODY-FORM IS ILLUSION.
IT CAN BE SEEN AS AN INTERLUDE,
AN INTERRUPTION,
A DISTURBANCE OF REALITY.

My Master, Nisargadatta Maharaj, states: "You are Reality". Apart from you, there is nothing else. Reality does not exist elsewhere. He summarized these teachings in one sentence: "There is no God, no *Brahman*, no *Atman*, no *Paramatman*, no Master, except Selfless Self", ie, there is nothing except the FORMLESS YOU. There is nothing except your Selfless Self. Apart from Selfless Self, there is nothing.

THERE IS NOTHING,
EXCEPT FOR SELFLESS SELF.

4. *Three Stages*

Q: You mentioned that there are three stages: First Self-Enquiry, second, Self-Knowledge and third, Self-Realization.

Maharaj: There are three stages, and at the same time, there are not. In fact, there are no stages. These are just the words we are using for guidance at the beginning. For teaching purposes, we can say that there are three stages. They are not clear-cut or linear, as in one, two, but are useful as a loose framework.

Self-enquiry leads to Self-Knowledge, and then, that Self-Knowledge leads to further Self-enquiry, etc. So it is more like a process of moving forward and then retracing one's steps, a kind of to-ing and fro-ing. But, yes, you can say, roughly speaking, that there are three set stages.

Put simply, when the Spirit clicked with the body, and the human being appeared, he had great fear. Out of that fear and confusion, he did not know who he was. This led to the following dilemma: "Who am I? I am in a body-form! But if the body is not my Identity then, who am I?" This is the root of Self-enquiry and man's eternal quest. He is trying to find out "Who am I?" and "Why do I have so many needs?"

The question arises because there were no needs prior to body-knowledge. At the initial stage, he is trying to find out "Who am I? What is the meaning of 'I'?" This is basic Self-enquiry.

As he searches for answers, he begins to gather knowledge from different sources: Books, friends, courses, retreats, workshops, teachers, maybe Masters. Through this knowledge, he comes to the realization, he comes to know, "I am nothing". He learns that in spiritual language, this 'nothing' is called *Brahman, Atman, Paramatman* or God. This knowledge that the seeker has found is literal knowledge.

The body is a material body and the knowledge that the body has been gathering is also material knowledge. This knowledge has been found from man-made sources that had no existence prior to beingness. It is therefore body-knowledge. Book-knowledge or second-hand knowledge is not Knowledge. Knowledge is Spontaneous Self-Knowledge, and that means knowing oneself in a real sense.

When the Knowledge you already have is absorbed, that you are *Brahman,* and not the body, then this Knowledge turns into Conviction. You may have reached the conclusion a long time ago, that the body was not your Identity, and had accepted this fact intellectually. But you need to go deeper. "Know Thyself!" Here, I will share the Knowledge that my Master has shared with me, and show you your Reality. You will be rid of fear, and get to know yourself in a real sense.

**WHEN KNOWLEDGE TURNS INTO CONVICTION,
IT BECOMES SELF-KNOWLEDGE.
SELF-KNOWLEDGE MEANS THAT YOU ARE
ABSORBING THE KNOWLEDGE THAT,
"I AM NOT THE BODY".**

You found out from spiritual books and other secondary sources that, "You are not the body".

**WHEN THIS KNOWLEDGE IS ABSORBED,
THAT IS THE STATUS OF SELF-REALIZATION.**

To recap, Self-enquiry leads to Self-Knowledge. With the help of the intellect and some words, you gained the knowledge that "I am not the body,
and I have been called *Brahman, Atman, Paramatman*, God, etc." But this is just literal knowledge. You will reach the stage of realization when this literal knowledge is absorbed. At that stage, there will be nothing remaining: no experience, no experiencer, no witness, no witnesser, nothing.

**THIS MEANS THAT,
AT THE STAGE OF SELF-REALIZATION,
YOU WILL BE COMPLETELY UNCONCERNED
WITH THE WORLD.
HOW YOU WERE PRIOR TO BEINGNESS
IS THE STAGE OF SELF-REALIZATION.**

Q: So the process is not a linear one because, as you say, Self-Knowledge then takes you back to further Self-enquiry, and vice versa. So we are constantly going from Self-enquiry to Self-Knowledge in this process, that in some ways never ends. There is always more and more knowledge being revealed, more to uncover.

Maharaj: As I said, Knowledge means just to know oneself in a real sense. We are knowing ourselves in body-form. This is not our Identity. To assist with the process, the Master prescribes the 'Medicine of Meditation' to overcome all physical, spiritual, mental and egoistic problems. After a period of strong and deep concentration, Spontaneous Conviction will arise, and Reality will appear within you.

**THERE WILL BE A HUGE SURPRISE!
A MIRACULOUS EXPERIENCE,**

A DRAMATIC AND MAGICAL EXPERIENCE!

When this happens, you will feel, "I am not concerned with the body at all. The body is not my Identity". And though you are living in the body, you will stay unconcerned, uninterested, uninvolved.

MEDITATION MAKES FOR A PERFECT FOUNDATION.

Everything is within you. It is all there, but buried, covered with ash, covered with layers of illusion, concepts. Burst that balloon of concepts. It will happen automatically and explode spontaneously.

5. *You Are Not the Body, You are the Holder of the Body*

Q: You said that we are knowing ourselves in the body-form and that we need to know our real Identity. So what is our Identity, our Existence?

Maharaj: Your Existence is Spontaneous Existence, Spontaneous Presence. Your Spontaneous Presence is Silent, Invisible, Anonymous, Unidentified Identity. The world is projected out of your Spontaneous Presence.

YOUR SPONTANEOUS PRESENCE IS SILENT, INVISIBLE,
ANONYMOUS, UNIDENTIFIED IDENTITY.
THE WORLD IS PROJECTED OUT OF
YOUR SPONTANEOUS PRESENCE.

You are totally unborn, but you are thinking, "I am born and I am going to die". These are the concepts, the illusionary thoughts.

YOU ARE UNBORN!
YOU ARE ULTIMATE TRUTH!

I am inviting the attention of the Silent, Invisible Listener in you.

I AM INVITING THE ATTENTION OF THE SILENT,
INVISIBLE LISTENER IN YOU,
THAT IS ULTIMATE TRUTH.

It is Ultimate Truth, it is unborn. It does not know death and birth. Prior to beingness, you did not know about death and birth. You did not know anything about 'God'. It was only when the Spirit clicked with the body, that beingness came along with all the concepts and illusions: Your father, your mother, brother and sister, to name a few, are all body relations that came out of this body feeling.

You were told, "God exists! Almighty God is here, or there. He is to be found in this religion, or that one, in this church or that temple". When there was no body feeling, there was no beingness. Prior to beingness, there was nothing. No other, no relations. Nothing.

YOU ARE NOT THE BODY, YOU WERE NOT THE BODY,
YOU WILL NOT REMAIN THE BODY.
OPEN FACT.

Here is a simple example: Your parents told you, "This body is called 'boy', and that body is called 'girl'." You accepted this information. They gave you a name, say, 'Ravi' or 'Sita', 'Susan', 'Paul', etc, and you accepted this identity without question. You went through the stages of the body, from a young man or woman, to middle-age, to old-age. Along the way, you asked many questions such as: "Am I just this body with a name tagged onto it? And, if not, who am I?"

Now that you have come here, you can go deeper. Stop and look within! Find out what you are! Get rid of illusion, then your Reality will be uncovered! Self-enquire! Use discrimination! Everything is within you.

**MASTER SAYS: "YOU ARE ULTIMATE REALITY,
ULTIMATE TRUTH, ALMIGHTY GOD".
YOU HAVE TREMENDOUS POWER AND STRENGTH,
BUT YOU ARE UNAWARE OF YOUR POWER BECAUSE
YOU HAVE ACCEPTED THIS BODY-FORM.**

The Master says you are Reality, God! You are to accept what the Master says. Spirituality aside, you know the body is not your Identity because it only lasts for x number of years. The Master is showing you your Reality.

Q: So what you are saying, Maharaj, is that we are to listen to the Master and accept his teachings, and stay focussed on Reality. But, in the beginning, is it not necessary to put some effort into dissolving illusion?

Maharaj: Yes, at the beginning, you have to do some work to eliminate the illusions and establish Reality. You see, when you came across with all these concepts, you accepted them blindly. For example, "I am a man, or a woman". I belong to this religion, or that religion". We are swimming in a world of concepts: sin and virtue, salvation and damnation.

There are endless concepts of hell, heaven, *moksha*, *prarabdha*, birth, death. All these are to be found in the scriptures, books, from Gurus, teachers, Masters. Illusion everywhere! There are so many concepts that make you feel you are in bondage, when, in fact, you're not. You are not in bondage, you are free as a bird.

**ALL THESE CONCEPTS CAME WITH THE BODY.
PRIOR TO BEINGNESS, THERE WERE NO CONCEPTS.
THERE WAS NO 'KNOWING'.
WE DID NOT KNOW ABOUT HAPPINESS OR PEACE.
AFTER THE INVISIBLE PRESENCE [SPIRIT]
TOUCHED WITH THE BODY, ALL CONCEPTS STARTED.
ALL REQUIREMENTS STARTED.**

Everyone is afraid of death. We will do anything to stay alive. But, instead of holding onto this fear, why not ask yourself the question: "What is death?" When you go to sleep, are you afraid to fall asleep? You say, "Let me sleep, don't disturb me." What difference is death? It is the same! Self-enquire! Every day, you may hear of, read about, or even have been with someone who has died. The death of the body is a certainty, unavoidable. The dead bodies are then buried or burned.

**THE BODY WILL GO, IT IS INEVITABLE.
BUT YOU ARE NOT GOING ANYWHERE.
YOU ARE NOT THE BODY,
YOU ARE THE HOLDER OF THE BODY.**

You are not the body, you are the holder of this body. You are Spirit and totally different from the body. The body is only the external part of flesh, blood and bones. Who is acting through the body? Who is experiencing such thoughts as "I have very bad thoughts. I have some awful dreams"?

WHO IS WITNESSING ALL THESE THINGS?
IT IS THE SILENT, INVISIBLE, ANONYMOUS,
UNIDENTIFIED IDENTITY,
CALLED 'ULTIMATE TRUTH'.

Q: I will ponder on that! Over the years, I have read a number of spiritual books, and I also meditate. When I visit a teacher or attend a *Satsang*, the experience is quite uplifting. I feel happy while I'm there, sitting quietly in the moment, but that feeling doesn't seem to last.

Maharaj: OK, so you have read some books, listened to some Masters, and you've done a little meditation. Take stock! What effect has all this had on you? Have you found complete peace? Are you tension-free? Are you fearless? Do you have happiness? If the answer is 'No', then you have to do Self-enquiry, so that you will find real and permanent happiness. I am talking about complete Happiness without any material cause.

If you are continuously reading books that are adding more and more external knowledge, you need to pause, stop for a moment, and ask yourself: "Is this knowledge giving me happiness and fulfilment? Am I fearless?" Be truthful with your Self-enquiry. "Will this knowledge help me when it's my time to leave the body?"

If the knowledge you are gathering now is not bringing you peace and happiness, then that means it is not working for you. Simple! If it is not helping you now, how is it going to help you on your deathbed? Therefore, of what use is all this knowledge?

FIND OUT WHOSE STORY
IS BEING NARRATED IN ALL THESE BOOKS,
IN THE NAME OF SPIRITUALITY!
THAT IS SELF-ENQUIRY.

Q: What do you mean by whose story?

Maharaj: It is your story! I am not relating, I am not telling you a story about *Brahman*, *Atman*, *Paramatman* or God.

I AM NARRATING YOUR STORY.
IT IS THE STORY OF THE LISTENER, THE INVISIBLE LISTENER,
THE ANONYMOUS LISTENER IN YOU.
IT IS THE STORY OF SELFLESS SELF,
YOUR SELFLESS SELF.

My Master, Nisargadatta Maharaj, clearly stated that there is nothing except for Selfless Self. Apart from Selfless Self, there is nothing. Selfless Self alone is Ultimate Truth, Final Truth. In his words: "Except for Selfless Self, there is no God, no *Atman*, no *Brahman*, no *Paramatman*, no Master".

THIS RARE KNOWLEDGE,
ENLIGHTENMENT,
WILL HELP YOU REALIZE WHAT ULTIMATE TRUTH IS,
WHAT FINAL TRUTH IS.
YOU ARE THAT!

6. *You Are a Millionaire, Not a Beggar*

Maharaj: To find out, and KNOW in a real sense, that you are Ultimate Truth, we have to go to the root, and question: "How were you prior to the body-form? What were you like prior to beingness? How were you? How were you prior to beingness?"

Q: I don't know.

Maharaj: That is right. And what will you be like after leaving the body?

Q: I don't know.

Maharaj: "I don't know" is the right answer.

**"I DON'T KNOW", MEANS THAT YOU KNOW
YOUR PRESENCE WAS THERE,
BUT NOT IN ANY SHAPE OR FORM.**

There is no cognizance of it, but you know that the Invisible, Silent Presence was there. As a matter of fact, the root of Knowledge, Ultimate Truth, is within you, but you have been ignoring and neglecting this Truth. You have been underestimating yourself. In other words, though you are a millionaire, you have been behaving just like a beggar.

To use the story of the beggar boy: A boy was begging on the street. One day his uncle approached him, and asked: "Why are you begging? You are not a beggar, you are a millionaire!" Naturally, the boy did not believe him and replied: "You are joking, you're trying to make a fool of me. You're lying! It's not possible!"

Eventually, the uncle persuades him to go with him to the bank, where he shows him an account in his name, stacked with millions! With all the evidence laid out before him, the beggar boy is finally convinced, and accepts his new-found status.

In a similar way, the Master says: "You are *Brahman, Atman*", but you are not believing or accepting the Master's words. You may not verbalise it, but somewhere in the background, a tiny little voice is maybe there, that says: "Me? No! You are joking".

How can you be convinced? In order to have Conviction, you need the process of meditation. The meditation will have the effect of dissolving all the illusory layers. Then, you will come across your Perfection: "Oh! I Am That!" [Master gestures with pleasant surprise.] The Master is perfect. He is showing you Ultimate Truth and because of this, he is deserving of your respect.

So, to have this Conviction, and to know your Perfection, meditation is essential. It is the only way to absorb Knowledge, while at the same time, erasing illusion. This is your time to stop begging, and to get to know your worth.

**YOU ARE A MILLIONAIRE, BUT YOU ARE LIVING
AND EXPRESSING YOURSELF JUST LIKE A BEGGAR,
SAYING: "OH GOD, DO SOMETHING, BLESS ME, HELP ME".**

Asking others for blessings and grace may give you momentary peace, momentary spiritual happiness, just like taking the odd painkiller, but it will not bring you fulfilment and lasting contentment. Now is the time to be strong. Be firm! This is your time, the time to know your own strength and power. Know your strength, and uncover your power.

Master says, "You are no longer handicapped". Your existence is full of Knowledge. You are the Source of Knowledge, but you are unaware. You are unaware that you are Ultimate Truth, Almighty God.

YOU ARE ALMIGHTY. ALMIGHTY GOD, OMNIPRESENT.
YOUR PRESENCE IS EVERYWHERE.
YOU ARE BEYOND THE SKY.
THERE IS NO INDIVIDUALITY.

Q: [Laughing], I find it hard to believe that this 'little me', is all of that! If I am all of that, as you say, how is it that I am not aware of this? And if I'm not, then how can I start becoming aware of my Self?

Maharaj: How can I? There is no 'I' at all. There is no 'You' and there is no 'I'. Everything is just like the sky. You see, even when the Master tells you that you are Almighty, that you are Ultimate Truth, Final Truth, you are not accepting it. You are not able to accept that Truth because you're caught up in all sorts of illusionary thoughts. You are considering yourself as 'little me', and that is making you blind to your Innate Power.

The remedy for this, a very simple remedy for this, as I have said, is meditation. Meditation is the anti-virus for illusion. It is one of the best remedies at the initial stage. It is like a potent medicine which takes time to go through the whole body. Then, the benefits will become apparent. How long this takes to run its course, and self-cure, depends on the spiritual body. Disciplined meditation will help dissolve all the body-knowledge, so that in time, everything will be completely erased.

UNLESS YOUR BODY-KNOWLEDGE DISSOLVES
AND DISAPPEARS COMPLETELY,
YOU WILL NOT BE ABLE TO KNOW YOURSELF
IN A REAL SENSE.

This is very important, so listen again: Unless your body-knowledge dissolves and disappears completely, you will not be able to know yourself in a real sense. I am telling you this to give you a jolt, so that you will throw yourself wholeheartedly, into the business of dissolving illusion.

This means, everything has to disappear, dissolve and vanish, everything! Including all the impressions, conditionings and memories from childhood till today!

Q: Maharaj, I had to come here to be reminded that I am Ultimate Truth.

Maharaj: YOU ARE Ultimate Truth. YOU ARE Ultimate Truth, but because of the long association with the body, Reality is not being accepted by you. You give a nod, and maybe say, OK, OK, OK. But what is needed, is your total involvement. It is not difficult, it is really very simple. Think about it, Self-enquire!

THE BODY IS NOT YOUR IDENTITY.
THIS IS AN OPEN FACT.

Your body-knowledge will be dissolved and erased with the help of meditation. At the same time, you must want to find out, "Who am I?" You need motivation, some impetus, fire! You need to be driven to find out, "Who am I?" Casual spirituality alone, will not do.

Q: My self is very strong, Maharaj, it shows no sign of dissolving.

Maharaj: That is because you have so much attachment to the body and the mind, ego, intellect. You are supplying energy to the mind, ego, intellect. All the time you are supplying energy to the mind, ego, intellect.

AS A MATTER OF FACT, YOU ARE THE MASTER,
BUT YOU ARE ACTING AS A SLAVE
OF THE MIND, EGO, INTELLECT.

Q: I've been interested in spirituality all my life, you know, searching for peace and happiness. It's disappointing and a bit depressing to have got to this stage in my life, and I've still not found what I was looking for.

Maharaj: All these problems with depression, disappointment, confusion, conflicts, etc, all these things are body-based concepts. Expectations grow because you think and consider yourself to be an individual, a 'somebody else', separate from the Reality that you are. "I want peace. I want happiness. I want to be spiritual". When you come to know 'spirituality', you will find that, it, too, is illusion.

WHY IS SPIRITUALITY REQUIRED?
BECAUSE YOU HAVE FORGOTTEN YOUR IDENTITY.
THAT IS WHY SPIRITUALITY IS REQUIRED.

Prior to beingness, there was no spirituality. There are so many books on spirituality, so many Masters of spirituality, claiming, "I am an exceptional Master". Where were all of these prior to beingness? The need for spirituality arises because you consider yourself as the body, as the body-form. When all the illusionary layers are dissolved, then,

YOU WILL COME ACROSS YOUR PERFECTION:
"OH! I AM THAT!"
SPONTANEOUS PERFECTION: "OH! I AM THAT!"

7.   *Why Keep Travelling, When You Are the Destination?*

Q: When I meditate, Maharaj, how should I meditate?

Maharaj: I will teach you a technique, but you must have strong faith in yourself. And, after you have been shown what to do, there should not be any temptation to go anywhere else. This is your last journey.

WHY KEEP TRAVELLING
WHEN YOU ARE THE DESTINATION?

This is the terminus. There is nowhere else to go. If you follow the practice with deep self-involvement, you will get a one-hundred per cent result. You will get a one-hundred per cent result back from your efforts.

Q: These teachings sound simple because you don't use many words. I like the simplicity, and I feel it is not really verbal at all. Something is happening on a different level.

Maharaj: If you have a background, then you can understand the language. The language used here is simple, simple language, with a simple and direct approach. Sometimes I use references in story-form, just to illustrate a certain meaning, or give some indication to help the understanding.

In this day and age, people have 'at-home' spirituality. They are reading a lot of books, listening to many different Masters, and performing different rituals or practices. This is OK for a while, but, then, there must come a time when one pauses, and stops to assess, weigh things up, and ask:

I MUST KNOW WHY I AM DOING ALL THESE THINGS.
WHAT AM I GETTING OUT OF ALL THIS READING?
WHAT AM I GETTING OUT OF LISTENING TO THESE MASTERS?
WHAT AM I GETTING FROM VISITING ALL THESE HOLY SITES?

You must know the purpose behind your actions. Why are you doing all these things, all these activities? The answer will generally be: "For peace and happiness", or "In order to have a fearless life, a tension-free life".

BUT WHO WANTS THIS?
WHO WANTS A FEARLESS LIFE?
WHO WANTS PEACE?
WHO WANTS A TENSION-FREE LIFE?

Q: Me! I do!

Maharaj: Who is this 'me', this 'I'? Ask the question again.

Q: I do ask this question, but the answer seems to be beyond words.

Maharaj:
AFTER SELF-ENQUIRY,
THE ENQUIRER ARRIVES AT THE SELF-CENTRE
WHERE THERE WILL BE EXCEPTIONAL SILENCE,
AND THE ENQUIRER WILL DISAPPEAR.

Number one: Ask yourself, "That 'me', that 'I', What is it like? How is it? Can you locate that 'me'? Answer: 'No'.

IT IS ANONYMOUS, INVISIBLE, UNIDENTIFIABLE.

Number two: All these needs and requirements that we have, in order to obtain happiness and peace, "Were they needed, prior to beingness?" Answer: 'No'.

And three: "Will they be needed after the body disappears?" Answer: 'No'.

IT IS ONLY BECAUSE YOU ARE HOLDING THIS BODY THAT ALL THESE NEEDS STARTED.
IT FOLLOWS THEREFORE, IT MEANS THAT ALL THE KNOWLEDGE THAT WE HAVE IS
BODY-BASED KNOWLEDGE,
AND BODY-RELATED KNOWLEDGE.

'You' are utterly and completely unknown to yourself because of the body relations that have separated you from your Reality. This illusory separation has made you think that you are apart and different from the Source that you truly are. "I am a somebody, an individual", you may think. "I am a man or a woman, *Brahman* or *Atman*, *Paramatman*, God".

Q: I like the sound of '*Brahman*' and "I am *Brahman*". It feels right, and it suits me. I have been repeating that over and over again, like a Mantra for years.

Maharaj: It does not matter what you call yourself by, or which names you prefer. '*Brahman*' is only a word. We have to use some words, some language to communicate. These are only 'names', and therefore, all one and the same.

Q: I still prefer '*Brahman*'.

Maharaj: OK, OK, as long as you remember that WE gave the names to different things. We created the alphabet of ABC. Names have been ascribed to everything, "This is D.O.N.K.E.Y", and "that is G.O.D", but remember:

**THESE NAMES WERE NOT IN EXISTENCE
PRIOR TO BEINGNESS.
THIS MEANS THAT THE 'SPONTANEOUS, INVISIBLE EXISTENCE'
WHICH IS NAMELESS,
HAS BEEN GIVEN THE NAMES
'BRAHMAN', 'ATMAN', 'PARAMATMAN', 'GOD'.
THIS IS THE WAY OF SELF-ENQUIRY.
THE ENQUIRER BECOMES SILENCE, INVISIBLE.
AND THAT 'LITERAL KNOWLEDGE' BECOMES REALITY.**

8. *The Entire World is Your Spontaneous Projection*

Q: And what about the world? The world is *maya*, illusion, yes?

Maharaj: You are totally different from this whole world because the entire world is your Spontaneous Projection.

**THE WORLD IS PROJECTED
OUT OF YOUR SPONTANEOUS PRESENCE.**

Without your existence, without your Presence, you cannot see the world.

**YOU ARE PRIOR TO THE WORLD,
PRIOR TO THE UNIVERSE, AND PRIOR TO EVERYTHING.
TO SAY, 'BRAHMAN', 'ATMAN', 'PARAMATMAN',
'GOD', 'UNIVERSE', 'SKY', etc.
YOUR PRESENCE IS REQUIRED.**

Your Presence has no limitations. It does not have a time limit, nor any circle around it. It is beyond the circle. This is simple knowledge.

**YOU ARE GOING ROUND AND ROUND
WITHIN THE CIRCLE OF BODY-KNOWLEDGE. WHY?
COME OUT OF THE CIRCLE!**

Q: How do I come out of what you call this 'circle of body-knowledge'? Is it not too difficult, too firmly established? How can I change?

Maharaj: By accepting that you are not the body, you were not the body, you are not going to remain the body. You are unborn. You are Ultimate Reality, Final Truth.

Put spirituality aside for a moment. Stand back a little, and take a cool, rational look. Use discrimination! You know that the body is not your Identity, because you have seen the changes taking place, from a young child to an old lady. So how can this be your Identity? It is not permanent.

Q: That's true. So what you are saying, is that if I accept that "I am not the body", that "I am unborn", 'Ultimate Reality', then that is the way forward?

Maharaj: Yes, yes, with discrimination and detachment.

Q: Even if I don't quite fully believe it, or feel it, and have questions about it?

Maharaj: Yes, yes, it will come. The Conviction will come, but it is a Spontaneous Conviction. All questions that arise are simply body-based questions. All this conflict, confusion and doubt is body-based, all body-related.

PRIOR TO BEINGNESS, THERE WERE NO DOUBTS,
THERE WAS NO KNOWER.
DOUBTS STARTED WITH THE BODY.
BUT YOU ARE NOT THE BODY.
THE BODY IS NOT GOING TO REMAIN, NOT AT ALL.

You are Ultimate Truth, but you have forgotten the Ultimate Truth. You now think that you are somebody else, an ordinary man or woman, who has to ask someone else to, "Please bless me. Put your hand on my head and bless me". Why?

Q: You say that it will happen by itself?

Maharaj: It is very simple, but total involvement is a must. To know this principle in you, to find out more about Ultimate Reality, Ultimate Truth, there has to be earnestness, self-involvement, like an unquenchable thirst, or a fire burning inside, that makes you want to find out, that pushes you to know the Reality.

DEVOTION IS STRIVING TO KNOW REALITY UNCEASINGLY.

I will give you an example: If someone abuses you, using really horrible and nasty language against you, then, these words will automatically be reflected inside you, in each and every cell. When someone is abusive, strong waves of feeling can, and do erupt. We all know this feeling: "Somebody has spoken against me. I will take revenge. Let him come near me, and I will get him back. I will do something about the way he has treated me. How dare he!" and so on.

DEVOTION IS LIKE THIS.

Q: I understand, [laughing]. You need determination and full involvement, like you can't think of anything else! I've experienced that a few times!

Maharaj: So, like this, complete involvement while trying to know yourself in a real sense is essential, the only way. Complete dedication in the pursuit of Self-Knowledge is devotion. You are not going to keep quiet and forget about it. You have to find out. There is no stopping you: "I want to know. I have to know who I am!"

THROW YOURSELF FULLY INTO SELF-REALIZATION.

When you say, "I am a man", or "I am a woman", this is not true. And even when you say, "I am *Brahman*", it is not true. You are neither *Brahman*, nor *Atman*, nor *Paramatman*. These names have been assigned. They are good names, but they are used only to indicate your Ultimate Truth, your Ultimate Identity. These words, '*Atman*', '*Brahman*', '*Paramatman*' have limitations.

THEY ARE ONLY WORDS, JUST WORDS.
YOU ARE BEYOND WORDS.

9. Godly Essence

Q: I am attached to the thoughts, feelings and emotions and so, I feel like a body.

Maharaj: All these feelings are flowing because you are holding the body. Presence does not know who Steven is, or whether he is a man or woman because Presence is invisible, just like sky, not knowing its name, any name.

Truth is placed before you, but unfortunately you are not accepting it. You are accepting all these sad and fearful feelings, tense feelings. You are accepting them very deeply. And because of this, these feelings are, so to speak, giving colour to that Presence, and this results in, 'I am somebody else'.

We are trying to invite attention of the Invisible Listener within you. You are Almighty God. You are Omnipresent God, everywhere.

**THAT GODLY ESSENCE HAS NO EXPERIENCE
OF BEING AN INDIVIDUAL.**

You have accepted Steven as 'somebody', but if the body and the Presence were absent, then who is going to talk about this 'Steven'? The body cannot have any activity without the power of Spirit. The Spirit-body combination is essential. This is very Direct Knowledge.

**PRESENCE DOES NOT KNOW ITS OWN EXISTENCE.
PRESENCE IS WITHOUT KNOWLEDGE.
IT HAS NO EXPERIENCE,
NO EXPERIENCER,
NO WITNESS, NO AWARENESS.**

The moment the Spirit clicks with the body you say, "I am". The fan will only work if there is electricity. Without the current of power - no electricity! Your Power is like invisible electricity, but you are only viewing the body, instead of the Power.

What we need to do therefore is erase all the memories, all our body-based memories. This will take some time. There will be total silence after everything has been erased.

You must have a strong foundation for this understanding, this Knowledge. To make your foundations strong, you are to undergo the discipline of meditation. Literal knowledge will not help you. Bookish knowledge is not enough, as it is just a body-based attempt at indicating your Identity.

**EVERYTHING WILL BE CLEAR
WHEN ALL FOOD-BODY-KNOWLEDGE DISSOLVES.**

Q: When the body-knowledge disappears, will all these intense emotions disappear too?

Maharaj: Yes! Spontaneously! I am using words like 'erase' and 'disappear', just for communication, but this process is a spontaneous process which will uncover your Omnipresence, indicating your Presence everywhere. All illusory thoughts will go, and everything will disappear.

In dreams, you sometimes see good things, sometimes bad things. On awakening, you may say, "What have I done?" Once you know the Reality, all concepts will dissolve. You will know when you awaken, that you have nothing to do with these dreams, and you did not do anything. Similarly, through Knowledge, you will realize that what you took yourself to be, what you thought you were, was in fact, not the case. It was a dream!

Q: Because I measured myself in body-form?

Maharaj: Correct! If you stop supplying food to the body, the body gets thin. Who is consuming that food? It is food for the flesh, just like when the oil in a lamp dries up, and stops burning. When the oil runs out, the light goes out. Food is just like the oil. Who is using the oil?

Q: The fire within you. Am I feeding my Spontaneous Existence?

Maharaj: You are not doing anything. I am just giving examples. If the lamp is burning, there is oil. Your Presence will be noticed until you stop supplying food to the body. If you stop taking food and water, the body will go. Where does the light from the lamp go? To heaven or hell? Your Presence will be felt until, like the light, the body expires.

Light is everywhere, all that is needed is a touch, like a matchbox and stick. All that is needed is a touch, and out of that touch you will see the flame. Light is everywhere, fire is everywhere, but with a touch, you can see it. It is invisible, but a mere 'click' makes it visible.

PRESENCE IS OMNIPRESENCE,
THE FIRE THAT IS EVERYWHERE.

The click brings it into focus for a time, for the lifespan of the body, and then when the oil runs out, it disappears again.

Q: Like a visible fire, a flame?

Maharaj: Your Spontaneous Presence is invisible fire. It is only because of this combination, the click of Spirit and body, that you can say 'I'. You know your Presence through the body. With it, you can say 'I'.

After knowing this Reality, you will have spontaneous courage and be totally fearless. You will be out of this fearful atmosphere of death and birth, so that when you leave the body, there will be no fear around.

Q: Does this feeling of fear come with the body?

Maharaj: I have to use some words.

THIS SPONTANEOUS FEELING, THIS FEAR IS AROUND
BECAUSE OF YOUR LOVE FOR THE BODY.

When you know, "I am not the body", there will be no fear! If you have something in your pocket, you will be afraid of the thief. If your pockets are empty, then there is nothing to be afraid of.

YOU ARE WORRIED ABOUT DEATH
BECAUSE YOU THINK YOU ARE SOMEBODY.

All your earnings, your assets, make you think that you have got so much to lose.

Q: So what you are saying is that I don't have this Knowledge because of the fear?

Maharaj: Yes, you have to undergo the meditation to get rid of all this illusion. The moment that Knowledge is digested, you will see the effects, and miracles will appear within. It will take a little time.

Q: Ramana Maharshi had an experience of death. After this, he was Realized. Is it necessary to go through this experience or not?

Maharaj: No. Everybody has different experiences, different experiences. Forget about Ramana Maharshi and any other Master.

THE EXPERIENCER IS ONE AND THE SAME.

FOCUS ON THE EXPERIENCER,
NOT ON THE EXPERIENCE.

The experiences may be different, they are not important. I am inviting the attention of that Experiencer which is Invisible, Anonymous.

LOOK AT YOURSELF,
NOT AT OTHERS!

This life is like a big ocean. So many are drowning. Everything has become dark. You are looking for ways to come out of this illusionary world, this illusionary ocean. You are following others and hoping their methods will work for you. Don't go looking here and there. You are to escape from here and there!

STOP PAYING ATTENTION TO THE WAY HE IS SWIMMING,
OR HOW SHE IS SWIMMING,
OR YOU WILL DROWN.

You have been thrown into the ocean of this illusionary world, now you have to swim out of this illusionary ocean.

THE MASTERS HAVE TOLD YOU HOW TO ESCAPE.
THEY HAVE SHOWN YOU HOW TO SWIM. DO IT!

First save yourself, then save others. The *Naam Mantra* is a technique that teaches you how to swim comfortably and easily. Half-knowledge and depending on others, borrowing from others is always dangerous.

Q: Maharaj, talking about half-knowledge... For years, I have been looking around for a proper Realized teacher, someone like you. There are loads of self-proclaimed teachers out there, but they are all what you would call Neo-Advaitin, or part of the *Satsang* culture.

I have found that these Neo-Advaitin teachings are insubstantial and confusing because they don't offer a detailed road-map, or show you the bigger picture. They can give pointers, but their knowledge remains superficial because there is a lack of Self-Knowledge. They are just showing you part of the elephant. The approach is commercial, with lots of money changing hands and some are very expensive. I'm so pleased to have found you at last. From my own research, you are the only one who is speaking from the Realized State.

Maharaj: I am glad you came here. This is your terminus, final stop!

10. Who Wants to Live Forever?

Q: I have been practising self-abidance.

Maharaj: These are only words. All of these concepts are layers on your Presence. Prior to the body, there was no self-abidance, no self at all. There was no self at all prior to beingness. This concept of abidance appeared simply because of the body.

DON'T SWIM IN THE SEA OF SPIRITUAL WORDS.
SEE YOUR SELFLESS SELF.

It is Open Truth.

Q: But difficult?

Maharaj: It is not difficult at all! This body is not your Identity, so what is difficult about that? It's Open Truth. Can you postpone your own death? Not at all, so where is the difficulty? Do nothing. Your seeking is disturbing you. Just be!

JUST BE WITH THE 'JUST BE'.
JUST SEE YOURSELF,
AND HOW YOU WERE PRIOR TO THE BODY!

These words like 'self', 'myself', 'himself', 'no self', are just words that appeared. The concept of self appeared in front of you, when the Spirit clicked with the body.

YOU ARE ALREADY FINAL TRUTH
WITHOUT IMAGINATION,
WITHOUT CONCEPTS.

All these words are used to indicate your Final Truth. These spiritual words are nothing more than indications that will cause confusion, and add more ego.

THERE IS NO SEPARATION,
NO INDIVIDUALITY.
WHEN YOU ARE ONE WITH THE ULTIMATE TRUTH,
THEN WHAT MEANING DOES 'SELF-ABIDANCE' HAVE?

Sky does not know itself or anything. Your Existence, Presence is beyond sky. We have been receiving impressions from body-knowledge since childhood till today. A child immediately accepts what the parent says as he is very open and impressionable. Adults are more suspicious, and twist and analyze everything, so they don't accept so easily. Tens of thousands of concepts are engraved inside us, and that is why the *Naam Mantra* is needed to erase them all.

Q: Is the *Naam Mantra* not self-abidance?

Maharaj: Total Conviction is Self-abidance. The *Naam Mantra* is inviting the attention of the Invisible Meditator that you are Ultimate Truth:

YOU CAN'T SAY IT IS ABOUT
HOW YOU WERE PRIOR TO BEINGNESS,
BECAUSE YOU WERE UNKNOWN TO YOURSELF,
AND THEREFORE YOU DON'T KNOW.
KNOWLEDGE CAME AFTER.

Prior to your existence in the body, Presence was there, invisible and anonymous. Prior to your existence, fire was there, but it is only with the click of the Spirit and body, that the flame can be seen. The combination of a matchbox and stick produces fire with just one strike. Likewise, the combination of Spirit and body is needed to say 'I'.

Q: Is Spontaneous Existence the flame or the potential flame?

Maharaj: The existence of fire is there but it is unknown. You click, and you see it, then it disappears. It is not going anywhere. The moment the Spirit clicked with the body you say, "I am". But don't measure yourself in the body-form. The basic principle of spirituality states that you are not the body. The body is subject to birth and death, not you.

WHEN THE TIME COMES TO LEAVE THE BODY,
THE BODY-FORM IS EXHAUSTED
BUT YOUR PRESENCE IS NOT.
PRESENCE CONTINUES.

Your Invisible Presence has exceptional importance. Your Invisible Presence has exceptional importance which you are ignoring. You are underestimating this. You are giving importance to external things. Look at you, look within you, see within you. Serious involvement is necessary with your meditation practice, and then all questions will be solved within yourself. Your Inner Master is very powerful.

So strong involvement is required.

THE POWER IN YOU
IS THE SAME AS THE POWER BEHIND MY TALKING.

Bodies are different, Spirit is One. As I have already said,

TOTAL CONVICTION IS SELF-ABIDANCE.

Just like you cannot remove a bucket of water after it has been poured into the sea, everything will be crystal clear after you recite the Mantra.

This is very, very simple spiritual knowledge. You must have trust in your Selfless Self and at the same time, trust in your Master.

YOU ARE BEGGING: "OH PLEASE, HELP ME!"
BECAUSE YOU DON'T KNOW YOUR GREATNESS.

Every creature struggles for survival because Spirit only knows itself through the body. The Spirit wants to keep the body because it is afraid of death. This is true from the biggest creature to the smallest. Look at the ants for example, they too, wish to survive. Once they know the taste of sweetness, they cling to life.

There was once a saint with foresight. He told his devotees that on such and such a date and time, he would leave his body. "I am taking birth, in a village nearby. I am feeling the pressure of some animal, it is a boar. When you see me as this boar, come and kill me! I don't want to remain in that boar form. Remember that! Kill me, cut me!"

So later on, he dies, and takes birth as a boar. His disciples go to this village, and as told in his story, the boar is there. They catch hold of it. The boar squeals, "Please, don't kill me, I like this body. Forget what I told you, forget what I told you, don't kill me! I want to remain".

This illustrates the human condition. Spirit is attached to the body-form. Spirit, the principle behind life, likes the body-form and wishes to remain in a particular body. Spirit does not know its Identity. It only knows itself through the body. The Spontaneous Presence is Unidentified Identity. In spite of this, every living being wishes to ensure its own self-preservation in body-form. It wants to live forever!

11. There is No Experiencer and No Experience

Maharaj: We know ourselves from a body-based perspective.

THIS BODY-FORM KNOWLEDGE HAS TO DISSOLVE.
THIS IS THE PRINCIPLE BEHIND SPIRITUALITY.

Though you may know, "I am not the body", that Knowledge needs to turn into Conviction. People say, "I am not the body, I am *Brahman*, I am *Atman*, I am *Paramatman*, I am God". It is very easy to say, but this Knowledge has to be real, established, totally established.

It is true that everyone knows the body is not our Identity because it undergoes change. We see the changes: first comes the child, then the young man, then the old man. And then, some day or other, willingly or unwillingly, we have to leave these bodies.

THE BODY IS NOT OUR IDENTITY,
THIS IS THE ESTABLISHED TRUTH.

Q: Yes, I know that. It is obvious.

Maharaj: You say it is obvious, but are you living like that? We are not accepting this Truth. We have a lot of love and affection for the body. This has to dissolve.

Q: Because we are too attached to the body?

Maharaj: King Bharat once asked his Minister: "Who has the strongest love for another? Is it the mother's love for the child, or the sister's for the brother, the husband's for the wife, and so on, who?" The Minister replied: "Everyone loves himself the most. People love themselves the most."

There is another story on the same theme of a mother monkey, and its infant. One day they were sitting, happily playing in the water pond. Suddenly, the water started to come in and rise. The mother monkey quickly lifts the infant out of danger. Then as the water continues to rise, the mother raises the infant even higher to prevent it from drowning. The water keeps on rising, till finally, in desperation, the mother monkey releases her protective hold of her infant, in order to save her own life. She sacrifices the baby for her own survival. This story is used to illustrate that no one loves another more than himself.

Q: Self-love?

Maharaj: Nobody loves anyone else more than himself. There is a lot of love and affection for the body, mind, ego, intellect. Therefore, it follows that our expectations are often so high, that they cannot be met by others.

Q: Is that love all for the body then?

Maharaj: Yes! But do take care of your body, don't neglect it. But at the same time, know that the body is not Ultimate Truth. As long as you view yourself as the body, you will be under the illusion of fear, and all the rest of it.

Q: If I am not the body, then who am I? I have had experiences, like bright lights in my head, astral travel, premonitions, visions, and feelings of spiritual warmth and so on. I know that I am much more than this body. I'm beyond, something beyond. It is hard to explain.

Maharaj: Experiences are not so important. When you get closer to Selfless Self, you will discover that there is no experiencer and no experience, and no witness and no witnesser either. Don't measure yourself in the body-form!

YOU ARE ULTIMATE TRUTH,
YOU ARE FINAL TRUTH,
YOU ARE *BRAHMAN, ATMAN, PARAMATMAN*, GOD.

Q: So how do I experience *Brahman*?

Maharaj: Brahman is invisible, anonymous, unidentified.

THERE IS NO EXPERIENCE, THERE IS NO EXPERIENCER.
THERE IS NO EXPERIENCE, THERE IS NO EXPERIENCER.
THERE IS NO WITNESS, THERE IS NO WITNESSER.

We have to forget the physical body, the biological body. We have a spiritual body which is invisible. It is not a biological body or a physical body. All the questions that you have are related to the physical body.

THERE ARE NO QUESTIONS
AT THE SPIRITUAL LEVEL.

Q: The questions will keep coming, as long as I consider myself to be the body-form?

Maharaj: Yes, yes. In reality, you were not the body, prior to beingness. You are not going to remain the body. Beingness started, and instantly you said "I". Prior to "I", your Presence was there.

So all these questions, along with 'spirituality', came after, when, one could say, Ultimate Truth attracted you. Remember that these words I am using are only words, so don't cling to them.

Q: It is the body then that has caused all the problems?

Maharaj: The body, in fact, offers an opportunity for you to know yourself. Reality became unknown to you when the body suddenly created a big illusory distance, which made you forget your Identity.

Be strong, have courage, don't live a cowardly life. Be like a lion! Do you know the story of the lion? A lion cub was brought up in a flock of sheep. The lion cub started to think it was one of the sheep. It was afraid of dogs, afraid of wolves. Then one day, a second lion appeared and tried to befriend the first one. The lion cub started bleating: "Don't hurt me, please, I am a sheep".

The second lion takes the cub to the bank of the river and says: "Look at yourself in the water, see your head! See the rest of your body. I'm showing you, I am serious, you are a lion just like me!". With just one glance, the cub sees its reflection, first the neck, then the body, each part, "OH! AH! OK!".

By doing this, it realizes and accepts, "So I am just like you! There is no difference! All this time, I was living as a sheep but I am not a sheep at all!" It looks at its reflection once again and roars, "I am a lion!" Convinced, it runs off as a lion, and not as a sheep, which it never was.

The Master is saying the same thing: "You are not a man, you are not a woman, you are *Brahman*". Why fear when you can roar!

THIS MEANS THAT,
AFTER KNOWING THE REALITY,
YOU GO TO YOUR ORIGINAL PLACE.

It is a nice story that indicates the Spiritual Lion. We are coaxing you to come out, and start roaring: "I am a lion. I am That!" You are already a lion but you forgot your Identity. Because of the long association with the body, you started considering yourself as "I am somebody".

Master tells you, "You are Ultimate Truth". You say, "How can I be?" So he explains. This is called Knowledge. These stories, which give confidence, are suitable for the initial stage. You are to accept the principle of the story. You have got to teach yourself not to fear, not to be depressed or affected. Don't take the touch. You are suffering because you are taking the touch.

Q: On a personal level, I have experienced quite a lot of suffering.

Maharaj: Who is the sufferer? Pay attention to what I am trying to convey! You have a sense of separation, alienation and distance from your Source, which has made you feel that you are something separate, somebody else, with an independent existence.

SPIRITUALITY IS THEREFORE REQUIRED,
MEDITATION, *BHAJANS* AND KNOWLEDGE TOO.
WHY?
BECAUSE YOU FORGOT YOUR IDENTITY.

Q: And so, when my memory comes back, and I remember my identity?

Maharaj: It is not like that. It has nothing to do with remembering or memory. Don't take my words literally! Every day I am saying the same thing. I am not talking about forgetting and remembering in a literal sense.

It will happen spontaneously when you KNOW. The moment the Unidentified Identity is known, then, that is Conviction, Spontaneous Conviction.

WHEN THIS SPONTANEOUS CONVICTION HAPPENS,
THE INDIVIDUAL WILL NO LONGER BE THERE,
BECAUSE 'THIS' IS BEYOND TALK.

At present, when we are talking together, we see ourselves as two bodies, a disciple and a Master. If you pour a bucket of water into the sea, you will not be able to remove that water because it has merged with the sea. This is called the 'Merging Process'. When there is Realization, it is like this.

If one is absorbed in the Reality - the bucket of water poured into the sea - you can't, then, extract the bucket of water from the sea. It is an impossibility. There is no individuality with that bucket of water. This happens in a similar way in the process of merging and absorbing one's Ultimate Truth. You are Ultimate Truth, Final Truth.

Q: How long does the merging process take?

Maharaj: Spirituality is needed for as long as there is that span of experience, of beingness and absorbing beingness, dissolving beingness. When we came across with this illusory world, all needs started. The moment you are convinced that this illusory world has no base, you will know that it is the Spontaneous Projection of your Spontaneous Presence.

THE WORLD
IS THE SPONTANEOUS PROJECTION
OF YOUR SPONTANEOUS PRESENCE.
IT IS INVISIBLE,
ANONYMOUS,
UNIDENTIFIED IDENTITY.
JUST TO KNOW THIS IS ENOUGH.

The body is not our identity at all. Open fact. All body relations are illusionary concepts. You can use your body, but don't give it so much attention. Don't depend on the body-form so much. The body has its own time-limit.

12. *Meeting Nisargadatta Maharaj*

Maharaj: Any questions?

Q: Maharaj, can you tell me a little about how you came to meet Nisargadatta Maharaj?

Maharaj: In 1962, I was staying with relatives. At that time, I was unemployed, searching for work and in a little bit of poverty. My sister said, "You are sitting here idle, come with me to see Maharaj". I wasn't sure, but this is how it happened, how I came to Nisargadatta Maharaj.

In those days, he did not give new visitors the *Naam Mantra* immediately. He used to observe you to see how much devotion you had. So, after going to Maharaj's home, sitting on the floor, and meditating on the name of a Deity, about a month later, on 2nd October, 1962, Nisargadatta Maharaj gave me the *Naam Mantra*, the Guru Mantra.

Subsequently, he came to know that I was somewhat poor and out of work. He asked everybody and anybody if they had a job for this 'poor boy'. He was just like a father, asking on my behalf. When I managed to find a temporary job for a few days, he suggested I should have a bank account. He opened one for me. He also purchased a watch for me. His kindly actions felt like parental love and affection.

I continued to go to his home every day, morning and evening. At that time, I was not able to understand what he was talking about because it was beyond me. But he used to say, "Listen to me, listen to me!", and I did.

He also helped by giving me some useful and practical tips, and like that, slowly, silently, slowly, silently, I absorbed that Knowledge to some extent. Then I went on to College and University, took a job in a bank and got married. I was back on my feet. About ten years later, I came to KNOW what he had been saying, what he was telling me back then.

When Nisargadatta Maharaj visited us at home, he used to say "Knowledge is part of you". He was a very simple and straightforward, down-to-earth character. Earlier, I was restless, and changed my jobs many times. My first job paid one rupee a day. At that time, I used to walk ten kilometres for one rupee. The reason I am mentioning this, is to impart knowledge, so that you know the importance of struggle and the vital role that it plays.

IT IS NOT EASY TO STRUGGLE IN LIFE,
BUT IT IS VERY IMPORTANT.
STRUGGLE IS A TEACHER BECAUSE
IT DEMANDS TOTAL INVOLVEMENT.
IN BATTLE, YOU MUST HAVE STRONG INVOLVEMENT.

Likewise, with spirituality,

YOU MUST STRUGGLE TO KNOW YOUR REALITY:
"I WANT TO KNOW MYSELF.
WHO AM I?
I HAVE TO KNOW."

Q: With many of the saints, the need to know became a matter of life and death.

Maharaj: I keep telling people that casual involvement, casual spirituality will not do. You must be driven, you must want to know the secret of "Who am I?" Am I just this body?"

In my childhood, some thoughts had arisen like, "Where was I prior to my birth?" This was around the age of eight, nine and ten. Some thoughts like these appeared, but answers were not forthcoming. So in this way, you have to struggle and search within yourself. Then, finally, with true Knowledge, the search will be over, truly over.

YOU ARE LOOKING TO FIND ANSWERS OUTSIDE OF YOURSELF,
YET THE FINDER IS IN YOU.
YOU HAVE FORGOTTEN THE FINDER.
YOU ARE ULTIMATE TRUTH.

What I am saying is very subtle. We have a lot of attachment to the body, a lot of affection and attachment, even though we know the body is not going to survive for a long time. Everybody knows this! Yet still, we continue to attend numerous pilgrimages, and go here and there for spiritual entertainment. Many continue with these casual pastimes, right up until it's time for the Spirit to go, when the body can no longer function. Then it is burned like any other common material. Lifespan ended! Missed opportunity!

The body is only alive because of the Spirit. This Power, this energy is called *Brahman*, *Atman*, *Paramatman*, God. Knowledge means just to know yourself in a real sense, to know that you are Ultimate Truth.

Up until now, we were knowing ourselves in the body-form, as the body-form. Knowledge must be absorbed: "I was not a body, I am not a body, I am not going to remain as a body".

It's the Truth, the Naked Truth, Open Truth known by everybody, and yet at the same time, a Truth that everyone prefers to ignore. Every day we hear of people dying, it is inevitable.

Knowledge of Ultimate Truth, Ultimate Reality means that there will be complete peace, without help from any material cause. Generally, the three causes of happiness in human life are considered to be publicity or power, money and sex. So many people are after publicity and will do anything to be famous, to be powerful. They will kill for power, they will kill for money and they will kill for sex. Human beings are always trying to extract peace and happiness from these three things.

BUT, WHO IS ENJOYING THAT PEACE?
YOU WILL SAY, "OH, I AM",
BUT THAT HAPPINESS IS BASED ON A MATERIAL CAUSE,
AND THEREFORE IT IS TEMPORARY.

No material cause whatsoever is needed for happiness and peace. You can have Spontaneous Happiness and Spontaneous Peace without money, sex or publicity which is just "Om Shanti". This is not artificial. This is real, this is Spontaneous Peace with no worries, no tension.

Why have tension? We have it only because we have body attachment. You need to grow in tolerance and patience.

Q: So how can I change? I tell myself that "I am *Brahman*", all the time.

Maharaj: Change will happen. It is not difficult if you have strong devotion, a strong will, and are prepared to make a little sacrifice. This is a very important time for you. Every moment in your life is very, very important.

DON'T SEEK AFTER THE ULTIMATE TRUTH

IN A CASUAL MANNER.
EVERY DAY, EVERY MOMENT,
IS IMPORTANT.

Do your job and be practical. Sitting idly, saying "Oh, I am *Brahman*, I am *Brahman*," this is not knowledge. You are searching for God somewhere else, hoping and searching for a God somewhere in the sky, a God that is administering the whole world. This is a concept, it is all illusion.

GOD IS NOT IN THE SKY RULING THE ENTIRE WORLD,
PUNISHING THOSE WHO ARE DOING BAD THINGS
AND BLESSING THOSE WHO ARE DOING GOOD.
THIS IS A CONCEPT,
AN ILLUSION.

No religion is bad in itself, but the way religion is implemented by so-called Masters of Religion, is not good, as it is basically done for selfish purposes. Be practical! This is the proper time. It is the right time for you. The ghost of fear is surrounding you.

BREAK THE VICIOUS CIRCLE OF THIS GHOST OF FEAR,
AND ACCEPT THAT
"I AM NOT DYING. I AM NOT BORN".
BIRTH AND DEATH RELATE TO THE BODY ONLY,
TO THE FOOD-BODY ONLY.
THAT CONVICTION IS MOST IMPORTANT.

You will need to undergo a process that will make it easy for you to accept the Conviction, and let it deepen. This process will include reciting the *Naam Mantra*, meditation, *bhajans*. This is a golden opportunity for you, so do not waste it!

13. The Listener's Story

Maharaj: Your involvement is most important. Just listen, and then forget it. What I am communicating, talking with you about, the words I have spoken, try to know the principle behind the words.

DO NOT ANALYZE THE WORDS.
THE WORDS ARE NOT IMPORTANT.
CONCENTRATE ON THE MEANING BEHIND THE WORDS,
TRY TO KNOW THE PRINCIPLE BEHIND THE WORDS.

I am talking to you, narrating the Listener's story, not the individual person's story. I am talking about the Invisible Listener within you.

I AM NARRATING YOUR STORY,
THE STORY OF THE INVISIBLE LISTENER WITHIN YOU.

Q: So it's an experience but it's an experience without the experiencer?
Maharaj: In the beginning, 'experience', 'witness', all these words are there, but YOU are beyond experience. Your Presence is behind every experience. Even if you say, "I am *Brahman*", it is also illusion because

Presence is needed to say *Brahman*. The name '*Brahman*' has been given, '*Atman*' has been given, '*Paramatman*' has been given, 'God' has been given, all these names have been ascribed to 'Ultimate Truth'.

HOWEVER, THE WORDS ARE NOT ULTIMATE TRUTH.
THIS IS THE MISTAKE MANY PEOPLE ARE MAKING.
THEY TAKE THESE WORDS TO BE THE ULTIMATE TRUTH.
THE WORDS ARE NOT ULTIMATE TRUTH.

We gave meaning to all these words. We have created all these words, through which we can understand, through which we can talk and converse with each other.

Q: So it is not about using the words to get clarity, it is more about always being in that silent place where questions are answered?

Maharaj: Yes, all the answers to all the questions are within you.

THE QUESTIONER ITSELF IS THE ANSWER.
THE INVISIBLE QUESTIONER ITSELF WITHIN YOU,
IS THE ANSWER.
WITHOUT THE QUESTIONER, YOU CANNOT QUESTION.

Q: This has stopped me in my tracks! So that is the answer to all my questions. That's definitely a place to go to with all this. That's what makes it tangible, really clear for me.

Maharaj: Now try and digest and absorb what has been said. This will give you Spontaneous Happiness and Peace. Happiness, Peace, everything is within you. You have just forgotten that you are the Source of it all.

We have lost our Happiness because we are measuring ourselves in body-form. In brief, you are underestimating yourself all the time, thinking, "I am somebody else. I am one of the family members, I'm a person in the world".

Q: Can I ask about duty to the family? You said, "Do your duty to the family", and I read that Nisargadatta Maharaj went back to his family when he understood that. Can you explain that a little more please? I am having a little difficulty understanding that.

Maharaj: If you are acting in a drama, you know that you are not concerned with the drama. You know it is a role you are playing for two or three hours. Your Presence is Spontaneous. Along with the Presence came family members, society, the world. You do whatever duties you are required to do but at the same time, you are supposed to remain unconcerned with the world because prior to beingness there was nothing.

PRIOR TO BEINGNESS,
YOU WERE UNCONCERNED WITH THE WORLD.
THERE WAS NO FAMILY LIFE,
NO ASSOCIATION OR INTERACTION
WITH ANY OTHER PERSON.

This whole dream began the moment the Spirit clicked with the body. Just like if you are in a deep sleep, and in your dream you are acting as somebody else. You see your big family, you are on holiday by the sea, the sun is shining. You see different landscapes, etc. After awakening, this whole dream world just vanishes. What happened to that family? What happened to that holiday?

Likewise, every day you see different dreams. This life is just a big dream, a long dream! It is open fact, open fact. Prior to body-knowledge, where were you? Prior to beingness what was your existence?

After the body dissolves, after the disappearance of the body, or after death, are you going to ask, "What has happened to my family? Where did the world go? Where did my knowledge go?" Knowledge means just to know oneself in a real sense. We know ourselves in body-form, and that is the cause of all our confusion and conflicts.

Q: Thank you.

Maharaj: So there should not be so much attachment to this material life which may drive or propel another dream. This will be the last dream. This will be the last dream. There should not be another dream.

Know yourself! This body has given you a real opportunity to know yourself in a real sense. If you lose this opportunity, well, we can't say. Do you want to see another dream, and another dream? If not, come out of it all.

COME OUT FROM ALL THESE DREAMS.

For this, Conviction of Reality is most important.

Q: Conviction?

Maharaj: Conviction, Conviction of Reality.

Q: So with meditation, and even beyond the meditation, you have to stay with that Conviction, and through that Conviction the rest falls away?

Maharaj: Through meditation you are reminding Selfless Self, the Meditator, that "You are *Brahman*, you are *Atman*". You are reminding your Selfless Self.

Q: The meditation helps the Conviction to grow, and the Conviction then becomes its nature?

Maharaj: You can take it in your own way, but keep in mind that you are Ultimate Truth. You are Final Truth. It is your story. I am narrating your story, your Reality, not what you have read in books.

I AM NARRATING YOUR STORY, YOUR REALITY,
NOT ALL THAT YOU HAVE READ IN BOOKS.

It is the Listener's story, the story of the Invisible Listener in you. When you are reading books you should read them as if it is the Reader's story in them.

WHEN YOU READ SPIRITUAL BOOKS,
THEY ARE NARRATING THE STORY OF
THE INVISIBLE LISTENER IN YOU.
YOU ARE TO READ THEM,
AS IF YOU ARE READING ABOUT YOU.
IT IS YOUR STORY, THE READER'S STORY.

When I am talking with you, I am not talking to you as a body, I am talking with the Invisible Listener within you. People make the mistake of reading spiritual books as if the books are telling the story of '*Brahman*' and '*Atman*', a story about something other, something separate from the reader.

Q: I think that's one of the main things you have done Maharaj, is taken away a lot of the book knowledge, and the emphasis on certain kinds of body-practices and reading. That comes through very solidly from you, and that in itself is a very important kind of emphasis. That's a big difference, a different experience to what we have been used to.

It also brings a new perspective and more faith in the process. To trust that process is not an easy thing. All the words that are out there from all the Masters are filtered when you read them. But you have put an emphasis beyond that which is very clear and helpful.

Maharaj: It is Open Truth, Final Truth.

Q: Wonderful!

14. *Meditation is Boring*

Q: I had a very profound experience last year, and I felt I must be at the last stage.

Maharaj: There is no last stage. Whose stage? Who is measuring? There is no stage at all. This is the impact of all your reading. What you read is reflected.

Q: If this world is just an illusion, how important are experiences? As I said, this spiritual experience was very profound. I have lost a lot of friends, and have diminishing interest in the world because of it. Should I force myself to take an interest in the world as I used to before this experience? I used to be active in social causes and charity work.

Maharaj: Who is acting through the body? Your Identity is covered with the body. So what you are doing is being done with the body-knowledge base. In spirituality, we say, "You are not the body, you are not going to remain the body. Therefore, who is acting through the body? You say you are talking, you are seeing, you are doing.

YOU SAY, "I AM DOING SOMETHING".
WHO IS SAYING THAT?

The Seer, the Speaker, the Invisible Speaker is your Identity, which is called *Brahman*, *Atman*, God, Master, or any other name. But since you are believing yourself to be the body-form, you are therefore unable to know yourself in a real sense. So all your questions are body-related questions.

Your social work, your friends, your relatives are body-related. Prior to beingness, what kind of social work did you do? None! After the body dissolves, what kind of social work will you be doing then? None! Do social work, but don't relate it to the ego. Subtle ego is a great problem. Do it if you wish, do normal things, but at the same time, try to know yourself in a real sense.

YOU ARE FORMLESS.
YOU ARE NOT THE BODY-FORM AT ALL.
WHERE WAS THIS BODY PRIOR TO BEINGNESS?

Keep doing Self-enquiry: Who is acting through the body? Who is listening? Who is reading? Who is looking at me? The whole world is projected out of your Presence, Spontaneous Presence. That is the principle of all this spirituality.

SPIRITUALITY JUST MEANS TO KNOW YOURSELF
IN A REAL SENSE.

Q: I am torn between caring about the body and neglecting it.

Maharaj: Don't neglect the body. Take care of the body. The body is a medium. Just try to know that prior to all this body-knowledge, prior to the existence of the body, your Presence was there. It was Invisible,

Anonymous. I am talking about that Presence prior to beingness. Out of your Presence, the entire world is projected. What you are talking about is related to the body only.

YOU ARE TOTALLY SEPARATE FROM THE BODY.
YOU ARE TO CONVINCE YOURSELF OF THIS REALITY.
IT IS OPEN TRUTH.

So whatever knowledge you have, whatever spiritual knowledge, whatever you are doing, these are all body-related actions.

YOU CANNOT DO ANYTHING.
PRIOR TO BEINGNESS, THERE WAS NO 'I'.
WITHOUT YOUR PRESENCE, YOU CAN'T SAY 'I'.

I am talking about that Invisible Presence, that Anonymous Presence, which we call *Brahman*, *Atman*, *Paratmatman*, God. There is no limit. It is beyond sky. It is not encircled or confined. It is without limitations.

Q: With the meditation, should I just concentrate on "I am *Brahman*"? Is that all I should do?

Maharaj: You can do this. Be clear, meditation is bringing you closer and closer to Selfless Self. Meditation is a must. It is a medium.

Q: I am pretty sure the meditation I have been doing is wrong. I have been doing a Buddhist meditation where you just observe the flow of thoughts. It is like watching the thoughts. You are not doing anything, the thoughts just carry on as they will. Like Zen meditation, disciplining the body and letting the thoughts flow. That is all. It is not doing me any good at all. Very boring. It is so boring that I fall asleep.

Maharaj: Meditation should bring happiness. The purpose of meditation is to forget the entire world. You are measuring it, saying it is boring. Since you are measuring yourself in body-form or as an individual, that is what is making it feel boring.

There is no 'boring'. Who is bored? Concentrate on "Who is boring?" You are to concentrate on the meditator. Concentrate on the meditator when you are meditating, and eventually the meditator will disappear.

CONCENTRATE ON THE MEDITATOR,
AND EVENTUALLY THE MEDITATOR WILL DISAPPEAR.

Q: I don't believe in happiness or sadness, or emotion any more.

Maharaj: Happiness, sadness, emotion, peace, tension, depression, these words never existed prior to beingness. There was no happiness, no peace, no boredom, no depression.

Q: I am not looking to be happy or anything. I am looking to find out who or what I am, that is it. I don't care about peace or anything like that. Can the mind ever be still? Is it impossible to still the mind?

Maharaj: You have given birth to the mind. There is no mind, no intellect. I am inviting your attention as to how you were prior to body-knowledge, how you were prior to beingness. That is your Identity. It is because we came across the body-knowledge, that all these problems started. Mind, ego, intellect, happiness, unhappiness, depression, tension, boring, all these words appeared. We have given the meanings to these words. What do you mean by boring? What do you mean by depression? Who is bored? What do you mean by peace?

WHO WANTS PEACE?

Q: The body-mind wants peace.

Maharaj: The mind just means the flow of thoughts. The mind does not have any identity. You have given birth to the mind, the flow of thoughts. You know that you are witnessing the thoughts. You are totally different from the thoughts. All this mind, ego, intellect. When did you first learn of these words?

Q: Probably from useless books.

Maharaj: You came across the words when you came across the body. Prior to beingness, you did not know, "Who am I?" Your Presence was there, but you were unknown to that Presence. All this talk of my mind, my ego, is all body-based knowledge. I am trying to drive you away from body-based knowledge.

Q: So I just have to let go of everything, let go of all of that, completely?

Maharaj: Don't do any physical exercise, don't do any mental exercise. Try to know yourself in a real sense.

Q: I will listen to you one hundred per cent. I can see where I am so stuck. From talking with you, I can see how I have become so stuck.

Maharaj: Don't stress the brain. Be normal.

15.   The Body is the Neighbour's Child

Q: Maharaj, I have some severe problems.

Maharaj: All the saints like Jnaneshwar, Tukaram and Nisargadatta Maharaj faced many, many problems. They knew that all the difficulties that came their way would quickly vanish. Everybody says, "My problem is a great problem, bigger than everyone else's". These saints all faced challenging problems at some time or other, but they did not concern themselves with them because of their strong Conviction. The problems were seen as just passing clouds for the body.

Nisargadatta Maharaj used to share this good story: Next door, the neighbour's child is suffering from a high fever, a severe fever. You feel sorry for that child, very sorry. The child's temperature is very high, but you are helpless. You feel for the boy and his family, but at the same time, you know, "This is not my child, this is the neighbours' child". Similarly, this body [your body], is to be viewed and considered as if it were the neighbour's child.

Q: So your body is like the neighbour's child? You are to see it as if it were not your own, but someone else's?

Maharaj. Yes, this body, made of five elements, is the neighbour's child. You feel something unpleasant, sadness maybe, pity even, but at the same time, you understand, that this is not your child. "I am separate from all this". You are to convince yourself in this way because you are your own architect and your own Master.

Therefore, see the body as your neighbour's child. All feelings and all concepts are rooted through the body only. You are witnessing this, experiencing that. Prior to the body, there was nothing.

Spirituality teaches you how to emerge from all the problems that keep showing up. Prior to the body there were no problems. After the body there will be no problems. Presently, while holding the body, it will not be difficult to come out from all these problems, if you put this into practice.

**STAY WITH THE PRINCIPLE OF ULTIMATE TRUTH
THAT YOU ARE.
YOU ARE THE SOURCE OF THIS WORLD.**

You are the Source of this whole world. Firmness is needed, and Conviction that, "I am nothing to do with this world". Don't borrow thoughts from others, as this will only create problems and disturb your stability.

BE WITH YOU, AND LISTEN FROM THE ALL.
READ YOUR BOOK.
YOUR EDITION IS FINAL!

Everyone has different concepts. Ignore everyone else! You are Final Truth! Why have ego? Why let jealousy in? Why struggle? All these aspects affect Ultimate Truth. Spirit is sensitive. Spirit is very sensitive. If you put red dye in water, or blue dye, it will become those colours. Spirit is like this. Ignore what is to be ignored. Mould yourself in this way.

If you pay serious attention to all that is happening in this illusory world, you will be seriously disturbed.

YOU ARE THE ARCHITECT OF YOUR OWN SPIRITUAL LIFE.

If you follow this simple principle, then nothing is impossible. The 'Himalayas' are within you only. Why roam here and there? You are ignoring your own Master, and begging from other Masters.

STAY WITH YOUR INNER MASTER,
ONLY THEN WILL YOUR QUESTIONS DISSOLVE.

There are layers on your Invisible Presence. You know yourself through the body only, without knowing, "Who am I?"

Q: What does "I am" mean? Is it behind everything?

Maharaj: It is not behind! There is no behind! It means that you are to keep your attention on Ultimate Truth. Through it, you are experiencing your Spontaneous Presence. Without the Spirit, without *Atman*, you cannot experience your Selfless Self.

SPONTANEOUS EXISTENCE IS NOT BEHIND.
YOU ARE EVERYWHERE, LIKE SKY.
IS SKY BEHIND OR IN FRONT?

Measuring yourself in the body-form means that you are not aware of your existence. Everything is indicative of your Presence. Without your Presence, you can't see the world, or utter one single word. You are totally unknown. Then, all of a sudden you feel "I am".

THERE CAN BE NOTHING WITHOUT
YOUR INVISIBLE PRESENCE.
WITHOUT PRESENCE, YOU ARE POWERLESS AND
INCAPABLE OF TALKING ABOUT THE WORLD.
THIS IS THE MEANING OF
"EXCEPT YOUR SELFLESS SELF THERE IS NO GOD... ".
SELFLESS MEANS WITHOUT 'I',
WITHOUT SELF, LIKE SKY.

The great saint and philosopher, Shankaracharya says "I am not the body, I am *Mahatma*, the Great Soul". There has to be this Conviction.

You are the cause and consequence of the entire world, but unknown to yourself. 'Witness' is just a name that has been given to the Ultimate Truth. The witnesser or experiencer does not have any form.

This life is just a long dream, like a video shoot. But who is shooting the video, or taking these pictures, or capturing these images? We say, "I don't know", because we are unknown to ourselves. We are not in any form. Whose memories? Whose feelings? No one's! These are all bodily feelings, the wrong bytes that are on our hard drive.

THE BODY MAY BE SUFFERING, BUT NOT YOU.
I AM INVITING ATTENTION OF 'THAT':
AND HOW YOU WERE PRIOR TO BODY-KNOWLEDGE.

Q: Is the Invisible Presence in manifestation or not?
Maharaj: Neither! This is not a debate. There is nothing to analyze. Everything is calm and quiet.

BE CALM AND QUIET.

16. Escape from Body-Knowledge

Q: Maharaj, how can I escape from all this knowledge? I want liberation right now. Is there any exit from the mind, feelings, life, everything?
Maharaj: Of course! Why not? You are, and you have, nothing to do with any of this. What you are talking about are simply layers on your Spontaneous Presence. Even though you are living in this body, you are completely separate from it all. You say, "I want liberation right now". That's up to you. You want instant happiness, like 'fast food'.

WHEN YOU ACCEPT THAT YOU ARE NOT THE BODY,
ALL THESE FEELINGS YOU TALK ABOUT WILL DISAPPEAR.

These needs are orientated through the body. Who'll be wanting happiness and peace when Presence disappears?

HAPPINESS IS ALREADY WITHIN YOU.
YOU HAVE THE KEY,
JUST LIKE ALI BABA'S 'OPEN SESAME'.
THE CAVE OF JEWELS IS THERE FOR THE TAKING.
I AM NURTURING YOUR HAPPINESS AND MAKING IT GROW.

The purpose of spirituality is to exit the body in a happy mood. Who is leaving the body? Why? Don't take this literally. There is no point in applying the intellect when everything is Spontaneous Presence. I have to use words to convince you.

YOU ARE UNBORN, IMMORTAL, IMMORTAL.

We are removing all unwanted files from your hard drive. There are so many viruses inside, like fast-spreading bacteria. Meditation is your anti-virus software.

ONCE IT IS INSTALLED,
IT WILL LAST FOREVER,
NO ANNUAL SUBSCRIPTION!

Q: This Invisible Presence that you talk of, is it love?

Maharaj: You are in love with yourself. Love and affection started the moment the Spirit clicked with the body. Prior to beingness, there was no love and affection, nothing. All these terms came afterwards.

This body is the dirtiest body, but covered with nice skin. What is inside? Machinery. All the machinery does its own job: heart, lungs, liver, with power supplied to each organ. If the Spirit were not there for one second, the body would deteriorate. Therefore, you are wholly separate from this body.

YOU ARE NOT THE BODY,
YOU ARE FORMLESS,
SO, WHO IS LOVING WHOM?

You are just like sky or space. The word 'love' came when your Presence was limited to the body-form. 'Love' and 'affection' are body-related terms relevant only to the body-form.

YOU ARE NOT IN THE BODY-FORM,
THEREFORE THERE IS NOBODY THERE
TO TALK ABOUT LOVE AND AFFECTION.

Q: There is a lovely quote from Nisargadatta Maharaj that talks about wisdom and love.

Maharaj: Forget about what others say!

IT IS WHAT YOU SAY THAT IS ALL-IMPORTANT.
THIS IS THE ONLY THING THAT COUNTS.

I have told you that,

NOBODY IS GREATER THAN YOU.

If you are firm and have strong faith and involvement, you will be able to face the difficulties that keep coming.

Spirituality is not about clapping hands and placing some garlands here and there, it is a framework for daily living. Watch the ego, it is always creating problems, like "I am a spiritual man". There is no need of struggle, of jealousy, because your Presence is everywhere. Be calm and quiet and unconcerned with the world.

WHEN YOU ARE ONE WITH YOUR DEVOTION,
YOU ARE ONE WITH YOUR SELFLESS SELF.

This means your strength is coming out, a kind of spiritual intoxication. But you are not to take any ego from this, or misuse your power.

YOU WILL SEE THE PROGRESS.
THERE WILL BE TOTAL AND COMPLETE INNER SILENCE.
YOU ARE BEYOND THIS WORLD.

Sometimes you may fall victim to external circumstances via money, power or sex. Just remember that when the body expires, we will not be taking anything with us from this world. Great power will come from your devotion. Whatever you say, will happen. Be sincere, true to yourself, and be sincere with your Master.

I AM NOT EXPECTING ANYTHING FROM YOU.
I AM ASKING YOU TO
GIVE COMPLETE DEVOTION TO YOURSELF.

My happiness comes from your spiritual progress.

SHINE!
BE SHINING,
AND MAKE OTHERS SHINE!

Be happy and make others happy. And don't waste this Exceptional Knowledge. After having Ultimate Truth, you will be happy and you will want to share that happiness with others. Don't be selfish. Share it out. Don't waste the delicious food. After consuming the food, if anything remains, you have to distribute it to all these people who are needy. At the same time, exercise caution! Watch out for people who are feeding your ego: saying, for example, "You are a great man!"

YOU ARE NOT TO EXPECT OR ACCEPT
ANY BODY-RELATED CONCEPTS BECAUSE
EVERYTHING IS IN YOU.
THERE IS NOTHING EXCEPT SELFLESS SELF.
NOBODY IS GREATER THAN YOU.
THE ENTIRE UNIVERSE IS WITHIN YOU.
OPEN TRUTH!

17. *Erase All Memories*

Q: Maharaj, apart from the ego, there is also the subtle ego?

Maharaj: The subtle ego is connected with the body-knowledge. The existence of the ego, mind, intellect, these are all illusory concepts. Prior to beingness, there was no ego, there was no subtle ego. Because we are posing ourselves in the body-form, the subtle ego appears. The moment the body-knowledge dissolves and disappears, there will not be any ego. Meditation is required to reduce the force of the ego. 'Subtle ego' and so on, again, these are just words.

THE EGO ITSELF IS ILLUSION BECAUSE THERE IS NO 'I',
THERE IS NO 'YOU', THERE IS NO 'HE' OR 'SHE'.
THERE IS NOTHING THERE.
THE SCREEN IS COMPLETELY BLANK.

Q: And what about the mind?

Maharaj: There is no mind at all. Mind does not have any existence of its own. It is just the flow of thoughts. No mind, no ego. You have given birth to the ego. Before birth, there was no ego at all. Prior to beingness, no ego, no mind. Nothing!

THE 'STATE' WAS ONE IN WHICH WE WERE
UNKNOWN TO OURSELVES.

Where does the ego go after leaving the body? We are talking ego, mind, intellect, so many things that are within the circle, the burden of body-knowledge.

I draw your attention to the words of Shankaracharya: "To say 'I' is illusion, to say 'You' is illusion, to say '*Brahman*' is illusion. The entire world is illusion". So where is the ego? Where is it located?

Q: If one person is humble and another person is full of ego, does that mean that it's easier for the humble one to get rid of ego? And often, I have noticed, with those who consider themselves to be humble, the subtle ego is at work, whether knowingly or unknowingly.

Maharaj: The body is there and the ego is there, but there is no body and no ego. Don't pay special attention to the ego or the subtle ego, or to whether the ego is small or big. Why do you want to measure and compare if you have a bigger ego than me?

Keep one principle in mind: The body is not your identity, the body was not your identity, the body is not going to remain your identity. Meditation, knowledge and *bhajans* - why are they necessary? Because along with the body, you started considering yourself in the body-form, as a separate individual. This has led to a strong attachment to the body, with the result that you now have a lot of love and affection for the body-form. It has become very dear to you.

JUST THINK ABOUT IT.
PRIOR TO THE BODY,
THERE WAS NOTHING.
THERE WAS NO NAME, NO REQUIREMENTS, NO DEMANDS.
WE DID NOT KNOW HAPPINESS OR UNHAPPINESS, OR PEACE.
THERE WAS NOTHING AT ALL.

Q: You say that the mind is just the flow of thoughts. My problem is that I have a lot of thoughts going round and round in my head. They never seem to stop. They seem to carry me along, sweep me away. What can I do?

Maharaj: It is natural. Don't give it so much importance. Thoughts are going to flow, but you have not to give them cognizance. It is simple:

PRIOR TO BEINGNESS, THERE WERE NO THOUGHTS.
THE MOMENT YOU CAME ACROSS WITH THE BODY,
THOUGHTS STARTED FLOWING.

Now, you know better! You know that the body is not your identity. So, use the thoughts that appear useful, and restrict the thoughts that are not useful. It is simple!

Q: I do know better. I am beginning to change my view of things, but I think it takes time. Even though I know different, I still get depressed and feel anxious about things.

Maharaj: This happens to the body because it is affected by the external atmosphere and the internal atmosphere.

BUT YOU ARE TOTALLY APART FROM ALL THIS.
YOU ARE ENTIRELY DIFFERENT TO ALL OF THIS.

Today's feeling or mood may not be tomorrow's mood. Happiness or unhappiness are veils on your Presence. Since you are holding the body, it is bound to be affected by the atmosphere. So this type of experience, these feelings, or layers of feeling happen, but they will not remain constant.

TODAY, YOU ARE FEELING A DEPRESSION,
TOMORROW,
YOU WILL BE FEELING HAPPINESS,
BUT THE WITNESSER IS THE SAME.

THAT PRESENCE THAT IS WITNESSING
HAPPINESS OR UNHAPPINESS IS ALWAYS THE SAME.

Put simply, 'happiness' is the name given to good feelings that come from things that you find tolerable. Conversely, things which you cannot tolerate, and produce negative feelings in you, we call 'unhappiness'. For example, when you have a headache, you think, "I am not comfortable". But if you take a tablet, a painkiller, then, relief: "Oh! I am comfortable". Thoughts and feelings are momentary illusions and undeserving of your attention.

SO, FOR TIMES LIKE THESE,
YOU HAVE TO TAKE A SPIRITUAL TABLET
TO REMIND YOU OF YOUR IDENTITY.

When you are in some pain, you will immediately take a tablet which will relieve it instantly. Likewise, if you feel a depression or lethargy or unhappiness, take your spiritual medicine, quickly. That way, you will feel, "I am unconcerned with these feelings of depression, anxiety, or lethargy".

BLACK CLOUDS ARE COMING,
BLACK CLOUDS ARE GOING,
THE SUN IS, AS IT IS.

Q: And the spiritual tablet is?

Maharaj: The spiritual tablet means turning your attention to the fact that:

I AM NOTHING TO DO WITH THE BODY-FORM.
I HAVE NOTHING TO DO WITH THE BODY-FORM.
I AM NOT THE BODY, I WAS NOT THE BODY,
I AM NOT GOING TO REMAIN THE BODY.
WHATEVER IS HAPPENING TO THE BODY IS UNCERTAIN.
IT IS NOT REALITY.

Q: We are to turn our attention away from the seen, and bring it back to the Seer. Stay with the permanent, not the impermanent?

Maharaj: Yes! So let's be clear about spirituality, and why we are doing what we are doing here. We are reading, we are listening, we are studying, meditating, singing *bhajans*. Why?

WE ARE TO ERASE ALL THE MEMORIES
FROM THE TIME THE SPIRIT CLICKED WITH THE BODY,
RIGHT UP UNTIL TODAY.

You have to undergo the process of meditation, *bhajan* and Knowledge, so that you can absorb Open Truth. These activities are also illusion, but they are the basics, and therefore necessary in the beginning. Bhausaheb Maharaj stressed the importance of innocent devotion, without concepts, ego, intellect, mind.

THESE PRACTICES ARE LIKE LADDERS, STEPS,
TO LIFT YOU UP.
ONCE YOU GET THERE, YOU CAN THROW THE LADDERS AWAY.

With various words, in different ways and from different angles, the Master is trying to convince you of your Reality.

YOU ARE ULTIMATE REALITY.
YOU ARE ULTIMATE TRUTH.
YOU ARE FINAL REALITY.

18. *You are Formless*

Q: Can I reach this Final Truth by myself, without meditation?
Maharaj:

MEDITATION ACTS LIKE A LADDER, OR LIFT.
CAN YOU CLIMB TEN FLOORS WITHOUT A LIFT?

Meditation is not needed after Conviction because when you have Conviction, you will KNOW. This body is called 'John'. Do you need to keep repeating your name? No! Your name was given to you by your parents, and it is fixed. You have the Conviction that you are John.

It is the same here. After Conviction, you will KNOW that "I am *Brahman, Brahman*". After some time, without your knowledge, twenty-four hour reciting will be happening automatically, spontaneously. The Mantra is needed to forget the body identity.

Q: What about other Mantras from other traditions?
Maharaj: Forget about other Mantras! What happened to me can happen to you, too. When you embrace the Reality fully, you will be able to talk spontaneously like me! Bodies are different but there is no difference between the Spirit. John is the name of the external cover. Do we talk about Indian sky, Chinese sky, Russian sky? No! Sky is the same.

YOUR SPONTANEOUS PRESENCE HAS
NO EGO, INTELLECT, MIND.

The sole purpose of meditation, and all this listening to Knowledge, is to dissolve knowledge. You must have a strong will and internal strength. You have hidden power. Be calm and quiet.

DON'T THINK IT!
DON'T APPLY YOUR INTELLECT, MIND!
BE WITH YOU.
DON'T BE WITH MIND,
EGO,
INTELLECT.

Be your own teacher. You know you are Ultimate Truth, beyond happiness, beyond silence. Forget and forgive because you are the Source of this world. Think of these discourses as stories that are all connected with your Selfless Self.

LIVE AS YOU WERE PRIOR TO BEINGNESS.

Q: But I don't know how that was.
Maharaj: No, you don't! "Don't know" means you are not in any form. It means you are formless like sky. And like the sky, you cannot die. When I say, "I don't know", I am saying "I am not in body-form". If I say, "I know", then some illusion is there. "I don't know" is the perfect answer. You can enjoy this now and then go

deeper and deeper and deeper. Enjoy swimming! It is rare, very rare.

Q: But we need patience and practice?

Maharaj: The question of patience never arises because you are not a patient. Patience is only required for the patient!

Q: Daily talks are like an injection. They really work!

Maharaj: The grace of my Masters.

Q: We are very honoured.

Maharaj: It's the rare and the rarest Knowledge.

Q: And the Knowledge has to dissolve too.

Maharaj: Yes, yes.

So, listen carefully. Presence is required to say, "I am". But this Spontaneous Presence does not have any individual identity because it is Anonymous, Unidentified Identity. Except your Selfless Self, there is no God, no Master, no *Brahman*, *Atman*, No *Paramatman*. This Conviction is supposed to appear spontaneously.

AT PRESENT, ALL THAT YOU KNOW,
HAS ONLY BEEN KNOWN BECAUSE OF THE BODY.

The "I don't know" answer has many meanings. The Spontaneous Presence came into existence in the body-form. Most importantly, "I don't know" communicates the fact that your Presence was there prior to beingness, but not in any form. You are formless.

Egoistic knowledge creates confusion and conflict. Spiritual Knowledge indicates one's Unidentified, Invisible Identity. Routine life carries on as normal, but one can live peacefully after knowing the Reality. Of course, there is no obligation to accept this Reality. You can act on it, or react to it. It is up to you! Reality is Reality, and not up for debate, discussion or argument.

Q: You say you must have faith.

Maharaj: Yes, you must have faith in yourself. If I am a man, I accept it, like that.

FAITH IS RELATIVE TO WHAT IS BEING IMPRESSED ON YOU.
HAVE FAITH
THAT YOU ARE ULTIMATE TRUTH.
KEEP FAITH IN THE MASTER'S WORDS.

With these talks, I am presenting you with your Truth, your immovable Truth. You are *Brahman*, *Paramatman*, Absolute Truth. You cannot move sky from America to India, can you?

Q: You are moving us from India to the Absolute!

Maharaj: Nobody is moving! Nothing is moving, there is no moving.

WHEN YOU ACCEPT THE MASTER'S WORDS ABSOLUTELY,
THAT IS CALLED FAITH.

Master says this is not your identity. You are just like the sky. Your Presence is everywhere.

WHATEVER I HAVE TOLD YOU SO FAR, DIGEST IT.
IF I GIVE YOU AN OVERDOSE,
IT WILL NOT BE POSSIBLE FOR YOU TO DIGEST IT.

19.   The Secret of Spiritual Life

Maharaj: One boy, Eklavya wanted to learn archery. The Master Dronacharya was a great archery teacher. He used to teach the King's family. Eklavya was about twelve years old, and came from a lower caste. He observed Dronacharya teaching some small boys. He approached this Master and asked him to teach him archery. The Master dismissed him, saying the boy would not understand his instructions.

Eklavya was determined. He decided to make an idol, a statue of Dronacharya, and took him as his Master. He put all his faith in the Master, and learned the skill of archery from that namesake. This statue was empowered by Eklavya's faith in the Master.

Guided by his Master, he practised archery every day. He asked the statue: "Am I aiming this correctly or not?" The inner voice said, "Yes, correct my boy!" In this way, through Direct Knowledge, he perfected the skills of archery.

Sometime later, there was a contest. Dronacharya made an announcement: "See that dog over there, it will keep its mouth open. You must fire the arrow straight in, in such a way that it doesn't touch anything or cause any harm". Arjuna was the first to fire. He had learned from his Master. He fired the arrow, but it did not hit the target. Eklavya's turn came. He fired the arrow perfectly and won the contest.

Dronacharya was amazed. He asked Eklavya: "Where did you learn such skill?" Eklavya replied: "Master, you have given me this knowledge". Dronacharya said, "No you did not learn this from me!" Eklavya explained that he had made an idol of his Master, and that was how he received the knowledge.

The next part of the story is most important. Dronacharya said, "OK, you are now my disciple, but you have to offer me something". "I will give you anything you ask", he said. To test his faith, Dronacharya demands Eklavya's thumb. [Here, cutting off the thumb means acknowledging the Source of Knowledge: it is the Master's Knowledge, and not his own.] Eklavya obeys.

This story has deep meaning. You must have strong faith in the Master, whether he is in the body or not. With full concentration, full faith, full trust like Eklavya, Spontaneous Knowledge will arise. This is an example of inner dialogue which happens when there is full self-involvement. It is the highest devotion, the last devotion, 'Talking with Selfless Self', (*Atma Nivedanam Bhakti*). You have to convince your Selfless Self. It means address yourself, ask yourself inwardly.

ADDRESS YOURSELF,
ASK YOURSELF INWARDLY.

Inner questioning and answering take place. You are convincing yourself. Questions and replies are appearing instantly, without anybody's help. This happens because the Master is already within you. It is conversation with Selfless Self.

Your trust and faith are essential, so that your Conviction can grow and become like that demonstrated by Eklavya. Complete faith in you and in the Master cannot be stressed enough. In India and elsewhere, miracles happen to many people who have this kind of strong faith in stone idols. You may wonder how this is possible?

THE STONE IS ONLY A NAMESAKE.
MIRACLES HAPPEN BECAUSE YOU ARE THE PRINCIPLE.

FIRST HAVE FAITH IN YOU,
AND THEN FAITH IN GOD.

You can talk about everything under the sun with the use of the intellect.

BUT WITH STRONG FAITH,
YOU CAN MAKE SOMETHING MANIFEST.

Real faith means to serve the Master without any ego. Don't misuse your power. Sometimes things may happen that you have willed to happen. If this occurs, don't take any ego for it will spoil your spiritual life. Individuality is supposed to melt away.

IF YOU HAVE COMPLETE FAITH IN YOURSELF,
THIS MEANS THAT
YOU BECOME ONE WITH THE UNIVERSE.
IT IS SELFLESS DEVOTION.

All the great saintly people had immense faith in their Masters, so much so, that nothing could affect them. Be devoted to your Selfless Self and watch the miracles unfold. Don't share these with anyone, as it will allow the ego to take hold of your spiritual body and then you might say, "I've had this and that experience". This will lead to a feeling of superiority, and you will think or say, something like: "You don't know anything", and start making comparisons. This is not good for the Spirit and will spoil and complicate your devotion. Have faith and trust in this simple Knowledge.

20.   The Guru is More Than a Mirror

Maharaj: It is very rare to find a Master with Direct Knowledge who can show you that you are Reality, Ultimate Truth, Final Truth. Nisargadatta Maharaj says, "I am not making you disciples, I am making you Masters". Swami Vivekananda searched for such a Master.

Q: Yes! I know the story very well. I read that Vivekananda looked for some time, asking various Masters if they had experienced God, and could show him God within him. No one said 'Yes', including, Devendranath Tagore, [Rabindranath's father]. But he did say, "You have the eyes of a Yogi, and you are most certainly going to self-realize in this lifetime".

It was only when he met with Ramakrishna Paramahamsa, that he finally got the answer he was looking for. Ramakrishna said, "Yes, I have seen God. I can show you".

Maharaj: Nisargadatta Maharaj says: "The Master is already within you, but you are unaware".

Q: So, is the Master sleeping?

Maharaj: You have forgotten your identity because of external forces. You have become unaware of your Reality because of the many and varied experiences and impressions throughout your lifetime.

Q: So the active role of the Guru is to enable or assist, and encourage the awakening of that which is already in you?

Maharaj: The Master, or Guru, is encouraging you and impressing Reality in you. He is placing before you your Ultimate Reality, which you have forgotten. You are underestimating yourself.

YOU ARE THINKING THAT YOU ARE SOMEBODY.
YOU ARE NOBODY,
AND YET,
YOU ARE EVERYBODY.

That Knowledge should be spontaneous, a Spontaneous Conviction. It can happen, like it happened with Nisargadatta Maharaj. It is not difficult, especially with your deepness, your strong faith. Realize this Truth - it is open fact. For example, [Maharaj lifts up a handkerchief], this is called a 'handkerchief'. I know! Likewise, when you realize the Reality, you will say 'I know!' just like that.

YOUR SPONTANEOUS PRESENCE
IS CALLED *BRAHMAN*, *ATMAN*, *PARAMATMAN*, GOD.
THIS BODY IS ONLY THE EXTERNAL COVER.

Once you know the Reality, you will carry on as before, living with the body, but at the same time knowing, 'It is not my identity'. The effect of this Self-Knowledge will leave you fearless. You will not have any fear of death at all, and all those body-related concepts of hell and heaven will also go.

Q: Is the Guru not like a mirror, so that we can see our reflection, that which we clearly are?

Maharaj: The Guru is more than a mirror. A mirror only has one side, the Guru shows you all sides.

Q: You remind us of our true Identity, by helping us to discriminate between the true and the false, the permanent and the impermanent. With discrimination, we become less attached...

Maharaj: Forget all that you have read! It is a big story. Forget this body-form with all its knowledge. You have just been playing with the words, with all these literal names that you found in books. You have just been playing with dolls! You have been amusing yourself, playing a children's game in your little world that is full of colourful literal words.

YOU ARE ULTIMATE! YOU ARE UNBORN!

Q: What is the relationship between the Guru and the disciple, or the Master and the student?

Maharaj: As a matter of fact, there is no 'Guru' and no 'disciple'. There is no relationship. There is only 'Selfless Self', 'Oneness', 'Ultimate Truth'. I have to step down, as it were, and take the role of the 'Guru', in order to teach, while you take on the role of the 'disciple'. But we are only posing as these for a time. Ultimately, there is no Guru and no disciple. Nisargadatta Maharaj used to say:

EXCEPT [FOR] YOUR SELFLESS SELF, THERE IS NO GOD,
NO *BRAHMAN*, NO *ATMAN*,
NO *PARAMATMAN*, NO MASTER.

Q: I feel that when you are talking, and teaching, something is happening on a deeper level that is hard to explain. If it is not to be understood as a 'relationship' between the Guru and the disciple, then what exactly is happening?

Maharaj: There is only Selfless Self. Your Spontaneous Presence is Invisible, Anonymous, Unidentified Identity. For understanding purposes, we can say that:

THE MASTER IS THE INVISIBLE SPEAKER AND
THE DISCIPLE IS THE INVISIBLE LISTENER.

The Master is addressing the Invisible Listener in you. They are one and the same: Ultimate Reality.

After all, there is only ever Oneness.

I AM NOT TALKING TO YOU,
I AM ADDRESSING THE SILENT INVISIBLE LISTENER IN YOU.

Q: I don't understand why, but in your Presence, Maharaj, there is a feeling of peace and happiness.

Maharaj: Don't try to understand! The Invisible Listener, call it Spirit, if you wish, likes to hear its own story. The Master is refreshing the memory of its Identity and prompting it to reawaken.

YOU MAY NOT UNDERSTAND,
BUT THE INVISIBLE REALITY DOES.

And it is One with the Master's words. You are covered in ash. Underneath the fire is burning. Master removes the ash.

Q: What you are saying, Maharaj, is that our True Identity has been buried under lots of layers, layers of illusion?

Maharaj: We are unaware of our importance, our real value. Since childhood, we have received non-stop impressions. All these have given us a false picture of ourselves, a false identity. You perceive yourself as something else, a separate entity who is apart and different from Reality. It is not true.

And even those of you who claim to have spiritual knowledge, that knowledge, is really of little use, because it is only literal knowledge.

TO SAY, "I AM *BRAHMAN*" IS ALSO ILLUSION,
BECAUSE YOU ARE CONSIDERING YOURSELF TO BE '*BRAHMAN*', USING THE MEDIUM OF
THE BODY-FORM.

'*Brahman*' is only a name.

ALL THIS KNOWLEDGE MUST BE ABSORBED.
ALL THIS KNOWLEDGE MUST BE ABSORBED.

The musk deer is famous for the scent it produces. It will sometimes go mad over its own powerful fragrance. It chases everywhere after the intense scent, not knowing that the perfume is coming from itself. The deer has that fragrance. However, because it is unaware, it is trying to find out the location, the source. The disciple behaves like the deer, until someone, [eg, the Master], comes along to bring enlightenment, and says: "This fragrance is coming from you".

YOU ARE THE PRINCIPLE, YOU ARE THE MASTER.
YOU ARE EVERYTHING. YOU ARE UNLIMITED.

We need to keep saying the same thing in many different ways, just to establish Ultimate Truth. You are Final Truth. OK.

21. The Master Regenerates Your Power

Maharaj: The Guru or Master KNOWS. He does not see or measure himself in the body-form. He is out of the circle of body-knowledge. He is Ultimate, and from that position, he is inviting attention of the Invisible, Anonymous Listener in you, and reminding you of Reality: "You are Ultimate. You are Final Truth". The Master tells you that there is nothing to fear because you are the Source. Therefore, when all activities end, full stop, dead, the search is over.

IN FACT, THERE IS NO SEARCH BECAUSE
THE SEARCHER IS ALREADY THE ULTIMATE.

Q: But all these years of seeking? I have been a seeker, a searcher, for as long as I can remember.

Maharaj: There is no 'seeker' or 'searcher', so don't try to find the searcher through body-knowledge, either intellectually, logically, or egoistically. There is just Spontaneous Reality. It is your Spontaneous Reality. It does not think, "Oh! I am *Brahman*, I am *Atman* or *Paramatman*". It is Spontaneous Reality. And, you are to maintain this Reality so as to prevent external forces, which will always be circulating nearby, from distracting you.

Q: That is why it is important for you to keep hammering, and repeating the same things over and over again.

Maharaj: Same, yes, because it is necessary. The Master is regenerating your power. The Power is there, but it is covered with ash. Master removes the ash that is in the form of illusory thoughts and concepts, etc.

Q: During the day-time, thoughts trouble me more than at night-time. What about time? Today is the last day of the year.

Maharaj: There is no day-time and there is no night-time. The limitations of time do not apply to you. As you know, you are not the body, so why give attention to day and night? Your day is someone else's night and vice versa. Time is connected to the body alone. So many concepts come through the body. Was there time prior to beingness? No, there was nothing. Be convinced and have Conviction.

There were no concepts, no need of God, no need of food prior to body-knowledge. Where was the mind, ego, intellect? Nowhere! There was nothing! There was no need of a Master either because there was no disciple. You were not a disciple. The 'Master-disciple' concept came when your Presence appeared in the world.

Q: But we do need a Master now?

Maharaj: A realized Master is essential at the initial stage.

THE MASTER IS BASICALLY A MEDIUM, A CHANNEL,
A MEANS THROUGH WHICH YOU CAN KNOW YOURSELF.

Without him, you would not be able to know yourself in a real sense. The Master is inviting attention of the Silent Invisible Listener: You are *Brahman*!

Q: Before we came over to see you, Jenny said to me "We have to get a Guru". I disagreed, as I have always done on the subject of Gurus, saying, "No, no, no, you can do it yourself like Ramana Maharshi did, or the Buddha". She asked me how many, apart from Ramana Maharshi, had Self-Realized? I had to agree that it is a very rare thing to be able to do it by yourself. It is almost impossible, isn't it?

Maharaj: You have come to the place where the Knowledge is Direct. Knowing oneself in a real sense is Knowledge. I am not talking about second-hand knowledge, and all the knowledge that you have accumulated through learning and study. No! This knowledge will not help you.

WHAT IS THE USE OF ALL THIS KNOWLEDGE?
WHO IS IT FOR?
IT IS FOR THE 'UNBORN CHILD'.

Everything is within you. You are the Source of Knowledge. I am talking about that. I am talking about your innate Knowledge. You may be a spiritual Master. You may have read thousands of books and achieved mastery over words. You may be a Master of spiritual words, but:

WILL THIS KNOWLEDGE HELP YOU?
WILL ALL THESE WORDS HELP YOU,
WHEN THE TIME COMES FOR YOU TO LEAVE THE BODY?

Q: I don't know. I have read a lot, so I hope so, fingers crossed!

Maharaj: Now is the time for you to find out. Don't leave it till it is too late! Do Self-enquiry and find out where you stand! Stop! Put the books away. Go within. Read your own book.

Q: I know, I know! I will! I'll do more. Maharaj, people say that spirituality is anti-life and things like that because you are sort of turning away from the world and going within, aren't you? You are looking inside, and everybody's looking outside, not everybody, but many.

Maharaj: There is no inside, no outside, no side at all! It is not necessary to make any deliberate effort to know yourself. You need not make any effort to know yourself. This is a direct approach. Everything is Spontaneous.

But in the beginning, to reach this Ultimate Truth, to have this Ultimate Truth, you have to undergo the discipline of meditation. There is no difference between the Invisible Speaker and the Invisible Listener.

AFTER CONVICTION,
THERE WILL BE ABSOLUTE PEACE,
COMPLETE PEACE.

You will be totally free in yourself. Then you will see:

MY PRESENCE IS EVERYWHERE.
MY PRESENCE IS IN EVERY BEING.

Be simple and humble! Beware of any disturbance from the mind, ego, intellect, with such thoughts as: "Soon, I will be self-realized", or "I am an enlightened person". Beware of difficulties that threaten to pull you back into illusion.

Nisargadatta Maharaj used to say, "When unpleasant circumstances appear in life, you go to the Ultimate Truth". He therefore saw difficulties as challenges to be welcomed. He used to say, "I invite unpleasant atmospheres, and unpleasant things. If I am fortunate, I will welcome all these difficulties".

Q: Well he was fortunate to meet Siddharameshwar Maharaj quite late.

Maharaj: He only spent about three years maximum with Siddharameshwar Maharaj.

Q: So he was lucky to get in before...

Maharaj: The foundation was already there in him, so everything just clicked into place. To say 'just clicked' is accurate because he had exceptional knowledge. When he listened to the lectures of Siddharameshwar Maharaj, he was so greatly impressed, that he accepted it all totally and completely. He had high, high faith in his Master. He had such a strong faith in Siddharameshwar Maharaj, that he would say, "My Master is Ultimate".

Later on, when well-read foreigners used to ask him some very tricky questions, he answered them immediately, and spontaneously, without any difficulty. He replied instantly, saying, "This is happening by the grace of my Master".

Q: Amazing, yes, absolutely fantastic. I mean, that's what got people going in the West. It was like anybody could come and ask, you know...

Maharaj: Maurice Frydman used to ask some very tricky questions because he had also studied different philosophies and spiritual disciplines. He had gone through so many Masters, Ramana Maharshi, J. Krishnamurti, and all the rest. He was very impressed by Nisargadatta Maharaj and said, "This is exceptional knowledge".

Q: The Master's Knowledge?

Maharaj: You will never find this Knowledge in any books. Books go round, taking you round and round. Here, this is a Direct Approach, Direct Knowledge.

Q: And Siddharameshwar Maharaj himself gave all credit to Bhausaheb Maharaj, so it is a very strong connection right through the whole Lineage?

Maharaj: Siddharameshwar Maharaj had a deep faith, a strong faith in Bhausaheb Maharaj. This Knowledge is Spontaneous Knowledge, it is not bookish knowledge, it is Spontaneous Knowledge.

Q: And the only variation is?

Maharaj: Of course, of course, the words are different, the style of speaking is different, but the principle is the same: There is NOTHING BUT your Selfless Self. There is no God, no *Brahman*, no *Atman*, no *Paramatman*, no Master APART FROM your Selfless Self. You are the Source. Everything is within you. The fire is there but it is covered with ash. The Master removes the ash.

Q: And then there will be an explosion, 'Boom', a big fire!

Maharaj: Yes! It is the merging process, like the bucket of water and sea idea that I mentioned. If you pour a bucket of water into the sea, you will not be able to remove that water because it has merged with the sea. It is like that when you Realize.

WHEN YOU REALIZE,
YOUR INDEPENDENT IDENTITY WILL NOT REMAIN.
WHEN YOU REALIZE,
THE INDEPENDENT IDENTITY OF SOMEONE ELSE
WILL NOT REMAIN EITHER. IT DISSOLVES.
AT THAT MOMENT, AT THAT PARTICULAR STAGE,
YOU WILL FORGET YOUR ENTIRE IDENTITY.

Your Presence is. Your Presence is there. Your Presence is not somebody or something else. Without neglecting the body, you will know. You will know, in this way:

I AM LIVING IN THIS HOUSE. [ie the body]
THIS IS MY TEMPORARY DWELLING PLACE,
BUT I AM ETERNAL.

Using different angles and dimensions, the role of the Master is to try and convince you of your Reality. Your role is that of accepting what the Master is trying to convey, and also of convincing yourself.

Q: I wanted to ask one more thing, about the *Aarti* part of the worship. I came in late this morning, and a few people were making a fuss because I was about to cross to the other side of the room, at what must have been an important part of the worship.

Maharaj: First of all, lighting the fire and its significance, the *aarti* ritual, is a custom, a concept. It is the custom not to cross the line that is marked down the middle of the hall, when the fire is lit, because all these deities, many deities are present here in a very, very subtle way. So you have not to disturb them, by crossing the line at this time. Like the *bhajans* and meditation, this is an aspect of devotion, concentration. You are reminding yourself that you are Ultimate Truth.

22. *Visit Your Own Website*

Maharaj: Without Presence, who can study philosophy or spirituality, *lakhs* of words, the *Brahman*, *Atman*, God, Master, disciple? No one! When did you come across all these words? What is the use of all these words? Self-enquire! Find out! Don't just keep reading, reading, reading.

"How were you prior to beingness? What will happen to you after the beingness is dissolved? Who requires peace and a fearless life?" These questions need to be cleared up, and that is why you are undergoing philosophical study, and knowledge and spiritual knowledge. But you must go deeper.

YOU HAVE TO GO DEEPER TO THE ROOT CAUSE,
INSTEAD OF THINKING ABOUT THE CONSEQUENCE.
GO TO THE ROOT CAUSE AND FIND OUT
WHY YOU ARE READING ALL THESE SPIRITUAL BOOKS.
GO TO THE ROOT AND FIND OUT
WHY ALL THIS SPIRITUAL KNOWLEDGE IS NEEDED.

The purpose of knowledge is a body-based purpose. The knowledge is needed for the body-base. Body-based knowledge is only for the body. Now that you know you are not the body, you will come to realize that the purpose of all your spiritual reading and knowledge was simply to lead you to knowing yourself in a real sense. It was leading you to your Identity. What is your Identity?

YOUR EXISTING IDENTITY IS UNIDENTIFIED IDENTITY.
YOUR EXISTING IDENTITY IS UNIDENTIFIED,
INVISIBLE, ANONYMOUS IDENTITY.

Then you will ask yourself, "Why all this reading?" YOU are not to be found in books. YOU are not within words. All you have to do is accept and know that "You are Ultimate Reality". Everything is within you, so:

KNOW THYSELF, AND BE WITHIN SELFLESS SELF.
Know Thyself and be within Selfless Self.
LOOK WITHIN YOURSELF.
READ YOUR BOOK. VISIT YOUR TEMPLE.
SEARCH YOUR WEBSITE.

Spiritual knowledge gives you an indication of your Ultimate Truth. It is not Ultimate Truth.

YOU ARE ULTIMATE TRUTH.

You must have this Conviction. You are prior to everything. Knowledge came after. Prior to all this knowledge there was your Presence. To even talk about this Knowledge, your Presence is required. Your

Presence is Invisible, Anonymous.

Q: You are talking about a mystery, of something that is beyond understanding?

Maharaj: It is not exactly understanding, it is Reality.

**WHEN YOU UNDERSTAND SOMETHING,
IT IS SEPARATE FROM YOU.
YOU ARE REALITY.**

When you use a word like understanding, which means that you understand something, remember that your Presence is behind all that. I am inviting the attention of that Spontaneous Presence, through which you are talking, through which the entire world is projected.

**WITHOUT YOUR PRESENCE
YOU CAN'T UTTER A SINGLE WORD.
YOU CAN'T TALK ABOUT ANY SPIRITUAL KNOWLEDGE.
YOU CAN'T TALK ABOUT ANY SPIRITUAL MASTER.**

You have become a victim of words. As I told you before, we assigned meanings to all the words. Where was the alphabet prior to beingness? I am talking about how you were prior to beingness. There was no confusion, no conflict, no words, no language, nothing. You were, but not in any visible form. I am talking about 'That' - prior to beingness.

**BOOKISH KNOWLEDGE IS NOT ULTIMATE.
THOUSANDS OF *LAKHS* OF BOOKS ARE OUT THERE,
HOW MANY READERS OF THESE BOOKS
HAVE SELF-REALIZED?**

I'm trying to simplify the knowledge using various examples.

Q: You are succeeding.

23.   Swim in the Sea, Not in a Puddle.

Maharaj: All experiences are progressive steps and not Ultimate Truth. Whatever is experienced is not Ultimate Truth.

LOOK AT YOU!

And how you were prior to beingness. The basic Truth is that you are *Atman, Brahman, Paramatman*. You forgot your Identity.

With the help of meditation, we are inviting the attention of the Ultimate Truth which is already within you, but covered with the body-form. When Reality eventually comes out, it will be an exceptional experience: "I am Everywhere, Immortal, Omnipresent". By then, all concepts will have vanished and will not dare to enter the spiritual life.

Q: So it will be like pure Presence without any concepts?

Maharaj: Correct. No experience, no experiencer.

Q: Why are external things still causing problems?

Maharaj: Because you are still measuring yourself in the body-form. Difficulties will be there, let them come and let them go. Things are moving just like in the movies. The screen is blank but so many things are happening on the screen. Afterwards you get up and walk away from the movie. In this way, you have to convince yourself. You are to just walk away. Whatever goes on in the circus, Reality is unmoved by the show. I will hammer you again:

ALL EXTERNAL THINGS APPEARED
UPON YOUR SPONTANEOUS PRESENCE.

Your Spontaneous Presence is free of concepts. Prior to beingness, there was no external, or internal. All these questions are just related to body-knowledge. After leaving the body, again, there will be no external, no internal. Body-knowledge has to dissolve. This is the basis of spirituality.

ACCEPT THE TRUTH THAT YOU ARE ABSOLUTE,
WITHOUT UTTERING A SINGLE WORD.

Q: You often say that literal knowledge is not enough.

Maharaj: Literal knowledge means connected with words, theoretical knowledge. All your questions are related to literal knowledge.

I AM TALKING ABOUT PRIOR TO KNOWLEDGE.

Literal knowledge is connected to books that offer some indications. Books are worldly knowledge, theoretical knowledge. Theory and practice always differ. You may understand the theory behind swimming, therefore you know how to swim, but you still can't actually swim, in a practical sense.

There are libraries full of books that inform you about spiritual knowledge. They may be indicating some truths to you but:

YOU ARE TO INVOLVE YOURSELF,
AND THROW YOURSELF INTO THIS SPIRITUAL OCEAN.
ONLY THEN,
CAN YOU SAY THAT YOU ARE SWIMMING.

Word knowledge is simply theoretical knowledge.

There is a story about a German-made printing machine that broke down in Bangalore. Different employees and engineers tried to fix it, without success. They could not get the machine to start. Eventually, they called an employee with simple knowledge and common sense. He said: "Get me a hammer!" He hits the machine with the hammer and gives it a jolt. Immediately, it starts working. Countless engineers were unable to repair the machine, but one simple man, with hands-on experience succeeded. That is practical knowledge!

Literal and bookish knowledge is not practical knowledge. There are numerous Masters talking about spiritual books, *Vedanta*, etc, but they have no practical knowledge.

PRACTICAL KNOWLEDGE MEANS
YOU HAVE THE CONVICTION THAT
"I AM NOT THE BODY".

Practical Knowledge! Spontaneous Conviction is not literal conviction. Just like you are living as 'John'. If someone writes your biography, it may be perfect, but it is nevertheless you alone who can live the life of John. Or, if someone sees Nashik Ashram, and he writes something about his knowledge of it, this is very different from your every day, hands-on, practical living in Nashik Ashram. You know! You have practical knowledge! What I am talking about is practical knowledge, not bookish knowledge.

AT PRESENT,
YOU ARE STANDING ON THE SEA SHORE,
YOU ARE NOT SWIMMING IN THE ACTUAL SPIRITUAL OCEAN.

24. *Stand on your Own Feet*

Maharaj: When you meet a Realized Master, he will confirm what you have already read in books, and tell you that the entire world is illusion. He will prove this to you by placing the evidence before you.

There are two kinds of awakening: physical and spiritual. The physical wake-up is when the Spirit clicks with the body, and you see the world. The spiritual wake-up means that from the beginning, you have been under the influence of the illusionary world.

You believed in a concept of God as some kind of supernatural power who governed the world. Who is God? What is God? You don't know. You have some idea of God as somebody who is controlling the entire world, punishing the bad and blessing the good. There is no harm in this, except that:

YOU DON'T KNOW WHO YOU ARE.
YOU DON'T KNOW WHAT GOD IS.
YOU ARE LIVING YOUR LIFE UNDER THIS INFLUENCE,
SOMETIMES PEACEFUL,
SOMETIMES DEPRESSED.
YOU DON'T REALLY KNOW WHAT IS GOING ON.

As soon as you come across a Realized Master, he will enlighten you, saying, "You are living in an illusory world. The body is not your identity. You are different from all this.

YOU ARE THE MASTER OF MASTERS.
YOU ARE THE FATHER OF THIS WORLD.
YOU ARE THE FATHER OF GOD.
GOD IS YOUR REFLECTION.

You do not know your existence which has tremendous power. You are unaware of your Reality and so you are neglecting your Spontaneous Existence. You are living under illusionary forces, illusionary influences as a depressed person, or an unhappy person who is always struggling, trying to find happiness, peace, a life without fear.

When you meet a Realized Master, he hammers you with Reality, telling you again and again, that you are nothing to do with all this illusion because you are unborn. You are measuring yourself in the body-form, and that is illusion. You are not the body, you were not the body, and you are not going to remain the body.

THE BODY IS THE MEDIUM THROUGH WHICH
YOU CAN KNOW YOURSELF.
WITHOUT THE BODY, THERE CAN BE NO AWAKENING.

Without the body, there is no existence and therefore you cannot know yourself. The combination of the body and Spirit, or Presence, call it what you wish, is the catalyst.

YOU ARE NOT THE BODY AT ALL. OPEN FACT.

THIS REALITY HAS TO BE ENGRAVED.

THIS CONVICTION IS SUPPOSED TO BE THERE.

When this Spontaneous Conviction arises, you will know that your Identity is Invisible, Anonymous Identity, and any fear that was there, will vanish. There will be no fear of death because you will know that you are unborn, just like the sky. Sky has no feeling, no brother, no sister. Who is God, the Master, the disciple? Who is the husband, the wife? All relations are body-related.

Q: So what you are talking about here is the second wake up?

Maharaj: These are just words I am using to communicate. Don't take them literally! There is, in fact, no first or second wake-up. The second wake-up gives you Knowledge, the first wake-up does not exist. The first wake-up is connected with body-knowledge, the second one is connected with spiritual life.

Q: Can we say that prior to meeting a Master, we were under the impressions of the illusionary world?

Maharaj: These are the concepts. When you visit the Master, awakening happens.

THIS AWAKENING TAKES PLACE BECAUSE YOU ARE RECEIVING KNOWLEDGE,

AND ARE BEING GIVEN SIGHT

THROUGH WHICH YOU CAN SEE THE WORLD.

IN THE LIGHT OF THIS KNOWLEDGE, YOU CAN SEE YOURSELF.

"YES! I AM NOT THE BODY!"

The body is just a material body that goes through a process of child, young man, old man, finish! If I am not the body, then I am unborn. All this fear of death and birth is connected to the body only, just like your external clothes. If anything goes wrong with them, you throw them away. Siddharameshwar Maharaj used to say the body is your external part, like a '*dagla*'... a large outer thick woollen protective coat. The body is a *dagla*.

Knowledge is within you, like fire that has been covered with ash, covered with concepts. Keep the flame burning, the spiritual fire. The *Naam Mantra* will remove these concepts so that the fire can burn brightly.

BE STRONG AND TAKE COURAGE.

You have a lot of inner strength, but you are still considering yourself to be impaired, disabled, needing help. You can walk on your own two feet. Stand on your own two feet! You must get rid of this habit of always feeling dependent, and constantly looking for assistance out there, and relying on concepts of God, *Atman*, *Brahman*.

Q: Nisargadatta Maharaj said: "Know the false as false and then Knowledge will come through".

Maharaj: I will tell you about this subject. One night, King Janaka had a bad dream. He was tossing and turning. He was a great king, but this night, he dreamt he was a beggar in the forest. When he awoke, he was very confused. This dream puzzled him greatly. What did it mean? He wanted to know: "What is the Truth? Who am I? Am I a king in this palace ruling this kingdom, or am I this beggar lost and starving in the forest?"

He wanted to find out, so he invited all the scholars from near and far. The king wanted answers to these questions, so he made an announcement: "Whoever can answer these questions satisfactorily will be rewarded with my kingdom!" He asked: "Is this true, or is that true? The dream state or the waking state?"

Nobody could come up with an answer. Eventually, one youth arrived at the great hall after getting past the guards who were blocking him. This young man had multiple deformed joints, and because of this, he was named Ashtavakra, [Eight Bends]. "I want to give a reply to the question!" he shouted. When these stalwarts of the Royal Palace saw him, these 'wise' men began to laugh, and make derisory jokes about his deformities. King Janaka told him to come forward and speak.

Ashtavakra started to laugh as well, as he looked around the assembly and said: "Oh, King Janaka these are all cobblers! I thought I was in the company of wise men, but now I realize that they only see the outside of me, the skin".

The king asked him, "Am I a beggar or a king?" Ashtavakra replied: "Neither is true. They are both illusion. If this is true or that is true, then this is also false or that is also false".

A beggar or a king? Which is the truth? Is suffering truth or non-suffering truth? It is an interesting question! Ask yourself these questions. Self-enquire. Use discrimination. Stay with the Seer.

PRIOR TO BEINGNESS,
YOU WERE UNKNOWN TO YOU.
WHEN YOU STARTED SEEING,
WHEN YOU CAME ACROSS WITH THE BODY,
YOU STARTED SUFFERING.

People are suffering, bad situations, good situations. Without your Presence, you cannot view this world. Indirectly or directly, the entire world is your Spontaneous Projection. That which has seen the false is not false. And for that, all this spiritual Knowledge is necessary.

25. *Churn, Churn, Churn*

Maharaj: It is very simple. You have tremendous power but you are unaware of it. At the beginning with the meditation, the ego, intellect, mind will fight against the Mantra and kick off. But after, if you keep at it with determination you will conquer the mind, and it will begin to turn around and accept, "I am *Brahman*, *Brahman* I am".

Put simply, digest what I have told you. I am repeating the same thing all the time. I am repeating, repeating, repeating, the same thing. Words may be different but the principle is the same.

The moment the body feeling disappears, everything disappears. The moment the body feeling disappears, existence disappears. So long as the feeling of 'I am' is here, the world is here. Saint Kabir said, "The moment 'I' disappears, the entire world disappears".

ALL OUR TALKING HERE,
THIS IS JUST ENTERTAINMENT.

Shankaracharya's approach was also direct: "To say 'I' is illusion, to say 'You' is illusion, to say '*Brahman*' is illusion, the entire world is illusion".

You are not in the body-form. This Conviction will appear spontaneously within you. You and I have to use some words to talk about it.

I AM ADDRESSING THE LISTENER,
THE SILENT INVISIBLE LISTENER WITHIN YOU
WHICH DOES NOT HAVE ANY SHAPE.

No man, no woman, nothing, nothing, just that, just 'I', [Master holds his hands up in a trance-like state]. At the Ultimate stage, there will be no experience, no experiencer, no witness, no witnesser, nothing. Through the body, we are knowing ourselves as "I am somebody" - man, woman, *Brahman*, *Atman*. All these are concepts. There are so many concepts around.

YOU ARE NOTHING. YOU WERE NOTHING.
YOU ARE NOT GOING TO REMAIN AS ANYTHING.
OUT OF NOTHING, YOU SEE EVERYTHING.
NOTHING WILL DISSOLVE INTO NOTHING.

Who is the witness? Who is the witnesser? There is no experiencer.

THIS IS RARE KNOWLEDGE, EXCEPTIONAL KNOWLEDGE.
IT IS THE INVISIBLE LISTENER'S KNOWLEDGE.

I will say it again: To establish Truth, you have to undergo a certain discipline.

TRUTH IS WITHIN YOU. TRUTH IS THERE.
YOU ARE AT THE DESTINATION.
YOU JUST FORGOT YOUR TRUE IDENTITY,
SEARCHING HERE AND THERE:
"WHERE IS MICHAEL?
WHERE IS MICHAEL?"
YOU ARE MICHAEL.

You are to teach yourself. After reading spiritual books and approaching various Masters, you have a lot of knowledge, but:

YOU MUST KNOW THAT THE MASTER'S
ESSENCE IS WITHIN YOU.
THE MASTERLY ESSENCE IS IN YOU.

You just forgot about this. As Nisargadatta Maharaj used to say, "I am not making you a disciple, I am making you a Master". This Knowledge is very easy to listen to - anyone can listen to it - but it is a little bit difficult to absorb. And that is why perfect dedication is required. Part-time commitment will not materialize into anything.

YOU HAVE TO DISCERN SELFLESS SELF,
TOTALLY, DEEPLY.

A little ego will create problems for you. A little ego will create problems, thinking, "I am somebody". Your experience of the *Brahman* and God is also an illusion. There is no experience. *Brahman*, God, etc, are only the polished words we are using for discourse. You are the principle. Stick with the principle expressed by Nisargadatta Maharaj, which says:

THERE IS NOTHING APART FROM SELFLESS SELF.

**EXCEPT FOR YOUR SELFLESS SELF,
THERE IS NO GOD,
NO *BRAHMAN*, NO *ATMAN*, NO *PARAMATMAN*, NO MASTER.**

26. *Spontaneous Power*

Q: I have heard you say that some people can spend twenty or thirty years with the Master. I am only here for a week. Is there greater benefit from spending more time with the Master?

Maharaj: Whose thirty years, forty years? Talk about you only. When did you start counting the years? We are counting years since the moment the Spirit clicked with the body. The moment you go to the Masters, realized Masters, enlightened Masters, It is instant. There will be Conviction instantly .

Q: Yesterday, I was so involved with a family problem that I was back in the world. I had lost my detachment. There was no distance from what was going on, and I felt annoyed with myself for falling back in the hole. To top it all, I had a really bad headache. What can you do in these circumstances?

Maharaj: Be normal! Be comfortable! No strain, no stress! What happened or did not happen has gone. Don't keep carrying it! Don't think about it. Everything happens spontaneously, therefore keep quiet.

You want to know how to behave? You will find the answers from within you. All questions arise in you automatically, and they will be solved automatically.

Don't think! Be normal! Be silent!

**DONT THINK SO MUCH!
FORGET IT!
YOUR INTERNAL POWER WILL TAKE CARE OF YOU.
YOU HAVE TREMENDOUS POWER.**

Q: You say that we have this amazing power, can it be used in a physical way? And if not, what is the point of having it? Why do we need it?

Maharaj: Why do we need this power if we cannot use it? You are still viewing yourself as the body.

THIS BODY IS A DEAD BODY.

You are still considering yourself in the body-form. You are not the body! You are the holder of the body! You are asking these questions from the stance and perspective of the body-form.

**WHO WANTS POWER?
YOU ARE NOT THE BODY,
SO WHAT DO YOU WISH TO USE THIS POWER FOR?**

No, no, you cannot use it in this way! The power of the Master acts automatically. He does not think about making something happen with his Power. If you want to use this power, then that means you are taking ego, and posing yourself as a body.

I have told you that this is illusion. The Master does not think about making something happen. What happens, happens spontaneously. In the eyes of the Master, everybody is equal. He does not grant special favours to anyone.

THE MASTER IS NOT USING THAT POWER.

IT HAPPENS BY ITSELF,
OUT OF DEVOTION.

The Master's Presence is everywhere in the world. If one of his devotees finds himself in difficulty, he will be there to take care of him. The Master does not consider himself in the body-form. This is the quality of enlightenment.

SINCE YOU ARE EXPECTING SOME POWER,
THIS MEANS THAT
YOU ARE STILL TREATING YOURSELF AS THE BODY-FORM.

You are understanding that the power is something different from you. It is not like that. The sun has vast power and shines throughout the whole world. There should not be any expectations of power.

DON'T EXPECT ANY POWER.
DON'T EXPECT ANYTHING.
THE BODY-MIND IS ALWAYS TRYING TO TRICK YOU.
THOUGHTS ARE COMING, WITH THE EFFECT THAT
THEY ARE DISTRACTING YOU FROM THE RIGHT PATH.

To combat this happening, you must have complete faith in yourself and in the Master. Don't expect anything like power. It is there already. Be calm and quiet!

People used to say to Nisargadatta Maharaj, "This and that happened because of your power". He replied, "I have no power. This power is not mine, it is my Master's power. It is Siddharameshwar Maharaj's power". Likewise, if power comes from your devotion, do not misuse it or take ego from this.

IF YOU DO,
THIS WILL BE YOUR DOWNFALL,
AND THE EGO WILL AGAIN TAKE POSSESSION
OF YOUR SPIRITUAL BODY.

You have to struggle for spiritual power to grow. Sometimes if you are enticed by an attraction, you will fall down. When this happens, it may be difficult to resurface.

A true devotee will not use his power, talk about it, or show it off. He will say, "This is not my power, but that of my Master". This is the way of humility, because he does not consider himself as the body-form. Don't be a victim of the mind, ego, intellect. The mind, ego, intellect are always trying to attack the spiritual body.

27. Mind, Flow of Thoughts

Q: Today I feel relaxed and quiet, so much better than yesterday. Sometimes thoughts travel faster than at other times.

Maharaj: Good! Ignore the thoughts, don't struggle! Let them flow. Let the flow of thoughts just be. Watch! Don't pay any attention to the thoughts. They are just coming and going, coming and going. You are separate from the thoughts. Stand back, be a spectator, and watch.

Q: Now I am aware of the thinking processes. I notice it. But then I ask, "Who is noticing, and who is thinking?"

Maharaj: Your Selfless Self. It is coming from you alone, coming out of you spontaneously. You are altogether separate from the thoughts, the thinking processes and the flow of thoughts. Everything is projected from you, and you alone, so don't give any attention to the flow.

You are Final Truth, Ultimate Truth. This is the Conviction. I am showing you the shortest way to Ultimate Truth, Final Truth, Naked Truth. You cannot understand this intellectually. Everything can be understood intellectually but intellectual understanding will not serve your purpose. The Conviction will become full Conviction. All concepts, all body-knowledge need to dissolve.

To establish the Ultimate Truth, you have to undergo meditation, *bhajan* and concentration for the body-knowledge that you have to date, to subside. When various thoughts are trying to pressurize you, don't give them any cognizance because you are behind that.

Your Spontaneous Existence is there. Don't measure yourself in body-form. Your external appearance is just like these clothes. Be silent! Do your normal duties. There's no hard and fast rules. Keep the focus on YOU rather than on others.

LISTEN TO YOURSELF AND NOT TO OTHERS.
LISTEN TO YOUR INNER VOICE.
THE SPIRIT IS NOW OPEN.
BE CALM AND QUIET.

You can see that your Unidentified Identity is totally separate from this world. Using words, I am addressing, speaking to your Unidentified Identity. You are the Source of all the strength and energy.

DON'T LOOK FOR POWER IN THE WORLD,
AS THE WHOLE WORLD IS
A REFLECTION OF YOUR POWER AND ENERGY.
YOU CAN SEE THIS OPEN SECRET.
I AM PLACING THIS OPEN SECRET IN FRONT OF YOU.
IT IS YOURS.

Therefore you are entirely separate from the body. There is no mind, no ego, no intellect. At the Ultimate stage, the experiencer and all experiences will be dissolved, along with the fears around 'death'. You are strong, so don't underestimate yourself.

THERE IS NOBODY IN THE WORLD GIVING YOU
THIS KIND OF LIVING, DIRECT KNOWLEDGE.
THEY WILL JUST KEEP TALKING
ABOUT THE *BRAHMAN, ATMAN*.

Dry spiritual discussions will not give you happiness. Be practical! I'm giving you practical knowledge.

I'M THROWING YOU IN THE SEA
AND TEACHING YOU HOW TO SWIM.
I'M NOT JUST TALKING ABOUT IT.

So have some courage! Be happy! Be firm! Don't be a victim of anyone's thoughts. Wherever you are, be strong with your Ultimate Truth. There's nothing wrong with you, or missing. You are not weak at all. You are Perfect.

I'M DOING NOTHING.
I'M SHOWING YOU YOUR ULTIMATE TRUTH.
I AM TRANSFERRING TO YOU THAT SAME KNOWLEDGE
THAT MY MASTER SHARED WITH ME.

He, [pointing to the picture of Nisargadatta Maharaj], is doing everything. I am not doing anything. I am only a puppet, my Master's puppet. I am just a skeleton! This body is a dead body. I am not doing anything.

Your spiritual life has high value. Don't waste your time. Power, money and sex will not give you permanent happiness. Now you have come to the right place. You are to be unreservedly fearless, so that when the time comes to leave the body, you will say, "Come on now. I'm happy!" You will be in a happy mood when leaving the body.

Q: Is it only possible to die while alive?

Maharaj: Death just refers to the body. There's no death, no birth. Death and birth presuppose a figure or form. Something must be there to die. You are formless. You are figure-less.

THERE IS BUT A GLANCE OF 'I AM' IN THIS BODY,
JUST A GLANCE.

You are completely invisible. Consider the elephant for a moment, the big elephant walking. If the Spirit were not there, a crane would have to be used to move the big beast. That Spirit has tremendous power, so there is no need to fear anything.

Q: So everything exists because of this Spirit alone?

Maharaj: Perfectly said! If there is no Spirit, who can say "I am, *Brahman*, *Atman*, God"?

YOUR SPONTANEOUS PRESENCE IS PRIOR TO EVERYTHING.

Every day you see the same sun, moon, people, but prior to that, you first see yourself. The moment you see yourself, you see the world. If that Seer disappears from the body, then there will be no one to talk about this world, the mind, ego, intellect, the gods and goddesses. In the morning when you wake up, who sees the world? If there's no awakening in the morning, who is going to say that the world is there? The seen and the Seer's projection are false. Only the Seer is true.

Your Presence is everywhere. Wherever you go, it is taking photographs. Like automatic photography, Presence is there, twenty-four hours a day, recording everything. Not only that, it is also photographing your dreams. Images of your each and every action are being captured. Non-stop video shooting is going on.

The Seer is that Invisible Presence that is so subtle, even subtler than space and sky. You are beyond sky and space because you can SEE sky and space. So who is taking these videos? Some force is there, some Spirit is there which is called Ultimate Truth, Final Truth, *Brahman*, *Atman*, *Paramatman*, God.

The body is nothing but an instrument, a medium. The eyes by themselves don't have any power to see the world. The ears and the mouth are only instruments.

WHO IS MAKING THE HANDS MOVE?
WHO IS SEEING OUT OF THE EYES?

**EVEN WHEN YOU ARE DREAMING,
YOU CAN SEE THE WORLD.
WITHOUT EYES, WHEN YOUR EYES ARE SHUT,
YOU CAN STILL SEE.
IN A DREAM, YOU ARE TASTING DIFFERENT FOODS.
WHO IS TASTING? WHO SEES THE DREAM WORLD?
YOU DON'T KNOW.
THAT IS YOUR SPONTANEOUS PRESENCE.
THAT IS EVERYWHERE.**

Your Existence is Spontaneous Existence, Spontaneous Existence. You are always measuring yourself in body-form which is causing the confusion. Come out of all this illusion!

28. *Only You Are, Only You Are!*

Q: I am not a *jiva*, I am not Shiva.
Maharaj: These are words. Who is saying these things? "You are" or "You are not" - you are neither of these.
Q: My tongue just says this...
Maharaj: Because the body is there. To say "You are" or "I am", somebody is there.
Q: Nobody is there. I am only watching.
Maharaj: Shiva is the name given to external things.
Q: OK. I am nothing. I have not to say, *'jiva'* or 'Shiva'.
Maharaj: No! To say "I am nothing", you have to take on ego.
Q: It is just for communication purposes. I finally understand. The 'I' is false and does not exist.
Maharaj: Very good! And who understands this? Be clear, you are neither Shiva nor *jiva*. You are something else that cannot be defined.
Q: So is it not possible to make deliberate effort?
Maharaj: I have already told you that what is going on is for the food-body. It is food for life!
Q: With effort?
Maharaj: Yes effort, but effort without ego. For example, like I am lifting this cup of tea just now, and then putting it down. Don't dwell on actions, don't linger. Everything is spontaneous. It happens. If you find some thoughts useful to you, then keep them, if not, don't.
Q: What if I find some spiritual thoughts useful?
Maharaj: OK, use them! But know that these spiritual thoughts are not Ultimate. Your spiritual life is entirely different from this. I told you, everything is behind your thoughts, spiritual thoughts or any other thought.
**YOUR PRESENCE IS BEHIND EVERYTHING.
WITHOUT YOUR PRESENCE, YOU CANNOT THINK.**
Don't register the thoughts, e.g. "I had this thought or I had that thought". After using a thought, forget it! Since we are holding the body and have the five elements and three *gunas*, numerous thoughts are bound to be flowing inside.

Problems arise because we are fighting with the thoughts: "I want this thought only. I don't want that thought". Be a spectator rather than continuously saying, "Why are these thoughts coming to me all the time?" Let it be! It is natural. When you are sitting, say at a shopping centre, many people will pass by. You are not taking any cognizance of them. So when something that you don't like happens, you are giving it too much attention. Forget it!

Some kind of energy is needed for thoughts to flow. Without energy, the light will not work. Electricity is needed. Likewise, that power or energy is behind everything. Out of that energy, something is projected, reflected out.

WE ARE FOCUSSING AND THINKING ABOUT THE PROJECTION,
INSTEAD OF THE PROJECTOR.
STAY WITH THE ROOT CAUSE,
THE SOURCE FROM WHICH, THE PROJECTION IS PROJECTED.

When you know yourself, you will know that you are primary, and everything else is secondary.

YOU ARE PRIMARY,
YOU ARE THE PRINCIPLE.

Use your body for routine life. Yesterday we had a meal, and today we don't remember it. This morning we have tea. Don't think of all the preparations, the making of the tea. Take tea, then move on!

In your routine life, do your job, but don't register it, don't engrave it inside you. This engraving causes irritation. But don't live just like a beggar, learn something, do something with your life. Blindly following spirituality is meaningless, "Oh, I am a spiritual man, how can I work?" To live, you need to work. If you just sit down and say, "I am Brahman", what is the use of that? Who will feed you if you have no money? This is not the way. Live a practical life, but at the same time, just know yourself in a real sense.

YOU MUST BE IN TOUCH WITH YOUR SELFLESS SELF
ALL THE TIME.

This is the purpose behind singing the *bhajans*. Bhausaheb Maharaj says that regular singing of devotional songs will keep you tied to yourself, in touch with Selfless Self. This way, so-called *maya* will not dare to attack you.

Q: If there are many people attending these festival days, I feel some disturbance. The more people, the more distraction. But afterwards, the vibration is stronger. If there are fewer people, the vibration is weak.

Maharaj: They are not weaker or stronger vibrations, they are just vibrations. They are all coming from you, and you are calling them 'strong' or 'weak'. Your Presence is behind the vibrations. Out of that Presence, when you get closer and closer, it will be burning brightly. When you get close to Selfless Self, you will feel it strongly. These are just words I am using for communicating information.

When you come close to Selfless Self, there will be exceptional happiness and exceptional silence. At that stage. there won't be any questions, only exceptional peace. You will not feel any body, mind, ego, nothing, nothing at all.

ONLY YOU ARE,
ONLY YOU ARE.

Except yourself, nothing is there, "Just I". No type of covering will remain.

At present there are still some layers: mind is one layer, intellect is another layer, ego another. There's so many layers.

WHEN YOU GO DEEP AND DEEP,
YOU WILL SEE THIS POWERFUL, FIERY ENERGY.

You are not separate from the energy, but because of the body, there appears to be some separation. When you get closer and closer, at that moment, at that particular moment, there will be exceptional silence.

Q: You are describing the *samadhi* state.

Maharaj: It is not *samadhi*, it is beyond *samadhi*. With *samadhi*, there is still an experiencer. You are experiencing *samadhi* saying, "I had a good *samadhi*". Remember once again, *samadhi* is only a word, don't get caught up in it.

This 'state', where you are unknown to yourself, what you are calling *samadhi,* is momentary. What I am talking about is lasting. There is no attachment to the world, where you say "I'm a man". At the Ultimate stage, the Spirit is acting spontaneously. It is not saying "I am *Brahman*". Through meditation, your Reality is impressed in you, and growing, until: "So that I!"

SAMADHI MEANS THE WAY YOU WERE PRIOR TO BEINGNESS.
IN THAT PRIOR TO BEINGNESS 'STATE',
THERE IS NO EXPERIENCE.

"I'm not the body, I'm not the mind, I'm not the ego, intellect. I'm nothing". This will be your Reality. You will know that the entire world is your projection. "I used to think I was in the world, now, after realization:

"I KNOW THE WORLD IS WITHIN ME".

So don't measure yourself in body-form, with mind, ego, intellect. Your Presence is there. I'm inviting attention of that Presence, where there is no witness and no witnesser.

WHAT IS LEFT IS SOMETHING THAT IS EXCEPTIONAL
AND INDESCRIBABLE.
ONE CANNOT EXPERIENCE ONESELF AT THE ULTIMATE STAGE.

Though you are living in the world, you will be unconcerned, as if you are acting. It will be like acting in a dream and watching the dream pass by. Your Inner Master is your Teacher. When you get closer and closer to Selfless Self, instructions will come from your internal Master because of your strong belief in the Master.

A dialogue will take place with your Inner Master. This is called Self-devotion. Out of this dialogue, you will teach yourself and become your own Master. That is what Nisargadatta Maharaj meant when he said: "Except your Selfless Self, there is no God...", therefore, be quiet!

29. Clean Out Your House

Maharaj: To say "I am realized", to say "I am enlightened", you have to take ego. But, your Presence is Spontaneous, there is no witness. No words are there, no world is there. W-o-r-d-s and w-o-r-l-d. No world, no words. So when all these questions are absorbed within you, and replied within you, you are calm and quiet.

There is no anxiety and no temptation.

Where do you wish to go to, and why? Wherever you go, the sky is the same. If you go to America, India or China, the sky is same. You will not find sky different anywhere. Is American sky different from Australian sky? Where will you go to find the sky? And likewise, where will you go to find the *Brahman*? People go to this Master, that Master, that Master, that Master, and then they go to the Himalayas, and so on.

All this is an unnecessary waste of time because everything is within you, but, you are ignoring this fact. You are not paying attention to your Selfless Self. I am repeatedly inviting attention of the Invisible Listener that you are Ultimate Truth.

ULTIMATE TRUTH IS NOT BEING IMPRESSED ON YOU
BECAUSE OF ILLUSORY CONCEPTS
THAT ARE ALREADY CROWDED WITHIN YOU.

The importance of your Ultimate Truth is being overshadowed by *lakhs* of concepts.

REALITY IS BEING CROWDED OUT.

I will tell you a true story, just to illustrate this: I used to go for a morning walk in Bombay National Park, and sometimes I would stop and talk with a friend who owned a big property in Pune. At that time he was not married [and didn't need all the rooms], so he said to his friend, "You can stay here on the ground floor. It's all right. There's lots of space". So his friend stayed on the ground floor, and he himself stayed on the first floor.

Then my friend got married and had children etc, this, over a twenty year period. The time came when he realized he needed more space. He asked his friend: "Please vacate and go somewhere else now. I will give you some money. The existing premises is not big enough for me and my family". The tenant was reluctant to go, saying, "How can I go? I can't go. I have tenant's rights. I am not going". The landlord asked politely, but still, his friend refused to go.

Subsequently, my friend in the park was always in a depressed mood. When he went for his morning walks, his friends would ask him why he was so agitated? After he had told them the story, they asked about this tenant friend: Was he of *Brahmin* caste? And was he taking non-veg food etc? "No, no, no he is not taking non-veg". [ie he was a strict vegetarian].

One of them suggested that he get some smelly, rotten dried fish. In those days, there was a big hot water tank and burner next to the ground-floor flat. Everybody used to go there to heat the water, and stoke it with dry wood. He followed his friend's suggestion, and put one kilo of this dried fish in the burner when the water was steaming hot. The tenant could not tolerate the smell. He grew extremely irritated. He was gone within a week!

What this story shows is, how hard it is to get rid of unwanted tenants. They are reluctant to go.

IF YOU ARE POLITE, THEY WILL NOT GO.
SOME FORCE IS NEEDED.

The mind, ego, intellect are these tenants, all illusion! In order to remove them, you'll need the help of other illusions. We are using the help of meditation, *bhajans* and Knowledge to make the environment unbearable for unwanted tenants.

These 'tenants' will abuse you as they go. Some depressive thoughts will still be around, just like the stinking fish. It is a cleaning process. When you are cleaning your house there can be a foul smell, bad smell, but afterwards the house will be perfectly clean.

It is a big house. The body is a big house, with thousands of concepts. The only way to remove them is with meditation, Knowledge and *bhajans*. After meditation, everything will be melted: the ego, intellect, mind - all these concepts. You will be entirely free from concepts. I am trying to simplify all this, just like you would for a child. When you remember this story, you will say, "Oh yes, these things are happening because of the cleaning process".

Until the entire premises is vacated, you must be serious and determined. The unwelcome guests are there, so you have to keep on cleaning the house. Later on, it will be automatic. You will have some difficulty in the beginning as negative thoughts arise, but it is just a necessary part of the cleaning process. Unless the entire place is clean you will not be able to function.

IF YOUR SLATE IS COMPLETELY COVERED,
YOU WON'T BE ABLE TO WRITE ANY NEW WORDS ON IT.

The *bhajans* sustain alertness by creating vibrations inside you. These vibrations banish the unwanted and unpleasant things, and they will disappear. The thief is put off!

This is a simple thing, forget about spirituality. Suppose you are blowing something like a musical horn, or a trumpet in the house, this will alert the thief. He will know that somebody is inside. He will think twice about coming in. Even when he is at the back door, he will be alerted to your presence and will not dare to come in. Similarly, with the *bhajans*, meditation, Knowledge, these are constantly sounding out that Presence is there, and therefore, any wrong thoughts, illusionary thoughts will not attempt to gain entry.

Q: My mind is very active with thoughts going here, there and everywhere. Obviously not a good thing.

Maharaj: You keep talking about "My mind". "My mind" has to be erased! It will disappear. There is no 'mind', no 'ego', no 'intellect', no 'I'. All these are just thoughts related to the body. 'I', 'mind', *'maya'*, 'illusion', *'karma'*, *'parmartha'*. All these words and meanings belong to the circle of body-knowledge, and keep you in that illusory circle.

PRIOR TO BODY-KNOWLEDGE, THERE WAS NOTHING.
WHATEVER KNOWLEDGE YOU HAVE NOW
WILL VANISH ALONG WITH
THE DISAPPEARANCE OF THE BODY.
SO WHAT IS THE USE OF ALL THIS KNOWLEDGE,
WHEN EVERYTHING IS EVENTUALLY GOING TO DISAPPEAR?

Q: But we need the mind, ego and intellect to function? How can I not use the mind?

Maharaj: You can use the mind, but use it like pickle... you know pickle? When you use pickle, you use it sparingly, and not all the time.

Q: OK! Got that!

Maharaj: It is like when you are in the wrong kind of company. You are in the wrong company with the mind, ego and intellect. Don't keep the company of these boys. You are keeping bad company. As a parent, you might tell your child, "Don't mix with bad company. That so-and-so, that boy, he is a bad boy". This is what you teach your child. You are giving your child guidance, using simple psychology, so that he can develop.

In a similar way, the Master talks to you about the mind, ego, intellect, as if they are naughty boys, naughty elements. You say, "my mind, my ego, my intellect". But who is saying this? Who says it?

WHEN YOU SAY "MY MIND",
IT MEANS THAT YOU ARE NOT THE MIND.
MY HAND, MY LEG, ETC.
IT MEANS THAT YOU ARE SEPARATE FROM THAT.
'MY' IS NOT 'I', SAYS THE MASTER.
'MY' IS NOT 'I'.

Why become a slave to the mind, ego and intellect? They are your babies. You have given birth to them. You are supplying food to them. You are supplying power to them, yet now you are afraid of them. Why?

MIND, EGO, INTELLECT - STOP SUPPLYING FOOD TO THEM,
STOP SUPPLYING POWER TO THEM,
AND THEY WILL GROW DUMB.
THEY WILL BE SILENCED.

Q: My mind is always very active, very busy. I don't know how to stop my mind racing.

Maharaj: You need to clean out your house, give it a good clean-out! Take the broom of Knowledge, and sprinkle some anti-germ powder over the germs.

We are the victims of thoughts because we are accepting them blindly. "Oh! I am depressed, I am unhappy, I am in a mood, so leave me alone, leave me alone". Why? Because:

DIRECTLY OR INDIRECTLY,
WHENEVER A THOUGHT APPEARS WITHIN THE BODY
YOU ARE ACCEPTING IT.

Accepting thoughts indiscriminately results in your entire physical body, your entire mental body, your entire spiritual body being affected. Then the confusion starts, conflict starts, and you grow restless and become agitated.

Why? Because in spite of knowing that you have nothing to do with all these thoughts, that you are, in fact, separate from all these thoughts, some subtle ego remains.

THE SUBTLE EGO IS STILL THERE, STILL FEELING,
"I AM SOMEBODY, SOMEBODY ELSE".
AND THEN, OUT OF THAT EGO,
THOUGHTS ARE ACCEPTED WITHOUT YOUR KNOWLEDGE.

Here is a very simple example. Say a dog is barking outside. The barking is unbearable. The effect is instant. You don't like it. You go out, throw a few stones and shout at the dog. This means that the dog's barking has been accepted. It has become troublesome for you. Yet, it is in the nature of a dog, it is a dog's nature to bark. But you are paying attention to the dog, and thinking, "Oh! Why is it barking and giving me trouble?"

SO THERE, AT THIS POINT,
YOUR SUBTLE EGO IS TAKING BIRTH.
YOUR MIND IS BARKING. YOUR MIND IS BARKING,

BECAUSE YOU ARE PAYING ATTENTION TO THE BARKING DOG

Q: So, don't give attention or accept the thoughts?

Maharaj: If you don't accept the thoughts, then they will not create any trouble. They will not affect you. Now, you have to motivate yourself. You have to motivate yourself in this way:

"I USED TO THINK THAT I WAS THE BODY-FORM.
NOW I HAVE COME TO KNOW THAT I WAS NOT THE BODY,
I AM NOT GOING TO REMAIN THE BODY,
MY BODY IS NOT MY IDENTITY. THEREFORE,
I AM NOTHING TO DO WITH THIS WHOLE ATMOSPHERE.
I AM UNCONCERNED WITH THE WORLD".

Forget about the body-base! Forget about the body-base!

YOUR PRESENCE WAS THERE PRIOR TO THE BODY,
BUT IT WAS INVISIBLE, ANONYMOUS, UNIDENTIFIED -
THEREFORE YOU ARE UNKNOWN.

You started measuring life when the Spirit clicked with the body. When you came across the body, you started thinking like this: "My age is such and such years. I am a woman. I was born in 1975 and therefore my age is forty years old. I am forty years of age".

The moment the Spirit clicked with the body, you started measuring the years, but prior to that, your Presence was there. Let go of the body, let go of the body-form.

YOU ARE NOT A WOMAN.
YOU ARE NOT 'SITA' WHO IS FORTY YEARS OLD.
NO! YOU ARE UNBORN.

30.   *Meditation is the Anti-Virus For Chronic Illusion*

Q: How to control the mind? How can I ignore all the mental activity? It does not seem possible.

Maharaj: Anything is possible. For cases like yours, for treating cases of chronic illusion, the Master prescribes the Medicine of 'Meditation'. Meditation is the anti-virus software. Meditation is the basic foundation for cleaning the field, for clearing away all illusory thoughts. Meditation means complete concentration.

MEDITATION MEANS COMPLETE CONCENTRATION.
THE MANTRA IS AN INSTRUMENT, A TOOL.
WHILE USING THE MANTRA, YOU ARE ENGAGING YOUR MIND,
AND AT THE SAME TIME,
YOUR SPIRIT IS FLOWING INSIDE WITH KNOWLEDGE, REALITY.

Q: When you engage the mind and recite the Mantra, what happens? How does it work.

Maharaj: **MIND ACTIVITY STOPS.**
INTELLECTUAL ACTIVITY STOPS,
AND EGOISTIC ACTIVITY STOPS,

SPONTANEOUSLY WITH THE CLICK OF THE MANTRA.

These days everybody has computers and laptops. All of them catch viruses at one time or another. To resolve this problem, we need to use an anti-virus programme. Likewise, unless your viruses are fully erased, dissolved, Ultimate Reality will not be realized.

Q: How do we get rid of years and years, layers and layers of illusion? It seems an impossible task?

Maharaj: **NOTHING IS IMPOSSIBLE!**

Meditation has an effect on the spiritual body. The Spirit is very sensitive and has absorbed a lot of impressions. Whatever is impressed upon it is immediately reflected. Since childhood, the Spirit has considered itself as the body-form: "I'm somebody [else], I'm born, I'm going to die". Then there were all the impressions and conditioning, upbringing, environment, 'tradition', 'conduct', 'culture', 'good deeds', 'bad deeds', '*prarabdha*', '*karma*', 'rebirth', 'heaven', 'hell', and all the rest of the concepts.

We have signed blindly, and accepted everything without question.

THESE CONCEPTS WILL DISSOLVE WITH MEDITATION.
THROUGH MEDITATION,
YOU ARE REGENERATING YOUR POWER,
AND REFRESHING YOUR MEMORY OF ULTIMATE TRUTH.

Q: That sounds wonderful! It sounds almost miraculous.

Maharaj: [smiles] Remember! Don't take my words literally. You forgot your Ultimate Truth and embraced the body. And because of all the illusory concepts, you are living as the body, under the pressure of an abundance of illusory concepts from childhood till today.

Not only this, but you are also under all those fearful impressions and accompanying anxieties, such as "What if something happens to me? What if so-and-so dies tomorrow? What will happen in the future? What is happening in the present? What happened in the past? If only this, if only that," etc. You are always worrying about something or other. Meditation is therefore required to dissolve this whole illusory package.

Q: I am listening to what you are saying, but at the same time, wondering if meditation is really necessary, if you read and study a lot, like I do?

Maharaj: Reading books and studying is not enough. Who is reading? Who is studying?

READING BOOKS IS NOT ENOUGH.
STUDY IS NOT ENOUGH.
WHO IS READING?
WHO IS STUDYING?

People are always on the move, visiting holy sites, going here and there. Why?

VISIT YOUR OWN SITE,
NOT SOMEONE ELSE'S.
FIRST, CLEAN OUT YOUR OWN HOUSE.

Q: I have never been very good at meditation. When I hear the word, I tend to go green. I always end up giving up. I don't seem to be able to concentrate for very long.

Maharaj: The first thing is concentration. Concentration with deep involvement is essential. This Knowledge, this Reality will only open up to you with the help of meditation. It is the 'Master Key' to enter the House of

Self-Knowledge. The Master Key will open the door to Self-Knowledge.

Q: How do I meditate?

Maharaj: The *Naam Mantra* is most important. If you do not have the *Naam Mantra*, then use another Mantra or the name of a deity you believe in, and concentrate on that. Full concentration is necessary. For example, "I am Brahman, Brahman I am" or *"Aham Brahmasmi"*.

Q: What is the *Naam Mantra*?

Maharaj: In our Lineage, some sacred words are given for meditation. The *Naam Mantra* is the Master Key, therefore, the Master, Shri Bhausaheb Maharaj, founder of the Inchegiri Navnath Sampradaya, insisted that beginners first undergo meditation. After a period of meditation, the practice will become spontaneous. Take two hours a day for yourself.

Because the Spirit is very sensitive, it is receptive to the vibrations of the *Naam Mantra*, and will absorb these like a sponge. At first, you will need to make some effort to recite it because the ego will put up a fight to resist it. Issues will surface at the beginning, so you may have to struggle to keep the Mantra going. Afterwards, however, it will run automatically.

**THE MEANING OF THE *NAAM MANTRA* IS
"*I AM BRAHMAN, BRAHMAN I AM*".**

Meditation is a process, a corrective process that acts as a reminder of who we really are. By cleaning out the layers of illusion that have built up since childhood till today, the Spirit is regenerated. The words of the meditation, the meaning of the Mantra is, as I have said: "I am *Brahman*, *Brahman* I am". We are hammering these words into you, your Reality into you, until you accept them.

Q: You were saying that the ego will try and resist the practice. Is that because it thinks it's the boss, and doesn't want to be dethroned?

Maharaj: It does not know any better.

Q: You were talking about illusion, is meditation not also an illusion?

Maharaj: Yes, meditation is also illusion, everything is illusion, but we have to use one thorn to remove another thorn. At the advanced stage, there will be no need for any meditation, so you can forget about it. But, in the beginning, to dissolve and erase illusion, you need the help of another illusion.

**THROUGH THE MEDITATION,
WE ARE REFRESHING YOUR IDENTITY.
YOU FORGOT YOUR IDENTITY,
THEREFORE WE ARE REGENERATING YOUR POWER,
REMINDING YOU OF YOUR TRUE IDENTITY
WHICH ISINVISIBLE AND UNIDENTIFIED.**

31. *My Presence is Everywhere*

Maharaj: Bhausaheb Maharaj, the Lineage Founder, was a Spiritual Architect. He had foresight where meditation was concerned, and planned for all eventualities. He realized that a little at a time, is all that is needed to make knowledge digestible, just like a mother feeding her child. The sparrow feeds its young a little bit at a time, so that it will grow strong. If it is stuffed full, then it will not be able to digest the food.

Nowadays, you don't have to leave the house for spiritual knowledge. You don't have to learn in a secretive environment either. There were many restrictions before but now there is freedom in spirituality. You are very fortunate to have it so easy. Be serious and meditate! Meditation is needed until you find your spiritual body.

Q: How long will it take? How much time?

Maharaj: How long? Why do you say, "How long?" There is no time. After continuous concentration, you will come to know, "Oh! I have nothing to do with the body. I was not the body. I am unborn".

THE BODY COMES AND GOES.
THE BODY HAS AGE FACTORS, LIMITATIONS OF TIME.
BUT FOR 'ME', THERE IS NO TIME LIMIT.
I AM EVERYWHERE.
MY PRESENCE IS OMNIPRESENCE.

Q: Can this happen quickly?

Maharaj: Instantly! It is up to you. Don't struggle with the mind. Thoughts are coming and thoughts are going. Accept those you want, and refuse those you don't want. You have good thoughts, you have bad thoughts.

AFTER A TIME, THEY WILL ALL BE GOOD THOUGHTS.

Q: I will try, and see how it goes.

Maharaj: This kind of "see how it goes" casual spirituality will not do! To have perfection, we need a perfect foundation. And for this, we need meditation. Out of this meditation, you will forget your external identity and your internal identity. You will come to know:

"YES! THIS IS MY ULTIMATE TRUTH.
MY SPONTANEOUS INVISIBLE PRESENCE
PROJECTED THIS WORLD.
PRIOR TO THIS BEINGNESS, I WAS NOT AWARE AT ALL".

Q: It sounds amazing. But I am still thinking that it must take time to know, to really know the Reality?

Maharaj: You are giving too much attention to the thoughts. Listen to the Master! Accept what the Master is saying about you.

LISTEN TO YOUR STORY!
ACCEPT THE REALITY,
YOUR REALITY.
YOU ARE ULTIMATE, YOU ARE FINAL TRUTH.
MASTER SAYS THAT YOU ARE ULTIMATE TRUTH,
FINAL TRUTH.

As I have said already, meditation is like an anti-virus software. Through this process of meditation, everything will be cleared out, made clean, cleansed, removed. You will arrive at the Stateless State, Thoughtless Reality.

Q: Do I have to sit in a lotus position? I can't do that. I could when I was younger, but not now.

Maharaj: That's OK. If your body or old age does not permit you to sit in the meditative position, then it's OK.

Concentration is more important.

Q: So, the purpose of the meditation is concentration?

Maharaj:
YOU WERE NOT THE BODY.
YOU ARE NOT THE BODY.
YOU ARE NOT GOING TO REMAIN THE BODY.
THE BODY IS NOT YOUR IDENTITY.
THAT CONVICTION IS SUPPOSED TO APPEAR
OUT OF THE MEDITATION.
THIS IS THE GIST OF THE MEDITATION,
THE RESULT OF THE MEDITATION.
THEREFORE AT THIS INITIAL STAGE,
CONCENTRATION IS MOST IMPORTANT.

Q: I hear you.

Maharaj: Meditation will bring you Knowledge, your Knowledge.
JUST TO KNOW YOURSELF IN A REAL SENSE,
THAT IS KNOWLEDGE.

You are Ultimate Truth. You are Final Truth. Don't play with the words, with the spiritual words. There are thousands of spiritual words.

YOU ARE DROWNING IN IGNORANCE.
YOU ARE DROWNING IN A SEA OF WORDS.

Remove all the external clothing, all these illusory layers, and see yourself. You are total, complete. Everything is within you. You forgot your Identity, that is all. But you have to undergo certain disciplines at the initial stage.

In the beginning, you do have to remember to repeat the Mantra, but once you accept your Reality, it will flow naturally by itself.

YOUR MASTER SAYS:
YOU ARE *ATMAN*, YOU ARE *BRAHMAN*,
YOU ARE GOD.
AT THE SAME TIME, YOU ARE REPEATING THE MANTRA
WHICH HAS THE SAME MEANING.
EVENTUALLY, THERE COMES A MOMENT WHEN
IT WILL BE ACCEPTED TOTALLY.
BUT, UNTIL THAT CONVICTION IS ESTABLISHED,
YOU MUST FIGHT.
YOU HAVE TO BATTLE ON.

Accept that you are Ultimate Truth! With some people, the Conviction happens immediately, for others, it takes longer because impressions have not been erased properly. Meditate with deep and full involvement!

32.   *Naam Mantra – The Master Key*

Maharaj: The Masters in our Lineage initiate sincere seekers with the *Naam Mantra*. You must not disclose it to anyone. This is one of the rules. Do you understand?

Q: Of course! I respect that.

Maharaj: Here is a little about the background, a few words about our Lineage. It goes back to Dattatreya, who is regarded as the head. Revanath Maharaj, was a disciple of Dattatreya, along with the Nine Nath, the nine deities. These direct disciples of Dattatreya were instructed to give spiritual knowledge, share it with others, in order to make them enlightened. From Revanath Maharaj, the same Knowledge was shared from disciple to disciple, passed on, in succession.

The Inchegiri Navnath Sampradaya begins with Shri Bhausaheb Maharaj, then Shri Siddharameshwar Maharaj, and more recently, Shri Nisargadatta Maharaj and Shri Ranjit Maharaj. This is just a brief description of our Lineage. Now here in this ashram, we are following the same traditions of the Lineage, and sharing 'Direct' Knowledge, 'Selfless Self' Knowledge with you.

Q: This sounds fascinating! It means that all the Knowledge and Power of these wonderful Masters, is being passed on and continue down the line as 'Living Knowledge', so to speak. It is amazing! The way I see it is that the *Naam Mantra* is empowered by the whole Lineage. I feel very privileged to be part of all this, Maharaj.

Maharaj: After receiving the *Naam Mantra*, you must keep up the discipline. As I told you, the Spirit is very sensitive, so, in view of its sensitivity, these secret words are passed on. When these sacred words have done their job and impressed themselves on the Spirit, Reality will be exposed.

REALITY WILL COME OUT.
ALL KNOWLEDGE WILL FLOW.
THIS IS NOT INDIVIDUALISTIC KNOWLEDGE,
THIS IS SELFLESS SELF KNOWLEDGE.

The activity will soon work automatically, but, for now, dedication is most important. As you go about your physical duties, at the same time, you must keep in touch with your Selfless Self.

Q: What is the best way to do that?

Maharaj: You are to spend at least a minimum of two hours, a minimum of two hours. You may split the time into two one hour practices or four half-hour slots, whatever suits your daily routine.

The Master, Shri Bhausaheb Maharaj, used to devote ten to twelve hours per day, sometimes standing in a well where he tied his pigtail to the water-wheel. He did this to keep him awake, so that if he dozed off, his head would collapse forward, and he would be woken up with a jolt.

These Masters forced themselves to do intense and strenuous practice. They endured so much hardship in their day. It is because of their struggles that we have it so easy nowadays. They have made it very, very easy for us.

Q: We have benefited from their dedication and struggle.

Maharaj: They all made such tremendous efforts in the Lineage. With strict discipline and determination, they tried to find out the secrets of 'Selfless Self'. They were very, very strict. Afterwards, Siddharameshwar Maharaj reduced the required period of meditation to two hours a day.

Due to their perseverance, we are now able to share this high and rare Knowledge in a very simple and direct way.

Q: I can only say that I'm glad I live in the twenty-first century! The practice today sounds easy by comparison.

Maharaj: We are fortunate that these Masters did not care very much about the 'body'. Instead, they were driven to share the Knowledge with others, to enlighten as many people as possible. They made sacrifices, rare sacrifices but they did not care because they had such high power.

THIS POWER WAS WITH THEM ALWAYS,
AND MADE THEM FORGET ABOUT THE BODY-FORM.
THEY USED THE BODY,
ALWAYS KNOWING THAT THEY WERE TOTALLY DIFFERENT FROM THE BODY.
THEY KNEW THEY WERE ULTIMATE TRUTH,
AND THEY LIVED LIKE THAT.
THEIR KNOWLEDGE
WAS REAL
AND PRACTICAL.

Now receive the Master Key, through which previous Masters achieved Perfection. The Master Key is the base, the foundation for the Realization of Ultimate Truth.

33. *Make Meditation an Obsession*

Maharaj: It is very easy, but at the same time, it is very difficult.

What is meditation? If somebody abuses you, someone insults you, you will say: "I am going to get revenge. How dare he! Where is that man?" And for the next twenty-four hours, you will be thinking of that particular man who has insulted and abused you. You feel fiery! You are fired up, incensed and want to get back at him. You are absorbed in ways of doing this.

Similarly, you need to have the same fire and passion for the meditation. All the time, for twenty-four hours a day, you are trying to find out who you are. You are determined and obsessed with self-discovery. Your involvement is very deep and absolute.

YOU NEED TO FIND OUT WHO YOU REALLY ARE, AT ANY COST.
NOTHING IS GOING TO STOP YOU!

Each and every cell in your body is on fire with what that abusive person has said. "I'll show him! I will get revenge".

Q: With every fibre of your being?

Maharaj: Yes! Your entire body is boiling! You can only focus and concentrate on this one thing.

THIS IS MEDITATION!

Q: I see! We have to be completely involved because we have a lifetime of these impressions, like scripts that keep saying, "I am Chris", with all the associations and baggage that comes along with 'Chris'. So I will have to work at it continuously and be one-pointed. What you are saying, Maharaj, is that it has to be a full-time pursuit?

Maharaj: All these great saints, [pointing to the pictures on the wall], they were all advancing meditation.

Q: And what about meditating while walking or whatever?

Maharaj: You don't have to sit to meditate. Meditation can be practised while you are working, relaxing, at any time, anywhere. Reciting will continue by itself. It will continue by itself. The meditation will continue in the background. Spirit is very sensitive, whatever is impressed on it is reflected.

REMEMBER THAT YOU ARE DOING ALL THIS MEDITATION
FOR YOURSELF, FOR YOUR BENEFIT,
NOT FOR THE MASTERS.

Casual spirituality will not work. Part-time involvement? No! Absolute and complete self-involvement is needed. Then you will notice dramatic changes happening in you. Meditation just means "Concentrating on the Concentrator". In this way, you are staying with Selfless Self at all times.

Q: I have a question about the devotional aspect of the meditation.

Maharaj: In the beginning, there is not really devotion. Here, devotion means surrendering and accepting. What is needed is non-stop devotion.

DEVOTION IS SACRIFICE:
"I WANT TO KNOW MYSELF.
I WANT TO KNOW WHO I AM".

Q: So, as well as fighting and struggling, you are also surrendering?

Maharaj: Yes! Because in order to remove this body-knowledge, to come out of body-knowledge, devotion is needed. It is a deliberate act. At the initial stage, you see yourself as a devotee. In order to reach Ultimate Truth you are to undergo devotion.

FIRST OF ALL, YOU ARE A DEVOTEE,
THEN YOU UNDERGO DEVOTION, PRACTISING, MEDITATING.
AFTER DEVOTION, "YOU CAN REALIZE THE DEITY".

Therefore the movement is one from Devotee, to Devotion, to Deity. But, remember that these are only words. Don't fall into the trap of taking the words literally. In reality, there is no devotee, no devotion, no deity.

Q: I understand that now, but I have to keep reminding myself because the mind has the habit of grasping, and I am aware of occasionally saying to myself, "I've got it". I am trying not to do this. It is tricky too, because the whole subject area you are talking about, Ultimate Reality, that we are, has no language. It is prior to language, prior to everything.

Maharaj: When you come here as a devotee, you say, "I want to know myself. I want to know who I am". The Master says, "You are Ultimate Truth, but you are not having faith in the Master because of the long association with the body." Your faith, your trust is wavering, shaky, not firm. There is no stability. You are told by the Master that you are *Brahman, Atman, Paramatman*. You are to recite the Mantra so that this Reality can penetrate and be absorbed.

Q: To go back to what I was saying earlier about language, if we created the words which are all illusion, how can these words that we recite work, or have any real and lasting effect on us?

Maharaj: Yes, the words are illusion, but again we have to use one illusion to erase another, ["I am *Brahman*" replacing "I am man"]. Considering the sensitiveness of your Spirit, what you impress on that Spirit, is reflected.

Q: So it definitely works?

Maharaj: Of course! As long as you have total self-involvement, one hundred per cent. It is a well-proven, scientific, systematic method. Ultimate Truth is being impressed in you through the Mantra. And then you will know, "Oh! So I am That!" There will be exceptional silence. Exceptional, Spontaneous Silence will be there.

Q: That sounds wonderful!

Maharaj: Where all thoughts end, there you are. In the thoughtless stage, even 'I' also ends. There is no 'I', no 'you'. But this state is not an unconscious state. Though you are living in the body, you are fully and completely separate from it, unaware of the world.

I am placing before you the Listener's Truth, your Truth. You can do it! Have some courage! Nothing is impossible! There is no difference between the Speaker in me and the Listener in you, except for the body-form.

NOW YOU ARE TO CONVINCE YOURSELF.
OPEN FACTS HAVE BEEN PLACED BEFORE YOU.
YOU HAVE THE KEY, NOW YOU HAVE TO OPERATE IT.
THE DISHES HAVE BEEN SERVED,
NOW EAT!

34.   The Master is Not a Miracle Man

Maharaj: Now you have been given the key. The Lineage Masters' Mantra is now your Mantra. I have told you how to operate it, now, it is up to you. It will be very easy for those of you who are serious, for others, with a more casual approach to the meditation, it will not be so easy. It all depends to what extent you are taking cognizance of this. It all depends on how important you view and value it.

Try to remember that:

EACH MOMENT OF YOUR LIFE IS VERY IMPORTANT.
IT WILL NEVER BE REPEATED.
AND, UNLESS YOU KNOW YOURSELF IN A REAL SENSE,
THERE WILL BE LOSS OF PEACE,
LOSS OF CONTENTMENT,
AND IN ITS PLACE, FEAR AND TENSION.

Q: I know what you are saying, Maharaj. Seize the moment and don't be casual. Just put some effort in, and do the practice.

Maharaj: This practice is necessary because of our body-attachment. When there was no body-attachment, nothing was needed. Look at it this way: It is a matter of fact, that there is NOTHING there. There is nothing at all.

WHEN THERE WAS NO BODY,
THERE WAS NO NEED OF GOD,
NO NEED OF *BRAHMAN*, NOTHING.

Q: Is it nothing and fullness at the same time?

Maharaj: These are words and this is your imagination. I know! You do not! It is like the story of a man on top of a hill, waving his arms. The man below shouts up and asks, "What is it like up there?" The man on the hilltop says: "You will have to come up and see for yourself".

Q: Yes, I was using my imagination, what you call body-knowledge, to try and grasp something, whereas your Knowledge is arising spontaneously. It's direct.

Maharaj: All needs, all requirements, all demands started with the body. Prior to 'beingness', we did not know the meaning of God, Master, disciple, brother, or sister. No names, no meanings! All relations are body-related. You know that some day, willing or unwillingly, you will have to leave this all behind. We can't take the body along with us.

IT IS ONLY BECAUSE OF SPIRIT THAT WE ARE ABLE TO TALK,
THAT WE ARE LISTENING, SEEING.
THE ENTIRE WORLD IS THE PROJECTION
OF YOUR SPONTANEOUS PRESENCE,
CALLED ULTIMATE TRUTH, *BRAHMAN*, *ATMAN*, GOD.
OPEN FACT.

But do not strain your brain, wondering, "Oh how can this be?" It is very simple. Very, very simple. The moment your body-attachment dissolves, it will be seen. Then you will know, that there is nobody there. I am telling you, hammering the same thing, over and over again:

TREMENDOUS POWER IS ALREADY WITHIN YOU,
BUT YOU ARE UNAWARE OF THAT POWER.

How the process works is also very straightforward. The Spirit is very sensitive. Considering the sensitivity of the Spirit, the *Naam Mantra*, the Guru Mantra is given as a tool. It has a dual function: It erases your body-knowledge, and at the same time, reminds you of your true Identity.

Here is a simple example: Suppose someone has forgotten his identity, say, he has lost his memory, and he's suffering from amnesia. We need to remind him, so we give clues, provide him with events and memories from his past, in order to refresh his memories.

If a child forgets something, we remind the child. Similarly, the Master is reminding you of a memory. The memory is:

YOU ARE *BRAHMAN*, YOU ARE *ATMAN*.
YOU ARE *BRAHMAN*, YOU ARE *ATMAN*.

You are not a man. You are not a woman. This is the preliminary stage, the beginning stage. Afterwards, when the Conviction is established, you will not need further disciplines. From that moment on, everything will happen spontaneously. Also, you will not feel the need to go searching elsewhere after Conviction. You will no longer find it necessary to speak using the polished words, such as 'Brahman' or 'Atman'.

JUST TAKE A LOOK AT YOURSELF
MINUS THE BODY-FORM,
AND SEE HOW YOU ARE.

Forget about the mind, ego, intellect. Remove everything, peel off the layers of illusion, one by one. What is left after removing the layers of an onion?

Q: What is left? Nothing!

Maharaj: 'Nothing' is correct! And, what is the polished word for 'nothing' called? We call it *'Brahman'*.

Q: So we are doing all this practice, doing everything, to discover nothing? Hmm! Another question, if you say everything is illusion, then why do we have to do meditation, sing *bhajans*, etc? I KNOW that I am *Brahman*!

Maharaj: That is good if you know, but literal knowledge is not the way. That Knowledge has to be absorbed. Anyone can say, 'I am *Brahman*'. It is not the words that are important, but what is behind the words, the essence, the gist of meaning that the Master wishes to convey. What is conveyed is most important.

If you have any doubts, then say. Don't just nod your head if you are not sure. There should be no doubts remaining, otherwise the foundations will not be firm. Follow?

Q: Yes, I follow!

Maharaj: You can only remove one illusion, by using another illusion. It is like taking a thorn to remove another thorn. Don't stop the meditation until you have perfect absorption of the Knowledge. You have the habit of questioning everything. This is the effect of literal knowledge: "Why do this?" or "What is the point of that?" No! Don't analyze the Master's instructions.

THE TIME WILL COME WHEN YOU WILL BEGIN TO RECEIVE
SPONTANEOUS INSTRUCTION FROM WITHIN,
GUIDING YOU FORWARD AS TO WHAT TO DO NEXT,
AND WHAT NOT TO DO.

In spiritual language this is called your Inner Master. In spiritual language, we talk about the 'Inner Master', and the 'Outer Master', or the 'Internal' and 'External' Master. These are just words, just the words I'm using to communicate and explain. The Outer Master is in the body-form; the Inner Master is the 'Invisible Listener'.

THERE IS NO DIFFERENCE AT ALL BETWEEN YOU AND ME,
EXCEPT FOR THIS BODY-FORM.
OUR BODIES ARE DIFFERENT
BUT THE LISTENER AND THE SPEAKER ARE FORMLESS.

So everything is within you, but you are unaware. That is why we are inviting the attention of this Greatness in you, the "Silent Invisible Listener within you". Look at you and decide what this 'I' is. By itself, this body, has no value. The moment the Spirit is not there, we say, "Take it, take it away. It is finished".

Remember! Every moment is most important! But this does not mean that you are to avoid your duties and say: "Oh I am a spiritual man, how can I do these menial tasks?" Carry out your duties. Do your job, and do not neglect your health. You have to convince yourself in this way, and then there will not be any questions.

ALL THE ANSWERS TO YOUR QUESTIONS

ARE WITHIN YOU ALONE.
THAT IS WHY THIS MASTER KEY IS GIVEN
TO ASSIST YOU WITH SELF-KNOWLEDGE.

Operate that key systematically, and all your questions will be solved spontaneously and automatically. There will be no questions remaining. You will also talk the way I am talking. You will do this. It will happen. But stay cautious and humble because there is a chance that the ego will rise up and claim: "Oh! I am an enlightened person".

I am not a miracle man. I do not have a magic wand. The power I am talking about is your power. It is already in you.

YOU ARE FREE FROM ALL BONDAGE.
YOU ARE A FREE BIRD,
YOU CAN FLY!

You were bound by so many concepts and tied up with worldly concerns. Now you have been untied. All bondage has been removed. You have been unwrapped and opened up. Now you might feel freer, with feelings like, "I can fly with my own wings!", "I am totally independent, totally free!"

YOU ARE NOT DEPENDENT ON ANYONE ELSE.
BUT THAT INDEPENDENCE HAS TO BE
DIGESTED AND ABSORBED.
DIGEST AND ABSORB THIS KNOWLEDGE
WITH THE HELP OF THE SACRED MANTRA.

35. Sick Patient

Maharaj: Inner Master, Outer Master, OK, these are terms that are used for understanding purposes only. There is no external, no internal. To say 'Internal Master', 'External Master' means that there is a division, duality, something that separates. You are dividing the world in two: "I am inside, I am outside", or "The Master is separate from me, and I am somebody else". There is no such thing!

WE HAVE CREATED ALL THESE WALLS.
BREAK DOWN THE WALLS.

Q: There is no inner and there is no outer?

Maharaj: Unless you accept what the Master says totally...

Q: That's right. There's no inner and no outer. No external, no internal, no inner, no outer.

Maharaj: If you say 'outer', that means you are considering yourself with shape, as a form. I'm somebody, and there's a living Master over there.

YOUR PRESENCE IS JUST LIKE A LIVING MASTER.
YOU ARE A LIVING MASTER.

Your Presence is just like a living Master. You're a living Master.

Q: I'm a living Master? Is there any difference between the living Master in you, and the living Master in me then?

Maharaj: There's no difference at all.

Q: Is it the one Master?

Maharaj: What is this one Master, two Masters, three Masters, four? We are not in a counting game. This is just for understanding. When you teach a child, you use these words. There is no one Master, two Masters, three Masters there. In reality, you are the Master.

Q: So why do we bow to you, Maharaj? Is it because we realize you're the Master, and we are not realized yet?

Maharaj: What do you mean by realization? You are realized, but not paying attention to the realized state. You know better that *Atman*, *Brahman*, *Paramatman* is your Ultimate Truth, but you don't give any attention to this. You have no Conviction and therefore you are coming to me. After knowing the Reality, after Realization, Enlightenment, call it what you will, you will know yourself in a real sense. Realization means just that, to know oneself in a real sense, not in the body-form.

You are Final Truth. You are not the body, you were not the body, you are not going to remain the body. The question of 'I', 'you', all these terms are just used for discussion.

BODIES ARE DIFFERENT
BUT SPIRIT IS ONE.

Houses are different, sky is one. This is a cottage, this a building, Russia, India, America – these are the names – sky is one. Sky is not different anywhere. We have given the names: this sky is America, that sky is Russia, England. Sky is sky.

Q: We are here because you, Maharaj, are realized. You can assist us in reawakening because we have forgotten our Reality. And if we do the practice of Self-enquiry, using the Mantra and the teachings, and anything else that is non-verbal in the presence of the Master…

Maharaj: Nisargadatta Maharaj says:

JUST TAKE ONE STEP,
AND I WILL TAKE THE NEXT STEP FOR YOU.

Q: If you lift my leg up for me then maybe I can start running. So there is co-operation between the two then? The Master and devotee are related?

Maharaj: It's not one-way traffic. Since you are a doctor, you will understand. When a patient comes to see you, he should co-operate with you. There will only be a cure if he co-operates with you.

Q: Yes, if he follows my advice.

Maharaj: Say a patient has some problem or other. You know that if the patient does not co-operate, then the treatment will not work. In your line of work, it is a two-way thing. It's the same here.

Q: Here, I am the patient, and I am very sick actually. I have many problems. Can you help?

Maharaj: Ask any questions!

Q: Oh! For example, money problems.

Maharaj: There are no problems. Problems are physical problems, mental problems, intellectual problems, logical problems. All these problems are body-based problems. All these problems only appeared when you started knowing yourself in body-form.

When thoughts are flowing, accept the useful ones for your routine life. If thoughts are not useful, then throw them out. Don't pay any attention to them.

Q: It is very easy to be in your company, to feel free of these problems, but when you go home, problems arise and then you don't always know how to deal with them.

Maharaj: No, No! You see, the world is your entire home.

THE ENTIRE WORLD IS YOUR HOME.

It is not America, not England, not India. Does sky have its own home?

Q: That's right, not anywhere. There's no separation between here and England.

Maharaj: Does sky have its own home? Does the sky say, "My home is in India?" No! Because sky doesn't know its own identity. Because you are measuring yourself in body-form, you say, "My home is in America". Don't measure yourself in body-form. All these troubles are coming from your doing just this.

YOU ARE THE CAUSE OF YOUR OWN TROUBLE.
YOU ARE THE VICTIM OF YOUR OWN THOUGHTS.
BECAUSE YOU ARE PAYING MORE ATTENTION
TO THE THOUGHTS, THAN TO YOUR SELFLESS SELF.

Thoughts happen: Good thoughts, bad thoughts, and then some words are spoken. We call all this 'mind'. Mind is the continuous flow of thoughts for twenty-four hours. There are thoughts in the present, memories of the past, thoughts of the future. All memories cause problems.

Say something distressing happened ten years back, and then, in a flash, it is remembered. All of a sudden, everything that happened then is remembered vividly now, with every little detail. Memory pulls you back into the past, and back into the ditch. You re-experience the pain all over again, saying, "Oh! Oh dear!" Then without noticing it, you feel depressed once again, and suffer fresh torment. All this because of a memory.

Thoughts are flowing because you have forgotten your Presence. You are not witnessing the thoughts, but unfortunately, accepting them. Therefore these thoughts are causing you problems.

You are to train yourself and decide which thoughts to accept and which to reject, where to pay attention, where not to pay attention. You are a doctor, you know only too well when to pay attention, and when not to pay attention.

Q: I do well with my patients, but as far as I am concerned, not so good. My habits are too strong.

Maharaj: You can cure yourself. You are your own doctor. Those things that are intoxicating, we call 'habits'. Develop the habit of spirituality. Be completely intoxicated with spirituality. Be addicted! Teach yourself! Self-medicate.

Q: I am very happy to have a practice that I can now do. I can already feel the strength of the Lineage.

Maharaj: Truth is placed before you. Reality is placed before you. Now the choice is yours: which thoughts to accept, and which ones to refuse. Here is a simple example: There is a big dish of foods with many different things to choose from. Some things on the dish don't agree with you. They are too rich maybe or fatty, so you say, "I don't want this, I don't want that". Those disagreeable things that you don't want are removed, and the things which you want, you accept. It's not complicated. In the light of this, you are to train yourself, train yourself. You are your own Master.

Q: The Mantra should help me too?

Maharaj: Yes, of course, of course.

Q: And the more faith I have in the Mantra...

Maharaj: Definitely!

Q: The more likely I am to conquer difficult situations.

Maharaj: The Master Key has been given to you. It is up to you how to operate it. The food has been served to you, now you are to eat it. You are the architect, your own architect, your own Master.

36.   *When it Rains, Use an Umbrella*

Q: I have problems at work which are causing me some anxiety and stress. I try not to give them any attention but it's still difficult.

Maharaj: The first thing you must do is concentrate on the meditation. You know you have nothing to do with all these happenings. You are to view them like your dreams and stay unconcerned. If you have a bad dream or a good dream, you don't take any notice of it. You don't let the ego take over. If you can ignore what is going on, ignore it. Don't accept another's thoughts. Act according to your strength and ability. Use your own willpower! You are strong!

Q: I don't feel very strong. It is very difficult to ignore this situation.

Maharaj: Be strong! Meditation will make you stronger so that you grow fearless. All your problems will dissolve with meditation. You will acquire spiritual strength which will empower you, so that you can escape from unpleasant atmospheres. You will become internally strong and be fearless in any circumstance.

Everyone is under pressure, of the mind, ego, intellect. As your power is regenerated slowly, silently, permanently, you will even begin to welcome problems. Your power will be regenerated when the bodily impressions and effects begin to dissolve, making you feel at one remove from worldly things. When you have Conviction, you will know that all thoughts are body-related, and therefore all illusion.

AS LONG AS YOU HAVE LOVE AND AFFECTION FOR THE BODY,
PROBLEMS ARE BOUND TO GIVE YOU TROUBLE.

You are to accept and establish this fact: "You are not, were not, will not remain the body". This means that "You are Ultimate Truth". All worries, all unpleasant atmospheres are body-related. Be calm and quiet! Don't get irritated by feelings. Don't give them any importance. Are you giving attention to every barking dog?

Problems did not exist before beingness, and they will not exist after leaving the body. This means you are unborn. This very basic knowledge is to be the foundation of your spiritual life. Know yourself in a real sense. Don't measure yourself in the body-form. Be strong internally and externally.

DON'T BE A SLAVE OF YOUR MIND,
EGO, INTELLECT.
GO AGAINST THE FLOW!

Develop inner strength and a commanding nature. This will come with the continuous reciting of the *Naam Mantra*. You know Reality! You are a Master! Let that Masterly Essence in you guide your decisions. This guide is leading you forward. It is your Inner Guide, the Listener's Ultimate Truth.

Q: I was feeling hopeless earlier, now I feel good!

Maharaj: The climate has changed, not you! You are not changing, it is only the climate that is changing: happy mood, sad mood, anxious mood, peaceful mood. You are just like sky. Clouds of happiness, restlessness, anxiety, peacefulness, depression, bliss all come and go, but you remain the same, as it is, just like sky.

SEASONS COME AND SEASONS GO,
SEASONS CHANGE,
YOU DO NOT CHANGE.

When it rains you use an umbrella, and when it is cold, you use a sweater. Different thoughts come and go. Clean your hard drive and you will get results. Your laptop is jam-packed, congested with viruses of illusory thoughts. I have given you the anti-virus software, the *Naam Mantra*.

I HAVE GIVEN YOU THE DISK,
NOW YOU HAVE TO INSERT AND INSTALL THIS PROGRAMME.

Wait and watch! After digesting this Reality you will observe the changes. Take your multi-purpose medicine. The *Naam Mantra* is a multi-vitamin that will get rid of all the viruses in your body and build your immunity. Your problems will be solved if you follow the instructions written on your prescription.

Using different angles, I am trying to convince you. Don't worry, deposit your mind, ego, intellect and all your problems in Nashik ashram, then go! It's very simple, very simple.

THE MASTER SAYS,
"THROW YOURSELF INTO THE DEEP OCEAN, THE DEEP SPIRITUAL OCEAN.
THEN YOU WILL BE A GOOD SWIMMER.
WE ARE GIVING YOU TRAINING IN DEEP-SEA DIVING.
WE ARE TEACHING YOU HOW TO DIVE IN THE DEEP SEA,
NOT IN SMALL LAKES OR PUDDLES".

Ignore any problems you encounter in the beginning. Just keep powering on! Around the time when Nisargadatta Maharaj met with Siddharameshwar Maharaj, so that he could have the experience of Knowledge, he suffered many losses. He faced many problems, family, money, health, but because of his Master's power, he rose to the challenge and faced all these problems head-on, while continuing to lead a very simple life. This may happen to you, too.

WHATEVER THE MASTER TELLS YOU,
DO IT AND SEE THE EFFECT.
STRICTLY FOLLOW EVERYTHING YOU HEAR,
AND THEN YOU WILL NOTICE,
AND BE SURPRISED AT THE EXPERIENCES
THAT ARE HAPPENING INTERNALLY.

Q: I look forward to that, but at the moment I am finding it difficult to concentrate. I don't know why, but I am feeling a lot of anger.

Maharaj: The cleaning process has begun! Supposing your stomach feels irritated and clogged up, you will take an appropriate remedy, like fig juice, to try and clean it out. Afterwards, everything will be fine, settled.

Similarly, you are to remove your old files, wrong files with your new *Naam Mantra* programme.

Once this new programme is up and running, its vibrations will take effect and produce complete peace, complete silence. The anger and irritation that you are now feeling means that the programme is working.

You have to persevere because some feelings are very stuck, very rigid because of the long association with the body. But after the melting, melting, everything will be silenced.

Q2: I woke up several times during the night and it felt like dawn. It felt like dawn each time. There was a strong and a very new and fresh state of 'awakeness'. Very fresh!

Maharaj: You will feel some dramatic changes happening inside as you get closer and closer.

Q1: Is the Mantra an object of concentration?

Maharaj: Yes! *Brahman* is the name given to Ultimate Truth. There is no form. It will take some time and patience. Wait and Watch! When you plant seeds you cannot expect the plant to grow immediately. It will take some time. Don't worry!

The Master says, "You are just like the sky. Your Presence is everywhere". But until you have this Conviction, it is necessary to keep doing the Mantra.

Q1: But will the Mantra really work? It would be great if it did!

Maharaj: Let me tell you a story, the secret Mantra story regarding the importance of the *Naam Mantra*, the Guru Mantra. One Master was at Nisargadatta Maharaj's birthplace, his native village. Simple country folk, with little education lived there. The Master was with a disciple he had just given the secret Mantra to. He was told not to disclose it to anyone else.

The next day, the disciple wandered down to the river to bathe. When he got there, everybody was repeating the same word, his secret Mantra! He was somewhat bemused! "My Master is not here and everybody is using my Mantra, something is wrong. What is going on? My Master told me this was a secret, and yet everyone here knows it. How can this be?"

Very confused, he went back to the old Master and said: "What kind of secret word is that? I went by the river and everyone is uttering the same words?" The Master smiled and then gave a stone to his devotee, a shiny round stone. "Just try to know the value of this stone. See if you can find out its value".

The disciple wandered afar for the next fifteen to twenty days, in search of the stone's value. The subtle games of the Master were causing him much hardship. He was naturally full of questions, and filled with confusion, but nevertheless, he followed the instructions of his Master.

First he reached the cottage where his grandmother lived. He asked her: "Mother, I got this stone. What do you think it is worth?" She said, "One or two rupees for that". Then he went to a small local goldsmith. "I have a stone, I want to know the value of it". The local goldsmith looked very dryly at it, and said, "I'll give you four hundred rupees!". "No thank you", he replied. Then moving on to a small city, he asked the owner of a jeweller's shop: "I do not know the value of this stone." The shopkeeper there looked closely at it, and said, "Mm, possibly two thousand rupees!"

Yet another shopkeeper in a wealthier district exclaimed, "Two *lakhs* rupees!" Finally, the disciple carried on his travels to a very big metropolis such as Bombay or New York, and called in at an exclusive and lavish jewellery store, the largest shop he could find. The owner there questioned him excitedly, "Who gave you this? It is invaluable! Unique! Exceptional value! Worth more than this whole shop!"

You can see from this story, that those who understand the real value of something, will have more knowledge of it, and so appreciate its full value.

It's the same with the *Naam Mantra*. Different values are placed on it by different people. Those who know the value of the Mantra rate it highly, and give it immense importance.

THOSE WHO KNOW ITS TRUE VALUE,
GIVE IT THE GREATEST IMPORTANCE.

I am stressing that the *Naam Mantra* has high value, like in this story.

THOSE WHO ARE REALIZED BY IT
HAVE PLACED THE HIGHEST VALUE ON IT, SUCH AS MY MASTER.

For those who take it casually, it has little, or no value. It will not work.

37. *Playing with Dolls*

Maharaj: Do you know the story of the elephant and the blind men? A number of blind men gathered round a huge animal. They were told it was an elephant. The blind men asked, "What is the elephant like?" And so, they began to touch its body. One of them said: "It is like a pillar". He had only touched its leg. Another man said, "The elephant is like a husking basket". This person had only touched its ear. Similarly, those who touched its trunk or its belly talked of it in very different ways. If your view of something is limited, then you will only get a little knowledge of it, which leads to misinformation and confusion.

Here, the Master is showing you the whole elephant. Everybody is struggling, struggling to find Reality, struggling to see the complete elephant, the Ultimate Truth. This is happening all over the world. Each blind person feels a different part. They are all unable to see the entire elephant, the whole picture.

It is advisable not to mix with people with only half-knowledge. They are partially right. But since you have seen the entire elephant, you are not to argue with them, OK? When you know your Ultimate Truth, the Ultimate Secret of your Presence, Invisible Presence, why struggle with others? If you are stable, solid, firm, nobody in the world will be able to distract you.

I don't know about the West, but in India, people are travelling far and wide and shutting themselves away in caves for long periods of time, isolating themselves, trying for some kind of '*samadhi*' experiences, seeking bliss and other such things.

DID YOU PUT YOURSELF IN A CAVE
PRIOR TO BEINGNESS?

Q: I guess not!

Maharaj: They are going here and there, growing long beards, long hair, shaven heads. There are people with garlands, beads, wandering around counting beads. One person recently came from Europe dressed in long robes. He was counting beads to the name of a God. I asked him:

"WHY ARE YOU PLAYING WITH THESE DOLLS?"
WHAT IS THE USE OF COUNTING BEADS?
NOTHING WILL HAPPEN.
YOU ARE NOT GOING TO MAKE ANYTHING HAPPEN.
IT IS JUST A FINGER EXERCISE.

This kind of thing happens a lot because nobody is telling anyone exactly what is what. They are unaware of Truth, Final Truth. Someone says: "Do these things", and they are doing these things, without knowing the purpose behind them. What is the purpose?

What is the point of doing such things? What is the outcome? One should ask oneself and not just follow things blindly. If someone asks you to do these things, ask him what for, what is the purpose? What will I get? What are the benefits? Will it give me happiness? What is the use of counting beads? This is child's play, just children playing with dolls!

Here, the process is one of Self-Conviction, or Self-Realization, or Self-Enlightenment. The names are unimportant. Spiritual science says that the body is made of five elements and three *gunas*. This is body-knowledge, material knowledge, body-knowledge, material knowledge. Spiritual science is body-knowledge, material knowledge. Unless this material knowledge dissolves, you will not be able to know yourself in a real sense.

This body is just a cover, a big cover made of bones, blood and flesh. It is a food-body. If you don't eat for a week, it will waste away. Who is eating the food? Say your body weighs sixty kilos, if you don't eat for a week, it will be fifty-five kilos. So what has happened to the five kilos? Who has taken it?

THIS IS A FOOD-BODY, JUST LIKE A LAMP WHICH NEEDS OIL.
THE MOMENT THE OIL DISAPPEARS,
THE LAMP GOES OUT.
THIS IS VERY, VERY SIMPLE KNOWLEDGE,
BUT PEOPLE MAKE IT COMPLICATED.

This is Direct Knowledge with no in-betweens.

EVERYTHING STARTS FROM YOU,
AND ENDS WITH YOU.
THE ENTIRE WORLD IS PROJECTED
OUT OF YOUR SPONTANEOUS INVISIBLE PRESENCE.
THE MOMENT YOUR BODY DISSOLVES,
THE ENTIRE WORLD DISAPPEARS.

After Conviction, your attachment to this material body will be reduced, and naturally, there won't be any fear.

Q: I am going back to the UK next week. I suppose I am feeling some anxiety.

Maharaj: It is natural to be a little concerned, but at the same time, remember that you are not going anywhere. What is with you, is always with you, and that is Presence.

38. Your Presence is Like Sky

Maharaj:

WHO IS DYING? WHO IS LIVING?
JUST SELF-ENQUIRE.
NOBODY IS DYING, NOBODY IS TAKING BIRTH.

Nisargadatta Maharaj defined the principle of spirituality in one sentence: "Except your Selfless Self there is no God, no *Brahman*, no *Atman*, no *Paramatman*, no Master". This statement has the same meaning as the *bhajan* we sing here every morning. '*Chidananda Shivoham Shivoham*'.

Q: That is a beautiful *bhajan*.

Maharaj: They both say the same thing: there is no mother, brother, no sister, no Master, no disciple, no relations. All relations are body-related relations.

PRIOR TO THE BODY, PRIOR TO BEINGNESS,
YOUR PRESENCE WAS THERE, BUT NOT IN ANY FORM.
AFTER BEINGNESS, YOUR PRESENCE WILL BE THERE,
BUT NOT IN ANY FORM.

If you want to compare yourself to anything, compare yourself to sky. Sky is everywhere, omnipresent. You are Final Truth, you are Ultimate Truth. Therefore, "To say 'I' is illusion, to say 'you' is illusion, to say '*Brahman*' is illusion. The entire world is illusion", said Shankaracharya.

Q: That is quite challenging! It rejects everyone and everything we think of, and view as our reality, and everyone we hold dear.

Maharaj:

YOU HAVE GIVEN SHAPE TO THIS WORLD.
THE MOMENT THE SPIRIT CLICKED WITH THE BODY,
THE DREAM BEGAN. THIS 'LIFE' IS JUST A DREAM.

It is like when you are sleeping, and dreaming. This is a dream. You are acting in this dream as someone, a man or a woman. In the dream, you are seeing gods, seas, oceans, temples. You see many people, many vistas.

After waking from the dream, when everything fades and disappears, ask yourself, "Where did all these people go? Where did all the scenery go?" What happened to the people you were involved with in the dream? Did they go to heaven, or did they go to hell?

Q: I suppose that when we wake up, we just accept that we were dreaming.

Maharaj: Yes, when you wake up after dreaming, do you start weeping, saying, "Oh my friend is gone. I have lost my friend?"

Q: No, because I know it is just a dream.

Maharaj: You know it is a dream, so even if you are dreaming of close friends, and have an attachment to these people in the dream, when you wake up, they are quickly forgotten. Correct?

Q: Yes!

Maharaj: Pay attention! When you awaken from the dream, that whole dream world just disappears. Likewise, this world is just a dream, a long dream which will also disappear. Absorb what I am telling you:

THE WORLD IS A PROJECTION
OF YOUR SPONTANEOUS PRESENCE.
THE WORLD IS A PROJECTION
OF YOUR SPONTANEOUS PRESENCE.

This Knowledge has to be absorbed completely. It is not intellectual knowledge. It is Reality.

THIS IS YOUR KNOWLEDGE,

NOT THE KNOWLEDGE OF *BRAHMAN*.
IT IS THE LISTENER'S KNOWLEDGE,
THE KNOWLEDGE OF YOUR INVISIBLE, ANONYMOUS, UNIDENTIFIED IDENTITY,
THAT CANNOT BE DEFINED USING LANGUAGE,
THAT CANNOT BE DEFINED USING ANY WORDS.

This is called Direct Knowledge. There is nothing in-between. It is Spontaneous and Direct, without long-winded examples and explanations that take one round and round in circles, adding confusion.

These Lineage Masters were just ordinary people, like you and me. They accepted the Reality without reservation from their Masters. The Knowledge came from their struggle and determination to find Reality, and uncover the Knowledge of Selfless Self. They had strong dedication, strong involvement, and a very strong faith, very strong faith.

Be absolutely fearless! When you come to know yourself in a real sense, you will be fearless. Why all this fear of death and birth?

THERE IS NO DEATH AND BIRTH.
YOU ARE UNBORN.

Have some courage! Not egoistic courage, not mental courage, not intellectual courage, but, Spontaneous courage, like, "Yes! Now, I know. I Am That!"

With this new understanding that you now have, you will know that it is not necessary to go begging to others for anything. Why would you do that, when you know that everything is within you? Why go begging when you know that the root of everything is in you?

One saintly person came to me last month. He said: "Please put your hand on my head". "Why?", I asked. "You can put your hand on your own head. We are the same!"

Q: [Smiling], When I first arrived, that's what I wanted to ask you for, but I was too scared. I had some anxieties, a little fear about a particular issue in my life, so I thought a blessing from you would help.

Maharaj: It happens when you are unaware of your own power!

Q: And also when you think that you are separate from it?

Maharaj: Yes, yes, like this saintly man that I may have mentioned. He had studied for about forty or fifty years. This man was full of questions from all his reading of scripture and spiritual books. He had some fears, impressions that had left their mark on him. These impressions had caused him to project his fears out there.

Q: It is like you create your own monster, and then you grow scared of it?

Maharaj: Consequently, this man was afraid of certain deities, and had a fear of God. I asked him:

"WHY ARE YOU AFRAID OF CERTAIN GODS?
YOUR PRESENCE IS NEEDED FOR YOU TO SAY 'GOD'.
WITHOUT YOUR PRESENCE,
THERE IS NO GOD.
GOD IS YOUR CHILD".

Your Presence comes first. Your Presence has to be there before anything else, everything else.

WITHOUT YOUR PRESENCE,
THERE IS NO SUN, NO MOON, NO SEAS, NO OCEANS,

NO PEOPLE, NO OTHERS, NO WORLD, NO GOD.

Suddenly, his face lit up. The Truth was beginning to dawn on him! Again we go back to my Master's statement: "Except your Selfless Self, there is no God, no *Brahman*, no *Atman*, no *Parabrahman*, no Master".

Q: Ah! These are bold statements, very unorthodox, most controversial. But in all truth, I have to say that what you have just said is extraordinary! Not just this, but all of the teachings are radical. I have read a lot, but I have never heard this kind of knowledge expressed in the way you do. It is so clear! Amazing! I feel like saying "I've got it!", but then I know, you will pull me up and say, "Who has got it?"

Maharaj: It is rare Knowledge, high teachings. Nisargadatta Maharaj used to say that when you understand that there is only Selfless Self, you will stop hurting 'others'. You will not despise anyone. There will be no feelings of hatred or jealousy for anyone, because you will know that there is no enemy anywhere in existence. You will know that you are everywhere. At that time, you will know.

YOU KNOW THAT YOU ARE NOT THE BODY-FORM,
SO THERE IS NO QUESTION OF JEALOUSY,
ENMITY OR HATRED.
THE SPIRIT THAT IS WITH YOU
IS THE SPIRIT THAT IS WITH EVERYBODY, WITH EVERY BEING.
THEREFORE, ASK YOURSELF:
WHO IS GOOD? WHO IS BAD?
WHO IS GREAT? WHO IS SMALL?

You have been looking here and there, like a person wearing a blindfold. There is no need for this any more. Don't be afraid, and don't run away from your life. Be fearless!

Yes, difficulties will be there, at times unpleasant atmospheres, but no problem, just let them come and let them go. You are steady, you are firm. OK? Now sit and meditate! Absorb this Knowledge.

Q: Thank you, Maharaj.

39. Are You Realized?

Q: I have been going for Satsang and visiting various so-called 'Neo-Advaitin' teachers for the last few years. But, it has still left me hungry. It's hard to put into words, but the knowledge that is being given from you is absolute, complete and fulfilling. It strikes an inner chord of truth that leaves me satisfied and at peace.

I don't know if being in your Presence has something to do with it, but I find that I can't stop smiling. There is a tangible sense of spiritual nourishment in the atmosphere and a ring of truth to everything you say. I just know it's Truth. The Knowledge that you share here is very fresh, rare and alive, also perhaps because it is spontaneous....

Maharaj: Knowledge means just to know oneself in a real sense, and not in the body-form. It is basically True Knowledge of Oneself, Self-Knowledge. So identify yourself in a real sense. You know yourself with the mind, ego, intellect, and all the concepts, but you are beyond that.

YOU ARE BEYOND ALL OF THAT.
YOUR PRESENCE IS NOT THIS.
THIS KNOWLEDGE IS A DIRECT APPROACH

TO THE INVISIBLE, ANONYMOUS LISTENER.

How long have you known yourself as a body-form? How long is this body-form going to last? OK, we have certain information, but this knowledge is body-knowledge, dry knowledge. Unless you know yourself in a real sense, Knowledge will not be there.

Nisargadatta Maharaj says, "All these things, all these words that are used about God, about spirituality, this life, the afterlife, so many things... about this, about that, about the future. All these words and concepts, all of them are solely related to body-knowledge".

Q: What you are saying is that everything that we have learned, studied and experienced, all the knowledge we have amassed over the years, is not real knowledge, not true knowledge. It is all just what you refer to as 'body-knowledge'?

Maharaj: Of course, of course. You see, prior to beingness, you were totally unaware. You were totally unaware of anything and everything. You did not even know the word 'knowledge', because you did not know yourself. You were not bothered with the body-form at all. But the moment the Spirit clicked with the body, self-identification began. Conditioning started when, eg, Mom said, "You are a girl. You are a boy called Ravi. This is Sita, there is John", and so on.

And as you heard the various statements that were made about you, they defined you to a large extent, and you accepted them without question. Over time, these layers of impressions that were formed since childhood, moulded you. And what happened is that you bought into the illusory world of body-knowledge, and took it all for real.

So what we are doing here is inviting the attention of the Silent, Invisible, Anonymous Listener within you. We are addressing your Reality, prior to beingness, and prior to the formation of illusory layers that were, say, put on top, or superimposed on your Reality.

Q: Reality was covered over by a blanket of illusion, which we then mistook for Reality?

Maharaj: Remember, don't take my words literally. What I am trying to convey is most important. We are inviting the attention of the Silent, Invisible, Anonymous Listener. You are Ultimate Truth, you are Final Truth.

THE SILENT,
INVISIBLE, ANONYMOUS LISTENER - REALITY.
YOU ARE THAT.

Though you cannot really indicate Ultimate Truth, we need to use some words that come close to pointing to that Reality. But don't buy into the words.

When we are talking in conversation, or having a discussion, you have to use words to get the sense, the principle, the gist, the essential meaning of words. What does a particular word wish to convey? People come here and they want to discuss things and hold a debate. There is no debate.

THE KNOWLEDGE THAT IS SHARED HERE IS DIRECT, TRUE,
AND NOT UP FOR DEBATE.

Q: I hope you don't mind me asking, Maharaj, but, are you Realized?

Maharaj: This is a silly question. How are you going to assess if someone else is Realized or not? You have to see whether you are Realized, instead of comparing this Master, with that Master, with that other Master. This question is an unnecessary question, a body-based question.

Q: Sorry, I thought it was, but I could not stop myself from asking.

Maharaj: Instead of asking this, focus on you! What is your purpose? You have to come out of this whole illusionary world. And when you know yourself, when this happens, the world, all this body-knowledge, will gradually get less and less. It will have little to no effect on you. But for this, serious involvement is required.

So you have to question, Self-enquire! You have to come out of the illusionary picture, the illusionary world. Things which are not present, that do not exist, you blindly sign up for, and accept as real.

Q: So, how do I become Self-Realized? What I mean is how do I get there?

Maharaj: There is no 'becoming'. There is no 'you'. And, there is nothing to 'get'. In the first instance, all body-based knowledge has to dissolve. Then, only after clearing out all this knowledge, will Ultimate Truth emerge and come out.

What I'm telling you just now will come out of you spontaneously, without your knowledge, and you will exclaim, "Oh! This Knowledge is flowing". It will just happen.

Stop considering yourself as the body-form. The impressions from childhood till today, and all the conditioning must be dissolved and erased.

**YOU MUST HAVE COMPLETE TRUST IN YOURSELF,
AS WELL AS COMPLETE TRUST IN YOUR MASTER.**

This is basically what is needed. Nisargadatta Maharaj had strong faith in his Master, Siddharameshwar Maharaj, and he, too, in his Master before him. So don't stress your mind or the brain, for it will happen spontaneously.

Q: Yesterday, when you were speaking, Maharaj, there was a clarity, and what was said was just right for that moment. You were speaking direct to the... which I wasn't fully aware of, but then afterwards... it was like "Aha!" You know? You said the right thing, at the right time. It felt like Direct Knowledge. But it wasn't just what was said...

For a moment, it was as if the listener and the speaker united, merged, and there was a pause of Oneness. It went beyond words.

Maharaj: Beyond words, beyond worlds. Plain Truth is being spoken here, there is no hide and seek. This Knowledge is Direct Knowledge and this approach is a direct approach.

**THIS IS NOT AN INTELLECTUAL APROACH,
NOT A LOGICAL APPROACH,
NOT AN EGOISTIC APPROACH,
AS ALL THESE THINGS CAME AFTER YOUR PRESENCE.**

40.   *Food-Body-Knowledge*

Maharaj: Because we are not looking inwards, we are ignoring the Searcher and the Finder, and running here and there instead. Everybody is running here and there for happiness, for peace. Everyone is misguided, some going this way, some going that way. People are searching, looking outside themselves, always looking for answers outside of themselves, in other people, in books, in holy places.

Q: We are looking for things from external sources, instead of trying to find answers from within?

Maharaj: Yes, you must have a strong will to enquire, to know, to find the answers to these Ultimate questions. "Who am I? What does death mean? What do you mean by birth? How was I prior to my beingness?" These unsolved questions need to be solved. Unless you go deeper and deeper, you are not going to be able to know yourself.

Q: I suppose most of us just get on with life. We put up with the ups and downs, and get carried along. Most of my friends are like that, too.

Maharaj: Forget about others! Talk about you!

Q: I suppose, I don't manage to find enough time to do much Self-enquiry.

Maharaj: Time is connected with the body only. There is no time at all. So forget about all these concepts! Prior to beingness, there was no time, nothing was there. All concepts appeared along with the body. You must be aware of that. Be convinced and have Conviction.

Q: I will! I will try and remember.

Maharaj: Everyone has different kinds of fear, and at times, find themselves shaking and trembling with fear, in unpleasant atmospheres. Even when a small tremor of confusion appears, you become disturbed and depressed. Train yourself not to fall into illusion!

All you have to do when there is an upset is find out, ask yourself, "What is the cause of my depression?" "Who is disturbed?" "What is causing the unhappiness and dispeace?" "How can I be tension-free?" "How can I be fearless?" These questions have to be solved. All the answers to these questions are within you, but you are trying to find the answers from out there, from the material world.

YOU ARE TRYING TO FIND HAPPINESS AND PEACE
FROM MATERIAL SOURCES
OUTSIDE OF YOURSELF.

People are often misguided in spirituality. They listen to whoever they meet. They are told to do this thing, do that thing, perform this sacrifice, donate some money, go here, go there. There are so many rituals. It is not just in India, it is the same all over the world.

People are seeking happiness and peace from sources outside of themselves, but they do not know their own Identity. They are wandering, travelling, roaming here and there, trying to find out where this happiness and peace is, with no success. To some extent, they are deceived by spirituality, in the name of spirituality.

Q: That is true. Spirituality is a commercial business these days, a commodity. I have lost a lot of my friends to so-called Neo-advaitin teachers. These friends don't seem to realize that it is *maya* at work. They are even paying for so-called 'Truth'. This is surely a bad start, a very shaky foundation for spirituality and truth. These teachers encourage dependency for financial gain. I can't speak for all of them, but...

Q2: Well, I know that the Neo-Movement often does not go very deep, but at least they are making people aware that you and the world are unreal, like there is no body there, nobody there you know...

Maharaj: OK. Here, the Master is making you Masters, not disciples. He is making you independent. You don't need anything from the outside. Everything is within you. You will find lasting happiness and peace, without any material cause.

BECAUSE OF THIS FOOD-BODY,

BECAUSE OF THIS FOOD-BODY-KNOWLEDGE,
WE HAVE FORGOTTEN OUR IDENTITY.

And so, because you have forgotten your Identity, that is why you must undergo the practice of meditation and Self-enquiry. One must have the Conviction that, "I am nothing to do with the food-body-knowledge and the food-body. It is only because I am providing food, that the food-body survives". But, more importantly, listen carefully, if the Spirit is not there in the first place, this body will not be able to function.

THIS BODY CANNOT WORK WITHOUT SPIRIT.

Q: Is 'Spirit' the same as Spontaneous Presence?

Maharaj: Yes, yes, but these are just the words, just the names. Don't grasp the words, grasp the meaning behind them. Come out of this vicious circle of body-knowledge. Come out of death and birth. Know yourself in a real sense because the body is not your Identity. I am repeatedly telling all of you:

YOU ARE NOT THE BODY,
YOU WERE NOT THE BODY,
YOU ARE NOT GOING TO REMAIN THE BODY.

The body only has value because of your Spontaneous Presence, Anonymous Presence, Invisible Presence which is unaware of its own Identity.

THAT SPONTANEOUS PRESENCE,
INVISIBLE PRESENCE,
IS UNAWARE OF ITS OWN IDENTITY
BECAUSE IT IS VAST,
ALMIGHTY,
OMNIPRESENT,
JUST LIKE SKY.

The sky does not know that, "I am sky". You say, "This is sky", "This is space". The sun does not know, "I am sun", or "I am moon", or "I am water". Your Identity is beyond, beyond that, beyond that.

There are many limitations because of the body. You have to come out from the circle of body-knowledge. You are the architect of your life. You are the Master of your life. Have some courage!

Q: When you give this kind of direct teaching, Maharaj, this peaceful feeling comes over me. But then I wonder, "What is the feeling? Who or what is feeling that?"

Maharaj: The Listener is listening to its own story. The Invisible Listener is listening to its own story, and therefore it is feeling wholly at peace. If someone talks about you and narrates your story, like your name, your place of birth etc, when this happens, you will say, "This is my story!"

The Invisible Listener is listening. Knowledge is being absorbed when this Invisible, Unidentified Identity listens. And then you forget your identity. You forget your individuality. There is Spontaneous Peace. You have become absolutely unconcerned with the whole body-form and all its related body feelings. Though you are holding the body, you are totally unconcerned, and so, there are no feelings, no feelings of 'I'.

Keep doing the practice, go deeper and deeper and deeper. Only then, will you find exceptional happiness without any material cause.

THERE IS ONLY ONE SOURCE.

YOU ARE THE SOURCE.
THERE IS ONLY SELFLESS SELF.

As Nisargadatta Maharaj said about the gist of spirituality, the summation, the principle of philosophy and spirituality:

"EXCEPT YOUR SELFLESS SELF THERE IS NO GOD,
NO *BRAHMAN*, NO *ATMAN*, NO *PARAMATMAN*,
NO MASTER".

41.   *The Master is Ultimate*

Q: What is faith, Maharaj?

Maharaj: Faith is a simple thing, it is complete acceptance. Put spiritual knowledge aside for a moment! Here is a simple example. Suppose I gave you the directions to get to a place. With faith, you will follow the instructions and go in that direction. If you have faith and trust, you will not be misguided.

Faith is simple devotion. If illiterate people can reveal spiritual knowledge, why is it difficult for you? You went to college, you are educated. They were not so qualified, but they had strong faith in the Masters, like in the following story of a fisherwoman.

It was the rainy season, and at this time there were evenings of lectures and kirtans taking place in the neighbourhood. A fisherwoman wished to go, in spite of the stormy weather. The lecturer said: "Keep the name of Lord Krishna on your lips, and you will get to the lecture safely".

The boatman who was to take her there, was a little anxious and reluctant to go out in the stormy seas. The fisherwoman reassured him. She was fearless. They set off. Throughout the journey, the fisherwoman kept the name of Lord Krishna on her lips. The boat managed to avoid the high waves. She arrived at the house safely.

The lecturer looked surprised to see her. He said: "How did you come through the flood?" She answered, "You told me to keep Lord Krishna on my lips, and all would be well".

The fisherwoman did not apply her intellect to the situation, just simple INNOCENT DEVOTION. This story is a good example of how, if you have complete faith, you do not need anything else.

FAITH MEANS
FAITH IN YOU.
YOUR INNER MASTER WILL REGENERATE YOUR POWER,
AND GIVE YOU GUIDANCE.
INSTRUCTIONS WILL APPEAR SPONTANEOUSLY.
IF I TELL YOU, YOU ARE *BRAHMAN*,
YOU ARE *ATMAN*,
YOU MUST ACCEPT WHAT THE MASTER HAS SAID.
YOU MUST HAVE FAITH IN THE MASTER'S WORDS.
THERE SHOULD NOT BE ANY DOUBTS.

Siddharameshwar Maharaj used to tell this story about a saint who told his disciple to, "Go down and give that grass to the cow". So the disciple went away and looked for the cow. There was no cow, he could only see a dog standing there. He knew that when his Master instructed him to feed the cow grass, he had to give the grass to the dog, maybe believing the dog was a cow.

So he fed the grass to the dog. He passed the test because he did not question his Master. He followed his Master's instructions. He had good faith, complete faith in the Master. That is faith!

Q: So even if you find the instructions a little strange, you have to carry them through because they have come from the Master?

Maharaj: Yes! As you know, in our Lineage, we give a Mantra. You must have faith in the Master, faith in the Initiation and faith in the Mantra. There should not be any doubts arising in you. You are to completely accept that Knowledge, that Reality, without any question, without any confusion.

HAVE COMPLETE LOYALTY TO THE MASTER,
AND TO SELFLESS SELF.

If you do not have faith, you will be easily influenced, and then conflict and confusion will arise, and create problems for you.

Q: When you say you must have faith, do you mean faith in God?

Maharaj: In this life that we are living, we must have faith in something, maybe God, maybe a Master. Having faith and trust is essential.

Q: And you need to believe in yourself, too?

Maharaj: Of course. You must have faith in yourself. If you don't, you will not have faith in others. If you yourself are confused, you will not have faith in others. For example, if your parents told you not to do something, you would not do it. You know they are instructing you out of good intentions, a good motive. If you go against their wishes, then this is a sign of disrespect.

So somewhere in your life you have to keep faith. At the same time, there needs to be alertness. That's why I am telling everyone not to nod their heads unless they are convinced, "Oh! Maharaj said.... Oh, I don't know about that", and you start questioning. No, this is not the way. If you accept Knowledge and you still have doubts, this will only create conflict and problems.

Q: Faith in the Master has to be complete, or not at all?

Maharaj: Yes! When you accept someone as your Master, you must have dedication, a co-relationship. You must have perfect dedication, to the extent that you feel very strongly that:

THIS IS MY MASTER
AND THIS IS THE ULTIMATE.

If you go to the doctor and he prescribes medicine for you, you must have some faith. Faith is acceptance, but it is not blind faith.

Q: And what is blind faith?

Maharaj: Magic and that sort of thing, where people are looking to others for miraculous experiences. People who claim to be performing miracles, and those who buy into what they are selling, that is blind faith. You may go on a fast, deny yourself, or torture the body because you have faith that this sort of thing might bring about change in your material life.

After accepting the Master, you should not mix with others who may distract you. Nisargadatta

Maharaj warned us. He said, "You are devotees of your Master. The Master has given you Ultimate Truth, the entire thing. After that, you should not come across people with half-knowledge or those who will distract you".

Q: Therefore faith in the Master means being committed to the Master for life?

Maharaj: Nisargadatta Maharaj said:

EVEN IF GOD APPEARS BEFORE YOU, YOU SHOULD NOT GIVE ANY RESPONSE BECAUSE YOUR MASTER IS ULTIMATE.

Q: Because the Master is Ultimate! That is beautiful!

Maharaj: Nisargadatta Maharaj used to tell this story about a great saint from the Himalayas. He sent one of his disciples to ask Nisargadatta Maharaj if he would receive this saint's powers. The saint said, "You are the only person to whom I can offer my power which I have gained after long, long, practice." He was very old and feeble.

Nisargadatta Maharaj said, "Tell your Master, 'Swami, I am not a widow'. It means, even though my Master is not physically alive, he is with me, he is my power". [This was shortly after his own Master Siddharameshwar Maharaj had left the body.] "Go tell your Master." The Himalayan Master was getting very irritated because his offer was rejected, and he was being so bluntly refused. He felt insulted.

The saint sent another message, this time with threats: "I will do something to you, something wicked with my power". Again Nisargadatta Maharaj said, "You can't do anything. My Master is very great, the greatest". The saint listened and then, he said: "Oh! This boy is truly Realized!"

Nisargadatta Maharaj was not at all tempted by this great saint offering his power. He had complete faith and trust.

THERE IS NO COMPROMISE WITH FAITH AND TRUST.

This is a sign of a Realized One. You have trust and faith in yourself, and in the Master.

On another occasion, the then Prime Minister, Indira Gandhi sent some people to invite Nisargadatta Maharaj to visit her. He refused. He never bowed down to anyone else because of expectations, or money, or honour. If someone pointed out and said to my Master, "Here is a great saint!", he would not flinch, and showed neither happiness nor sadness. So that same quality is to be established in you.

I am sharing the same thing with everybody. Some people like the teachings, some people do not. Important people, unimportant people, that is irrelevant. I am placing before them their own Truth, Final Truth. You may or may not accept it.

See the daily dramas as a test of your Knowledge, and you will gradually be drawn in less and less by any attractions. Even if God appeared before you, you will know that God is a projection of your Presence.

THE FIGURE OF GOD IS YOUR REFLECTION.

To say God, your Presence is required. God does not have an independent identity. This is straight power. I learned so many things from my Master.

42. *The Rope and the Snake*

Q: I think I understand that the core of the practice is faith and Conviction that the Spontaneous Presence is the Reality, and that is where you stay. And that continues to annihilate the body-knowledge, the mind-knowledge?

Maharaj: We are using words like 'spontaneous' just to invite attention of the Invisible Listener. Yet, the Listener does not have any language.

If you are strongly dedicated it will not be difficult to absorb the teachings. Now you know better. You know that this external identity is not going to remain constant. Conviction is essential for spirituality, the Conviction that you are not the body.

Your Spontaneous Presence is Anonymous, Invisible, Unidentified. You can call it Spirit, or Power, if you like. The names are not important. Some Spirit is there through which we are talking. Some power is there working in the background when we are looking, when we are listening. All activities are for the body, all activities are for the body.

THERE IS SOME POWER, SOME STRENGTH,
SOME SPIRIT THERE, JUST LIKE ELECTRICITY.
IT IS INVISIBLE, ANONYMOUS AND UNIDENTIFIED.

It is that which enables us to feel. Without it, you cannot utter a single word. Without it, you cannot even raise your hand. You are using the body, but the body is not using you. Without your Spontaneous Presence, you can't even lift a finger. Without the power, without the Spirit, there can be no movement. That Spirit is called *Brahman*, *Atman*, *Paramatman*, God, *Parabrahman*, Master.

That Spirit, that Invisible, Anonymous and Unidentified Presence, has been called by many different names.

THAT YOU ARE!

Q: What is this Presence, this Spirit?

Maharaj:

IT HAS NO DEATH,
IT HAS NO BIRTH
JUST THAT, JUST THAT.

Q: After the death of the body, what is left?

Maharaj: Simple, simple:

THERE IS NOTHING.
NO EXPERIENCE,
NO EXPERIENCER.
NO KNOWLEDGE.
NOTHING.
NOTHING IS LEFT.

Q: We are always just Presence, so after the body disappears, are we still Presence?

Maharaj: Nothing is there before and nothing is there after. When a person's body disappears, how will his world appear then?

Q: Without the beingness, without the body, obviously, there is no appearance, no world. There's nothing.

Maharaj: Yes, because the world is the Spontaneous Projection of your Spontaneous Presence! Therefore, no body, no world! Nothing. We are using these words just for the purpose of communicating. So, the 'something' that appeared as the body, then disappears. That something is then merged with nothing. Something is merged with nothing. They are interrelated. Put simply:

OUT OF NOTHING
THERE IS SOMETHING.
THEN THAT SOMETHING
GOES BACK TO NOTHING.
NOTHING MERGES WITH SOMETHING
SOMETHING MERGES WITH NOTHING.

Q: But, there is no 'something' in reality. That something is illusion because there is only Spontaneous Presence?

Maharaj: Yes, yes. With this understanding, we want to have the Conviction which says:

"I AM TOTALLY UNCONCERNED WITH THE WORLD".

Q: You mean, view everything in a new light, with a new perspective?

Maharaj: Don't make any effort, it will happen spontaneously. The Conviction is Spontaneous. The Conviction is Spontaneous.

ALL NEEDS,
ALL RELATIONS AND EXPECTATIONS
ARE BODY-RELATED.

We want peace. Who wants peace? We want happiness. Who wants happiness? We want a tension-free life. What is a tension-free life? What is the meaning of happiness? What is the meaning of peace?

WE DID NOT KNOW THESE TERMS PRIOR TO BEINGNESS.
THEY CAME WITH THE BODY AND
THEY WILL GO WITH THE BODY.

These are the bodily requirements, not YOUR requirements. The body dissolves. Open fact! You have fear, everybody has some fear because of attachments to the body.

NO ONE WANTS DEATH.
EVERYONE IS AFRAID OF DEATH.
BUT WHEN YOU COME TO KNOW THE TRUTH ABOUT DEATH,
YOU WILL NO LONGER HAVE ANY FEAR.

Ask yourself, "Why do I fear death?" Unless you know the Reality, this fear will carry on murmuring and multiplying. The fearless state at the time of death is real knowledge, pragmatic knowledge, Ultimate Truth.

Q: And how long do you think it will take to know, really know and accept the truth about death?

Maharaj: Why do you say, "How long?" It is instant! You know the famous story of the rope and the snake?

Q: Yes.

Maharaj: Therefore, if you know, you will also know that it is instant. At first, you are afraid of what you perceive to be a snake. There is fear. Then, in the light, when you see that it is only a rope, the fear disappears in a second. It is a matter of fact that there is no snake, that it is just a rope!

SIMILARLY, WHEN WE KNOW THAT WE ARE UNBORN,
THAT DEATH IS ONLY APPLICABLE TO THE BODY,
THAT FEAR OF DEATH THAT WE HAD,
BECAUSE WE DID NOT KNOW ANY BETTER,
WILL DISAPPEAR.

It will simply vanish because now we know better.

Q: I can see how I have carried certain fears around with me. I know there is no death. I have known this, but maybe only intellectually, I suppose. At the same time, I have been aware that I am very attached to the body which has caused fear and anxiety.

Maharaj: Yes, yes, it happens. That is why I insist on, I keep telling everyone:

SELF-ENQUIRE!
YOU MUST KNOW YOURSELF IN A REAL SENSE.
YOU ARE NOT THE BODY-FORM.
WHO IS DYING? WHO IS TAKING BIRTH?
SELF-ENQUIRE! SELF-ENQUIRE! SELF-ENQUIRE!

You are the root of all Knowledge. You are not the body. You are the root of this whole world. The Invisible Listener is the root of this whole world. The entire world is projected out of your Spontaneous Presence.

Q2: Maharaj, you often stress the importance of having a solid foundation. Well, while I was reciting the Mantra, there was a sense in which the formless 'me' was taken deeper. An image of a cave appeared. It was a very deep dwelling. I was going deeper and deeper inside myself.

It is hard to talk about. Eventually the bottom was reached. It was like solid stone, a strong base. That was the lowest or deepest that I could go. Then I saw myself standing at the very bottom of this cave. It was like the formless looking at the form. I recognized a solid foundation was there, an indestructible base for the Knowledge to be built on.

There's a lot happening at the moment, spontaneously. Just before falling asleep last night, Bhausaheb Maharaj appeared in deep blue. The energy coming from him was very strong. He was floating in front of my eyes for some time. Then I noticed Nisargadatta Maharaj standing at the side as well. It was amazing!

Maharaj: It happens. The Masters are encouraging you.

43. *Everything Comes Out of Nothing*

Maharaj: Everything comes out of nothing. Your Presence was there prior to beingness.

Q: What about consciousness. I notice you don't talk about consciousness?

Maharaj: Consciousness came afterwards. In order for you to say 'consciousness', your Presence has to be there first. Presence is Anonymous Presence, Invisible Presence. Even your 'I' is not present there. Presence is needed for you to say 'I'. Without using the body you cannot say 'I'.

So names, labels, pointers, all words came afterwards. Prior to these, your Presence was there. I am inviting attention to that Presence, that Invisible Anonymous Presence.

YOU ARE ANONYMOUS BECAUSE "YOU ARE",
WITHOUT YOUR KNOWLEDGE.
YOUR REFLECTION IS THERE.

There is no mind. This came afterwards. The moment Spirit clicked with the body, the entire world was projected out. Prior to that, there was your Spontaneous Invisible Existence. I am inviting, drawing your attention to That. There is no reason, there is no meaning to it all. We are not talking about awareness. When you say 'awareness', it implies the existence of some thing, some form being there. You are formless.

What is the use of the mouth, the eyes, the ears? You can't speak, or see, or hear without Presence. Without Presence, they are just holes. It is most important to understand this teaching. Have full concentration, full involvement, and then you will understand. We have become victims of body-knowledge.

All these are words. I am inviting your attention to Reality, using some words, but Reality is beyond words. We have created the words and have given them meaning. However, what we are trying to talk about is beyond words. We say 'mind', 'awareness', 'consciousness'. These are just the various words: this is 'A', this is 'B', 'C' and so on. Therefore don't take the words literally.

You are to go under the direction of the Master, and listen to the direct teachings. It is simple. Dry discussion will not serve the purpose. A Master is needed, any Master of your choosing, but when you do go and see the Master, you must have strong faith, complete faith in that Master.

I mentioned the great saint who offered his powers to Nisargadatta Maharaj. He refused. Why did he refuse? Because he had complete faith and trust in his Master. Even if God appears before you, you will say "Sorry, No". This Conviction leads to the Reality. My words here are also illusion, but what I am trying to convey, will lead to the Reality. Conviction!

Q: About the meditation, Maharaj. When you are meditating, you start reciting the Mantra slowly at first, and then it goes even slower and slower. I want to ask you if what I'm doing is correct. After a long time, the Mantra gets fainter, but it is still there. You feel your body relaxing, you feel your mind quietening. And then you get to a point where you are in between awake and asleep, just on the edge. So on the website you have the picture of the egg with light coming through. Is that crack the same as what is going on in my meditation? Is that it?

Maharaj: Everything is illusion! What you see after your Presence is illusion.

EVERYTHING YOU SEE AFTER YOUR PRESENCE IS ILLUSION.

Everything is illusion. Even if you see God, your Master, it is illusion. There is nothing! There is nothing but concepts.

I told you that the Spirit through which you are talking, listening, accepting everything is very sensitive. It is its nature to accept everything spontaneously. If your involvement is deep and full, then that is reflected or projected.

Suppose you have strong faith in the Master and have become one with him. You are living elsewhere and encounter a problem. Because of your faith, even though you are living elsewhere, Spirit can take the form or figure of the Master. You may see me there, just like one devotee who was undergoing a seven hour operation saw me standing nearby. Later, he asked me, "How did they let you inside the operating theatre, Maharaj? It was a miracle!"

I told him that he saw me because he is One with me in Spirit. Master is there to protect you at any and every moment. Out of that Oneness, Spirit projects the Master and takes shape.

When a Master who has left his body appears to a disciple, this does not mean, as has often been misunderstood, that the Master has taken rebirth. No! The Masters are free. He has not taken rebirth or appeared as a dead Master.

WHEN YOU BECOME ONE WITH SELFLESS SELF,
YOUR IDENTITY IS FORGOTTEN.
WHEN YOU ASK FOR SOMETHING,
YOUR IDENTITY THEN POSES AS YOUR MASTER.
IT TAKES THE SHAPE OF YOUR MASTER.

Problems will come your way, but if you have deep love and remember your Master, or God in whatever form, your problems are quickly forgotten.

GOD HAS NO IDENTITY.
YOUR SPONTANEOUS PRESENCE IS TAKING SHAPE.

Then you say, "Oh, I have seen God". This is *Darshan*. When you have faith and trust in the Master, you get the Master's touch.

Q2: Talking about Masters appearing. I was sitting quietly on my own recently. It was a peaceful afternoon at home and the Mantra was silently humming away in the background, without my deliberately reciting it. I became aware of something. I looked to the side and there was Ramana Maharshi sitting on one of the chairs! I was amazed! And that wasn't all. I looked across to the couch, and both Nisargadatta Maharaj and Siddharameshwar Maharaj were sitting on it! Nothing was said, but their Presence was there.

The next day I was thinking back on what happened, and wondering where you were Maharaj? Then I realized that you were within me, that we are One, and that is why you did not appear with the others. But it was pretty extraordinary!

Q: That's very interesting. I used to think that the Masters returned, like *bodhisattvas*, to help us.

So, what I was saying about meditation, earlier, is it good to stay there in the in-between stage?

Maharaj: Yes, because this is the process. You are inviting the attention of the meditator. Don't overemphasize it, meditation is just the process. You are getting rid of all the deeply engraved illusory impressions that you have a lot of love and affection for.

As you get closer and closer to Selfless Self, you forget your identity. You forget everything. The whole world is illusion, and God is illusion because in order to see something, your Presence must be there. Without Presence, nothing can be seen. This is very high Knowledge, top Knowledge. You won't find this anywhere. Meditation is the process, and *bhajan* is also part of the process to help you forget your external identity.

Q: Are the physical reactions to meditation normal, like headaches?

Maharaj: Don't pay so much attention to this!

DON'T STRESS OUT
AND BE SO INTENSE WITH IT ALL,

saying: "I have to do meditation, recite the mantra, sing the *bhajans*". When you are emphasizing it in this way, and 'stressing-out', you are taking ego.

Carry on as normal! All activities, including spirituality, should be normal. There should not be any subtle ego either. It is very easy, but also very difficult because you have read a lot of books that have left a lot of impressions. You have listened to many people: "So-and-so says this, and So-and-so says that", and then you analyze and compare them.

Everything is within the circle of your Presence. Don't analyze things like a computer does. Who is going to talk about the world, meditation, Masters, God, if Presence were not there? Therefore, spirituality is itself illusion. When Conviction comes you will find this out, "Yes, everything is illusion, including spirituality".

BE WITH YOU,
ALL THE TIME.
BE NORMAL WITH IT ALL.

Reality is before you. Live a simple life, a humble life. "Oh I've got knowledge!" No! Knowledge is no knowledge. Everything comes out of nothing and everything dissolves back into nothing.

44.   *Reality is Engraved in the Invisible Listener*

Maharaj: The Master is placing the *Naama Mantra* in your spiritual computer. You have to follow it seriously. Once you realize that you are nobody, you will be completely unconcerned with the body, with the world. You will feel totally indifferent.

YOUR PRESENCE IS SPONTANEOUS
JUST LIKE THE SKY.

The entire world is projected out of Presence. Without our Presence, we cannot see the world. We can't see anything.

THAT PRESENCE IS
ANONYMOUS, INVISIBLE, UNIDENTIFIED IDENTITY.
IT IS CALLED *BRAHMAN, ATMAN, PARAMATMAN.*
AND FOR THAT PRESENCE,
THERE IS NO DEATH AND NO BIRTH.

When you accept that you are unborn, that you are Ultimate, all these questions about heaven and hell will no longer arise. They have no relevance.

THERE IS NO NEED OF SALVATION EITHER
BECAUSE YOU KNOW
THAT THERE IS NOBODY THERE TO BE SAVED.

All this talking about *karma* and *prarabdha*, has proved pointless.

Q: Surely there must be *prarabdha*?

Maharaj: The concept of *prarabdha* is only there to pacify people. There is no individuality and therefore no *prarabdha*.

Q: And religion?

Maharaj: Religion? We created religion, just to give some peace and contentment to the people. It is there to give them an identity. It is there to control the masses. Forget about all these concepts. Forget about everything. All these things are body-related. All this knowledge is body-form knowledge.

Q: I don't know what to say, Maharaj. It feels like the more I listen to the teachings, the more you are stripping away, taking everything away from me. I will have nothing left to hold onto which makes me feel a little nervous. You have a knack of wiping out everything we seem to value, everything by which we live.

Maharaj: You are to use discrimination to separate Reality from illusion. Also, you are to erase all body-knowledge. Remember what I told you:

**ULTIMATE REALITY WILL NOT COME OUT UNTIL
ALL BODY-KNOWLEDGE HAS BEEN DISSOLVED.**

It was only after beingness, that you came across all these things that you have become attached to. 'This' thing, 'That' thing, it is all body-knowledge, second-hand knowledge. These illusory concepts came with the body-form. Prior to the body-form, were you familiar with the word 'illusory'?

Q: I guess not.

Maharaj: And prior to beingness, did these names of individuals belong to anyone? Were you called 'Michael' prior to beingness?

Q: No! I know, there were no names, no individuals, nobody!

Maharaj: Religions and the principle of religion were formed just to stimulate a peaceful life. The principle of praying was formed as well. It is OK, as long as:

**YOU KNOW AND UNDERSTAND
THE SECRET OF YOUR LIFE.
YOU MUST REALIZE WHAT IT MEANS.
ONLY THEN, WILL YOU BE TOTALLY FEARLESS.**

Self-enquire! "Why should I fear death when it is common to us all?"

Q: That is true!

Maharaj: You may think that no one can escape from the concepts of 'death' and 'the dead', but find out, "Who is dying? Who is living?" Just Self-enquire! I will repeat this again and again. With direct hammering, you will eventually get the message:

**NOBODY IS DYING,
NOBODY IS TAKING BIRTH.
NOBODY IS DYING, NOBODY IS TAKING BIRTH.
YOU ARE UNBORN. YOU ARE UNBORN.**

The problem is that we are thinking from the point of view of the body-form, and we have blindly accepted all these concepts, all these illusory concepts: "I'm a man", or, "I am a woman". "I belong to this religion", or, "I belong to that religion". "My last birth was like this, and my next birth will be like that". Present birth, last birth, next birth, rebirth... We are caught up in the circle of illusion, going round, and round, and round.

Q: So the problem is that we have accepted concepts, belief systems, philosophies, etc, without giving too much thought to any of it?

Maharaj: We have blindly accepted, and blindly signed, without question. We continue to sign and accept all these illusions... say, it is like, you may not have committed any crime, but you are still signing a confession that states, "I am a criminal".

The Master says you have not committed any crime. You cannot, but still you accept the concepts, the illusions, and say, "It is OK. I am a criminal". The Master is making you enlightened. You were never a criminal. You are not a criminal.

YOUR MASTER IS YOUR REFLECTION.
AS A MATTER OF FACT, THERE IS NO MASTER,
THERE IS NO DISCIPLE.

The totality of all our 'knowledge' has been formed out of 'body-knowledge', and framed around the body and body-relations:

WHICH YOU ARE NOT, WHICH YOU WERE NOT,
WHICH YOU ARE NOT GOING TO REMAIN.

Q: What is the best way to get rid of the body illusion?

Maharaj: You are the architect of your own life. You will come to know that all this is a dream. Compare it to acting in a drama, playing the hero or heroine or the villain. You know that you are acting. You know better. For a few hours, you are playing a particular role. You know this is your role.

Similarly, we are playing these roles, "I am a man", or, "I am a woman". We have been accepting all these concepts, yet, we have nothing to do with all or any concept whatsoever.

YOU ARE UNBORN.

To know Reality, the basics are required. And that is why you have to undergo the disciplines of meditation, Self-enquiry, and *bhajans*.

Q: Alongside all these, there is also being in the presence of the Master, and listening to the Knowledge. This is a really potent cocktail. You could say, it is the elixir of immortality because by drinking the nectar, there is Self-Knowledge. You get to KNOW, really KNOW that you are unborn?

Maharaj: You will be intoxicated! I am placing the same principle before you: What we call 'God' does not exist outside of you. Everything is within you. I am using different words, different ways, different angles, different dimensions...

Q: In order to hammer home the truth?

Maharaj: Yes! It is direct hammering, direct hammering. The message is always the same. There is nothing else:

EXCEPT YOUR SELFLESS SELF,
THERE IS NO GOD, NO *ATMAN*, NO *BRAHMAN*,
NO *PARAMATMAN*.

This is the message. Sometimes I give simple examples to establish the Truth in you. It is like telling stories to a child. In order to relate the principle behind a story, you have to, first of all, present it in story-form. The mother or father will tell a story and then explain its meaning.

Likewise, the Master is presenting you with your Ultimate Truth in story-form, using certain language, certain words.

Once the Master has presented you with the Ultimate Truth, the rest is up to you.

Q: You mean it is up to us to keep up the practice?

Maharaj: It is like a jigsaw puzzle. You have the Knowledge. In order to have Conviction, and to know what to do, or not to do, the next step is up to you. You have to fit the pieces together.

**BECAUSE YOU KNOW YOUR SELFLESS SELF
MORE THAN ANYONE ELSE.
YOU KNOW YOUR SELFLESS SELF BETTER THAN ANYONE.**

Spontaneous Conviction will come,

**WHEN YOU BECOME ONE WITH THE FINAL TRUTH.
THIS IS CONVICTION,
ENLIGHTENMENT,
REALIZATION.
YOU CAN CALL IT BY ANY NAME.
THE NAME IS NOT IMPORTANT.**

Through a process of direct hammering, the Conviction will arise. You will know, "I am unborn, so why have any fear of death?" After realizing that there is no birth and death, you will exclaim, "All my fear has gone". No fear will remain. This is the result of direct hammering.

Q: Sometimes, while I am listening to you Maharaj, I might not hear, really hear what is being said. But, at other times, when I listen, there is a surety, a 'Yes!', a click of understanding.

Maharaj: The Invisible Listener in you is listening quietly and calmly.

**THE INVISIBLE LISTENER WITHIN YOU
IS LISTENING QUIETLY AND CALMLY.
REALITY IS ENGRAVED IN THAT INVISIBLE LISTENER,
WHICH CANNOT BE REMOVED.**

Perhaps you are not aware, or maybe you will not understand some things, but nonetheless, the Silent Listener is accepting everything, just like a recorder.

Q: I like the sound of that!

Maharaj: Silently, the process of recording is going on. Silently, the process of analyzing is going on, without your knowledge, without the mind, ego, intellect.

NO EGO, NO INTELLECT, NO MIND.

Q: The mind, ego and intellect try to block…

Maharaj: These are all external layers. You can use them, it's not bad. Use them, as and when, you like. You can use them, but do not become their slaves. Excessive use of anything is poison. Excessive use of anything will be poison. If you take more food than is necessary, it is poisonous. Anything taken to excess will be poison.

Q: Too much mind, too much mental...

Maharaj: There is no mind at all!

THIS IS EXCEPTIONAL KNOWLEDGE.
THIS IS REALITY.
IT IS NOT BOOKISH KNOWLEDGE.
IT IS NOT LITERAL KNOWLEDGE.

Q: It is beyond all the knowledge I have come across, and I have read tons of spiritual books.

Maharaj: It is beyond everything.

IT IS BEYOND KNOWLEDGE,
BEYOND EVERYTHING.
BEYOND WORDS,
BEYOND WORLDS,
BEYOND IMAGINATION.

Nisargadatta Maharaj used to say, "Remain how you were prior to beingness, remain as it is". How were you prior to beingness?

Q: I honestly don't know.

Maharaj: That is right. You were "not knowing". You were completely unaware of anything. You did not know anything at all. But since you came across with the body, you started knowing so many things. Therefore,

MIND IS BODY-KNOWLEDGE.
WHAT REMAINS? THE FOOD-BODY.

You are neither the mind nor the body. There is no mind and the body is a food-body. So what remains? Some day or other, you will leave this body. It is not your identity.

45. *Concentrate on the Concentrator*

Q: I have heard that Nisargadatta Maharaj initiated very few 'Westerners' into the Lineage because he considered them to be 'spiritual travellers'. You are one of the very few, if not the only one, who is offering the *Naam Mantra*. What made you decide to do this?

Maharaj: To make seekers enlightened. To share Knowledge with them, and remove them from the illusionary world.

Q: Do we really need to meditate?

Maharaj: A lot of people ask this question. You see, from childhood until now, there has been a lot of attachment to the body. There is a lot of love and affection for the body, and all body-related relations. This has to be dissolved. Of course, meditation is also an illusion, but we need to use one thorn to remove another thorn. This is only needed at the initial stage for focus and concentration.

CONCENTRATE ON THE CONCENTRATOR.

The body is not your Identity. You are 'Final Truth', 'Ultimate Truth'. But, in order to have this outright Conviction, all concepts and body-knowledge need to dissolve.

WE MAY UNDERSTAND EVERYTHING INTELLECTUALLY,
BUT INTELLECTUAL UNDERSTANDING IS NOT ENOUGH.

Therefore, you have to undergo the meditation. It is essential at the beginning. Later, at the advanced stage, it is no longer required.

In our Lineage, the Inchegiri Navnath Sampradaya, we give a Mantra, but not to those who have a Master already. One must remain faithful and loyal to one Master only.

Q: How does the Mantra work?

Maharaj: The Mantra produces vibrations in you. Through these vibrations, you will come to know the Reality.

SLOWLY, SILENTLY, AND PERMANENTLY,
YOU WILL FEEL SOME CHANGES HAPPENING INSIDE.

Your body-knowledge will be dissolved. You will be totally fearless because you will know, "I am not the body". Every day I am saying the same thing:

ALL NEEDS ARE BODY-RELATED NEEDS:
NEED OF GOD,
NEED OF FOOD, NEED OF HAPPINESS, NEED OF PEACE.
THESE ARE ALL BODY-RELATED.

When you came across with the body, all needs started.

PRIOR TO BEINGNESS, THERE WERE NO NEEDS,
THERE WAS NO FEAR.

Q: So, meditating regularly will help to bring about a shift, a change?

Maharaj: Meditation is the basis, the starting process to ensure that a perfect foundation, a strong foundation is laid. As you recite this Mantra,

YOU ARE REMINDING YOUR 'UNIDENTIFIED IDENTITY',
THAT YOU ARE *ATMAN, BRAHMAN, PARAMATMAN.*

You know Reality, but you have forgotten Reality. Everybody has the Knowledge of their Reality within them.

THIS PROCESS OF MEDITATION IS NEEDED FOR CONVICTION,
TO ESTABLISH AND ABSORB THE KNOWLEDGE.
DRY KNOWLEDGE, BOOKISH KNOWLEDGE,
LITERAL KNOWLEDGE IS NOT SELF-KNOWLEDGE.
MEDITATION ALONE
WILL LEAD TO SELF-KNOWLEDGE.

Q: Maharaj, when reciting the Mantra, the question sometimes arises, "Who is reciting?"

Maharaj: Ah! Who is reciting? The question comes because of body attachment. There is no 'Who?' and there is no 'He', or 'She'. There is nothing. These are just the terms, the body-related terms.

WHO IS RECITING THE MANTRA?
THE CONCENTRATOR, THE INVISIBLE PRESENCE.
WHY ARE YOU RECITING IT?

BECAUSE YOU HAVE FORGOTTEN YOUR IDENTITY.

How does it work?

WHILE YOU ARE RECITING THE MANTRA,
YOU ARE INVITING THE ATTENTION OF THE
INVISIBLE PRESENCE,
YOUR ULTIMATE TRUTH.

At the initial stage, you have to make some effort to recite it. Thereafter, it will happen spontaneously, without your knowledge, twenty-four hours, during waking, dreaming, sleeping, all the time. Knowing yourself in a real sense cannot be done via the intellect, logic, inference or guesswork, or any other mind-related activity. Why?

BECAUSE YOUR EXISTENCE IS SPONTANEOUS EXISTENCE.

How were you prior to beingness? How will you be, after leaving the body? What is your identity? Here, we conclude, that the Identity has stayed the same. It is the same today, as it was prior to beingness.

THE ONLY DIFFERENCE IS THAT
YOU ARE HOLDING THE BODY.

So, again, I repeat:

BODY-KNOWLEDGE HAS TO BE ERASED COMPLETELY.
FOR THIS TO HAPPEN, YOU HAVE TO MEDITATE.
MEDITATION IS ESSENTIAL.

Q: Maharaj, I have been reciting the Mantra for some time now, and it is now happening spontaneously, just as you said it would. Also, the effects of the meditation are now showing. There's an almost tangible quality present, such as stunning silence and peace and emptiness. To use your word, 'CleaReality'. There is just Spontaneous Happiness that is causeless.

Maharaj: You are operating the Master Key, the *Naam Mantra*, with deep involvement, and so it is bringing you closer to Selfless Self. This Spontaneous Happiness is the fragrance of Selfless Self. This means that the Knowledge is being absorbed. Very nice! Embrace Selfless Self, and go deeper and deeper. You see, when you go deep and deep within the Selfless Self, you will find so many things, beyond your imagination. You will forget this external/internal Identity.

YOU WILL REMAIN UNKNOWN TO YOU.
NO KNOWLEDGE IS KNOWLEDGE.
NO KNOWLEDGE IS KNOWLEDGE.
WHATEVER KNOWLEDGE IS ROOTED TO THE BODY
IS ILLUSION.
YOUR KNOWLEDGE OF *BRAHMAN, ATMAN, PARAMATMAN*
IS ALSO ILLUSION.

These are just the words, only the W-O-R-D-S, [The Master spells it out]. It is OK, it will maybe give you some pleasure, momentary happiness, a little entertainment, but,

IT IS NOT ULTIMATE TRUTH.
IT IS NOT ULTIMATE TRUTH.

46. *Words are Only Indicators*

Q: What is the meaning of Presence, Maharaj?

Maharaj: Presence means 'That' which enables you to live, to talk. When the questioner in you is asking, "What is Presence?" That is Presence.

Q: So my Presence will be there after my life?

Maharaj: There is no 'after my life' because Presence is just like the sky.

Q: So that is what I am, just Presence?

Maharaj: Of course, of course.

Q: And is that the same as Ranjit Maharaj's 'I am He'?

Maharaj: All these words are indicators, not Ultimate Truth. 'I am That', 'That, you Are', 'I am He', you can give any name you want. People come here and make this mistake. The indicators, pointers, are taken for the real thing, when they are only the W.O.R.D.S that we created. These are simply the names that we have attributed to 'Ultimate Truth', 'Ultimate Reality' or whatever we wish to call it, for understanding purposes only.

DON'T TAKE THE MASTER'S WORDS LITERALLY.
YOUR PRESENCE IS SPONTANEOUS,
SILENT, ANONYMOUS, UNIDENTIFIED,
THEREFORE, 'I AM HE' IS SIMPLY A CLUE, AN INDICATION.

Q: I prefer, 'I am He'...

Maharaj: That's OK, OK, as long as you understand, that this phrase is only an indicator, a clue, an intimation. Don't take it for 'Ultimate Reality'.

Q: If it is anonymous and imperceptible Presence, how does anyone get to know about it?

Maharaj: Forget about 'anyone'. Talk about yourself!

Q: OK. How can I get to know about this Presence, then?

Maharaj:
YOU ARE THE SOURCE OF KNOWLEDGE.
YOU HAVE EXCEPTIONAL POWER.
YOUR INNER MASTER IS ULTIMATE TRUTH.
YOU AND ME? WE ARE BOTH THE SAME.

Q: You say that measuring ourselves in the body-form is illusion. Is that because Selfless Self is not perceptible?

Maharaj: When you try to see it, the Seer will disappear.

WHEN YOU TRY TO SEE IT, THE SEER WILL DISAPPEAR.

Just see how you were prior to beingness! Be as you are! Be as you were prior to beingness!

THESE CONCEPTS: PERCEPTIBLE, IMPERCEPTIBLE,
KNOWLEDGE, MAN, WOMAN, BIRTH, DEATH.
THIS IS ALL BODY-BASED KNOWLEDGE. FORGET IT!

Everybody says, "I am *Brahman*", "I am *Atman*", but that Knowledge has to be fully absorbed within you, in a real sense. You are Master of Masters. At the moment of Conviction, you will forget about your identity. But, remember, this Conviction is spontaneous. Don't use force! It will appear spontaneously.

47. *Everything Starts and Ends with You*

Q: Maharaj, you say that I am a Master. I don't feel like a Master.

Maharaj: The body is the cause of tension. We are basing everything at the body level. But the body was not your identity. The body is not your identity. The body will not remain your identity. So why bother about feelings: a cloud of anxiety or a cloud of bliss, fearing this or that, fearing death? You have forgotten your Identity.

Q: So how can I remember it?

Maharaj: In our Lineage, we give some words like a Mantra for you to recite. The Spirit is very sensitive. Whatever is impressed upon it, is reflected. Put in a simple way,

THE INVISIBLE LISTENER FORGOT ITS IDENTITY.
THROUGH THE PROCESS OF MEDITATION,
WE ARE ABLE TO REMIND THE INVISIBLE LISTENER.

Meditation is like a ladder. Once it has been used, it can be thrown away. It is only necessary in the beginning.

Q: Can I ask you a little more about Selfless Self? If you look for the Selfless Self from the mind, would you say that you cannot see?

Maharaj: This is a body-related question. Mind! Don't try to look. This will bring the ego. It is Spontaneous.

YOU ARE TRYING TO GUESS THE PRESENCE IN SOME FORM.

We are using names like *Brahman* and *Paramatman*, just to identify this Unidentified Identity.

IN REALITY,
THERE IS NO EXPERIENCE, NO EXPERIENCER,
NO WITNESS, NO WITNESSER,
NOTHING.

Q: I suppose, the mind is just trying to know.

Maharaj:
PRIOR TO BEINGNESS
AND AFTER THE BEINGNESS
THERE IS NO MIND,
NO EGO,
NO INTELLECT.
IT IS A KIND OF DREAM.
AFTER WAKING UP, THE DREAM DISSOLVES.

This life is just like a dream.

SELFLESS SELF MEANS AFTER THE DREAM.
AFTER THE DREAM IS OVER, ALL HOUSES COLLAPSE.
THEY ARE DEMOLISHED AFTER THE DREAM,
AND ALL THAT IS LEFT IS SKY, SPACE.

Q: So how was the Presence before?

Maharaj: Prior to the world, your Presence was there, but it was 'unknown Presence'. Since you started knowing, "I am", you took on some subtle ego.

BUT IN REALITY, YOU ARE NOBODY,
AND THAT MEANS, YOU ARE EVERYBODY.

Q: So the mind?

Maharaj: Intellectually, we know everything, but we are ignoring the Reality because of the pressure of the mind, which we mistakenly take to be true. With meditation, all the Knowledge can be put into practice.

Q: So what happens? What is it like once you know the Reality?

Maharaj: After knowing the Reality, you remain quiet in your Selfless Self. It is a kind of spiritual intoxication. At that time, you are completely unconcerned with the body. There is no trace of an ego that says, "I am the doer".

Q: So, I am *Brahman*!

Maharaj: You are neither man, woman, nor *Brahman*.

TO SAY "I AM *BRAHMAN*", IS ALSO ILLUSION.
WORDS ARE ONLY INDICATING YOUR HIGH VALUE,
YOUR GREATNESS.

Q: How can I combine this knowledge with living in the world?

Maharaj: There is no combining! Who combines?

Q: Is it undisturbed by living in the world?

Maharaj: Prior to beingness, was there any disturbance? Who is disturbing who? We are applying the intellect, and trying to grasp this knowledge intellectually.

YOU ARE FATHER OF THE WORLD AND FATHER OF THE WORD.
IT IS THE SEER'S REFLECTION,
THE SEER'S PROJECTION.
WITHOUT THE SEER, YOU CAN'T SEE THE SEEN.
EVERYTHING STARTS FROM YOU, AND ENDS WITH YOU.

48. Who Wants Darshan?

Q: Maharaj, I am afraid I cannot stay here for very long because I wish to go and see Mother Amma.

Maharaj: If you feel that you will get happiness with Mother Amma, then go to Amma. I am not restricting your activities. If you are not happy here, OK you are free to go anywhere, but going to Amma is a different kind of knowledge. You are looking for happiness in and for the body-form.

IN OUR LINEAGE,
WE GIVE DIRECT KNOWLEDGE
TO YOUR INVISIBLE REALITY,
NOT TO YOUR BODY-FORM,
WHICH IS NOT YOUR IDENTITY.

Be stable! Be stable and steady! If you keep chopping and changing wives, you will spoil your spiritual life. Go anywhere you wish to go, but then you have to stay there. If you find peace with one Master, stay with that Master.

Instability and a wavering mind are unhealthy for your spiritual life. Stability is most important so that you can come out of the circle of body-knowledge, and get rid of problems and depression. You may have faith in, and worship an idol, a stone, any idol, in fact. It does not matter what it is, as long as you remain loyal to that idol.

POWER IS NOT IN ANY MAN OR WOMAN, STATUE OR STONE.
POWER IS IN YOU ALONE.
YOU ARE THE MOST IMPORTANT IDOL, THE ONLY IDOL.
THEREFORE BE FAITHFUL TO YOURSELF.

Strong self-involvement is most important. All this travelling is no good: expecting happiness from elsewhere, underestimating your Selfless Self. It is pointless.

BECAUSE YOU DO NOT KNOW THE TRAVELLER
WHO IS WANTING PEACE,
YOU ARE NEGLECTING YOUR INTERNAL POWER.

Q: When I repeat the Mantra, the body starts to feel weak.

Maharaj: This is a consequence of the vibrations. You are feeling weak because you cannot tolerate your own power. Don't worry! Continue reciting!

Q: When I first received the Mantra, the initiation was so powerful, that I felt completely obliterated by it. As a result, I completely forgot the Mantra and had to ask you again for it, as you know! But then there was peace and harmony. Now there's a change, and I don't feel the same peace of mind, but a slight disturbance instead.

Maharaj: These are the effects of the body. It should not be like this! You are not remembering what I have told you, what I have been hammering again and again. Listen to me! Whose mind? Whose feelings? Whose harmony? Whose disturbance? These are the external parts. You are a victim of your own concepts.

YOU ARE STILL CONSIDERING YOURSELF
TO BE SOMEBODY ELSE,
SEPARATE AND OUTSIDE OF SELFLESS SELF.

Who is expecting happiness? Who wants peace? Who is fearful? You are not the body! Are you this body? Spiritual science says you are not the body. As long as you are attached to the body, you will experience all these feelings. Come out of this vicious circle!

YOU MUST KEEP UP THE DISCIPLINE OF MEDITATION.

It is the only way you will have Conviction. You are feeling depressed because you still have a lot of love and affection for the body.

Q: If you are realized, do you get feelings of depression?

Maharaj: You will remain untouched even with the feelings. If a dog is barking, you are not going to struggle with it. Similarly, the mind, ego, intellect is barking, because you are paying attention to it. Paying attention to thoughts and feelings, giving them importance, causes suffering. Good things or bad things should be the same for you. If you keep giving attention to the barking, you will suffer!

The Mantra has tremendous power, however, it is only when you are sincere, that Reality will open up. With these sacred words, you are reminding the Spirit of its Identity: its Unidentified Identity, Invisible Identity, Anonymous Identity. Slowly, silently, permanently, you are impressing your Ultimate Truth [the

Master claps]. At the moment of Conviction, you will stay aloof from the body-knowledge and everything will begin to unfold.

Wait and watch, wait and watch. It is like watering a plant. The water does not flow immediately. It is first, absorbing, absorbing, and then it begins to flow. It is the same with the meditation - absorbing and absorbing, and then - I have told you the results. Deposit all of your physical mind, ego, intellect in the ashram, then there will be no fear.

IF YOU HAVE SOMETHING IN YOUR POCKET,
YOU WILL BE AFRAID OF THIEVES. IF YOU HAVE NOTHING,
THEN YOU WILL NOT WORRY ABOUT BEING ROBBED.
EMPTY YOUR POCKETS
AND YOU WILL NOT FEAR THE PICK-POCKETS.

Q: Can you say why going to see someone for *darshan* is not such a good idea?
Maharaj: Who wants *darshan*? Have your own *darshan*! Give yourself *darshan*.

WITHOUT YOU,
THERE CAN BE NO *DARSHAN*.

To say 'Amma' your Presence is required. To say 'God' your Presence is required. You are the father of Amma, the mother of Amma. Without your Presence you can't see Amma because the entire world is projected out of you.

YOU ARE GIVING IMPORTANCE TO THE SEEN,
AND NOT TO THE SEER.

Without the Seer, who can see the seen? Through these sacred words, you will be able to identify yourself. You need a phone number to open an account. You have forgotten your number. The Master has given it back to you.

YOU NEED TO LEARN THIS CODE BY HEART
BECAUSE IT IS THE MASTER KEY,
WHICH WILL KEEP YOUR ACCOUNT OPEN.

I am trying to convince you of your own power. You are feeling weak and depending on others because you are attached to the body. You feel that going here and there for *darshan* will give you strength. Everything is within you.

ALL GODS AND GODDESSES ARE IN YOU.
THE WHOLE WORLD IS YOUR SPONTANEOUS PROJECTION.

Unless you know the traveller, your travelling will be meaningless. When you know the traveller, the travelling ends.

If you are slowly getting to know God, or whatever you wish to call it, and finding peace at Home, then why go to others? Why go elsewhere?

FOR HOPE?
WHO HOPES?
THERE IS NO HOPE.
BE STRONG AND HAVE COURAGE.

Listen, listen! Recite, recite! Then everything will come clear. How you think, behave and act depends entirely on you. If you go the wrong way, it is up to you. You are Ultimate Truth, you are not in the body-form. Spiritual words are only indicators, not Ultimate Truth.

Do more Self-enquiry. Probe deeply and ask yourself what exactly it is that you want? Explore the fears, depression, tension, fear of death.

Q: That fear of death isn't there any more. It used to be in everything, an intense fear of death. I know there is no death, this doesn't die. This wasn't born, and what I am isn't affected. This experience just came.

Maharaj: The question of death never arises because you are unborn.

Don't just visit places and Masters out of habit, or so that you can tell others that you have been. You must know why you are visiting here and there. Self-enquiry is essential. Why are you going to Amma? Who is expecting happiness? Without Presence, you are a dead body. You are giving so much importance to the seen. Stand on your own feet! How long are you going to keep going for blessings?

BLESS YOURSELF!
DON'T TAKE FROM ANYONE ELSE.
TAKE FROM YOURSELF.
YOU ARE WHOLLY INDEPENDENT,
COMPLETE.

49. *You Are Covered in Ash*

Maharaj: Every day I am repeating myself, and telling everybody the same thing: "Don't take my words literally". What the Masters are trying to convey is what is important - the essence, the meaning, the gist. We are not here to have a debate, or to study the exact words that are spoken, or compare teachings or make a comparative study of the Masters. Listen to me!

I AM NOT SPEAKING TO YOU,
I AM ADDRESSING
THE SILENT INVISIBLE LISTENER WITHIN YOU.

Q: Is the presence of the Master and the conversation only a kind of game?

Maharaj: At the first stage, the Master is needed to give Direct Knowledge and remind the 'disciple' that he, too, is a Master. He imparts the Conviction that there is no difference between them. The Master begins the process of convincing the disciple, and then the disciple continues with the process by convincing himself.

The Master is speaking from the Ultimate. He has transcended the limitations of the body-form and is free from illusion. The Master KNOWS because his Knowledge is Self-Knowledge, first-hand Knowledge. The Master reminds the disciple of his true Identity by prompting him, saying, for example:

"THE MASTER REGENERATES YOUR POWER",
"YOU HAVE FORGOTTEN YOUR TRUE IDENTITY".
"YOU ARE NOT THE BODY,
YOU WERE NOT THE BODY,
YOU WILL NOT REMAIN THE BODY".

"YOU ARE COVERED IN ASH,
UNDERNEATH THE FIRE IS BURNING.
MASTER REMOVES THE ASH".

In fact, there is no 'you', no 'I', no 'he', no 'she', no 'disciple', no 'Master'. We have to play at being the Master and the disciple, in order to remove the layers of ignorance and illusion, and to get back to the Source, and
uncover Reality.

Q: If you discriminate between Self and ego, is that not a kind of duality?

Maharaj: The world is projected out of your Spontaneous Presence. Mind, ego, intellect are our babies. By themselves, they have no independent reality.

Q: If the mind and its content is illusory, does that not mean that all words, including the knowledge given by the Masters, must be untrue as well? Ranjit Maharaj and Siddharameshwar Maharaj say that knowledge is the greatest ignorance.

Maharaj: The Masters are beyond mind. They speak from Thoughtless Reality. They speak from the bottomless bottom of Reality. We are not talking here about body-knowledge which is ignorance. The Masters' Knowledge is Selfless Self Knowledge, not second-hand book knowledge or experiential knowledge. Even when you read spiritual books, you are reading them as if they are stories about someone else or something else, different from you.

Book knowledge is not enough. Knowledge has to be sourced from within. When all body-knowledge is dissolved, then the door of Knowledge will be open to you.

Q: What is enlightenment?

Maharaj: Enlightenment is the CONVICTION that, "You were not the body. You are not the body. You are not going to remain the body". It is the Conviction that you are beyond *Brahman, Paramatman*, that you are Selfless Self:

IT IS SELF,
EMPTY OF ALL CONTENT AND BODY-KNOWLEDGE.

Selfless Self is that which can only be pointed to, and cannot be described. "You are the Spontaneous, Invisible, Anonymous, Unidentified Identity".

Q: It is impossible to stop the flow of thoughts, the 'mind', completely. Do you agree that it is sufficient to know for sure, that it is illusion?

Maharaj: First, you have to be a Master of the mind, ie, witness the thoughts flowing, without being affected by them. At the advanced stage, there will be no thoughts. The illusory thinker will disappear.

Q: Can you confirm, that I am the base of all experiences, but as such like a void, without action, time, space and any kind of perception?

Maharaj: Again, these are words: void, time, space, action, perception - all just a reflection of your Spontaneous Presence. In the Ultimate stage, [there are no stages, but this is used for teaching], there are no experiences, no experiencer, no witness, no witnesser. There is nothing. It is the state of not knowing, unknowing. You are unknown to you. Nisargadatta Maharaj used to say, "How you were prior to beingness - stay like that". No needs, no requirements, no Master. No knowledge!

YOU DID NOT EVEN KNOW THE WORD 'KNOWLEDGE'.

Q: As Nisargadatta Maharaj used to say, "All that is perceivable and conceivable is not that."

Maharaj: Yes, yes. It is easy to understand intellectually, but this Knowledge has to be absorbed, so that it can be applied to your daily life. It is pragmatic knowledge. Also, you have to BE the Conviction that you are Ultimate Reality, Final Reality, so that when the time comes for the body to go, there is no attachment left.

50. *The Melting Process Is Marching Towards Oneness*

Maharaj: Watch and wait! The melting process has started. So many experiences will happen that will make you strong. Don't think, or even try to identify what Ultimate Reality is, and what it is not, wondering, "Is this it?" or "Is that it?" Forget about the words 'Ultimate' or 'not Ultimate'. Remove these words.

Your Spontaneous Presence is Ultimate, your Spontaneous and Invisible Presence is Ultimate and beyond that. Experiences have appeared upon your Spontaneous Presence.

Whatever you are experiencing during this dissolving process, whatever is happening is correct, it is right. But do not question what is happening or not, as this will interfere with the spontaneous unfolding.

IT IS THE MELTING PROCESS
MARCHING TOWARDS ONENESS.

Some types of layers of experiences are happening during this melting process that will dissolve you. At the Ultimate stage, the witnesser, the witness and the witnessing will all be completely dissolved. When this happens, you will not be able to witness anything. It will happen. This is the outcome of the meditation.

Q: Does the meditation really work as an eraser of body-knowledge and memories?

Maharaj: Of course! The reason I emphasize meditation is because so many thoughts were impressed upon us since childhood till today. The melting process will take some time, and that is why I keep stressing the meditation. It is essential.

THE MELTING PROCESS WILL TAKE SOME TIME,
AND THAT IS WHY MEDITATION IS ESSENTIAL.

You must have strong dedication towards yourself, and strong dedication towards the Master because he has shown you that Unidentified Identity.

Q: So the Master is necessary, really important?

Maharaj: It is only because of the Masters, that we have the Teachings. Without my Master, Nisargadatta Maharaj, I would not be able to speak one single word. Instead, I would still be going to one or other of these God-temples, looking for happiness and peace. Because of the Masters, we now have strong foundations. What Nisargadatta Maharaj says is:

"THERE IS NOTHING EXCEPT YOUR SELFLESS SELF.
WHEN I SEE MY SELF,
THERE IS NOTHING THERE".

Q: Can you say more, Maharaj?

Maharaj: What more do you want me to convey? There is nothing more to say. It is crystal clear: Except for your Selfless Self, there is nothing. So why keep looking for something else, or something more, elsewhere, when all the power is in you?

There is nothing more to convey. Then, it will be open. The door of Knowledge will completely open up. This dedication, this Conviction, is what Nisargadatta Maharaj says is perfect.

Remember the story of the beggar boy who is told by his uncle that he was a millionaire, and was convinced after being given the proof? He accepted his new-found status immediately. Likewise, the Master says: "You are *Brahman*, *Atman*". Why do you not believe it? Somewhere in the background, there is a little voice that says, "No, you're joking?" It is not so easy to convince you, and that is why we need the process of meditation. The meditation will have the effect of dissolving all these illusionary layers.

WHEN ALL THE ILLUSIONARY LAYERS ARE DISSOLVED,
YOU WILL COME ACROSS YOUR PERFECTION,
"SO I AM THAT!"
ALL THESE LAYERS WILL DISSOLVE SPONTANEOUSLY.

All these layers will dissolve spontaneously.

Have faith in the Master and what he is telling you. Have strong faith as he has shown you your Identity.

THE MASTER IS PERFECT, THEREFORE,
YOU ARE TO RESPOND TO HIM
WITH THE GREATEST REVERENCE
BECAUSE HE HAS SHOWN YOU YOUR ULTIMATE TRUTH.

Faith in the Master is not blind faith. It is only because of him that you have been able to 'catch' Reality. It is only because of the Master. You realize that if you had not come across a Master, you would most likely still be a 'spiritual tourist', journeying here and there. You would still be searching for some kind of knowledge or other, still searching for some person, Guru, this Master or that Master.

THERE IS NOTHING
APART FROM YOUR SELFLESS SELF.
STOP WITH YOUR INNER MASTER.
STOP WITH YOUR INNER GURU.
BE STRONG!

[The Master gestures with clenched fist.] Accept! It is an open fact.

Q: What is the best way of accepting it?

Maharaj: Slowly, silently, permanently.

51. There is No 'My Past'

Maharaj: In our Lineage we serve a cocktail of Knowledge, meditation, *bhajan*. It is very potent. We also give little sweeteners in the form of stories. Knowledge is just like antibiotics. Sometimes the antibiotics produce acid. To absorb this Knowledge, an anti-acid medicine is prescribed. The anti-acid is meditation. Then that anti-acid might cause some weakness, so for that weakness, a tonic is needed. This tonic is *bhajan*. *Bhajan* is the B-complex.

THIS IS STRONG KNOWLEDGE,
SO YOU HAVE TO DIGEST IT.

To help the process of digestion, meditation will help, also devotional songs, *bhajans*. The combination of all three is important.

Q: It comes together as one. In *I Am That,* Maurice Frydman says this Lineage is the best of all, as it combines Devotion, Knowledge, Action and Meditation. He refers to this as the 'Royal Road to Liberation', because it leads directly to Realization.

Maharaj: It makes for a strong spirituality, mixture, a strong medicine. You won't be lured by anybody's thoughts with this spiritual medicine, so that:

EVEN IF GOD APPEARED BEFORE YOU,
YOU WOULD KNOW THAT FOR THIS TO HAPPEN,
YOUR PRESENCE HAS TO BE THERE FIRST.

I see from my Presence. If my Presence were not there, can God be seen? No! This is not egoistic talk, this is logical, Spontaneous Talk. But to have this Knowledge, you need to put in some deliberate effort.

Q: Why? Why do we have to make effort, if I know I am *Brahman*?

Maharaj: Because it is not so easy. It is very easy to talk using literal knowledge. You have to absorb the Knowledge. That is the difficult part.

Q: Because of years of conditioning and brainwashing?

Maharaj: Yes, yes. But here, with these disciplines, we are cleaning out all the memories so that your Reality will appear.

Q: Like washing the brain. Washing everything away, the whole of my past?

Maharaj: There is no "my past"! Deliberate effort is needed especially at the beginning, so that there is full alertness, full-blown concentration.

Bhausaheb Maharaj after intense meditation and in depth Self-enquiry and investigation knew that this discipline was necessary. He understood psychology and human behaviour very well. He had great insights into the weaknesses of the human being.

YOU WILL COME TO KNOW ULTIMATE REALITY
THROUGH USING THE TOOLS
OF KNOWLEDGE, THE MANTRA AND THE *BHAJANS.*

He instructed Gurudev Ranade, a scholar of philosophy, to select the *bhajans* that contained the highest of meanings.

Q: What you are saying is that this cocktail of Knowledge, meditation and *bhajans* is a proven method that, if followed, will guarantee enlightenment?

Maharaj: It will work. It is inevitable, as long as you put in some effort.

At the initial stage you are to undergo all these disciplines deliberately. These practices are all illusion, as well as our talk of *Brahman, Atman, Paramatman,* 'God'. At the advanced stage, you will not need any discipline because the practice will continue by itself, without your knowledge.

So I am asking everybody to be serious, because unless you are serious about knowing the Reality, and just carry on reading as before, using the mind and intellect, you are not going to get it. Bhausaheb Maharaj came to the *bhajans* early morning, every morning and meditated for long periods throughout the day, without fail.

Q: Was all this really necessary though?

Maharaj: You need to be alert so as not to forget your Identity. Be intense at the beginning, so that you are staying with Selfless Self all the time.

Q: I can understand the need for Knowledge and meditation, but the *bhajans*? Maybe it is because we are not used to singing these in the West, so I don't see them as an important part of the practice?

Maharaj: Singing *bhajans* is part of the process of gaining Conviction to establish your Ultimate Truth. The Spirit likes the *bhajans*, the spiritual *bhajan*. These devotional songs will help open the door of Knowledge. Then Reality will open Spontaneously.

REALITY WILL OPEN SPONTANEOUSLY.

Spirit is so sensitive that it makes people dance. The Masters used to dance, they were moved by the Spirit. They did not suddenly get up and decide to dance, no, they were moved. During the *bhajans*, Nisargadatta Maharaj, even in his early seventies, was dancing. It happens spontaneously. So *bhajan* is part of the process of spirituality. It is necessary and fuels the Knowledge.

Q: The words are extremely powerful, beautiful, uplifting. They are almost like a meditation in themselves. It's important for us to understand the words. They are very strong when you understand the meaning.

Maharaj: Yes, very touching, very touching.

Q: Today I was tired when I came, but when I started singing, the tiredness just went. The meanings are so powerful.

Maharaj: Everything is connected with Selfless Self. As I said, Bhausaheb Maharaj instructed his disciple Gurudev Ranade to select *bhajans* with high meaning. High meaning in the sense that they were elevating and touched the bottom of your heart. That way, the meanings are deeply impressed.

Each and every *bhajan* has high meaning that reflects your Selfless Self-Knowledge. Therefore, the reading, the Knowledge, the meditation, the *bhajans* all serve one purpose. The principle behind all of this is just to establish your Ultimate Truth. The foundations are perfect!

Q2: I quite often sing the *bhajans*, and find it a good *sadhana*. It makes the Spirit more receptive, open.

Maharaj: *Bhajan* is most important because:

THE INNER SPIRIT GETS SPONTANEOUS HAPPINESS
FROM THE *BHAJANS*.

Even though you don't know the language, you can sing them. Read the meanings, the language is exceptionally high language. So, yes, *bhajan* is most important.

THE WORDS BEHIND THE *BHAJAN*S
ARE SINKING DEEPER AND DEEPER
INTO YOUR SELFLESS SELF,
TWENTY-FOUR HOURS A DAY, SEVEN DAYS A WEEK.

Q2: I can understand about the spontaneity. It is like when you hear music that stirs something inside, and then before you know it, you are swaying from side to side.

Maharaj: When you get closer and closer to the Unidentified Identity, individuality is getting absorbed, little by little. When this happens, you cannot afterwards remove the part of that individuality that was absorbed. No! Remember I told you about the bucket of water poured into the sea? Even if you tried to remove it, you cannot.

Q: Because it has merged into the sea? The process of Oneness, if you can call it that is irreversible. The individual can't come back, so to speak?

Maharaj: There's no individuality. We are just using some words to communicate. Come out of the illusory circle! We are talking spirituality, so as to come out of illusion and disappear. But some indirect, concealed illusory concepts will still be there. These concepts have appeared out of illusion. With the practice, you will begin to notice these hidden, concealed concepts, like when you say 'my' and 'yours'. Be careful!

IF THE BASE OR FOUNDATIONS ARE WEAK,
A SMALL LEAK WILL APPEAR
WHICH WILL DESTROY EVERYTHING.

That is why it is most important to make the foundations strong. I know that meditation is an illusion, the *Naam* is also illusion, Knowledge and *bhajan* too - because all of these practices have come out of body-knowledge. But still, we need to use them to establish your Ultimate Truth.

52.   *This is a Long Dream*

Q: Where do questions come from? All these questions where do they come from? Why all these questions? What is the source of all the questions?

Maharaj: You are the Source. Your Spontaneous Presence is appearing with some questions and answers. So your beingness is Spontaneous. Your beingness is Spontaneous. Out of beingness, the Spirit clicked with the body. Questions and all needs, all questions are coming out spontaneously.

Prior to beingness, there were no questions, no questions, nothing. You were totally unknown to you. You were totally unknown to the world. So it is only through the body that you know yourself: "I am somebody", and through which intellectual questions arise: "Who am I? Where am I? Where did I come from?" Therefore all questions are body-related questions. These questions will dissolve after leaving the body.

Spiritual science says your Identity is not the body. The body is not your Identity and will not remain so. It is just this spontaneous appearance. There is no reason to any of it at all. It is just like a dream. We don't decide which dream is going to appear. The dream is spontaneous. Today's dream may not be tomorrow's dream, likewise this is a dream.

ALL QUESTIONS ARE SPIRITUAL, INTELLECTUAL,
EGOISTIC QUESTIONS.
AT THE ULTIMATE STAGE
THERE ARE NO QUESTIONS,
THERE IS NOTHING.

Prior to beingness, you had no experiences, you had no questions. You were unknown to you. You have some information and knowledge, but this is because of the body, therefore this knowledge is illusion.

The body is not your permanent identity. On leaving the body, nothing will remain, there will be no questions left.

Questions are created spontaneously, and you are asking them because of the mind, ego, intellect. We are separating ourselves from Reality when asking questions. We ask questions as if we are separate 'individuals'. But who or what is supplying the energy to raise the questions? Who is experiencing the questions? Who is witnessing the questions? Who is supplying power to the questions?

THAT YOU ARE.
ULTIMATE TRUTH,
FINAL TRUTH.
IT CANNOT BE DESCRIBED IN ANY WORDS.

My Master said: "If you want to compare yourself to anything, compare yourself to sky". Does sky have any questions? Does sky ask, "Where do I come from?" Sky is everywhere. Likewise, your Presence, your Spontaneous Presence is everywhere, but you are measuring yourself in body-form, and that is why there are so many questions.

Q: Thank you. Maharaj, you talk about knowing oneself in a 'real sense' that's not intellectual, and not through words. Can you tell me again what you mean by real sense?

Maharaj: Again I have to caution you: These are just the WORDS that we are using. There is no 'real', there is no 'unreal'.

WE ARE DISCRIMINATING BECAUSE
WE HAVE A BODY-FORM.

Is there a someone who can talk about the real and the unreal? No! Nobody exists, nothing is there. It is only the unborn child who asks these body questions of real or unreal. You are the unborn child, therefore reality and unreality are merely connected to logical thinking.

NOTHING HAS HAPPENED.
NOTHING IS HAPPENING.
YOU ARE ASKING ABOUT ILLUSION,
YOU ARE TALKING ABOUT THE UNBORN CHILD.
YOUR PRESENCE IS TOTALLY UNIDENTIFIABLE.
IT IS UNIDENTIFIED IDENTITY.

You are trying to identify Reality through the body, and as I keep telling you all so many times, the body is not your permanent identity. It will vanish like a puff of smoke. This Knowledge, this Reality has to be engraved, absorbed within you, so that after knowing the Reality, you remain unconcerned, uninterested, uninvolved with the world, just like you are unconcerned with a dream.

THIS IS A DREAM WORLD.
THIS IS A LONG DREAM.

King Bhartri was lost in a long dream. He had many wives, but Pingala was his favourite, the love of his life. Pingala reciprocated his love. She had been overheard saying, "If anything ever happened to my beloved, I would die".

The king decided to test the veracity of her love. One day, he sent a messenger to inform her that the king had been killed by a tiger on a hunting trip.

On hearing this terrible news, Pingala was broken-hearted, and took her own life. When the king heard of the tragedy, he was beside himself with grief, filled with remorse: "Oh! What have I done? How am I going to live without my Pingala? I want her back. I cannot live without her". He had played such a foolish game, a cruel and dangerous game, and now his beloved Pingala was gone.

He spent his days grieving at the cremation ground, weeping and groaning out loud for his dear Pingala. Many people joined him in his unending sorrow.

One day a Yogi was walking close to the king in the cremation grounds, when he dropped his clay pot. The pot broke and smashed into many pieces. The Yogi began to cry, he started sobbing heavily, even more loudly than the king who was crying nearby.

The king was annoyed: "Stop your weeping! For goodness sake, stop weeping! I will buy you a hundred new pots". "No! No!" wept the Yogi, "I want my old pot back." "What nonsense said the king, what is gone is gone".

The Yogi stopped crying and said, "Oh wise king, if you know this, then why are you still crying? Your Pingala is gone and will never return."

The king replied "You cannot compare my loss to yours. I have lost my beloved, my beautiful Pingala that I loved so dearly, with all my heart. You have just lost a meaningless earthen pot".

The Yogi replied: "They are both made from the earth, and what comes from the earth must go back to the earth." He then created one hundred identical Pingalas and asked the king to point out his special Pingala. Naturally, the king was unable to identify her. He understood that Pingala was part of the dream he had projected out of his Spontaneous Presence.

All of a sudden, the king became enlightened. He realized that he had been crying over a dream, for something illusory and impermanent. He was so ashamed because he had taken the dream for Reality. Shortly after, he renounced his kingdom and became the Yogi's disciple and awakened to Reality!

53. Be Independent and Fly!

Maharaj: The Master is not giving you anything that does not belong to you. He is just reminding you of what is already within you, but was somehow forgotten. You know the Reality, now you just have to exercise caution.

When a son or daughter leaves for college, the parents will warn them to be careful of their new surroundings, a different atmosphere. They tell them to study and not be diverted by the exciting new environment. Likewise, you are to stay on high alert at all times to all possible threats and difficulties, right up until the physical body dissolves.

Q: I was depressed for some time. Illusion was all around me. I used to visit different churches and temples and explored different faiths. I did not really know what I was doing or looking for. I meditated in my own way, but still I was surrounded by *maya*.

Maharaj: There is no *maya*. *Maya* is a concept just like *Brahman* is a concept.

As long as you see yourself in body-form, attractions will be near and affect you. Spirituality can help you at every moment of your life. Dissolve the concepts!

YOUR EXISTENCE IS INVISIBLE,
EVEN THOUGH YOU FEEL IT.
IT IS JUST LIKE HOW YOUR PRESENCE WAS INVISIBLE,
PRIOR TO BEINGNESS.

Q: I'm glad I found you, Maharaj, because you keep me on the straight and narrow. And now, I know I can come and see you when I need to. When the distance between us starts to grow, that's when I know I have to be in your presence. I don't like feeling this kind of separation.

Maharaj: Yes, but remember that the Master is not the form. Don't be dependent on the form of the Master. The Master is formless. You must have complete faith in yourself and in your Master, but not the Master in physical form. This 'body' [points to his chest] is not Master, the speaker is Master. The Invisible Speaker speaking, and the Invisible Listener listening, is the Master. Bodies are different, Spirit is One.

THE MASTER IS FORMLESS.

He has given you power. How long are you going to remain at the Master's side, sheltering under his wing?

FLY ON YOUR OWN WINGS!

The Master has given you everything. Be independent and fly!

When I was young, I did not understand all that my Master, Nisargadatta Maharaj, was saying, but later, on reflection, I understood. He said, "If you need to do something, do it alone. Don't expect any help from anyone. You have not to remain in anyone else's haven, you have to be strong and:

TAKE REFUGE IN YOUR OWN SANCTUARY.
WALK ON YOUR OWN TWO FEET.

The Master gives you advice now and again, sometimes even expressing a little anger. But this is not real anger, it is just 'tough love', like a parent endeavouring to make his child strong. What the Master wishes to convey is most important. See yourself as formless and see the Master as formless, then there will be no separation.

54. *Engrave Reality Like a Tattoo!*

Q: You spoke about strong foundations. Can you explain?

Maharaj: The conclusion of knowing that you are not the body is "Who am I?" First you undergo Self-enquiry. Then spiritual science says, "You are Ultimate Truth", which is the theory, the theoretical knowledge. The next step is to find out how to establish this Truth. Knowledge is established through meditation. This way, your foundation will be strong. Foundation here means that you are convinced that the body is not Reality.

The next question may be, "How does one accept it?" The spiritual ground should be cleared and cleaned before planting any seeds. Then you do the practice which gives you that strong confirmation that is needed, to make you detached and unconcerned with the body. Final outcome: Exceptional Happiness and Peace.

ILLUSIONARY LAYERS ARE LIKE VEILS, SUBTLE VEILS.

WHEN ALL THESE LAYERS,
WHEN EVERYTHING DISAPPEARS,
THAT IS THE BASE, THE FOUNDATION.

So, read some books, recite the Mantra, listen to the medium of the Master who is convincing you that you are Ultimate Truth.

BECAUSE YOU ARE FINAL TRUTH,
YOU WILL REALIZE THAT EVERYTHING IS WITHIN YOU,
THAT THERE IS NOTHING EXCEPT YOU.
EVERYTHING COMES OUT OF NOTHING,
AND EVERYTHING DISSOLVES BACK INTO NOTHING.

You will no longer take the touch of material things, nor the help of any material cause to give you happiness. When you no longer require happiness, you have reached the destination. All these entertainments out there! What are they doing? Making money!

YOU ARE THE SOURCE OF THE WORLD.
YOU ARE FORMLESS. NO 'I'.
YOU ARE EVERYWHERE.
THIS TRUTH HAS TO BE ESTABLISHED.

You are Ultimate Medicine. Beyond your Selfless Self, there is nothing. Even though we know the Truth, the influence of body-knowledge creates subtle expectations. Be alert! Be Involved.

Q. Does *karma* have any importance?

Maharaj: People ask about *karma* a lot. It is meaningless illusion. I have told you many times that prior to beingness there was nothing. Nothing means nothing, yet people still say, "Yes, OK, there was nothing, but what about *karma*?" Prior to beingness there was nothing. All this *karma*, *prarabdha* is illusion. Forget about all these illusions!

Q: In the practical life, maybe there is no *karma* for the Realized Master, but for the ordinary person, there may be bad deeds, *karma*?

Maharaj: Prior to the body-knowledge, nothing was there. You are to forget about everything. These are the influences of illusionary aspects and impressions. These are the layers upon the Ultimate Truth, the layers upon the Ultimate Truth.

Can a dead body have any illusion? Listen to me, carefully! The foundation is "I am not the body, I was not the body, I will not remain the body". Everything comes out of you and dissolves back into you.

After knowing the Reality, forget about your existence. To do this, you need full faith in the Master.

FORGET THE PAST! THERE IS NO PAST.
PAST, PRESENT AND FUTURE ARE CONCEPTS.
STOP MEASURING YOURSELF IN BODY-FORM.
THAT IS THE GREAT ILLUSION. IT IS A GREAT SIN.

Because you have a body, you need God. We have created the word G.O.D. out of imagination! You can fly on your own wings, but you are not making any effort. Your expectations of miracles shows that you are still considering yourself in the body-form.

YOU ARE TO ENGRAVE REALITY LIKE A TATTOO.
AFFIX REALITY LIKE A TATTOO, SO THAT IT WILL NOT VANISH.

Remove all concepts that you have accommodated from childhood till today. Delete all the bad files, wrong files. Clean your hard disk. Keep the good files for yourself.

Q: I sometimes feel that I have no control over what is happening in my life.

Maharaj: That is why you need meditation. When everything ends, there you are. There is no beginning, there is no end. We are just talking like this for understanding purposes. All spiritual discussion is in respect of the unborn child. Nothing is happening because you are unborn.

WHEN THE INVISIBLE PRESENCE IN YOU DISAPPEARS,
IT GOES EVERYWHERE.

Where does God go after the body is burned? Everywhere! When everything dissolves, there is nothing.

55. *Enjoy the Sweets of Knowledge*

Maharaj: When the Spirit clicked with the body, it came under the constant pressure of all sorts of illusions. To dissolve these, various disciplines are needed. On the way, you will have experiences which are no doubt progressive steps, but they are still to be considered as illusion. When no 'I' remains there will not be anything to describe.

THERE WILL NOT BE ANYTHING TO DESCRIBE
BECAUSE THERE WILL NOT BE
ANY DESCRIBER OR EXPERIENCER.

This is very simple Knowledge, and after knowing this Reality, there is nothing left to go looking for. You are free.

Q: Do people still go searching after being here? I would find this hard to believe because your teachings say it all.

Maharaj: It happens, it is a habit they have of talking about illusionary things, and comparing Masters like Nisargadatta Maharaj, Siddharameshwar Maharaj, Ramana Maharshi.

THERE IS NO BONDAGE.
YOU ARE ALREADY FREE.
PEOPLE SAY THEY WANT SALVATION.
THIS IS A CONCEPT.
YOU ARE FREE.

Conviction has to be there: firm, strong, solid, immovable. I am always hammering the same thing. It is open fact: "Except your Selfless Self there is no God, no *Brahman*, no *Atman*, no *Paramatman*". Be calm and quiet.

Q: Are there any other aspects to devotion apart from *bhajans*?

Maharaj: Devotion means involvement. You are told that you are not the body-form, that you are Ultimate

Truth, Final Truth, *Atman*, *Brahman*, that that is your Unidentified Identity. You are accepting this absolutely. You are absorbing it all. Absorb!

ACCEPTANCE IS DEVOTION.
ABSORPTION IS DEVOTION.

It is very simple with Self-Conviction. You are to be convinced that the Seer is Ultimate. The Seer is the Ultimate Truth.

'THAT YOU ARE' - WITHOUT SAYING IT.

Q: Why "Without saying it"? I often say it aloud as a reminder, "I am *Brahman*", I am *Brahman*".

Maharaj: In order to say something, you have to take ego. It is enough to know, so be quiet.

Q: OK, and I suppose if I say it, it brings in duality, too?

Maharaj: You will absorb this Knowledge with the help of the Mantra, and meditation and *bhajan*. All these saints gave instructions without any bondage. You are a free bird.

IN THE BEGINNING A LITTLE INTENSITY IS GOOD.

Q: Is that because the practice is new and there will be some sort of resistance to it?

Maharaj: Yes, yes. From childhood till today you have been besieged by illusion, so you have to fight a little.

AT THE SAME TIME, YOU CAN ENJOY THIS KNOWLEDGE!
IT IS NOT DRY KNOWLEDGE.

I have given you a bag of sweets, now you have to consume them, eat them. You are not to ask "How is this sweet?" No! Don't ask!

Q: What you are saying is, don't ask what it all means, don't dissect the Knowledge that has been shared. Just suck it.

Maharaj: You just have to eat it. Knowledge has been given to you. Knowledge means Reality. Knowledge and Reality are both ONE and the same.

KNOWLEDGE MEANS REALITY.
THIS IS THE FINAL DESTINATION.
THERE IS NOTHING BEYOND.

This is the conclusion of all our discussions. I am using words to try and convince the 'Invisible Listener' within you.

Q: I understand! We are using aids, tools to get to - not to get to because you already are - but to help us know and establish Ultimate Reality?

Maharaj: Before coming here you had been searching here and there. Maybe you had a few addresses from books that gave you pointers, or teachers that gave you clues. Now that you have come to the destination you can throw away those addresses. They are no longer of any use to you.

Q: Yes, I follow. Maharaj, I was going to ask you a question concerning the *bhajan*s. Back home, is it possible to try and sing these *bhajan*s in English because I am struggling with the Marathi, even though it is written phonetically?

Maharaj: Of course, whatever you find easier. It's the same, same process.

Q: But are they not more powerful being sung in Marathi rather than in English?

Maharaj: Language was created by us. With the *bhajan*s, it is not the words that are so important, but the rhythm. The rhythm creates some vibrations inside you, like an atmosphere. When you are cooking something, you might add a little salt, this herb, that spice, and like that, you are giving it some atmosphere. You know *gunas*?

Q: Yes, the three *gunas*?

Maharaj: All *gunas* are connected with the body only. I am talking beyond that. But for simple understanding, there are three *gunas*: *sattva guna* applies to someone who is disposed to worship, devotion, prayer, devotion to God. Devotion and the singing of *bhajan*s create a *sattvic* atmosphere.

Q: So that is why we do it?

Maharaj: I have told you. When you are singing the *bhajan*s, you forget about the body-form. The rhythm creates vibrations that the Spirit likes. Remember not to take any words literally!

Q: I know, I know. I am aware of a tendency to sometimes try and grasp what you are saying so as I can slot it in a compartment, if you know what I mean.

Maharaj: *Raja guna* is about finding enjoyment through various material causes. *Tama guna* is related to, say, criminal concepts, criminal thinking. But all *gunas* are connected with the body only.

I am talking beyond that. In fact, there are no *gunas*. This is called *nirguna*. And now, forget all about this talk! You see all of this spiritual language, spiritual knowledge is connected with the body alone. It is all body-knowledge, body-related knowledge. I am talking beyond all that, beyond knowledge, no knowledge, nothing.

KNOWLEDGE MEANS SELF-KNOWLEDGE,
AND DEVOTION MEANS
THE PERFECTION OF THAT KNOWLEDGE.

56. Who is Counting the Years?

Q: Is a Master or Guru really needed?

Maharaj: In order to come out from all these concepts, a guide is required.

WE KNOW THE ENTIRE WORLD,
BUT WE DO NOT KNOW OURSELVES!
WE MAY KNOW EVERYTHING ABOUT THE WHOLE WORLD
BUT WE DO NOT KNOW OURSELVES!

We can talk and talk about anything, about work or spiritual matters, but,

WE ARE NOT ENTERING OUR OWN FIELD OF REALITY.

We are ignoring that. Therefore,

THE MASTER IS INVITING THE ATTENTION
OF THE INVISIBLE LISTENER.
YOU ARE ULTIMATE TRUTH,
YOU ARE FINAL TRUTH.
THE BODY IS NOT YOUR IDENTITY.

I am shouting this out every day. The body is not your identity. The 'I' never remains. Even if you want to protect it with the help of a doctor, the maximum he can do is maybe postpone death. But he cannot do anything to prevent death.

Self-enquire! What is the secret of death? As you go deeper and deeper, you will find that there is nothing to be afraid of. There is no death for you. You know the story of the rope and the snake?

Q: Yes! I had a similar experience once. In a darkened room, I saw a huge black snake on the floor. I was really scared. I ran for help. My friend switched on the light to see this terrifying snake, and then the truth was revealed. It was nothing but a thick black belt lying curled up on the floor. The fear left in an instant, and I started laughing.

Maharaj: That was a good experience. When you see in the light that it is a rope, and not a snake, you are no longer frightened. It is the same with the fear of death. "I am unborn so why should I have fear of death?"

I WAS NOT BORN AT ALL.
THE BODY IS NOT GOING TO REMAIN MY IDENTITY,
BECAUSE I AM WITNESSING ALL THIS.

Q: So for thirty-plus years I have been living with all these concepts and...

Maharaj: Who is counting the years?

Q: That's right! Age is a concept as well, I suppose.

Maharaj: Correct! When Spirit clicked with the body, the concepts entered. Nobody thinks about the facts. Instead, we are under the pressure of all these thoughts, and accept illusion over the Reality that we are. You must know the Reality.

Q: And you, as the Master, will help me to do this?

Maharaj: You must have some courage to know the Reality. Nothing is impossible, [pointing to pictures of Lineage Masters - Bhausaheb Maharaj, Siddharameshwar Maharaj, Nisargadatta Maharaj and Ranjit Maharaj].

ALL THESE SAINTS ARE OF THE SAME SPIRIT AS YOU.
ALL THESE GREAT SAINTS
ARE WITH THE SAME SPIRIT THAT IS IN YOU.

Q: When I see these pictures of the Masters here in the hall and feel their presence, I pick up 'The Ant's Way' meditation from Bhausaheb Maharaj; *I Am That*, earnestness and strength from Nisargadatta Maharaj; 'I am He' and 'Everything is zero', from Ranjit Maharaj; and 'The Bird's Way' from Siddharameshwar Maharaj. And then from yourself, direct, down-to-earth, simple, 'going for the jugular', cutting through it all, radical and absolute.

Maharaj: The teachings are the same, only the expression is different.

Anyway, stop underestimating the Spirit. You accept, "I am a man or a woman", and every day you are depending on somebody else, something else. We depend upon God, depend upon God. We say, "God bless me, Oh God, bless me!" People talk about God, which God? Have they seen God? No! Have you seen God? No! You haven't seen God. Yet everyone says, God is there, God is there. But 'God' is not in any form.

EVERYBODY SAYS GOD IS THERE,
BUT GOD IS THERE ONLY BECAUSE
YOUR SPONTANEOUS PRESENCE IS THERE FIRST.

We have become victims of words, slaves of concepts. We enjoy playing with the words.

Q: That's true! I am guilty of that.

Maharaj: So you have to accept this Truth and not give in to the pressure of illusory thoughts such as: "What will happen? What is going to happen?" etc. Nothing has happened. Nothing is happening, and nothing is going to happen. Then the secret will no longer be secret, but open. It is very simple! But you have enclosed yourself in a circle of concepts, in a balloon. It is a vicious circle. You must come out of this circle of body-knowledge.

Q: Or burst the balloon?

Maharaj: Correct! So all of these thousands of spiritual books, what do they indicate? You have to find out through Self-enquiry. Just enquire, ask yourself: "After reading so many books, after approaching several Masters, after travelling to so many different places, what is the outcome of it all?"

WHAT IS YOUR CONCLUSION?

Q: Conclusion? I don't really know. I guess I am still trying to work it all out.

Maharaj: For example, when you are doing Self-enquiry, find out if the books you have read have given you peace, fearlessness, brought you out of confusion. If your inner voice says 'No', this response will then lead you to knowledge. You have to ask these questions. There has to be a full stop, otherwise there is only aimless drifting, swimming in a sea of thousands of words.

Q: I see what you are saying.

Maharaj: If your Inner Master says 'No', then, this means full stop.

THERE MUST BE A FULL STOP.

Then you will need to change tracks, and get on the direct line to Self-Knowledge.
It is very simple!

IF YOUR SPIRITUAL PURSUITS HAVE NOT LED YOU
TO SELF-ENQUIRY AND SELF-KNOWLEDGE,
THEN THE CONCLUSION IS
THAT IT HAS ALL BEEN ONE BIG ILLUSION.

We are trying to know ourselves through the body-form. We are trying to know through the medium of the body-form.

THE BODY IS ONLY THE MEDIUM.
OPEN TRUTH IS WITHIN YOU.

You are ignoring that. You are Final Truth.

THE ENTIRE WORLD IS PROJECTED OUT OF
YOUR SPONTANEOUS PRESENCE.
AND THE SAME THING WILL HAPPEN IN REVERSE,
WHEN THE PROJECTED WORLD IS TAKEN AWAY.
ACCEPT THE REALITY.

Q: I think I'm really beginning to hear what you are saying. The penny is beginning to drop, and I'm feeling excited.

Maharaj: We are under so many impressions and pressures from the body, imbalance of mind, no peace, a lot of confusion and struggle. Why?

BECAUSE WE ARE NOT ACCEPTING THE REALITY.

BECAUSE WE ARE NOT ACCEPTING THE REALITY.

So all this will come to an end when you know yourself in a real sense.

YOU ARE,
WHEN EVERYTHING DISAPPEARS.
WHEN EVERYTHING DISAPPEARS,
THERE YOU ARE.

I am trying to convince the Invisible Listener in different ways, using various words, that you are Ultimate Truth, *Brahman*, *Atman*. There are many different words for the Reality, therefore the *Naam Mantra* is given.

Bhausaheb Maharaj found that it was very easy for anyone to say, "I am *Brahman*", but it was not practicable. He said:

WE ARE KNOWING THE TRUTH THROUGH WORDS.
WE ARE NOT KNOWING THE TRUTH DIRECTLY.
WE ARE KNOWING THE TRUTH
THROUGH ILLUSORY THOUGHTS.

Q: And if we only know the Truth through words, then that means it is not Direct Self-Knowledge? So we will not be able to know ourselves in what you call a 'real sense'?

Maharaj: Correct! So be calm and quiet. Don't be subjected to the impressions of any illusory thoughts.

57. Good Files Are Corrupted

Maharaj: As I said, the first step is for you, [pointing to a new visitor], to undergo meditation. Why? Because your entire laptop is crowded with the wrong bytes. The good files are corrupted, so we have to clean up this laptop completely. To do this, meditation is most important, as necessary as taking a daily bath, or washing your clothes.

Your spiritual body needs to be cleaned every day with meditation. Meditation is just like the soap which you use for bathing every morning and evening. It is the soap for cleaning the spiritual body.

The approach used here is a scientific approach, which shows you how to absorb the Knowledge which you already have.

Q: When you say 'scientific', what do you mean, Maharaj?

Maharaj: Well, scientific means that it is systematic. It is a proven method that has been used and brings results. At the initial stage, I ask you not to mix with people who may misguide and distract you.

Q: Because of the newness of the practice which makes you vulnerable?

Maharaj: You need to be strong, so keep good company. One boy about your age, came here for some time. He was paying good attention to the teachings. He suddenly changed because he visited his old friends. I feel sorry for these people. After being shown the Reality, they are influenced by others, and once again they become victims of these illusory circumstances.

Q: I find it hard to believe that after listening to the highest teachings, and hearing the highest Truth, so to speak, you could just drop it all like that?

Maharaj: It happens! Don't throw it all away for an illusory dream. For what? The Master is always alerting you. There are very, very few devotees that accept the Reality.

VERY, VERY FEW DEVOTEES ACCEPT THE REALITY.

When I have shown you the Reality, why would there still be a need to go here and there? You are not handicapped at all. You are not dependent at all. You are independent. To maintain this Reality, meditation, *bhajan*s and Knowledge are essential. Then you will be totally fearless. You will know that "I'm wearing this [points to his sweater], just like I am wearing this body".

WHEN THERE WAS NO BODY THERE WAS NOBODY.
NO NEEDS WERE THERE,
BECAUSE WE ARE UNKNOWN TO OUR SELFLESS SELF.
IT IS OPEN FACT.

Any questions?

Q: You were saying that there are no needs?

Maharaj: All needs are body-related because when you came across with the body it all started: food, God, happiness, unhappiness, peace.

PRIOR TO BEINGNESS:
NO NEED OF PEACE OR HAPPINESS, UNHAPPINESS.
NO FEAR OF DEATH, OF BIRTH.

Q: So meditating regularly will help?

Maharaj: It is the base. Everybody has literal spiritual knowledge. Meditation is needed to absorb this knowledge. This is an opportunity! This is a golden time! But if you ignore it? It will be gone. So aim high!

Q: I find that people at work, and in life generally, can pull you away from...

Maharaj: You have to be indifferent! Stay strong and ignore difficult people. They behave according to the circumstances they were brought up in, with all their unique impressions.

HOW YOU WERE PRIOR TO THE BEINGNESS,
AND AFTER BEINGNESS DISAPPEARS,
IS THE ULTIMATE TRUTH.
YOU ARE TOTALLY UNAWARE OF YOUR EXISTENCE,
TOTALLY UNAWARE OF YOUR EXISTENCE.

Q: Is it not possible to remember?

Maharaj: It's an open fact. People make the mistake and think I am talking about memory. No! The words have not to be taken literally. What I am talking about has nothing to do with memory. Remembrance comes after existence. Prior to the existence, where is the remembrance? In order to remember, something would have to be there to do the remembering.

Your Presence is Invisible, Anonymous, Unidentified, so the question of memory never arises. Does sky remember itself? Look at it! The spectacles of Knowledge have been given to you.

THE SPECTACLES OF KNOWLEDGE ARE YOURS.
YOU CAN SEE YOURSELF WITH THEM
BECAUSE YOU ARE FINAL TRUTH.

It is open fact that the entire world is projected out of your Spontaneous Presence. And we are giving importance to the projection, instead of the Projector.

You are Ultimate Truth. Absorb the Knowledge! So many words are out there, so many books, all of which belong to, and are part of, this illusory world. All knowledge that is conveyed by language is illusion. It is literal knowledge, dry knowledge. It will not serve you.

REAL KNOWLEDGE IS SELF-KNOWLEDGE,
BEYOND WORDS AND BEYOND WORLDS.
YOU ARE BEYOND WORDS
AND BEYOND WORLDS,
BEYOND IMAGINATION,
BEYOND THE BEYOND,
BEYOND EVERYTHING!

58. *Oneness Has No Mother, No Father*

Maharaj: Shankaracharya was eight or nine years old when he was told that his mother had died. He asked all the relatives and people in the village for help to carry the body to the funeral site. "Please help me!" he said, but no one wanted to help the young boy. At that time, there was a lot of hatred towards saintly people.

The mother was of heavy build and he was just a thin, small boy. He had to remove the body all by himself. To do this he had to cut up his mother's body into manageable pieces. Using a sharp blade, he closed his eyes and did the necessary. Then he carried the pieces to the funeral pyre all by himself. This was an exceptional feat!

He composed the words to *Chidananda Sivoham Sivoham.* The song has a very high meaning. It is exceptional, and really the summary of our philosophy: No mother, no sister, no brother, no Master, no disciple, nothing. No witness, no witnesser, no experience, no experiencer. Everything is illusion.

The Ultimate Truth is in you, but some body-attachment is not allowing you to be close to your Selfless Self. It's not impossible. This song, *Chidananda,* reaches the inner part of the body.

AFTER LISTENING TO ALL THIS SPIRITUAL TALK,
A MELTING PROCESS WILL FOLLOW.
ONLY THEN WILL THERE BE COMPLETE PEACE.

The ego, intellect and mind will melt completely, and then there will be love and affection towards the Selfless Self, spiritual love, spontaneous love! There will be no hatred, no duality, just complete calm and quiet. Bodies are different, but the Spirit is one.

ONENESS HAS NO MOTHER, NO FATHER,
NO BROTHER, NO SISTER, NO MASTER.
THESE ARE BODY RELATIONS.

All relations were formed when you came across with the body: God, *Brahman*, *Atman*, Master, brother, sister, mother.

ALL THESE RELATIONS ARE BODY-RELATED.

YOUR PRESENCE IS EXCEPTIONAL PRESENCE.
WORDS CANNOT REACH YOUR EXCEPTIONAL PRESENCE.

Be calm! Be quiet! Forget all that you have been told about *karma*. At the last stage, when you are leaving the body, at that time exceptional happiness will appear within you. It cannot be explained by any words. Complete Calm and Peace will be there, absorbing totally, totally, totally.

Saintly people like Shankaracharya faced a lot of difficulties. There are so many rules in each and every religion. To a certain extent they are right, but what is taught is not Ultimate Truth. What I am saying is that the Power is in you. That powerful Spirit is within you! It has tremendous Power, but you are ignoring it. Therefore we are inviting the attention of this Power in you.

THIS POWER THAT IS IN YOU,
USE IT TO COME OUT OF ALL IGNORANCE.

After listening to this Knowledge, absorb it completely and thoroughly. All these saintly people faced a lot of difficulties but they had established good Knowledge, Perfection. Achieve that Perfection! Don't ignore it. Don't take it casually. Know that what you are doing in this body-form is not Ultimate Truth.

This body is on a timer. Be serious! It is not difficult, not impossible. Perfect humility is a must. Don't say: "Oh! I am someone, somebody, something!" Far better to say,

"MY PRESENCE IS EVERYWHERE.
MY PRESENCE IS THERE,
IN EACH AND EVERY BEING".

Bodies are different and actions are different, but the actions are made possible only because of the Spirit.

No ego, no mind. You can use the mind, ego and intellect, as and when they are required, but don't become a victim or slave of the mind, ego and intellect. The mind, ego, intellect are co-relations. Thoughts come in the mind, the intellect instructs, "Do this!" And the ego says, "Yes!". They are interconnected. Without these, you cannot live your life. They are instruments for knowledge. They are not Ultimate Truth. They are to be used as and when required, and then forgotten.

59. Say 'Boo!' to the Ghost of Death

Q: Maharaj, I wanted to ask you about death and dying. You don't really talk about death.
Maharaj: There is no death, only for the body. Everyone wants to survive in the body. From the biggest animal to the tiniest insect. Why? Because they like the body. They enjoy the sweetness. Take the ant for example. If you pour a drop of water near an ant, it scurries away as if its life depended on it. Human beings are the same as the ants.

Spirit only knows itself through the body. It has become attached to this identity, and doesn't want to leave. The concept of death creeps slowly towards you, and then, one day, willingly or unwillingly, you will have to leave this body. The body has a time limit. Open fact! But, you are not the body. You were not the body. You are not going to remain the body. You are unborn. So, who is dying? Who is living? Just Self-enquire.

NOBODY IS DYING. NOBODY IS TAKING BIRTH.

You have a golden opportunity to make sure that when you leave the body, it will be a very happy time.

Q: So, how can I make sure?

Maharaj: Do Self-enquiry and get to know yourself in a real sense, then you will see that there is no death, and you can say, "Boo!" to this ghost of death. Every moment in your life is very precious, never to be repeated. Now is the time to find out.

How are you to see the existence of the world? It came out of non-existence. Existence disappears into non-existence. Look at you! What is this? Then, ultimately, you will be totally fearless. "Ah!" Nothing is going to happen. Nothing has happened. Why fear a shadow? Because of your Spontaneous Presence, there is this fearful shadow that you are so scared of. It is only your own shadow, your principle!

Q: I am listening to what you are saying, and things are falling into place, with lots of 'Aha!' moments, such as, "I am not the body". I believe you. But I still have some fear about dying.

Maharaj: Who is afraid? Self-enquire! It is not a matter of belief. So many people claim to have spiritual knowledge. They will say "I am not the body", I am *Brahman*, I am *Atman*", BUT when something unexpected happens, like an accident or illness, or suffering at the end of life, then all these Truths just vanish. And then they are dying, trembling, "Ooh, Ooh", with fear. By then, it is too late to do anything.

THIS MEANS THAT THE CONVICTION THAT
"YOU ARE NOT THE BODY" DID NOT GO VERY DEEP.
IT WAS NOT ESTABLISHED, AND THEREFORE,
IT WAS NOT A REALITY,
NOT REAL CONVICTION.

Any spiritual knowledge that you have must be real Self-Knowledge. Self-Knowledge has to be pragmatic, so that when the time comes to leave the body, you will be strong, courageous and fearless. There must not be any body-attachment left. You are not the body, you were not the body, you will not remain the body. Open fact! Therefore accept this Truth.

Q: It does take time to fully absorb and be accepted in a pragmatic way.

Maharaj: Why time? There is no time. Was there time prior to beingness? You accept that you are a woman, and that you were born in such and such a year. You count the years and say you have fifty something years old. You accept all this illusion. Then, when I share with you the Knowledge shared with me by my Master, you don't accept it.

Think on your existence! Take a look, contemplate! No one is thinking, just accepting everything blindly. If you are not the body, what are you? You are unborn. Make Self-enquiry, and then you will find out that you ARE nothing to do with the body.

USE DISCRIMINATION!
I REPEAT: THIS IS NOT AN IDEA,
BUT THE TRUTH.
YOU WERE NEVER BORN,
SO HOW CAN YOU DIE?

There is no birth and there is no death. When you know the Reality, you will see that all your fears had no basis. They were built on false self-identifications, on body attachment, on illusion. But now you know better.

There is a story of a boy called Nachiketa. He was full of curiosity and was a little bit naughty because he was always asking his father questions. There was no end to his questions. His father was a saintly person, something of a hermit, but his son was slowly driving him crazy with his persistent questions.

At the end of his patience, the father asked Yama, the God of Death, to come and take his son away. When Yama came, his father said, "Please, please take this boy away. He is harassing me asking all these questions". Yama took him. On their way out, the boy started asking Yama a string of questions. He said "So you are the God of Death. What do you mean by death? If you are taking the souls of all the ordinary people, who is going to take away your soul?"

Yama replied: "I will give you anything you want but please stop asking me these questions". The boy said "No, no, I am not going to stop asking you, just answer them!"

This example indicates the need to know Reality. We are constantly asking questions about things which have not happened. We are asking about the prospects, the future, the destiny of the child that is not born, the unborn child. You must know the Reality!

Your Presence is Silent, Invisible, Anonymous, Unidentified. Your Presence is the same now as it was prior to beingness. It will be the same after beingness. The only difference is that you are holding the body. You are the holder of the body, but you are not the body.

**YOU ARE THE HOLDER OF THE BODY,
BUT YOU ARE NOT THE BODY.**

60. Where Was Your Family Prior to Beingness?

Maharaj: You are living like a sheep when you should be roaring like a lion. "I am That!" Why fear, or be depressed? If something happens, it happens. It will come and go. You are suffering from involvement, over-involvement. Just ignore these passing things. Don't take the touch or the bite, or you will suffer.

Q: I have taken the sting a lot in this life, and I do get involved with the family and worldly things, as you say over-involved. Now that I have taken the *Naam Mantra*, and I'm doing the practice, how can I handle these family relationships?

Maharaj: Carry on as before, as usual, normally. Family relations need not be a blockage or hurdle to spirituality. Just be normal. When did you first come across the family? The 'family' came with the beingness and all the rest of these concepts. When the Spirit clicked with the body, all these concepts started: the people, the family, the places and the world. Carry out your normal duties. There's no problem.

Q: I thought maybe that I needed to distance myself from the family for the sake of the practice?

Maharaj: Not at all! Most of these saints had a family, [pointing to the pictures of the Masters], and were married, with children, and doing their business. Ranjit Maharaj was employed in a shop until the age of 73. Nisargadatta Maharaj owned his shop for many years. Siddharameshwar Maharaj was also employed, and before him, Bhausaheb Maharaj. So they all carried on with their duties and family life without any problems.

Through the Master, you are being reminded of your Reality. The Master is inviting the attention of that which is Ultimate in you, without body-knowledge. The body is not Ultimate - it is Spirit that is important. If the Spirit goes away, the body dies.

Death? A dead body? What is the value of this passing body? What then is the relationship with your Mom? Who is mother? Who is father? Who is brother? Who is sister? Who is God? Who is Master? Who are friends? Who is wife, son?

ALL RELATIONS ARE RELATED TO THIS BODY ONLY.
IT IS AN OPEN FACT. IT IS AN OPEN FACT.

After death, what do these relations mean? Where are these relations? There are none! No relations, no family life. Therefore all these relations have come out of this body-knowledge alone.

THIS BODY IS A FOOD-BODY.
AS LONG AS YOU SUPPLY FOOD TO THE BODY, IT WILL LIVE.
THE MOMENT YOU STOP SUPPLYING FOOD,
THAT WILL BE THE END OF THE BODY.

Q: What if a conflict arises between the teachings and the family? Suppose the family does not agree with the teachings?

Maharaj: When did you come across the family? It's a simple understanding. The moment you came across the body, the family started. After leaving the body, where is that relationship? In the *Chidananda Sivoham Sivoham*, it says there is no mother, no father, sister, no brother, no friend, no death, no Master, no disciple, nothing, nothing.

THE ENTIRE WORLD IS YOUR SPONTANEOUS REFLECTION.
YOUR SPONTANEOUS PRESENCE IS BEHIND EVERYTHING.

Without your Presence, you can't see, you can't talk, you can't do anything. So just know yourself in a real sense. This is a dream world. In this great drama of the world, the director is invisible. You are that director!

Q: So you would say not to worry about the family, but focus on knowing yourself in a real sense?

Maharaj: Why worry about the family? There is no conflict, no problem.

Q: But sometimes there is disturbance. Even close family members can make things tough.

Maharaj: That is because there is so much affection for the body, so much affection and love. Spirituality doesn't tell you to ignore your family life. The Masters have not run away from their family duties. Family is not a hurdle, not an obstacle, not a blockage.

61. Who is Suffering?

Q: I visited a teacher once. He talked about the 'pain-body' to describe personal pain and collective pain. He said that all our emotional pain is collected and stored, and as a result, it has almost become a kind of entity, like a ball of pain that you carry around with you. He went on to say that the only way to stop this pain from damaging us, is to live fully in the present, because the 'Now' has a lot of power.

Maharaj: This is all body-knowledge, imagination! You are not the body! The body by itself has no power, so how can there be an entity of a pain-body? It sounds like someone has created a little monster to frighten you. Whose pain? Whose pain-body? Whose 'Now'?

You are unborn! This is a long dream! There is no past and there is no future. There is no present, and no 'Now'. All Power is in you. As my *Sadguru*, Nisargadatta Maharaj messaged: "Except for your Selfless Self, there is no God, no *Brahman*, no *Atman*, no *Paramatman*, no Master".

Q2: But Maharaj, I seem to move from one problem to another, physical, or emotional, it brings suffering.

Maharaj: Problems grow because we give so much importance to the body. This is body-knowledge, just like when you face problems in a dream, and then after waking up, the problems have gone. The saints always faced their problems with courage. Because of their strong Conviction, they did not concern themselves so much with their problems, even when they faced serious losses, illness and unexpected tragedies.

Consider the tragic story of Saint Jnaneshwar. His mother and father threw themselves into the Ganges and left the children destitute, all because the father had become a *sannyasin*, and then, contrary to *Brahmin* law, had returned to his family. "According to you, I have committed the fault so why are you punishing my children?" The father stated that he himself should be punished, but he begged that his children should not be. The *Brahmins* ignored his pleas, and so the parents threw themselves into the sacred river, in the hope that the children would fare better and be looked after. There were four small children, three brothers and one sister.

The orthodox religious Masters would not allow the four children to beg. People had a lot of hatred in those days. They suffered a lot and asked humbly, "Please help". The orphaned children were ignored by their relatives, treated as outcasts. Nobody helped them. And so they took to travelling to various places looking for a place that would welcome, accommodate them. At some places they were met by the orthodox religious leaders who would not accept them.

Jnaneshwar approached the learned *Brahmins* to try and clear the family name. "God is everywhere in each and every heart", he proclaimed. The *Brahmins* asked him to prove this and said "OK, make this buffalo recite the *Vedas*!".

As soon as Jnaneshwar placed his hand on the animal's head, it started singing the *Vedas,* as good as the *Brahmins*! A big crowd gathered to listen to and witness this miracle. The people were so surprised with the power he had, that they bowed down. The orthodox priests were forced to accept the greatness and supernatural power of Jnaneshwar.

This story shows the importance of struggle.

**IF YOU LISTEN
TO THE SOURCE OF YOUR KNOWLEDGE
WITH COMPLETE FAITH,
THERE WILL BE SPONTANEOUS ARISING
OF YOUR INDWELLING POWER.**

Be determined like Jnaneshwar! Now you have maturity, Knowledge, Reality, so don't keep coming back downstairs to the body-level. Use the body like an instrument, like a middle-man.

You have a body, and therefore you are going to have physical, mental, spiritual problems. Everybody thinks his problem is the greatest, but if you look at the big picture, there is always someone who is

133

suffering more than ourselves.

View your problems as a test of your spiritual life. Bring that Knowledge into practice. Don't give undue importance to problems which come and go just like clouds. Unbearable things become bearable with established Truth. You have good knowledge. But it is not put into practice, and that is the real problem. The Finder is missing. You have a lot of assets but you are not using them and because of a lack of planning, it's not giving you a result. You have to use the property, the asset, and with good planning, you will enjoy the benefits.

Q: You said body-knowledge should be dissolved totally.

Maharaj: Spontaneously!

Q: Maharaj, I wanted to tell you that I had experience of "I am That, I am everything".

Maharaj: That's very good because this kind of spiritual experience is a progressive step. I am not saying it is Ultimate Truth, but it is a progressive step and therefore encouraging.

EXPERIENCES ARE PROJECTED FROM YOUR PRESENCE.
WHEN THE EXPERIENCER AND THE EXPERIENCES DISSOLVE,
THERE YOU ARE.

It will happen spontaneously, then you will have the Conviction that you are nothing to do with the world. You will know that whatever happens in the illusory world, whether good or bad, has nothing to do with you.

THE SEER REMAINS ALOOF FROM ALL THAT IS SEEN.

If I say that "I am *Brahman*", it is the Seer's reflection. The Seer's existence in the world is Spontaneous, Shapeless.

Q: As long as there is body-knowledge, it is impossible to understand my Spontaneous Presence.

Maharaj: The Seer is one, dreams are different. Are you taking ego from all these dreams? No! You just forget about them. Forget this dream also! What you see is the Seer's projection/reflection, not anything 'good', or 'bad'. You are still viewing yourself as separate from Reality.

When you accept Reality Spontaneously, you will be able to face any problem with courage. In human life, there is no escape from problems, how you handle them is up to you. People are undergoing devotion, reading books, but not doing any Self-enquiry.

The problems you are describing are what you have seen. You are ignoring the Seer. Without the Seer, you can't see the seen.

WE HAVE CREATED THESE CONCEPTS,
AND THEN WE ARE TRYING TO LIVE
WITHIN THE CIRCLE OF THESE CONCEPTS.

You can talk about swimming but you cannot swim.

Q: Maharaj, I realized that I was reading for twenty years, and then I suddenly stopped. I suddenly realized I did not know why I was reading.

Maharaj: You do need to know how all this book-knowledge is helping you, otherwise it is a pointless exercise.

When you know the Reality, you will undergo a complete inner change. If you are aggressive, you will become calm and quiet. You can review the changes so that you know where you stand. Nisargadatta Maharaj says: "I am making you Masters not disciples". The Masterly essence is already in you.

THAT MASTERLY ESSENCE IS ALREADY IN YOU.

62. *Itchy Feet*

Maharaj: So you want to go travelling again, still tempted to go begging elsewhere? If you want to go anywhere, go deep within yourself.

GO WITHIN, AND BE WITHIN THE SELFLESS SELF.
PRAY TO YOUR SELFLESS SELF.
LOOK AT YOU!
TRY TO SEE THE SEER.
AS YOU TRY TO SEE THE SEER,
THE SEER WILL DISAPPEAR.

You will find that all sense of individuality will vanish and there will be nothing left. How you were prior to beingness is not known, not known in the body-form, not known through words. You are to surrender yourself. If there is any ego loitering, body-knowledge, hidden fears and doubts, etc, they all have to be cleared up and dissolved.

KNOWLEDGE WITH EGO WILL CREATE PROBLEMS.

Turn your attention inwards and give it to your Selfless Self. When you are searching, the Searcher will disappear. I have told you therefore that no knowledge is knowledge.

NO KNOWLEDGE IS KNOWLEDGE.

All these words are body-related. Compare yourself to sky! Become your own Master, a Master of Masters! The Masterly essence is in you, but the body impact of mind, ego is not allowing you to be your own Master. You need spiritual courage, internal courage, strong involvement, only then, will you be fearless. Let anything happen to the body! You are not concerned at all.

View your body as if it were your neighbour's child. You have a fever, but you know it is not happening to you. It is the neighbour's child who is suffering. View your body like the neighbour's child. You feel sorry, but you are at one remove. You can view the body in this way because the body is not Truth. You are ignoring this fact. All things are within you only. Don't be a tourist!

Q: I went round Arunachala and I found it very beneficial. Strong energy!

Maharaj: What did you achieve from going to Arunachala? Good and strenuous exercise maybe! And all this visiting is just adding more and more ego, and distancing you from yourself. All the time you are travelling away from yourself, instead of towards yourself.

YOU ARE NOT APPROACHING YOUR OWN MASTER.
YOU ARE NOT VALUING YOUR OWN PRESENCE.
YOUR PRESENCE IS INVALUABLE, INCOMPARABLE.
SO WHY GO HERE AND THERE?

THE SEARCHER WHO IS SEARCHING, IS ULTIMATE TRUTH.

You are Ultimate Truth. You are That which you were searching for. The Searcher who was searching is Ultimate Truth.

63. *"I am Somebody" is Very Dangerous*

Maharaj: You have the Knowledge, but it is not secured, not fixed down.

Q: So how do I fix it, secure it so that it is solid and permanent, and sticks to me like super glue?

Maharaj: I have told you, the only way is to have a solid foundation. Meditation is the base. You need to do the practice to make the Knowledge live. Meditation, devotion, Knowledge, prayer, all these will give you a solid base.

YOU CANNOT ESTABLISH A SOLID BASE IF BODY-KNOWLEDGE IS NOT DISSOLVED.

The questioner, the Invisible Questioner who is asking, is asking so many questions because you forgot your Identity. You are asking so many questions, yet at the same time, ignoring the Questioner. You have a lot of questions because your knowledge is body-based.

The Master says you are to undergo meditation. Meditation is concentration. Concentrate on the Concentrator, that Invisible Presence, Invisible Truth, Final Truth.

Q: In the beginning, I suppose we will be guessing, imagining the Presence?

Maharaj: Yes, correct, because when we are asking, "Who am I?", we are using our intellect. Intellectually, we know "I am *Brahman*", but this Truth is not established and therefore we feel depressed, and questions arise. The purpose of meditation is to think on your Selfless Self. By constant thinking, thinking on your Selfless Self, after some time, the thinker disappears. Meditate on the Meditator, the Invisible Presence that you are.

Q: Is that not duality? Meditation, meditator, is that not duality?

Maharaj: There is no duality. Meditation is just the process because the Meditator, the Invisible Meditator in you, forgot its Identity.

THAT MEDITATOR IS YOUR MASTER.
THAT INVISIBLE MEDITATOR IS YOUR MASTER.

You ask yourself, "How can I be God?" because of your strong ego and attachment to the body. We are under so much pressure from the ego. If you pay so much attention to this ego dictating terms, it is going to be your downfall. The ego with its commanding nature of "I am somebody", is very dangerous. You will come to know the Reality only when the ego is dissolved.

KNOW YOURSELF IN A REAL SENSE, NOT AS AN INDIVIDUAL.
YOUR SPONTANEOUS PRESENCE IS THE LAST DESTINATION, THE FINAL STOP.

Dissolve everything else. Be involved with Selfless Self. Casual spirituality or dry discussion will not help you. Visiting so many different places will not help you, visiting so many Masters will not help you.

VISIT YOUR OWN MASTER.

THIS WILL TAKE YOU HOME.

We don't know what *Brahman* is because we are hearing it from books. We are wholly innocent and totally unaware of the Reality. We don't know who God is. This is not our fault. But, after knowing the Reality, the concept of God will be dissolved.

YOU WILL KNOW THAT WITHOUT YOUR PRESENCE,
TO EVEN TALK ABOUT GOD IS AN IMPOSSIBILITY,
NEVER MIND BEING ABLE TO SEE GOD.
ANY AND EVERY PICTURE OF GOD
IS YOUR REFLECTION ALONE.

We are in search of miracles and therefore approaching different Masters who may make them happen. Miracles are not Ultimate Truth. Your Spontaneous Presence is a miracle. Unless your ego dissolves, you will not be able to know yourself. Keep up the practice! That means forget everything that is associated with "I am somebody else", and "I am a separate body".

BE LOYAL TO YOURSELF. BE LOYAL!
YOU ARE YOUR OWN TRUSTEE, THE TRUST-HOLDER.

This morning one of the elderly devotees with a heart condition fell down. He just said "I'm OK", and got up. There was no fear. This is an example of courage, a living example of Knowledge Absorbed.

Tremendous power is in you which, in turn, will instil tremendous confidence. We are insulting ourselves with this lack of faith, lack of trust. Therefore these talks are necessary to give you courage so that you can be a real devotee, a true disciple.

After the Spontaneous Conviction of "I am *Brahman*", without saying it, you can use your body as before, but at the same time, the Conviction, Reality is there. "I am not the body, nothing to do with the body. I am beyond that, beyond that...". It is not logical inference, it is not guessing, it is Reality.

Your Invisible Presence is Reality, but because of the influences of the body, you are not accepting it. All these thoughts that you entertain, you are trying to work out which ones are true. There is no true and false! Everything is within you. Now it is up to you.

Q: It is not only me, I think most people have a resistance when it comes to doing practice, meditation and the likes.

Maharaj: Practice is needed. You are creating difficulties. You want miracles but you are not prepared to put in any effort. When you have grown up, you will not need spirituality.

Q: Practice for whom? For the ego?

Maharaj: These are intellectual questions. The practice is needed at first to forget the body-knowledge.

Q: Is it required to dissolve the ego?

Maharaj: It will dissolve spontaneously. You have knowledge, but not practical knowledge. You are still asking all these body-related questions. The questioner has to look to the questioner, the Invisible Questioner. You can't guess! Full Spontaneous Conviction, "I am *Brahman*" is non-intellectual. The intellect came with the body.

Q: It is not known intellectually?

Maharaj: No intellect, as this is connected with body-knowledge. The practice is necessary to remove all these illusory concepts.

**YOU HAVE TO KEEP TAKING THE MEDICINE
UNTIL YOU RECOVER FROM THE DISEASE.
ONCE YOU HAVE MADE A FULL RECOVERY,
YOU WILL HAVE NO FURTHER NEED OF THE MEDICINE.**

64.   'You' Are Disturbing the Peace

Maharaj: The purification stage will start with meditation. Purification means that all concepts will dissolve, slowly, silently and permanently. Initially, there will be a lot going on at the body level. Just for a moment, put spirituality aside and look at the facts.

**FORGET ABOUT SPIRITUALITY.
PRIOR TO BEINGNESS, YOU DID NOT KNOW ANYTHING
ABOUT THE WORLD, THE FAMILY, OR GOD.**

All needs and demands were orientated through body-knowledge only. If there is no body, there is no family, no need of wife or husband, no child, no father, no Master, no disciple, no God. The moment that the Spirit clicked with the body, you started a big list of wants: "I want happiness, I want peace", etc. These are concepts. Who wants peace? You do not know what peace is. "I want peace". "You want peace of mind". These are concepts, just concepts. When did you come across this 'peace'?

**THERE IS PEACE. IT IS YOU WHO ARE DISTURBING THE PEACE.
PEACE IS THERE,
BUT YOU ARE DISTURBING THE PEACE.**

Q: When working in the world, I get absorbed in it. I forget Selfless Self and then I get upset. How do I stay…?

Maharaj: This is talk on a mental level. The moment you realize that the entire world is illusion, you will see that these upsets and depressions are just happening on a mental level. Sometimes there is a disturbance if what we are expecting does not go according to plan.

Wife, son, daughter, father, anybody, all these are part of the circle of expectations. If you act within the circle, [according to expectations], you are viewed or seen as a nice person. If you go beyond the circle then, "Oh! He's not a nice person".

If your parents say, "You are a good boy", you say, "Oh! I am a good boy", but if your parents say, "You are a bad boy", you feel bad. This is all mental. It is what is going on at the mental level.

THERE IS NO BAD, AND THERE IS NO GOOD.

This type of thing happens in the beginning. Later on, everything will dissolve during the melting process. Reality is supposed to be fully absorbed within you. For this to happen, complete involvement, complete devotion is needed. Then there will not be any more problems.

**PRIOR TO ONE HUNDRED YEARS,
DID YOU HAVE ANY PROBLEMS?
AND WILL THERE BE ANY PROBLEMS**

AFTER LEAVING THE BODY?

Q: Yesterday, you said that the Spirit doesn't know itself, so what can I do to help the Spirit know itself?

Maharaj: Don't make any efforts, your Spontaneous Existence is there. Spirit is only a word I am using, just to know yourself. It's what I want to convey that is most important. It is your story, the Listener's story. Read the book *I Am That*. Sometimes at a delicate point, if you are vulnerable, and something happens to challenge you, like an attraction or sickness or upset, this may cause unsteadiness, trembling, and the shaking of your foundation. And as a result, the Conviction just crumbles.

If possible, take a look at the *Dasbodh* also. This was written by Swami Ramdas, an eminent Marathi saint and poet. There is an excellent translation of this book by Dr Ghaisas. It gives guidelines: The Nine types of devotion. How to approach, see your Selfless Self. With each reading you will get more information.

So yes, the Questioner is the answer to all questions. The Questioner is the answer to all questions.

YOU ARE IGNORING THE QUESTIONER.
YOU ARE NOT SEPARATE FROM YOUR OWN IDENTITY.

It is only because of the body that you say, "This is *Brahman*, this is *Atman*, this is Spirit". All these words were created just for communication purposes, discussion, so as to give attention to, and address the Invisible, Anonymous Spirit.

YOU ARE THAT SPIRIT, THAT ' I ',
WITHOUT SAYING IT,
OUT OF WHICH THE ENTIRE WORLD IS PROJECTED.

Therefore your Presence was there prior to everything. Prior to everything, your Presence was there. It cannot be defined. We are trying to impress Reality, the Listener's Reality. The Listener is not in any form. If you were to try and compare it to something, it is just like the sky. Sky does not know it's own existence. Sky does not know it's own existence. This is very simple knowledge. Don't stress your brain, don't stress your memory. Whose memory? Who am I? Who am I not?

WHEN ALL THINKING PROCESSES HAVE STOPPED,
THERE YOU ARE,
IN THE THOUGHTLESS STATE.

Depression, confusion, unstable mind, mind, ego, intellect, these are all part of the subtle body that you have embraced. You have got to emerge from it with the Conviction that "I was not a body, I am not a body, I am not going to remain a body".

"THE QUESTION OF DEATH AND BIRTH NEVER ARISES.
I AM UNBORN."

It's an open fact that you are unborn. We are measuring ourselves in the body-form therefore it is difficult. All the time, we are measuring ourselves in the body-form. You are underestimating yourself. And the result is that you go begging elsewhere looking for somebody else's blessing. Your ego is creating problems. Your ego is sticking in, saying, "I am somebody else". Humility is required.

KNOWLEDGE WITH EGO IS MEANINGLESS.
A COMPLETE MELTING IS WHAT'S NEEDED.

All these saints were very humble, very, very humble. They were not self-discriminating, saying, "I am a great Master". The ego is therefore a blockage, a hurdle in the way of your Knowledge of Reality. You have knowledge but it is with ego. The subtle ego is there saying, "I am somebody". Humility is not there.

Everything will be easy with humility. First respect yourself and then respect others. Respect yourself, then respect others. Respecting yourself doesn't refer to the body or to your status.

THE TRUTH IS "I AM NOTHING", SO WHY SHOULD THERE BE ANY EGO?

All the saints are very pious, very calm and quiet. They do not show irritation, or disturbance, or conflict. Follow their example! This is the Spontaneous Reaction that will appear in you when you see yourself in the real sense. There will be unlimited patience at all times, no matter whether someone is angry, or saying good or bad things. Nisargadatta Maharaj used to say, "If anybody says good things, I am not happy. If anybody says bad things, I am not unhappy".

Happiness-unhappiness is body-related. So this will take a little time because there is some physical ego, mental ego there. But don't look back! Forget the past, don't try to remember the past, because your Spontaneous Presence is your target.

This also means, "Don't go anywhere". You have to attain the highest position. In spiritual life the highest position means you are Spontaneously forgetting the body identity. After knowing the Reality, you will be fearless.

FORGET THE PAST, FORGET EVERYTHING.

~~~~~~

PART TWO: *SELF-KNOWLEDGE*

65. *Spirit Does Not Know its Own Identity*

Q: Maharaj, you said that Spirit does not know its own Identity.
Maharaj: Correct! Spirit only knows itself in the body-form. Yes! We are in the body-form. In the body-form, there are some feelings of happiness and peace. There is a need to find happiness and peace, but basically, you were not the body, you are not the body, you are not going to remain the body. Therefore the Spirit does not know its own Identity, that it is Ultimate.

SPIRIT DOES NOT KNOW ITS OWN IDENTITY,
ITS ULTIMATE, STATELESS STATE.

This body is a material body, and as a material body, it needs all sorts of things, everything. Its needs are endless. Because we are holding the body, and therefore in a different form, the material needs grow, as the body searches for peace and happiness. The body thinks it is something else, independent, someone else, [other than Spirit Identity], therefore all these needs appear in the body-form.

SINCE YOU ARE HOLDING THE BODY,
YOU WANT TO EAT FOOD,
YOU NEED TO BE ENTERTAINED.
PRIOR TO THE MATERIAL BODY
THERE WERE NO WANTS AND NEEDS,
NOTHING AT ALL WAS NEEDED.

So while you are in the body-form, this material body, you are searching for things that will bring you peace. You are searching for these things outside of yourself. Existence 'in the body' means that you are under a lot of pressure and tension. You cannot find lasting peace and happiness because of the bodily pressures, fears and tension. Even small things create conflict and confusion which then drive further tension.
Q: So how do I stop feeling all these bodily pressures?
Maharaj: To overcome this you must convince yourself in this way:

THOUGH I AM HOLDING THE BODY,
I AM UNCONCERNED WITH THE BODY-KNOWLEDGE.
PRIOR TO THIS BODY-KNOWLEDGE,
MY EXISTENCE WAS THERE,
BUT WITHOUT ANY FORM.

Q: What was it like without a body?
Maharaj: Formless! We do not know what type of existence was there. It is beyond imagination, beyond intellect. Spiritual science says many things, books too, when as a matter of fact, we know nothing about prior

to body-knowledge.

THERE WAS NO KNOWINGNESS.
IN THAT STATE NOTHING WAS NEEDED
BECAUSE YOU WERE FORMLESS.

The moment the Spirit clicked with the body, all requirements, demands started: We want happiness, we want peace, a tension-free life, a fearless life. All these needs are only connected with body-knowledge.

At the moment of Conviction, when you KNOW that, "I am not the body, I am not going to remain the body, I was not the body", at that time, everything will simply vanish. It is open fact. As long as we are concerned with the body-form, all these requirements will remain. We need Masters, we need some God or other.

'GOD' IS THE WORD GIVEN TO THE UNKNOWN POWER.
'GOD' IS ONLY A WORD.

We do not know what God is but we have an image, a picture of God administering the entire world. This is a concept.

Q: Like the God who sits in judgement and punishes us for our sins?

Maharaj: A God who exists and is administering the entire world. He punishes those who are doing wrong, and rewards those who are doing good. These are the concepts, just concepts to offer a little comfort and happiness, but it is momentary happiness. What is the Reality?

YOU SHOULD DIG IT OUT FROM WITHIN YOU.
FIND OUT!
WHAT IS YOUR REALITY?

Prior to body-knowledge, prior to beingness, we did not know any of these words. We did not have any of this knowledge: What is God? What is *Brahman*? The moment the body disappears, everything disappears.

WHAT IS THE USE OF YOUR KNOWLEDGE?
DOES IT HAVE ANY IMPORTANCE?
NO, NONE!
IT HAS NO IMPORTANCE BECAUSE
FIRST, YOU SEE EVERYTHING OUT OF NOTHING,
AND THEN, NOTHING DISAPPEARS INTO NOTHING.
NOTHING DISAPPEARS INTO NOTHING.
NO FORM!
WHERE IS YOUR SHAPE THEN?

Q: What you are saying Maharaj, is that the knowledge we have from books etc, is body-knowledge and not true knowledge?

Maharaj: You are formless. The body is only the external part, the food body.

YOU ARE TRYING TO KNOW ULTIMATE TRUTH
FROM WITHIN THE BODY-FORM.

You are using books and language and words to find your Reality. You are taking these words to be true, the truth. They are not! Words are only indicators.

YOUR VIEWPOINT WILL CHANGE
WITH CONVICTION.

It is a fact that this body is impermanent. We don't need any knowledge or spirituality to know this. Every day we hear of people 'dying', and people 'taking birth'. This life is a long dream. There is no birth, no death. Forget about spirituality! Think simply, and ask yourself, "How was this world, when I was not in the body-form? What was it like?

You don't know! "Don't know" is the perfect answer. Not knowing means that, "I am not in any form. I am totally unaware. I don't know who I am". When the body disappears, everything goes, everything disappears, just like the disappearance of a dream.

In dreams you can see everything, the sun, moon, people, and sometimes you even see yourself as a man, instead of a woman. But then at the awakening stage: What happened to those people? Everything has just vanished. People, places, events, scenery - everything has simply vanished!

THIS LIFE IS A KIND OF DREAM.
AWAKENING MEANS THAT
YOU KNOW YOURSELF IN A REAL SENSE.
THAT IS THE AWAKENING STAGE.

You must have the Conviction that you were not, you are not, you will not remain the body. I am hammering this home all the time. Once it is established, you will remain totally unconcerned with the 'world appearance'. It's simple, simple talk, but you have to absorb it.

IF YOU ARE IN A CROWD OF PEOPLE,
YOU WILL BE THE SAME AS IF YOU WERE ALONE.

I will give you an example: Maurice Frydman, and an American Ambassador friend of his once went to Sri Ramana Ashram and stayed overnight. Maurice slept calm and quietly, but his friend could not sleep. In the morning, he said to Maurice, "What a crowd, there was so much noise!" Maurice replied, "Oh! What noise? I slept deeply." Maurice was not aware of any noise. He slept peacefully as he was completely unconcerned with the world - mental, physical, anything. But his friend was paying more attention to externals, and maybe even brought some psychological baggage along with him. He felt uneasy and disturbed.

Q: So the noise was coming from inside his mind?

Maharaj: Yes, There was no noise at all. It was the internal noise of the mind. He was complaining to Maurice, who said he was not aware of it. So this example shows, that out of your Spontaneous Existence, if you give more attention to external things, then there will be problems. If you ignore everything that is happening externally and internally, if you ignore what is happening internally, externally, only then will Reality be exposed. So tell yourself over and over:

"I AM UNCONCERNED.
I AM NOTHING TO DO WITH THIS WORLD
BECAUSE MY PRESENCE IS PRIOR TO THIS WORLD".

66. One in a Billion

Maharaj: There is a Marathi story about Lakshmi, the goddess of wealth. She knocks at your door but you do not recognize her. You pick up the broom and say, "Get lost!" Similarly, the Master appears with Knowledge, but since you do not know the significance of the Masters, you minimise their importance. You will say, "OK, there's a Master in Nashik!"

Generally speaking, ninety-nine per cent of people come here, saying, "Give me the Mantra, give me the Mantra. Here is my son! Here is my daughter! Bless them!" They are keen to get the Mantra because they are looking for miracles. They have expectations that after receiving the Mantra, they will come into money, employment or marry. Very few people are really interested beyond having these expectations.

There is a story of Lord Shiva. Thousands of people had gathered at the Shiva Temple. They were dancing and praying: "*Oh Lord Shiva, Om Nama Shiva*".

One of the ancient sages, Narada, asked Lord Shiva: "Why are you not giving these people *darshan*? They are simple devotees. All your devotees are becoming 'One with That'. They are chanting your name and praising you. Why are you neglecting them? You are cruel. You should go to them".

Shiva replies: "With great difficulty, I will come, but on one condition: I will be standing five miles away. Tell them to come to me". Narada went to the temple and announced: "Oh devotees! Lord Shiva has come into the world and is going to give you *darshan*. So come along with me".

Half of the people said, "What a foolish man! It's impossible for Lord Shiva to come into the world. What a fool!". Some people said, "Maybe he will be there, we can test him".

Fifty percent of them went with Narada. On the way, they came across sellers of copper, copper utensils and copper vessels. This attraction occupied them fully. Half the group said, "Oh! These are very good. I must take these home now". So they parted, and said, "Bye-bye, Ta-Ta".

The rest of the group continued the journey until they came across a display of silver vessels. Some of them exclaimed: "The copper back there was OK, but this is silver, and it is very nice". As a result, half of them deserted the group, choosing instead to take the vessels home with them. Again, the group proceeded until one person spotted something glistening nearby: "Oh, look! Gold! Golden vessels! What an opportunity! I am going to get some of these".

By this time, there was only a trickle of people left. All but one of them entered a high-class jewellery store, with some excitement. There they took their time and perused the sparkling diamonds.

Finally, one devotee reached Lord Shiva. He said, "You see, all these devotees had expectations. They were all looking for something. I came here just for one, one real devotee".

The principle behind the story is the same. Everyone goes to the Math, temple or ashram, but they are not interested in spirituality. They are visiting so many places, tasting something here, and something there. They are really just on vacation, visiting India for five or six months, living in ashrams, but not interested in Knowledge. They are going from ashram to ashram, from the south to the north.

Nisargadatta Maharaj used to say: "They are tourists, not seekers". They are not real seekers. Therefore,

I AM ASKING YOU NOT TO BE TOURISTS.
THIS IS AN OPPORTUNITY FOR YOU.
IF YOU WASTE THIS OPPORTUNITY,
IT WILL NOT SURFACE AGAIN.

And once more, you will find yourself with struggles and difficulties.

REALIZED MASTERS COME AFTER GREAT DIFFICULTY.
SUCH RARE KNOWLEDGE!
THERE ARE MANY MASTERS,
BUT THE MASTER WHO ENLIGHTENS THE DISCIPLE,
IS VERY RARE.

Nisargadatta Maharaj said: "I am not making you a disciple, I am making you a Master". Such a Master is very, very rare. He has no frills, no publicity, no glamour.

It is very difficult to find such Masters.

AFTER FINDING ONE SUCH MASTER,
DO NOT WASTE THIS CHANCE.

Do not let it slip through your fingers.

Beware of *maya* and external attractions! Everyone is tempted to go here and there for worldly happiness. There are always going to be external forces trying to distract you from the Reality, with the result that you will slip. To avoid these snakes, we are giving you cautionary tips.

Bhausaheb Maharaj recommended early morning *bhajan*, morning *bhajan*, evening *bhajan*, meditation. There are no rules or conditions, except that you keep in touch with your Selfless Self. The practices are illusion, I know, but without them, you cannot keep in touch with your Selfless Self. You will be attacked by body-knowledge in one form or other. Therefore,

KEEP ALERT AND LIVE A SMOOTH LIFE.
YOU WILL HAVE NO DIFFICULTIES.

67.   Who is Good and Who is Bad?

Maharaj: You have a lot of attachment to the body and all body-related associations and relationships: my husband, my wife, my brother, my sister, my son, my daughter, my relatives, etc. Everyone has a different God. Religions have thirty three million gods, but nobody sees.

NOBODY SEES.
NOBODY IS LOOKING WITH OPEN EYES,
WITH THE EYE OF KNOWLEDGE.

There are many spiritual people wearing long faces. Why? Be happy! Nisargadatta Maharaj used to say, "Those saintly people with all their knowledge, they should never be serious". Be happy because you realize that this life is illusion and spirituality is also illusion. This is a dream, and that is a dream. Both are false. You are to laugh at the whole thing, then everything will be calm and quiet. Be strong, be strong!

REMAIN IN TOUCH WITH YOU ALWAYS.
ALWAYS REMAIN IN TOUCH WITH YOUR SELFLESS SELF.

Don't have blind faith. Find out, "Who am I? Why this life?" People say, "Last *prarabdha*, this *prarabdha*. Whose *prarabdha*? What is the meaning of good fortune? What is the meaning of bad fortune?" No fortune! Good or bad? This is the circle of body-knowledge.

FIND OUT WHO YOU ARE.
THIS IS DIRECT KNOWLEDGE.
NO COMPLICATIONS.
OPEN SECRET!

You have become attached to the body. You have much love and affection for it. You know that the body is not your identity and need to have this Conviction. In order to establish the Conviction, you must undergo the disciplines of meditation and *bhajan*s. Then slowly, silently and permanently, the entire Truth will be absorbed. And then, "Aha!"

You consider yourself a dependant, unaware that you are totally independent. If you want to compare yourself, compare yourself to sky or space. And you are beyond sky, beyond space. The sky has some boundary lines, you do not.

WE ARE NOT ACCEPTING THE FACTS,
THE REALITY,
BECAUSE OF THE PRESSURES OF
LOVE AND AFFECTION FOR THE FOOD-BODY.

You accepted all these thoughts, illusionary thoughts blindly. If you depend on somebody's thoughts, this means that you are not believing in yourself. You are not having faith in you. You don't know your power, your own tremendous power. Instead, you are always expecting somebody's help to take care of you. Why?

EVERYTHING IS WITHIN YOU.
YOU ARE THE SOURCE.

Knowledge must be absorbed within you, to the extent that you remain completely unconcerned with the world, calm and quiet, forgetting and forgiving. There will be patience, and no struggle or hatred. Why struggle? Why hate? Who is the enemy? There is no enemy. Who is bad? Who is good? You are supposed to be totally changed.

There is a simple story in the *Mahabharata* when Lord Krishna sent two brothers on an errand. He instructed one to go to the village, and find out if there were any bad people living there who were committing sinful actions. He did as he was told, visiting many houses, checking for unsavoury folk.

When he had done the rounds of the village, he returned and reported to Lord Krishna: "No one is sinful. Everyone is good. I did not find one person who was meddling in sin or messy things like that".

Then Lord Krishna asked his brother to visit the village, and investigate if any of them were doing wrong, and committing sinful acts. When he eventually returned, he shared his findings with Krishna: "Everybody in this village is bad! I could not find a single good person!"

These two differing viewpoints illustrate true Knowledge. There is no 'good' and there is no 'bad'. It all depends on the viewpoint, the stance that is taken.

IF YOU PAY ATTENTION TO THE SEEN,
YOU WILL BE DRAWN INTO THE ILLUSION.

As long as the illusion is taken for real, there will be this duality of good and bad, right and wrong.

STAY WITH THE SEER.

After enlightenment, when you know yourself in a real sense, you will be changed completely. The feeling will be one of: "I am everywhere". My Presence, Spontaneous Presence, Invisible Presence is everywhere, in every being. When that time comes, you will not view others in the body-form.

THE SAME SPIRIT IS HERE,
THE SAME SPIRIT IS THERE.
THERE IS NEITHER
GOOD NOR BAD.

When this happens and you see your Presence everywhere, there will be no jealousy, no enmity. You will treat everybody as equals. Meditation will alter your view and change your perspective: You will see everybody like I do. These changes are taking place in the internal body. This will bring exceptional Happiness and Peace, simply, yet, profoundly, because you are not viewing everyone as if they were different. Lord Krishna says, "I am everywhere. My Presence is there in every being". Your view will be changed in this way. A shift like this will occur.

Q: In *I Am That*, I seem to remember Nisargadatta Maharaj saying something about this. He said, "There is no good and no bad". People were very shocked because they had never even thought about this.

Maharaj: Yes! Good and bad are related to body-knowledge.

Q: They were absolutely shocked. With all of the wars, all the troubles in the world, all the murders and that kind of stuff...

Maharaj: Because we are measuring ourselves in body-form, we see good and bad. The fact is you were never the body, you are not the body, you will not remain the body. This is the Ultimate Truth. There's no birth and death. These are all concepts. All concepts. There is no birth, no death, no salvation, no bondage.

Q: No wars, no heaven?

Maharaj: There is nothing. As I told you, everything comes out of nothing, and will be absorbed, merged with nothing. It's open fact. All memories will disappear with the body. We know this, but still we are under the impressions and pressures of this body.

Though we know the Reality, we are not accepting it. You have to undergo this process to dissolve body-knowledge. The first lesson is meditation, then everything will open out because your existence is Spontaneous Existence.

YOUR EXISTENCE IS SPONTANEOUS.
YOU ARE NOT PART OF THESE CRAZY AND MISGUIDED NOTIONS LIKE,
"I WILL TAKE BIRTH IN AMERICA,
OR ENGLAND, OR CHINA, OR ELSEWHERE".
YOU CANNOT DO THESE THINGS.

Embrace Reality and not the body-form. To embrace this Reality, you must have strong faith and strong dedication to the extent that, even if so-called God, appeared before you, you would not stir.

GOD IS THE REFLECTION OF YOUR SPONTANEOUS PRESENCE.

Q: I have never heard anything like this before! It is amazing!

Q2: I accept everything you are saying! You know, Maharaj, when I said these words just now, they happened intuitively. They were spoken spontaneously, without my even having to think about it.

Maharaj: Just like, when you see the world in a dream, God, everything.

Q: Where is this God?

Maharaj: Your Presence is essential to say God, to say anything. If your Presence is not there, how can you see the gods and goddesses? Your Spontaneous Invisible Presence lies behind everything.

REALITY IS BEYOND IMAGINATION,
BEYOND INTELLECT.

Final Truth, Ultimate Truth, Exceptional Truth, you may use any word. Words only act as a medium, a channel or instrument.

Q: For communication?

Maharaj: We have given birth to the words, created an alphabet, joined up the letters, made the words and given them meaning. Literal knowledge is therefore not sufficient.

Q: A few words may come close?

Maharaj: Some indications can be found in these words. They do give a message. But basically we have invented the alphabets and given meaning to the words. Spirit is in body-form, therefore, we have to use words to communicate.

We cannot know ourselves through words, books, even the finest literature. We are prior to words, prior to language. We can only know ourselves through Self-Knowledge. The principle of spirituality means: Know yourself in a real sense:

"I AM TOTALLY AND UTTERLY UNBORN".

Only then, will you become fearless. You are like sky. We are constructing all these walls, and yet the sky is there. When the walls collapse, where does the sky go? This is the way to convince yourself. The Master Key has been given to you, now you have to operate it. This is the Listener's Truth.

THIS IS THE LISTENER'S TRUTH.
THE INVISIBLE, ANONYMOUS LISTENER
WHO SEES THROUGH THESE EYES,
LISTENS THROUGH THESE EARS,
TASTES WITH THIS TONGUE.
SPIRIT MAKES ALL THESE ORGANS ACTIVE.

If Spirit were not there, you would not be able to see through these eyes, smell through this nose. Nothing!

What is the conclusion of all this knowledge? Except oneself, there is nothing. There is nothing beyond Ultimate Reality. So don't go looking for thoughts, feelings, experiences or another Guru.

Q2: Earlier, it was really strange because words came out of my mouth without my knowledge so I was very surprised to listen to myself say that I accept everything you are saying.

Also, this morning during the meditation, there was a strong indication of what you have just been talking about, that there is only Spirit.

My eyes were closed. Then a light appeared, which turned into a fire burning brightly. The message was that this pure sacred fire is always alight, always burning brightly. It was like the eternal flame of Spirit.

Maharaj: You are having good experiences but they are not Ultimate Truth.

68. *Polished Words*

Maharaj: All these words, all these concepts are compromising you. All these illusionary thoughts are related to the body only. The Master is inviting attention of the Silent Invisible Listener. You are Ultimate Truth, you are unborn, but because of the impressions of the body-knowledge, the food body-knowledge, the material knowledge, we are ignoring Reality.

Mind is nothing but the flow of thoughts. You are witnessing that flow of thoughts. You are witnessing the dream. This is a long dream. It is just like a long dream. You are wasting every day with so many dreams, different types of dreams.

THE SEER IS THE SAME.
THE ATMOSPHERE OF EACH DREAM IS DIFFERENT.
THIS IS TODAY'S DREAM,
AND TOMORROW,
A DIFFERENT DREAM.

You are not to give any importance to what is happening in this dream. This is the Conviction you are to hold. This is Ultimate Truth. It is the Final Truth because you are unborn.

ALL THAT YOU CAN SEE IS ILLUSION.
WITHOUT THE SEER,
YOU CANNOT SEE ANYTHING.
WITHOUT YOUR PRESENCE, NO ONE CAN SAY ANYTHING
ABOUT *BRAHMAN*, *ATMAN*, GOD, MASTER.

Your Presence is behind everything. It is Spontaneous Presence, Invisible Presence, Anonymous Presence.

Q: You are saying, 'behind' the Presence?

Maharaj: Don't take the words literally! There is no 'behind' and no 'in front'. These are words. I am just using these words to communicate, to try and put the Knowledge into words. Listen to these teachings, my words are very important: Spontaneous Presence, Invisible Presence, Anonymous Presence. There is no name for this.

FOR THIS, THERE IS NO NAME.

It cannot be defined, described. Without this nameless Power, we cannot see.

IT IS THE SPONTANEOUS UNIDENTIFIED IDENTITY.
YOUR PRESENCE IS UNIDENTIFIED IDENTITY.

This Presence has high value. It is invaluable. Don't underestimate yourself. All godly saints, Masterly saints are secondary to you. They can only appear after you. Your Presence comes first.

To say something, anything, your Presence is essential. For example, "He is my father". To say, "He is my father" your Presence is required. "This is God"! To say 'God', your Presence is required.

THE ENTIRE WORLD COMES OUT OF YOUR PRESENCE ALONE.
WITHOUT YOUR PRESENCE,
WHO CAN SAY THE WORLD IS TRUE OR FALSE?
WHO CAN SAY ANYTHING?

Your Presence is Invisible, it's everywhere, it cannot be defined by any words. Words are merely communicators of knowledge. We are the inventors of the words, and now we have allowed them to compromise us.

Q: I think that for most people, words and language have become our Masters. We have allowed all these millions of words to control, confuse and compromise us. We get caught up in the words instead of the Truth, or we think the words are the same as the Truth.

Maharaj: Because we are in body-form. All these words *Brahman, Atman, Paramatman* are OK at a certain level, as indicators, but after this, they are completely meaningless. People go here and there, finding different Masters, reading more spiritual books. And at the same time, what they are really doing is adding more and more ego.

YOU TALK ABOUT *BRAHMAN, ATMAN, PARAMATMAN,*
BUT YOU ONLY KNOW THESE AS NAMES, AS WORDS.
YOU DO NOT KNOW WHAT THEY MEAN.
I AM NOT TALKING ABOUT THE KNOWLEDGE OF *BRAHMAN, ATMAN, PARAMATMAN,*
I AM TALKING ABOUT YOUR KNOWLEDGE.

You are the architect of your own life, your spiritual life. It is up to you how to mould your spiritual life. I am trying to simplify this Reality, using simple words, without any complexities.

All your questions are appearing out of your body-knowledge: "I am somebody, I am a Master, I am a knowledgeable person". These are egoistic thoughts. You are nothing! Everything comes out of nothing and dissolves back into nothing. What do you say?

Q: Yes, absolutely. And the way you communicate the teachings is so simple. No frills, no messing!

Maharaj: You have to be strong because there are so many concepts and words out there to confuse you. We get lost in them: birth, rebirth and future, past life, future life, salvation, hell and heaven, so many words, Mumbai, California, etc. What do you mean by salvation? What do you mean by hell and heaven?

Innumerable words have been created, and then we try and find their meanings through even more words. Whatever knowledge you acquire will disappear along with the body.

Ask a simple question: "Will all this knowledge be useful to you at the time of leaving your body?" If there is some subtle fear remaining, then what is the use of this knowledge, all this polished knowledge? It means you have been collecting colourful currency that has turned out to be unmarketable. You have accumulated a bundle of dollars or pound notes, but they are fake notes. You cannot use them.

So you may have a lot of knowledge about spirituality, *Brahman, Atman,* God, and you can even talk about these and deliver lectures eloquently, but,

MAKE SURE THE KNOWLEDGE IS REAL AND PRACTICAL,
OTHERWISE IT IS MEANINGLESS.

You may know this story about Albert Einstein, the famous scientist. He used to tour and give lectures at various universities in the States. He was always accompanied by his chauffeur, Harry, who would attend each of these lectures, and sit at the back of the hall. One day, after Einstein had finished giving his lecture, Harry said, "Professor, I've heard your lectures so many times, I am certain I could deliver one perfectly myself!"

"Very well," replied Einstein, "Next week, we are going to Dartmouth. They don't know me there, so you can deliver the lecture, and I'll be Harry!" So Harry delivered the lecture perfectly, without a word out of place, while Einstein sat in the back row, dressed in his chauffeur's uniform, dozing off. Just as Harry was about to leave the stage, one research assistant stopped him, and asked him a very tricky question, one that involved a lot of complex calculations and equations. Harry replied quickly: "Oh, that's easy! It's so simple that I'll let my chauffeur Harry answer it!"

This story is used here to illustrate that anyone can quote from books and Masters parrot-fashion, but they cannot answer questions unless they themselves have Self-Knowledge.

BE A MASTER OF REALITY,
AND NOT JUST A MASTER OF PHILOSOPHY AND SPIRITUALITY.
A PROFESSOR MAY TEACH BY TALKING ABOUT TRUTH,
WHEREAS A MASTER LIVES IT.

Nisargadatta Maharaj once told a visitor, a Doctor of Philosophy, who was asking many questions: "Just minus [negate] what you have read, and listen! Subtract everything you have ever read since childhood, and then just listen".

IF YOU WANT TO KNOW NOTHING,
ALL THESE SPIRITUAL BOOKS ARE AVAILABLE.

We are talking about the unborn child. Nothing happened. Nothing is happening.

Q: Maharaj, we must have hundreds of books in the loft space at home. They are all on spiritual matters. We put them up there a few years ago because we were finished with books. These books insulate and keep the house warm in winter!

You were saying that when you die, all these books will be of no help. You could have all these books beside you, when you are on your deathbed, but they're not going to help, are they, even if you read them all?

Maharaj: You have to mould yourself in the light of all this spirituality. Again I am repeating the same thing, meditation is the base. I cannot stress the importance of meditation enough. Considering the sensitivity of the Spirit, the meditation impresses Reality on Spirit: "You are *Brahman*, you are *Brahman*".

Reciting the Mantra is very effective. I will give you an example. When police officers are trying to catch a criminal, in the beginning, he might say, "I haven't done anything". But then, after a little pressure and maybe some torture, he gives in, and admits to his crime: "Oh, OK, OK, I will tell you everything, I confess".

Similarly, in the beginning, it feels like you are torturing yourself with "I am *Brahman*, I am *Brahman*". There is a threat to your existence. The ego rises, it reacts and revolts. But then it surrenders, and there is acceptance: "Yes! I AM *Brahman*", and all the secrets open up to you.

You are to use this anti-virus software all the time, so that no virus will dare to enter your laptop. So do your practice, and forget about the past.

THERE IS NO PAST, NO PRESENT, NO FUTURE.
THERE IS NO GOOD, NO BAD.
THINGS WE FIND TOLERABLE,
WE CALL 'GOOD THINGS'.
THINGS WE FIND INTOLERABLE,
WE CALL 'BAD THINGS'.

What is not tolerable is 'I Am'. 'I Am' is intolerable. For this, [to cope with this], Presence requires entertainment. When the child has taken birth we give it some honey, sweet things like that. We cannot bear beingness, we cannot stand it without entertainment.

WHAT KIND OF ENTERTAINMENT DID YOU HAVE PRIOR TO BEINGNESS?
THERE WAS NOTHING.

Now it is a different story. We want food, this thing, that thing, so many things. Take a bath every day, brush the teeth. Prior to beingness, nothing had to be done, there were no teeth to brush, no soap was required, no sweets were required, no food was required. There were no requirements. We did not know God, *Brahman, Paramatman, Atman*.

THIS KNOWLEDGE IS VERY, VERY SIMPLE,
BUT IT HAS BEEN MADE COMPLICATED BY ENDLESS BOOKS.

Nisargadatta Maharaj used to say, "The gist of it all is that You are Ultimate Truth, You are Final Truth". Talking about books, he used to say, "Read books, but don't let them drown you. Read them, but don't drown yourself in them".

WHILST READING THESE SPIRITUAL BOOKS,
YOU MUST KNOW THAT IT IS THE INVISIBLE READER'S STORY,
THE INVISIBLE READER'S STORY.
THERE IS NO DUALITY,
NO INDIVIDUALITY.

No duality, no individuality. Go deeper and deeper within and you will see, and find exceptional happiness. Then you will exclaim: "Oh, I was a fool! All that I was doing was using a system of beliefs". If you glance at your past, you will see that it was foolish knowledge, that what you were doing was completely silly. When you know as a grown-up, and you think back to the things you did as a child, you feel silly. It is like this. Now you are a grown-up, you know yourself.

69. Almighty God

Q: What does Nisargadatta Maharaj mean when he says that you have to go beyond 'I am God'? If everything is God, how can one go beyond God?

Maharaj: God is a concept. God, *Brahman, Atman, Paramatman*, these are concepts, created by us. You do not know what this God is, or what you mean by God. What do you mean by *Brahman*? The moment your Presence appears in the world you say, "Oh God, bless me", or "Please do me a favour".

Where was God prior to your beingness? Did you know about God? No! Nothing! Or *Brahman*? Nothing. The entire world came out of nothing. The whole world came out of nothing and will be merged with nothing. Follow? It remains nothing.

The Spirit clicks with the body, and you see the world. The body is the cause, and the world is the consequence. If there is no body, there is no consequence. The body cannot work independently. It needs Spirit to function, like a fan needs electricity. To have action, for any action to happen, body-related action, some Spirit, some power is required.

Q: And that power is *Brahman* or God?

Maharaj: Well, these are the names: *Brahman, Atman, Parabrahman*, God. These are the names we call this power by, but it is YOUR POWER. That Power does not know its own Identity. That power does not know its own Identity. We give names such as *Brahman, Paramatman*, God, etc, simply for us to be able to identify it, just for us to know.

YOUR UNIDENTIFIED IDENTITY IS BEYOND THAT.
THIS UNIDENTIFIED IDENTITY,
THIS ANONYMOUS IDENTITY,
INVISIBLE IDENTITY CANNOT BE DESCRIBED.

I am using various words to convince you that you are Ultimate Truth, and you are using various words to convince yourself of the same thing, without any ego. This is not logical thinking, not intellectual thinking. There are no mental concepts. There is no mind, no ego, no intellect.

Q: What about 'I am' and making sure, trying to make an effort to stay with that feeling of 'I am'?

Maharaj: Why stay with the feeling? You have not to make any effort. 'I am' is Spontaneous! You are already 'I am' so you don't have to try anything.

Q: But Nisargadatta Maharaj said that we were to hold on to the 'I am'.

Maharaj: Again, you are taking the words literally. The Masters are using words to indicate something. They are giving indications through words. Don't be a victim of words! We are to make ourselves free from all this illusory bondage.

YOU ARE TRYING TO GRASP THIS KNOWLEDGE WITH THE MIND.
YOUR KNOWLEDGE IS PRIOR TO MIND.

There is no bondage at all. You are already free and independent.

Q: With your grace, Maharaj, I will be free.

Maharaj: I have told you that you are already free, but you are always thinking you are dependent, handicapped and expecting grace from someone else. Because we are unaware of our own importance, we are measuring ourselves in body-form.

This is nothing but illusion because you were never in body-form prior to beingness, and you are not going to remain in body-form.

It's Open Truth, open fact, very simple. But you are not giving any cognizance to your Selfless Self. You are not giving any cognizance to your Selfless Self.

YOU HAVE TREMENDOUS POWER,
BUT YOU ARE MEASURING YOURSELF IN BODY-FORM.

THIS IS NOT YOUR IDENTITY.
HOW CAN IT BE WHEN IT CHANGES ALL THE TIME?

You're a small child, that child grows up: a young man, an old man, and then some day or other, [the Master claps his hands], you will leave the body. Consider this seriously! Understand and convince yourself.

We have a lot of attachment to the body. It's bound to be there because of the lengthy association. Attachment is bound to be there because as I have told you, the Spirit only knows itself through the body. Therefore that Spirit, the *Brahman*, does not wish to leave the body.

Q: Because it thinks it is something else rather than Spirit, something separate from Spirit. It thinks it is the body?

Maharaj: You can say it any way that you like. That Spirit is attached. All it knows, is "I am the body. I am somebody". But you are nobody. As a matter of fact, you are nobody. This body likes to say, "I am somebody".

YOU ARE NOBODY.

Likewise, to say, "I am *Brahman*" is illusion.

TO SAY "I AM *BRAHMAN*" IS ILLUSION.

You want to give it some name, when there is no name.

YOU ARE NAMELESS.

Q: I understand! This is mistaken identity. We have identified with the body since childhood, and taken it to be our identity. So that kept us in the circle of body-knowledge. Afterwards, even when we looked for our true identity, when we looked for it, say, within, or in books and elsewhere, we did this while we were still identified with the body, still trapped in the circle of body-knowledge.

This meant that the knowledge we found was sourced from this illusory world, acquired by this illusory person, this illusory mind, this illusory ego - Me?

Maharaj: Why do you cry for the perishable when your Identity is not perishable? Your eternal power is greater than all these things. You have tremendous power, the power, the force to create this world. You are giving importance to the seen and not to the Seer. To say 'God', your Presence is needed. You are the Father of that God. You are unaware, you are not known to Your Power. The body only has importance because of your Presence.

Know the secret of your life. All secrets are within you only. And since you are not realizing your importance you are running here and there. Try to understand your valuable existence, Presence. What I am telling you is an open secret. It is the Listener's story. You, the Listener, are not in any body-form. You are nothing to do with the whole of this world.

YOU ARE ALMIGHTY GOD,
YOU ARE ALMIGHTY GOD.
YOU ARE GOD ALMIGHTY.

[Long silence follows.]

Q: Maharaj, I felt wiped out when you spoke these words. They hit 'me' so powerfully. I felt they penetrated and went deep inside and through this body. The weight of truth, the power, the meaning seemed to explode both outside and inside me. I am amazed and humbled at the same time. It is hard to explain.

Maharaj: There is no outside and no inside! You are nothing to do with this world. So remain unconcerned with the world, unconcerned with this whole atmosphere.

Clouds are coming, clouds are going, thoughts are coming, thoughts are going. Whatever thoughts are useful for you, you can accept them. If they are not useful, you can throw them out. This flow of thoughts is the nature of the body-form coming out of the five elements. Thoughts are coming, various thoughts are coming and enacting the three *gunas* (*tama, raja, sattva*). The body belongs to the five elements, so ups and downs are bound to be there.

This is just spiritual science, some information that is not important for us. We are beyond the *gunas* because we are not the body. This language is only used for the purpose of understanding. It can indicate and convince you of the Reality but your spiritual science is limited. The bottom line is:

YOUR UNIDENTIFIED IDENTITY
IS ALMIGHTY GOD.
YOUR UNIDENTIFIED IDENTITY
IS ALMIGHTY GOD.
EMBRACE THAT REALITY.

70. The Universe is In You

Q: Last night, I was reciting the Mantra. Then an image of musical notes in the air appeared. They were floating notes. I felt something stirring inside, and there was this wave of happiness. All the Lineage Masters were gathered and standing behind me. They were also very happy and were clapping. Their energy was invisible, but there was a knowingness that it was the Presence of the Masters.

I just wanted to tell you that. I was going to ask you about singing the *bhajans*. Should I practise the singing of *bhajans* regularly every day, like with the meditation?
Maharaj: Yes, daily practice! All this is necessary to absorb knowledge, but only at the initial stage. 'Initial stage' means until you have Conviction. Until that happens, you have to undergo the discipline of meditation and *bhajan*. Then it will be Spontaneous.

TO ESTABLISH TRUTH, YOU NEED A FOUNDATION.
AND UNLESS YOUR FOUNDATION IS PERFECT,
YOU WILL NOT BE ABLE
TO KNOW YOURSELF IN A REAL SENSE.

If you follow this discipline, it will be automatically projected within you. What I am relating is the Listener's Knowledge, the Invisible, Anonymous Listener's Knowledge that is already in you. But you are unaware.
Q: I am unaware?
Maharaj: I am not speaking to the body-form of Michael, I am addressing the Anonymous Listener, the Invisible Listener within you. That which I am addressing is being addressed to the Invisible Master within you, that is not in any form. Follow? It is the Invisible Listener, the Anonymous Listener.

So after hearing and dwelling on the Knowledge, the Reality will automatically be impressed, and

Knowledge will be engraved. Then at the Ultimate Stage when you fully realize, you will say, "Yes, I have found what I have been struggling for. Got it!" Reality is your own property. You forgot your wealth, your own property.

REALITY IS YOUR PROPERTY,
NOT THE PROPERTY OF *BRAHMAN*, *ATMAN*, GOD.

The Silent Invisible Listener in you has been called by different names - *Brahman*, *Atman*, *Paramatman*, God, Master. They are just words but you have become attached to them. A lifetime of illusionary thoughts have been impressed on you. The *Naam Mantra* and meditation is the best way to remove these.

Q2: Is it appropriate that I should be initiated by you when my Guru is Nisargadatta Maharaj? Is this a problem?

Maharaj: No problem! All is One.

Q2: Exactly! But is it a problem that he is not in the body?

Maharaj: There is no individuality. Indian sky, European sky, Russian sky, Australian sky - there is no difference. Is there any disagreement, fighting or conflict between the Indian sky and the American sky? Not at all.

There are no individuals. We are all One: Nisargadatta Maharaj, Ranjit Maharaj, myself, yourself. The only difference lies in the body-form. We are saying that Nisargadatta Maharaj is separate, Ranjit Maharaj is separate, Siddharameshwar Maharaj, separate.

BODIES ARE SEPARATE,
ULTIMATE TRUTH IS ONE.

There is no sense in making an issue about the different Masters. Why are you making a problem out of it?

Q2: What about in the intensity of contact with the Master? If the Master is not in the body, but one is very certain and one hundred per cent devoted, is that contact just as good and as powerful, as contact with a living Master?

Maharaj: There is no difference between the Inner Master and the Outer Master. If a temple collapses, the sky is still there.

Q2: So I need not have any doubts, everything is OK?

Maharaj: These doubts are appearing because of the impressions of illusory thoughts. As long as you are considering yourself as 'I am in body-form', questions and doubts are bound to be there. The moment your body-form, food body-knowledge dissolves, at that time, you will become the vast universe, instantly. The entire universe is within you.

Q2: The entire world is within me? How?

Maharaj: Because out of your Spontaneous Presence, you see the world. Out of your Presence you see the world. The moment that Presence disappears, all this disappears. You are discriminating between a living Master and a non-living Master. Where did it all go? What happened to it? [claps his hands].

We are measuring ourselves in this body-form. It is illusion, it is not going to remain constant, but Spirit will not go anywhere.

**IF A HOUSE COLLAPSES THE SKY DOES NOT GO ANYWHERE
BECAUSE IT IS FORMLESS.
YOU ARE FORMLESS.**

Again, I am repeating the same thing. To have this Conviction, you have to undergo this discipline. There is no Conviction because you have strong faith in the body-form, the body feeling.

**EVEN THOUGH YOU SAY, "I AM *BRAHMAN*",
THE BODY-FEELING IS STILL THERE.
CONVICTION IS NOT TO BE HAD OR FOUND WITH THE BODY, OR IN THE BODY.
IT IS SPONTANEOUS.**

Q2: So strict discipline is needed to that point of Absolute Conviction.

Maharaj: Absolutely!

Q2: Build that Absolute Conviction that "I am not the body"?

Maharaj: Spontaneous Absolute Conviction, Spontaneous.

Q2: Will it happen alone by itself?

Maharaj: Not intellectually, not mentally.

Q2: The Conviction is not mental but it is something Spontaneous. I don't understand. It comes somehow?

Maharaj: It is like you accepted this body as a man's body. You are a man. Once you knew of the body, you started to think that you are a man. You don't say, "I am a woman" because you have the conviction that you are a man.

Similarly, the Master says, you are Ultimate Truth, you are *Brahman*, but you are not accepting it because of body-form impressions. Unless the body-form dissolves, you will not be able to know yourself in a real sense.

We are sleeping in a dream world. You see yourself in a dream as a man or a woman. As long as you consider yourself to be somebody else, all knowledge will be meaningless. This body is an opportunity for spiritual life, spiritual happiness. Happiness is being lost.

Your Spontaneous Presence is Unidentified, Anonymous, Invisible Identity.

**PRESENCE IS THERE,
BUT NOT IN ANY FORM,
NOT IN THIS FORM.**

Q2: And what does it mean when Nisargadatta Maharaj says, "The first concept is the feeling 'I Am'? Is it something that originates or started at the moment of conception of a human body?

Maharaj: Correct! The moment Spirit clicked with the body. The moment that Spirit clicked with the body you could see the world. Prior to that, there were no concepts. Where were the concepts? Prior to birth, there were no concepts, there was no illusion, no God, no *Brahman*, no *Atman*.

All these polished words, they are very fine words, but there were no words prior to beingness. All these talks and words are inviting the attention of your Spontaneous Presence. Reciting the Mantra does the same!

Q2: So during the meditation, when I use the Mantra, am I stopping the mind?

Maharaj: There is no mind! How many times do I have to tell you. Mind is just the flow of thoughts. After practising the Mantra, reciting the Mantra, you will forget your external identity. What remains is just, say, [again remember these are just words, not Reality], 'I am' without words, without feelings, without any witness. Ultimately everything disappears: the witness, witnesser, experience, experiencer, everything, including 'I am'.

Q2: Even though I have read Nisargadatta Maharaj and studied the books, it is very different from being in your Presence, and listening to these teachings.

Maharaj: Your base is supposed to be strong. You need base knowledge, strong foundations. Meditation will make your foundation very strong. A boiling process takes place through meditation. All the concepts will be boiled.

THE MOMENT YOUR FOUNDATION IS STRONG,
IT WILL BE VERY EASY TO BUILD AN ENTIRE BUILDING UPON IT.
IF THE FOUNDATION IS WEAK,
THEN ALL THE KNOWLEDGE YOU HAVE WILL JUST COLLAPSE.

Q2: Because there are too many cracks, too many attractions in the world?

Maharaj: There are three types of attraction: publicity [power], money and sex. You have to leave all temptation and entertainment behind.

Q: I think I read somewhere that Nisargadatta Maharaj had a hobby writing devotional poetry. The story goes that Siddharameshwar Maharaj one day told him to stop because he was enjoying it too much! Maybe he was becoming too smart, maybe the subtle ego was getting involved. Obviously, he stopped immediately, as he did everything His Master asked.

Maharaj: Don't think so much! Be normal! Natural. This is your Knowledge so don't stress out, wondering, "Where is *Brahman*? Where is *Atman*?" Talking about *Brahman*, *Atman*, *Paramatman*, is nothing but spiritual entertainment.

Any doubts?

Q: I think that all the doubts that I am aware of have gone. They have been washed away. I think I have to remember the important things you said. You have to have very strong devotion, be disciplined, and this will lead to strong Conviction. Everything else is simple.

71. *Nothing is Happening*

Q: I feel really good here, but when I go back home, I don't know what's going to happen.

Maharaj: After going home, what will happen? What can happen? Nothing is going to happen because your Presence is not a physical Presence.

YOU ARE UNBORN.
NOTHING HAPPENED,
NOTHING IS HAPPENING,
NOTHING IS GOING TO HAPPEN.

Your Presence is not physical Presence, not mental-level Presence, not intellectual-level Presence. Presence is Spontaneous. But since it is in the body-form, you think you are something, somebody else.

Presence does not have any body, any shape, any form.

There is no consciousness, no unconsciousness, there is no awareness, no unawareness. There's no witness, no witnesser. There's no experience, no experiencer. It's the Final Truth. It is open fact.

YOU ARE TO ACCEPT THESE FACTS.

Q: When you are with other people who don't understand what you've just said, but consider you to be 'Chris', or whoever, then back home, other people won't recognize this new-found status.

Maharaj: Forget about other people, just talk about you. When did you come across other people? When did you come across other people? There's so many people in a dream. What has happened to them? How many people have come and gone to hell or heaven? Are you counting? When did you notice that other people were there?

IN ORDER FOR YOU TO SAY, "OTHER PEOPLE",
YOUR PRESENCE MUST BE THERE.
TO SAY ALL THESE THINGS, PRESENCE IS NEEDED.

As I have already told you, the entire world is your projection. The moment you wake up early, [claps hands], you say 'I'. Instantly, the world is projected. So recognize yourself, see yourself.

Q: With all that has happened, and considering my age, I don't think I can change my habits which are very ingrained.

Maharaj: Nothing has happened. You have to motivate yourself. You have to motivate yourself. Forget about habits!

When you know the Reality, your view will change, Therefore you are to motivate yourself in a particular way like: "I was considering myself in body-form, now, I have come to know that I was not the body, and I am not going to remain the body. My body is not my identity. So I am nothing, and have nothing to do with this whole atmosphere. I am unconcerned with the world, so I will forget about the body-base".

THE WORLD IS MY SPONTANEOUS PROJECTION.
SO IF YOU GO TO AMERICA, OR ANYWHERE IN THE WORLD,
YOUR SPONTANEOUS PRESENCE WILL BE THERE.

I will put this in a very simple way: This body is called 'man'. If you go to America, do you forget that you are called 'man'? This body is called man, or this body is called woman. If you go to America, or London, do you say, "Oh, in India, I was called man or woman? What I am telling you is the established Truth. Very simple.

YOU ARE THE *BRAHMAN, ATMAN, PARAMATMAN*, GOD,
THE ESTABLISHED TRUTH.
WHERE IS THE QUESTION OF FORGETTING YOUR IDENTITY?

Are you forgetting that 'I am man'? No! You are not forgetting that because this body called 'man', is the apparent established truth which you accepted. Now you know that the body is not your identity.

BRAHMAN, ATMAN, PARABRAHMAN, GOD
IS THE ESTABLISHED TRUTH.
IT IS THE HOLDER OF THE BODY,
LISTENER OF THE BODY,

EXPERIENCER OF THE BODY,
WITNESSER OF THE BODY.
I AM INVITING ATTENTION TO THAT.
THEREFORE, YOU ARE THAT.

Forget all that you have read. Forget all that you have listened to! Now you have come to the Final Destiny. Surrender yourself and absorb Ultimate Truth. You are finding it a little difficult.

Q: Why is that? Why is it difficult to absorb Truth, Maharaj?

Maharaj: Because with great effort, you have collected so many fake notes, colourful notes, but fake notes. This means that you have accumulated multiple colourful thoughts. "I read the great Ramana Maharshi. I read Jiddu Krishnamurti. I read...". But all the time you were adding ego, ego, ego... polished ego, colourful ego. You have knowledge, granted. Knowledge is there, "I read this book, I studied that course, I wrote that book".

BUT WHAT DID YOU GET FROM EXPLORING ALL THIS?
WHAT DID YOU GET
FROM READING THESE SPIRITUAL BOOKS?

Q: Good question! I guess I would have to think about that.

Maharaj: Self-enquire! Find out! Was it helpful? Was it useful to your Ultimate Truth? Has the knowledge given you courage? Do you have any fears?

Q: Of course! Everyone is afraid of something.

Maharaj: Well, get a move on! When it is time to leave the body, there should not be any type of fear. There should not be any fearful thoughts inside you. If there is still fear around, this means that whatever you have read is meaningless, like collecting fake notes, dummy notes. It is important to know this. You understand?

Q: Yes, Maharaj.

Maharaj: You are to forget everything you have ever read and listened to. Their job is done, over. Listen to me:

YOU ARE TO FORGET EVERYTHING YOU HAVE EVER READ, AND LISTENED TO.
THEIR JOB IS DONE, OVER!

Wipe the slate clean. Accept this!

Q: So I won't need to read any more books or big tracts?

Maharaj: They brought you here. All this reading and listening brought you here. Now there will be no further temptation to search for anything.

THE MASTER PLACES THE SEARCHER BEFORE YOU.
YOU ARE SEEING THE SEARCHER.
THIS IS THE TIP, THE EDGE.

Nothing is impossible. Don't be afraid of what will happen when you go back to America. Nothing is going to happen. Take some photographs of the ashram, and remember the teachings. Sit alone, concentrate on this Knowledge.

LET IT TOUCH THE BOTTOM OF YOUR HEART.

I don't think you will have any problems because I have given you commando training.

72. *Washing the Brain*

Maharaj: After listening to the Master, there should be Spontaneous Conviction: "I am Ultimate Truth" without ego. Your spiritual existence is beyond everything. That Conviction is supposed to be established permanently, because it is your Ultimate Truth, Final Truth, called *Brahman*, *Atman*, *Paramatman*.

As long as you stay in the circle of illusion, and keep on separating yourself, thinking that who you are, and what *Brahman* is, are two different things, until then, you will have difficulties, and experience unpleasant illusory atmospheres.

WHO YOU ARE, AND WHAT *BRAHMAN* IS,
ARE NOT TWO DIFFERENT THINGS.

You may have fear, feel confused and experience different moods. You may feel sad or depressed. All these depressions come from an imbalance that is connected with the body-knowledge. Therefore, I will say it again. Accept what the Master is saying:

YOU HAVE TO ESTABLISH THAT YOU ARE NOT THE BODY.
IT IS AN OPEN FACT. YOU WERE NOT THE BODY,
YOU ARE NOT THE BODY,
YOU ARE NOT GOING TO REMAIN THE BODY.

The body you are holding is not your Ultimate Truth. The Listener within you, the Anonymous Listener, the Invisible Listener is totally formless. There is no form. You are listening, with the help of this body, but the Listener is Silent and Invisible. I am inviting the attention of the Silent, Anonymous, Invisible Listener.

Q: Who is listening?

Maharaj: The Invisible Listener within you. Concentrate! That is your Ultimate Truth, Ultimate Identity. But all the time, because of the pressures of body-knowledge, we are considering ourselves as somebody else.

Until the time comes, when all your body-knowledge has been dissolved, till then, you will feel unstable, experience change, fluctuations. This is Open Truth, it is Open Truth, Final Truth.

WRONG ASSOCIATIONS WITH THE BODY
ARE PREVENTING YOU FROM ACCEPTING THIS TRUTH.

Q: How do I get rid of these associations?

Maharaj: Meditation is the only way. It is like cleaning a film and erasing the thousands of images that are on it. Meditation will clean the film of illusionary thoughts, illusionary concepts: "I am born, I am dying". All these concepts have to go: happiness, unhappiness, loneliness, hopes and fears, the past, memories, everything has to dissolve.

THE MOST IMPORTANT CONCEPT IS
"I AM GOING TO DIE".
EVERYONE IS FEARFUL OF DEATH.
NOBODY LIKES DEATH.

The body will undergo death. But go deeper and ask yourself, find out, "If I am unborn, if I was never born, then who is going to die? Who is dying?" Death and birth are related to the body only. The body is not my identity. It is Open Truth. The body will one day be buried or burned - guaranteed! Inevitable! Forget about spirituality!

This is rational, logical thinking. If you accept that the body is not your identity, then along that line of thought, there is no death. Such a deduction is unquestionable. So why should you fear death?

YOU ARE UNBORN, WITHOUT SAYING IT.

This Final Truth has to establish itself in you. This will happen through meditation, through conversation, through listening, through reading.

SLOWLY, SILENTLY, PERMANENTLY,
YOUR FORGOTTEN IDENTITY IS BEING IMPRESSED IN YOU, ENGRAVED IN YOU:
'I AM ULTIMATE TRUTH, I AM FINAL TRUTH',
WITHOUT SAYING IT.
THIS CONVICTION WILL APPEAR WITHIN YOU.

If you follow the instructions, your practice will result in Conviction, the Conviction that you are Final Truth. As I have told you, the practice is essential because unless you prepare the ground, and clear the entire field, one hundred per cent, you will not be able to know yourself.

People come here and say the same thing all the time: "Why should I recite the Mantra and do meditation?" To which I say the same thing all the time: "Because you have forgotten your identity".

THE PRACTICE IS ESSENTIAL
BECAUSE YOU HAVE FORGOTTEN YOUR IDENTITY.
YOU ARE *BRAHMAN*, YOU ARE *ATMAN*,
YOU ARE *PARAMATMAN*,
YOU ARE GOD, YOU ARE MASTER.

You have to undergo this practice, until it happens spontaneously.

Q: And what will be the benefits for me if I do all this practice?

Maharaj: For me? Forget about 'me'! Attachment will go, so that wherever you are, and whatever you may be doing, you will be distanced from, removed and unconcerned with all the activities of the body.

You will, just like before, be acting as a body, doing your job, but you will not be affected by anything. You will feel completely indifferent, totally and utterly unconcerned with the world.

Q: Because you know who you are?

Maharaj: Because Conviction is there. You will know: "Whatever I see, it is not my identity, including the body. Whatever I see is the world". Seeing is not my identity. The Seer is the Identity. Without the Seer, you can't see the world.

WHATEVER IS SEEN IS NOT YOUR IDENTITY,
INCLUDING THE BODY.
WHATEVER YOU SEE IS THE WORLD.
SEEING IS NOT YOUR IDENTITY. THE SEER IS THE IDENTITY.
WITHOUT THE SEER, YOU CANNOT SEE THE WORLD.

Q: What is that Seer like?

Maharaj: Anonymous, Invisible, Unidentified. It is known by different names that point to and indicate

Ultimate Reality. *Brahman*, *Atman*, *Paramatman*, God, Master, are just names that have been given to identify it. Just like you were once given the name 'John', and now you are stuck with this name. If a thousand people say 'John', you respond as John. In a similar way, the Master tells you, and keeps on telling you, hammering all the time:

YOU ARE *BRAHMAN*, YOU ARE *PARAMATMAN*,
YOU ARE GOD.

But you are not accepting it so easily. Meditation will help you accept your Ultimate Truth.

MEDITATION IS
THE CONSTANT REPETITION OF YOUR REALITY,
UNTIL IT FINALLY SINKS IN.

We are giving you psychological treatment, hammering the same thing all the time, "You are *Brahman*. You are *Brahman*", until it is fully embraced.

Q: I was just thinking that the process, not that there is really any process, is partly psychological, in that you are replacing an old perspective with a new one. And you are doing this via a kind of brainwashing. I am not saying it is brainwashing, but you are using a technique of repetition by hammering, hammering, hammering. It is an accepted fact that if you tell someone something often enough, he is going to believe it. Do you know what I mean?

Maharaj: Were you not brainwashed as a child by your parents, when the identity of 'boy', or 'girl' was reinforced by them. Or when you were given the name 'John' or 'Susan', and given a toy train or a doll?

When you were told that you were a Christian and belonged to that Christian religion, was that not brainwashing? And so it went on and on, with so many concepts that were accepted blindly. All illusion!

Q: That is true! And then while we were growing up, there were also the influences and impressions from school and peers and television. And this was followed by my identity in the field of work. Also as a 'husband' and 'father', etc. I can see how it all unfolded. And to be honest, Maharaj, I really am benefiting from your brainwashing. I am not talking about it in the sense of being indoctrinated, and then becoming like a zombie. No!

Since I have been here, I feel an almost physical, you could say, 'washing of the brain', a cleansing, a clearing out of a lot of stuff, useless concepts. It is hard to explain. There is less baggage, and I feel empty, in a good way. So whatever you're doing, keep doing it, because it is working.

Maharaj: Suppose a patient is suffering from memory loss, and then goes to see a psychologist. He tells the psychologist that he cannot remember anything, and because of this he feels lost and anxious. The psychologist tries to remind him of his forgotten identity. He tells the patient his name, the name of his family members, his work, his hobbies, etc. He is hammering the patient with the facts.

The Master is also treating 'patients' who are suffering from delusion and considering themselves to be men and women. These patients will say things like "I have done good things and bad things. I am under so much pressure. My mother is dying and I can't cope. I feel guilty because I hurt someone". They are always under the pressure of feelings and uncomfortable atmospheres. So here, the Master is the psychologist and convinces his patients that they are suffering from a case of mistaken identity.

"YOU ARE UNBORN.

ALL THESE PROBLEMS ARE AN ILLUSION, BECAUSE YOU ARE NOBODY, AND NOTHING HAS HAPPENED."

Q: Once there is the Conviction, then all these concepts will just go?

Maharaj: After Conviction, all concepts will dissolve completely. It is up to you. As long as you are considering yourself as an individual, "I am somebody", you are not going to know yourself in a real sense. This body is just a cover, like clothes. It is not going to remain. Forget about spirituality, it is a simple fact.

Q: I can't argue with that.

Maharaj: We can't preserve this body forever. One day, willingly or unwillingly, we will lose this body identity. It is called 'death'. But you are not dying. When it's time to leave the body, at that time, there will not be any feeling of, "I am dying", because you will know, truly know, that "I am nothing to do with this body. My body is just an external cover", just like these clothes. If we remove our clothes, do we feel "Oh dear, I am dying?"

73. *The Missing Truth Has Found You*

Maharaj: In dreams, when you are doing good things or bad things, you don't have any ego attachment to these good or bad things. Nisargadatta Maharaj said: "If you kill a thousand cows in your dream, do you wake up saying, Oh! I did a very bad thing? No!"

You are not taking ownership of this because it is a dream. How you were acting, how you were behaving then, was just a dream. You are unconcerned about it, as it is a dream. You are not a killer. You are not taking on ego that, "I have done something".

YOU CANNOT DO ANYTHING.
THERE IS NO DOER, THERE IS NO DEED.
THERE IS NO SEER, THERE IS NO SEEN.
THERE IS NO EXPERIENCE, THERE IS NO EXPERIENCER.
THERE IS NO WITNESS, THERE IS NO WITNESSER.

This is exceptional Knowledge. We have to use various words just to explain, as without them, we can't convey anything. We have given the meanings to the words.

PRIOR TO BEINGNESS, THERE WERE NO WORDS AT ALL.
YOU WERE TOTALLY UNAWARE OF 'YOU'.
YOU WERE NOT ASKING "WHO AM I?"
TO SAY 'I AM' YOUR PRESENCE IS REQUIRED.

Listen carefully! This is deep Knowledge. Your Presence does not know its own Identity. You have got tremendous power. Why behave like a coward?

Q: When you have such power?

Maharaj: You say: "Oh I don't know what to do! I don't know what is going to happen". You are a Master! You are your own Master! Therefore when you know this, when you know yourself in a real sense, all fear, dependency, temptations will come to an end. The search will be over.

IN FACT, THERE IS NO SEARCH.
IT IS YOU THAT IS MISSING.

BUT NOW THE MISSING TRUTH HAS FOUND YOU!
THE MISSING TRUTH HAS FOUND YOU.

Q: We were missing our own Truth. We were so busy doing our searching, that we forgot about the Searcher?

Maharaj: Where is John? Where is John? Where is he? You are here. John is here. He has been here all along. All the time you were looking for truth, you were looking for yourself. Now you know better.

Q: It is a joke really!

Maharaj: Some patients forget their identity and have to be reminded and convinced. Similarly, I am trying to convince you.

YOU MUST HAVE STRONG FAITH WITHIN YOU,
STRONG TRUST WITHIN YOU THAT,
ALL THAT I HAVE TOLD YOU, IS YOUR STORY.
IT IS THE TRUTH THAT YOU ARE.

Accept it and recognize it like, "Aha! This is my story! Now, at last, I know who I am!" We are always thinking about the body. OK, you can use your body, but it is not Ultimate, it is not Final Truth.

Q. Recently, Maharaj, I have been experiencing some fear, even a little panic.

Maharaj: Nisargadatta Maharaj used to tell this story. There was once a big house, and so the owner decided to take in some tenants. After a while, he wanted to kick the tenants out. They started shouting abuse at the owner. They had become used to the house and very comfortable in it, so they were not going to leave willingly, without a struggle.

In this house, [pointing to the body], there are so many tenants, so many concepts. But why fear? Who is fearing? What is the fear about? Prior to beingness there was no fear. This fear and panic you talk about is good.

THIS FEAR IS A GOOD SIGN.
IT MEANS THAT THE CLEANING PROCESS HAS STARTED.
ONE BY ONE, THE TENANTS ARE LEAVING.
THEY ARE HAMMERING YOU ON THE WAY OUT.

Q: Eject the squatters, they are hiding in corners!

Maharaj: Does the sky have any fear? You are fearing your own shadow, you are scared of your own shadow. Why fear your own shadow? Who is fearing? What is fear? Go deeper and find out. Know this fear and who is fearing!

THOSE THINGS WHICH ARE UNPLEASANT AND UNBEARABLE CAUSE FEAR.
BUT THERE IS NO FEAR,
BECAUSE YOU ARE NOT THE BODY.

So don't worry, everything will go, including all these illusory fears. Birth and death are related to body-knowledge only. Your Ultimate Identity is unborn. Why fear your shadow, your own reflection?

Q: What do you mean shadow?

Maharaj: Out of your Presence, this whole world is projected. So what is projected is reflected as your shadow. Your body-knowledge, experience, everything is your reflected shadow because behind that, there is your Presence. The entire world is your Spontaneous shadow. Why fear that shadow? You have embraced the shadow as reality, and therefore there is fear.

Q: It is only because of the body then, that these feelings come up, this fear and worry?

Maharaj: The body is a material body therefore many things are going on. Thoughts come, old thoughts and new thoughts. Sometimes there is unhappiness and depression. But you are absolutely not concerned with what is happening inside because you are separate from the body.

You can see, look at, witness the struggle that is going on and expressing itself. It is only the body, the three *gunas* body. Unpleasant thoughts, depressing thoughts, good thoughts, bad thoughts, subtle thoughts, all sorts of things are there.

BUT YOU ARE WITNESSING THESE THOUGHTS,
JUST LIKE THE CLOUDS THAT ARE COMING AND GOING.
THE SUN IS THERE ALL THE TIME.

In spirituality they say, there is the sun and there are the clouds that come and go. Sometimes you have doubts, sometimes you have fear. Why fear?

WHAT IS THE CAUSE OF FEAR?
WHAT IS THE ROOT OF FEAR?
THE BIG FEAR OF DEATH.
THE BIG FEAR OF DEATH.
WHO IS DYING?

Why fear? We have done nothing wrong. If your fear is great, can it preserve the body? You can't preserve this body. It does not matter how many doctors you have.

ACCEPT THIS REALITY BECAUSE THE
BODY IS NOT YOUR IDENTITY.
WE HAVE ESTABLISHED THAT ULTIMATE TRUTH.
YOU ARE ULTIMATE TRUTH.

Q: So if negative feelings and thoughts come up, we should not give them too much attention. Just let them pass by like passing clouds. Because if you give them attention, they will just get bigger and bigger, but if you just let them go and keep doing the Mantra with determination, you will not get drawn in.

Maharaj: Correct! You are paying so much attention to body-knowledge. There are so many layers of illusionary thoughts. When these thoughts are dissolved, you will feel the difference. Don't be put off by fear, or by any feelings that may arise that will try to distract you from doing the Mantra.

It is just like a sculptor who is hammering a stone. After the hammering, a big statue is revealed. The statue was already there, all that was needed was to remove the unwanted parts, some jaggy parts that were there. The Master helps you remove the unwanted parts so that the Deity can be revealed in all its Purity.

74. *You Are Truth*

Q: I want to know the truth?

Maharaj: You are Truth.

Q: I know, but…

Maharaj: The Knower is Truth. The one who wants to know, who is expecting Truth, That is Truth. Because we have been under the impressions and influences of the body since childhood, we find it difficult to absorb the Knowledge. We have accumulated knowledge, through hearing and reading, but we have not absorbed the Knowledge.

You know you are *Brahman*, *Atman*, but to absorb this, you need systematic meditation, using the *Naam Mantra*. Then all these illusions that are wrapped around you will dissolve.

What is the value of this body? Forget about spirituality! As long as Presence is there, everyone is bowing down, saying, "Oh, you are great, you are great". But the moment Presence, or Spirit, disappears, people say, "Take it away, take it away". It is open fact.

**THERE IS NO BIRTH AND DEATH
FOR YOUR SPONTANEOUS PRESENCE,
WHICH IS CALLED *BRAHMAN*, *ATMAN*, *PARAMATMAN*, GOD.
I AM INVITING THE ATTENTION
OF THAT INVISIBLE LISTENER WITHIN YOU.**

You are Ultimate Truth, you are Final Truth, you are Master. But, the influence of the body has to dissolve. Nothing is impossible. If the Seer is not there, who will talk about the seen? If the Seer is absent, who will talk about the world?

We are begging all the time, "Oh, God bless me. Master, please bless me and do something for me". When you come to know that Godly essence within, you will not go begging for any more blessings from anybody!

**YOU WILL BLESS YOURSELF.
BLESS YOURSELF!
YOU WILL BOW DOWN TO YOU.
BOW TO YOURSELF.**

The Master has given you a new pair of divine spectacles. Now you have to wear them because you are Final Truth.

Q: How to dissolve the mind?

Maharaj: I have told you that there is no mind! Mind is just made up of some illusionary concepts. Because we have given so much importance to it, we have followed all its instructions telling us to: "Do this, do that, do this, do that".

**WHAT HAPPENS IS THAT THOUGHTS COME INTO THE MIND,
THEY ARE DIVERTED TO THE INTELLECT.
THEN THE INTELLECT ASSESSES THEM,
MAKES A DECISION, AND FINALLY
THE EGO PUTS THESE THOUGHTS INTO PRACTICE.**

You have been blindly obeying this internal government, and blindly following its instructions. Not any more!

**YOU ARE A MASTER, YOU ARE THE BOSS.
NOW YOU HAVE TO DICTATE THE TERMS.**

Q: Most everyday thoughts that we have can be avoided, about ninety-five per cent of them, but there are certain tendencies, which come in a cyclical way, and when they happen, it happens so quickly that the habitual response happens immediately.

At that moment, we cannot identify with Presence, and then we get lost. Before we realize it, a few days have gone by. Gradually the effect is reduced, and then we think, Oh God! What have we been doing? I recognize that we have been lost for a few days.

Maharaj: That is why alertness at all times is needed. The Knowledge, meditation and singing are all aids to help you stay alert to illusion. These are your tools, your equipment.

WHEN YOU ARE WEAK, WHEN YOU ARE UNAWARE,
THE ENEMY WILL GAIN ACCESS,
AND ENTER VIA THE BACK DOOR.

If you are alert, no one will dare come inside. I told you, meditation is the anti-virus software. You have to install it. That way, you are always keeping in touch with your Selfless Self. It is a powerful compound that will keep you strong till there is Absolute Conviction.

If you are weak, the mind will attack you, the enemy will attack you. But if you are strong, and have, say, the appearance of a body-builder, flexing your solid muscles, nobody will dare fight with you.

You have to grow spiritually strong. Strength is within you. What is lacking is willpower, confidence and courage. Meditation will regenerate your power.

Teach yourself! You have the basics. Master has given power, but it is up to you to use it now. Absorb this Knowledge. You are Truth!

75. *Whose Heart?*

Q: Is there anything else that I need to know?

Maharaj: Why? After reaching the destination, why are you needing more addresses? It is not necessary!

Q: I do have a question about the heart. People talk about spiritual Masters having an open heart, and there is also Ramana Maharshi, saying the mind dissolves into the heart.

Maharaj: Whose heart? There's no heart at all. Some subtle part of the body needs some Presence.

Q: What about a cosmic heart, universal heart?

Maharaj: You are naming all this. When did you come across the universe? All these words are there: heart, universe, cosmos. We have an Invisible Anonymous Existence, but we are measuring ourselves in body-form, and therefore attempting to measure things, using words like 'heart'.

Q: A couple of visitors recently said that the Master had an open heart.

Maharaj: In the beginning, open heart is used because they are under the pressure of ignorance. After reaching Ultimate Truth, after having Ultimate Truth, after Conviction, there are no such words. Who created all these words?

Q: And love?

Maharaj: Who is loving whom? Who is loving whom? Love, affection, loyalty, faith, trust are the literal words of the body base. Activity is Spontaneous.

You are loving yourself more than others. Self-love, love, affection, attraction, all these are body-based. Prior to the body, prior to beingness, did you know about love, affection, trust, faith? No, nothing!

The moment the body disappears, what was all this love about? Where has the love gone, who was loving whom? Who is the lover? Who is loving? There are no objects. This object I'm loving... this somebody else... this something... I'm loving this, I'm loving that, I'm somebody else, this is all duality.

Q: And God is love?

Maharaj: This is a child's game. You are no longer a child.

Q: And they say, God loves you?

Maharaj: Nisargadatta Maharaj used to say, "Without your Presence, God cannot exist". Since coming into worldly existence, you are having some illusion that you are somebody in the world. Then all these terms 'love' and 'affection' started. Prior to hearing this Knowledge, you were considering, "I am within the world, within love, the universe".

NOW, YOU SEE WITH THIS EYE OF KNOWLEDGE,
THAT THE UNIVERSE IS WITHIN YOU.

This is how it came.

I gave you the example of the dream-world. You are sleeping, and the entire universe is there. How did the universe come into that dream? You see the sea, ocean, sun, moon, sky, numerous people, the forest, the whole world projected. How can this be? Just a click of 'I'! A click of Presence that sprouts to see the world.

The same thing happens here. This 'life' is a long dream: "The day I sat by the sea, my holiday, my wife, my relatives, my son, my friends". It is a long dream! There are no relations!

Q: Like in the *Chidananda bhajan*, "I am not...

Maharaj: In *Chidananda* there are some words that identify the illusion. Remember! Don't cling to any words. "I am not" is also an illusion. To say "I am not", some Presence has to be there first. Where was *Chidananda* prior to your Presence? Where was *Chidananda*, happiness, unhappiness? Nisargadatta Maharaj used to say:

"THE REAL IS VERY UNKNOWN TO YOU.
SO LIVE LIKE THAT
AND IT WILL NOT BE A PROBLEM FOR YOU".

When you are not identifying yourself in any form prior to beingness, when you are not identifying in any form prior to beingness, you won't have a problem. So try and live like that! No attraction, no love, no universe, no God, no *prarabdha*, no nothing.

WHEN EVERYTHING ENDS, THERE YOU ARE.
WHEN EVERYTHING ENDS, THERE YOU ARE.

Q: So we have to live like we were prior to beingness?

Maharaj: These are only words. It is your story. These are the indications.

I AM INVITING THE ATTENTION OF
HOW YOU WERE PRIOR TO BEINGNESS.
THESE ARE ONLY WORDS,
IT IS YOUR STORY.
PRIOR TO BEINGNESS YOU WERE UNKNOWN.

THEREFORE 'UNKNOWN' CANNOT BE EXPERIENCED.
NO KNOWLEDGE, NO KNOWER.

Q: No!

Maharaj: Mind, ego, intellect, knower, knowledge, devotee, Master, God. We came across these terms when we came across the body. The body is not your identity, neither is mind, ego, intellect, Masters, God. Open Truth. Read if you so wish, but don't drown yourself in an ocean of reading.

Be convinced, and convince others. We say 'others', just to communicate. There are no others. They are not knowing themselves, and so they are still thinking they are 'other'.

Q: They are others because they are not knowing themselves?

Maharaj: They are the cause and the consequence of each entire world.

YOU ARE THE CAUSE AND CONSEQUENCE
OF YOUR ENTIRE WORLD.

You cannot realize the world without your Presence.

BE CALM AND QUIET.
EXCEPTIONAL SILENCE IS THERE.
NO STRUGGLE, NO TEMPTATION, NO ENTHUSIASM.

Q: You are not going after things, ideas?

Maharaj: Calm. Full stop. No more running! Finished! Running is over.

Remember what I told you, when everything ends, there you are. When everything ends, there you are:

WITHOUT ANY SHAPE,
WITHOUT ANY BODY, WITHOUT ANY FORM.

Q: I have one more body question, Maharaj. You said that Spirit finds beingness intolerable. Was it Spirit that projected the seeker, the searcher?

Maharaj: This is for understanding only. Spirit is not different. Since we are holding the body, some unpleasant things do happen to the body. Sickness comes. So if you are unaware of your Identity, it is intolerable. After knowing the Reality, 'I' becomes tolerable because you remain unconcerned.

UNBEARABLE THINGS BECOME BEARABLE
WITH ESTABLISHED TRUTH.

You are to live with the body, as if it were your neighbour's child. Sometimes you try to be sympathetic, but you know you have nothing to do with your neighbour's child.

Q: The body is to be viewed in a detached way, like the neighbour's child? That is helpful, it creates distance.

Maharaj: The Conviction is there. You know that this is my neighbour's child, and you have nothing to do with it. If you know it is the neighbour's child, you are not having to put up with pain.

So be careful! Don't be a bookworm! Just remember that while reading spiritual books, the content that is connected with the Ultimate Truth is about you. It is your story: That you are! This is the Conviction.

THESE ARE THE MEDITATIONS:
SPONTANEOUS, CONTINUOUS ALERTNESS
THAT WE ARE ULTIMATE TRUTH, ULTIMATE IDENTITY.

76. *Trying to Catch the 'I'*

Q: I have been asking questions since childhood. I was a Zen Buddhist, and then I discovered Nisargadatta Maharaj and Ramana Maharshi. For years, I have tried to concentrate on the 'I', trying to catch the 'I'. While working, eating, meeting with others, hearing, I have always tried to concentrate on 'I'.

Recently there has been a stronger feeling of suffering, and more attachment than before. I try to put it all aside, but it is very difficult. I am despairing a little because of the suffering and this ego, this strong attachment. I want so much to be a pure devotee.

Maharaj: You need scientific meditation. You are using so many different pills and medicines. Your knowledge has come from reading books and listening to Masters.

**ALL THIS CONFUSION IS HAPPENING
BECAUSE OF A LACK OF FOUNDATION,
A LACK OF A SPIRITUAL FOUNDATION.**

In our Lineage, we teach: "How to concentrate on the Concentrator". If you undergo scientific meditation, your confusion will disappear. What has happened is that because of the influence of the body, the influence of reading various books, visiting various Masters, this has caused great confusion. Every Master has something to say, and says it in a different way.

**SCIENTIFIC MEDITATION MEANS THAT THERE SHOULD NOT BE
A SCATTERED MIND, DIVIDED MIND, DIVIDED FAITH.
THERE SHOULD ONLY BE ONE TARGET.
ONE MASTER, NOT TWO MASTERS, OR COMPARING MASTERS.**

Changing Masters will not bring you happiness. You must have strong faith in your Master. A strong faith in your Inner Master will regenerate your power. Your Inner Master will empower and teach you spontaneously. But you must not have a wavering mind. Meditate with full faith and trust. What is meditation?

**MEDITATION MEANS FORGETTING YOUR IDENTITY.
RECITING THE *NAAM MANTRA* HALF-HEARTEDLY,
AND WITH SOME SUSPICION IS NOT MEDITATION.
WHAT IS IMPORTANT IS THE QUALITY OF THE MEDITATION:
FULL CONCENTRATION, PERFECT INVOLVEMENT.**

Q: I have been a devotee of Ramana Maharshi for a long time. Every year I go to Arunachala for a retreat. Is this confusing? Should I decide on one Master?

Maharaj: You see, there are all these Gurus. The physical bodies are different. You are identifying them in body-form. Spirit is one. Ramana Maharshi, Nisargadatta Maharaj, Siddharameshwar Maharaj, there are many saintly people, but Spirit is one.

**YOU HAVE TO PAY STRONG ATTENTION
TO THAT SPIRIT ALONE,
AND NOT TO THE BODY-FORM OF THE SAINTS.**

You have been doing various practices which is good. But at the same time, these practices are inflating the ego, and because of the ego, you are not getting the happiness you are seeking. You feel sorry, depressed, and some fear is also there.

But the moment you become one with Ultimate Truth, there won't be any of these feelings.

YOU ARE UNBORN,
SO DON'T MEASURE YOURSELF IN THE BODY-FORM.
THIS IS NOT YOUR IDENTITY,
IT IS JUST YOUR EXTERNAL COVER.

Q. It is hard to be devoted, so difficult to be a good and pure devotee.

Maharaj: There is no difficulty. You must have complete faith in your Master, whether he is alive or not. Reading books and changing Masters will not help.

YOU ARE TO GO TO A REALIZED MASTER,
NOT TO ANY OLD MASTER
WHO IS DOING IT FOR COMMERCIAL PURPOSES.

When you accept someone as your Master, you are supposed to be wholly loyal to that Master. Therefore in any circumstances in life, you should stay loyal to your Master. The Master is there to take care of you. Sometimes there are tests.

Q: So many tests!

Maharaj: There should not be any dual mind, or ill faith towards the Master under any circumstances. This is the quality of spirituality. Confusion and fear is with you because you are listening to different teachers, talking about destiny, *karma*, *prarabdha*, etc. There is no destiny, no *prarabdha*.

ALL THESE THOUGHTS ARE APPLICABLE TO THE BODY ONLY,
NOT TO YOU.
WHY ACCEPT SOMEBODY ELSE'S ILLUSORY THOUGHTS
AND HAVE YOUR BLOOD PRESSURE INCREASE?

Your search has to come to an end because there is no search. Where everything ends, there you are.

CONCENTRATE ON THE SEARCHER, NOT THE SEARCH.

At the moment you are scattered. Your strength is divided. Your faith is scattered like the sun's rays. Be the sun! Power is within you but it is scattered here and there. Using one finger only, you cannot do very much, but with five, you can clench your fist and give a firm blow. That power is divided between ten fingers. If all fingers come together, nothing will dare attack you.

Dry discussion of knowledge will not help. Practical knowledge is needed. Theory and practice always differ. You know how to swim theoretically, but unless you jump in the water, you are not swimming in the ocean of spiritual knowledge.

77. *Fake Currency*

Q: One difficulty I see is with past *karma* and tendencies, *prarabdha*. Of course this is body identification, but we do have a tendency towards living the external life in a particular way, and that can cause problems. How can I overcome this?

Maharaj: Don't make any deliberate effort. There is no *prarabdha*. Whose *prarabdha*? Your existence is Spontaneous Existence.

**DID YOU DECIDE WHICH BODY TO BE BORN INTO
PRIOR TO BEINGNESS?
ALL YOUR TALKING IS CONNECTED TO THE BODY ONLY.**

What's going to happen after leaving the body?

**PRARABDHA, KARMA, HELL, HEAVEN,
ALL THESE CONCEPTS CAME ALONG WITH THE BODY,
AND WILL DISSOLVE ALONG WITH THE BODY.**

All this that we are talking about in-between the 'prior to' and the 'after', is illusion. We are talking about the unborn child.

**IF YOUR BODY IS NOT YOUR IDENTITY,
THEN WHOSE DESIRES ARE YOU REFERRING TO?**

Saint Kabir said, "Everything goes away along with the body". Therefore all this talk, what we are talking about is for the 'in-between' unborn child.

**WE ARE PLAYING DURING THIS 'IN-BETWEEN' ILLUSORY STAGE,
FROM SO-CALED BIRTH, TO SO-CALLED DEATH,**

because we are measuring ourselves in body-form.

**SO WHAT YOU HAVE READ AND WHAT YOU HAVE LISTENED TO,
FORGET IT!
IT IS FAKE CURRENCY!**

Q: Truth is just emptiness Maharaj, it is just like sky.

Maharaj: Ah! It is OK, it is very nice because when everything ends there you are - quality-less!

Q: I have a feeling of emptiness, nothing.

Maharaj: It is a kind of magnetic experience. The Invisible Listener in you becomes one with the Ultimate Truth, so everything else goes away. When you feel emptiness, your body identity dissolves. It is a good sign. We have to maintain this with meditation.

Q: We have to hold onto this emptiness?

Maharaj: Do not hold on! It is Spontaneous. Do not make any deliberate effort to do something. Once my Master told me, "If you take a drop of poison, you don't have to find out its results. It happens automatically". Similarly, when you take the *Naam Mantra*, everything happens spontaneously. You do not have to try and find out what's going to happen, or even try to make something happen.

In the beginning, you have to recite the *Naam Mantra*, the Guru Mantra because as I have told you, it is the anti-virus software. There are lots of viruses: concepts, *prarabdha*, greed, desire, illusions.

We were all raised in a unique atmosphere. We grew up in different atmospheres which have influenced our spiritual body.

**YOU ARE NOT THE BODY.
WE ARE HAMMERING THIS ALL THE TIME.
THE NAAM MANTRA HAMMERS YOU IN THE SAME WAY.**

Any more questions?

Q: I am busy following your teachings.

Maharaj: Very good! The Invisible Listener is listening to my talk. Spontaneous recording is taking place. So be brave, have courage.

FORGET ABOUT ALL KNOWLEDGE.
THAT IS KNOWLEDGE.

No knowledge is knowledge.

Q: Many times I prayed to get courage and bravery. Can you give me courage?

Maharaj: Courage is already within you. Bodies are different but Spirit is one. Clothes are different but Spirit is one. It is as if you are asking to compare the Indian sky to the Chinese sky or the American sky. Sky is sky. Stop measuring in body-form! These are the words, very beautiful words, courage, peace, and bravery, very nice.

BUT WHEN DID YOU START NEEDING COURAGE AND PEACE?
ONLY WHEN PRESENCE
CAME INTO EXISTENCE IN BODY-FORM.

78.   *The Nectar Tree Has Been Planted in You*

Maharaj: Just remember what I have told you, just remember it. Forget the past. Forget the past. What we have discussed over these days, just remember it. It is your story. Nisargadatta Maharaj said, "I am not making you a disciple I am making you a Master" because the Masterly essence is within you. We are talking about the same thing, again and again. The same thing, again and again! We are discussing one principle.

THE *GITA* DESCRIBES SO MANY DIFFERENT WAYS,
BUT YOU HAVE ALREADY WON YOUR DESTINATION.
YOU HAVE ALREADY CROSSED THE FINISH LINE.

To know oneself in a real sense is Self-Knowledge. So be calm and be quiet. Deposit all your worries in the ashram. Just deposit all your worries, temptations, difficulties in the ashram, then go. Go quickly.

Q: Sounds good to me!

Maharaj: There is one last thing. We are demanding something from you.

Q: Oh?

Maharaj: Deposit your ego! Deposit your intellect! Deposit your mind! And then you can go. People are prepared to pay for teachings and spiritual instruction, but they will not deposit their ego, intellect, mind. [Master laughs].

I am not presenting anything new. It is an open secret. You can easily glance within you, but you are under pressure of various thoughts, illusionary thoughts. You are living under the pressure of illusionary thoughts. Your lifestyle was completely controlled by the impressions of all these illusionary thoughts. But now that you know better, you can change your lifestyle.

Q: I am going to.

Maharaj: Start with forgetting all that you have learned. What you have listened to, forget it! It is gone. Forget the past. It is the mind measuring things - twenty years ago this memory, some fifty years ago, that memory. Something happened twenty years ago, and still you remember it today, and even re-experience the pain of it all.

FORGET THE PAST!
THERE IS NO PAST, NO FUTURE, NO PRESENT.

Q: No present? I can accept there being no past and no future, but no present? What about the 'NOW', the present moment? There has to be a present!

Maharaj: Whose present?

SINCE YOU ARE NOT THE BODY,
THEN WHOSE PAST?
WHOSE PRESENT?
WHOSE FUTURE?

No present, no past, no future. Does sky have a past, present, future? Nisargadatta Maharaj used to say, "If you want to compare yourself to anything, compare yourself to sky". Your Unidentified Identity is just like space. There is no feeling. Accept this Truth, Your Truth.

WHAT ARE WE DOING HERE?
WE ARE NOT DOING ANYTHING.
WE ARE REMOVING THE ASH,
SO THAT THE FIRE CAN IGNITE.

The fire is there, but it is covered by a heap of illusion, heaps of illusions. Keep the flame burning, the spiritual fire. Keep the Mantra going, otherwise you will stay covered with the ash of illusion. The cleaning process has started. Meditation cleans everything. Meditation cleans everything. It is a cleaning process.

Q: I will persevere with the meditation, Maharaj, I could do with a good clean-out.

Maharaj: You have to have some courage for this. But nothing is impossible. Past, present, future are related to the body-knowledge. Spiritual science says, you are not the body, you were not the body, and you are not going to remain the body. It is open fact.

IN ORDER FOR YOU TO HAVE A PAST,
PRESENT, FUTURE,
SOMETHING HAS TO BE THERE IN THE FIRST PLACE.
THERE IS NOTHING THERE.
YOU ARE FORMLESS.
NOTHING IS THERE.
EMBRACE YOUR POWER.

Why not embrace your Power? Be natural, be simple, be humble. You have the Key, now you are to operate it. You must have complete faith in yourself and in the Master.

Be like the examples of the saints and stalwarts I told you about. They had such strong faith in their Masters. They were not educated, not qualified. How did these spiritual words appear and come out of their mouths? Who was speaking for them?

I saw a number of foreigners coming to Nisargadatta Maharaj. They were asking so many complicated questions. Maharaj gave simple answers.

THIS COULD HAPPEN TO YOU.
THE SAME THING CAN HAPPEN TO YOU, TO ANYONE.
BODIES ARE DIFFERENT,
ROADS ARE DIFFERENT,
SPIRIT IS THE SAME.
IT IS OPEN TRUTH.

Have I convinced you?

Q: Yes Maharaj!

Maharaj: **NOW YOU HAVE TO CONVINCE YOURSELF.**

Thoughts are flowing, it is the nature of the body, but don't struggle with the thoughts. Fully accept the useful thoughts. Correct? [hand clap].

Q: I'm hoping that the Mantra will gradually become more automatic.

Maharaj: One hundred per cent subject to how great your involvement is. It is up to you!

Q: The more you put in, the more you get out. You have to put effort in at the beginning, especially at the beginning?

Maharaj: You are to make some deliberate efforts at the beginning. Then it will happen spontaneously. All your actions and reactions will be Spontaneous. You will remain unconcerned with the world.

REMAIN UNCONCERNED WITH THE WORLD.

Q: This is a good time to remain unconcerned with the world, as I have nothing else to do except recite the Mantra.

Maharaj: Reciting is most important. Reciting and sitting for meditation. Many people do not have a knowledge-base. You are well-read, so you have a good base, a very good base.

New people come, and they are all from different backgrounds, at different levels. They have different levels of understanding. If they are not very educated, or don't have a very good knowledge base, then I will use some stories to convey the teachings. There is something for everyone in the stories.

Everyone has their own particular standard of understanding, and they are taught according to their level. It is a technique of the Masters. When Siddharameshwar Maharaj delivered lectures, he had to decide how to teach, depending on who was there. And when any newcomers came, he immediately changed the pitch. Old devotees know the Reality, but when new people come, they need you to talk to them in a simple way.

Siddharameshwar Maharaj used to say, "For you, I am taking ego, I have to step down, so that I am Master and you are disciple. There's no difference between you and me but when I am teaching you, when I am talking with you, when I am delivering lectures to you, I take the ego of the Master, and you are the disciple".

So don't worry. You have a good base. Deposit all your worries, all your difficulties, everything in the ashram. You have a lot of luggage!

Q: Both literally and metaphorically!

Maharaj: Leave all your luggage, and go alone.

JUST BE WITH YOU!

BE WITH YOU ONLY.

Q: And would you say it is a good thing not to look for results, like doing the Mantra without expectation?

Maharaj: That's correct. Don't do meditation with the expectation that maybe you will get an experience, a sign, that something out of the ordinary may happen.

Q: Like bright lights or something?

Maharaj: It will be Spontaneous. It will come to you. After a time, maybe you will feel that you have some power. These subtle expectations are bound to be there, it happens. But you are to give time for meditation. Devotion without expectation. Then only, will you find your deity within you.

DEVOTION WITHOUT EXPECTATION LEADS
TO KNOWING THE DEITY WITHIN YOU.

So with various words I am hammering, I am placing your Ultimate Truth in you, I am implanting your Ultimate Truth in you.

NOW YOU HAVE TO MAKE IT GROW
WITH FERTILIZER AND WATER.
THE NECTAR TREE HAS BEEN PLANTED WITHIN YOU.
HOW ARE YOU GOING TO TEND IT?
WITH WATER AND FERTILIZER.
THE FERTILIZER IS
THE POWER OF *BHAJAN* AND MEDITATION.

After listening to all of this, read *I Am That* again. It will be much clearer! Nisargadatta Maharaj was a very rare personality. The statements he made had so much force. He spoke with exceptional force. So I am myself very, very fortunate. It is only because of him, that I am talking like this. I am very, very fortunate to have had such a long association with my Master.

Q: And now we are benefiting from that association.

Maharaj: I am sharing the same knowledge with you. The language may be different, the approach may be different, the principle is one.

I SEE MY HAPPINESS IN YOU.
I SEE MY HAPPINESS WITHIN YOU.
IF YOU ARE HAPPY,
I AM HAPPY.

So there must be a full stop somewhere. Don't be a spiritual traveller. I have seen so many people coming here, discussing the teachings then saying, "OK, OK, now I have to go and see someone else". So my shouting has all been wasted. I feel sorry about that.

Q: You don't know, maybe in a few years, down the road, something will click. Yes! Because you are planting seeds. It takes time.

Maharaj: Yes, you must have patience.

Q: If it is young people, all sorts of things happen they get married, etc.

Maharaj: So be happy, and make others happy. Be realized and help others come out of illusion.

Q: I notice you don't use the words 'get' realized, but 'be' realized. Am I right in thinking that getting is like a commodity?

Maharaj: Again, these are the words. You are already Realized, but you are unaware of your realization. You are already Realized, but you are unaware of your realization. Since you are forgetting your Identity, we are inviting attention of that Invisible Listener, your Ultimate Truth. Knowledge is already with you, it's just that you have forgotten.

79.   Do We Need a Master?

Q: When you became self-realized, why didn't you start teaching then? Why did you continue with your work? What's more important?

Maharaj: They happen at different times. Realization happens spontaneously. It is different from teaching. When Nisargadatta Maharaj was realized, he was not teaching for some time. He was avoiding it. First reason, it is a big responsibility, and secondly, it depends on the circumstances, and how many devotees wish to come. If they have strong devotion and involvement, then it will happen. People forced me! Ranjit Maharaj had left his body, and so they said, "Who is next? You must do something. What about our children?" It happened spontaneously.

Q: I am so grateful to you Maharaj.

Maharaj: Everything happens because of my Masters. I was a small boy, and then a young man in my early twenties, earning one or two rupees a day. And then it ended like this! All miracles!

It can happen to everyone, it just depends on your involvement. You talk of 'realization', 'enlightenment', these are the words. You are already realized, but you are unaware of that. Everything is within you, but you are unaware, that is all.

WE ARE MAKING YOU AWARE.
THROUGH OUR TALKS, WE ARE MAKING YOU AWARE.

Don't underestimate yourself. Be strongly involved with deep devotion.

Q: Maharaj, I wanted to ask you what the meaning of devotion is?

Maharaj: Devotion means complete involvement with our Selfless Self. Devotion means absolute involvement with our Selfless Self, without any ego. Spontaneous involvement in Selfless Self, not deliberate action.

Q: Some seekers say that you don't need a Master to self-realize. How necessary is the Master?

Maharaj: When the doctor prescribes medicine, he does not tell you to take all the tablets at once. He prescribes maybe one or two tablets at different times of the day. Similarly, the Master is there to prescribe, instruct and give guidance for you to follow. Without the Master you are trying to find your way in the dark. At the beginning stage, a Master is needed.

THE MASTER PRESENTS THE SEEKER
WITH HIS UNIDENTIFIED IDENTITY.
THE UNIDENTIFIED IDENTITY IS PLACED BEFORE HIM,
THROUGH THE MEDIUM OF THE MASTER.

The Master is there to indicate and point to your Reality. He is there to show you, convince you, so that you know the Reality. Then you will ask, "Who am I?"

Q: What happens after the body goes? What's left?

Maharaj: At present you are holding the body. Prior to beingness there was no body. After the disappearance of the body, you will be unknown to yourself. So whatever knowledge, whatever spiritual information you have now, will disappear along with the body. There's nothing left.

Q: So what's the point of all this spiritual knowledge then?

Maharaj: Spiritual knowledge is needed because you have forgotten your identity.

**YOU HAVE FORGOTTEN
HOW YOU WERE PRIOR TO BEINGNESS.**

Q: What is knowledge then?

Maharaj: You are jumping about erratically from one question to the next without stopping.

Q: Sorry, Maharaj, I guess I am just excited to be here.

Maharaj: It is OK, but this knowledge is not intellectual knowledge, it is Direct Knowledge. Knowledge means just to know oneself in a real sense. We know ourselves in body-form. This is not your identity.

**KNOWLEDGE IS SELF-KNOWLEDGE.
DEVOTION IS THE PERFECTION
OF SELF-KNOWLEDGE.**

Q: Is Conviction blind faith?

Maharaj: Conviction just means to realize Ultimate Truth. A simple example is: This body is called 'man', so I have accepted that this body is called 'man'. That is Spontaneous Conviction.

Q: I sense from what you have been saying that in order to have that Conviction, meditation is crucial?

Maharaj: Meditation is the base because through meditation only, will these illusory thoughts, these wrong thoughts, wrong concepts, be dissolved. Since childhood till today, *lakhs* of illusory thoughts have developed in the body. Meditation is therefore necessary to erase all of them. In the beginning, you are to make an effort, then it will happen without your knowledge.

80. Vision of the Master

Q: I'm having a lot of spontaneous happenings during meditation that you sometimes refer to as 'landmarks'. This morning the Masters had prepared a pyre for me! I took this as guidance for me to make greater effort to completely surrender the ego, so that it could be burned away with the rest of the illusion that I am. But I was talking to another devotee, and he did not seem to be having any experiences of any kind.

Maharaj: That is fine! At the beginning, when you are getting started, it is different for everyone. You may have experiences, or you may not. It depends, some people don't have experiences at the start of the practice.

Some have many experiences out of their meditations, out of their total involvement, as they are getting closer and closer to Selfless Self. Others experience miraculous occurrences.

Briefly, spiritual science says you can experience God in three ways, seeing, hearing and touch. You may see your Master with whom you have total involvement. You may feel the touch of your Master. Or you may hear your Master talking with you.

WHEN THERE IS TOTAL INVOLVEMENT,
YOUR SPIRIT TAKES THE SHAPE OF YOUR MASTER.

I will give you an example of a saint named Hemvabai, just to illustrate the Oneness. She was a disciple of Bhausaheb Maharaj. She was suffering from incurable plague, and was banished to the forest to avoid spreading the disease. There she prayed to her Master. She prayed in such a deep way, with such devotion, that Bhausaheb Maharaj took shape before her in body-form. She was cured of the plague.

He told her to go to the ashram at Bagewadi. She was nervous, and told him she would be treated like a ghost. He said, "When you pray, I will be there, but invisible to all except you". She went to the ashram and told the people that Bhausaheb Maharaj had given her *darshan*.

The local people tested her. Prasad was brought, and shortly afterwards, Bhausaheb Maharaj appeared, and cleared the plate. Eventually, the people took Hemvabai's *darshan*. This kind of miraculous thing happens. As a matter of fact,

THE SAINT DOES NOT ACTUALLY TAKE FORM.
WHEN YOU ARE TOTALLY INVOLVED
WITH YOUR SELFLESS SELF,
THE FORM IS PROJECTED.

This is not Ultimate Truth. It is a good experience, yes, a landmark, but it is not Ultimate Truth. There are many miraculous events happening all the time.

I will tell you another: One of the elderly devotees needed to have a major operation. His son asked him if he were afraid of the operation? He answered, "Why should I be afraid? I am the Master of death". During the operation, he saw his Master. He was present with the doctors. This happened because of his strong faith.

MIRACLES ARE NOT ULTIMATE TRUTH.
THEY ARE THE SEER'S REFLECTION, THE SEER'S PROJECTION.
IT IS YOUR REALITY TAKING SHAPE.

The Spirit is very sensitive. If you think about your Master seriously and deeply, and you forget about your identity, your Master will appear before you. It can happen! The Realized saints do not encourage miracles. Nisargadatta Maharaj said, "Do not disclose these happenings because it gives people the wrong message".

Miracles happen, they happen out of your Spontaneous Presence. You have got tremendous strength. You have got tremendous strength, tremendous power, but you are underestimating that power, and trying to find that Reality somewhere else. Be independent!

81. *Wordless Reality*

Maharaj: You are covered by so many garments, layers of illusion. You have to remove them, one by one. You will know the classic story of the disciple who asked his Master: "How is *Brahman*?" The Master said, "*Brahman* is just like an onion".

It is just like an onion or a cabbage. If you remove the layers one by one, then eventually there will be nothing left. Likewise, if you remove all these illusory thoughts, then nothing will remain. But in that nothing, there is everything.

IN THAT NOTHING, EVERYTHING IS THERE.

In various ways, various language, with various words, various sentences, we are trying to convince you of the Reality.

NOTHING WAS THERE PRIOR TO BEINGNESS.

After the dissolution of beingness, there will be nothing.

All this talking that we are doing is just like talking about the unborn child. Talking about this philosophy and the *Brahman*, *Atman*, and other words, is just like talking about the unborn child – Nothing!

WE ARE TALKING ABOUT THE UNBORN CHILD.
WE ARE TALKING ABOUT NOTHING.

Everything will leave with the body, so how will *Brahman* be then? If the body is no longer there, how will *Brahman* be for you, for anyone? The moment the body disappears with so-called death, what will this *Brahman* be like? Where will this *Brahman*, *Parabrahman*, *Atman*, God be?

THERE WILL BE NO WORDS.
THIS IS THE REALITY.
SO WHY ALL THIS ATTACHMENT TO THE WORDS?
YOU HAVE A LOT OF AFFECTION FOR THE WORDS.
TRY TO FIND THE REALITY,
YOUR REALITY.
REALITY WITHOUT WORDS.

Why continue hanging onto all these words? "Why does this saint say it like this? Why does that saint say it like that?" It is not about the 'saying', it is the meaning that is the most important thing. People are addicted to words. What do we mean by *Brahman*? What do we mean by *Atman*, *Paramatman*, God, Master, *Maya*, *Brahman*? So many words! We have created the words. We are creating the words.

We have made an alphabet a, b, c, d, and created the words. 'DAD' - Oh! That means 'father'.

WE ARE ADDING THE WORDS,
GIVING THEM MEANING,
AND THEN TALKING AND FIGHTING WITH THE WORDS.

Words naturally serve a purpose, without them we can't transact with each other, we cannot converse with each other. But we are to go deeper into the words.

GO DEEPER AND DEEPER
INTO THE MEANING OF THE WORDS.

I appear in this world as a man or a woman. Is this true? Having the sex of a man or woman, is this external cover true or false?

Say the same metal, gold or silver was used to create two statues: one of God and one of a donkey. If you were to go to the goldsmith and say to him: "This is a statue of God! It should be more valuable than the statue of the donkey!" You will not get more for the gold 'God', than for the gold 'donkey'. The value is in the weight of the gold or silver, and not in the name, shape or form.

So likewise Ultimate Truth is Ultimate Truth. You are Ultimate Truth. So you have to convince yourself. You have to motivate yourself. You have to mould yourself.

DIRECTIONS HAVE BEEN GIVEN TO YOU.
GUIDELINES HAVE BEEN GIVEN TO YOU.
SO THINK ABOUT THEM,
USE THEM,
AND REGENERATE YOUR OWN POWER.

Don't neglect yourself, don't underestimate yourself. Have some courage to face the external and internal things. Waves are coming and going, thoughts are coming and going. Accept and reject, accept and reject. Simple! You are your own Master.

Q: I can understand these things, but doing them is something else. I am the Master of my world. I can understand that, but putting it into practice is a different thing.

Maharaj: It just means putting the Knowledge into practice. The facts have been presented to you. The facts are placed before you. Open facts are placed before you. Open Truth is placed before you. The rest is up to you, what you do with it all is entirely up to you.

ULTIMATE TRUTH IS PLACED BEFORE YOU.
IT IS YOUR TRUTH, YOUR FINAL IDENTITY.

What happens is that when you read books, particular words influence you. You analyze them: Ramana Maharshi says it like this and Nisargadatta Maharaj, like that. You are making a comparative study of various words, while at the same time,

YOU ARE IGNORING THE SPIRIT
THAT IS TRYING TO MAKE THIS COMPARATIVE STUDY.

Various words are indicating your Ultimate Truth. Accept that only! Don't play with the words!

82.   *You Are Smiling Now*

Maharaj: How simple this Knowledge is!

Q. Simple but hard.

Maharaj: I am bringing to your attention what is already in you. All you have to do is accept with complete confidence, complete trust. Examine it, by all means! Don't have blind faith. Examine every Master's teachings, and discern if he has given you proper, or improper information.

Q: Maharaj, I am aware of what's going on more. When something unpleasant arises, I understand just to be with it, not to fear, and then it just goes.

Maharaj: Good, correct. Spirituality is commando-training, beyond soldier-training. Have you packed everything? Any final questions?

Q: No None! The difficulties have gone, the sadness gone! [laughing].

Maharaj: Very good, very good. Be normal! Complete silence. You don't have to keep thinking. Whatever is happening, just let it happen. You are seeing a picture on a screen, momentarily you are becoming happy or unhappy because of the scene or the story. Then when you leave the auditorium you forget it.

This is a big auditorium with thoughts flowing, pictures flowing. This is a dream. Watch the dream, and forget it. Be ordinary, simple, be humble. Be ordinary, be simple, be humble.

DON'T TAKE ANY NOTICE OF WHATEVER IS HAPPENING AROUND YOU.
DON'T REGISTER ANYBODY'S THOUGHTS
THAT ARE HAPPENING AROUND YOU.

Your happiness is my happiness. You are smiling now and laughing, it is very nice. When you came you were serious and sad.

It is very simple, very, very simple, don't stress, and don't be drawn by attractions. Sometimes you will feel tempted, but you will be guided and receive instructions from your Inner Master: "Don't do this, this is *Maya*, illusion. Over here, do this". It is a little like the children's game of snakes and ladders.

IN SPIRITUALITY,
WE ASK THAT YOU FORGET ABOUT THE PAST.
DON'T THINK ABOUT THE PAST BECAUSE,
YOUR SPONTANEOUS PRESENCE IS YOUR TARGET.
YOUR SPONTANEOUS PRESENCE IS YOUR TARGET.

Don't become a slave of somebody else's thoughts and views. Forget about bookish knowledge, literal knowledge! Be a completely blank slate. Remove all the wrong files, illusionary files, and insert your new programme. Just change your vision, change your specs. It is your story. I am inviting attention of the Invisible Listener within you.

COME TO KNOW SELFLESS SELF.
SO INSERT THE PROGRAMME 'SELFLESS SELF',
AND LET IT TAKE CARE OF
ALL YOUR COMPUTERS AND LAPTOPS.

83. *Ultimate Reality Has No Face*

Maharaj: You can live a fearless life. Why is there fear? Because we have attachment to this body. Suppose you had a lot of money in your pocket, and you went outside, you would have some fear of being robbed. So you are looking around, anxiously and fearfully, with your hand in your pocket. You are afraid of a thief. If there is nothing in your pocket, your arms will be relaxed by your side.

SIMILARLY, YOU ARE FEARFUL BECAUSE OF
YOUR ATTACHMENT TO THIS BODY.

If nothing is dear to you, then there is nothing to fear.

NO DEAR, NO FEAR!

As long as there is a trace of conviction left that you are somebody, then this egoistic knowledge will continue to cause problems and conflicts. Therefore some dedication is needed, if you are to know yourself in a real sense. Think on yourself! This is very simple Knowledge. Forget about spirituality for a moment. You are a small child, you grow to a young man and then to an old man.

THESE ARE THE STAGES OF THE BODY, NOT YOUR STAGES.
YOU ARE THE WITNESS TO THE SMALL CHILD,
YOU ARE THE WITNESS TO THE YOUNG MAN,
YOU ARE THE WITNESS.

The witness is not changing, the thing which is witnessed is changing. The body changes, not you.

YOU ARE CONSTANT.

Even when we know that, "I am not the body", in spite of that, some fear is still there, some subtle fear and anxiety about what is going to happen. If anything goes wrong with the body, you plead, "Oh doctor do something, give me an injection to survive!" Why?

BECAUSE IT IS THE NATURE OF SPIRIT.
BECAUSE SPIRIT KNOWS ITSELF ONLY THROUGH THE BODY.

We are calling it Spirit, *Brahman*, *Atman*, *Paramatman*, but Spirit is yourself. You are Selfless Self. The combination of the Spirit and body, the illusion of the mind, ego, intellect, identifying yourself as someone separate, have all contributed to this dream world.

When you wake up from a dream, you are not taking any cognizance of that dream. Similarly, you are not to take any cognizance of this world. This is a dream world. Follow?

Q: I have often read that everything is '*maya*' and I have understood this intellectually. But the way you are telling it now is so down to earth, that I really, really understand it. It sounds not only true, but pragmatic.

Maharaj: The Conviction will come. Gradually, all these illusionary layers will be melted completely. The melting process has already started. Slowly, silently and permanently, body-knowledge and how things affect the body will lessen, dissolve and disappear.

Q: What will be there instead?

Maharaj: That exceptional Peace without any material cause. At present, we are trying to extract peace and happiness from material causes. We are reading the scriptures, this is a material cause. We are eating good dishes, that is a material cause. Temporary!

THIS HAPPINESS THAT I SPEAK OF CANNOT BE DEFINED.

All concepts are illusion.

YOU MUST FIND OUT HOW YOU WERE PRIOR TO CONCEPTS,
PRIOR TO BODY-KNOWLEDGE,
PRIOR TO BEINGNESS.

We undergo this process to find this out. This process is also illusion. Knowledge is also illusion. But, you have to use knowledge just like a ladder or an address card. After reaching the destination, you can throw away the directions.

In *I Am That* and *Master of Self-Realization,* these Masters are trying to convince you, the reader, of your Ultimate Truth, Final Truth. In the light of that knowledge, you have to convince yourself, so that "I Am That".

THIS IS A MATERIAL BODY.

YOUR PRESENCE IS INVISIBLE, EVERYWHERE.

Ultimate Reality has no face. You have to have Self-Conviction. It is up to you to convince yourself. The Master has placed your Identity before you. Now it is up to you to accept it.

YOU HAVE TO CONVINCE YOURSELF.

IT IS UP TO YOU ALONE.

Just like if someone brought you a good dish, you wouldn't just describe it like, "Oh! What a very good dish", you would eat it! You would consume it. Similarly, with the teachings, with this Knowledge, don't just say, "Oh very good, very good, what is next?" Eat what has been given, and digest it! What do you say?

Q: Yes, absolutely! I am eating everything voraciously!

Maharaj: It is a beautiful journey. It goes deeper and deeper depending on the devotee. Take all the teachings. Take everything. Take all the riches, not just a couple of rupees!

84. *Master Shows You 'God' in You*

Maharaj: Everything is within you, so you don't have to go and search anywhere else, either physically or mentally. You need to do the practice to gain this Conviction.

THE EXPECTATIONS YOU HAVE THROUGH SPIRITUALITY

WILL BE FULFILLED BY THE EXPECTER

THAT IS ALREADY WITHIN YOU.

That expecter is called God, *Atman, Brahman, Paramatman*. When the Spirit clicked with the body, your expectations started: I want peace, complete happiness, peaceful life, tension-free life.

These expectations started in childhood. The child is crying, crying because it can't explain or make sense of what is going on. In our country when the child cries, we give him honey. Once the sweetness is tasted, the child is happy.

Similarly, after entering the so-called world, we expect so many things to bring us happiness, to make us sweet. Why? Because the Spirit, the Presence finds beingness intolerable, insufferable, unbearable.

BECAUSE PRIOR TO EXISTENCE, PRIOR TO BEINGNESS

THERE WAS NO UNHAPPINESS OR HAPPINESS.

Q: That's interesting! This morning I was meditating, and Bhausaheb Maharaj's Presence was there. He spoke, saying, "Surrender all your joy and happiness!" At the time, I did not know what to make of it. Why should I give up what was positive in my life? Surely joy and happiness are not problems! No! I'm keeping that, I thought. If he had said, "Surrender all your pain and suffering", I would have obeyed, instantly! But now, I get it. Prior to Beingness there was neither happiness nor unhappiness. Happiness or joy is body-knowledge, so it has to go!

As a barometer to gauge spiritual progress, I have looked for peace, joy, bliss, happiness, not realizing that all this is part of body-knowledge.

Maharaj: No happiness or unhappiness. Everyone is struggling for peace, travelling here and there. You have come all the way here to find peace and happiness. Happiness is unknown to you. You try to find it through entertainment, money, sex, power, and even through spiritual experiences and so on. But in spite of all these different sources, it escapes you.

HAPPINESS IS UNKNOWN TO YOU
BECAUSE YOU ARE UNKNOWN TO YOURSELF.
THE ROOT PRINCIPLE OF HAPPINESS WITHIN YOU
REMAINS HIDDEN FROM YOU,
UNKNOWN TO YOU.

You accept this unbearable body-knowledge, and the subtle body-form of mind, ego, intellect, and then you look for ways to find peace. You approach Masters, go to temples and holy places. This may give you temporary happiness, and relief like painkillers, but nothing permanent.

And then you visit another temple, and another, like a travelling circus. Someone says, "Go here, go there. Do this, do that". And still, in spite of all this roaming, all this travelling, nobody is showing you that God is within you.

NOBODY IS SHOWING YOU GOD IN YOU.

There is no need to go searching here and there any more. Now you are at the destination, you have reached the Final Destination. This is the Ultimate Truth. So you have to stick at it. You have to mean it, and take it seriously.

THE PREVIOUS JOURNEY IS TO BE FORGOTTEN.
NOW YOU ARE HOME YOU NO LONGER NEED THE ADDRESS
OR THE ROUTE THAT WAS TAKEN.

Time has gone, years have gone, and confusion has been added. Every day confusion was added. But now, you have come to the Direct Destination, it is already within you.

YOU NEED NOT GO SEARCHING
BECAUSE YOU ARE NO LONGER A BODY.
ALL YOUR WORRIES STARTED WITH THE BODY.
NOW GO TO THE ROOT.
EVERYTHING IS ROOTED WITHIN YOU.

Q: In my head I know that, but I have difficulty going to the root, and I am still very attached to Anthony.

Maharaj: Body-related knowledge will not give you happiness. You can say: "I am *Brahman, Atman, Paramatman,* God", if you wish, but this is all body-knowledge. You are neither *Brahman, Atman, Paramatman,* nor God. These names are given for the beingness. They are good names, but your Existence is beyond that. Your Presence is beyond that.

YOU ARE ULTIMATE TRUTH,
YOU ARE FINAL TRUTH.
YOU ARE THE FATHER OF THE WORLD.

Q: Maharaj, how do I realize that Ultimate Truth that I am?

Maharaj: We are giving some processes, medicines to keep your head strong.

Q: Sounds good!

Maharaj: Do you have any Master?

Q: Not any more. I had a Master for a long time, and I loved sitting at his feet.

Maharaj: What was your conclusion after being with this Master? What did you realize or understand?

Q: I don't know if I had any understanding, I just felt how much love was there. It was very nice being with him. I felt a lot of love coming from the heart.

Maharaj: Knowledge is essential in order to help you understand and realize your true Reality. After reaching the destiny, forget the address. You must have strong faith because if your faith is lacking, thoughts will continue forcing you to go here and there. There is no stability with the continuous flow of thoughts. It is restless, distracting, encouraging you to keep going here and there.

Q: That's true!

Maharaj: How long are you going to be going to different Masters for? Why are you going to so many Masters? What have you achieved? Approach the kind of Master who will show you God within you, as Ramakrishna Paramahamsa did with Swami Vivekananda. Exceptional! He had spoken with so many other Masters, before finally meeting a true Master. A rare occurrence!

Approach the kind of Master who will show you God within you, as we do in our long Lineage. This is empowered by the sacred *Naam Mantra*, the Master Key. You will never find this Direct Knowledge anywhere else.

So stop! Stop! Make sincere efforts, so that you don't become a victim of the mind again.

STAY WITH ONE MASTER ONLY.

Have some faith! Mind is always tempted to 'text-message' you, "Go here! Go there! Come on! Time to move on!" There needs to be a full stop.

HOW LONG ARE YOU GOING TO SEARCH FOR PEACE?

Who wants peace? Who wants happiness? Try to find out. Ask your Inner Master questions like, "For the last fifty years I have been struggling for peace. What did I find? Who was struggling?"

LOOK AT YOU!
LOOK AT YOU!
LOOK AT YOU!

85. *Your Hard Drive is Choked*

Maharaj: The concept of death is coming slowly, slowly to frighten you. And the body is becoming old, older and older. Act according to your spiritual age. Spirit knows itself through the body only, and wishes to live for a longer time.

Be your own Master, your own teacher. The moment you KNOW perfectly, there won't be any fear of death. This body does not belong to you. If anything goes wrong with it, you are to be unconcerned. Every day we read of people dying in the newspapers, some accident, xyz dies, we don't bother too much. If a close relative dies you are crying, weeping because you have some attachment to that person.

Similarly, you have a lot of love and affection for this body. You try to protect the body and you have a very close relation with it. You don't want anything going wrong with it. If this happens, you will do your best to protect it. You will make great efforts to protect it. You will go to the doctor so that he can get rid of your suffering, and of course, even prolong your life.

Q: I see a lot of suffering in my line of work. When people are dying, some of them who have faith, lose it. They ask, "How can God allow so much pain?"

Maharaj: We have created the world. In the dream, you see so much suffering.

ALL THESE STICKY CONCEPTS
THAT ARE STUCK TO THE BODY MUST BE MELTED.

Let them all melt, and place yourself prior to beingness. Let yourself be Selfless Self.

Q: I think that for me, faith is difficult because I am getting old, and I have gone into so many different teachings. And still my mind gives me no peace.

Maharaj: These are all thoughts. Forget all you've read and listened to. You are like a big computer. It should be completely blank. Your house is overcrowded, your house is overcrowded. Yes?

Q: That's true. My mind is too active.

Maharaj: Forget your mind, when did you come across with the mind?

YOU ARE THE WITNESS OF YOUR MIND.
YOU ARE THE FATHER OF YOUR MIND,
BUT YOU ARE NOT THE MIND.

You know what thoughts are going on inside. You are witnessing the thoughts of the mind, good thoughts, bad thoughts. You say 'my mind'. You are not the mind. You say 'my mind', 'my hand', 'my body'. You are not the body.

You are not the body, the hand. 'My finger' means that "I am not the finger". You see everybody talks about my finger, my body. You are indicating my body. So like that, my mind, my ego, my intellect, all this stuff is totally separate from you.

You say, my child, my father, my brother. You are totally different because you are witnessing: "my father, my child, etc." So you are not that. All these are relations: mind, ego, intellect are related. They came after. They came with the body.

You are following the instructions of all these relatives. You are following instructions of all these relatives - mind, ego, intellect, which you are not.

If you have any doubts, then clear them. In spirituality, this is very important. Don't accept knowledge with doubt. You have to be perfectly clear. If there is any doubt, just ask.

IF YOU ACCEPT THE KNOWLEDGE
AND STILL HAVE DOUBTS,
THERE WILL BE CONFUSION.

If you accept the knowledge with doubts, there will be confusion.

Q: I think for me, getting rid of my doubt is not that easy. I am old. I have gone on so many different paths, and none of them have really been what I was looking for.

Maharaj: First you have to convince yourself. You are a good doctor. You know what is good and what is bad. So being a good doctor, you can cure yourself, you can cure yourself. You are your own doctor, with all the drawbacks, problems, you know where you stand. What to do, what not to do?

First you need to remove all the wrong bytes from your computer. Everything should be cleared out.

If the hard drive is full up with information, you cannot try anything new.

Q: That's true. It's choked. The hard drive is full, and it doesn't work properly.

Maharaj: Overcrowded with thoughts. So what I have been talking about, remember it, and then try to find out what is Ultimate Truth. And then it will come, the realization that "I am the Ultimate Truth, without any body-form".

Q: So, Maharaj, will you help me empty my hard drive?

Maharaj: If you are interested, then it is not a problem. But what happens is that many people are coming to me with some problem or other. I am telling them all this that I have been telling you, but then, after leaving here, they come across another Master who influences their wavering mind once again! I feel sorry for them because they have missed an opportunity.

Q: I think I am different, because I had virtually given up, and was disappointed because I could not find what I was looking for. I am serious! I mean business. I have travelled halfway across the world. After seeing the website, something resonated in me, so I am not going anywhere else after here. This is the terminus.

Maharaj: This is the last stop, the terminus. OK, today I will give you some instructions on how to meditate, and how to make yourself happy without any material cause. I am not doing anything special,

I AM SHOWING
THE ULTIMATE TRUTH WITHIN YOU.

And then there will be no need to go anywhere, just like in the story of the beggar boy. When he came to know that he was rich, he stopped begging instantly. I am telling you this in order to convince you.

When you come to know that what you are searching for is the God, the *Brahman*, *Atman*, *Paramatman*, that is within you, you find that the God, Master, *Brahman*, *Atman*, is your own reflection, your projection without the body.

WHY TRY TO FIND GOD,
OR MASTER OUT THERE,
WHEN YOU ARE YOUR OWN MASTER?

Nisargadatta Maharaj says, "I am not making you a disciple, I am making you a Master".

Q: I have heard that. Yes, it is beautiful. It stops you running, it stops the chase for something supposedly out there. You know it is already inside.

Maharaj: You must be sincere about receiving the *Naam Mantra*.

Q: I think I am sincere. But of course, then the mind comes in and says, "Maybe you are not really sincere".

Maharaj: The mind, ego, intellect, everything will be erased.

Q: Sounds good! I wanted to share with you Maharaj that I lost my husband of many years just last year. I guess my heart is still heavy with sadness.

Maharaj: It happens with everybody. Those who enter this world are to, willingly or unwillingly, leave this world, [He claps]. Relations are formed along with the body. When you were not the body, were there any relations? When we were not the body, we were not knowing our son, our father, mother, husband, wife, nothing like this.

Did you have any brothers, sisters, mothers a hundred years ago? And what sort of relations will be there after a hundred years? All relations are body-related relations. Even the Master-disciple relationship is body-related.

Q: When Nisargadatta Maharaj's wife passed, he carried on teaching as normal.

Maharaj: What courage! The same thing happened in the case of Guru Ranadev, when he was told his only son had died. He was about to deliver a lecture in a big auditorium at the university. He gave the philosophical lecture regardless. Afterwards he said: "God has given me a gift, now he wants to take it back". So, even in that instance, which is really beyond imagination, his ability to control what he must have been going through was so very impressive.

Q: That's a wonderful story, powerful!

Maharaj: Where does this courage come from? It comes out of this spirituality because you KNOW. You know that the entire world is illusion. In order to have that courage, there is the discipline of meditation. It bestows great courage and opens up the Knowledge.

EVERYTHING IS WITHIN YOU.
REALITY WILL OPEN UP.
YOU NEED NOT GO ANYWHERE AGAIN.

86. *These are Only W.O.R.D.S.*

Q: I have been studying and following the teachings of Nisargadatta Maharaj for years, but I feel stuck. I don't seem to be making any progress.

Maharaj: You have expectations of making spiritual progress with the help of body-based knowledge. Through the intellect and subtle ego, you are expecting spiritual progress. Even when you are staying with a great Master like Nisargadatta Maharaj, you have to accept what he says, and not just go along with the literal knowledge.

UNLESS YOU ERASE YOUR BODY-BASED KNOWLEDGE,
YOU CAN BE WITH A MASTER FOR A HUNDRED YEARS,
AND IT WON'T MAKE ANY DIFFERENCE.

You have accepted the body-mind identity, and through it, you are expecting some progress towards the Ultimate Truth. You won't get it. These are open facts, you are not the body, you were not the body, you are not going to remain the body. "Except your Selfless Self, there is no God, no *Brahman*, no *Atman*, no *Paramatman*, no Master".

THESE ARE WORDS ONLY.
FIND OUT THEIR MEANING!

What kind of progress are you expecting? Miracles, publicity, money, sex? What progress? Unless you know yourself in a real sense, your so-called progress will not have any meaning.

HERE, REAL PROGRESS MEANS
THAT TRUTH IS ESTABLISHED TOTALLY WITHIN YOURSELF,
WITH THE RESULT THAT, YOU HAVE NO EXPECTATIONS.

No happiness, no unhappiness, no experience, no experiencer. No witness, no witnesser. If at all you have to compare, compare yourself to the sky. Sky does not have its own feeling 'I am'. This 'I am' feeling is also illusion because your Identity is beyond that, beyond imagination. There are no limits. So, what progress are you expecting? Progress is related to the body-knowledge.

WHO IS EXPECTING PROGRESS?
IF YOU ARE LOOKING FOR MIRACLES
OR YOU WANT TO SEE GOD, IT WON'T HAPPEN.
EVERYTHING IS WITHIN YOU,
EVERYTHING IS PROJECTED OUT OF YOU.

The moment there is awakening, you see the world. The world is fresh, Presence is fresh. Presence disappears, world disappears.

Q: When I meditate, I have not had any of the signs that you speak of, which makes me feel that I am at the very beginning. No progress!

Maharaj: Absorbing is going on, even when you feel nothing is happening.

DON'T EXPECT ANY EXPERIENCE.
YOUR PRESENCE IS GREAT EXPERIENCE.

Who wants progress? You know better now. You are no more an individual. What is the progress of sky? Sky has no individuality. Similarly, you were knowing yourself in the body-form, but now you know better. When the Master places before you the Ultimate Truth, your Ultimate Truth, little by little, you will be less concerned with the body-knowledge.

It is ego that says, "I stayed with Nisargadatta Maharaj for ten years, twenty years". What have you learned? What did you learn? Did you come to learn or think about the Master in a body-form? It is the ego that says, "I stayed with Nisargadatta Maharaj, or with some other famous Guru". This happens because you are thinking something like, "I must get some power from the Master!" You need to use discrimination. Don't expect anything.

At the initial stage, you are a devotee. After that, at the last stage, you are Deity.

DEVOTEE AND DEITY. DEVOTEE AND DEITY.
NO SEPARATION.
DEVOTEE AND DEITY, NO SEPARATION.
DEITY KNOWS THROUGH DEVOTEE.
DEITY LIES WITHIN THE DEVOTEE.

You are viewing the deity and the body as two separate entities because you are still considering yourself to be an individual. This is OK in the beginning. At the advanced stage, you will realize, "Yes, I am Deity". You will Realize Deity.

Q: Why is the Master important?

Maharaj: Because the Master is converting - These are only W.O.R.D.S - the Master is converting the Listener to the Ultimate Form. The Master is already within you. You are considering yourself to be a devotee until you know the Reality. Master says, "You are Deity".

People who stay with a Master for many years with high or low expectations, will not realize. They will not realize because they are looking for some so-called realization in the form of miracles, power and so forth, for the ego.

YOU HAVE TO GO TO THE MASTER,
TOTALLY HUMBLE,
AND SURRENDER.

That Spontaneous Presence is not within the circle of body-knowledge. The body is only the external part.

THERE IS NO BIRTH AND NO DEATH.
YOU ARE UNBORN.

How long are you going to be a devotee for, still seeking, looking, wanting, grasping? You are to surrender yourself to the Master, without any expectations. You are to surrender yourself to the Master, then everything will be fully absorbed.

THE MASTER IS USING DIFFERENT WORDS
TO TRY AND CONVINCE YOU,
BUT THE DEVOTEE IS STILL NOT ACCEPTING IT.

I will tell you again: reading spiritual books, and living with the Masters for long periods will not help you find out what the Master wants to convey, what he wants to say.

Suppose you wanted to go to a certain place. You have an address, so on your way there, you pass certain landmarks like a swimming pool, statue, etc. You are going the right way to get to the destination. On reaching the destination, you are there. Once you are there, no more progress is needed.

When you talk about progress, some individuality has to be there. Progress is body-related. But you are not the body. Does sky have any progress? It is as it is. Everything is within you. You have not to search because there is 'NO WAY'.

ALL WAYS COME FROM YOU, AND GO TO YOU,
BECAUSE YOU ARE ALWAYS WITH YOU.

All ways start from you and end in you, because you are always with you. [Master chuckles.] No maintenance needed. It is always there.

YOU HAVE TO COME FORWARD,
COME FORWARD AND SURRENDER
TO THE MASTER.

If you put this process into practice, then you will find happiness within you.

GO DEEPER AND DEEPER.

87. *Insect Justice*

Q: I don't want to leave. It is difficult. I am happy here. I don't want to go home.
Maharaj: We are already with you.

YOUR HOME IS NOT AMERICA OR INDIA OR ENGLAND.
YOUR HOME IS THE WORLD.
YOUR PRESENCE IS LIKE SKY, BEYOND LIMITS.
YOU ARE EVERYWHERE.

Q: I can feel that connection between us Maharaj.

Maharaj: You are welcome to return. We are expressing our Knowledge. It is not a particular type of knowledge, not bookish knowledge. This is an opportunity for all of you to know yourselves. This is the final outcome, the Final Truth.

There should not be any type of temptation to go anywhere because this is the terminus. So, strictly, and with full confidence, accept this Truth. With full confidence, accept this Truth. It is Reality. Your Reality. You are no longer concerned with the body because you never came across the body prior to beingness. You are not going to remain in the body-form. You are not going to remain in the body-form. Correct? Why worry?

That means it is a logical deduction. You are not this, you are not that, (*Neti-Neti*) you are not... so, "Who Am I? I am Ultimate Truth." It is a process of induction and deduction. Logic. Induction, deduction, logic. This is not, this is not, but this is... So, it helps you.

Accept the Truth. Don't be a victim of concepts.

WE LIVE WITH CONCEPTS,
FROM THE START OF BEINGNESS,
TILL THE END OF BEINGNESS.
BUT THERE IS NO START FOR SELFLESS SELF.
NO END FOR SELFLESS SELF.

Prior to beingness, you were totally unaware of all this illusion. During the span of beingness, you have been under the pressure of all these concepts and stuck in the circle of body-knowledge.

YOU HAVE TO GET RID OF ALL THESE CONCEPTS
BECAUSE THEY ARE NOT ULTIMATE TRUTH.
IF YOU DON'T,
THEY WILL FOREVER CROWD YOU,
TILL THE END OF BEINGNESS.

Prior to beingness your Presence was there, but it was Invisible Presence. After the disappearance of the beingness, your Presence will still be there. Invisible. So you are no longer concerned with the body, and no longer concerned with the world. It is open fact. Why fear? You know that the body is not your identity, so why fear?

I am hammering home the same teachings again and again because you still have some confidence in, "I am somebody", which is giving you trouble all the time. "I am somebody else, man or woman. I am *Brahman, Atman, Parabrahman*, God and so on". These never-ending concepts keep creating problems for you, like an insect that keeps on stinging you.

This sting is difficult to reject completely because you have been trained to react in this way from childhood. It comes from a need to protect the body. This behaviour has to be unlearned.

In India, we tell the story of insect justice. A big insect makes its house in a wall. He then captures and puts a small innocent baby insect inside this hole in the wall. The large insect begins making the sound, "whoo, whoo, whoo!", to instil fear into the imprisoned insect, and then stings it. The vulnerable imprisoned insect suddenly experiences really strong fear for the first time in its life. It quickly learns how to protect itself by making the same sound, and stinging the big insect back.

So the insect's behaviour is learned. Likewise, our behaviour is learned, and because of vulnerability and fear, the ego starts to protect itself. Conditioning and impressions were imposed on Spirit like illusory layers.

As a result, the survival instinct becomes stronger and stronger over a lifetime: "I don't want to die, I am afraid", etc. Out of this conditioning, the Spirit starts accepting wrong knowledge and says: "I am I! I am somebody! I am very important!" This is mistaken identity. Come out of this whole illusionary world! There is no birth and there is no death.

Q: You were saying that the state of beingness is intolerable, and that is why we need happiness and go looking for peace out there?

Maharaj: All unhappiness, happiness, peace, temptation, concepts of birth, rebirth, death came along the moment beingness started. Prior to beingness, you were unaware of everything and anything. [Master claps].

I AM INVITING ATTENTION,
DRAWING YOUR ATTENTION
TO HOW YOU WERE PRIOR TO BEINGNESS:
NO SHAPE, TOTALLY UNKNOWN,
TOTALLY UNAWARE,
NO CONSCIOUSNESS, NO UNCONSCIOUSNESS.

Q: No knowledge, no concepts, no problems.

Maharaj: No experience, no experiencer. There were no problems. The problems came when beingness began. Your existence, your Identity is prior to beingness. Since you started considering yourself as, "I am somebody", a form, body-form, all these problems arose.

SO COME OUT!
COME FORWARD!
HAVE COURAGE!
THE THINGS WHICH ARE NOT,
YOU ACCEPT WITHOUT QUESTION.

Why are you accepting all that when you know it is illusion? Take courage from this, strength. You have immense strength and power, but you are not using that power. What to do, what not to do, what will happen? What will not happen? Why worry? What will happen? Nothing will happen. Nothing has been happening. Nothing is going to happen. Nothing!

Q: I do not realize all this yet, but I think you were saying that if I continue practising the Mantra, then the Knowledge will come.

Maharaj: Don't worry! Nisargadatta Maharaj's speeches and lectures were very touching, but at that time, I was not able to understand the teachings fully. He used to say, "Listen to me! Listen to Me!" In time, I gradually realized what he was saying.

Self-Knowledge! Knowledge of your own Identity! What do you mean knowledge? Just to know oneself in a real sense, that is Knowledge. To know oneself in a real sense is Knowledge. All that we know about ourselves is in body-form. This is not your Identity. You were never a body, you are not going to remain a body.

Whichever body you are holding now has an end. It is not your Ultimate Truth. Some day or other, you are to willingly or unwillingly leave this body, therefore body is not your identity, and all concepts, body-related concepts are illusion.

Simple, simple knowledge. Knowledge is also illusion. There must be a knower to know knowledge.

THERE IS NO KNOWER, THERE IS NO KNOWLEDGE.

Listen to me, listen to me! Concentrate on what I am telling you, and record it within you. Your Inner Master is a good recorder. The recorder is always on. Record it!

Q: What about meditation?

Maharaj: I told you that meditation is a must. Meditation and *bhajan*s. Meditation and *bhajan*s will help you melt, and dissolve your strong concepts, illusionary thoughts. Very simple. Don't stress your mind, don't stress your brain. You won't need to go elsewhere if you do the practice. If you continue to talk about 'last *prarabdha*', 'last *karma*', 'next *karma*', then this means that you are still misguided.

There are so many Masters in the world whose teachings are misleading. They say you have taken birth because of your last *karma*. They are anticipating all sorts of illusionary, imaginary things, and trying to pressurize you.

YOUR ROAMING DAYS HAVE FINISHED.
AM I CLEAR?

Q: Very clear, thank you Maharaj.

Maharaj: Don't worry! Deposit everything here. Deposit all of your ego and intellect. You are a free bird. Fly! Sky is the limit.

Q: Sky is the limit? [laughing]. No limit! Beyond the sky! Beyond that!

Maharaj: You can fly with your own wings and go anywhere because you are omnipresent. You are omnipresent.

88. *Bless Yourself*

Q: What about experiences while meditating? Things like lights, flashing lights, white lights, different coloured lights, different phenomena, visions that you might have in meditation? Are they a part of the body, aspects of the mind? Is that right?

Maharaj: All experiences are progressive steps. They are not Ultimate Truth. Without the Presence of the experiencer, no one can experience anything? Without the Presence of the experiencer who is experiencing? Your Spontaneous Presence is needed for you to say, "This is a good experience, or bad experience".

WITHOUT YOUR SPONTANEOUS, INVISIBLE PRESENCE,
YOU CANNOT WITNESS WHATEVER IS TO BE EXPERIENCED.

Therefore, your Presence is most important. It is coloured with the body-form, and that is the illusion. Meditation is the first lesson to erase or dissolve the body-form. You will overcome all this material knowledge with this discipline.

Q: Maybe you could speak about the concept of the self identifying with the body. Siddharameshwar Maharaj says, "That which has no bondage is having bondage", and you said that, "the Spirit clicks with the body". It sounds like the mind has ambushed the body, and that the mind somehow needs to be convinced to commit suicide, and that's the practice?

Maharaj: All the saints talk Reality. Instead of analyzing their statements, pay attention and accept what they wanted to convey. We are not here to analyze the statements of Siddharameshwar Maharaj, Ramana Maharshi and other Masters. It is what they wanted to convey that is most important, that Reality, and how it is connected with your Selfless Self.

Don't quote anybody's statements, we are not analysts. Analyzing what the Masters have said, and comparing their statements is the cause of debate. We are not here to debate anything. We are not here to analyze the sayings of various saints. I am hammering the ego. It is the ego that enjoys these comparisons and analyzes.

What the Masters conveyed, the Reality they shared through their statements, or lectures or through their advice, is what is most important, truly important.

Q: Which is the Conviction.

Maharaj: Of course!

Q: Again the Conviction that all this is unreal is what seems to be the most....

Maharaj: It is not intellectual conviction, it will be Spontaneous Conviction, just like this body is called man, or this body is called woman. You are not dreaming as a woman, and she is not dreaming as man, because there is Conviction that this body is called man or woman.

So like that, your Ultimate Truth is *Brahman*. This is the Conviction so that even when you are talking, discussing or completely involved in doing something, you still know that, "I am beyond that. My Presence is beyond that. I am no longer connected with the body-form". That is Spontaneous Conviction.

Q: So really all these questions, all this analysis, all these are really dissolved or answered through the meditation?

Maharaj: There is no question of analyzing. All this confusion, all this conflict, all this illusion is supposed to be dissolved completely. When will it be dissolved? As you draw closer and closer to your Selfless Self. That means, "I no longer have any connection with the body. I was not having any connection with the body, therefore the body is not my identity. That is Ultimate Truth".

This will be accepted spontaneously. It is called Conviction. Though you are living in the body-form, you are totally unconcerned with the body-form. This is a golden opportunity through which you can realize, through which you can be enlightened. Self-Enlightenment, Self-Realization.

THERE IS NOBODY BLESSING YOU.
THERE IS NOBODY GRACING YOU.
BLESS YOURSELF.
YOU HAVE TO BLESS YOURSELF.
YOU HAVE TO GRACE YOURSELF
BECAUSE YOU ARE ULTIMATE TRUTH.

You are fully and totally independent. The dependent one will say, "I am going to see a famous Guru who will bless me, and give me grace". This is all imagination that has come from conditioning, brainwashing, culture. All illusion!

Slowly and silently and permanently, the Reality that you are Ultimate Truth will be realized. After having this Conviction, there won't be any fear of death and birth because you will KNOW that you are unborn.

Q: Does speaking with you fortify that Conviction? Our paying attention to you and your teaching, does that bring us strength?

Maharaj: I am sharing the Knowledge that was shared by my Master, Nisargadatta Maharaj.

Q: Yes, thank you, it is a wonderful grace.

Maharaj:
MAINTAIN, NURTURE AND PRESERVE
WHAT YOU HAVE LEARNED.

What you have heard, maintain and retain. Your involvement is most important. Dry discussion on spiritual knowledge alone will not help. You have to implement the Knowledge in a practical way. Practise in the sense that you press down on your Identity. Churn over your Identity, your Invisible Identity which is called *Brahman, Atman, Paramatman,* God, Master.

Spiritual Knowledge will give you the courage to face problems, material problems or otherwise. All problems are related to the body-form, physical problems, mental problems, intellectual problems, logical problems, egoistic problems, there are so many problems. All problems are connected with the body-form.

Prior to beingness there was no problem, no family, no world, so there was no question of family.

FAMILY LIFE STARTED THE MOMENT
THE SPIRIT CAME ACROSS WITH THE BODY.
WHY GIVE SO MUCH IMPORTANCE TO THE FAMILY?
OKAY, TAKE CARE OF YOUR FAMILY,
BUT THERE SHOULD NOT BE SO MUCH ATTACHMENT THERE.

Do your duties and carry out your responsibilities, without any expectation. Don't be too involved with family as it will divert you from the Reality, and take you back to the illusion. It is better not to connect or link family problems to spirituality. Just remember what we have discussed, remember and absorb it.

Q: Yes, we will. The teachings are very clear. The way you communicate them is very simple.

Maharaj: So now you have to bring this Knowledge and put it into practice. Don't mix family life with spirituality. Spirituality has its own aspects, and family life has its own aspects.

THE SPIRITUAL LIFE HAS NO CONNECTION TO FAMILY LIFE.

Where will your family be after the body disappears? Where will your family be? Prior to beingness, nothing was there. I am repeating the same thing to everyone. Prior to beingness there was nothing: No family, no world, nothing. After the body dissolves, nothing will remain.

WHATEVER WE SEE IN BETWEEN,
IS THE PROJECTION OF YOUR SPONTANEOUS PRESENCE.
WHATEVER WE SEE WITHIN THE SPAN OF BEINGNESS
AND DISSOLUTION OF BEINGNESS,
IS THE SPONTANEOUS PRESENCE,
THE PROJECTION OF THE WORLD.

YOU ARE THE FATHER OF THE WORLD.

Q: So, what we experience and what we go through is our own projection?

Maharaj: Yes, of course, because without your Presence you can't experience anything.

Q: So we have to realize that we are creating whatever we go through?

Maharaj: Your Realization should be Spontaneous, natural, and not intellectual realization. Realization means just to know oneself in a real sense. It is the absorbing of the Reality, of Knowledge, your Knowledge.

You are completely separate from this world. You are separate from the whole family, and separate from the body. Without Presence, you can't visualise the world. So how you were prior to beingness, and how you will be after the dissolution of beingness, that is your Spontaneous Identity, Invisible Identity, where there are no words or worlds.

WHERE THERE ARE NO WORDS AND WORLDS,
THERE YOU ARE,
SPONTANEOUS, INVISIBLE.

Your Spontaneous Presence has given birth to each and everything. Unless you see yourself, you can't see the world.

Q: And that is the Conviction?

Maharaj: After knowing this, Spontaneous Conviction will appear in you. It will be Spontaneous: "I am the Final Truth, Ultimate Truth which is called *Brahman*, *Atman*, *Paramatman*, God. That is my Invisible, Anonymous Identity". You will be totally fearless.

89. Who Is Falling In Love?

Q: I spent ten years or so with a Sufi Master. I practised meditation and felt a close connection in my heart to this Master. After that, I became interested in Zen Buddhism and spent a few months meditating with the monks, and generally I felt it was very beneficial. But even after all this, I was still left feeling the need for something other, something more, and that was when I found Siddharameshwar Maharaj.

Maharaj: What was your conclusion after making these efforts and practices?

Q: The ego needs to be annihilated completely, and when that happens along with the mind, there is nothing left but love, but the divine, the Self. I believe and feel very devoted to that and the practice.

Maharaj: All these efforts, all these exercises, all this knowledge, they are only related to the body. You see, basically, you were not a body, you are not a body, you are not going to remain a body.

The moment the Spirit clicked with the body, all these different philosophies were needed. Why? Just to have peace, happiness, a tension-free and fearless life. Everybody's making lots of effort reading Buddhism, Zen, the Sufi Masters, other religions and philosophies. There is a vast amount of spiritual knowledge out there.

BUT YOUR IDENTITY IS UNIDENTIFIED IDENTITY.
PRIOR TO BEINGNESS,
YOU DID NOT NEED ANY KIND OF SPIRITUAL KNOWLEDGE.

All these needs came after, along with the beingness. And all these religions, philosophies, practices are connected with the body. It does not matter if they are ancient or modern, they are all body-knowledge, without exception.

Q: So, really, anything that we identify as having to do with the body-knowledge, anything material, I should just discount? There is nothing to ponder over or consider, or know except the fundamental question, "What is prior to that?"

Maharaj: Just know yourself. What we know of ourselves is in the body-form. What is your fundamental identity?

WHEN YOU ARE CONVINCED
THAT THERE IS NOTHING EXCEPT YOUR SELFLESS SELF,
THERE IS NO NEED OF ANY KNOWLEDGE.

Q: The concept that I came to understand with Sufism and other spiritual practices was beyond words. Really the basis of a lot of that practice was falling in love with the Master. Becoming one through love with the Master led to being free.

Maharaj: Who was falling in love? You are not an individual. Since we started considering ourselves as individuals all this overcrowding of so-called knowledge has projected so many concepts. Just to know yourself is enough.

Knowledge, spiritual knowledge or any knowledge has its own limitations. It is simply messaging, conveying that, "Except your Selfless Self there is nothing". But you are not in any form. Your Selfless Self is not in any form.

What we are talking about, we are considering it with form, like, "I am a Master, or disciple or devotee". We are taking ego that, "I am somebody". But after having Ultimate Truth, you realize that you are nobody, because you are everybody. So stop measuring yourself in body-form.

Q: One of the differences I find with this way, your way, Maharaj, is that the Master leads you to realize what is in you, what you are naturally. With the other orientation, what I experienced was like you were merging with something outside yourself, which is maybe only a subtle difference or distinction, but it feels significant. To take something that you already are, and realize something that is right within you, as opposed to merging with something that is outside yourself.

Maharaj: We are using so many words but behind all that is your Presence.

WITHOUT YOUR PRESENCE
YOU CAN'T UTTER A SINGLE WORD.
YOU ARE PRIOR TO EVERYTHING.
KNOWLEDGE CAME AFTERWARDS.

90. Forget All You Have Read!

Q: I am not a very relaxed person. I am thinking, thinking all the time. I am saying, "Why? Why? Why?"

Maharaj: Stop thinking! There is no 'Why?' at all. There are no questions. Better to stop thinking. Thinking is the cause of your depression, the cause of your feeling bored. There is so much thinking because you are very, very sensitive.

Q: I am very sensitive. And I know that my 'sensitivity' is an illusion too. It is just the body and mind consciousness. But I do, I am always analyzing things, you know.

Maharaj: Forget all these words, all these concepts: consciousness, body, mind. Forget it. Everything you have listened to and learned, you are to forget. Forget it all entirely.

FORGET EVERYTHING YOU HAVE EVER
LISTENED TO AND LEARNED.

Q: A clean slate, wipe it off? Yes that sounds great! I feel like crying because I have never had that kind of closeness of understanding before. I always read books, read, read, read, useless!

Maharaj: Whatever you see is illusion. Whatever you see is illusion. But the Seer is not illusion. In the absence of the Seer, how can you see the whole world? In the absence of the Seer, how can I say, "I can see, I can see". Who is the Seer? The Seer is the Invisible Self within you, taking images of what you see.

Q: I can feel the truth in your words. Dissolving...

Maharaj: Just relax. Stop thinking. Don't stress your mind or your intellect. Just be very, very simple and humble. Forget about all that you have read and heard before.

Q: No more books for me!

Maharaj: Forget about all your spiritual words. Consciousness and mind and ego... nothing was there. You are prior to all that, prior to everything.

Q: How long should I meditate for?

Maharaj: There is no time limit. After reaching the destination, why do you ask, "How long should I meditate for? Addresses are used to try and find the way. After reaching the destination, you no longer need the address. Meditation is like that. After you have the Conviction, meditation is not needed.

Q: You have cleared up so many concepts. Right now, I am overwhelmed to speak with you, and with all this truth and clarity. As I work through what you have told me, I am sure questions will arise. I had this experience and now I have lost interest in the world.

Maharaj: Make a note of your questions for next time. This is all a kind of mental entertainment, physical entertainment, spiritual entertainment. Your Identity is beyond that. Because you are fixated with "I am a body", you need a lot of entertainment, like visiting places, going to the movies, going out for dinner. All this entertainment is to make the bodily feelings bearable. Did you have any entertainment prior to beingness? Prior to beingness you were unknown to you. After the body dissolves, you will remain unknown to you. Were you watching the movies prior to beingness?

BEINGNESS IS UNBEARABLE BECAUSE
YOU DO NOT KNOW YOURSELF IN A REAL SENSE.

Knowing yourself in the physical body, the mental body, the spiritual body, is illusion. The entire world is illusion because it is projected out of your Spontaneous Presence.

But you are not paying so much attention to the Reality. You are paying so much attention to the body-form, the mental form. You are thinking, always thinking and creating great problems all the way through, making them rooted to this thinking, of depression, boredom, lack of interest, the body, all these things. So much energy is wasted at this mental level, intellectual level, physical level. Your Identity is beyond that.

SO MUCH ENERGY IS WASTED AT THIS MENTAL LEVEL.

Q: I used to love to eat, but now that's gone, everything is gone. I take each day as it comes, and I don't concern myself too much. The experience was like an explosion!

Maharaj: Human beings are struggling with petty, petty matters. They are miserable! Just see how you were prior to beingness, no individuality! After dissolving the body, after leaving the body, no struggles. Stop thinking! Don't think so much. Thinking appeared after, along with problems, stress, confusion, struggles. Prior to body-knowledge there was no thinking. Who is thinking? The Invisible Thinker is there.

YOU ARE NOT CONCENTRATING ON THE THINKER,
THROUGH WHICH YOU ARE THINKING.
YOU ARE CONCENTRATING ONLY ON THINKING.
YOU ARE CONCENTRATING ON THINKING
INSTEAD OF ON THE THINKER.

In the absence of the Thinker, you can't think. The Thinker is the Unidentified Identity. The Thinker has no shape. It is Unidentified, Invisible.

Q: I still look at myself as an individual.

Maharaj: Everything is within you, but you keep forgetting that, and again and again return to the body-based knowledge. Be normal. Don't think so much!

Q: I know I do! But I understand something better now. Having a glimpse of the truth is not the Ultimate Reality. So no matter what I have been through, it is not Ultimate Reality. I am the Ultimate Reality. Even if I was taken to heaven to see God!

It doesn't matter what I go through. I understand it is all part of the illusion. It is all part of a game. I understand now, that I took that experience and made myself the experience. And that is where I made the mistake.

Maharaj: Now you are to absorb this understanding, absorb it fully within you.

Q: I also realize how helpful Self-enquiry can be. Who is unhappy? Who is the thinker? Yes, I got a lot of my mind cleared up.

Maharaj: There is no mind. Again and again you are talking of the mind. Mind is your baby. You have given birth to the mind.

QUESTION YOURSELF,
DON'T QUESTION ANY OTHER.
YOUR INNER MASTER IS VERY POWERFUL.

Question that Master: "I read so many books, I meditate for six to eight hours. What is the outcome? What is the result?" Ask yourself these questions. This will lead to knowledge.

What you are doing at the moment through body-based knowledge is illusion. That 'I' is creating so many problems. Your problems will not disappear until that 'I' is erased. So many problems came along with 'I'. When there was no 'I', there were no problems.

Q: I feel so refreshed, thank you, Maharaj.

91. My Master is Great

Maharaj: How long are you going to be without limbs, saying, "Oh God, Oh God! Help me, God"? God does not have any existence without your Presence. Without your Presence, God cannot have any type of existence.

YOU HAVE GIVEN BIRTH TO GOD.

You have given birth to God. Your Presence is needed for you to say 'God'. You have a lot of importance, therefore don't underestimate yourself.

Live as an ordinary man, a humble man, without ego. You are not to stress your mind and intellect. Live a very simple life. All sense of individuality will go, after knowing the Reality. No ego!

Q: No need to entertain the mind?

Maharaj: We are entertained by so many different concepts that we have created: *Brahman, Atman*, God, *maya* and so on. We go around with the chest sticking out, so proud, saying "I am *Brahman*". All this talk is about nothing. We are talking about the unborn child.

Nisargadatta Maharaj used to say, "If good things happen, I am not happy, if bad things happen I am not discouraged. If someone speaks eloquently, I am not impressed. All thoughts don't apply to me because I am not the body at all".

Know that you are not the body. Your Presence is like the sky or space. The sky does not know its own identity. If you abuse the sky, does the sky retaliate? Sky does not know its own existence. Sky does not know its own Presence.

Q: With actions, is it helpful to offer everything to *Brahman*, or remember *Brahman* in everything?

Maharaj: What actions were there prior to beingness? Action and reaction came after beingness, not prior to. There is no action. You need an actor for any action. There is no actor at all. No actor! There is no actor. See, and listen, I already told you that you are not the body. It's very easy, but also very difficult.

Therefore you must have complete faith within you, and equally, you must have complete faith in your Master. Nisargadatta Maharaj and Siddharameshwar Maharaj both had a lot of faith in their Masters. They would say, "My Master is great". There was never any compromise.

YOU MUST SURRENDER TO THE MASTER.
HAVE COMPLETE FAITH IN YOUR MASTER.
LET IT TOUCH YOU: "MY MASTER IS GREAT".

Q: Unreserved belief in the Master.

Maharaj: Visitors to Nisargadatta Maharaj asked some difficult questions. Maharaj replied instantly. He always attributed this to his Master, saying, "It is only by the grace of my Master, Siddharameshwar Maharaj, that I am talking". It is the same here now. I am only talking now because of my Master Nisargadatta Maharaj, because of him only.

Q: Are questions only used to eradicate doubt?

Maharaj: Questions are there because the body is there. Prior to the body there were no questions.

Q: So there is no need to ask questions?

Maharaj: Ask questions! The Master is talking about the spiritual life, your existence, Spontaneous Existence, your own story. You are to convince yourself.

Q: What is Conviction?

Maharaj: Conviction means what you are not.

CONVICTION MEANS WHAT YOU ARE NOT.

At present, we are knowing ourselves in body-form. The body-form is not your Identity. After knowing that, Conviction means: "I am beyond the body-form". What you are cannot be defined.

WHAT YOU ARE, CANNOT BE DEFINED.

92. *Commando Training*

Maharaj: Daily practice is essential. Always be on your guard. You should always be alert and maintain your armour. That is why we are giving you commando training. There should not be any type of temptation because there is nothing more to know.

Prior to beingness you were not in any form. Prior to beingness you were not in any form. And after the body dissolves, you are not going to remain in any form. Totally formless.

Spiritual knowledge is to be listened to, so that all your memories will be erased.

ALERTNESS IS REQUIRED.
BE UNSHAKEABLE!

Don't become a slave to someone else's thoughts. So many stalwarts are around trying to impress their own ideas on you, to do this thing, that thing.

Q: What you are saying is don't be bullied?

Maharaj: People are exploiting spirituality. It has become a profession. Be wary and careful of those who are taking advantage of vulnerable seekers in the name of spirituality, and extracting money from them. After Conviction, after knowing the Reality, be firm, don't be swayed by others, by anyone. After having this Knowledge, you must maintain it continuously.

Q: OK, OK.

Maharaj: You say, OK, OK. Protect yourself. The moment you leave the premises, there will be all kinds of influences around vying for your attention. So be strong, be alert, constant, disciplined, determined, courageous. And don't mix with the wrong company.

BE YOUR OWN SECURITY GUARD.

Q: For twenty-four hours.

Maharaj: So that if at any moment you are distracted, you will be alert.

IT TAKES A LONG TIME TO GROW A TREE,
BUT IT ONLY TAKES FIVE MINUTES TO CUT IT DOWN.

Nisargadatta Maharaj once said to me: "If anyone takes a drop of poison, he does not need to think about what the effect of that poison will be because it will act spontaneously".

Similarly, this drop of nectar in the form of the *Naam Mantra*, will lead to Reality. It is already inside you. You do not have to think about it. The body-form that is covering the Invisible Listener will be erased. It is a fact that you were not the body, so all illusory concepts will dissolve. Reality will open out.

Q: I had a dream last night, Maharaj, that I was going off to die. There was a small tear about to fall from my eye. And in that tear, I could see images of the suffering of the 'human condition', as it were, down through ages. It was about body-knowledge. There was awareness of what was going on, and the tear and death were seen for what they were, both illusion.

There was knowingness within the dream, that this was the effect of the meditation and practice coming through, self-revealing in the dream state. And of course, the whole purpose of the practice is to be awakened to the fact that you are not the body, you never were the body, there is no death, you are unborn.
Maharaj: Correct.
Q: And the death of the body should really be a happy event, not a sad event.
Maharaj: The Reality will be absorbed. When that time comes, you will forget all about your body identity. As Nisargadatta Maharaj used to say, "This is a food-body". So just continue with the meditation. Continue with the cleaning process.
Q: I am working hard with the meditation and being disciplined.
Maharaj: As I told you, the Spirit is very sensitive. It is just like if you throw a ball against a wall, it will come back to you with double the force. Similarly, when you are meditating, it will come back, rebound with double the force. Conviction will come back double the force. But strong meditation is needed. If you throw a ball with full force, immediately it will rebound. Similarly, if you are meditating with full force it will rebound with the Thoughtless State. It is very simple.

Therefore reciting of the Mantra is a must and thereafter it will be spontaneous. Even in deep sleep there will be meditation. You sense, you see some vibrations with the reciting of the Mantra. It is spontaneous. You can listen through the internal ear, not this ear, but the internal ear. Miraculous experiences are often related. There is exceptional happiness. Maintain the continuity of practice.

93. *You Are Subtler Than Sky*

Maharaj: Now for our revision of Reality.
Q: Yes Maharaj, you were talking about keeping bad company. Bad company is the ego, intellect and mind, so even on your own, you can be keeping bad company.
Maharaj: The ego, intellect, mind represent the inbuilt bad company within the body, the physical body and spiritual body. Publicity, money and sex are the bad friends. Greediness, attraction and jealousy are also bad friends. They can all distract you from the Reality and cause body-based conflicts. But this kind of talk is only for beginners. You are no longer a beginner.
Q: Sometimes there is a sense of progress, and I think: "Oh, I have done this". I watch it and witness it occurring. I do see it as illusion, and know that I am not the doer, that my Spontaneous Presence has to be there first, for anything to happen.
Maharaj: Yes, your Presence is essential for everything: to say something, to do something, anything. If your Presence is not there, who will talk about the world? Who will talk about the ego? Who will talk about God? Who will talk about the Master and the disciple?
YOUR INVISIBLE,

ANONYMOUS,
UNIDENTIFIED PRESENCE IS EVERYWHERE JUST LIKE SKY,
AND YOU ARE SUBTLER THAN SKY
BECAUSE SKY IS WITHIN YOU.

You are sleeping, the dream begins, and suddenly your Presence comes into focus - projection. Instantly, the whole world is projected. The dream world came out of you, because it is within you alone. The dream world came out of you because of your Knowledge that lies within. Similarly,

THIS WORLD CAME OUT OF YOU SPONTANEOUSLY,
AND YOU BECAME VISIBLE.
THEREFORE EVERYTHING IS SOURCED IN YOU.
SEE EVERYTHING AS COMING FROM WITHIN YOU.

You are a Master. You are your own Master. You are Ultimate. This is Open Truth.

Q: I understand that the body offers an opportunity to self-realize?

Maharaj: Correct! The body is an opportunity to realize. It is like a ladder, a medium, call it what you will. By itself, the body cannot work. By itself, the Spirit cannot function. It is the combination that is crucial, significant, important. The combination of Spirit and body enables you to say, 'I'.

IN ORDER TO SAY 'I',
THERE HAS TO BE A BODY,
AS WELL AS THE SPONTANEOUS PRESENCE
THAT WE CALL 'SPIRIT'.
WHEN THESE ARE JOINED TOGETHER,
YOU SAY 'I'.

Using the simple example of a matchbox and a matchstick. By itself, the stick cannot produce fire, neither can the box do it alone. But with one strike, a click, there is fire. But for that fire, some combination, some direct effort is needed.

Fire is everywhere, but it is unknown, invisible. Similarly, your Spontaneous Existence is everywhere, but you are only knowing yourself through the body.

Q: You often say, Maharaj, "This is the Invisible Reader's or Invisible Listener's story"?

Maharaj: When you read any spiritual book, your attention should be like this: Know that what you are reading is your story, the Reader's story, the Reader's Knowledge, and not the Knowledge or the story of the *Brahman, Atman, Paramatman,* God, Master.

IT IS YOUR STORY.
LISTEN TO THESE DISCOURSES AS YOUR STORY,
DESCRIBING YOU.
IT IS THE LISTENER'S STORY,
THE LISTENER'S IDENTITY,
THE LISTENER'S IDENTIFICATION.

You can use any words you like. Just remember, it is an open fact, that you are not the body. This is a food-body. You have to give it food for it to be effective. If you don't feed it, then you can say, "Ta-ta".

94. The Finder is Ultimate Truth

Q: I have been a seeker for the past twenty years, but I have never met someone to help with my search. The only way I have gotten help is through books mainly. Maharaj, you are the first person, the first teacher I have ever met. For the last twenty years, I have been reading books, that is all.

Maharaj: Where do you stand, after reading these books?

Q: I have come to the final realization that I am not a person, I am not a mind, I am not a body. And there is something around me, around. No, not outside, but around here, that is the real path. Sometimes I can feel it very, very strongly, but sometimes I don't get that feeling. I was meditating this morning and it was very powerful. I could feel the power, the presence. The body was almost not there. But when I come back to my daily routine, it seems to fade.

Maharaj: Very good. You need not make a lot of effort. What you understand through your reading is supposed to turn into Conviction. We are holding the body, and through it we are acquiring and collecting a lot of knowledge. What is the purpose of knowledge? What we call knowledge, has been formed out of illusory concepts.

EVEN AFTER READING THESE SPIRITUAL BOOKS,
WE ARE NOT FINDING REALITY
BECAUSE THE SO-CALLED KNOWLEDGE IS BODY-BASED KNOWLEDGE.
THERE IS EGO.

Conviction has to be established fully. Only then, will you come to know the Ultimate Truth.

WHATEVER YOU FIND,
REMEMBER, THAT THE 'FINDER' ITSELF IS ULTIMATE TRUTH.
THE FINDER IS THE VERY TRUTH
THAT YOU ARE TRYING TO FIND OUT.
THE FINDER ITSELF IS REALITY, GOD.

There are concepts everywhere. Without the body, you cannot have beingness. And without your beingness, you cannot recognize God. If your Spontaneous Presence were not there, then no one can speak of God. Your Presence is needed for you to be able to say, 'God'.

This means that the concept of God was created by you, just for your happiness. But you are unknown to yourself. You are unknown to your Power, you are neglecting your power, your energy. You are underestimating your energy.

GOD IS A CONCEPT
THAT WAS CREATED BY US FOR OUR HAPPINESS.

Conviction will come through meditation. Meditation means concentration. Concentration means concentrating on the Concentrator, until both disappear. When you forget your body, there will be Exceptional Silence. The aim is to be completely in touch with Selfless Self.

In brief, you are Final Truth, Ultimate Truth. You must have this Conviction. This is the shortest way to Ultimate Truth, Final Truth, Naked Truth.

YOU CANNOT UNDERSTAND THE REALITY INTELLECTUALLY.

We understand everything intellectually, but intellectual understanding will not serve your purpose. It has to be out-and-out complete Conviction. And for this, all concepts or body-knowledge need to be dissolved. You will not find any difficulty because you have a good base.

Q: You know Maharaj, all these things came to me spontaneously, because it was not that I knew anything. I am a Christian, and I never thought of this in my religion. Jesus Christ said the same thing many times, for example, he said "Before Abraham was, I am". Now I realize. It came spontaneously.

Maharaj: "I belong to this religion, that religion". There is no religion. There was no religion prior to beingness. All religions have been created to establish a peaceful society.

Q: I like going to church when it is quiet, and sitting in the silence. I can usually sit for quite a long time, and do my own meditation.

Maharaj: It is not a problem. It does not make any difference. When you go to church, just remember that there is nothing except for your Selfless Self.

THERE IS NOTHING EXCEPT FOR YOUR SELFLESS SELF.

So don't look for anything else, don't look for something more. There is nothing.

EVERYTHING IS WITHIN YOU.

You are just like the sky. Your Presence is just like the sky. Sky does not have any feeling. Sky does not have any fear. Sky does not know whether it was born or unborn. Therefore, your Identity is totally unborn.

Q: I have read all the Nisargadatta Maharaj books, and his Master Siddharameshwar Maharaj's Teachings, also the *Dasbodh*. Intellectually, I have read all these. I really get a lot of strength from these books. Every night I don't go to bed, without reading at least a little from them.

Maharaj: Very nice, I am happy. Now, this knowledge which you have grasped intellectually has to be absorbed spontaneously within your Selfless Self. You have got a good background, foundation. You will not find it difficult.

Q: I am searching through all my waking hours.

Maharaj: Full self-involvement is essential.

95. *You Have Made the 'Reader' Separate*

Maharaj: Don't depend upon book knowledge, bookish knowledge. You have sufficient literal knowledge. Reading spiritual books, books on philosophy followed by dry discussions may give you momentary happiness, entertainment, but nothing more. All bookish spiritual knowledge, literal knowledge is dry knowledge.

Yes, it is related to the Unidentified Identity, but when you are reading, you are separating the reader from the knowledge: "I am the Reader".

WHEN YOU ARE READING,
KNOW THAT IT IS THE READER'S KNOWLEDGE.
WHEN YOU ARE LISTENING,
KNOW THAT IT IS THE LISTENER'S KNOWLEDGE.
IT IS YOUR KNOWLEDGE.

THERE IS ONENESS, NOT DUALITY.

Read as if someone wrote your biography: "Oh, this is my biography! My story!". This is the way, so that there is no separation, no duality.

You are reading your own story in these spiritual books, not a story about something different, something separate that is called *Brahman* or *Atman*, *Paramatman* or God. These are concepts indicating Reality, your Reality. It is very important to know how to read, and how to listen. This is the greatest story ever told, your story!

EVERYONE IS READING BOOKS,
BUT IN THE BODY-FORM,
WITH THE MIND, EGO, INTELLECT.
THEN THEY ARE ANALYZING THE WORDS
AND COMPARING THE TEACHINGS AND THE MASTERS.
THIS IS DRY KNOWLEDGE.
LET THE INVISIBLE READER, READ THE BOOKS.
LET THE INVISIBLE LISTENER, LISTEN TO THE MASTER.

Unless there is the Conviction of Oneness, the knowledge is pointless.

THE AUTHOR OF THE BOOK, THE WORDS,
AND THE READER, ARE ONE.

This is Reality. You can go on talking and talking about the same thing, using different words. I am placing before you, your Reality, not the Reality of *Brahman*, *Atman*, *Paramatman*, God.

'THAT', IS NOT IN ANY FORM.

Knowledge, what did the knowledge point to? Don't try to analyze it or scrutinize the words. There are so many words out there, that we can easily get lost in a maze.

You have a good base. You have good foundations. You have some maturity and Conviction but you are 'coming down', taking ego by analyzing and making comparisons with everything you read. The Invisible Speaker in me, and the Invisible Listener in you are One and the same.

THE SPEAKER, [here, the Master]
WHO IS GIVING KNOWLEDGE IS SIMPLY IMPARTING
THE INVISIBLE SPEAKER'S KNOWLEDGE.
THE LISTENER IS SUPPOSED TO LISTEN TO
THE INVISIBLE LISTENER'S KNOWLEDGE.

Forget worldly identity! As I told you, you are not a body and you are not going to remain a body. Whatever you listen to, whatever you read is coming from your Presence alone.

After beingness, you started identifying with 'God', saying, "God is great". Prior to beingness you did not know the word 'God'. "What is *Brahman*? What is God? God is a concept. You did not know anything about 'Master' and 'disciple'. All these concepts came the moment Spirit clicked with the body.

I AM DRAWING YOUR ATTENTION
TO THAT WHICH IS PRIOR TO BODY-KNOWLEDGE.

After reaching the destination, throw away the address. Nisargadatta Maharaj used to say: "This is not a way, this is the Ultimate Truth, Final Truth, the Final Destination.

YOU ARE FINAL DESTINATION. THERE IS NO WAY.
WHERE ALL WAYS END, THERE YOU ARE.

When my Master told people to forget everything they had read, and then talk, what he meant was that he did not want you to talk from within the circle of bookish knowledge, literal knowledge.

THIS KNOWLEDGE IS MATERIAL KNOWLEDGE
BECAUSE THIS IS A MATERIAL BODY.
THE BODY IS A MATERIAL BODY.

You are Ultimate Truth. Now convince yourself.

96. *God's Spectacles*

Q: If you say that the awakening is sudden, then does that mean it is not profound?

Maharaj: That is not so. You must have complete faith in yourself. When you come to know the Ultimate Truth, that, "I am Selfless Self", the door will be open, and no effort will be needed.

When you come to know that "I am a rich person, not a beggar", this is a sudden realization. The change happens instantly. The beggar does not carry on with his stories about being a beggar for the next fifteen years. That person who was once a beggar has gone.

Q: This person disappears?

Maharaj: He is gone! There won't be any person. Don't measure yourself in body-form. It is an open fact. Forget about spirituality. I have told you, first you are a small boy, then older and older. These changes apply to the body only. There is no person!

Q: So as a child you think of yourself as on a journey. Even as a grown-up you think you are on a spiritual journey, when there is no 'you' in the first place. So it is mistaken identity. There is no journey, no....

Maharaj: It is the deer and musk story.

Q: Jumping about, looking for itself.

Maharaj: It is like that. We use so many stories to establish Ultimate Truth. All these stories just to establish your Ultimate Truth. You are Final Truth. You are unborn.

Q: Are you established in Ultimate Truth?

Maharaj: What can I say? There is no 'you', there is no 'I' at all. It reflects. By the grace of my Masters, I am not thinking. Instant answers appear spontaneously. It can happen to you also, [said with voice raised]. What I am telling you can happen to you also, but unless you are Self-Absorbed you will find it difficult. The Master is giving you spectacles to wear, God's spectacles, eyes to see through the illusory world.

Don't take my words literally. Words are only a necessary medium. What we are talking about is the Listener's story. But the Listener is Anonymous, Invisible. When I say something, you are listening. There is some analyzing taking place spontaneously. Who is the analyst? Who is discriminating? It happens spontaneously.

I am inviting attention of that analyst who is analyzing my thoughts which you are questioning. Who has created the thoughts? Behind the thoughts is your Invisible Presence. Out of that Presence, thoughts are projected instantly.

I say something, then the questions come, answers come, thoughts come. How did that thinking process start? It started out of your Spontaneous Presence. Thoughts are projected out of that Presence. Out of that Presence, thoughts are projected. You started thinking, "I am somebody". You are nobody.

Q: How long is a Guru needed for?

Maharaj: For as long as you are a disciple. The Presence of the Guru is already within you, but you are viewing yourself as a body. You consider yourself in body-form. A Guru is therefore needed. You had an address, and this address brought you here. After arriving at this ashram, you no longer needed the address. It has served its purpose.

YOU HAVE ARRIVED.
YOU HAVE ARRIVED AT THE DESTINATION
BECAUSE YOU ARE FINAL TRUTH, YOU ARE ULTIMATE TRUTH.
UNFORTUNATELY,
YOU ARE NOT ACCEPTING THE ULTIMATE TRUTH,
AND THAT IS THE PROBLEM.

The same principle, the same thing is being placed before you again and again, in different words, different sentences, using different stories, but the principle is one. "Except your Selfless Self there is no God, no *Brahman*, no *Atman*, no *Paramatman*, No Master".

You are your own Master. You are your own *Paramatman*. But since you are measuring yourself in the body-form, you are unaware of your Ultimate Truth.

You have to stand on your own feet. You are not handicapped. All this body-knowledge has made you view yourself as disabled, disadvantaged, incapable. The Master says, "You are not disabled at all. You can walk using your own legs. Remove these artificial limbs. You have to learn to stand on your own two feet".

You must have courage! It is a lack of courage and a lack of confidence that leads to problems: "Oh I am weak". Jump in and swim! This is the only way you can be strong. The swimming teacher throws the child into the water, and then, next moment, he is swimming. His confidence grows. The Master is creating confidence in you.

THE MASTER IS BUILDING CONFIDENCE IN YOU.
YOU ARE HOLDING ALL THIS POWER,
BUT YOU ARE UNAWARE OF IT.
YOU ARE UNAWARE OF YOUR STRENGTH.
YOU CAN FACE ANY CHALLENGE.

Have courage, like this: "Let any circumstances come to me, and I will face them head on". This is how you should be. Don't run away from difficult circumstances. Thoughts are coming and going, coming and going.

YOU ARE ON THE BANK OF THE RIVER
WATCHING THE RIVER FLOWING.
YOU ARE CALM, UNDISTURBED,
AT PEACE.

97. Should I Give Up My Work?

Q: When we are on the quest, is it helpful for us to disengage from our activities, say, for example, give up my profession?

Maharaj: Don't concern yourself with this matter. This has nothing to do with your bodily activities. You can carry on as normal.

Q: No, but my work requires thinking, so I have to function as the mind-body.

Maharaj: As long as you are considering yourself as a somebody, an individual, all these questions will keep coming. You are nobody at all!

YOU ARE NOBODY, AND BECAUSE YOU ARE NOBODY,
YOU ARE EVERYBODY.
BECAUSE YOU ARE NOBODY, YOU ARE EVERYBODY.

You have had this body-knowledge your whole life. You have been conditioned by a continuous stream of concepts, so many rapid endless thoughts, like an express train. It happens. But now you must take courage and stop. Stop thinking so much! Concentrate! Concentrate on the Concentrator. Everything is within you. This is Open Truth. You can accept or reject it.

Q: But why don't we give up something?

Maharaj: The complete Truth, in full, is within you. Have absolute confidence in that! Why these questions? You are trying to cure some weakness, some weakness of mind, weakness in confidence. Unless that weakness is removed, you will keep coming up against all kinds of difficulties.

You believe you are weak. You are not weak at all! Nothing is impossible for you. Why compromise? Have courage! Have some faith in yourself!

THIS IS TRUTH, OPEN TRUTH, FINAL TRUTH.
WHATEVER TRUTH IS THERE,
I AM PLACING BEFORE YOU.

I am sharing this knowledge, given by my Master. I am placing your knowledge in front of you. You may accept it or not, that is up to you.

Nisargadatta Maharaj used to say the same thing to me: "You must have courage. Don't waste your life. Listen to me, listen to me", he would say.

THE INVISIBLE LISTENER IS RECORDING EVERYTHING
WITHOUT YOUR KNOWLEDGE,
AND THEN THAT KNOWLEDGE
WILL BE EXPOSED AND REVEALED TO YOU.

I had faith in my Master, total faith. So I am now talking to you from Direct Experience. I realized that nothing is ever impossible.

Q: When I first came across Nisargadatta Maharaj in *I Am That*, one of the phrases that really jumped out at me was when he said to some visitors from America or wherever: "I am beyond all this! Beyond the world, beyond the sky, beyond the universe, beyond all this". And I thought, Wow! That is really impressive! And for him to have this Conviction, was even more impressive. That is what got me in.

Q2: I found Ramakant Maharaj through Facebook, and my friend heard about him through the website. Your teachings are very absolute. They are not for everybody because as you say, "All body-knowledge has to go". But then again, if someone is ripe, the teachings are perfectly suited.

Maharaj: Time is very short. Each and every moment of your life is valuable.

BE WITH YOU!
DON'T LEAVE YOURSELF BEHIND
TILL THE END OF YOUR LIFE.

Try to know yourself in a real sense now, otherwise the concepts, illusions, thoughts will keep on pressurizing you. Your life will end in confusion and conflict.

Have the courage to face the concept of death. There is no death for you, only for the body. Your life should be fearless. It can be fearless: just remove the ego! Literal knowledge is not useful. Literary knowledge is not useful. This is all little knowledge. You are not little, you are great. You are Almighty! You are Great! Therefore find out your Greatness! Self-discover, uncover your own Knowledge. Then you will find Great Knowledge in abundance.

INTELLECTUAL KNOWLEDGE IS NOT ENOUGH.
YOU ARE TO GO TO THE ROOT.
GO DEEPER AND DEEPER.

Books may give you some temporary relief from worldly pain, but you need to go to the root and find out who you are. Go to the Source and Realize your Power. You are underestimating yourself all the time. Listen to me and accept what I am saying:

YOU ARE GREAT,
YOU ARE ALMIGHTY.

Now is the time to be serious, to look within, to go to the root. The moment of death should be a happy moment.

98. There is No 'I' in Sky

Q. I have a question about working on the ego, making an effort to dissolve the ego. What can I do?

Maharaj: As long as we are considering ourselves in body-form, all these questions will arise.

Q: Even though I try, it seems impossible to do anything to get rid…

Maharaj: It will happen automatically. Nisargadatta Maharaj says if you take one drop of poison you need not ask, "What will the consequences be?"

SIMILARLY, THIS SPIRITUAL KNOWLEDGE
IS A DROP OF NECTAR
WHICH WILL AUTOMATICALLY TAKE ITS COURSE.
IT IS ADDRESSED TO THE INVISIBLE LISTENER,
AND NOT TO YOU.

Don't bring the 'I' in. You need not think about what may, or may not happen.

Q: It just works on its own?

Maharaj: This is addressed to the Silent Listener, and not to you.

Q: I just want to disappear.

Maharaj: Be careful not to get mixed up with that 'I'. You are just like the sky.

Q: Yes, I know, even beyond sky…

Maharaj: Sky is everywhere. English sky, American, Indian sky, it is not different. We have divided the sky by naming it: 'English sky', 'American sky' or 'Russian sky', but there is no difference at all because sky is sky. Likewise, with spiritual knowledge, *Brahman* is *Brahman*. It's not the case that James' *Brahman* is different from Michael's *Brahman*, because *Brahman* is *Brahman*.

Ultimate Truth is called *Parabrahman*, or *Atman* but we are discriminating with the use of this mind and intellect. So don't use your mind! Forget about it! Mind came after. It does not have its own independent existence. You are supplying power to the mind. It is only because of your power, that the mind functions.

THE MIND WORKS WITH YOUR POWER.
IT IS YOUR POWER ALONE
THAT MAKES THE MIND WORK.

The ego functions with your power. If there were no power, what would happen to this body? The fact is you are Final Truth and therefore you are unborn. In order to have this Conviction, you have to undergo this process. The Knowledge has to be absorbed. If you have any questions or doubts, do not keep them to yourself. Clear all doubts.

Q: I know all this. I know this is the Ultimate, completely, but still there is some subtle individuality remaining.

Maharaj: When you say "I know this", it is illusion. Prior to beingness, you did not know anything. Prior to beingness, you did not know that you were *Brahman*, *Atman*, or *Parabrahman*, God. You did not know anything. It was just like, "I don't know". "I don't know" is the perfect answer. You are your own Master, and you will be able to answer all questions.

Q: I can't dissolve myself and I get frustrated. I know I don't exist. This "I don't exist" is just like a thought. 'I' comes in and then it goes.

Maharaj: Stop thinking! Just remain! Be! The poison is acting, that drop of nectar has already gone inside. Don't worry about what may or may not happen, or about any of the consequences. The mind is a crazy mind. The mind is very crazy.

IT BECOMES SILENT FOR SOME TIME,
AND THEN IT WILL FIND A WAY OF COMING BACK.
IT IS LIKE THE DOG'S TAIL WHICH IS INSERTED INTO A TUBE
IN ORDER TO STRAIGHTEN IT.
BUT THE MOMENT THE TUBE IS REMOVED,
IT CURLS UP AGAIN.

Q: When the mind becomes silent, I don't think it is dissolved, maybe just hiding.

Maharaj: Listen to me! I am hammering the same thing:

MIND DOES NOT HAVE AN EXISTENCE OF ITS OWN.

WE HAVE GIVEN BIRTH TO THE MIND.

Where is the mind? For this discussion we are using the mind. It took birth the moment the Spirit clicked with the body, and you started saying, "This is my mind". We have given birth to the mind. Open fact.

Q: But this I? When you say "my mind", "my ego", is this "I" the ego?

Maharaj: All this confusion is caused by the words. And as I told you, there were no words prior to beingness. Why do you give so much importance to these illusions? 'I', is also an illusion and that's why I told you: "No 'I', no mind, just sky... no 'I', no mind, just sky". Does the sky have an ego?

The impact of all this body-knowledge must dissolve. To do this, you are given the meditation practice so that, slowly, slowly, slowly, you will come to the Ultimate Truth. "Ah! So that I! I Am That".

I am knowing myself in body-form. This body is a food-body. Who is acting in this food-body? This food-body is not going to survive. It has an age limit, a time limit. If you want to know yourself in a real sense, you have come to the proper place. Are there any questions? I am here to answer any questions.

Q: So much to absorb! I just want to kill the 'I'.

Maharaj: This is nonsense talk.

THERE IS NOTHING TO KILL.
I HAVE TOLD YOU
THE 'I' IS ILLUSION.

Do your practice and develop your base knowledge as well. Read *I Am That* again and again and *Master of Self-Realization*.

The notes from Siddharameshwar Maharaj's lectures were taken down by Nisargadatta Maharaj, and these became the book *Master of Self-Realization*. In those days, there were no tape recorders. Parts of these talks might be missing, but Nisargadatta Maharaj managed to write down the majority of them, because he had a strong base. He was able to understand what Siddharameshwar Maharaj wanted to convey, and therefore this book is very effective.

All this Knowledge is very simple, very simple Knowledge, but people have made it so complicated, that now it appears as if it belongs to someone else, and not to you.

YOUR KNOWLEDGE HAS BECOME ALIEN,
EXTRANEOUS.
IT DOES NOT BELONG TO SOMEBODY ELSE!
IT BELONGS TO YOU!
IT IS YOUR KNOWLEDGE!

Q: Sometimes I feel very connected to what you are saying, and every word speaks, but at other times, it's not so clear.

Maharaj: As I told you, this happens because of a lot of impressions on your subtle body. This causes an imbalance of thoughts. But just remember that the mind, ego and intellect came afterwards.

Compare yourself to an actor in this world. We are acting as a man or a woman in the drama of life. But you are neither a man nor a woman. In this way, try and convince your Unidentified, Anonymous, Invisible Identity.

99. Self-Love

Maharaj: Maurice Frydman put in a lot of effort for the book *I Am That*. He was in his seventies. A frail, small man, he had great command of a lot of spiritual teachings, and had been with Ramana Maharshi, Krishnamurti, the Dalai Lama, Gandhi, etc. His last stop was Nisargadatta Maharaj. He found my Master's Knowledge exceptional and felt compelled to bring awareness of these teachings out into the world. He used to bring his tape recorder and film camera with him, and spent hours listening to Marathi, English, Hindi translations. He was very, very humble. OK, any questions?

Q: Not at this moment. I have been absorbing, trying to take things in. Yesterday you spoke about self-love?

Maharaj: Self-love has to do with the body. Prior to beingness, there was no love, no affection. There was nothing. It's because of body attachment that you love, that you love yourself the most.

Q: Do we have to transcend self-love or be with self-love?

Maharaj: It should not be body-orientated love, mind-orientated love, ego- orientated love.

SPONTANEOUS SELF-LOVE
MEANS HAVING COMPLETE PEACE.

We are using words to try and impress the Reality. When we came across with the body, we came across love. When we came across with the body, we came across love, affection, ego, intellect, mind. Prior to that, there was nothing.

It is natural, love is bound to be there because we are attached to the body, and have a lot of affection for it. We have body relationships with our mother, wife, husband, sister, brother, father, therefore affection is bound to be there. If someone close 'disappears', and dies suddenly, you feel sad. It's quite natural. Suppose your close friend or father, sister, mother pass away, it is natural for you to feel some sadness, because of that love, that established love. Though we know this body-love is not permanent, even so, this feeling is bound to be there.

With spirituality, that attachment remains only momentary. Immediately, we come to know that this world is illusion. Everybody is going to have to leave this world willingly or unwillingly. So out of that Knowledge of Reality or Ultimate Truth, you derive courage. You say, "OK, it happens". And you get this feeling just for a second. "Today it is him, tomorrow it might be me". Your attachment has to dissolve.

THIS NON-ATTACHMENT WILL HAPPEN SPONTANEOUSLY
WHEN THE ULTIMATE TRUTH IS
ESTABLISHED IN A REAL SENSE.

Real sense means not in the body sense or the mental level, intellectual level. All these are coming and going, coming and going. Be the witness!

Suppose you love someone in a dream, and then in that dream, she dies. When this happens, you start weeping. But as soon as you wake up, you say, "Oh, it was just a dream!" What has happened to that dream and your loved one? In the dream you were crying and weeping, but when awake, it was all quickly forgotten.

Spirituality means awakening out of illusion, illusionary thoughts and feelings. It means having the Conviction that the entire world is illusion, including your food-body. All food-body-knowledge needs to be dissolved. One should not make any deliberate effort, just understand, try to understand.

YOU JUST HAVE TO KNOW THE REALITY,
ACCEPT THE REALITY,
YOUR REALITY.

Prior to body-knowledge, your Presence was there. After dissolving the body-knowledge your Presence will be there, but not in any form. If you want to make comparisons, compare yourself to the sky. During an earthquake, the houses that were standing collapse. Does anything happen to the sky?

The sky appears not to be there when we live within walls that seem to block it. Sky is present, but we say, "This is a temple, this is an ashram, this is a kitchen, these are rooms". We give them names. "This is England, this is Russia". Can you bring a little bit of America to India? No! The names are causing you problems and creating separation and illusion.

COME OUT OF THESE COMPARTMENTS.
IF THERE IS A HUGE TREMOR, ALL THE HOUSES COLLAPSE.
BUT WHAT HAS HAPPENED TO THE SKY?
NOTHING, IT HAS NOT BEEN AFFECTED!

Similarly, your Spontaneous Existence does not know itself, whether 'I am', or 'you are'. This is the Ultimate Stage: no 'I am' or 'you are'. Just listen to me, because of body identity we know each other, but if the body identity disappears, it remains just like sky.

To realize this, you have to keep up the practice, step by step. Little by little, you will know everything. The Knowledge must be established with Conviction. Conviction! Conviction! Then there will be complete Peace. You will be talking, doing your job, looking after the family, but without involvement, detached and casual.

100. There Must be a Full Stop!

Q: Maharaj, it is very important for me to get initiation from you and get the *Naam Mantra*.

Maharaj: First of all, do you have any Guru or Master?

Q: I have! My Guru is Nisargadatta Maharaj, and you are his disciple. For me it is the only way to get initiation into this Lineage. And this is why I have come to meet you.

Maharaj: To give you the Mantra is not a problem but only if you intend to undergo strict discipline. Without meditation, you will not be able to realize Ultimate Truth.

You already know, "I am *Atman*, *Paramatman*, *Brahman*, God, everything". However, to establish the Reality within you, strong dedication is required. Some people are taking the Mantra and not concentrating, not taking it seriously. Then they go elsewhere because of a roaming mind and lack of Conviction.

The Mantra is not a miracle tool, it is not a magic wand. The magic wand is in you. We are regenerating your Power. Power is there, but you are unaware of your Power. You have tremendous Power in you.

Q: So during the meditation, I should concentrate on the Mantra and have the feeling that I am *Brahman*?

Maharaj: Don't feel! Don't feel during the meditation. You've not to feel. Don't make any deliberate effort, it will be Spontaneous. Don't do anything, just follow it. Don't think anything, like, "I'm *Brahman*, I am *Atman*", it will happen automatically, spontaneously.

Whatever Mantra is given, just recite it. Repeat the Mantra. Don't think: "What will it do for me?" Don't think at all, anything. It will automatically happen, spontaneously happen. It is the Master Key.

Knowledge is in you, not outside you. Everybody has knowledge, but you are unaware of the Reality, therefore you are begging for blessings. "Oh God help me, bless me, do something!" And going to different places to see various Masters.

We have created very, very sweet words like *Brahman*, *Atman*, *Parabrahman*, God, but they are still only words. Fine words, fine stories in spiritual books.

WHOSE STORY IS IT?
WHAT IS BEHIND *BRAHMAN*?
GO DEEP AND DEEP AND DEEP. NO BLIND FAITH!

Q: I don't know what happened there during the *bhajans*, but I could not stop laughing. I felt I was just going higher and higher, and filled with so much happiness, that the laughter just exploded. I was trying to contain it, but I could not stop myself.

Maharaj: It is nice! The *bhajans* bring a lot of Spontaneous Happiness. The vibrations are very strong, with high meaning.

Q: I really like the evening ones, there's a line that goes, "Always meditate on the Guru who is Absolute. Don't forget to worship him because he's the only one who gives the correct understanding". And then something like, "He is all knowledge. Sing the *bhajans* because he is the illuminator". Just wonderful!

Maharaj: The meditation and the *bhajans* together are a very good combination. *Bhajan* and meditation are most important because with *bhajans* the inner Spirit gets Spontaneous Happiness. Bhausaheb Maharaj said:

"YOU WILL COME TO KNOW ULTIMATE REALITY,
THROUGH THE MANTRA AND THE *BHAJANS*".

Nisargadatta Maharaj said, "There must be a full stop to all this searching. This is the full stop, the Ultimate, the Final Truth". You won't have any temptation to go elsewhere. After Realization, you won't be drawn or pulled in a different direction. When you realize that Godly essence, that the Master is in you, without ego, intellect, mind, it will be Spontaneous. You are *Brahman*. You are prior to that, you are prior to the world.

WHAT I SAY IS TRULY GOING ON INVISIBLY, SILENTLY,
PERMANENTLY IN THE BACKGROUND. REALIZE THIS!

A wandering mind is not the way. You must have complete faith, strong faith in yourself, and not go with any other Master. Complete faith, complete dedication is essential. Which books have you read?

Q: Lots of books: many on Nisargadatta Maharaj, parts of the *Dasbodh* and *Yoga Vasistha* which I like very much.

Maharaj: You have a good base. Whatever you read, you have to put into practice. Intellectual spiritual knowledge is only a pastime!

THERE ARE MANY SPIRITUAL BOOKS OUT THERE.
THE LISTENER, OR READER OF THESE BOOKS

IS ULTIMATE REALITY.

Don't take it as just another story of *Atman, Brahman*.

When you read spiritual books, you must have the understanding, the Conviction that, "This is my story", ie, the story of you as Formless Reality. It is open fact that you are not in body-form. The body is the external cover, with a time limit, an end.

You must be aware of your Ultimate Truth. Everything is within you but you are unaware of that Reality. I am reminding you, inviting attention of the Invisible Listener in you, that You are *Brahman, Atman, Paramatman*. But the mind, ego, intellect is not allowing you to keep that faith. It says, "How can I be *Brahman*? I am so and so".

Q: It is very important for me to hear this from you. It is encouraging and strengthening to hear this directly from you, so thank you very much.

Maharaj: Nisargadatta Maharaj had exceptional power. I am sharing the same knowledge with everybody. It is the proper time, the right time. Every single moment will never come back again. Plus, you have to come out of all these illusionary thoughts because in Reality, you are totally unborn, you were never born. So birth and death only apply to the body, which you are not, and you were not.

Prior to one hundred years you did not have a body. Death will happen to the body only, which you are not, and which you were not. After one hundred years you will not know your body. That means: How you were prior to this body-knowledge, and how you will be after dissolving this body-knowledge, THAT is your Ultimate Truth, Final Truth, *Brahman, Atman*, God, Master. You may use any words.

HOW YOU WERE PRIOR TO THIS BODY-KNOWLEDGE,
AND HOW YOU WILL BE
AFTER THIS BODY-KNOWLEDGE DISSOLVES,
THAT IS YOUR ULTIMATE TRUTH, FINAL TRUTH.

101. *Addicted to Words*

Maharaj: After listening to the Master, you are to come out of this world of concepts. Dedication is needed for this task. Numerous books exist. It is not enough to read, so if you are reading spiritual books, you must at the same time, keep up the practice.

ALWAYS REMEMBER,
THAT THE LISTENER/READER OF BOOKS
IS ULTIMATE REALITY.

Don't look upon these spiritual books, as if they are just stories of *Atman, Brahman*. When you read books, you must have the understanding, the Conviction, "This is my story", [not in any body-form]. It is open fact that you are not in body-form. The body is the external cover, with a time limit, an end.

You are like me. [The same as me. He gestures with hand.] Forget about this, [points to his garment], the body is just a layer, a covering! So you are to accept it like this.

WHEN THE MASTER IS TELLING YOU SOMETHING,
YOU ARE TO ACCEPT IT AS YOUR TRUTH,

YOUR REALITY,
BECAUSE IT IS YOUR STORY.

You are to listen and understand the teachings in this way: "This is my story", as if someone has narrated your life story from the beginning till now.

WHAT I AM NARRATING IS YOUR BIOGRAPHY,
YOUR STORY.
IN THIS WAY, YOU ARE TO ABSORB THIS KNOWLEDGE,
SO THAT YOU KNOW YOURSELF INSIDE OUT.

All spiritual books offer indications. The majority of seekers depend upon bookish knowledge. This can give you happiness to an extent, but when the time comes to leave the body, the depths of this knowledge will be tested. Recently, one of the devotees here suffered a loss. He was shaking and trembling. His foundation, [Knowledge], was weak. I am always stressing this to everyone who comes: "Your foundation must be strong".

WHY BOTHER ABOUT MEDITATION, THE MANTRA, *BHAJANS*?
BECAUSE THESE ARE THE FOUNDATION STONES
THAT ARE NECESSARY TO ESTABLISH REALITY
WITHIN THE UNIDENTIFIED, INVISIBLE IDENTITY.

Nisargadatta Maharaj used to say that, whereas some people found the Master's language difficult to understand, those disciples who were real disciples, true disciples were able to understand his teachings. The child understands the language of the mother. The mother knows what the child needs. Mother knows!

Therefore be simple, be humble, and don't stress your brain. I'm placing before you, your Truth, Final Truth, your Ultimate Truth, YOURS! The Invisible Listener's, the Anonymous Listener's Truth. No complications, no confusion, no conflicts.

So many individual thoughts and concepts have appeared since the beginning of childhood. There are so many thoughts inside you. You have not committed any crimes or sins in your last lifetime. Who is guilty? Whose *karma*? Whose *prarabdha*? We have created endless words and imaginary thoughts, which have been impressed upon us and accepted blindly.

YOU ARE DROWNING IN A SEA OF ILLUSORY WORDS, THOUGHTS, CONCEPTS.
THIS IS ALL IMAGINATION!

A Perfect Foundation, a solid base is needed for spirituality, so that Oneness will be there in whatever you read, listen to, or study. Without a foundation, duality will continue. All this knowledge that you have now is related to the body, all body-knowledge. You are grasping knowledge intellectually. Your reading is intellectual reading that is done with the subtle ego: "I am somebody [else], and I'm reading this book. I'm somebody [else], and I'm reading this book".

You are trying to understand and grasp with your body-based knowledge and understanding. I am bringing this to your attention again because it is very important. When you are reading a book about an aspect of *Atman*, *Paramatman*, God, you are reading it through the medium of body-knowledge. Maybe you do understand, but:

ALTHOUGH YOU ARE GRASPING EVERYTHING INTELLECTUALLY,

IT IS NOT BEING ESTABLISHED IN YOU,
BECAUSE YOU ARE NOT ONE WITH THE ULTIMATE TRUTH.

You are separate from THAT when you're reading. You are separate from THAT when you're listening, and when you are approaching various Masters, you have separated yourself from Ultimate Truth!

YOUR FOUNDATION AND STARTING POINT IS BODY-BASED.
YOU ARE COMING FROM A BODY-KNOWLEDGE BASE.

This means that the spiritual knowledge that you are acquiring is piled on top of that fragile and illusory body-base.

IN YOUR SPIRITUAL PURSUITS,
YOU ARE USING THE MIND, INTELLECT, EGO,
WHEN ULTIMATE TRUTH IS BEYOND ALL OF THIS.

You did not stop to ask, "When did the mind, ego, intellect appear?" You did not Self-enquire and find out that the mind, intellect, ego came after, along with the beingness, and therefore could not serve you, could not be instruments for finding Ultimate Truth.

HOW CAN THE MIND FIND THAT WHICH IS PRIOR TO IT?

The moment the Spirit clicked with the body, you started "I am". And out of "I am" all these concepts came. Your base therefore was formed out of illusory concepts.

One thing is clear and simple, if you ponder on it: Prior to beingness, we had not come across any, say, *Brahman, Atman, Paramatman,* God, happiness or peace. There was nothing. All these terms and conditions came into existence, when your Presence came into existence along with the body, ie spirit clicked with body.

Presence alone does not know happiness, peace or existence, it is the combination of the body and Presence, like, say, a fan and electricity that causes this illusion. The body can't say 'I', the Spirit can't say 'I'. The light is on, or the fan is turning because of the electricity.

Likewise, when the Spirit clicked with the body, you instantly said, 'I', and then along with the 'I', there appeared all these expectations, demands and needs: "I want happiness. I want peace. I want something more".

SO TRY TO KNOW YOURSELF.
WHERE WAS YOUR PRESENCE PRIOR TO BODY-KNOWLEDGE?
HOW WAS YOUR PRESENCE?

Prior to body-knowledge, you did not know anything, and you did not have anything. In the light of this, you should have the Conviction that, "The body-form is not my Ultimate Truth".

What about heaven and hell? There is so much fear around these concepts. Again, you had no knowledge of heaven or hell prior to beingness. You acquired this spiritual knowledge afterwards.

WHAT IS THE USE OF SPIRITUAL KNOWLEDGE
WHEN THERE IS NO KNOWER?
IF THERE IS NO KNOWER,
THEN WHAT IS THE USE OF ALL YOUR SPIRITUAL KNOWLEDGE?

The illusory Knower came across with the body. The Knower is Invisible, without form, without shape. There is neither 'knower' nor 'not knower'. Therefore all this spiritual knowledge is only illusion.

Q: If all this spiritual knowledge that we have is illusion, then how can I find Ultimate Truth?

Maharaj: You have forgotten your Identity. When the Spirit touched with the body, you forgot your Identity. Therefore Knowledge is required just to establish Truth within you that, "You are Ultimate Truth. You are Final Truth".

KNOWLEDGE ACTS AS AN ELEVATOR,
TO TAKE YOU TO THE TOP FLOOR.

Once you get there, you will no longer need it.

Don't depend on body-based knowledge that will disappear along with the body. You are neither *Brahman*, nor *Atman*, nor God. In fact, you are nothing. Your base must be strong.

SO MUCH SPIRITUAL KNOWLEDGE AROUND!
WHATEVER YOU READ SHOULD BE POWERFUL KNOWLEDGE.

People who read endless books, may be Masters of books, Masters of philosophy, but all this Knowledge has a time limit. The moment the body goes, everything goes, therefore Knowledge is also illusion. Knowledge is not Final Truth, it is just a medium.

WHAT IS KNOWLEDGE?
KNOWLEDGE MEANS JUST TO KNOW ONESELF
IN A REAL SENSE.

You are knowing yourself in body-form: "I am a man. I am a woman. I am *Brahman*". This illusion, that illusion, this illusion! "I am doing this activity, that activity, adding ego, ego, ego". You are totally caught up in egoistic concepts. "I'll do this activity. I've done something". You can't do anything.

YOU CAN'T DO ANYTHING WITH THAT BODY
BECAUSE THAT BODY IS NOT YOUR BASE.
IF YOU FIND YOUR BASE,
THEN YOUR FOUNDATIONS WILL BE PERFECT.

Q: What is my foundation?

Maharaj: Your foundation will be established after you clear away all body-knowledge. I am hammering the same thing. Listen carefully! Prior to beingness, there were no needs. Peace, happiness, fear, *Brahman*, *Atman*, all these concepts came after.

It's a very simple thing, so just take a look and ask yourself: "Where do I stand after reading all that body-knowledge?" We have become addicted to all these concepts. We have become victims of our own concepts, blindly signing this, signing that, "I'm a man, I'm a woman. I have done bad things. I have done good things". Now it is time to wake up and Know the Reality!

KNOW THE REALITY.
REALITY IS PLACED BEFORE YOU. IT IS AN OPEN SECRET.

Try to come out of the circle. You are not in bondage. Knowledge is limited, only useful while you are living. There is no knowledge, no knower, no concepts. This is the Final Truth. No disciple, no Master, no God, no devotee. All this illusion started when you came across with the world. Now you know that the entire world is your Spontaneous Projection. To see this world, your Presence is required.

YOU ARE NOT WITHIN ANY WORDS.
YOU ARE NOT WITHIN THE UNIVERSE.
THE UNIVERSE IS WITHIN YOU.

The moment Presence clicks, you see the world. Without your Presence, you can't see the world. I'm inviting the attention of that Presence, that Invisible Presence, that Unidentified Presence. That You Are [pointing to the visitor].

Birth and death have nothing to do with you. This is Reality, your Reality. I am saying the same thing to everybody: "Don't analyze the literal meaning of these words, stop picking at the books, asking, "What is this? What is that? Ramana Maharshi said it like this, Nisargadatta Maharaj said it like that". Don't compare the books, the Masters, the teachings.

What they wanted to convey out of their statements is what's important. No comparisons! You are not studying spiritual knowledge.

WE ARE EXPECTING CONVICTION, NOT STUDY.

So many people come here saying what is the meaning of such and such? Asking, Why? Why? Why? What are you going to achieve with your comparative studies? It is not going to help you. You are to come out of this whole illusory world.

CONCENTRATE ON THE CONCENTRATOR.
DON'T SWIM AMONGST THE LITERAL MEANINGS.
STOP DROWNING IN A SEA OF WORDS.
YOU ARE NO LONGER AN ADDICT.

102.   All This Book Reading – Who is it For?

Q: You don't sound very keen on us reading spiritual books. Is it not helpful for the practice to read books?
Maharaj: You may read books, of course, read books that give you knowledge. But you must establish that your Ultimate Truth is not separate from you, while you are reading these spiritual books. What you are reading is the Reader's story.

The Reader is not in any form. When reading any spiritual books, read in such a manner that you know it is your story that you are reading, the Invisible Reader's story. Ultimately, it is your story without any form. Only then, will that Knowledge be established.

Q: You mean you have not to separate yourself from the content in the book. We tend to read in such a way that it is the individual, so to speak, that is using the mind to gather information, as a kind of intellectual exercise. This is duality. What you are saying Maharaj, is that the reader is invisible. It is like the Silent Listener speaking to itself, like God speaking to God?
Maharaj: When you read any books like *Master of Self Realization*, or *I Am That*, they are giving you a message which is the Reader's message, Your Truth.

This phrase, given by my Master, should be the conclusion of all your reading: "Except your Selfless Self, there is no God, no *Brahman*, no *Atman*, no *Paramatman*, no Master." This is the gist, the principle of all philosophical and spiritual books.

THIS PRINCIPLE HAS BEEN COLOURED
BY VARIOUS WORDS AND ENDLESS STORIES,
THAT HAVE OBSCURED THIS MAIN PRINCIPLE
WHICH INDICATES THE READER'S KNOWLEDGE.
THE READER DOES NOT HAVE ANY FORM.
THE READER IS THE INVISIBLE READER.

As I am talking with you about something, you are listening. Not only are you listening, you are also analyzing. And not only are you analyzing what is being said, you are witnessing that which you are analyzing. Instantly, things are happening which you are witnessing again. I am inviting the attention of that Witnesser, that Invisible Witnesser within you, which has been called *Brahman*, *Atman*, *Paramatman*, God, Master.

After reading a good number of books, there must be a conclusion. What's the outcome? What did you get from reading all these books? To what extent was the reading helpful to your Ultimate Truth? How useful was it all?

THERE MUST BE A CONCLUSION.
YOU MUST REACH A CONCLUSION,
OTHERWISE YOU ARE WASTING PRECIOUS MOMENTS.

Gathering knowledge, accumulating knowledge, this is dry knowledge and will not help you on your deathbed.

ALL THIS BOOK READING, WHO IS IT FOR?

Q: I guess I just love reading spiritual books.

Maharaj: If all you do is read books, if the only thing you do is read books, then all that will happen is you will become a 'Master of books', a literary Master, and not a Master of Reality. This will not help you.

Why do you want to keep knowing more and more, adding more and more ignorance? Books have already indicated that you are Ultimate Truth. You are to be established in that Ultimate Truth. So why this urge to read more and more, again and again and again?

Q: I understand! I have to let these spiritual books speak to the Invisible Listener in me rather than the mind?

Maharaj: Yes! Because you are no longer an individual. You know better! Don't be a book worm! You are Ultimate Truth, Final Truth.

WHILE READING THE CONTENT
THAT IS CONNECTED WITH ULTIMATE TRUTH,
KNOW THAT YOU ARE THAT ULTIMATE TRUTH.

This is your Knowledge, not book knowledge. "Yes, I am That!" This is the Conviction. This is the Meditation. Spontaneous continuous alertness that you are Ultimate Truth is necessary.

Q: You often say that we have not to take the words literally, or compare them to what we have read elsewhere. I suppose we get stuck on words and hang on to them?

Maharaj: Knowledge is there, but how to interpret it and put it into practice is the problem. If you do not use the knowledge in the right way, it will create problems for you. Anything in excess is poison.

Q: Some books like *I Am That* and *Master of Self-Realization* invite greater attention of the Invisible Listener than others. You are one with the content because it speaks directly to one's Ultimate Reality, so to speak.

Maharaj: Yes, yes.

Q: Thank you for that Maharaj. What you have said about the reader making himself separate from the reader's knowledge is really helpful. What you have pointed out is a subtle difference, but the more I reflect on it, it makes a huge difference. I realize that I have read many great spiritual classics, and said to myself "This is wonderful", but a part of me was separate. There was duality because although I could identify with the content, it did not really feel that it was "my story", not completely.

And that is where your approach is really helpful, Maharaj, in making us aware that these books about *Brahman* are not stories about *Brahman*, but "my story" because "I am *Brahman*", [without saying it, without ego]. To be one with the Truth that is being expressed is what, I believe, you are saying. It is hard to explain. I will get back to you on that, but something profound has taken place.

Maharaj: Very nice, very nice!

Q: And it is not just in relation to books. I am now listening to you, the Master, and what you are narrating, as my story. It is so Real and it's being accepted totally and completely. I know it is the Truth. I feel it deeply. I feel One with the Truth that you are conveying.

Maharaj: Very good! You have a deep involvement. Keep going deeper and deeper.

103. 'I Am'

Q: What exactly is 'I am' in simple words, and what is it not?

Maharaj: 'I am', is an indication of your Spontaneous, Anonymous Presence, but it is without any shape, without any colour. Names have been given to '*Atman*', '*Paramatman*', 'God', just to understand, to communicate. Reality is beyond imagination. There should not be any confusion. It sounds like some people have created a special house for 'I am'. At the advanced stage, 'I am' is also illusion.

Again, be clear, there is no 'I am', there is no 'You are' - these are simply w.o.r.d.s. Prior to beingness, you did not know what the 'I' or the 'You' was.

YOU ARE ARTIFICIALLY MOULDING YOURSELF,
SAYING, "I AM SOMEBODY",
AND IN THE LIGHT OF THAT KNOWLEDGE,
YOU ARE THINKING, MEDITATING ON 'I AM'.

You are limiting your Reality by naming it, enclosing it. Remember, 'I am' is a concept. We are just using words to try and understand, exchanging words through which we are inviting attention of the Invisible, Anonymous Listener within you. All words are used for the purpose of understanding.

TRY TO KNOW YOUR IDENTITY.
TRY TO KNOW YOUR UNIDENTIFIED IDENTITY.
THE KNOWER WILL DISAPPEAR.
WHILE TRYING TO KNOW ULTIMATE TRUTH,

THE KNOWER WILL DISAPPEAR.
NO KNOWLEDGE, NO KNOWER.

Q: The understanding is that 'I am' is very deep …

Maharaj: Who is understanding that? [Maharaj laughs]. 'I' am understanding. Who is understanding that? All this requires Presence, but your Presence is not any shape or form. It is formless. No beingness, no non-beingness, no consciousness, no unconsciousness, no awareness, no unawareness. No knower, no knowledge etc.

You are neglecting that which already exists within you, the Formless, Invisible, Unidentified Identity. You are That. You are *Brahman*, *Atman*. 'I' is just like the sky. Does the sky say "I am"? Sky is totally unaware of its existence. Likewise, your Presence is totally unaware of your existence.

All these words are body-knowledge. Beingness is also illusion. Who is saying beingness and non-beingness? When you came across with the body you created a big illusionary field: beingness, non-beingness, awareness, unawareness, consciousness.

YOU ARE ROAMING IN THE FIELD,
AND TRYING TO EXTRACT KNOWLEDGE.
COME OUT OF THE FIELD!
BE BRAVE,
BE COURAGEOUS!

Q: I sometimes think that the 'I Am' practice has been taken too literally and maybe grown out of proportion. Also there is a lot of confusion around it, a third of a century since Nisargadatta Maharaj's passing. It has perhaps ballooned into something...

Maharaj: What happens is that seekers, devotees or disciples read books, and on the basis of their reading, they form a square, and then they expect answers from within the square. So you have to leave all that.

WHATEVER IS REALIZED
FROM THE EXISTENCE OF THE BODY, IS ILLUSION.

You have brought yourself into the confusion field, using confusing words. You are a victim of your own ideas, your own concepts: 'I am' 'You are', 'He', 'She', '*Brahman*'...

Q: When we abide in 'I am', how am I to stay, or go beyond it?

Maharaj: Forget about spiritual talk. To say 'I' is ego. Why are you trying to remain in, or, as 'I'? It means you are taking some ego and saying, "I am something, somebody, somebody else. I am"! This means you think you are somebody else, and you are to stay like this, 'I', [with eyes closed]. This is duality.

You have not to make any efforts. In the beginning, you are to accept that your 'I am' is in existence, and that you know 'I am' through the body only. It is an open fact that the body is not your identity. But while remaining in the 'I am', you are considering yourself as somebody else and, with the subtle ego, you are staying as 'I am', and saying 'I'.

YOU ARE TRYING TO EXPERIENCE 'I',
TO BE *BRAHMAN*, *ATMAN*.
AND TO DO THAT,
YOU ARE HAVING TO BE SOMEBODY DIFFERENT,

SOMEBODY ELSE.

Q: So there is duality, there is a split.

Maharaj: Immediately, if you try to stay like that. Why try? I want to stay as John. "I am John". You are already John, so why to be, 'I am John'. John is the name which has been given to this body, it is not your Ultimate Reality. Similarly, your Spontaneous Presence, your existence is without shape. Don't make any effort. Don't take the literal meaning of these spiritual words, rather take what they are trying to convey.

You are your own Master. So whatever you listen to or read, to some extent, it is helpful but after reaching the final destination, you do not need an address. So don't take what the Masters say literally. What they want to convey is most important. You have created a balloon. Burst that balloon!

ALL YOU HAVE TO DO IS
REALIZE THAT THE BODY IS NOT YOUR IDENTITY.
WHEN YOU MEDITATE,
YOU ARE POSING AS SOMEONE ELSE,
AND THEREFORE THE MEDITATION IS DUAL.

The 'I am' is only an indication, so why are you analyzing it so much? All this meditation, concentration, knowledge, Self-enquiry - these are all only various steps, part of a process on the way to Final Truth. After having Conviction that you are not the body, there is nothing more to do. Your reaction will be Spontaneous action.

You are already 'I am'. You just have to know yourself in a real sense. Except your Selfless Self, there is no 'I am'. So why stay in this little world, this literal world of 'I am'? You are already there, together twenty-four hours. Why remain in something that's artificially created or imagined guesswork?

Don't struggle with words. They are just indications of Ultimate Truth and how that Truth is your Identity. But the Truth is Invisible and Anonymous. So stop imagining, guessing. Don't use logic or intellect.

YOU ARE TWENTY-FOUR HOUR PRESENCE,
SO NO NEED TO TRY, TO BE,
TO THINK OF 'I AM' AT ALL.

You are beyond the beyond.

104. 'I Am' is Illusion

Q: I have being doing my meditation regularly and trying to stay in the 'I am'.

Maharaj: When you come to know the Reality, why do you want to try and stay in the 'I am'? Be as it is. Very simple! Don't do anything. There is no deed, no doer so don't make any deliberate efforts. You are everywhere. Don't do, don't try to remain in 'I am-ness'. It is OK, but it is a child's game, and you are no longer a child. Everybody knows that 'I am' is the base.

BUT HOW LONG ARE YOU GOING TO KEEP ON SAYING,
"THIS IS THE BASE, THIS IS THE BASE"?

Q: Nisargadatta Maharaj says 'I am' is the first concept and…

Maharaj: Always remember that words are only a medium, an instrument that is used to indicate something.

Again, I have to repeat the same thing: Don't take the words used by the Masters literally. Don't take the words literally or logically.

What is the body? Just a sign of beingness, 'I am', a kind of feeling 'I am'. You feel 'I am', and out of this spontaneous feeling you see the world. In the early morning in the first moment, you get this feeling. At first, you do not have a body and then instantly you see the world, therefore 'I am' is an indication. 'I am' is the indication of your Spontaneous Invisible Unidentified Identity. This is the perfect phrase. Out of that Spontaneous Spirit, 'I am' is.

'I AM' IS THE INDICATION OF YOUR
SPONTANEOUS, INVISIBLE, UNIDENTIFIED IDENTITY.

Individuality, duality, we are fighting with the words. Don't fight with the words! I am placing Ultimate Truth before you. Forget about all that you have read and listened to.

HOW WERE YOU PRIOR TO BEINGNESS?
WHAT DID YOU KNOW ABOUT THE *BRAHMAN*,
***ATMAN*, *PARABRAHMAN*, GOD? NOTHING!**
WHAT DID YOU KNOW ABOUT 'I AM'? NOTHING!

Q: You talk about dissolving body-knowledge, does that include 'I am'?

Maharaj: The feeling of 'I am' is Spontaneous because it is body-knowledge. It is Spontaneous because through body-knowledge you know 'I am'. Prior to beingness, you were unaware of this 'I am'. So it is just a feeling of 'I' where there is no body, no intellect, no knowledge, nothing.

Prior to Spirit touching the body, you were unaware and unknown to you. This is your Identity. So why do you wish to remain in 'I am'? You are doing so artificially. You are already there. Your Presence is already there. If you are trying, it means you are taking ego. You are Final Truth but you have forgotten your identity, and so you are trying psychologically and mentally to stay in 'I am'.

Q: So in a sense the 'I am' can vaporise, dissolve...

Maharaj: 'I am' indicates your Spontaneous Presence. I have told you, to say 'I am', your Presence is required.

'I AM' IS PROJECTED OUT OF YOUR PRESENCE.
YOUR PRESENCE IS UNKNOWN,
ANONYMOUS, INVISIBLE, UNIDENTIFIED.

Q: I think that there is a confusion about the Presence, and what exactly 'I am' means?

Maharaj: You are giving this too much importance! These are just words, 'I am'. You are struggling with the W.O.R.D.S. You are prior to words, prior to 'I am'.

Q: So Presence is prior, before 'I am'?

Maharaj: Yes, yes, of course. Your Presence is, as Saint Tukaram, says, "Earlier, earlier, earlier. Prior to sky, God and all the deities. When there was no sky, no light, your Presence was there. When there was no light, no sky, your Presence was there. We are earlier than God and all these deities". Saint Tukaram was illiterate, as he only reached the second or third grade. His education was very poor. So how did this Truth appear in him?

TRUTH APPEARED FROM WITHIN HIM.
TRUTH MAY APPEAR FROM WITHIN YOU, TOO.
BUT YOU ARE NOT CONCENTRATING.

YOU ARE NOT PAYING ENOUGH ATTENTION,
YOU ARE MORE INTERESTED IN PLAYING WITH WORDS,
AND IN WHAT'S GOING ON IN THE BODY-FORM.

Who created language? Do you know this story of Bhausaheb Maharaj? Gurudev Ranade used to write in English, and then read out loud to his Master. Bhausaheb Maharaj did not know English, but nevertheless, he could point out a sentence and say, "This sentence is wrong!"

Gurudev Ranade said: "How do you know?" Bhausaheb Maharaj's reply was: "Who created language? Language is eternal. You are placing words next to each other but the meaning of these words lies internally. Language is known to Almighty Spirit, language is not a barrier".

Q: My own experience is that even though the 'I am' practice is supposed to be a gateway, it has proved to be a stumbling block. I feel you can get caught up too much in the words 'I am', and after all, it is still only a concept. You, Maharaj, don't really talk about any concepts, you go straight to the Absolute, and you stay there. It is an effective way of clearing everything up in one fell swoop.

Using few words, you simplify the highest Knowledge. Your Direct Approach works, and along with the method of hammering and repetition, there is great clarity. The teaching has a non-verbal element, too, because your Presence is very strong.

105. *Beyond Words, Beyond Worlds*

Maharaj: Prior to beingness, there was nothing. You were completely unknown to yourself. After leaving the body, what is going to be left? Nothing! So why do you wish to talk about this body-knowledge?

THIS EXISTENCE CAME OUT OF NOTHING
AND WILL BE ABSORBED BACK INTO NOTHING.

'I am' is a concept. Stop measuring yourself in body-form: What I am talking about is beyond 'I am', prior to 'I am'. Truth is truth, and is the same for all. Where you have come from there was no measuring tape. Why do you want to keep talking about body-knowledge?

Q: I have practised meditating on the "I am" and I am able to turn my attention to the feeling of being me, of being 'I am' regardless of any social or conditioned identity. It feels blissful. But that feeling of bliss comes and goes and so I get disheartened. What can I do?

Maharaj: All feelings are body-based feelings.

Q: So that Spontaneous Presence which I feel as me, that isn't real?

Maharaj: You are known to you through the body. Prior to the body, prior to beingness, you were unknown to you.

YOUR PRESENCE IS NEEDED TO SAY, 'I AM'.
YOUR PRESENCE IS ANONYMOUS, INVISIBLE, SHAPELESS.
THERE IS NO EXPERIENCE, AND NO EXPERIENCER.

Q: That experience of being no shape, does that sort of just happen? Would one experience it just like being free, free of everything?

Maharaj: You are totally free. You consider yourself in bondage only because of body-knowledge.

Q: I guess it is an experience of prior to the 'I am'?

Maharaj: Correct! Your Spontaneous Presence is prior to 'I am'. Prior to beingness, you were unknown to your Presence.

Q: I am not known to it?

Maharaj: Unknown to that Presence!

PRESENCE IS UNTRACEABLE.

The moment you came across with the body, you started knowing 'I am'. In brief, you are Reality. You are Ultimate Truth, Final Truth without any body-form.

Q: Does it take effort in the beginning to identify with this?

Maharaj: In the beginning you have to make some effort to know yourself in a real sense because so many thoughts and concepts have been wrapped around you. Illusory thoughts have crowded you, therefore to erase all this, you need some help in the form of spiritual knowledge, as well as the discipline of meditation.

Q: Sometimes I meditate on the feeling of 'I am', and at other times I meditate on 'Who am I?'

Maharaj: When you ask yourself "Who am I?", the answer is the questioner.

Q: The questioner itself is the reply?

Maharaj: The questioner is the Invisible Anonymous Questioner. Through the body-form you are asking yourself the question, "Who am I?" because you forgot your identity.

THEREFORE, WHEN YOU ASK THE QUESTION,
"WHO AM I?", THE REPLY IS
"YOU ARE EVERYTHING.
YOU ARE ULTIMATE TRUTH,
YOU ARE FINAL TRUTH",
BECAUSE YOU ARE NOT IN ANY FORM.

Without your Spontaneous Presence, you cannot utter a single word. So your Identity is beyond that, beyond beingness, prior to beingness.

Q: My question is, would you say that meditating on the 'I am' is helpful in this respect, in this understanding, or not?

Maharaj: At the beginning it is OK. But if you are concentrating on the 'I am', it means that you are using the body to help you. You are not the body. Open fact! You are Invisible Presence. Your Presence was there without any body-based knowledge.

CONCENTRATE ON THE CONCENTRATOR,
THEN SUBSEQUENTLY,
THE CONCENTRATOR WILL DISAPPEAR.

In this way, there won't be any 'I am'. Practise but don't make it a problem. Take it easy.

Q: I guess I am a little confused about the approach.

Maharaj: 'I am', 'I', these are concepts. This is OK when using a physical approach. But you are already 'I', so really you do not need to pay so much attention, to remember or know 'I' because you are already 'I'. So many people are saying, "I have to meditate on 'I am'", forgetting that it is just an indication of your Unidentified

Identity.

'I AM', IS JUST AN INDICATION OF
YOUR UNIDENTIFIED IDENTITY.

I keep telling everyone the same thing, "Don't take the words literally". We created the words: 'I', 'I am' and gave them meaning to communicate, in order to indicate, point to, identify something. But they are just words. You are being led astray by words.

YOUR EXISTENCE,
YOUR PRESENCE IS BEYOND,
BEYOND WORDS, BEYOND WORLDS.

See yourself spontaneously and then the meditator will disappear without your knowledge. The form will disappear, and with it, memory and 'I am'.

WHEN EVERYTHING DISAPPEARS,
THERE YOU ARE IN INVISIBLE FORM.

Q: So there is a point where all that goes, like swimming in a light or something?

Maharaj: You can use any words you wish, as long as you keep in mind, that you are Ultimate Truth, you are Final Truth. You are *Brahman*, *Atman*. You are *Paramatman*. You are God. You are Master.

ULTIMATELY, WHAT IS MOST IMPORTANT, IS THAT
THIS REALITY IS TOTALLY ABSORBED.

No individuality whatsoever will remain after Absorption. There will be nothing left.

Q: Really? Is it just peace, or is it bliss or non-bliss?

Maharaj: Peace belongs to experience. Peace and silence have to do with experience, bliss also. Prior to beingness, there was no peace, no happiness, no unhappiness, no depression. There was nothing.

WE NEED PEACE AND SILENCE
BECAUSE WE ARE IN A BODY-FORM.
WHEN ALL KNOWLEDGE DISAPPEARS,
THERE YOU ARE,
BECAUSE KNOWLEDGE, TOO, IS ILLUSION.

Q: I guess it seems to me like a really long path?

Maharaj: There is no 'path' and there is no 'long'. Your Spontaneous Presence is a miracle. You were unknown to you. Through the body, you started to know yourself, and then you wanted to survive in the body for as long as possible.

Q: Right! And so once that is seen or realized, it's all gone?

Maharaj: After Realization, there won't be any fear, no death, no birth because you will realize that 'I am unborn'. Remember one thing, all this talk, all our talking just now is about the unborn child.

ALL THIS TALKING IS ABOUT THE UNBORN CHILD.

Q: After all my struggles, [laughter]! Well that sounds just wonderful! I guess once you know that you are not the body, once you really know that you are not the body, that you are beyond it...

Maharaj: Stop this guessing! No guessing is needed. Be Spontaneous! Remain Spontaneous! When you guess, you are again taking the form of the body.

Q: Yes! OK.

Maharaj: Stay simple. Remain simple. Your Presence is very simple, without concepts, without imagination, without guessing, without any intellectual activity.

YOU HAVE GOOD KNOWLEDGE,
BUT YOU HAVE TO APPLY IT,
PUT IT INTO PRACTICE.
THIS IS CALLED CONVICTION.

After Conviction, you will not have any problems or questions. You are the questioner, and therefore the answer is within you. So be silent! Look at yourself and how you were prior to all this body-knowledge.

THERE WERE NO QUESTIONS, NO ANSWERS,
NO HAPPINESS, NO UNHAPPINESS, NO BIRTH, NO DEATH.
THEN EVERYTHING WILL DISSOLVE,
IN THE LIGHT OF THIS REALITY.

Spontaneous Happiness, Spontaneous Silence, Spontaneous Peace will emerge.

YOU ARE FORMLESS,
YOU ARE FORMLESS.
YOU ARE GOING TO REMAIN FORMLESS.
THERE IS NO FORM,
NO INDIVIDUALITY.

Q: I wish I had more questions, but I have reached a state where none of them are coming any more.

Maharaj: A good thing! This is a sign of Knowledge being absorbed, the merging of Knowledge. Contemplate on these talks. It will be helpful for you.

Q: I'm on fire! I really appreciate your teachings.

Maharaj: It is by the grace of my Master, Nisargadatta Maharaj, that I am sharing these teachings, the same teachings that my Master shared with me.

Q: Thank you, Maharaj. I feel very fortunate to have found you.

106.   *A Master to the Very Bones*

Maharaj: Remember what I have told you and practise it. Theoretically you know, you understand, but this Knowledge must be applied and lived practically. The recitation of the Mantra and the *bhajan*s will penetrate deeply, so that all illusory concepts dissolve with their vibrations.

I AM CONVINCING YOU.
YOU HAVE TO CONVINCE YOURSELF ALSO.

Convince yourself that you are not the body. This will make you fearless and ready to face any problem with full strength and power. Don't neglect your responsibilities and family duties. Live life happily! Practise what you read. Theoretical knowledge is not sufficient. Do the meditation and listen to your internal voice.

BE SIMPLE,
AND KNOW YOURSELF IN A REAL SENSE.

When Bhausaheb Maharaj's body was burned, some people said that the *Naam Mantra* could be heard coming from the bones. The *Naam Mantra* was sounding out through his bones. The Mantra had become totally one with his whole body. His whole body, each and every part of his body was spontaneously sounding out the Mantra.

ALL MIRACLES HAPPEN BECAUSE OF YOU ALONE,
WITHIN YOU ALONE.

When this Knowledge has been implemented in practice, and absorbed within each and every part of your body, your physical identity will just disappear.

In spirituality, you are to keep yourself empty, totally blank. People used to visit Siddharameshwar Maharaj and tell him, "I am *Brahman*". The Master would say, "Then why are you here?"

Use the Mantra to be liberated from all these concepts. 'Slowly' means that when you recite the Mantra, it is not so easy to remove the concepts. So it is done slowly, silently, permanently. Remove them one at a time, "This is not true, this is not true, this is not true", like removing obstacles that are blocking a road. You know spirituality intellectually, but not practically.

YOU ARE TO VALUE HIGHLY,
BOTH THE MANTRA, AND THE GURU.

The Guru plays a most important role. He can guide you because he has had first-hand experience of the process.

THE REALIZED MASTER KNOWS EVERYTHING, EVERY DETAIL,
BECAUSE HE WENT THROUGH IT HIMSELF.
WITH HIS PRACTICAL KNOWLEDGE THEREFORE,
HE CAN IMPRESS YOU WITH THE KNOWLEDGE, THE REALITY.

All that you know now, has been known via words only. You have literal knowledge. When you are reciting the Mantra, thoughts are coming, maybe you cannot concentrate so well. That's OK, slowly the Mantra will begin to work. Body-knowledge will dissolve and Knowledge will be absorbed. The Ultimate Medicine will take some time to digest.

ANYONE CAN SAY, "EVERYTHING IS ILLUSION",
BUT ACCEPTING THIS FACT, IS A DIFFERENT STORY.
PEOPLE DON'T ACCEPT IT.

This way, Knowledge will be absorbed. Sometimes, in order for water to reach a plant, a tunnel has to be dug. Only then will the water absorb, absorb.

IF I SAY, "EVERYTHING IS ILLUSION",
IT IS NOT ACCEPTED.

This way, it will be absorbed, absorbing, absorbing slowly, until the water has filled up.

First you need to approach a Master who is Realized, secondly, you must have complete faith in him. Siddharameshwar Maharaj says you need to take a step towards the Master. "There has to be co-operation". You have to come forward. It is not one-way traffic. You are to accept the Knowledge totally. Half-faith is neither sufficient, nor practical. You must have complete faith.

WE ARE EXPECTING TRUTH IN THE BODY-FORM.

When spiritual knowledge explodes and bursts inside you, there will be silent, spiritual intoxication. "Oh!" After knowing the Reality you will be very calm and quiet. If an enemy from the past resurfaces, you will respond in a different manner than you used to,

BECAUSE YOU SEE YOURSELF IN EVERYBODY.

You will forget the body-knowledge, and as long as you are involved, and keep thoughts at bay, you will be filled with Spontaneous Happiness. Total involvement is needed to stick with Ultimate Truth.

There are many Masters who are exploiting seekers because they know people are looking for happiness. We know this, but we are to have an attitude of indifference. Nisargadatta Maharaj did not criticize any Master. After enlightenment, there is no basis for any ill feeling like jealousy or anger.

EVERYONE IS NOT A DEVOTEE,
BUT THE MASTER HAS A DUTY TO SHARE THE TEACHINGS.

When people leave the ashram without problems, that is my happiness. My wish is to remove you from illusion. I have no expectations, just your peace and happiness. All saintly people made sacrifices to make others enlightened.

If, after knowing the Reality, you are still expecting something, say money or material gain from someone, this is an indication of your imminent downfall. Be cautious! The ego, *maya*, mind are trying to find a place once more in the spiritual body. *Maya* is there to make you a slave. *Maya*, illusion is a wrong concept. You are a Master. You can overcome illusion. You have self-decision. You are a Master.

YOU ARE *MAYA'*S MASTER.

Before Conviction, the mind was dictating to you, not any more. Now you have a commanding nature. Don't become anyone's victim, including God's.

KNOWING THAT "GOD IS MY BABY",
IS A SIGN OF REALIZATION.

The Master gives you courage. You are getting courage to overcome all these illusory influences. Courage comes from your involvement, devotion, the *Naam*. It comes from observing the devotion of the Masters. I am not talking about any egoistic Masters. You cannot be impressed by anyone because you know what God is, and you have seen yourself in the real sense.

YOU ARE NO LONGER A BODY.
'*CHIDANANDA SHIVOHAM SHIVOHAM*'.

After knowing the Reality, you must continue with the process of convincing yourself and absorbing the Knowledge. Siddharameshwar Maharaj used to say, "Chew the chocolate, chew the chocolate of *Brahman*. This will give you happiness".

No man can serve two Masters. Respect others! You are to change yourself internally, externally. Light and Power have been given to you. Power is yours, but don't misuse it.

"Your tongue is like a sword", said Nisargadatta Maharaj. Be careful how you use it. I am telling you to be cautious because you will have a little Power after devotion. Avoid misusing this Power, otherwise the ego will take possession of the spiritual body. Exercise caution!

In childhood, some impressions of spirituality may have appeared. But now that you are spiritually grown-up, your experiences will be mature because you have established Truth.

TRUTH IS ESTABLISHED IN YOU.
YOUR SPIRITUAL FOUNDATION
IS THE RESULT OF YOUR DEVOTION, YOUR INVOLVEMENT.

You know you have no business, no relations with the body: "My Presence without the body is Ultimate Truth". You know the Reality. Now you are to continue it, like doing yoga, and keep fit. This will make you spiritually fit.

CONTINUE TO STAY IN YOUR OWN ULTIMATE TRUTH.

Your Invisible Presence is very sensitive. It attracts everything instantly like a magnet. Your Invisible Presence is very sensitive. You are to be alert. Beware of external things. The effects are instant! Continue to remain in this atmosphere so that you won't be affected. That way you will stay indifferent to everything. Remain indifferent! If something happens at work, it won't have such a physical impact on you. Alertness!

"I AM UNCONCERNED WITH THE WORLD"
IS THE QUALITY OF THE ENLIGHTENED SAGE.

We are defining, "This is good, this is bad", yet prior to beingness, there was no good or bad. After knowing this, all concern simply evaporates.

IF YOU ACCEPT THE TRUTH TOTALLY,
IT WILL BE TOTALLY ABSORBED IN YOU.

You will have no other thoughts, no second thoughts, no doubt, no suspicion.

"I AM WHAT I HAVE BEEN SEARCHING FOR",
IS THE SPONTANEOUS CONVICTION.

And that Conviction keeps you quiet, without struggle, without doubt. Be doubt-free! A small mosquito of doubt will create trouble. Tremendous silence will be there, full and total silence. Nothing is going to happen. There are no differentiations. Become your own teacher, your own Master, standing on your own feet. You are no longer dependent. You are independent. Don't expect anyone's help, or any miracles.

THE MIRACLE IS IN YOU.
WITHOUT YOUR PRESENCE,
YOU CAN'T SEE ANY MIRACLES.

Q: You say that we should not expect help. Is the Guru not helping us?

Maharaj: The Guru is not helping you. He is showing you your Ultimate Truth, which you have forgotten. You are already rich. Everything is already in you.

Q: I feel the Guru is my father.

Maharaj: Siddharameshwar Maharaj says, "Don't expect anything from *maya*, illusion". You have given birth to *maya*. What is *Brahman*? You have given birth to these names. All these concepts are rooted to the body. Prior to beingness, what did you know about *maya*? For understanding purposes we are using all these polished words.

Q2: After spending some time in your Presence, Maharaj, I feel good for a couple of months, but then I start to go down.

Maharaj: You are still considering yourself as an individual. There is only Oneness. There is no difference between the Master and the disciple. Accept this truth. As long as you are considering yourself separate from Master, these feelings are bound to be there. You have to be in touch with your Selfless Self twenty-four hours.

Your own concepts are creating ash. Fire is always there. Sweep the ash with the broom of Knowledge. Your Spontaneous Presence is the sign of the Master. When you say, "My Master is in India", you are creating concepts and problems for yourself. The Master is not separate from you. He is not in the body-form, he is just like sky.

YOU CAN BE ANYWHERE IN THE WORLD.
THE MASTER IS EVERYWHERE IN THE WORLD.

The spectacles of Knowledge have been given to you. So don't think, "I'm different, and separate from my Master". Full self-involvement is needed. The Master is revealing your Identity, revealing your Power.

STOP BEING A DISCIPLE, AND START BEING A MASTER!

"I am far away from my Master". Don't think like this! Always stay in touch with your Selfless Self: "My Master says I am there!"

Contemplate on what you have listened to. Keep that fire alive, otherwise there will be more ash. Don't let temptation in! Your Spontaneous Presence has no words. Your Ultimate Truth has no words, nothing. Now maintain it! Remember the talks, read, do meditation. Be humble! Don't struggle! Stay simple!

Keep aloof from *maya*. Do not become a victim of your own illusionary ideas, concepts. If you take simple precautions, no one will dare come near you. You have Exceptional Power, Masterly Power. That Circle of Power is with you.

107.   Be Surrounded By Your Inner Master

Maharaj: It is really very simple: We are going to leave this body. What happens after?
SPIRITUAL SCIENCE SAYS THAT:
YOU ARE NOT GOING ANYWHERE.
YOU ARE GOING EVERYWHERE.

Swami Ramdas says, "After your body is burned, you are not going anywhere". You are like the sky. If a building collapses, what happens to sky or space? Nothing! Sky is everywhere. Likewise, the Invisible Speaker, the Invisible Listener is not going anywhere. When the body goes, the Spirit of the Listener does not go anywhere.

If Spirit is not going anywhere, then you are immortal. The Listener's Presence is Spontaneous, Invisible. We are, all the time, trying to guess what this Presence is like, using the intellect, and asking, "Why this? Why that? Why? Why?" It is not your fault because every day, we are living with the help of the ego, mind, intellect.

Thought, intellect, scrutiny, then instantly, the intellect passes on its instructions to the ego to implement the thoughts. This is the process, the natural function. By itself, the body cannot do anything.

Through the body, you see the whole world.

The invisible part that is in every being is the power which is called *Brahman, Atman.* Instantly, this power goes through the intellect, then the intellect decides if the thoughts are good or bad, just like a doorman. All this has to do with the body because we are unknown to ourselves. Prior to the body: no knowledge. Good and bad are different for different people. What I want to convey is:

THE ENTIRE WORLD IS YOUR SPONTANEOUS PRESENCE.
THIS IS THE CONCLUSION.
YOU ARE ULTIMATE TRUTH, UNBORN.

When the body goes, you will be unconcerned with the body and out of fear. The body is the medium through which you can know yourself. The fear of death will be removed. The mind will not create any fear - that will be gone.

What is the conclusion of spirituality?

YOU ARE ULTIMATE TRUTH.
WHEREVER YOU GO,
REMEMBER THAT YOU ARE ULTIMATE TRUTH.

When you travel and visit some place, know that the Invisible Visitor in you is the Ultimate Truth. Know yourself in a real sense. Know this and you will have a smooth, simple life. Don't neglect the family! Doing spirituality and forgetting about family members is egotistic spirituality.

ALL THE PROBLEMS STARTED
WHEN YOU BECAME KNOWN TO YOURSELF.
SO BE WITH YOU.
ALWAYS BE WITH YOU,
AND NOT WITH THE MIND, EGO, INTELLECT.
THEN YOU WILL GET REAL PEACE, REAL STABILITY.

A wavering mind is always dangerous. A suspicious mind is always dangerous. It will spoil your spiritual life.

BE SURROUNDED WITH YOU!

The world will be there for as long as you have Presence. When the body is gone, who is going to talk about God? The mind, ego, intellect are not accepting the Reality because of their own self-importance.

Q: It is not easy with the ego.

Maharaj: These are words that do not have their own Presence. It is because of your Presence that you see the ego, mind, intellect. Where does all that go when the body goes? Don't measure things in body-form. You are viewing things from the body-base. All these words are illusion.

Who created this dream-world?

YOU ARE THE FATHER OF THE DREAM-WORLD.
LIKEWISE,
YOU ARE THE FATHER OF THIS LONG DREAM-WORLD.

Q: It is difficult to live with this Presence!

Maharaj: It is not difficult. You just live a normal life. You know it is a dream. You are acting, reacting. The question of there being a doer never arises.

IF IN A DREAM, YOU DO BAD THINGS,
YOU DON'T ACCEPT OWNERSHIP IN THE DREAM.
SIMILARLY, BECAUSE WE ARE TAKING EGO FOR DOING SOMETHING GOOD OR BAD,
WE ARE TAKING THE CONSEQUENCES.
IN THIS DREAM, IF SOMETHING HAPPENS,
YOU WILL NOT BE CONCERNED AT ALL.

When these questions arise, it is the beginning of Self-enquiry. You are to find the answers within you, using discrimination. You are not to resolve the questions through ascetic practices. The *Sadhus* are torturing themselves. What are they trying to achieve? Who are they doing it for? For the body? The mind has to dissolve, be completely erased, then, there is nothing left to do, except to live a simple, humble life. Live a simple and humble life!

YOU ARE THE ARCHITECT OF YOUR OWN SPIRITUAL LIFE.
IT IS UP TO YOU HOW TO ACT, OR NOT TO ACT
IN THE LIGHT OF THIS KNOWLEDGE.

The saints are shouting, shouting at everyone who runs after happiness and peace. This happiness and peace is not separate from you.

YOU ARE RUNNING HERE,
RUNNING THERE,
BECAUSE YOU DON'T KNOW THE RUNNER.

The ego is not allowing you to, 'Be with You', because of pride. Surrender this ego that is stopping you from knowing yourself.

Q: There is also pride in intellectual knowledge.

Maharaj: There was no intellect prior to beingness. The ego, intellect, mind took possession of your whole body, and then administered it and ran the show.

HUMAN BEINGS ARE LIVING JUST LIKE SLAVES,
FOLLOWING THE INSTRUCTIONS OF:
EGO, MIND, INTELLECT.
THEY ARE USING YOUR POWER.
YOU ARE THE OWNER,
THE POWER.
YOU ARE THE SUPPLIER OF THAT POWER.

108. *You Are a Sadhu. You are a Master*

Maharaj: Your own story is written everywhere. You are Ultimate Truth. Spiritual books point out that you, as the Invisible Reader, are Ultimate Truth. But reading by itself is not sufficient because you are adding body-knowledge to the body-base. You are reading, reading, reading and confusing yourself.

The principle behind spirituality is to identify yourself. Knowledge is needed to forget your body identity, and for this a process is essential.

Reading books is not enough. People read thousands of books and they are still not making any progress. You need full confidence, full faith, full involvement. If the purpose is not clear as to why you are reading books, then it is a waste of time.

Make your mind strong for the last moment when there is often tremendous fear. Spirituality teaches you how to be strong, and reminds you that you are unborn. How long are you going to read for? What did you get from all these books?

I'M NOT SAYING, DON'T READ BOOKS,
BUT READ THEM WITH THE UNDERSTANDING,
THAT YOU ARE READING YOUR OWN KNOWLEDGE.
IT IS THE READER'S KNOWLEDGE.
THE READER IS NOT IN ANY FORM.

Change internally! There are so many Masters who are teaching nothing but knowledge that they have taken from books. And then they are charging for it.

WHY CHARGE? YOU ARE TRUTH.
I AM NOT DOING ANYTHING FOR YOU.
I'M JUST PLACING BEFORE YOU YOUR FINAL TRUTH THAT IS YOUR PROPERTY.
YOUR PROPERTY IS UNKNOWN TO YOU,
SO I AM SHOWING YOU YOUR PROPERTY.

Why should I charge for something that belongs to you? For something that you just forgot about? You need strong faith in yourself, and in your Master.

THE UNKNOWN CAME INTO EXISTENCE,
AND BECAME KNOWN THROUGH THE BODY.
THE UNKNOWN CAME TO BE KNOWN.
THE KNOWN WILL BE ABSORBED IN THE UNKNOWN.
SIMPLE TEACHINGS!

Question your Inner Master! Saint Janabai was devoted to Saint Namdev. She had staunch faith and used to say: "I catch hold of God and I see myself in every being". That is Conviction!

TOTAL INVOLVEMENT IS A MUST.

You need to be practical in this life because simple things will cause difficulties. You have to be practical.

Q: My doubts have gone, Maharaj. You have answered my doubts. Now there is only silence, hammering myself and practice.

Maharaj: Good! There are so many concepts that have the potential to cause anger and emotional upset. They all need to go, as they will distract you from Reality.

THIS KNOWLEDGE ACTS AS A SPEED-BREAKER
SO THAT WHEN EMOTION RISES,
THE IMPACT WILL BE REDUCED.

Reading books and a little meditation will not suffice. You have to go deep and deep into your

Selfless Self. The Masterly essence is with you. You are a *Sadhu*, you are a Master, but you are giving attention to external things.

There is nothing except your Selfless Self. You are Almighty God. This is your Knowledge, your right. Make yourself deserving of this Knowledge, and then accept it totally, not egoistically.

ACCEPT IT FROM THE BOTTOM OF YOUR SPIRITUAL HEART,
THROUGH WHICH YOU ARE LISTENING.
BE BRAVE,
FORGET THE WORLD: "SO THAT 'I'!"
SEE YOUR SELFLESS SELF,
AND THEN THE SEER WILL DISAPPEAR.
SEE YOUR SELFLESS SELF, AND THE SEER WILL DISAPPEAR.

The Seer will vanish like a bucket of water that is thrown into the sea. You are to throw yourself into the ocean of spirituality. You are unborn!

Q: You say you need a strong will, I also need a happy demeanour for my family.

Maharaj: You are considering yourself as an individual and that is why these thoughts are coming. Illusion!

LIVE LIKE YOU WERE PRIOR TO BEINGNESS!

Who wants happiness? View the body as belonging to someone else. The body is your neighbour's child. When Knowledge is completely absorbed, you will be able to tolerate all the unpleasant things that come your way.

109. No Up, and No Down

Maharaj: Knowledge is needed to minimise this painful life and dissolve all concepts, including "I am *Brahman*". All these processes exist for you to accept Reality spontaneously.

Q: Why is it that sometimes I feel I am getting closer, but at other times, it is as if I am going backwards?

Maharaj: You are feeling up and down. There is no up or down. I am placing Reality before you. When you feel up and down it is because you have strong faith in the body. You need to continue with the processes until you have Conviction. Be as you were prior to beingness.

WE ARE GOING FROM THE KNOWN, TO THE UNKNOWN.
PRIOR TO BEINGNESS, THE UNKNOWN BECAME KNOWN THROUGH THE BODY.
ONCE AGAIN, THE KNOWN WILL BECOME UNKNOWN
WHEN LEAVING THE BODY.
ALL THESE PROCESSES ARE THERE
TO ERASE THE BODY-FORM.

When you feel up and down, concentrate!

Q: So there is no up and no down?

Maharaj: I told you not to take the words literally. This is plain knowledge, straight knowledge. Meditation is needed, for as long as you are posing yourself in body-form. After leaving the body, there will be no need for meditation. There should not be another dream like this.

SPIRITUAL KNOWLEDGE IS THE KING OF SELF-CURES.
SELF-KNOWLEDGE MEANS SELF-CURE.

Siddharameshwar Maharaj used to say, "How long are you going to talk of this ABC, preliminary knowledge, the *Brahman*, *Atman*? It is just there for us to have a good basic foundation.

The Master says that you are beyond your assumed identity. Using different statements, the Master is trying to drive you, push you to the Ultimate Truth. You have to break the circle.

YOU HAVE TO DISSOLVE THE EGO, MIND, INTELLECT
AND BE AS YOU WERE,
PRIOR TO BEINGNESS.
SIMPLE!

You are not a baby any more. You are not in the kindergarten or school. This is a Postgraduate class!

HOW LONG DO I HAVE TO TEACH YOU THE ALPHABET FOR?
JUST FIND OUT, HOW YOU WERE PRIOR TO BEINGNESS,
AND THEN THE PAIN WILL GO.

Why is there pain? Because we forgot our Identity.

AFTER REALIZING YOUR POWER,
ALL YOUR PAINFULNESS WILL DISSOLVE.

I tell stories in this way so as to dilute the Knowledge, like giving food to small children. Our stories are a diluted diet. DILUTED DIET! Take a look! Glance at yourself, at how you were prior to beingness, and at how you are going to be after leaving the body?

THIS IS EXCEPTIONAL KNOWLEDGE.

A boy came here the other day wearing saffron robes. He had a fresh cut on his ear. His Master had instructed him to do this, as it was a sign of a *Sadhu*.

WHEN YOU ARE BORN,
DO YOU COME DRESSED IN SAFFRON CLOTHES,
WITH A CUT IN YOUR EAR?

This is body-knowledge!

IN OUR LINEAGE, WE DO NOT GIVE IMPORTANCE
TO OURSELVES AS MASTERS, BUT TO THE LISTENERS.
THEY ARE MASTERS 'IN POTENTIAL'.
ALL THE MASTERS IN OUR LINEAGE WERE VERY HUMBLE.

This visitor dressed in robes was a yoga teacher and karate instructor. I asked him if his training had made him fearless. It had not. He was still fearful about several things. Physical yoga is OK for the body, but at the same time, it has the effect of inflating the ego.

In our Lineage, we use a Direct Approach for teaching. Direct Knowledge with no in-betweens. Many Masters are impressing their illusionary knowledge, on seekers who do not know any better. Theirs may be a new version, but it is just another version of illusion. In our Lineage there are no *Brahman*, *Atman* concepts.

Q: When the Master is near, Knowledge is near!

Maharaj: No! Not so! I am not the form, I am already in your heart.

WHAT I AM PLACING BEFORE YOU,
IS SOMETHING EXCEPTIONAL.

In the light of Reality, you are to break this circle of illusory concepts. You are not the form, the Master is not the form. This is simple knowledge! Prior to beingness, you did not have a bodily form. Because of associations with the body, you accepted the form in yourself and in everyone else. This meant that you accepted a painful life.

Brahman, *Atman* are old dolls, polished dolls that you are still playing with. Put these dolls away!

Q: How can you be so patient? Can you give extra power to me?

Maharaj: Not so. 'Who' is asking for power? Self-enquire! Power is not separate from you! This will happen within you, the Inner Master. It will happen spontaneously in you, and then you will forget your external and internal identity. Forget about power as a concept!

LISTEN TO ME!
THOUGHTLESS THOUGHT WILL APPEAR.
WHY THOUGHTLESS THOUGHT?
THOUGHTS ARE CONNECTED WITH THE BODY.
THOUGHTLESS THOUGHT IS CONNECTED
WITH ULTIMATE TRUTH.

Every word has deep meaning. Thoughts are plain thoughts. They are connected with the body: mental thoughts, egoistic thoughts, intellectual thoughts.

THOUGHTLESS THOUGHT MEANS,
IT COMES SPONTANEOUSLY FROM WITHIN YOU.

That exceptional experience of the way you were prior to beingness, will appear in you, and then you will draw closer and closer to your Selfless Self.

ALL BEINGS ARE AFRAID OF DEATH.
HUMAN BEINGS NEED NOT HAVE ANY FEAR BECAUSE
THEY CAN KNOW THE REALITY.

There should not be any dreams. The door of Knowledge has been opened. The secret of Knowledge is yours. Be sincere and without suspicion. Don't take your eye off the peak of the mountain. After knowing the Reality, maintain it! There is nothing beyond.

People become victims of spirituality, *Sadhus* roaming in a world of confusion. With strong faith in your Master, there will be no temptations.

NOW YOU HAVE STATUS, STANDARDS.
KEEP IT UP!

How you behave is important: all your actions are supposed to be devotional. Devotion to Selfless Self with Spontaneous Conviction. You know the open secret. Silence will reign, even in unpleasant circumstances. We are giving you courage to face any unpleasant atmosphere.

This body is a magic box, a magic box! All Truth is in you! How you act and react is up to you. There are no questions and no answers. These were for the body-form.

FROM NOTHING,
TO SOMETHING,
TO NOTHING.

Something is everything, just words again... The basic principle of spirituality is to help you become fearless for the time when you must leave the body. The Spontaneous Conviction that "I am unborn" will make this happen.

Don't neglect the Spirit or adopt a casual approach. Be alert, cautious, with strong faith. Don't be anyone's victim, including your own. Who is leaving the body? You are not going anywhere. Our culture creates boundary lines: India, China, England. You are to convince yourself that there are no boundaries.

110.   The Ball is in Your Court. Smash it!

Maharaj: You are to stay at the highest level, that is why it is so important for the Knowledge to be absorbed. Remain at the top level. Everybody is under the influence of fear, and that is why the discipline of meditation and reciting the *Naam* is essential.

You have fear of birth, death, rebirth. You feel guilty about things you are supposed to have done. You are not guilty. You have not done anything.

NOTHING HAS HAPPENED, NOTHING IS HAPPENING,
NOTHING IS GOING TO HAPPEN.

Why accept things you don't know about? There is no rebirth. Throw out all the concepts and accept the Reality that you are Ultimate Truth.

DOES A LAMP TAKE REBIRTH
BECAUSE IT HAS RUN OUT OF OIL?

You are not the body, so why worry? Be calm, quiet, totally thoughtless, no good or bad thoughts. Presence is there, Silent Presence, Anonymous Presence. Glimpses of 'I', just 'I'. Glimpses of 'I', just 'I'. There is no consciousness, just 'I', just 'I', something that cannot be defined by words.

Q: Like 'I' without walls?

Maharaj: There is no experience and no experiencer. I have to use some words to communicate. You know the basic principle, now you have to accept it totally. Whose rebirth? Whose destiny?

"I AM IMMORTAL",
SO THERE IS NO FEAR OF ANYTHING.

You were free, you are free, and you are going to remain free. Now it is in your hands. The ball is in your court. Smash it!

FORGET ABOUT ALL CONCEPTS, AND STAY EMPTY.

Disease may come from stomach problems likewise, the mind is the cause of disease. Whatever you feel, whatever impressions are received are automatically reflected.

Q: It is difficult to accept it.

Maharaj: Final Truth is easy to accept, just like you accepted that you are a man. You will find it difficult only if you are accepting the dictates, and are pressured by the mind, ego, intellect.

J. Krishnamurti was once asked the question, "How is one supposed to live after sixty years of age?" He replied, "Just like a dead body, without consideration to the family, the universe, anything. Totally unconcerned". A dead body has no feelings, no requirements, no needs. It doesn't go, "Oh! I don't want to be buried or burned!" Being buried or burned makes no difference to a dead body.

THROW OUT, CAST ALL DOUBTS TO THE GROUND.
MAINTAIN YOUR STATUS
AT THE TOP LEVEL,
AND DON'T LOOK BACK.

Mountaineers are instructed not to look down. If you look down, you will fall down. Forget about the past! Your past is gone. There is no past, no future, no present. Sky does not have a past, future or present.

THIS IS REALITY, INVALUABLE REALITY,
THAT IS MAKING YOU STRONG
TO FACE ALL LIFE'S CIRCUMSTANCES.

It is up to you to accept, or not accept the Reality that has been presented to you. This Knowledge is open Knowledge.

In our Lineage, nothing is kept hidden. It is Open Truth shared freely without any expectations. There is to be no commercial abuse of this Knowledge. It is your property. I'm placing before you, your Truth. You may or may not accept it, that is entirely up to you.

111. *Dare to Live Without Concepts*

Maharaj: There is no difference between us, except for the body. We are the same. Spirit is One. Master knows his own Identity. The Listener has forgotten his Identity. There appears to be two bodies, two identities but the Spirit is the same. The Master knows himself in a real sense.

HE IS WITHIN THE SELFLESS SELF.

The Listener can know his true Identity through the medium of the Master. The Master says, "Don't analyze what I am saying. Don't take the words literally".

WHAT I AM SAYING IS ULTIMATE TRUTH.
CONCENTRATE ON THIS.

There is nothing wrong with reading spiritual books, as long as you accept that they are only indicators of Reality.

EVERYTHING YOU KNOW IS BODY-KNOWLEDGE,
AND THEREFORE ILLUSION.

You cannot say, "I am *Brahman*", without your Presence. Your Spontaneous Presence is essential. Without it, there can be no action and no reaction.

Q: I have been contemplating quite a lot on what you have been saying about reading spiritual books, and feel I have had a breakthrough. When I read books in the past, I accepted "I am *Brahman*", and stayed with that concept, if you like. I also had experiences around *Brahman*, which I valued and considered to be highly significant.

But now I realize that there was still a separation between the Reality of *Brahman* and 'my' Reality. What you are saying, Maharaj, is that behind the 'I am *Brahman*', behind everything, in fact, lies our Spontaneous Presence. And that Spontaneous Presence comes first. It has to be there to utter, "I am *Brahman*".

In brief, I was attached to the words or concept of 'I am *Brahman*' as the Reality. Now I know that my Spontaneous Presence comes first and is the Reality, the undefinable Reality.

Maharaj: Final Truth, Naked Truth. If the body is not my identity, then, who am I? '*Brahman*', '*Atman*'... these are just words. "Who am I?" These words and names are used to identify that Invisible Spontaneous Presence. Without your Spontaneous Presence there can be no action, no feeling, no thought, no books.

THEREFORE WHATEVER YOU SEE
AND UNDERSTAND IS ILLUSION.
IF YOU SAY, "I HAVE SEEN GOD",
IT IS THE SEER'S REFLECTION, THE SEER'S PROJECTION.

Prior to beingness, you did not know anything. Now we say: "This is called 'God', and that is called 'ghost'". These are layers on your Reality. "I have done something terrible and I feel guilty", is another layer of illusion. You have not done anything, and you are not guilty of anything. Do Self-enquiry and find this out for yourself.

KNOW THYSELF,
AND BE WITHIN THE SELFLESS SELF.

What is the purpose of spiritual knowledge? If you want this Knowledge to open up, then you must be disciplined. Meditation washes away all illusions. You can't see your face if the mirror is dirty. Likewise your mirror needs to be perfectly clean. Self-Knowledge leads to Conviction which is Self-Realization. You must have complete trust. No doubts!

THE SECRET OF FINAL TRUTH WITH ALL THE EVIDENCE,
IS BEING PLACED BEFORE YOU.
IT IS THE LISTENER'S SECRET, THE SPEAKER'S SECRET.

How can we describe that Listener? "Invisible, Anonymous, Unidentified". We need to use some words. You are to accept and absorb the Knowledge. It is not difficult at all.

Q: When I think of living without concepts, I have great fear.

Maharaj: After knowing the Reality, why are you swimming in the sea of concepts again?

THIS IS UNKNOWN TERRAIN. LET IT BE.

Explore, go deeper, self-discover, but remember it cannot be named, defined, compared.

Q: Recently, during meditation, I could not find my body. I was startled, afraid.

Maharaj: It happens. Don't worry! When you are involved in Selfless Self, many experiences happen. All these experiences are very good, progressive steps.

There are three types of experience: The *Darshan* of seeing, hearing, and touch of the Master. You may see the Masters or deities. You may feel someone touching you. You may hear the Master talking to you. These experiences happen. The Masters are manifesting out of your faith and Oneness with the Master. They are taking form, and talking with you.

For example, a disciple of Bhausaheb Maharaj had the plague. She prayed to her Master. Bhausaheb

Maharaj appeared, even though he was no longer in the body, and he cured her. That disciple had a vision of her Master because of her devotion.

SHE BECAME ONE WITH THAT,
ONE WITH HER MASTER'S IDENTITY.

This experience has nothing to do with the intellect. It is a progressive step, and encouraging. These miracles happen from your Presence. Here I'm talking about something more advanced, nevertheless, these experiences are indications of progress. Miracles do happen, when you have no doubt and strong devotion.

At the final stage - not that there really are any stages - all traces of body-knowledge will be gone. Until that time, just listen without suspicion, without a wavering mind that raises doubt. I'm trying my level best to convince you of the Plain Truth, Naked Truth, Final Truth. Strong faith is needed. Be sincere, don't say something, and then do the opposite. The entire Truth is placed in front of you.

Q: Talking about experiences, Maharaj, today I saw Nisargadatta Maharaj here in the ashram.

Maharaj: Nice! Good progress! It means that you are forgetting the body identity. Everyone has different experiences during the process of dissolving, merging and absorbing the Knowledge within Selfless Self.

Q: How many realized people do you know?

Maharaj: What do you mean by realized? People say, "Is he realized? Is she?" Realized means Spontaneous Conviction. There are no signs of Realization. Out of the Spontaneous Conviction, your whole vision, and all your actions change. There is no 'one big sign' of Realization. These are just words for understanding purposes.

HOW YOU WERE PRIOR TO BEINGNESS,
AND HOW YOU WILL BE AFTER LEAVING THE BODY,
THAT IS REALIZATION.

112. *Knowledge Beyond Miracles*

Maharaj: Sweet words like 'awareness', 'enlightenment', 'realization' and 'God' appear out of your Presence. These are not so important. I am placing before you 'Prior to Beingness'. Question yourself: "How were you prior to beingness?

Q: You can't fathom that, you can't even begin to imagine how you were.

Maharaj: Because your Identity is beyond imagination. Your Presence is beyond imagination. When you imagine something, you are taking ego from the body, when you are not the body at all.

Q: So the minute you talk, you are participating in a fiction.

Maharaj: Use words to establish your Ultimate Truth. Don't play with words! Listen to what the Master is conveying. Your Identity has nothing to do with the body. Your Identity is everywhere. You have no need any more of all this body-knowledge, of words like awareness, enlightenment, God. You know this talk is useless. You know better. No knowledge is knowledge. Everything came out of nothing. Everything dissolves into nothing.

Q: It's a cruel joke.

Maharaj: A cruel joke for whom? There is no past, no future, no present. No past, no future, no present. Spiritual books indicate your Ultimate Truth. Accept that only. People are influenced by words and get confused by them. Don't play with words. Doing this is like playing a game of cards for momentary happiness.

Q: When doing things is it worth offering all action to the *Sadguru*, your Inner Master or the Master himself?

Maharaj: Why are you offering? Again, you are taking yourself to be, "I am someone else, and I am offering something to my Master". You are considering yourself as different from me". There is no difference between us at all.

Q: The ego is tricky.

Maharaj: Tricky, yes.

Q: It sneaks in the back door.

Maharaj: The ego, mind, intellect are still playing tricks on you, and catching you out. You have to be alert, therefore keep up the meditation, Knowledge and *bhajan*. That way, you will not be deceived or cheated. External forces are there every moment trying to trick you. Maharaj holds up his hand, gesturing, 'Stop'! Keep the traffic at bay. Now you are the traffic controller!

Q: I wanted to ask you as many questions as possible while I was here. But now I don't seem to have any more questions to ask. Why is that?

Maharaj: All questions have been solved. Our Knowledge is very practical. Also, if you have complete faith and accept that the Reality is not separate from you, it is not difficult. You are to accept it.

Your lives were generally modelled on illusion. You were trying to find peace from illusion.

HAPPINESS IS INBUILT IN YOU.
YOU CONSIDER YOURSELF SEPARATE
FROM ULTIMATE TRUTH.
THIS CONFUSION IS REMOVED BY THE REALIZED MASTERS.

We are inviting attention of the Searcher. 'He' or 'She' is Ultimate Truth. The Searcher is the Source of this world. After knowing this in a real and practical sense, you will not have the need to go anywhere else.

Another confusion surrounds supernatural powers. People have the wrong impression. Miracles happen out of your Spontaneous Presence.

YOU ARE MISTAKINGLY GIVING CREDIT TO A GOD OR MASTER
FOR ANY MIRACLE THAT MAY HAPPEN.
YOU HAVE FORGOTTEN THAT YOU ARE A MAGICIAN.
INSIDE YOU, THERE IS A MAGIC BOX.
YOU ARE A MAGICIAN WITH YOUR OWN MAGIC BOX!

The Master is making you stand on your own two feet. You can do it! You must have guts, and at the same time, thoroughly follow the Master's principles.

AFTER CONVICTION, ALL THE SEARCHING ENDS.
ALL SEARCHING STARTS FROM YOU,
AND ALL SEARCHING ENDS WITH YOU.
THERE YOU ARE.

Your Knowledge is beyond any miracle. Some people are afraid of white magic or black magic because they don't know their own power.

THERE IS NO POWER OUTSIDE OF YOURSELF.

But you are still not giving enough importance to yourself. You are not always listening to, or accepting what I am saying.

THIS IS SIMPLE KNOWLEDGE
THAT IS TO BE ACCEPTED WITH YOUR STRONG WILLPOWER.
THE PRINCIPLE IS THAT
EVERYTHING STARTS FROM YOU,
AND ENDS WITH YOU.

Q: I was in south India and before I knew it, I was doing some *sadhana*.

Maharaj: When you know that this is the Reality, why do you still wish to travel to southern India, so you can stand on ice and torture your body?

Q: This time the practice happened, as if by itself.

Maharaj: Every practice has a purpose. You already know the Reality. This is a diversion, some entertainment or other.

You are here because you want to solve the mystery, the mystery of your Spontaneous Existence, because you are unknown to That. All your problems will be resolved after knowing the Reality. Nobody is good and nobody is bad. These are all body-related terms. Everything will disappear. Nothing will remain.

All actions are to be natural actions without any self-importance. Non-discrimination is a quality of saintly people. Everything is in you. You are the teacher, the student, the Master, the devotee. The worshipper and the worshipped! Engrave all this in you. If someone says, "God is standing at the door", just say "Sorry!" and ignore him.

THIS IS GREAT KNOWLEDGE,
NOT CONNECTED AT ALL TO BODY-BASED KNOWLEDGE.
"GOD IS A REFLECTION OF MY PRESENCE.
MY PRESENCE LETS GOD APPEAR".

113. *Swimming in a Sea of Fear*

Maharaj: You have to come out of this fear of death. You have no cause to fear! You are unborn and, like in the story of the rope and the snake, you are afraid of an illusion. You are unborn, immortal, therefore there is no question of birth and death!

When the time comes for you to say goodbye to the world, it should be a happy moment. Try to know the reality behind 'death'. Who is dying? Your Presence was there prior to the Spirit clicking with the body, prior to your beingness.

If Presence was not, how can there be any birth or death for the body? Spirit is unborn, it is always there as Presence. Spirituality is there, meditation, knowledge, prayer, etc, to establish the Conviction that, "You are unborn".

You read different spiritual books on XYZ, and then you analyze everything that has been said. Why all this analysis, when you, the Invisible, Formless Reader are Ultimate Truth? Unless food-body-knowledge dissolves, you will not be able to know yourself in a real sense, and there will be no Conviction.

YOU MUST KNOW THE PRINCIPLE OF SPIRITUALITY.
DRY KNOWLEDGE IS JUST SPIRITUAL ENTERTAINMENT.

You are swimming in an illusory ocean of concepts and fear, of sin and virtue. The principle of religion has been submerged, and converted into sets of rules by human beings. These rules have been created for selfish purposes to regulate society. Spiritual leaders, church leaders have created so much fear and illusion in people, obscuring Reality, making people dependent on them, religion and God.

Forget about all these man made rules. All these illusions have come out of your Presence. All actions are recorded from this illusory dream. Who is recording? Who is enjoying the dream? Find out! There is no snake and there is no death.

YOU ARE NOT GIVING THE SEER ENOUGH IMPORTANCE.
FORGET ABOUT THE SEEN,
IT IS YOUR REFLECTION ONLY.

Q: What you are saying, Maharaj, is that by becoming fully independent, you will be completely autonomous, without any conditionings?

Maharaj: This understanding is not logical understanding, it is Spontaneous Understanding, Conviction, just like knowing you are a man, without giving it any thought.

You have theoretical knowledge, but what is needed is practical knowledge. And this will only happen through meditation.

Q: Is the meditation like giving life, something like taking light away from the ego, and moving your attention to Reality?

Maharaj: A cleaning process is taking place through the vibrations. If the mirror is dirty, you can't see your image. All illusory concepts will dissolve, and then, "Yes! I am That!" We are always considering ourselves as handicapped, incomplete. This is not true.

Q: We have to be independent of all reinforcers of illusion?

Maharaj: Go deep and deep and deep...

Q: Could you say, 'accept' "prior to beingness", instead of "except", as in "Except your Selfless Self, there is no God...", etc?

Maharaj:

YOU ARE PLAYING WITH THE WORDS,
STAYING DRY AND SAFE BY THE SHORE,
WITH DRY KNOWLEDGE.

Don't live a cowardly life, swim. Dive into the sea and start living like a lion! Don't be afraid of the water! A person who fears every moment is a coward.

Q: We have to have the attitude that, "This is my Power", but at the same time, "It is not my Power", so that it is not misused?

Maharaj: This is dry discussion! Dry discussion will not help you. You are to put the Knowledge into practice!

114. Read Your Own Book

Q: I am digesting the Knowledge.

Maharaj: Very nice, it is a good sign. Now that you know Ultimate Truth, you are to maintain it. Continue with the meditation, this is most important. Sing the *bhajan*s during the day, they will give you Spontaneous Happiness. Do these practices regularly. They are essential, as necessary as your daily food.

The purpose of spirituality is to dissolve body-based knowledge. For this to happen, the cleaning process has to continue. Every day you are to refresh your Conviction.

DON'T READ ANY BOOKS,
READ YOUR OWN BOOK.

Your laptop has an account, password, phone number, all the details you need. You are a search engine, like Google or Yahoo! All websites are to be found in you. All websites are 'One' in you.

Q: Sometimes I get very distracted.

Maharaj: Don't give attention to this feeling. Meditation helps with concentration. All thoughts will vanish. Slowly, slowly all of them will vanish.

YOU ARE THE PRINCIPLE OF THE WORLD.

Because of a lifetime of impressions, these layers are not going to be removed immediately. It will take some time. Carry on with your work and do your job well and efficiently.

HAVE THAT VISION THAT YOU ARE EVERYWHERE:
NO MAN, NO WOMAN, ALL IS *BRAHMAN*.
SLOWLY, SILENTLY, STABILITY WILL BE ESTABLISHED.

Q: At the beginning, it is a little like living in a house that is full of squatters. Then you come to realize that you are the owner, and these are just the tenants.

Maharaj: When you come to know that you are the owner of this house, you will want to clean it. First you have to get rid of the tenants who like living in this building and don't wish to leave. Patience and firmness is needed at this time because they will abuse you while they are being kicked out.

Q: Then the tenants become subservient and even ask: "What do you want boss?"

Maharaj: Dramatic changes will take place. Wait and watch, slowly, silently permanently. Continue with the meditation, it is your foundation. Don't come under the influence of someone else's concepts. A weak mind is very dangerous. You know better!

Mental strength is very important so that you don't take on board anyone else's thoughts. Have self-confidence so that no one will dare come near you. Nobody will even try to teach you because you are Ultimate Truth. Who created the *Vedas*, *Upanishads*? They are your babies.

ALL SPIRITUAL KNOWLEDGE
CAME OUT OF YOUR SPONTANEOUS PRESENCE.

Maharaj: You are Master of this world. Open fact. Not egoistically!

Q: Old habits are very strong.

Maharaj: It is only natural because of the long association with the body. Don't see yourself as a patient in need of a psychologist. There was a lady who suffered from pain in her joints, at three o'clock on the dot, every day! She was advised to ignore three o'clock. When she followed this advice, her problem vanished.

Similarly, normal people are patients with psychological problems. Because of numerous illusory concepts that have been accepted without consideration, such as doing good or bad, sin, hell, guilt, etc, we feel we have done something wrong, and as a result we feel guilty and afraid.

The Master says, "You are not guilty at all. Why are you signing all these confessions and admissions of guilt at the Criminal Court? You have become a victim of your own thoughts and feelings, a victim of your own dream. And in that dream, you are crying and crying. The only crime you are guilty of is of wrongly thinking that you are a 'human being'.

YOU ARE *BRAHMAN*, NOT A HUMAN BEING.
THE CRIMINAL IS A HUMAN BEING,
BUT YOU ARE NOT A HUMAN BEING.
THEREFORE YOU ARE NOT GUILTY.
CASE DISMISSED!

Suppose someone takes a loan from you and they don't give it back. You say, "I loaned you some money, now you have to return it". You are constantly reminding him, saying, "I gave you a loan. Come on, pay up! You are cheating me. I need the money".

So likewise we are saying, "No, no! You are not the body at all, you are Spirit. You are *Brahman*, you are *Atman*. You are falsely trying to take my place. You are sitting on my throne. You are deceiving me, cheating me! Come on, get lost! "

IT IS A GREAT SIN TO ACCEPT THAT WHICH YOU ARE NOT!
AND, TO KEEP ON CRYING IN THE DREAM!

115. *Your Story*

Q: Often, people get hurt by close relations.
Maharaj: The spiritual person is not supposed to hurt anyone's feelings. You can ignore someone, but don't struggle with anyone. Forget and forgive! We all have the same essence, but different standards and upbringing. Unpleasant atmospheres will not remain constant. You are a spiritual being, not a human being.

If a tiger appears and you run, the tiger will run after you. If you face it, eye to eye, the tiger will run. If anyone tries to insult you, this will not touch you. Spirituality teaches you: your inbuilt teacher will instruct you. This will happen spontaneously out of your meditation. You become one with Selfless Self through the meditation. When temptations arise, you will get inner guidance on how to act.

SIMPLICITY IS THE BEST POLICY.
AVOID DIFFICULT PEOPLE!

Your own Master will teach you how to live in difficult circumstances. This is the highest kind of devotion, when questions and answers flow, like an inner dialogue. Don't ask why there are problems, that is just for children learning the ABC. Here you are becoming a Master of language!

This is a way of approaching your Selfless Self, listening, receiving prompts, and taking guidance. This Spontaneous flow is a sign of your Realization.

Q: What do you mean by "Reader's Knowledge", when you talk of reading spiritual books?

Maharaj: When reading these books, read them as your story, and not just a story about *Brahman*. It is the Reader's Knowledge, the Reader's Biography, your 'Spiritography'. Be calm and quiet! Whatever you listen to, use it to refresh your memories, nothing complex.

BE WITH YOU!
FORGET ABOUT THE WORLD.
DON'T GO LOOKING HERE AND THERE.

Spiritual Knowledge teaches you how to live and act in this world. Meditation is effective to calm the ego, intellect. When you know these feelings are coming, ignore them. Don't give them attention, just like ignoring a barking dog! You are teaching yourself. This is 'Self-Teaching'.

In the beginning, the disciple works at getting close to Selfless Self. He continues to move closer and closer to Selfless Self. Initially, deliberate effort and discipline is required to achieve this movement, using the tools of Self-enquiry, meditation, Mantra recitation, *bhajans*, and some spiritual reading, reflection, contemplation, The disciple is teaching himself, Self-Teaching.

After absorbing Reality, Spontaneous Awakening appears within the devotee. The devotee has Realized the 'Deity' within. He has 'Merged with the Ocean', so to speak, and no longer has to make deliberate efforts, or take any deliberate action.

All action occurs spontaneously from then on, as Selfless Self and devotee are ONE. Therefore, in different situations how to act, or what to do, is now automatic with no deliberate effort needed. There is Inner Guidance, a spontaneous flow of indications. We call this Self-Teaching without any deliberate effort. Prior to Awakening, to teach yourself, some effort was needed, now not so. The devotee has become a Master, a Master of Selfless Self, a Teacher of Selfless Self. Remember! These are words only. Look to the meaning behind them, the gist.

You are now a 'Teacher' of your Selfless Self. You are a 'Master' of your Selfless Self. Therefore use your spiritual Power, your spiritual Knowledge in every area and walk of life, whether it be your family, social, or spiritual life.

Q: You say don't be a victim, don't listen to others' concepts?

Maharaj: Nisargadatta Maharaj said that after knowing the Reality, you are not to be distracted. This is an illusionary world with people who will try to shake your faith and trust, making you suspicious once more. Now that you have Reality, maintain it with meditation. Other people talk bookish knowledge: "The *Vedas* say this and that", and they may distract you with their half-knowledge. This will bring about a downfall. Beware!

This is simple Knowledge, but essential Knowledge. Why do we need this Knowledge? Because the body is not our identity, and we are unknown to ourselves. We are to know ourselves in a real sense.

YOU NEED COURAGE TO SAY,
'GOODBYE' TO THIS ILLUSORY WORLD.

You know the Direct Source, Ultimate Truth. Now you are to digest, absorb this Knowledge with constant reciting and meditation. This way, your 'body memories' will be constantly refreshed by Reality.

When Nisargadatta Maharaj talked about Knowledge, he said, "Chew it like chocolate and the chocolate fluid will refresh it by itself.

Q: I was reading one of Ranjit Maharaj's books. He was talking about doing nothing, not speaking, not eating. Should we do these things, or not do them?

Maharaj: Why these imaginary tricks? It is OK for beginners, but at this particular level, when you know that your Presence is invisible, why ask this question? There's no 'I', so who is talking about, "I am not eating".

YOU HAVE HAD SO MUCH KNOWLEDGE,
YOU ARE NOT TO TAKE A STEP DOWN.
AFTER LISTENING FOR ALL THIS TIME,
I EXPECT YOU TO HAVE A BASE, SOME FOUNDATION.

But if you are getting happiness from this, then read it!

116. You Are the Trustee

Maharaj: The doctor needs some information from his patients, so that he can advise them and determine which medicines to prescribe. You are your own Master. All this Knowledge leads to Conviction. If you have a solid base, foundation, a good knowledge base, then all you need is a click, a touch from the Master.

But you need to come forward and surrender, so that you can be guided and get the right prescription, according to your spiritual maturity. Nothing is impossible, and everything is easy, when the foundation is solid. This way Knowledge will automatically be exposed in your Selfless Self. Your Knowledge is already there.

WE ARE DIGGING A WELL, REMOVING STONES,
REMOVING THE MUD, DIGGING, DIGGING,
REMOVING ALL THE UNWANTED STONES.

As I have told you, the meditation is creating vibrations inside. Slowly, silently, permanently, everything will be removed, in the light of these vibrations.

YOU NEED COURAGE TO THROW YOURSELF INTO IT.
I AM HERE TO PROTECT YOU.

You also have the three watchmen of Knowledge, Meditation and Bhajans to protect you 24 hours a day.

First thing you need is a good teacher, who teaches you slowly, slowly, how to be a good swimmer. Then you are to throw yourself into the ocean of spirituality. Bad thoughts are coming, bad concepts are coming. Carry on!

When you are digging a well, stones appear, then mud. After patience and perseverance, after digging, digging, you will eventually uncover pure water. Out of the vibrations, all unnecessary things, everything that is unwanted will be removed.

YOU ARE TO CONVINCE YOURSELF.
YOU ARE THE TRUSTEE.

You are the trustee of your own spiritual Knowledge.

In our Lineage, we have a method of meditation which is used for acquiring practical spiritual Knowledge, Self-Knowledge. In this way, the Knowledge is conveyed in an organized way, step by step, systematically, scientifically.

Everybody knows of different medicines that are available, but it is only the doctor who knows how to administer the dose. You may know the law, but you need a lawyer to implement it. You have studied many spiritual books, but not in a systematic or scientific way.

I am giving what you already have, and have forgotten. I am simply returning this to you. I have given you systematic Knowledge. All that was missing was a method of organizing this Knowledge. The Knowledge was not there. You now have strong Conviction. Everything is within you. You just have to click it, strike it, ignite it. The fire is already there.

ENGRAVE THIS KNOWLEDGE.
EMBRACE THIS KNOWLEDGE.
ACCEPT THIS KNOWLEDGE COMPLETELY.

Very few devotees involve themselves. Some come here to the ashram in a casual way. They don't even bow. I don't mind if they don't bow to me, but they should bow to my Masters, who are great saints. Don't respect me, but pay respect to them. Bow down to them!

Q: Bowing is a custom in every church, every religion.

Maharaj: Some visitors have travelled long distances. I have to share the knowledge with them. At the same time, I am expecting, at least, some respect for these great saints up on the wall.

Q: Someone was talking about dispassion earlier?

Maharaj: It means that you have no attraction to the world. After Conviction, there's no longer any attraction. Your Presence is there, but it is unknown Presence, Unidentified, Anonymous, Invisible Identity.

After knowing the Reality, dispassion becomes meaningless. When you were in the circle, you were expecting money, status, power. There was greed, as well. After knowing the Reality, you realized: "Who is going to use all this money? For how long? What is the use of all this greed when my existence is not body-based?" And you remain unconcerned with the world.

Knowledge is supposed to lead to Realization. When the Knowledge is absorbed, then nothing remains, no experiencer. You merge with your Selfless Self. When Knowledge has been totally accepted and absorbed, there is no evidence left. Everything vanishes, nothing can be seen. All concepts are dissolved.

THE 'ADVANCED STAGE' MEANS
THAT KNOWLEDGE IS ABSORBED TOTALLY.

But you are not quite ready yet to accept this Truth. Meditation is the necessary base. As I told you, if the foundation is weak, the entire building is weak. You will grow in courage and power, so that at the last stage there will not be any thoughts. Then there will be Spontaneous Silence, spiritual intoxication. You will remain in your own world.

Meantime, all concepts are to be erased, and the ego, dissolved. Use this Knowledge to erase all illusion. Everyone is equal. There is no need for competition! Who are you competing against? With the awakening of your Inner Master, all questions will be solved automatically. This is Self-curing, Self-healing, Self-teaching.

YOUR IDENTITY IS PLACED BEFORE YOU
THROUGH THE MEDIUM OF THE MASTER.

When you come to know your Inner Master, you will come to know that differences don't exist.

There are no differences between anybody and anything.

As long as there is body identification, where you identify yourself as an individual, you will find differences. There are no differences or distinctions. Accept this Truth. It is Final Truth. It is your story. That is the purpose behind spirituality, so that you can know your story.

117. Reality Should Touch Your Heart

Q: Recently, Maharaj, there were so many thoughts crowding me, that I couldn't meditate.
Maharaj: Don't struggle with them, just let the thoughts flow. It is natural, body-related. Witness them, see them, then ignore them.

You are completely unknown to Selfless Self. And Selfless Self is just like the sky. Sky does not know its own existence. You are formless. The meditator forgot its Identity and is measuring himself in body-form. You were never in body-form. Final Truth.

Your Spontaneous Presence flashes and from the Seer's reflection, you see the dream-world. Without the Anonymous, Invisible Seer, you cannot see the world.
EVERYTHING COMES OUT OF YOU.
THE SPONTANOEUS PRESENCE IS REFLECTED,
BUT IT IS FORMLESS, UNIDENTIFIED PRESENCE.
Q: Do things arise that push you further into meditation? My boss gets on my nerves.
Maharaj: All physical, and mental problems will dissolve with meditation. Research shows that a high percentage of people who meditate benefit from it. It has been scientifically proven that meditation reduces stress, and eases physical, mental and emotional problems. Spiritual Knowledge helps physical problems.

Through these discourses, I am presenting you with the Invisible Listener's Identity. You are Ultimate Truth, Final Truth. This Reality should touch your heart.
Q: And at some point it opens up?
Maharaj: In this world everything is illusion. Don't keep any doubts pending. Keep in 'mind' that this is an illusionary world. Everything is true and everything is false in this dream world.
REMEMBER, YOU ARE ULTIMATE TRUTH,
WITHOUT ANY FORM.
You know this, but still you stay in the circle of illusion, trying to extract peace and silence from it. Who wants silence? Does the sky want silence? In order to have this Conviction, all these disciplines are needed. These talks are not a circus, or a show of words. They are Reality, indicating your Invisible Reality.

Your strong ego is not allowing you to reach Selfless Self. Everybody is listening calmly and quietly but within the circle of illusionary knowledge, still thinking, "I am somebody else, I am *Brahman, Parabrahman*". You are embracing an identity which is not you at all.
THIS IS A LONG DREAM, AND IT IS NOT GOING TO LAST.
You have had thousands of dreams since childhood. Where did everyone go? Who captured all these images? What will happen after death? Who is dying, taking birth?
ASK SELFLESS SELF ALL THESE QUESTIONS.

They are supposed to be solved by Selfless Self.

The ego has to dissolve totally. You are to surrender to Selfless Self, only then, will Reality come forth within you. Your Spontaneous Presence projects Reality. Effort is not needed, just your involvement which is most important.

GET RID OF EGO.
AND THEN THAT REALITY THAT IS PLACED BEFORE YOU,
WILL TOUCH YOUR HEART.

It should touch your heart and move you. You should feel something like:

"I HAVE WASTED ALL MY TIME TILL TODAY.
BUT NOW IS THE TIME".

Then you won't feel sorry later on. If you ignore it, time will creep up behind you, and you will say, "Oh what have I done, or not done! I had the chance to do something and I ignored it". The attractions of the illusory world kept you in the circle.

118. *Mountain Peak*

Maharaj: When you get to a certain level, be cautious. Don't allow any thoughts back in. Keep body-knowledge out!

STAY WITH 'THERE IS NOTHING THERE'.

No suspicions, and no doubts. Keep your eye on the target, the top of the mountain. If you lose your concentration, hear a noise, or get drawn to an attraction, you will not be able to 'fly to heaven'! You are already there. You just have to convince yourself. If you pay attention to other people's thoughts, you will be distracted at the end of life.

THIS IS A DIRECT ROAD. THERE ARE NO BYPASSES.
WITH DIRECT HAMMERING,
YOU WILL KNOW THAT YOU ARE FINAL TRUTH.
YOU ARE FINAL TRUTH.

Once you hold a spiritual position, you need to be steadfast and alert. There was one devout devotee. I used to say to him, "You are nearly at the peak". Suddenly, he developed a physical problem and he stopped coming to the ashram. He threw everything away for some petty matter. There is no need to let physical or bodily problems take over. You have to stay as you were prior to the body, prior to beingness.

YOUR OWN THOUGHTS,
YOUR OWN FEELINGS ARE CREATING PROBLEMS FOR YOU,
WITHOUT YOUR KNOWLEDGE.

Q: You said, "Be like you were before, prior to beingness. I can't imagine that...

Maharaj: **THAT SPIRIT, WHICH CANNOT BE IMAGINED,**
                     IS SPONTANEOUS, INVISIBLE, ANONYMOUS PRESENCE.

Q: What should we think it is like?

Maharaj: It is beyond thinking!

AFTER KNOWING THE REALITY,
'THE WORLD IS WITHIN ME'.
ACCEPT THAT ULTIMATE TRUTH TOTALLY.
NOT PHYSICALLY, NOT MENTALLY, BUT SPIRITUALLY.

Q: Why is *karma* not explained in the *Gita* by Krishna?

Maharaj: Many things are explained. What *karma*?

Q: If you do something bad...

Maharaj: There is no bad, no good. What is bad for the animal is good for the butcher. Forget about the *Upanishads, Vedas,* Krishna, Rama. This is spiritual entertainment. I am talking about prior to beingness. All this literal knowledge is half-knowledge. Without your Presence, who is going to talk about the *Upanishads, Mahabharata, Vedas?* Stay with prior to beingness!

TRY TO SEE WITHIN YOUR SELFLESS SELF.
YOUR INVISIBLE PRESENCE IS
THE FATHER OF ALL THIS KNOWLEDGE.

I'm inviting the attention of the Invisible Listener in you. Prior to body-knowledge, did you know the *Vedas, Upanishads?* You offer *Namaskaram* to me. Who is that 'me'? Who is that me? It is that Invisible Presence. Throw out all illusion! All this external knowledge has disabled you.

Have you seen God, any God?

Q: Sometimes!

Maharaj: Only sometimes, not always?

Q: Some phenomenon.

Maharaj: Without your Presence, there's no God. You are not accepting this Truth.

THE DEVOTEE IS GOD ALL ALONG,
BUT WHEN HE REALIZES HE IS GOD,
THE DEVOTEE VANISHES AND ONE ALONE REMAINS.

After knowing the Reality, you are to erase all concepts. My Master used to say, "All that you have read and listened to, just minus it all, and then talk".

THINK OUT OF THE CIRCLE, OUT OF THE BODY ROOT.

Don't stress the intellect. This is very, very simple Knowledge. We have become victims, trapped in our own web of knowledge, *Brahman, Atman,* etc.

Who says these things?

I AM INVITING ATTENTION OF THAT QUESTIONER,
THROUGH WHICH THAT QUESTION ARISES.

Maharaj: Don't nod your head unless you are convinced!

Q: But that might take a hundred years!

Maharaj: If you had been sitting in a dark cave for years, and then suddenly you have light, are you going to say, "I'm not going to use the light just yet. I will wait for another hundred years?" No! The change is instant, immediate.

When you see the light, don't hesitate, don't postpone it and stay in the darkness. There is no tomorrow. Don't measure yourself in body-form. Just know yourself in a real sense. We have been depending on what we have read and listened to.

WE HAVE BEEN TRYING TO KNOW THE SPIRITUAL LIFE
THROUGH PHYSICAL KNOWLEDGE.

All these imaginary gods will dissolve, along with all the concepts, including hell and heaven. People are so afraid of concepts like hell, even though no one has ever seen it!

YOUR INNER MASTER IS VERY POWERFUL.
PLEASE YOUR INNER MASTER.
HE IS GOD.

Your external Master has told you that you are Almighty God, Omnipresent, Ultimate Truth. You are not accepting it so easily. Somewhere there is some doubt, "How can I be Almighty God?"

YOU SHOULD COME FORWARD WITH CONVICTION,
AND FEELING, THAT SAYS, "YES, I AM ALMIGHTY GOD".

You need complete faith in yourself and in the Master, and then you will come forward. No half-way measures. Complete involvement is a must! You know how to swim, so jump in, practise! You need to jump in with courage, strength, guts. Everything is in you, but you are not using your power. You can control bad thoughts with the Master Key.

CHANGE YOUR VIEW TO SEE YOUR SELFLESS SELF.

With courage, know and feel, "I am not the body, I am *Mahatma*". This Conviction leads to Knowledge. Forget about the *Vedas,* they brought you here. Literal knowledge indicated you are a Master, you are Ultimate Truth. No need to be so serious either. Be happy! Be happy because you know the Reality! The Searcher found what you were searching for.

WHAT YOU WERE SEARCHING FOR, WAS FOUND IN YOU.
IT WAS THERE ALL THE TIME!

"I went in search of God and I became God!", said Swami Vivekananda. Vivekananda used to wander around asking people: "Have you seen God?" He got no response until he approached Ramakrishna Paramahamsa and asked him the same question. Ramakrishna replied: "Yes, my child, I have seen God. I see Him as I see you here, only more clearly. God can be seen. One can talk to Him. I can show you God."

Swami Vivekananda was not only surprised, he was astounded. He knew that Ramakrishna's words had been uttered from the inner depths. "Oh! This is the first time I have heard anyone say this", said Vivekananda.

Vivekananda knew intuitively that he was face to face with a genuine Master. He was face to face with Reality. God was very much alive in him. Vivekananda had no doubt about this Master, as no one before him had spoken in such a way. He said,

"I HAVE SEEN GOD, AND I CAN SHOW YOU!"

That is something exceptional. The same thing was told by Nisargadatta Maharaj, "I'm not making you a disciple, because the Master is already within you. I'm showing you the Master in you".

119. The Master is God's God

Maharaj: You must have trust, strong trust in the Master, that he will make you enlightened. Nisargadatta Maharaj used to say that if it wasn't for his Master, Siddharameshwar Maharaj, coming into his life, he would have just been a common man, aimlessly running here and there from one temple to another.

There must be respect for the Guru, the Master. Saint Kabir says: "If my Master and God appear before me, I would give respect to my Master, for it is only because of Him, that I know God". So you must give importance to the Master, the Guru.

THE MASTER IS GOD'S GOD.
THE MASTER IS GOD'S GOD.

You can see the Lineage there, [Maharaj points to the pictures of the Masters, Bhausaheb Maharaj, Siddharameshwar Maharaj, Nisargadatta Maharaj, Ranjit Maharaj]. They were ordinary people but they had no ego, no big intellect, no expectations. They were humble. When this quality appears in you, it is a sign of enlightenment.

If something unpleasant happens in your life, the mind becomes restless and feels like, "Oh! something is wrong". So the discipline is very easy, but, at the same time, it is very difficult because body-knowledge, the 'food-body-knowledge' must be totally dissolved. This Knowledge is very simple knowledge which is beyond imagination. Your intellect will not help you. How were you prior to beingness? "I don't know", you reply.

YOU SEE, THERE WAS NO EGO, NO INTELLECT, NO MIND,
NO GOD. IT IS ONLY BECAUSE YOU ARE IN BODY-FORM
THAT THERE IS A NEED FOR GOD.

If there is 'nobody', where then is this God, this Master, this knowledge that you speak about, that you have found in books? You have forgotten your Identity, and therefore, we are inviting the attention of the Silent, Invisible Listener in you that is called *Brahman* or God.

Change will take place. With strong devotion, a strong will and a little sacrifice, it won't be difficult. Every moment is very important. This is your time.

BE EARNEST!
DON'T SEEK AFTER THE ULTIMATE TRUTH
IN A CASUAL MANNER.

There will be complete and Total Peace, without any material cause. Inner Peace without disturbance from mind, ego, intellect, from anything. Even if the external atmosphere is unfavourable, you will be at peace. Even when there is chaos, the enlightened devotee will have Complete Peace because he is always unconcerned with, and untouched by anything at all times.

TOTAL KNOWLEDGE IS ABSORBED IN ONENESS.
NO DUALITY.

Clouds are coming, clouds are going. The sun is as it is.

We can go on discussing philosophy for hours and years together. All you will get from this is 'spiritual entertainment', nothing more than that. To have strong Conviction, you need the discipline of various processes, meditation, *bhajan*, prayer, Knowledge.

You should be very serious and very eager, with an edge of concern and anxiety. After thinking, thinking about all this, one day, you will exclaim, "Oh! Now, I see!"

We are so fortunate to have had these Lineage Masters with such direct Knowledge. Although they did talk about *maya*, *Brahman*, *Atman*, *Paramatman,* there was less emphasis on these polished words. 'Last *prarabdha*', 'future *prarabdha*', all these words take you round and round and round in circles and entrap you. The focus has been shifted from these polished words to down-to-earth, direct parlance:

EVERYTHING IS IN YOU.
EVERYTHING IS IN YOU.

In order to get the direct attention of the Invisible Listener, Direct Knowledge is used. With the attention focussed on that Invisible Listener in you, we are telling you:

YOU ARE THE SOURCE OF HAPPINESS.
YOU ARE THE SOURCE OF PEACE,
NOT IN BODY-FORM.

Gradually, day by day, your attachments will loosen and reduce. You have a lot of attachment to the body, a lot of love and affection. When it is all dissolved, then you will come to know Reality. It is a known fact, open fact, Open Truth, Ultimate Truth, Final Truth.

Our Lineage Masters have shown us how it can happen. They have shown us that Self-Realization is possible. It happened to them, so it can happen to you.

Slowly, silently, and permanently with practice, illusionary thoughts will dissolve, until they vanish completely.

It's a cleaning process, just like when your laptop is crowded with unwanted files, which you then have to delete because of viruses. Meditation is an anti-virus software. This anti-virus software can control and guard, keep watch, and keep you alert.

Every day it is necessary to clean your house. Likewise, you have got to clean 'this house'. Every day with meditation, *bhajan* and Knowledge, and then it will be very easy. But you must be devoted:

DEVOTION, EXTREME DEVOTION,
EXCEPTIONAL DEVOTION,
EXCEPTIONAL INVOLVEMENT IS NEEDED.

Nisargadatta Maharaj used to say, "Casual spirituality will not help, casual spirituality will not help you find complete peace". Everything is within you, but still you are looking here and there, trying to find something else, something different, something more. While always busy trying to find, finding this, finding that, you are forgetting the Finder.

YOU HAVE FORGOTTEN THE FINDER.
THE FINDER IS THE SOURCE OF THIS WORLD.
BUT THAT FINDER IS INVISIBLE, ANONYMOUS.
IT CANNOT BE DEFINED IN WORDS.

It is possible to have Conviction, but you must have strong faith and courage. Difficulties will be there, they are bound to be there. So you must have complete faith, perfect foundations, strong foundations.

It's very simple Knowledge. Knowledge without any complications or complexities. This is Direct Knowledge. There is no need to go here and there, and read more and more books that confuse you more and more. You may read books, but don't become addicted to words.

STAY WITH THE PRINCIPLE.
YOU ARE THAT PRINCIPLE, BEHIND ALL THE WORDS,
AND ALL THE BOOKS.

Likewise, you are your own teacher, you are your own guide and the architect of your own life. See your Selfless Self. How can you see that Selfless Self? The Magic Key has been given to you. The *Naam Mantra*, the Master Key, will help you see your Selfless Self!

120. The Master Sparks the Fire

Q: When you give the *Naam* Mantra, is Shakti power given at the same time?

Maharaj: If you accept the *Naam* and the Master totally, some power will come along with the Mantra. If there is no suspicion or doubt, then that Power which is already in you will explode.

THE POWER IS WITHIN YOU ALREADY.

All that is needed is a touch. Through the Master, you are getting some touch. It is like I told you, fire is there, all that is needed to produce fire, is for the matchstick to touch the box. The moment the matchstick strikes the box, you see the fire.

Q. And if you accept the *Naam*, the initiation, and the Master totally... ?

Maharaj: Your Power will arise spontaneously because your Presence is spontaneous. Every action and reaction is connected with your Spontaneous Presence. This is a direct line to your Ultimate Truth. Reciting the Mantra is a little like spiritual torture at first: "I am *Brahman*, I am *Brahman*, I am *Brahman*." But now there is surrender, "Yes, I Am *Brahman*!"

Tukaram says, "People are drowning. I try to help them, but they are not accepting my help". Just as you have to ignore dreams, you have to ignore others as well because you know better.

WITH GREAT EFFORT, YOU HAVE ARRIVED
AT A CERTAIN STAGE. DON'T FALL BACK NOW!

You are near to the mountain peak. Neglect the external atmosphere. Go straight to heaven! Don't lose concentration.

A group of boys were learning archery, including Arjuna, the greatest archer. A few of them placed an artificial parrot on a big tree in the far distance. Then they asked if everyone could see this parrot. All anyone could see was the sky, as the target was so very far away. There was a commotion and much talking going on about this impossible task. When Arjuna was asked if he could see it, he said, "I can only see the eye, I don't see the parrot".

This has great meaning, deep meaning... "I can only see the eye". He aimed at the eye and hit the target. This illustrates that there are many devotees, but maybe only one who has Self-Conviction. Everybody says "I am *Brahman*, I am *Brahman*".

Everybody is a 'devotee', but lacking that strong devotion, that necessary total concentration - total concentration, total concentration. So slowly, silently and permanently, concentrate on your Selfless Self. Every moment, life is diminishing, diminishing, more and more, so don't take it lightly or casually.

MY MASTER TOLD ME,
"YOU ARE FINAL TRUTH",
THEREFORE, I AM FINAL TRUTH.

There is no ego, only a spontaneous feeling. You have to accept it. Have strong faith in yourself and your Master.

DON'T MEASURE THE MASTER IN BODY-FORM.
YOUR MASTER IS PART OF YOUR SPONTANEOUS PRESENCE.

Your Master is part and parcel of your Spontaneous Presence, of your Spontaneous Anonymous Presence which cannot be defined in words. Glance inside! Who is listening, talking? Strict meditation. Full concentration - only two hours' practice!

Q: When we recite the Mantra should we focus on the meaning?

Maharaj: Not on an intellectual level, just spontaneously. You must have full trust. Excessive use of the mind, ego, intellect will spoil your spiritual life.

ALWAYS BE WITH YOU.
BE WITH YOU ALWAYS.
THIS MEANS DON'T MIX IN THE WRONG
TYPE OF ATMOSPHERE.

These spiritual words will automatically implement Reality in you. Like poison, the consequences are already acting inside accordingly. It is a drop of nectar. "I Am That!" All illusion will be dissolved. Accept what I have told you. Don't underestimate yourself. Everything is in you.

Q: About two days after receiving the *Naam Mantra*, Bhausaheb Maharaj appeared. I was surprised because I didn't feel a connection to him, in fact, I knew very little about this particular Master. I felt strongly connected to Siddharameshwar Maharaj and Nisargadatta Maharaj.

The first time I saw Bhausaheb Maharaj, he appeared in a meditation, as a gigantic figure towering above me. He placed a crown on my head and said, "This is your rightful inheritance". I understood that he was referring to the Knowledge. Then, during another meditation, he appeared dressed in deep blue regalia, against a deep blue surrounding. There was a feeling of something opening up in me. Bhausaheb Maharaj spoke: "Grace is going through you". They were very clear visions of the Master, and a very strong empowering energy.

There's a lot going on, I'm sure, as a direct consequence of the *Naam Mantra*. For example, sometimes there are episodes of spontaneous laughter, and at other times, spontaneous crying. The tears were a kind of outpouring. Both the laughter and the tears were not related to any mood, like being happy or sad. So, anyway, there is a lot going on, and it's fantastic. What's happening feels really powerful and interesting. I express gratitude to the Masters for their strong Presence, and I ask them to continue to help with the process.

Maharaj: You do not need to ask them for help. Help is already there.

THE MASTERS ARE BEHIND YOU,

WORKING INVISIBLY IN THE BACKGROUND.

You are having good experiences, because you are deeply involved.

By taking the *Naam*, you are receiving the help and power from the Masters of this Lineage. You are One with the Masters. As you go deeper and deeper, you will find it very interesting. You can take it at different levels, it depends on your background. I am happy! Enjoy your spirituality!

121. *Maya Does Not Want You To Go To Ultimate Truth*

Maharaj: You can have great devotion, but when you get closer and closer to Selfless Self, at a certain critical point, if you lose concentration, you can fall right back down. Even a tiny hint of doubt can spoil or even ruin your whole position.

MAYA DOES NOT WANT YOU
TO REACH YOUR ULTIMATE TRUTH.

You have to stay alert, otherwise what you have earned will be lost!

USING VARIOUS STORIES,
I AM TRYING TO 'TALK' TO THE DESTINY,
THE PEAK OF THE MOUNTAIN.
DON'T LOOK BACK,
DON'T LOOK DOWN!

If something comes along to lure you, it will come between you and your target, with the result that there will be loss of concentration. Like in the children's game of 'Snakes and Ladders', you will slide down to the bottom. Also, in the world, a single slip, can send you plummeting down the mountainside.

I'M ALERTING YOU,
WARNING YOU!
SHOWING YOU
HOW TO ESCAPE FROM THESE SNAKES
CALLED ILLUSORY THOUGHTS,
GREED, EGO, MIND, ETC.

This is a material body, so there's bound to be worldly and material attractions there. After knowing the Reality, there won't be any temptations at all.

Be courageous and strong, help yourself. Since you are your own Master, you have to convince your Selfless Self. "I am Ultimate Truth without any ego. I am Ultimate Truth, I am Final Truth, says my Master". You have to believe in your Master, whoever he may be. Believe in your Master.

THIS KNOWLEDGE IS SUPPOSED TO BE ROOTED
THROUGH THE MASTER ALONE.
IF YOU JUST READ SPIRITUAL BOOKS,
THE KNOWLEDGE WILL NOT BE IMPRESSED IN YOU.

This Knowledge should touch you, it should touch you at the very bottom of your heart.

Q: Maharaj, I wanted to ask you a question about babies. If you're to take a newborn baby, and say, you started to teach this Knowledge from a young age, would that baby understand its natural state, or is it all predetermined?

Maharaj: Good question! What is impressed upon a child is reflected. The baby comes as a blank slate. Suppose a child is brought up in a criminal household. Will the child become a criminal? The spirit attracts everything like a magnet. Each and everything, memories, thirty years back, "Oh I know that". Like spontaneous automatic photography, Spirit records everything all the time, including dreams. The Spirit in a child is totally blank, like a brand new computer! So, yes, whatever is felt is reflected. Impressions will be engraved.

Q: So you are saying, that you can influence a young baby. Nisargadatta Maharaj seems to say that everything is predetermined from the five elements. Whether you are going to be enlightened or not, makes no difference.

Maharaj: There is no 'predetermined'.

WHO IS PREDETERMINING?

What you are talking about is body-based knowledge. You are beyond that. Who determined?

Q: The five element combination.

Maharaj: Was there a five element combination prior to beingness? Was there any combination?

Q: I meant after manifestation.

Maharaj: Did you know of the five elements prior? Nothing was known to you.

Q: All conceptual?

Maharaj: When we are teaching, we take ego. Through teaching, we are trying to invite the attention of the Listener that you are Ultimate Truth. What we are conveying is most important. Each and everything is recorded inside your big computer. Thousands of programmes are stored there. From childhood till today, bundles of programmes have crowded you, to the extent that you can reply instantly and automatically because of conditioning.

You still know of every person you have ever come into contact with since childhood. You are like a Magic Box, a very powerful computer. I keep telling you of your tremendous power. You have no need to go elsewhere.

You are Ultimate Truth, Final Truth, so don't measure yourself in body-form. Meditation is bringing change. You are on the right track.

Q: But sometimes I feel like I'm losing my mind.

Maharaj: Mind is only giving you trouble if you give it attention. When you know this 'mind', you ignore it, as it tries to divert you the wrong way. You know it is just playing tricks.

Q: This gives you a sense of power. *Maya* is tricking you.

Maharaj: Don't analyze the Master's statements. It is the secret of your Presence that they wish to convey. You are Ultimate Truth, Final Truth. Everyone uses different techniques, different words to do this.

Q: How can I investigate 'prior to beingness'?

Maharaj: Prior to beingness you were unknown to yourself. Then you pose as a man or woman, perhaps do a little Self-enquiry, and then leave the body. Nothing remains. Why spirituality? Because you forgot your Identity. How were you prior to beingness? Without form! No form! You were formless.

122. Hammering and More Hammering

Maharaj: We are hammering and hammering you! You will feel some pain as we remove the unwanted parts of the stone. The stone is *Bhagavan*, the Lord and Deity. The Master removes the unwanted parts of the illusory body to make a good statue of the Deity. The hammering is causing some pain just now, but it will be worth it. Afterwards you will smile and exclaim: "Ah! I am happy!"

BE SELF-INVOLVED!

Now that you have some Power and know the Reality, you can put the Knowledge into practice. There will be distractions, blockages, hindrances, difficulties, *maya* in different forms trying to drag you down. These material attractions may cause a brief imbalance, but you will be able to control yourself. You will be guided by your Inner Master. Your Inner Voice will say, "Don't do that", or "Do this!" or "Be careful", etc.

Q: In my professional life, there's a lot of politics going on in the office. I get dragged in.

Maharaj: Don't be discouraged! Do your duties and come home. Ignore people, even if they insult you.

BE HONEST WITH YOUR SPIRITUAL DUTIES.
BE HONEST WITH YOUR SELFLESS SELF.

Forget about your family, your circle of friends, social life where there is always competition. Here, you will get Perfection.

I used to have angry customers visiting the bank where I worked. The first thing I did was make them a cup of tea, and try and calm them down.

Q: Does the practical and professional life help the spiritual life?

Maharaj: Experience and practice will definitely help your day-to-day life. If you have patience and are not prejudiced, you will develop a positive approach. Your spirituality can help you to be tactful in the world, and teach you how to use the ego and intellect in moderation. You have to be the judge of thoughts, which ones to keep, and which ones not to keep.

Q: I have to be judgemental?

Maharaj: Use discrimination! You are the Master! Your existence lies beyond the mind, ego, intellect. It cannot be described in words.

REMAIN IN THAT!
BE IN THAT ULTIMATE TRUTH.

123. Bow to Your Greatness

Q: Is a Guru or Master needed?

Maharaj: Yes he is required to show you the Reality. You are like the beggar boy till you meet a Master, who tells you that you can walk on your own feet.

When you make an effort with spiritual life and practice, at first, you may fall, but you can pick yourself up again. The Master encourages you to keep trying. You are used to discouraging yourself, getting depressed because you lack confidence, because behind that, there is some ego, pride or dignity. These are enemies on the way, in the way of spirituality.

In Indian culture, people bow down when they go to the temples. Their action is your action.

YOU ARE TO SURRENDER,
SELF-SURRENDER INTERNALLY.
BOW TO YOUR SELFLESS SELF.
YOU ARE GREAT!

By doing this, you will get an indication of your greatness. The great ones are always humble, humble and kind, this is a mark of saintly people.

What happens in life is that people say, "I've got status, dignity". This is dry knowledge. This Knowledge should touch you. It should touch you at the bottom of your heart. It should touch the bottom of your heart.

The Master is alerting you. The Master is there to guide you. The Master has a commanding nature. The Master is giving Power through his commanding nature. Commanding Power! What is said by his Power, is put into practice. Be deserving of that Power.

ALL THAT IS GIVEN,
SHOULD BE DESERVED.
YOU ARE TO ACCEPT THAT POWER,
WITHOUT ANY DOUBTS.
IF YOU ACCEPT IT WITH SUSPICION,
IT WILL NOT BE FULFILLED.

Therefore everything is within you. All secrets are open to you - open secret. How to act and react is up to you. The Master has given you hints, clues, warnings of distractions, that will limit your chances, and of incidents that may divert you.

But people are ignoring the Master's guidance. Those who say, "I am a devotee", are ignoring the Master's words because the mind, ego and intellect are creating suspicions. The whole Truth is placed before you, therefore why have any doubt? So you are not to follow the instructions of the mind, ego, intellect.

OPEN TRUTH,
PLAIN TRUTH HAS ALL BEEN PRESENTED,
AND LAID OUT BEFORE YOU.
WE ARE TRYING TO DO OUR LEVEL BEST
TO CONVINCE YOU OF THE REALITY.

The Listener is under pressure, therefore, meditation brings surrender.

I am trying to convince you! We say, "God is Great", but the person who says, "God is great" is greater than God. If you give one hundred per cent marks to a student we say, "Excellent!". But that excellency comes from your excellency. To say "Beautiful!" means that the principle of beauty is within you. We say, "Very good!", that means that a very good nature is within you. "Good boy!" means there's goodness in you.

You are ignoring your own qualities, and not giving importance to your Magic Box. After a period of concentration, the Meditation Key will open your Magic Box.

124. You Have to Know the Secret, Your Secret

Maharaj: Ultimately, we have a lot of attachment to the body, a lot of affection which has to dissolve. Only then, will you be fearless. Every being is fearful because the Spirit called *Atman, Brahman* does not know its own existence. It only knows itself in the body-form.

When the Spirit clicked with the body, it accepted, "I am this", and it likes, enjoys and wants to survive through the body. Through this body, it derives happiness and peace. This Invisible Spirit is completely unaware of it's own existence.

THE SPIRIT'S EXISTENCE IS ONLY NOTICED
THROUGH THE BODY.

The body is its medium made of flesh, blood and bones. This body produces a family because of the Spirit. You have to know this secret, your secret.

THIS IS NOT GOD'S SECRET,
OR THE SECRET OF *BRAHMAN, ATMAN, PARAMATMAN.*
THIS IS YOUR SECRET, WITHOUT ANY BODY-FORM.
SO KNOW THYSELF, AND KEEP QUIET.

Stop battling with the words. This is not a debate. People are asking questions all the time, talking, talking, yet the entire world is illusion.

KNOW THYSELF AND KEEP QUIET.

How can you talk about the unborn child? The child is unborn. This child we are talking about all the time is illusion. Nothing has happened. Nothing is going to happen.

THE MASTER CONVINCES YOU OF YOUR REALITY,
THEN, YOU HAVE TO CONVINCE YOURSELF.

The Master persuades you, then you have to convince yourself, till you arrive at the conclusion, till you reach Conviction. Convincing leads to Conviction. Convincing leads to Conviction: "Yes! After all this wandering here and there, at last I am certain". You know you are the destination. You are Ultimate Truth, Final Truth.

YOU KNOW YOU ARE THE DESTINATION.
YOU ARE ULTIMATE TRUTH,
FINAL TRUTH.

One should see the Seer! But the Seer cannot be seen because the Seer is Invisible, Anonymous, Unidentified.

What do we mean by Spiritual Knowledge? Your spiritual eyes are your Spiritual Knowledge. 'I' disappears. There is nobody: No 'I', no you, nothing. You are totally detached, unconcerned with the world. No experience, no experiencer, no witness, no witnesser, no duality - nothing. No duality or individuality. This is rare knowledge. When everything disappears, there you are.

With self-involvement, through deep self-involvement, you will come to this. You will come to know first-hand, what I am saying now, as Self-Knowledge. This is Self-Knowledge.

WHAT I AM SAYING NOW,

YOU WILL COME TO KNOW
AND REALIZE DIRECTLY.
SELF-INVOLVEMENT BRINGS SELF-KNOWLEDGE.

When I first went to Nisargadatta Maharaj, I was not able to understand what he was saying. For me, it was like a foreign language, so he used a very direct approach because my mental, spiritual capacity was rock-bottom. But he encouraged me always, saying, "Listen to me, listen to me!" And now this Knowledge has been exposed. In time, the understanding came naturally, with ease.

Q: What age were you when you met Nisargadatta Maharaj?

Maharaj: I was around twenty-one years old in 1962. What often happens is that circumstances force you to go to Ultimate Truth. If you have a comfortable life, you will not go, but if there are difficulties, you will embrace it. A simple example is, say, when you are a child, and something frightens you. You scream, "There is a ghost!" and run to Mom. You embrace Mom because she is Ultimate, she is your protector. It is the same with the Master and the disciple. The Master is mother, the Master is father. The Master is everything. The Master is God.

Nisargadatta Maharaj used to say:

"IF I AM FORTUNATE,
MISFORTUNE WILL COME MY WAY.
DIFFICULTIES WILL COME TO ME".

He really had a lot of difficulties in life, so much suffering, so many losses. But he did not run away. He stayed firm and strong always, no matter what impossible situations he faced. He had many trials.

And even at the end, my Master continued teaching up until a few days before he passed. He was in such pain with throat cancer, coughing up blood, but he never complained. This shows you his greatness.

People generally tend to run away from problems. If they are doing meditation and other practices, they often ask: "Why have I got these problems?", as if there is some connection.

THERE IS NO CONNECTION BETWEEN THE SPIRITUAL LIFE
AND WORLDLY PROBLEMS.

Don't entangle body-knowledge with spiritual knowledge. They are not interrelated. Make your foundations strong, very strong, solid. This will lead to the Conviction: Except for this, there is nothing.

So don't let anyone or anything divert you from this valuable knowledge. Tests will come, so be alert and strong at all times. Do not be distracted by people or things. Other people can be under the pressure of illusion, and they will want to enforce their illusion on you. Maintain continuity.

Q: I have to keep things going and also be careful who I spend time with? Yes!

Maharaj: Of course, this is most important. Nisargadatta Maharaj used to advise his devotees and disciples: "Don't mix with the type of people who will disturb and distract you from your principle" - the principle that is Ultimate Truth. You have to be alert. Remind yourself, 'I know'. If the mind is weak then it will get distracted, so he guided them to be very careful. He used to say:

"DON'T BE SO CHEAP,
THAT THE WORLD CAN POCKET YOU".

He often gave us helpful tips. They were good because they were practical. "You must have self-respect", he would say. He was very down-to-earth, very practical. I received an education only because of my Master who arranged it for me.

ONCE UPON A TIME, I WAS REALLY SMALL, SO SMALL,
BUT NOW, I AM A MIRACLE.
I AM REALLY A MIRACLE.

I know my past. What I am today, all that I am today, is all due to my Master. It is only because of him. Dramatic changes have taken place in my life because of my great Master, Nisargadatta Maharaj. I am now sharing the same Knowledge with everyone.

HOW MANY OF YOU ARE WILLING TO ACCEPT IT?
IT IS UP TO YOU
WHETHER YOU ACCEPT IT OR NOT.
IT IS MY DUTY TO OPEN THE SECRET.

The cave of jewels has been opened for you. Your lost treasure has been found. Take it! Take from it as much as you want. Take what you can, take your fill, according to your capacity.

Q: I will take it all, not just a little! I will! I feel that I have been waiting so long to find this rare treasure, that my thirst and hunger has no bottom.

125. *Transference of Power*

Q: What is grace? I recently heard a few people asking for your grace.

Maharaj: Grace is a kind of support, encouragement. People say "The *Sadguru*, or Maharaj will grace you, or bless you". It means giving assurance that what you are expecting will materialize. There is a lot of superstition around grace, even today, around grace and curse.

If someone does not get what he wants, he may say, "I will curse you". But in our spiritual language, grace means that whatever we expect from our Selfless Self, will materialize. It will happen. Therefore to please the God, to please the Master, the devotee shows devotion, and expresses love. I am talking about Selfless love without expectation, not selfish love.

When the Master is pleased with his devotee, and can see that he is a true devotee, he graces him.

WHEN THE DEVOTEE SHOWS THE MASTER SELFLESS LOVE,
THE MASTER GRACES HIM WITH HIS POWER.

The Master has tremendous Power. I will present you with an image, for understanding purposes only, which you are to quickly forget. Indian philosophy speaks of the 'Transference of Power'. As you know, all Power lies within you. But just for understanding, such concepts exist, like 'Transferring the Power'.

You already have Power, energy, but you have forgotten. The Master is showing you that you have tremendous Power. He is therefore gracing you with this Power.

THE MASTER IS GRACING YOU WITH POWER,
THE SAME POWER THAT IS WITHIN YOU.

There is no difference between the Master and the disciple, except for the body-form, and therefore the Master is convincing you of your Power, via the use of various statements, repetition, discourse and dialogue.

IF YOU ARE COMPLETELY DEVOTED
TO YOUR SELFLESS SELF,
YOU WILL RECEIVE GRACE.

Q: The difficulty lies in being completely devoted, especially when you are living in the world with family, and problems with relationships, and things happening all the time.

Maharaj: Nothing is happening. This is a long dream, a long dream. Saint Samarth Ramdas says, "This is a long dream within which we say my mother, sister, my wife, my son". With a lot of emotion, and a lot of feeling, we say, "This is my mother, my father, my brother, my sister, my wife, my God". We say all this, and yet there's nothing. All these relations are related to the body-form.

Prior to the body-form, there were no relations, nobody, no brother, nobody, no sister, nobody, no Master, nobody, no *Brahman*, no *Atman*, nothing, nothing, nothing. You can understand all this literally, but it needs to be applied in practice. Only in that way, will it lead to Conviction.

You can understand it logically and intellectually, but this Knowledge has to be lived. You have to live like this. Nisargadatta Maharaj said:

"I AM LIVING THAT LIFE, THAT SPIRITUAL LIFE.
I AM NOT TALKING INTELLECTUALLY, OR LOGICALLY.
I AM TALKING FROM LIVING KNOWLEDGE".

Just like you are living Susan's story. We are narrating your story. You are Susan, so that when you hear the name, you exclaim: "This is my story". It is like reading your biography because the Master is telling you, not an imaginary story, but your real story, your true story. So grace comes if you are completely involved, completely devoted, when you know, "I am living that life".

All these processes of reading, meditation, Knowledge, prayer, etc, exist for the sole purpose of identifying your Selfless Self. All these disciplines are there, so that you can reach the conclusion.

Q: What is the conclusion?

Maharaj: That nothing is there! Just like an onion, after removing the layers, one by one, nothing remains. This is open secret. I am opening up the secret with you. This is not knowledge that explains things in a roundabout and indirect way. This is Direct Knowledge. Direct Living Knowledge. Just digest this, digest this.

THIS IS DIRECT KNOWLEDGE.
DIRECT LIVING KNOWLEDGE.

Q: There is an urge to say something, but there are no words.

Maharaj: Be quiet! Be silent!

126. *Spiritual Entertainment*

Q: What about the *kundalini* and *chakras*?

Maharaj: This *chakra*, that *chakra*, there is no *chakra*! This dry knowledge is momentary entertainment. There were no *chakras* prior to beingness. What do you mean by *kundalini*? This is just connected with the body. You are beyond that, beyond that.

269

Don't become a slave of literal knowledge. Look within you, everything is open. Thousands of books exist, thousands of concepts. Everybody is asking you to do this thing or that thing. Why? There is no deed, there is no doer.

THIS KNOWLEDGE IS EXCEPTIONAL, AND IT IS YOURS.
BUT THE EGO IS NOT ALLOWING YOU TO CLAIM IT.

It is stopping you from breaking the circle of illusionary thoughts. You are still looking for salvation. Why 'salvation' when you are already free? Why 'liberation'? There was no liberation prior to beingness. You are bound to your own thoughts and concepts.

Q: But we have to use the body to know Selfless Self, don't we?

Maharaj: You have to use the body, it is a medium. Spirit only knows itself through the body. It does not know that, "I am *Brahman*, God".

"I am not the body, I am *Mahatma*", said Shankara. He lived by his Conviction of being *Brahman*. This Conviction leads to Knowledge. Your Presence is very valuable. Don't waste your time with this *kundalini* talk and *chakras*!

Q: What is the meaning of *upasana*?

Maharaj: You are not a baby! Why do you want to know? What you are reading in books is not *upasana*. Don't be a slave of literal knowledge, you are not a beginner.

Q: Is time only in the memory?

Maharaj: Whose memory?

Q: Time must be in the memory because without the memory there's no time.

Maharaj: If you consider yourself in body-form, then there is memory, time, *karma*, etc. But prior to beingness was there any *karma*? Were you reading the *Gita*?

YOU HAVE TO BOW DOWN TO YOURSELF.
BOW DOWN MEANS BOW DOWN TO 'THAT'
THROUGH WHICH YOU KNOW YOUR SELFLESS SELF.
IT IS A SPONTANEOUS ACT.

When you talk about *mukti*, *upasana*, *chakras* or whatever, you are talking about the unborn child.

FORGET ABOUT THE UNBORN CHILD,
AND REMEMBER YOUR GREATNESS.

I told you, you are a Magician, you have the key to open the Magic Box to the whole world that is within you. These processes of meditation, *bhajan* etc, are there because you forgot your greatness. Even after knowing the Knowledge, you still want to go elsewhere. You are rich with millions of rupees and yet, you keep saying, "Give me one rupee".

THE GOLDEN PLATE HAS ALREADY BEEN GIVEN TO YOU,
BUT YOU ARE USING THAT PLATE FOR BEGGING.

Knowledge is there, Reality is in front of you, inside you, around you, everywhere.

How many times do I have to say the same thing! That is why continuous hammering is necessary. Listen to me! There is no *prarabdha*, *karma*, destiny. Through meditation and its vibrations, you will, like a baby chicken, peck through the hard shell and break through. You are *Brahman*, you are *Atman*!

ALL THIS SEARCHING, WHERE AM I?
WHERE AM I?
WHEN YOU ARE HERE ALL THE TIME.

Nisargadatta Maharaj used to say, "There's no way, no death, no ways, no path, you are always with you". Direct hammering! You are the Final Terminus. You are only adding confusion if you are still tempted to go elsewhere, after knowing the Reality. For how much longer are you going to keep visiting so many places, when you, the Visitor, are yourself Ultimate Truth?

THE VISITOR IS ULTIMATE TRUTH.
ALL YOU HAVE TO DO, IS VISIT YOUR OWN SITE.
THIS IS NOT INTELLECTUAL KNOWLEDGE,
IT IS REALITY.

Q: How are we to live? What is the best way?

Maharaj: I have told you how to live, live like sky. Sky does not know its own existence. It is unknown to itself. Your Presence is unknown Presence. Nisargadatta Maharaj used to say,

"THE REAL IS UNKNOWN TO YOU,
SO LIVE LIKE THAT,
AND IT WILL NOT BE A PROBLEM FOR YOU".

How are you to live? How will you be when the body dissolves? Forget the past also! No present, no future, no past! What you have done so far, just drop it! It brought you to your Final Destiny. Knowledge is not concerned with what you are doing, or what you are eating. Anything taken to excess is poison. Don't take the literal meanings! Don't get caught up in restrictions and struggles of do's and don'ts.

DON'T TAKE ON THE EGO OF BEING A DOER.
YOU CANNOT DO ANYTHING.

Q: This is a hard one to remember all the time.

Maharaj: It is not hard, it is simple. If your body wants food, feed it, but not excessively. Too much liberty is poison! Respect yourself and respect others. Be humble, and charitable to keep the subtle ego in check. Say 'No' to the ego.

All the saints are humble. Be like them!

ALL THE SAINTS ARE WITHIN YOU.

You are making them out to be separate and different from you.

ONENESS IS ALL THERE IS.

You are to teach yourself, just like you teach yourself Hatha Yoga. Realize that nothing is impossible.

ACCEPT THAT REALITY. IT IS WITHIN YOU.
THAT MASTERLY ESSENCE IS IN YOU.
THEN YOU WILL FINALLY STOP ROAMING.

The Master introduced you to God, showed you God, that is why Kabir bowed down to his Master. Don't be a slave to somebody's thoughts.

Q: I still see myself as 'me' and others as 'them'.

Maharaj: Can you see the Seer? You cannot see the Seer because the Seer is Ultimate Truth. This is body-related talk. There is no God except you. God does not have its own existence. Stop imagining the body-form, you are not the body, but the holder of the body. You are not to imagine the body-form.

YOU ARE NOT THE BODY-BUILDER,
BUT THE BODY-HOLDER.

Use your internal vision to see! Be spiritually strong. Your body-knowledge has to dissolve completely. Keep reciting the *Naam*!

You are the Projector of the world, not the projections. The Questioner is Invisible. The Questioner itself is the answer. Keep it simple:

TO SAY ILLUSION IS ALSO ILLUSION.
DON'T DO ANYTHING.
YOU DID NOT DO ANYTHING PRIOR TO BEINGNESS.
HOW CAN YOU KNOW YOUR PRESENCE,
IF YOU CAN'T USE THE BODY OR MIND?
SIMPLY LOOK AT YOU,
LOOK AT THAT WHICH IS WITNESSING ALL THESE THOUGHTS.

You are trying to know yourself with an illusionary body-base. Impossible! Know yourself as you were prior to beingness. How was that? You say, "I don't know". This 'negative' answer has come from a 'positive'.

"I DON'T KNOW" MEANS "I KNOW",
BUT I WAS NOT IN ANY FORM.
THE KNOWING IS THE PRESENCE, THE 'I AM'.
YOU KNOW, THAT YOU DON'T KNOW.

To put it simply, it is like the example of children playing, when one says "Knock, knock, who is there?", and the other child says, "No one!" Here, the one who answers 'nobody' or 'no one' means simply, that 'somebody' has to be there first, in order to say 'nobody'.

LIVE LIKE THAT ANONYMOUS, INVISIBLE,
UNIDENTIFIED PRESENCE!

People sometimes come here as if they are visiting a showroom. They sit like statues, completely untouched and unmoved. It is like they are gathering information in a cold manner, statistics for a survey. Their egos are not letting them come out of their circle, to wonder at the greatness of my Masters.

They show no respect to them. These talks, this Reality, should touch people's hearts. One visitor has been here for a week, and I don't see any effect showing on his face. He is still a statue. He is still here but I don't see any change taking place. He remains a statue.

127. *Falling Back Into the Ditch*

Q: One has to be alert, on guard, always, you were saying, because impediments appear all the time in many different forms?
Maharaj: During the process of spirituality, when you are very close to your Selfless Self, it happens. Some

illusory thoughts, attractions, some temptations are likely to be there, and they can distract you at a crucial moment.

THIS HAPPENS WHEN YOUR INNER POWER,
YOUR ORIGINALITY IS BEING EXPOSED,
AND REALITY IS EMERGING.

This is called *maya*. But in Reality, there is only Selfless Self, there's no *maya*, no *Brahman*, no *Atman*, no *Paramatman*. This happens when you are close to Oneness.

WHEN YOU GO TOWARDS THE SELFLESS SELF,
AND ARE ABSORBING THE KNOWLEDGE,
GETTING CLOSER AND CLOSER TO ONENESS,
AT THIS VERY MOMENT, HURDLES APPEAR
THAT MAY CAUSE CONFUSION AND CONFLICT.

At this time, some temptations or adversities show up. What happens is that after reaching a certain level of detachment, you may be drawn back in again, by some little attraction that offers momentary happiness.

Knowingly or unknowingly, in one second, you might forget about Reality, forget about everything, and fall back into the ditch, without thinking of the consequences. Then, afterwards, when you realize the mistake, you will regret it and repent: "Oh! What have I done?".

There are many examples of this in spiritual literature. One saint who had fallen from grace was the great sage Vishvamitra. The story goes that for sixty thousand years, this saint had intense and unwavering devotion. He was so powerful! Then one day, he came across an exceptionally beautiful lady, and all of a sudden, [Maharaj claps his hands], he became attracted, and he threw everything away, [he claps again].

THIS STORY ILLUSTRATES THE NEED FOR ALERTNESS
AT ALL TIMES.
ILLUSION IS ALWAYS THERE TO TRAP YOU.
SOMETHING HAPPENS, EITHER INNOCENTLY OR DELIBERATELY,
AND THEN, ALL OF A SUDDEN,
THE SPIRIT ATTRACTS TEMPTATION,
FOR NO REASON AT ALL!

For momentary happiness, you will forfeit everything: it may be publicity, or money, maybe sex. Without thinking of the consequences, you will throw it all away and lapse back into illusion. I feel very sorry when this happens. Listen to me!

THIS SHOULD NOT HAPPEN.
DON'T LET THE ILLUSIONARY WORLD BACK IN.
YOU ARE SO CLOSE TO SELFLESS SELF,
DON'T LOOK BACK.

It is like when you are climbing a mountain and you are very near to the summit, nearly at the mountain peak. You must not look back. Just keep going up, and up, keep going till you reach your goal. If you look back, you will lose your footing, and end up back at the bottom of the mountain.

At this advanced stage, therefore, some precautionary measures need to be put in place. I cannot stress it enough.

AFTER CONVICTION,
DON'T GIVE ANY COGNIZANCE
TO ANY KIND OF ATTRACTION OR TEMPTATION.
DO NOT PAY ATTENTION TO ILLUSION.
BE ON YOUR GUARD,
AND GIVE NO IMPORTANCE TO *MAYA*.

The Master is giving you a warning, that you are to take precautionary measures. If you exercise these measures and implement Reality, you will remain alert and prepared for these challenges, tests and obstacles.

NOW THAT YOU HAVE CONVICTION,
YOU KNOW BETTER.
YOU ARE NO LONGER AN INDIVIDUAL,
SO YOU CANNOT BE TEMPTED.

Q: If I am tempted or drawn into illusion again, does that mean the Conviction is not really there, or the foundations are not strong enough?

Maharaj: Correct! That is why you have to be serious about the practice. That is why I insist on the discipline of meditation. You need a perfect foundation, a strong foundation. Meditation is the base and the basis of everything. I have told you many times, that at the Ultimate Stage, meditation is also illusion, but it is necessary for dissolving the body-knowledge and establishing the Reality.

YOU HAVE TO CONVINCE YOURSELF,
WITHOUT ANY EGO, THAT:
YOUR UNIDENTIFIED IDENTITY IS ALMIGHTY GOD.
YOUR UNIDENTIFIED IDENTITY IS ALMIGHTY GOD,
BRAHMAN, ATMAN.
EMBRACE THIS REALITY,
EMBRACE THIS REALITY.

You are embracing the food-body instead of Reality, and therefore dependent upon everything. Prior to beingness, you needed nothing. Prior to beingness, you needed nothing. When there is no body-form, there is no question of happiness, unhappiness, peacefulness, tension-free life or fearlessness. This is the whole of Reality. This is the Final Truth.

128.   *Can You Empty my Hard Drive?*

Maharaj: The scriptures, books, Masters and others all say, "God is like this. You have to do this or that. Because of your *karma*, you must do so-and-so". This is all body-knowledge.

A MASTER WHO <u>SHOWS</u> YOU,
THAT GOD IS WITHIN YOU,

IS A VERY RARE MASTER.

When you have this Conviction, after establishing complete Conviction, you will finally know, and say, "Yes! All that I was searching for, and trying to find out, had nothing to do with the body. Now I KNOW that everything is within. I am That!"

WHY SHOULD I GO ANYWHERE
WHEN EVERYTHING IS WITHIN?

This is not egoistic talk. Out of the Spontaneous Conviction, it is realized that: "What I was searching for, what I was trying to know, trying to find out, the happiness I was seeking, is and was, within me all along." There is no longer the need to go anywhere.

WHY LOOK ELSEWHERE
WHEN YOU ARE THE SOURCE OF EVERYTHING?

There is a shift, a definite change after Conviction because you are convinced that you are not the body. Up until then, you considered yourself in body-form. And with this body-form, you were trying to find God, or happiness and peace.

YOU WERE TRYING TO FIND GOD,
OR HAPPINESS AND PEACE WITH THE BODY-FORM.

Go to the root cause! Stay with the root cause because the body is not a permanent thing. Willingly or unwillingly, we are to leave this body. So who wants happiness? Who wants the happiness? The Spirit finds the body intolerable. It feels unbearable in the body. When there was no body, there was no question of tolerance or intolerance, happiness, unhappiness, peace or dis-peace because nothing was required.

Q: So there were no needs, no problems, and nothing to look for?

Maharaj: As I keep telling you, before the Spirit clicked with the body, you did not know yourself. You were totally unknown to you. There was no 'I', no 'you', no 'he', no 'she'. All these needs, demands and expectations came with the body.

Stay with the root cause. After Conviction, you will realize that, "All these things which I am not, the things which I'm not, I had accepted, blindly, as if I were somebody. The body is not my Reality, it is not Ultimate Truth". You were innocently unaware of it.

YOU ACCEPTED THE BODY AS ULTIMATE TRUTH,
WHICH MADE YOU THINK, "I AM THE BODY".
THEN ALL YOUR PROBLEMS AND WORRIES STARTED.

Q: When illness comes to the body, or old age, the challenge is even greater. With good health you can keep the body in the background, and be more, as it were, truly centred in that which you are.

Maharaj: Your Presence is beyond all this body-knowledge. You are to maintain the practice. Here we are administering medicines to keep you strong.

Q: I think it is not that easy for me to get rid of all my doubts.

Maharaj: Your hard drive is full.

Q: My journey has been such a long one and I have seen so many Masters.

Maharaj: After reaching the destiny, you can get rid of the address. Forget about your journey. Now you have reached the terminus.

Q: I am feeling tired and old and wondering if I have left it all too late?
Maharaj: Who is tired? Who is old?

HOW OLD WERE YOU PRIOR TO BEINGNESS?
WHEN DID YOU START COUNTING THE YEARS?

These are all thoughts, illusion. Forget everything! The computer should be totally blank.
Q: Can you empty my hard drive, Maharaj?

129.   *Look at You! Look at You!*

Maharaj: Throw yourself wholeheartedly into Self-Realization. These teachings are direct. You have to keep doing Self-enquiry, it is not enough to think, "I am not the body". You need to know deep down. Similarly, deep down you have to know that you are *Brahman*. Now is all we have, never to be repeated.
Q: What do you mean when you say, "Every moment of your life is very important"? You say it quite often?
Maharaj: Because going along with body-knowledge may drive you into another dream like this one. To have that Conviction, you have to use each and every moment for knowing the Reality, because it is natural for obstacles to appear all the time. Therefore you need to stay alert, to absorb the Reality. Vishvamitra was distracted for just a moment, and in that moment, he lost everything.

YOU CAN REALIZE IN THIS HUMAN LIFE
BECAUSE YOU HAVE INTELLECT,
AND CAN KNOW THE REALITY.

Therefore be alert! Thereafter it will be Spontaneous, and you will forget about the body/world.
Q: Sounds very difficult not to be distracted even for a short time.
Maharaj: That is why we have the practice of meditation in our Lineage. This way, the Reality that was forgotten, is impressed and engraved in you.

YOU HAVE A WRONG FRIENDSHIP.
YOU HAVE MISPLACED YOUR FRIENDSHIP
AND MADE FRIENDS WITH THE BODY.
IT IS A MISTAKEN FRIENDSHIP.
YOU HAVE TO BE YOUR OWN FRIEND, YOUR OWN FRIEND.

When you are driving, you will usually try and avoid trenches and pot holes. If you don't, then you will fall in, or get stuck. Similarly, in life there are so many trenches, blockages which you are to avoid, without damaging yourself.

You are to teach yourself in various ways. You are your own Master therefore let Him guide you. If you ignore Him, then accidents will happen. You have to manoeuvre and take preventative actions. This body is accident prone!
Q: You say that I am not the doer, but I still feel guilty for some things that have happened in the past.
Maharaj: Prior to beingness, you hadn't done anything. No sin, nothing, so how can there be any guilt? You were totally unknown. No past life, no future life.

You are making some allegations that you are sinful, that you have done something bad, taken birth. You have adopted concepts of rebirth, hell and heaven. These are all false allegations. To overrule all these concepts, you are to see your Selfless Self. Go inside and try to know the Reality. You are going outside to different Masters for happiness.

YOU ARE NOT APPROACHING YOUR OWN,
VERY POWERFUL AND STRONG MASTER.

It is happening because of a lack of faith and trust in yourself. And this subsequently leads to a lack of trust in the Masters. Be like those Masters! You can have any Master you wish, but be loyal to him.

REACH A CONCLUSION!
LOOK AT YOU!
LOOK AT YOU!

Then the hidden door will open. If there is no effort or involvement, just listening to knowledge, will not serve the purpose.

YOU ARE TO COME FORWARD.
TAKE ONE STEP,
I'LL TAKE THE NEXT.

It is not one-way traffic. You must have a deep interest and not a commercial one. Take from the Master. This Knowledge is given free of charge, but should be valued. We are not expecting anything, but if you come here, you are to take the Knowledge seriously, and appreciate that it is deeply meaningful.

Q: I heard a strange story from the south, where there is a couple known as 'Mr & Mrs God', [Mr & Mrs *Bhagavan*], who charge per second and minute in euros. They invite foreigners saying, "I will give you peace or whatever you want".

Maharaj: They are taking advantage of the devotees, deceiving them with a promise of miracles.

Here, your happiness is our asset. Your peace is our asset, the Masters' assets. Take something from us! I am showing you the whole elephant! And when you know the Reality, just like the blind man and the elephant, you will not be impressed by anybody's statement regarding *Atman, Brahman, Paramatman*. Jewels are offered to you, but you are only taking stones, and continuing to beg.

WHEN EVERYTHING IS SHOWN TO BE WITHIN YOU,
WHY BEG?
ALERT! ALERT!
REALITY IS WITHIN YOU.

Don't be distracted from the principle. That is why every moment is important, to stop you slipping. If you miss that particular moment, a force will bring you down. Enemies are waiting, looking for your weaknesses, drawbacks. They will attack you when your guard is down.

And therefore, I am asking you to be alert, meditate. Keep the soldiers on duty, guarding day and night, watching. And make sure the border guards are alert too! If they ignore what is around them, then intruders, illegal immigrants will enter the country. It is a big country, so once they are in, it will be difficult to deport them. You are the captain, the colonel in charge of the soldiers, so be alert at all times. If you fall asleep, then who knows what might happen.

**IF YOU SURRENDER COMPLETELY,
IT WILL NOT BE DIFFICULT,
BECAUSE THE EGO WILL BE KEPT IN CHECK.
RESPECT YOUR SELFLESS SELF.**
Avoid pride! Avoid ego! You know better that pride is a sign of ego.

130. *No Countries, No Nationalities*

Maharaj: Spiritual science says that there are six desirable qualities. You can gauge your progress and see if you have these. They are forgiveness, patience, expectation of realization, desire to know, total devotion and lastly, faith in the Master.

Q: Indian people, generally speaking, have these, don't they? So I was wondering why there are not more enlightened people in India?

Maharaj: Don't consider other people. Don't be concerned with other people. Be concerned with yourself. I told you, this is a dream. The life you are living in this world is a dream.

**THERE ARE NO INDIAN, NO AUSTRALIAN,
NO ENGLISH PEOPLE.**

Prior to beingness, where was India, Russia, Australia? Did you say, "I will take birth in Australia, in China? "When you take a body, you start imagining countries".

You did not know of any countries prior to beingness. You are sky-like! Change your view! Your Presence is Ultimate Truth, just like the sky. Again you are disconnecting yourself in body-form, and wanting to see different nationalities.

**WE ARE NOT CONCERNED WITH THIS.
WE ARE CONCERNED WITH SELFLESS SELF.**

You cannot see India, Japan or anywhere without Selfless Self. The whole world is within you. The moment you wake up, you see the world. The whole world is a reflection of your Presence.

The Seer's Projection is Spontaneous, not deliberate. But what happens in this world, is that we are posing ourselves in the form of human beings. As I told you repeatedly, the body is only a covering, a dead body. All these countries came out of your Presence.

What you are seeing is the Seer's reflection in the form of the words and the world. Your Presence is behind all that, behind everything. Try to avoid all these illusionary thoughts. Look at you!

**I AM NOT IN THE BODY. I AM TALKING, YOU ARE LISTENING.
THE BODY IS ONLY A MEDIUM.
THE LISTENER IS INVISIBLE SILENCE.
THE LISTENER IS INVISIBLE, ANONYMOUS.**

That supernatural power is already within you. In between, there is a blockage of ego, intellect, mind, that is not allowing you to reach the Ultimate Truth.

EVERYBODY SHOULD BE ENLIGHTENED!

Look at you, and nowhere else! There is no India, no China, no countries. We have given names to sky, temple, toilet, kitchen, bathroom, dining-room. In one house we are giving different names to the one sky.

We are enclosing the sky within various walls - temple, kitchen, toilet. We do the same with countries, "This is Australia, India," etc. We have constructed these walls with our imagination. These people are Indian people, and those, Australian. Who is discriminating? I am talking in that sense.

Therefore you must have Conviction that you are not the body. After a certain time, you must say, "Bye-bye!" to the body, but never to your Presence. Sky is, was, and will be, and you are subtler than sky. Houses may collapse, but does the sky die?

This is very, very important. Look at YOU and see how this world is projected. We have created language from ABC and given meanings to words. I am not concerned with words and their meanings, I am inviting attention to That, that Ultimate Truth that you are.

THINK SERIOUSLY!
GO DEEP AND DEEP AND DEEP INTO THE SELFLESS SELF.
THE WHOLE SECRET OF SPIRITUALITY
IS HIDDEN WITHIN YOU. YOU ARE TO OPEN IT.
OF COURSE, STRONG INVOLVEMENT AND FAITH IS NEEDED,
FAITH IN YOU.

You must have trust, complete trust. Don't concern yourself with comparative studies of who is, or is not, realized or enlightened. After knowing the Reality you must have complete trust.

FORGET ABOUT OTHER PEOPLE. WHY?
BECAUSE THEY ARE DREAM PEOPLE.

The body is perishable, but because we are not accepting this fact, we are asking so many questions. Meditation is the base, the ABC that will dissolve illusion so that Final Truth is established totally.

YOU CAN VISIT ANY MASTER,
BUT AS I HAVE SAID MANY TIMES, YOU,
THE INVISIBLE VISITOR IN BODY-FORM,
ARE THE MASTER OF MASTERS.
THAT YOU ARE THE MASTER OF MASTERS,
HAS TO BECOME YOUR CONVICTION.
DON'T DENY YOUR OWN GREATNESS,
AND AFFIRM IT IN SOMEONE ELSE.

In Indian culture, you bow in temples, offering respect, and surrendering your ego. It is a good custom in any religion, going to church and bowing down, whether you are enlightened or not. Sometimes the ego does not allow someone to bow, like when some visitors come to the ashram, and they do not wish to bow to the pictures of these great saints in our Lineage.

Dry knowledge will not help. You can be a Master of words, giving Spiritual lectures from literature that you have learnt by heart. This is just rote learning and not practical Knowledge.

SO KNOW YOURSELF AND BE QUIET.
THINK IT! THINK IT!
BY THINKING, THE THINKER WILL DISAPPEAR,

AND THERE YOU ARE!

In your daily life, you are to be intoxicated with spirituality, this means you are to, "Be with you! Remain within you!" while you are acting in the drama. It is a nice drama, where the child says, "My father", the friend says "My friend", and the boss says, "My servant". All one, but different names.

YOU ARE TO VIEW YOUR SELFLESS SELF IN THIS WAY.
THIS REALITY IS ALREADY LYING WITHIN YOU,
BUT YOU ARE NOT LOOKING.

Q: Say, I wanted to go and see another Master, is that a sign that I have not accepted that everything is within me?

Maharaj: It happens because of a lack of confidence and faith in yourself, maybe doubt, ego, pride. Be practical with your daily life. Always go beyond the seen, look behind, and stay with your Invisible Presence.

When you see something happening, look behind that, with the knowledge that, "Nothing is happening". When you say something is happening, or not happening, go to the Source, "Who is saying that?" You are to train yourself in this way, so that your stance is, "Nothing is happening".

PRIOR TO BEINGNESS,
WHAT WAS HAPPENING OR NOT HAPPENING?
AFTER THE BODY DISSOLVES,
WHO IS GOING TO TALK ABOUT WHAT'S HAPPENING OR NOT?

Who decides what's good or bad? Everybody's understanding is different. Our views are different because of the body impact, and all the impressions that have been absorbed from childhood till today. Good, bad, right, wrong, how you see the world, all this body-knowledge needs to dissolve.

GO DEEP AND DEEP
WITHIN THE SELFLESS SELF.

You are already formless. There is no form!

Q: Sometimes I don't doubt it, and I feel it very strongly.

Maharaj: It is a Superpower which you are neglecting. You are forgetting your Reality because of body impressions.

YOU ARE TO STICK UP FOR REALITY,
THEN THE DOOR WILL OPEN,
AND THE WAY WILL BE CLEAR.

Q: The door will open?

Maharaj: These are just words I'm using. There is no door or way. Everything is open already. Be calm and quiet!

Q: If someone assaults you, Maharaj, you have to react.

Maharaj: Of course! If a snake tries to bite you, you will run away. You want to protect your body, and the snake wants to protect its body. The intention is one and the same. Everyone has difficult experiences, how to react to them will happen spontaneously. All instructions will be given by your Inner Master.

Q: I suppose the ego will have to dissolve so that you can hear the voice of the Inner Master?

Maharaj: There is no ego! What is your status in the world? The body has no status. The body has no value.

You are a Superpower with Supernatural Power but you don't know yourself yet. If, therefore, you still want to go travelling:

CONCENTRATE ON THE TRAVELLER WITHIN YOU.
THE TRAVELLER IS ULTIMATE TRUTH,
WHICH IS NOT IN ANY FORM.

This is truly exceptional Knowledge, exceptional Reality.

131.   Glance Within

Q: You say that it is very important to stay alert. Who is alert all the time?

Maharaj: It is Spontaneous, not deliberate effort. Your alertness will be Spontaneous. Don't depend on the stories, just remember the principle behind the stories, what they were conveying.

ALL CONCEPTS WILL BE DISSOLVED
WHEN YOUR OPEN SECRET IS PROJECTED SPONTANEOUSLY.

This is a world of illusion in which you are posing as a man or a woman. Prior to beingness, who were you? Digest this knowledge. Throw yourself into spirituality. This means total involvement.

GLANCE WITHIN YOURSELF.
THE POWER IS HIDDEN WITHIN YOU.

Everybody has different experiences according to their spiritual status.

Q: What do you mean by spiritual status?

Maharaj: It means how involved you are, and your approach. How seriously you are taking it all? Spirituality is not there so that we can become spiritual experts, Doctors of Philosophy on the subject. Its purpose is to get rid of all the illusion and fear, so that we can be happy when the time comes to leave the body.

Nobody dies and nobody is born. One year, two years, fifty years, eighty years are the ages of the material food-body. Sky is ageless.

The Seer is important, the seeing is not. You are emphasizing illusion more than Reality. We are trying to know ourselves in the light of all these concepts. Be determined like the baby chicken breaking through a very hard shell, like a solid door, so it can see the world. Likewise, you are to break through the hardened layers of illusory concepts.

You are accepting all this Knowledge through the intellect. It is to be accepted spontaneously. You did not decide you were a man, but you live alongside that name. Your Master has given you the name '*Brahman*', but there is still some resistance. It is all up to you. When the moment is gone, it's gone. You are ignoring your Inner Master, your own existence, your own Presence.

Q: Why are we ignoring all this?

Maharaj: Because of the pressure of body-knowledge. The secret is known to you.

EVERYTHING COMES OUT OF NOTHING.

Q: Is it not a natural process to think, "I am the body"?

Maharaj: Where was this natural process prior to beingness?

WE CREATED THE PROCESS.

PRIOR TO BEINGNESS, NO KNOWLEDGE, NO NOTHING.
No nature! Why this? Why that? All body-related!
WHATEVER KNOWLEDGE YOU HAVE GATHERED TILL TODAY,
MINUS IT, AND THEN TALK. IF YOU DO THIS,
YOU WILL FIND THAT YOU CANNOT TALK.

132. Burning to Know

Maharaj: Thoughts come into the mind and immediately they are reported to the intellect. The intellect then instructs, "Do this!" You are a Master therefore you can control the mind, ego, intellect. You can stop a thought on the spot, and not allow it to reach the intellect. If you do this, there is no action. But if you allow that thought to travel to the intellect, then there will be a hammering immediately.

You are a Master of all these subtle elements. You are beyond all these invisible bodies. Through meditation, you can control each and every thing. There are great benefits from the meditation which will give you great power, strength and alertness. If any unwanted person approaches you, you can stop him. If any unwanted thoughts appear, you can stop them: "I am the technician, not the mind, ego, intellect". In this way, you can easily control yourself, with the result that all activities will be controlled spontaneously.

Q: The only value I see in life is for consciousness to find its way back to where it belongs.

Maharaj: Did you know about consciousness or unconsciousness prior to beingness? Awareness, unawareness? These are the sweet words just for our understanding. Consciousness, realization, enlightenment, God, mind, ego, intellect. So many, many words! All these words appeared out of your Presence. I am placing before you 'Prior to Beingness'. Question yourself! How were you prior to beingness?

Q: I don't know. I can't even fathom that.

Maharaj: Your Presence is beyond imagination.

'This is my house! This is my body!' There is attachment to the body, even a kind of conviction that, "This is my house", and you are staying in your house. Your ego came along and declared, "I am the owner of this house". You are carrying out all your activities through this house.

You are looking at me, eating, walking, moving your hand. As you know, the body itself does not have any power. We are discussing, questioning, listening, thinking, using the mind, the intellect. But don't forget, it is the body and Power combined that enable action.

YOU MUST HAVE THIS CONVICTION.
THOUGH YOU ARE STAYING IN THIS HOUSE,
IT IS RENTED.
YOU KNOW THERE IS ANOTHER OWNER,
THAT IS CALLED *BRAHMAN*.

The owner is telling you to vacate the house now because in the future, you will have to vacate the body. Still, in spite of knowing this, there is still a lot of attachment to the body.

YOU KNOW THE TRUTH,

EVERYBODY KNOWS,
BUT TRUTH HAS TO TURN INTO CONVICTION
AND BECOME ESTABLISHED TRUTH.

The Conviction is not there, if you are tempted to go anywhere.

Q: The ego says, "I am the body".

Maharaj: This Conviction is rooted through the body, and is therefore not Conviction. Doubts are there!

Q: Why am I so attached to the body?

Maharaj: It is natural, not your fault. Spirit is very sensitive. Understand that your existence, Presence, is Ultimate Truth. This body is not. All comforts are needed for the body, not for you. Listen with full concentration because you have so many questions.

Q: Is Spirit independent?

Maharaj: Of course, but it does not know itself. It only knows itself through the body. The purpose of these talks is to convey your importance. You must have the will, a strong will, to accept it.

LISTEN TO ME VERY QUIETLY, AND WITH FULL CONCENTRATION.
LISTEN TO ME VERY CAREFULLY.
IT IS THE LISTENER'S PRINCIPLE, REALITY.

But again and again the ego rises, and with it, more questions come. You are to listen with attention. You have been reading books, focussing for a moment on what you have read, and then all is forgotten! Thirty years, forty years of spirituality, and still nothing is there. Why are you doing it?

Q: For spiritual experiences, maybe.

Maharaj: This is body-talk. There were no experiences prior to beingness. Now, everything is open. Accept it, or don't accept it. It is up to you. A casual attitude and excessive use of thoughts, will only cause difficulties and not move you forward. Meditation means that your whole body, your whole sense of being is burning to KNOW, and so you are thinking constantly about your Selfless Self.

IT SHOULD TOUCH YOUR HEART.
IT SHOULD GIVE A BLOW TO YOUR HEART.
REALITY IS SUPPOSED TO TOUCH YOU DEEPLY.

133. *Irritation*

Q: I have noticed that I cannot tolerate some things now that I could before.

Maharaj: Tolerance is connected to the body level, and the influence of the mind, ego. Now that you know Reality, identify those things that you find intolerable. Think about these triggers and why some things are intolerable. Remember, what you think is not your Identity. That through which you think is your Identity.

Because beingness is intolerable, you need a lot of entertainment: getting married, having a family, eating ice cream.

But because you have a spiritual background, and you know it is coming from the mind, you are to minimise the problem. Don't let it inside. It is a very bad thing to register these thoughts. So many things happen in life, but now you know the art of management.

The great Saint Eknath was challenged many times during his life. He grew in tolerance. One person used to spit at Saint Eknath every time he saw him. When this happened, the saint would take a bath. In the end, after spitting on him about forty times, this opponent bowed at the saint's feet and said, "I have not been able to irritate you". The saint said he was happy because he took forty auspicious baths!

This is tolerance. It was a test of his spiritual life. There are always tests, and when they come along, you are to view everyone as yourself! There is no difference between you and anyone else - friends or enemies are just words. This quality of seeing yourself in others is the way. It will be there spontaneously. Don't get irritated! Pacify yourself! Spirituality shows you how to act in difficult situations. Recognize that this life has a time-limit!

IF YOU IGNORE TODAY, YOU ARE IGNORING FOREVER.

Again you will find you are in another dream. This is an opportunity, so use it fully. Don't pay attention to these thoughts and feelings. Now is your time, be aware of it, or you will miss it, and that would be unfortunate.

Q: I should know this, but I am not taking it seriously enough, I suppose.

Maharaj: You will gain strength and power from spirituality. These incidents are momentary, so what is the use of getting annoyed. Stay strong! There will be many challenges, tests on the way. I am giving you commando training. It will make you an all-rounder so you can act smart in any circumstance.

134.   *You have Given Birth to the World*

Q: There is a feeling, some feeling there that the Master is reinforcing something that the disciple already knows.

Maharaj: At the initial stage, the Master and Disciple are two identities, but the Spirit is One. We say 'Master' and 'Disciple', for understanding purposes. Since you forgot your identity, the Master is needed to indicate your Formless Identity. The Master is placing before you your Ultimate Truth.

Q: So there is no experiencer, no experience, just experiencing?

Maharaj: Prior to body-knowledge there were no such words at all. We need to erase all these terms, and for this, the Master is necessary.

Q: Is the 'I am' like a pivot point? It seems to be the only choice, to go to ego, or to go to Truth?

Maharaj: Your Presence is needed to say, 'I am'. Without Presence, you can't utter a single word. All words came along with the body. After leaving the body, who is going to say, 'I am'. 'I am' is an indication of your Spontaneous Presence, not in body-form.

THE ENTIRE WORLD IS THE CONCENTRATOR'S PROJECTION,
THE ANONYMOUS, INVISIBLE CONCENTRATOR.
THE SPONTANEOUS PROJECTION OF THE CONCENTRATOR.

You cannot guess the nature of the Concentrator. You cannot imagine or infer. You cannot use logic to understand. Just see how you were prior to beingness. "I don't know" means you know yourself, but you know yourself as formless.

There can be no cognizance! You are to fix your Unidentified Identity in the light of these words.

Q: When you say "prior to beingness", is that the same as "prior to consciousness", meaning that we were separated from...

Maharaj: We are using all these words just to try and understand. Every time you use words, you are other than what you are.

You are to erase all body-knowledge.

Q: So the closest is experiencing?

Maharaj: You have given birth to the world. The world is the Seer's reflection. Without the Seer, you cannot know the world. Basically, you know the world through words, through the alphabet, joining up a string of letters ABC, and then giving these words meanings.

Q: So what you are saying, is that we have given meaning to everything that we call knowledge, and all of that, is really only body-knowledge, not Self-Knowledge? Therefore, what you are advocating is a process of reverse accumulation, or reverse conditioning to undo everything?

Maharaj: In a nutshell, you have forgotten your Identity! You need to know the Principle of Knowledge. This means knowing oneself in a real sense. You need a solid base to know yourself, to know Reality. You also need Conviction and confirmation from the Master.

135. Heart Love

Q: I take it that heart love and Selfless Self are one and the same thing?

Maharaj: Heart love is connected with the body. Heart love came along with the body. Where is the heart? Where is the love? Where is the affection? All these words came with the body. There was no such thing as 'heart love' prior to beingness because your Presence was unknown.

All this knowledge is body-knowledge. I am drawing your attention to prior to the body, prior to beingness. There is no heart, no love, no affection. We say 'Selfless Self' because 'self' is connected to the body. Selfless Self means without body, without mind, without ego, without intellect. That is called Selfless Self.

'I am' is a body-connected, body sense. Prior to that, there was no 'I am', no self. It is therefore called 'Selfless Self'.

NO KNOWLEDGE WAS THERE, NO IGNORANCE,
NO EXPERIENCE, NO WITNESS, NO EXPERIENCER.
YOU ARE JUST LIKE THE SKY, UNAWARE THAT "I AM SKY".
SELFLESS SELF IS JUST LIKE THE SKY.
NO IDENTITY!

Q: So there is no love?

Maharaj: That love came along with the body. Does sky love? Who is there to love, when all is One, Spirit is One? There are no differences, no separation, no individuals. Does the Australian sky love the Indian sky? All this love and affection talk started with the body.

Mind, ego, intellect, heart, love, affection are all illusory concepts, which you are using because you are measuring yourself in body-form. Prior to beingness, you were not connected to all these. You did not know, "Who am I?" Everything is behind your Spontaneous Presence, your Invisible Power. Your Presence is Invisible. These are just words I'm using to communicate:

THE SEER DOES NOT KNOW
THAT WHAT IT PROJECTS IS ITS OWN PROJECTION.
WHAT THE SEER SEES IS INVISIBLE,
ANONYMOUS, UNIDENTIFIED IDENTITY.

Therefore body-knowledge is supposed to dissolve. Your Spontaneous Presence does not need any food. Presence does not know, "I am the body", or "I am somebody". When the Spirit clicked with the body, you say, "I am". Spirit only knows itself through the body. Your Identity is Unidentified, Invisible Identity. You must have Conviction. Forget about all this love and affection, it is just body-knowledge.

The whole world is illusion. Your view should be something like this:

MY PRESENCE IS EVERYWHERE, IN EVERY BEING.
THEREFORE WHO CAN I HATE?
WHO CAN I STRUGGLE WITH?
THIS IS CALLED REALIZATION, SPONTANEOUS REALIZATION.

It is very easy, if you look at you. Remember all this that you have been listening to.

EVERYTHING IS WITHIN YOU ONLY.
'LOOK AT YOU'
REMEMBER THESE WORDS,
THEN APPLY THEM TO YOURSELF.
THIS IS YOUR KNOWLEDGE.

Your subtle ego is not allowing you to reach realization. 'Realization' is already there, but as yet unknown. Realization with Conviction is what's needed, Conviction of the Reality. You are Reality. Meditation is necessary to attain this. Dry listening without action is pointless.

THE KNOWLEDGE, THE TRUTH THAT IS BEING CONVEYED,
SHOULD TOUCH YOUR HEART.
YOU SHOULD BE SO DEEPLY MOVED BY IT,
THAT IT REACHES YOUR CORE.

Here, when I am talking about 'heart', I am talking about something that is deeply felt. A 'profound feeling'. If someone assaults you verbally with abusive language, you feel it deeply. Your heart, your very core feels it because your trust, your faith has been hurt or betrayed. I am talking about this heart.

Q: From what I have read, there is another meaning to heart. It is a conscious thing.

Maharaj: When you are told that, "You are *Brahman*", your response should be like a deep and meaningful turning point,

"YES! I AM TOUCHED AND MOVED BECAUSE I AM *BRAHMAN*".
YOU ARE TOUCHED BECAUSE
YOU HAVE LIVED FOR SO LONG AS A MAN OR AS A WOMAN.

When you started knowing 'I am', you suddenly embraced all concepts and other people. You have not to make any deliberate kind of effort. It is Spontaneous. Forget about others!

OTHERS EXIST ONLY BECAUSE OF YOUR PRESENCE.

Q: If you make a conscious decision to forgive someone?

Maharaj: No! It is Spontaneous, it will be a natural process. Up till now, you have been considering yourself as a guilty man. Meditation is the foundation. It cleans and purifies everything. Then, in the light, Knowledge will be planted.

Farmers burn the land and apply fertilizer so that the seeds will grow well. If other things are still there, like stones and weeds, unwanted things, these little seeds will not have a chance to grow.

THEREFORE, YOU ARE TO REMOVE THE CONCEPTS,
AND PLANT THE REALITY OF KNOWLEDGE.
KNOWLEDGE MEANS REALITY.
AFTER THAT, YOU ARE TO ENCOURAGE IT TO GROW
WITH MEDITATION AND PRAYER.

It is simple. Your involvement is most important. It is all that is needed.

GLANCE AT THE KNOWLEDGE
I AM TRYING TO IMPLANT IN YOU.
MAKE A NOTE OF WHAT YOU HAVE LISTENED TO.
REMEMBER WHAT HAS BEEN SAID.
ALL THIS KNOWLEDGE IS BEING RECORDED
BY YOUR INNER RECORDER.
THERE WON'T BE ANY QUESTIONS LEFT TO ASK,
NOR WILL YOU BE HAMMERED BY ANY CONCEPT.

You are to surrender the ego, willpower and trust. The ego, dignity and pride. Why let the ego dictate to you when it has no existence, and is not going to remain constant?

THE BODY IS JUST LIKE FIREWOOD,
TO BE BURIED OR BURNED.

Don't struggle through life. Be peaceful and live a peaceful life. Every being wants a peaceful life. You can have a peaceful life if you know your Selfless Self. If you don't have peace, then change your route and avoid people who are disturbing your peace. These people could be your family members. Avoid them!

YOUR PEACE IS THE MOST IMPORTANT THING.
YOU ARE ULTIMATE TRUTH.
YOU ARE FINAL TRUTH.

136. *Act in Your Own Movie*

Q: Even now, there are periods of confusion.

Maharaj: When there is confusion, ask, "Who knows the confusion?" It is really a good sign because it shows that you know the Reality. And when you know, you can shift the attention back to Selfless Self. When you are noticing some confusion going on inside, it is a good sign because you know what is happening.

THE KNOWER IS ALERT.
IT MEANS YOU ARE SEPARATE FROM THE SOMETHING,
THIS SOMETHING, THAT IS GOING ON.

Now you are separate from the body because you know that, "The body is separate from me". If something is going on in the house, you notice it. This means you are separate from the house, separate from the body. When there is something that is disliked, you can change your route.

Before, say, if you felt depressed, you just fell into it. Now you know what's going on. It is a good sign because you are coming closer and closer to the Seer. You know something is going on, and you can do something about it.

IT IS A SIMPLE FORMULA:
KNOWLEDGE AND YOU ARE ONE. THERE IS NO DIFFERENCE.

Your Selfless Self is separate from the body, separate from the world. Mood changes are bound to happen because this body belongs to the five elements. Any imbalance in the five elements is reflected. When you notice it, you will say, "Something is going on". The whole body is made up of the five elements. The same thing happens with the three qualities (*gunas*), when there is imbalance.

The '*Tama*' quality is the most dangerous: struggling with others, offending, criminality, etc. '*Sattva*' likes prayer and meditation, so it is good for spirituality. '*Raja*' looks for pleasure, enjoyment and therefore diverts you from Reality. If any of these qualities are carried to excess, there will be imbalance. Now forget the *gunas*!

YOU ARE BEYOND ALL THESE *GUNAS*.

Be aware and alert, and you will be OK. If you go closer and closer to Selfless Self, you will stay separate from the world, and these qualities will have no effect on you. Everything is within you. Where were the *gunas* prior to beingness? When did you come across such knowledge? This means you are beyond that.

Q: You mean I can choose the *guna*?

Maharaj: Why choose?

IN ORDER TO CHOOSE, THERE HAS TO BE SOMEONE THERE.
THERE IS NO ONE THERE!
BE AS YOU WERE PRIOR TO BEINGNESS.
REMAIN LIKE THAT.

There are no *gunas*! *Sattva* is good for establishing Truth, but it is not Ultimate Truth. Come out of all the *gunas*! It is elementary education, primary school level talk. No *gunas* and no body-knowledge!

BE AS YOU WERE PRIOR TO BEINGNESS - ULTIMATE TRUTH.

Total involvement is needed. If you want to swim in the deep sea, you have to dive deep. Everything has been taught to you, so don't be afraid. You are to create confidence in your Selfless Self.

YOU HAVE KNOWLEDGE.
HOW LONG ARE YOU GOING TO REMAIN AT THE BANK OF THE RIVER FOR?
NOW PRACTISE!

Q: What if someone can't swim, will he not die?

Maharaj: There's no someone, there is only yourself, your Spontaneous Presence.

WHEN THE KNOWER AND KNOWLEDGE DISAPPEAR,
THERE YOU ARE. NO FORM!

Why think of others? Will you be thinking of others when the time comes to leave the body?

DID YOU BRING A WIFE, OR ANY FRIENDS WITH YOU
WHEN YOU CAME INTO THE BODY?
FORGET ABOUT THE DREAM!
THE BIG FAMILY IS A DREAM!
YOUR HUSBAND IS A DREAM. YOUR WIFE IS A DREAM.
AFTER AWAKENING, WHERE DOES ALL THIS GO?

All replies and answers are inside you, but you are not glancing within. You are not looking with Selfless Self. Don't take what I am saying literally. The words I am using here, are just to help you understand, and indicate your Selfless Self.

WE ARE LIVING IN THE CIRCLE OF WORLDLY-KNOWLEDGE.

You forgot your Identity and accepted things that you are not. Have a conversation with Selfless Self. Make your Internal Master talk! You are the Questioner, and you are the Answerer. You are the Master and you are the devotee. There will be happiness and peace when you come to know that there is nothing. Why fight when there is nothing there? The entire world, including yourself is an illusion, so why fight?

No Knowledge is Knowledge. After knowing the Reality, you will realize that you were trying to hammer, strike, hit, batter, and fight with the air. There is no need to struggle because your 'I' is prior to beingness.

THIS IS A GOLDEN OPPORTUNITY.
SURRENDER COMPLETELY!
PARTIAL KNOWLEDGE IS NOT ENOUGH.

Practical spirituality means that you don't escape from problems, but face them head-on. For example, you don't abandon your parents. Abandoning them is not spirituality. Do your duty, and take care of your parents. Why go here and there in the name of spirituality? You know the whole world is illusion, therefore converting so-called bad situations and circumstances into good, is to be seen as a challenge and test of your spiritual Knowledge.

Live as if you are acting in a movie. Sometimes the movie is a tragedy, at other times, it may be a comedy. Sometimes you are the villain, but whatever is happening, you will always know, that it is illusion.

JUST VIEW YOUR SELFLESS SELF,
AND HOW YOU WERE PRIOR TO BEINGNESS.

137. Do You Want Another Dream?

Q: Maharaj, things are pretty clear now. I have a better idea of the practice.
Maharaj: You have to keep up the discipline of meditation. You don't want another dream. Whatever concepts you may have at the time of leaving the body, may be reflected. This reflection is what's termed, 'rebirth', but

there is no rebirth at all. So now you know!

DEMAND WHAT IS RIGHTFULLY YOURS.
DON'T JUST TAKE A LITTLE.
TAKE IT ALL!

You are your own Master. Your thinking is supposed to be positive thinking. Accept the Reality without any doubts. What will happen? Is that true or false? No! This is knowledge with suspicion. This is negative thinking, negative feelings, doubts. You are to think positively. Accept your Ultimate Truth wholeheartedly.

Through words, I am trying to convince the Silent Listener in you. The basic requirement is still the same: body-knowledge has to dissolve totally with meditation. There is no way round this.

Accept your Knowledge, your Reality. You now have the technique that will show you how to find out about your Selfless Self.

YOU HAVE THE FACTS AND FIGURES TO HAND,
NOW ALL THAT IS NEEDED
IS YOUR SERIOUS INVOLVEMENT.

The meditation will give you courage to accept it. You may be anywhere in the world, but always keep in mind that there is only Selfless Self. There is absolutely nothing else.

Your Presence is Spontaneous Presence. You will not find anything impossible, if you have courage and strong willpower. You know the Reality, now you need to dissolve the food-body-knowledge. Be spiritually strong! Be fearless because you are unborn. To establish this Truth, you are to come forward. Take one step in my direction - this process demands two-way traffic.

You must be strong-willed to want to know the Reality, and to not be tempted to go anywhere else. If you are still attracted to another Master, it means that,

YOU ARE MISREPRESENTING YOURSELF.
EVERYTHING IS WITHIN YOU,
THEREFORE THERE IS NO NEED TO BEG ANY MORE.

Q: Nisargadatta Maharaj said, "The child of a barren woman...".

Maharaj: Roaming in the circle of literal knowledge will not give you happiness. Don't analyze knowledge. What the Masters said is correct, but what they wanted to convey is more important. It is not a spiritual competition or debate or argument, counter-argument.

WHERE YOU STAND IS ULTIMATE.
THAT IS WHAT IS IMPORTANT.

You are no longer a student of your Master. This is the summary of spiritual Knowledge. It is the principle, the base, the gist of the Invisible Listener.

So think positively, and engrave this Knowledge.

ENGRAVE THIS KNOWLEDGE.

Don't let it disappear! Continue with it, engrave it permanently! If something is engraved in stone, metal, brass or gold, it will be very difficult to remove.

138. You are Separate From the World

Q: The question is, knowing how to live a spiritual life in the world, and how to stay aware?

Maharaj: Who says 'knowing'? This world is a dream-world. No excitement! Live a simple life, a quiet life. Nobody is a friend, nobody is an enemy. To know the Reality, you have to carry out the disciplines, then you will be totally at peace. The Mantra creates vibrations which will delete all body-knowledge files, including all the polished concepts like, '*chitta*', '*buddhi*', 'consciousness', 'awareness', etc. People love to play with fanciful names!

NAMES ARE NOT ULTIMATE TRUTH,
YOU ARE ULTIMATE TRUTH.

The *Naam Mantra* washes out everything that is surplus to requirements. My Masters said:

"THE BODY IS THE DIRTIEST BODY.
THE BODY HOLDER IS TOTALLY PURE -THE PUREST PURITY".

The body is important because of the Spirit. After Conviction, there will be complete calm and quiet, and no expectation or greed. The sign of Conviction is Absolute Knowledge, Omnipresence.

WE HAVE FORGOTTEN WHO WE ARE.
WE HAVE ACCEPTED ILLUSION AS TRUTH.

The aim of your life is critical, crucial. Give importance to Selfless Self because you are the root of this whole world. Don't follow any concepts, *karma* or "thirty years' seeking"! For what use is all this? Torturing your body, doing *sadhana*. Whose *sadhana*? Apply your spiritual intellect.

YOU ARE UNDERESTIMATING YOURSELF.
DON'T BECOME A CONCEPT SLAVE AGAIN!

What will you get from following a practice? Happiness, maybe peace? But the benefits will be momentary.

Q: My goal is to manifest the *sadhana*.

Maharaj: Who wants to manifest the *sadhana*? Who and what were manifest before beingness?

Q: Something happened with a friend of mine. I knew him socially. Anyway, he turned out to be dishonest. I don't like dishonest people. I'm telling you this because it has just appeared in the mind, at this very moment.

Maharaj: Social life is social life. Spiritual life is spiritual life. They are unconnected. Don't keep this incident in mind. Don't dwell on it. This kind of energy, excitement or agitation should be momentary. Don't keep hold of it.

THE TRICK IS TO FORGET IT QUICKLY.
DON'T RECORD EVENTS,
AND KEEP PLAYING THEM, AGAIN AND AGAIN,
LIKE A RECORD.

You should not keep remembering this kind of incident. It is not helpful. Don't carry thoughts, excitement, anger. It is not healthy!

IF YOU CARRY THESE MEMORIES AROUND WITH YOU,
YOU ARE MAKING THE EXPERIENCES LIVE AGAIN.

You are playing them over and over like a record. Something happened to you ten years ago, and you are still playing the same old record over and over! No! This is a bad habit. Your reaction was not wrong, but to carry the memory around with you is not good, not clever! Try to avoid adding ego, ego, ego. Apply your Spiritual Knowledge.

Q: As a Realized being, Maharaj, do you get angry?

Maharaj: Recently, a visitor to the ashram became agitated. He wanted to take his personal problems out on me. I kept quiet and tried to calm him. For me, it was nothing. No effect! Ramakrishna Paramahamsa, Swami Vivekananda's Master, was once with a companion. An insect, a scorpion was nearby. His companion said, "Why don't you kill it?" Ramakrishna replied: "It is its nature to bite. It does not know what it is doing". If someone is assaulting you verbally, just forget about it. Things happen all the time, ignore them, forget them!

YOU KNOW BETTER.
YOU ARE DIFFERENT FROM THE ORDINARY MAN.
HE KNOWS NOTHING ABOUT SPIRITUALITY.
IF WE GO ALONG WITH HIS NATURE,
THEN THERE IS NO DIFFERENCE BETWEEN BOTH OF YOU.

I told you the story of Eknath who was spat on about forty times. Not only did he bathe in the sacred water forty times, but he also took his opponent to lunch!

When unpleasant things happen, there is bound to be a little excitement, agitation, a moment's anger. But you have to control it, and forget about it the next moment.

The mind loves to chew over and over negative things. In dreams, you may harm, even kill, but you don't take on the emotions, the sting. Likewise, this is a dream, therefore don't carry any aggression. You are separate from this world. Godly essence is with you, the Masterly essence is with you.

WHEN YOU HAVE REAL DEVOTION, COMPLETE DEVOTION,
EVEN IF YOU ARE TEMPTED TO BE ANGRY,
YOU WILL NOT BE ABLE TO BE ANGRY.
YOU WILL BE FIRMLY ESTABLISHED IN REALITY.

Once, a visitor started shouting at my Master. He grabbed hold of Nisargadatta Maharaj's neck. He wanted to test him. My Master was calm and quiet. Other people in the room were agitated. It happened spontaneously.

All illusory concepts will dissolve. This is the effect the *Naam Mantra* will have.

Q: Is this Mantra the same as Nisargadatta Maharaj's?

Maharaj: Yes, back to Dattatreya. The Mantra is not for commercial use. Rural doctors use many different kinds of medicines. They do not charge because they believe that charging for medicines disturbs the knowledge. Similarly,

ANY ASSOCIATION WITH MONEY
WILL SPOIL THE *NAAM MANTRA*.

The *Sampradaya* does not demand anything.

I AM SHARING THIS KNOWLEDGE FREELY,
BUT I AM EXPECTING YOU TO FOLLOW THE TEACHINGS,

**TO COME OUT OF ALL THIS ILLUSION,
FOR YOUR OWN BENEFIT.**

Don't be a slave of your mind. The mind is always demanding, wanting a new house, car, holiday, money, and more money.

**WHAT WILL YOU DO WITH ALL THAT MONEY?
CAN YOU TRANSFER IT ALL TO THE BANK IN HEAVEN?**

Q: Maybe buy a plot in heaven!

Maharaj: If you want to give a meaningful offering, then deposit your ego, intellect, mind here with me.

139.   Tangible Silence

Maharaj: Now you are absolutely unconcerned with the body. You know you are not the body at all. Who is the holder of the body? Who are you? 'They' say it is *Brahman, Atman, Paramatman*, God. You may call it by any name. You are beyond whatever name it has been given.

**YOU ARE BEYOND THAT. YOU ARE BEYOND THAT.
YOU ARE BEYOND SKY.**

After knowing the Reality, illusory concepts will dissolve spontaneously. Spiritual knowledge means to know oneself in a real sense. We are knowing ourselves in body-form.

**AFTER HAVING THIS KNOWLEDGE,
THE BODY-BASED KNOWLEDGE WILL DISSOLVE COMPLETELY.**

First of all, you concentrated on meditation, now you are moving slowly to the advanced stage, where you will forget everything, including yourself.

**THERE WILL BE EXCEPTIONAL SILENCE
AND EXCEPTIONAL PEACE.**

Q: I wanted to say, Maharaj, that recently the Presence of the Masters during meditation has been very strong. Nisargadatta Maharaj yesterday and today Siddharameshwar Maharaj. It is as though they are helping and giving encouragement to the practice, paving the way and pushing me forward in a kind and gentle fashion.

Nisargadatta Maharaj, for example, opened the door and said "Come in!" He was waving his hand, beckoning me to come forward!

Maharaj: The Masters are helping you and guiding you all the time. Through the meditation, you are spontaneously identifying your Invisible Existence. Through the meditation, you are identifying your Unidentified Identity.

**THROUGH THE MEDITATION,
YOU ARE IDENTIFYING UNIDENTIFIED REALITY,
WHICH YOU ARE,
WITHOUT ANY SHAPE, WITHOUT ANY BODY.**

All the thoughts, and all the concepts related to the body, will dissolve. You will become totally fearless. You may have difficulties, but you will be working and handling your responsibilities, remaining totally unconcerned with any difficulties, as if you are acting in a dream.

Q: There is greater silence and peace. Tangible silence!

Maharaj: Exceptional silence, exceptional peace will be there which cannot be described using any words.

Truth is beyond "I am Brahman", beyond that, beyond silence. This can be realized through Selfless Self. There is no self. When self disappears, nothing remains. This is called Selfless Self. As long as there is a trace of self, you will be able to identify it. When everything goes, it is indescribable.

Q: While listening to the talks again, Maharaj, there is increasing absorption of all that you've said. And it is so good, wonderful! What is happening feels organic. It's growing like a plant.

Maharaj: It is by the grace of my Masters.

Q: Jai Guru! I am very happy and strong. The practice is becoming stronger and deeper. All is well.

Maharaj: Very good! Stay strong and courageous.

140. *Merge With the Sea.*

Maharaj: The basic thing to know is that Knowledge is already within you. Spiritual knowledge is already within you. You just have to refresh it, and remove the illusory concepts. And that's what the meditation is for. The meditation will reduce the forces of the ego, mind, intellect.

CHANGE WILL HAPPEN. IT WILL BE SPONTANEOUS CHANGE.
IT IS ALREADY INBUILT WITHIN, BUT YOU ARE UNAWARE.

The Invisible, Silent Presence was there before beingness. After the body dissolves, that Presence will be there, but without any witnesser or experience. Presence is everywhere, but we are limited by the body. It is only because of body attachment that you have so many questions.

IF YOU CONCENTRATE ON THE QUESTIONER,
YOU WILL FIND THE ANSWER.
CONCENTRATE ON THE SOURCE,
WHERE THE QUESTION ARISES,
AND ON THE QUESTIONER, WHO IS THE QUESTIONER?

At the same time, you are witnessing that question. This means you are both the question and the Questioner. You are both the Listener and the Speaker. But because of the food-body, you forgot your Identity. That is why meditation is needed, to refresh the memories of Reality, of Ultimate Truth.

In addition to the meditation, you need Knowledge. Knowledge, as I keep telling you, just means to know oneself in a real sense. Therefore after Knowledge, there will be Conviction: "I am the Ultimate. I am the Final Truth".

The next step following Conviction will lead to Absorption. Knowledge will be absorbed in the body. So Conviction means YOU KNOW. And this leads to Reality: "Yes! I know the Reality. I am the *Brahman*, I am the Ultimate Truth". But it is known by words only. It should be absorbed within your Selfless Self.

THE INDIVIDUAL GOES AFTER THAT.
KNOWLEDGE OF REALITY HAS BEEN ABSORBED.

THE INDIVIDUAL WILL BE GONE.

There will be no more duality. Your identity will disappear. Everything comes out of nothing and everything is dissolved back into nothing.

THE BODY, AND THAT WHICH WE SEE
WITHIN THE SPAN OF THIS LIFE,
THE SOMETHING WITHIN THE NOTHING,
IS DISSOLVED BACK INTO NOTHING.

Because of the body, you were seeing yourself, you were knowing yourself. You were trying to extract some happiness and peace through the body alone. But now you know better. You know your body is not your identity, that it is just the food-body, which will continue to survive, for as long as you are supplying it with food.

CONVICTION LEADS TO ABSORPTION,
WHICH MEANS MERGING.
EVERYTHING IS BEING ABSORBED,
AND MERGED INTO ONENESS.

The bucket of water that is poured into the sea becomes one with the sea, inseparable from the sea. It becomes sea. So after absorbing, there is merging. You can't remove or undo any of it, even if you wanted to.

Q: So let me see if I understand, Maharaj? First thing is meditation and Knowledge, then Conviction, which comes from the Master convincing us of the Reality, as well as from our own Self-Conviction. This is, 'active' Conviction because we are working at it to accept Reality.

After the Conviction, which means really 'knowing' that we are not the body, we go through a period of Absorption which means that all the Knowledge is absorbed in the body. And then, there is the final stage of Spontaneous Conviction, and this happens when it happens. Is that more or less accurate, Maharaj?

Maharaj: Yes, yes. And how is that Knowledge absorbed? I keep repeating the same thing, by doing the basics, the meditation. Meditation reduces the forces of mind, ego, intellect and that is why the secret Mantra is given.

WHEN YOU ARE RECITING THE MANTRA,
YOU ARE INVITING ATTENTION OF THE RECITER.
LISTEN TO ME CAREFULLY! THROUGH THE MANTRA,
YOU ARE SHIFTING ATTENTION FROM THE BODY,
AND REMINDING THAT RECITER THAT YOU ARE ULTIMATE TRUTH,
THAT YOU ARE FINAL TRUTH.

And after reciting, and continuously inviting the attention of the reciter, it becomes... "So that I!"

Your Spontaneous Presence is at first resistant to the Mantra because of the long association with the body. But as you will know by now, after continuous reciting, continuously inviting the attention of the Invisible Presence, the Ultimate... It suddenly happens, "So that I!" At this point, 'it' immediately becomes unconcerned with the world.

You forget your external identity, you forget 'I', you forget everything. You forget your Presence also. You are not concerned with any body-knowledge. You don't need any peace or happiness.

THERE IS SPONTANEOUS HAPPINESS,
SPONTANEOUS PEACE.
THERE IS NO TENSION,
AND NO FEAR,
BECAUSE YOU KNOW THAT,
"I WAS NEVER BORN".

So as I told you, your Conviction leads to the Absorption of Knowledge. After Conviction, Absorption is most important. It is a kind of merging. You are using your body but without any expectations, without any attachment, love or affection. You will function spontaneously.

THERE WILL BE SPONTANEOUS LIVING AFTER CONVICTION,
WHERE EVERY ACTION WILL BE SPONTANEOUS,
NOT DELIBERATE.
IT IS A SIMPLE THING.
EVERYTHING IS IN YOU.
EVERYTHING IS IN YOU.
TO PUT IT SIMPLY: YOU WERE INNOCENTLY UNAWARE.

This is simple Knowledge which has been made complicated by intellectualization and books. It is straight knowledge that is directly concerned with your Selfless Self. There's no need to go anywhere to find out, because the Finder itself is Ultimate Truth.

THE FINDER ITSELF IS ULTIMATE TRUTH.

We were looking for the Finder, searching here and there. The Searcher, the Finder, is the Ultimate Truth but it is covered with the body, the food-body. And because of the long association with the body, all our knowledge was egoistic knowledge. Now the ego is dissolving, dissolving.

141.   Nothing Means Nothing

Q: Whose Presence? As a child you grow up, become aware and gradually, hopefully, awaken. How would you describe Presence?

Maharaj: How do you see the entire world? How do you see the child, the man or woman, the world? It is all the reflection, projection of your Presence, your Spontaneous Presence. There is no individuality, just Presence which is very vast, everywhere. We have given it a word 'Presence', but the word, as you know, is also illusion.

Don't get caught up in words. Go behind the words. If we say 'child', 'awareness', 'beingness', 'consciousness', we are just using these words as a means of communicating. So, likewise, Presence is a word that is directing you to your Unidentified Identity. It is messaging your Unidentified Identity.

THERE ARE NO WORDS,
THERE IS NO EXISTENCE. THERE IS NO PRESENCE.

When we are talking about Presence, we are using egoistic, intellectual and logical thoughts. There is no logic, no intellect, no mind, no ego. There is absolutely nothing.

BUT OUT OF NOTHING, YOU SEE EVERYTHING.

WHEN NOTHING DISSOLVES, ABSORBS,
THERE YOU ARE.

Q: So, the Spontaneous Presence cannot be defined by any words?

Maharaj: The word is used just to point out, just for Conviction, just to know the Invisible Listener's own Identity which is like sky. You see the sky, you see the sea! It is the Seer's reflection. Your Identity is beyond that, beyond that.

Q: Who is awakening?

Maharaj: There is nobody awakening. There is no question of anything relating to the body-form. No awakening, no consciousness, no beyond consciousness, no before consciousness. These are the words that we use for understanding, just for Conviction. We have nothing to do with this world, nothing to do with individuality. All these explanations are used to invite the attention of the Invisible Listener, the Spontaneous Listener within you, which has no shape.

Q: You said that everything comes from nothing, and is absorbed back into nothing. So what is nothing?

Maharaj: Nothing is nothing! Nothing cannot be defined. Nothing is nothing. It cannot be defined. What is no knowledge? It is no knowledge. I have told you that we are talking about the unborn child!

WE ARE TALKING ABOUT THIS CHILD,
THE CHILD WHICH IS NOT BORN.
NOTHING, NOT BORN,
UNBORN.

Q: But is there still a something after the dissolution, something in the nothing?

Maharaj: No, no nothing, no something, no dissolution. All these are words. W.O.R.D.S. Again, you are talking through your body information.

Q: Yes! But you did say that there is still something. When everything disappears and there is nothing, there is a little...

Maharaj: Words are trapping you all the time! Don't take them so literally. I said "There you are" in relation to Conviction. We have to use some words.

Q: And, "There you are" is Spontaneous Presence?

Maharaj: Yes! You cannot see the world without your Spontaneous Presence that is Invisible, Anonymous, Unidentified. I am asking everybody not to analyze the words, but rather, to focus on what they are trying to convey. Don't take the literal meaning of what is being communicated.

Q: Nisargadatta Maharaj talks about when you are a small child, before you identify with the body and the name, you know like a baby. He talks quite a lot about that - the 'pre I am' state, before identification with the body.

Maharaj: Again, what he is saying has not to be taken literally. He is simply pointing to Presence, to convince you of Presence, from different angles and dimensions.

Q: Before 'pre I am'? Before the body?

Maharaj: This is your own anticipation. "What was there before 'I am'?" All this anticipation is related to the body-form. There are no words.

ALL WORDS END THERE.

NO LANGUAGE,
NO WORDS.

Even 'existence' is anonymous. It cannot be defined in words. All these questions are raised because of the body-form.

Q: The answers are in the silence.

Maharaj: Silence is the answer to all questions.

142.   Listening With Fresh Ears

Maharaj: There must be a knower, for knowledge to be there. In order to say 'knowledge', there must be a knower. When the knowledge disappears, the knower disappears. The knower does not have any identity. When you say, "I am *Brahman*, I am *Atman*, I've got knowledge", it means that you are separating yourself from Source. The subtle ego makes you see yourself as something else, something apart.

WHEN THE KNOWLEDGE AND THE KNOWER DISAPPEAR,
THERE YOU ARE.
WHEN THE KNOWLEDGE AND THE KNOWER DISAPPEAR,
THERE YOU ARE.

Knowledge is related to the Knower. The Knower and knowledge have no physical existence. The knower does not have any physical existence.

Q: I have faith that if I keep reciting the Mantra, it will quieten the fires of my mind.

Maharaj: 'My' is not 'I'. 'My' body!" You are separate from the body. 'My' wife, 'my' son, you are separate from them. 'My' God, 'my' Master, this is separate from me. Everything comes out of your Presence. Out of Presence, you are talking 'my this, my that'.

Q: When the mind goes, and the body goes, what's left?

Maharaj: There are so many words, there are thousands of *lakhs* of words just to make you understand, make you alert. But,

REALITY HAS NOTHING TO DO WITH ANY WORDS,
OR WITH ANY WORLDS.
REALITY HAS NOTHING TO DO WITH ANYTHING.

The Master is presenting you with your Ultimate Truth. He is impressing upon you that Ultimate stage, one in which you are totally unconcerned with the world because you know that your Presence is totally Invisible, Anonymous, Unidentified.

You know! You know better, but you are still not accepting it completely, and that is the misery of your life. Now you know everything, but you are to accept the Knowledge and use it, put it into practice in your daily life. You have good knowledge, but you are not implementing it.

The moment you accept this Reality, everything will vanish. I am talking about the moment you accept your Reality.

ACCEPT YOUR REALITY,
NOT THE REALITY OF *BRAHMAN, ATMAN, PARABRAHMAN*, GOD.

YOU ARE REALITY,
WITHOUT ANY FORM.
YOU ARE TOTALLY FORMLESS.

The Masters in our Lineage are trying to impress upon you the Reality of Ultimate Truth, 'That You Are'! The Master is within you but you are not fully aware. You are not fully aware of your importance, your greatness, so the only thing we are doing here is showing you 'That'. We are pointing out and showing you your greatness, your value and your importance.

Q: I am listening with fresh ears, Maharaj, and the more you hammer me, the more you repeat the same thing over and over, the easier it is becoming for me to accept my Reality.

Maharaj: The message is not a complicated one. I am simplifying and placing before you, your Truth, not the Truth of *Brahman*, *Atman*, *Paramatman*, God. These are the polished words, very polished words.

You can stand on your own feet. You are not handicapped at all. You never were. You are not dependent, you are independent. Throw out all these illusionary supports!

143. *A King on a Royal Throne*

Maharaj: When Maurice Frydman came to Nisargadatta Maharaj, he was involved in many good causes. He was helping the orphans, the animals and he was involved in various other kinds of social work. One day, Maharaj asked him: "How long are you going to keep helping others for? Help them, but don't take any ego from what you're doing. Never feel that you are doing a good job or your internal ego will develop. Go to the root cause and stay there".

"Who are you going to help after leaving the body? Who were you helping prior to one hundred years?" That is why I always say, do your job, but don't take ego. Self-enquire and make sure that there is no ego involved.

Q: Would you say that Self-enquiry has to continue? I have done a lot of meditation in my life but I must confess, I have not done a great deal of Self-enquiry.

Maharaj: Self-enquiry leads to Self-Knowledge and Self-Knowledge leads to Self-Realization, and vice versa. So, yes, keep the Self-enquiry going.

KEEP THE SELF-ENQUIRY GOING.

Don't be a coward! Everything is within you, but you have to look.

KNOW THYSELF!

Be brave like a lion and roar! Behave like a king! Behave like a king without ego. You are a king on a royal throne. You are not a beggar, you are a millionaire!

Q: That's good to know, Maharaj.

Maharaj: You are a millionaire, but you are unaware of your own property, your assets.

THIS PROPERTY, YOUR PROPERTY, IS SHOWN TO YOU
THROUGH THE MEDIUM OF THE MASTER.

You are a millionaire but you are not aware of your riches. You are shown your Reality via the medium of the Master. You see yourself as a beggar, and this is illusion. The Master removes this illusion. He shows you the Reality.

Q: Maharaj, you hold up the mirror to show me that I am a lion, and not a sheep.

Maharaj: Yes! We are trying to indicate your Identity in a simple way, using simple words and simple language. A plethora of words and books have complicated this very simple knowledge.

Live a practical life! Spiritual talk is very, very easy. You have to live in that state, as the holder of the body. When you have the Conviction, you will live like that. Why be a slave to the mind, ego and intellect when they are your babies? Stop supplying food and power to them, and they will eventually grow dumb and be silenced.

STOP SUPPLYING FOOD AND POWER TO THE MIND, EGO, INTELLECT,
AND THEY WILL BE SILENCED.

Keep on convincing yourself.

CONVINCE YOURSELF!

If you do this, your spiritual lifestyle will change completely. Your spiritual life will totally change. Don't rely on somebody else's statements about Reality. Listen to yourself, listen to you, not to others. 'You' means that Invisible Listener, that Inner Master that is your strength.

VISIT ONE TEMPLE ONLY,
YOUR TEMPLE.
THE TEMPLE WITHIN.

Q: I guess this is where the meditation will help with the process of eliminating all the impressions that have built up over the years?

Maharaj: Yes, you have to recite the Mantra to keep your house clean! The Masters of this Lineage all recited the same Mantra. Nisargadatta Maharaj, Ranjit Maharaj, Siddharameshwar Maharaj, Bhausaheb Maharaj. It is the only means, the only effective way to take you back to your Original State, and lead you to true Self-Knowledge.

RECITE THE MANTRA
AND IT WILL LEAD YOU TO YOUR ORIGINAL STATE.

This is a Direct Approach. We are using words to try and impress you with your Ultimate Identity. All words are directives, indications that communicate a message. Similarly, all books are like lighthouses. Their flashing lights indicate some message.

Q: The reciting of the Mantra is already happening spontaneously, Maharaj! It is there when I awake in the morning and it carries on throughout the day until I fall asleep!

Maharaj: Yes! Spontaneously! Keep strong faith in yourself and in your Master. I am placing before you the Final Truth. There is nothing beyond. You may agree, or you may not agree.

AFTER KNOWING THE REALITY,
WHY GO ELSEWHERE?

But, this is what happens, because people still have wandering minds, or they are still looking for miraculous experiences.

There are thousands of Masters, *lakhs* of Masters in the world, who are extracting money from people like yourself. We are not charging anything, but the irony is that those things which are free, seem to be given no value in today's society.

Bhausaheb Maharaj said, "In our Lineage, you are not to take any monies from devotees. Nisargadatta Maharaj never took a penny. Nothing! When 'Westerners' came to him, he told them, "I am not a commercial man". He was very strict.

Q: Truth is free, knowledge is free. Of course, it should be free!

Maharaj: With some effort, we are taking you out of the illusory ditch. But some people are jumping back in. What is to be done?

Before you go, take some photos to remind you of this atmosphere. They will flash up Reality, and remind you of the teachings.

Q: I notice that you come in from different angles every time. Sometimes I hear a message, and sometimes I don't. But when it is said in yet another way, there's the eureka effect, an 'Aha!' moment. And it is so powerful! But I think, Maharaj, you only have one message, and you say it in many ways, until finally, the understanding comes. Hammer, hammer, hammer!

Plus, we have to do our own bit. Work at our Self-enquiry, do the meditation, do the Mantra. It will work as you say, with co-operation from us. It's not just one-sided, I understand that. I have to do the work too, and then I get more help from the Master.

As you say, you are not creating disciples, you are creating Masters. I'm so happy to have found you, because there are so many teachers these days with little or no substance. You stand out! The teachings are solid and strong, with the whole Lineage behind them. These are rock-solid, and so pure, so very pure, and extremely powerful.

There's a lot of interest in Oneness in the States, but I am not sure that there are any strong teachers in America right now, or anywhere else, for that matter. I feel fortunate to have found you. Thank you, Maharaj. I bow to you.

Maharaj: My Master is giving you encouragement, [he looks at a picture on the wall, of a smiling Nisargadatta Maharaj], saying, "Don't worry, I am here". You see this picture over there, my Master is telling you, "Don't worry, I am here".

HE IS SUPPLYING THE POWER,
AND I AM TRANSMITTING THAT POWER INTO YOU.
When you leave, and return home, just remember that you are Ultimate Truth.
YOU ARE ULTIMATE TRUTH!

144.   *This is Not an Idea – You Are Final Truth*

Maharaj: Dry knowledge will not materialize in practice because it is grasped with the body-knowledge base, and therefore rooted through material knowledge. As a disciple, Direct Knowledge should not be rooted in, and through the body, it should be accepted by 'Selfless Self', 'Selfless Selfly'. In other words, by Selfless Self! This means that the body is only the medium, through which you can listen to the story of the Invisible Listener. [Maharaj claps his hands].

Though you are using the body, ears and intellect, the Conviction that you are to maintain, is that this Knowledge is the Invisible Listener's Reality. It is not the story of any body-based knowledge of *Brahman*, *Atman*, *Paramatman*.

IT IS THE REALITY OF THE INVISIBLE LISTENER IN YOU.

It is your Reality, Final Reality. The Listener has no shape, therefore don't use the subtle ego to try and grasp the Reality.

Q: Is it dry knowledge because you are using the mind and intellect to understand it? And that way it creates duality and becomes conceptual? The mind is at work rather than…?

Maharaj: Forget about mind! The mind has no existence, it is just the flow of thoughts. Let Selfless Self accept the Knowledge.

Q: So what you are speaking about is beyond knowledge?

Maharaj: Yes, yes, beyond knowledge, beyond words. We say 'beyond' just for understanding purposes alone, like we say 'prior to knowledge', or 'prior to beingness'. These are just words for understanding alone, for Conviction alone, for Realization. There is no 'beyond'. There is no 'prior', there is no 'nothing'. All this talk is for the purpose of communicating and illustrating Reality. Any doubts?

Q: No, Maharaj, none at all. With the practice, I feel like I am well-rooted in Reality.

Maharaj: All that you have listened to so far is the Listener's story, the Listener's Reality. It is the Listener's Ultimate Truth, Final Truth. After a while, as I have said, the practice will be spontaneous and automatic. When you arrive at the advanced stage, all Knowledge is absorbed. Nothing remains.

WHEN ALL KNOWLEDGE IS ABSORBED,
THERE WILL BE NOTHING LEFT.

Q: Like an onion, peel it all the way?

Maharaj: One layer, two layers, three layers, then nothing. When everything is finally removed, nothing will remain. When everything disappears, there you are. This is what all the practice is about, these progressive steps, these landmarks. When you reach the destination, the Final Terminus, all these landmarks will vanish. We are just using words to convince the Listener.

Q: I think you are giving a teaching that is beyond words.

Maharaj: You are Ultimate Truth. There is no 'beyond'.

THIS IS NOT AN IDEA. THIS IS NOT A CONCEPT.
YOU ARE FINAL TRUTH.
YOU ARE THE FINAL TERMINUS,
WHERE THERE IS NO BEGINNING,
AND THERE IS NO END.
NO BEGINNING, NO END.

If you say 'beyond', beyond implies that there is 'something' there! Beyond what? There is nothing there! Where everything ends, where everything comes to a full stop, there you are. There you are, formless.

WHEN EVERYTHING ENDS,
THERE YOU ARE:
FORMLESS.

Be strong, be firm. Don't pressure the mind or stress the intellect. Reality has nothing to do with these. When you leave the ashram, dump everything here. Deposit everything here. You can read books if you wish, no problem, as long as you don't ignore the Reader.

DON'T IGNORE THE READER.
DON'T UNDERESTIMATE THE INVISIBLE,
ANONYMOUS READER.

Any questions, doubts?

Q: It seems that since I started the practice, a lot of my old habits and addictions are coming up, and resurfacing again.

Maharaj: This is good, very good. Everything is melting, it is the melting process. You will visualise many changes inside. Slowly, silently, permanently, all concepts will leave, one by one, and there will be indescribable, exceptional Happiness, exceptional Peace. You will find what you have been struggling to attain for so long. Go ahead, go ahead! Go deeper and deeper.

145. *Open Secret*

Maharaj: Presence is untraceable. No knowledge is knowledge. No knowledge is knowledge.

Q: So now I am Ultimate Reality!

Maharaj: These are just words. Now you are to follow the Conviction. You are already there. This is the Open Secret.

YOU ARE ALREADY THERE.

You were there all the time, shapeless, formless, but you were unaware. This is the Open Secret. You were always in search of something external, like food for the body, or thinking for the mind.

WITH THE LIGHT IN YOUR HAND,
YOU WERE RUNNING AFTER THE DARK.

This is the Open Secret. This is your time. Now is your time. This is a Golden Opportunity. Total involvement is most important. Total involvement is most important. What more do you need? Stop looking for more explanations.

SEE YOUR GREATNESS!
USE YOUR SPIRITUAL EYES.

There is to be no more finding because the Finder has been found and has been exposed. This is the concluding part of spirituality, the concluding part of spirituality. You are Ultimate Truth, you are Final Truth. You are Spontaneous, Autonomous.

Q: You said yesterday that the Master talks from the bottom of Reality?

Maharaj: Yes, it is the Spontaneous Projection, out of the Spontaneous Presence. The secret will open up to you, as you identify the Unidentified Identity, prior to beingness. The secret will be opened up, as you identify:

YOUR INVISIBLE EXISTENCE PRIOR TO BEINGNESS.
AS YOU IDENTIFY YOUR ANONYMOUS,
UNIDENTIFIED IDENTITY,

THE SECRET WILL BE OPEN.

As I have told you many times, prior to beingness, your Presence was Invisible, Anonymous, Unidentified. There is no 'I'. There needs to be a somebody to say, 'I'. As a matter of fact, somebody is nobody because he is everybody. You must have strong Conviction. Beyond this, there is nothing.

Q: Maharaj, when did you realize this, that you were just the Selfless Self? Was it when you were with Nisargadatta Maharaj?

Maharaj: Forget about that! After the association with Selfless Self, in the light of a Guru or Master, the secret is opened up gradually, gradually and spontaneously.

Q: Am I right in saying that as well as the Silent Invisible Listener, these teachings are being understood by the long road travellers, the aspirants who have been searching for close to half a century? We know this stuff already but have not been putting it into practice. You are the agent for this. It is like a computer. There is a new programme, and then you have to push a button to activate it. You, Maharaj, are the one who is pushing the button to activate that programme?

Maharaj: You have to press the button yourself to activate the programme. The switch is in your hand. You may switch it on, or switch it off.

146. Creeper Tree

Maharaj: The *Naam Mantra* is very important. People say, "I have got knowledge, why do I need the *Naam Mantra*?" That's OK, but,

IF YOU WANT TO KNOW YOURSELF PERFECTLY,
THE *NAAM MANTRA* IS EXREMELY IMPORTANT.

If you want to identify yourself perfectly, the process of the *Naam Mantra* is extremely important. Humanity has a lot of knowledge about *Brahman*, *Atman*, *Paramatman*, all these things, but it is not pragmatic knowledge. It is dry knowledge for discussion purposes only.

Q: Some people claim that they have practical knowledge, without the *Naam Mantra*. They say that it is enough to read Nisargadatta Maharaj's books, and follow his instructions. They assert that they have found Absolute Knowledge, the Absolute State, without the *Naam Mantra*.

Maharaj: It is not a question of finding the Ultimate State, because:

WHATEVER IS FOUND,
IS FOUND AGAINST THE BACKDROP OF BODY-BASED KNOWLEDGE.

Here, [Maharaj points to his body], the body-based knowledge is inside. So, unless it is dissolved, whatever you build on top of it, is going to collapse. The basic, fundamental requirement is to dissolve the body-base!

Q: What you are saying, is that knowledge cannot be built on the body-base foundation?

Maharaj: Yes! People who are attending to spirituality, without the *Naam Mantra*, and saying, "I've got knowledge", that's OK, but it is only offering temporary relief.

Q: So we need to dissolve the body-knowledge first? What you are saying is that we need the help of the

Mantra in order to do this?

Maharaj: Yes! One should undergo this process. I will give you an example of this, from a great philosopher and politician, who was around seventy years old. He spent about five or six months discussing spiritual matters with Nisargadatta Maharaj. He was very well-read in philosophy, the *Vedas*, Jnaneshwar, Tukaram, etc. Then one day, he announced, "I know your knowledge very well, but, it is still not so impressed in me".

Nisargadatta Maharaj used the analogy of a creeper/climber plant to respond: "You know the creeper plant that grows on walls? How did it grow like that? It was able to grow because the seeds were planted in the correct spot. The plant grows close to the wall and grips itself to the wall for support as it gets stronger and grows higher.

SPIRITUAL KNOWLEDGE SHOULD BE ROOTED LIKE THIS,
THROUGH THE MASTERS ALONE, THROUGH THE GURU ONLY.

If you try and plant the creeper seeds elsewhere, it will not flourish". The Master is planting the plant of Reality in your Selfless Self. This is Direct Knowledge from the Invisible Speaker to the Invisible Listener. They are one and the same.

Maurice Frydman, on another occasion, told his Master that he could understand the Knowledge, but was unsure how to absorb and establish it. He was not getting it in a 'real sense'. Nisargadatta Maharaj again used this example of the creeper tree. The devotee must be rooted to the Master. The Master is the base and support. Knowledge can only be established through the Master.

You have to follow what the Master says.

USE THIS GURU MANTRA PROCESS AT THE INITIAL STAGE.
IT MAKES THE PERFECT FOUNDATION
FOR YOUR SPIRITUAL KNOWLEDGE.

But of course, everyone has different opinions.

Q: Did Nisargadatta Maharaj want people to take the Mantra?

Maharaj: No, he never insisted that anybody, whether ordinary, famous, foreign, or whatever, should do anything. He never ever said, "Take the Mantra and be my disciple". It happened spontaneously, like with the politician I mentioned. He decided for himself, and said to Nisargadatta Maharaj, "Now, I want to take the Guru Mantra". For him, it grew in importance over time, until it became necessary, essential.

Q: Are there other ways of getting there, of reaching the Absolute?

Maharaj: There are other ways, for example, if you have, [Maharaj makes a fist and shakes it in the air], strong devotion like Saint Eklavya. It is not impossible to do it using another method, but it is not so easy. You will not do it with just casual spiritual reading alone.

YOU MUST BE DRIVEN: "YES, I WANT TO KNOW THE REALITY.
I HAVE TO KNOW!"

You have to surrender totally to the Master, whosoever that Master may be. This is also very important.

Q: What if you are devoted to a Master who is no longer in the body, Maharaj?

Maharaj: His Presence may not be there in life, he may not be in existence, but if the involvement is very strong, then this way is also possible. However, perfect devotion rarely happens. It is difficult because there should not be any kind of dual mind, or trace of duality left.

Q: And Maharaj, do you want people to take the Mantra?

Maharaj: I am not insisting on anything. Many people are coming to me, but I am not insisting that they take the Mantra, the Guru Mantra, and be my disciples. No, not at all. With them, I am openly sharing all the spiritual secrets. I am not keeping anything to myself. I am giving them all the secrets.

It is then up to them to determine the effect of this Knowledge. Some people are deeply impressed, others not so much. Some people feel it is important to take initiation, whereas others are not interested. It is different for everybody. It also depends on their spiritual maturity.

147. *Priceless Mantra*

Q: Recently, I came across a passage about Nisargadatta Maharaj and the *Naam Mantra*. He said: Your parents give you a name, and call you by that. Similarly, the *Naam Mantra* is given to you. This is your real name, your real Identity.

He said: "The Mantra is very powerful and effective. My Guru gave me this Mantra and the result is all these visitors from all over the world. That shows you its power". So Nisargadatta Maharaj did give it great importance! The Mantra seems to have been ignored and overlooked since then. Western sources tend to play it down.

Maharaj: It really is up to you! If you value it highly, it will assist you powerfully. If you treat it casually, there will be no benefits. Those who have knowledge of something, understand its true value.

IT IS LIKE THIS WITH THE MANTRA.
DIFFERENT DISCIPLES GIVE IT A DIFFERENT VALUE.
I TELL EVERYONE THAT THE MANTRA HAS HIGH VALUE.
THOSE DISCIPLES WHO ACCEPT WHAT THE MASTER SAYS,
THEREFORE GIVE IT HIGH VALUE.

Disciples who have total faith in the Master, will value the Mantra highly, and benefit the most. The Mantra is the Mantra, but the value put on it is vastly different. For those who are taking it casually - 'No value!' It is up to you.

Q: A day or so after the initiation, I was meditating here in the hall. Over the years, I have not done so much meditation, but I have done a lot of motoring! Anyway, all of a sudden, during the meditation, I was in the driving seat once more. All I could see was this very muddy car windscreen flashing up before my eyes. I could not see out of it at all!

But with just one smooth silent 'swish' of a 'magical' windscreen wiper, in an instant, the window became completely clear. This clarity was serene, peaceful, immensely powerful, alive and unfathomable. Words cannot describe this transformation! This revealed the amazing benevolent power of the Mantra to me. This clarity is now continuous. I am so very grateful.

Maharaj: If you use the Mantra in the right way, you will notice dramatic changes going on inside, spontaneous changes. These changes happen on the physical and mental level. Spiritual experiences will also occur.

After meditating for some time, the sages talk about three types of experience via sight, hearing, or touch. You may see your Master in physical form. You may hear your Master talking to you. You may feel your Master's touch on you.

**THESE TYPES OF EXPERIENCES MAY HAPPEN,
BUT THEY ARE NOT ULTIMATE TRUTH.**

They are progressive steps. Everybody's progressive steps are different.

DO NOT STOP THERE!

Sometimes you may experience miraculous power, or find yourself saying something, and then, shortly after you have said it, that very thing happens! Power is being regenerated in you. But that is also not Ultimate Truth. Do not stop there!

Changes will take place spontaneously. This leads to Ultimate Truth. "Ah!" Total calmness, no desires, no temptations. Just, "Om Shanti, Shanti, Shanti". This is the Final stage. Your activities will be normal, but without ego. The 'I' has gone. Forget the past. Forget the past. What you have heard is Your Story!

148. Death

Q: Maharaj, what about death?

Maharaj: Who is dying? Death for whom? Death is an illusion. Why talk about death? Better to talk about who you are. That is far more important. Find out now, while you still have the opportunity. Ask yourself, "Who am I?" The concept of death creeps slowly towards you, and then, one day, willingly or unwillingly, you will have to leave this body. Open fact!

The body has a time-limit, but, you are not the body. You are unborn. Every day we hear of people dying.

**WAKE UP! YOU HAVE A GOLDEN OPPORTUNITY
TO MAKE SURE THAT WHEN YOU LEAVE THE BODY,
IT WILL BE A VERY HAPPY TIME.**

Q: You mentioned a few days ago how Bhausaheb Maharaj was clapping his hands with great happiness, during his last moments!

Maharaj:

**WHO IS DYING? WHO IS LIVING?
KNOW THYSELF.**

I am refreshing your memory. This fear of death came from your identification with the body. From the very beginning, we have been conditioned into believing that we are born, and that we are going to die. And we have accepted this information blindly, as FACT. We have become so strongly attached to the body, that now we are afraid to let it go. We find it very difficult to break free.

Many people claim to have spiritual knowledge. You say, "I am not the body", I am *Brahman*, I am *Atman*", BUT, when something unexpected happens, like an accident or illness, or you are suffering on your deathbed, all these truths vanish, as if they were mere affirmations. And all you can do is tremble full of fear. I am speaking generally here. This means that the Conviction that, "I am not the body", has not taken root. It is not real Conviction, and your 'spiritual' Knowledge, is not real Self-Knowledge. Somewhere in the foundations, there is a crack.

Q: So what can I do to ensure that there are no cracks?

Maharaj: For that, you have the Master Key. Keep using the *Naam Mantra*. It is good insurance. If you want to know yourself perfectly, the process of *Naam Mantra* is most important. This Mantra I have given you started from Dattatreya – It has a one thousand year history. It is more than words. It has science behind it and a long history. Humanity has a lot of knowledge about the *Brahman*, *Atman*, *Paramatman*, but this is all merely dry knowledge for discussion and entertainment.

You see, body-based knowledge is here [Master points to the body].

UNLESS BODY-BASED KNOWLEDGE DISSOLVES,
THEN WHATEVER IS BUILT ON TOP OF IT WILL COLLAPSE.

Q: Like building castles in the sand?

Maharaj: Those people who say, "I have knowledge without the *Naam Mantra*", well, that's OK, but it is still only acting as a painkiller, maybe offering some temporary relief. There is a lot of milk, [knowledge], around. But if you add just one pinch of salt, then all that milk will be spoiled. This means that if we have one small doubt, this little doubt will produce, a little tremor, then a crack, which will gradually be followed by an earthquake. And then, it is only a matter of time before the whole building collapses.

If we recite the *Naam Mantra*, it will give you a very good solid base, a very good start. Our foundation will be so firm, so solid, that nothing will affect or penetrate it. One hundred per cent guaranteed!

Q: So meditation is the prescribed medication for us all?

Maharaj: I have told you, meditation on the *Naam Mantra* is the 'anti-virus for chronic illusion'. You need the Mantra to dissolve all the body-knowledge, to clean and empty your hard drive of illusion. As well as cleaning everything out, the Mantra will regenerate your Power, by reminding you of your Reality: "I am *Brahman*, *Brahman*, I am".

Every moment of your life is very precious, never to be repeated. Now is the time to discover whether your foundations are solid or not. See! Examine! Find out! Are there are lingering doubts? Do Self-enquiry now! If you delay and leave it till the last moment, it will be too late.

THIS IS A LONG DREAM, A LONG MOVIE.
YOU ARE THE PRODUCER, THE DIRECTOR,
THE ARCHITECT OF YOUR OWN LIFE.
IT IS UP TO YOU
TO DETERMINE THE LAST ACT IN YOUR MOVIE.

Q: What you are saying, Maharaj, is that it is entirely up to us as to how the end is going to happen, how the final scenario is going to play out? We can either blissfully sail into the blue yonder, or, with trepidation, let the hungry 'grim reaper' devour us.

If we want a smooth exit, we need to seriously confront ourselves, starting now, and find out whether our knowledge goes deeper than 'skin-deep'?

Maharaj: It is entirely up to you. Self-Knowledge has to be pragmatic, so that when the time comes to leave the body, you will be fearless. There must not be any remaining attachment to distract you. I am hammering this again and again.

YOU ARE NOT THE BODY, YOU WERE NOT THE BODY, YOU WILL NOT REMAIN THE BODY, OPEN FACT! THEREFORE, YOU ARE TO ACCEPT THIS TRUTH.

If you are not the body, what are you? You are unborn. Find out for yourself, and then you will know, really KNOW that you are nothing to do with the body. Use discrimination, take a look, contemplate. Think seriously on your Existence!

Your Existence does not know itself. I am talking about that. I am placing before you a clear picture of Ultimate Truth, using short words, direct words. There are no in-betweens. In order to convince people I have to use phrases, without these how can you be convinced?

No one is thinking, everyone is just accepting everything blindly. Find out your weaknesses! You know your weaknesses better than anyone. Find out if you are on shaky ground. Maybe you have read a large number of spiritual books. Maybe, you have faith, a cherished belief, and you think that you are prepared. That's good. But, be certain, be sure.

Q: What you are saying, is that we should test ourselves, make sure that we have our feet firmly planted in Reality?

Maharaj: The Masters in our Lineage were all very practical in their approach. Ask yourself four questions: "Am I totally fearless? Am I totally peaceful? Do I have complete happiness? Am I tension-free?" If the answers to these questions come back a "No", then it seems that all your efforts, all your knowledge has been in vain, and for nothing. The currency you were buying has turned out to be dummies, fake notes, fake currency. [Master chuckles].

Ask yourself, "Where do I stand?" before it is too late. Better to face these illusory ghosts now, than wait till our bodies are nearing the end. At that time, you will be trembling with fear, going "Ooo, Ooo". There will be no peace, only fear.

Q: Yes, I understand. Real Spiritual Knowledge, Self-Knowledge, needs to be pragmatic. It has to be implemented into daily life. If it remains merely theoretical, intellectual knowledge as you say, then it is basically useless.

Maharaj: You know that there is no birth and death. You know that you are unborn. When you know the Reality, you will see that this overwhelming fear was baseless. That fear that followed you around, and haunted you from 'birth', was a big illusion. Now the balloon has burst!

YOU HAVE BURST THE BALLOON!

Q: We discover that all our fears were rooted in the greater fear of death. And that fear of death is just a body concept, body-knowledge, and therefore baseless, hot air.

I don't know why I am laughing, but it turns out that all our heavy baggage of dread and trepidation surrounding mortality, which we carried around from decade to decade, was completely unnecessary. What a waste! We, or I, expended all this energy on keeping at bay a gigantic monster. And this beast, this monster never existed in the first place. Oh well! It is gone now. The illusion is being dissolved. Better now, than not at all.

Maharaj: Self-enquiry leads to Self-Knowledge and Self-Realization. Real Self-Knowledge is so very important, for without it, the end will be painful, without mercy.

Ask yourself this, "Why do I fear death?" Unless you know the Reality, this fear is murmuring, the fear is multiplying. The fearless state at the time of death is Real Knowledge, Pragmatic Knowledge, Ultimate Truth.

[The Master smiles warmly]:

BE ALERT,
AND PREPARE FOR THAT HAPPY AND PEACEFUL MOMENT,
WHICH IS THE GOAL OF THE SERIOUS SEEKER.

Q: The great *Mahasamadhi*! Thank you, Maharaj.

149. *You Are Prior to God*

Maharaj: Siddharameshwar Maharaj used to say, "If you take one step, I will raise your foot and take the next step for you. One-way love is not effective, it has to be there on both sides. You must have strong faith in your Master, and remain loyal to him.

Years after Siddharameshwar Maharaj's passing, Nisargadatta Maharaj used to say, "My Master is alive. He may not be here physically, but my Master is alive. I am not a widow".

Q: Like he was still married to Siddharameshwar Maharaj?

Maharaj: Yes! He had the strongest faith. You must have strong faith in your Master, whoever he may be. Only then, will the Knowledge be implemented, converted and put into practice. Half-faith, half-trust is of little use.

EVEN IF GOD APPEARS BEFORE YOU,
YOU MUST HAVE THE COURAGE
TO RECOGNIZE AND DENY THIS, AND SAY:
"NO, NO, MY MASTER IS GREATER THAN YOU,
BECAUSE IT IS OUT OF MY PRESENCE
THAT YOU APPEAR AS GOD."

There has to be that Conviction. God cannot appear without your Presence. Your Presence comes first, and then, God. The Conviction is: "Out of my Spontaneous Presence, you appear as God. If my Presence were not there, then who can see God? So I am prior to you, God".

THIS SPONTANEOUS FEELING IS NOT A JOKE,
THIS IS THE STRONG FAITH OF THE MASTERS.

The Guru, the Master is greater than God. Kabir said, "If God and my Master appeared before me, I will bow down to my Master and not to God, because my Master has shown me God. The Master says, "This is God", so I trust my Master. I have complete faith in my Master. I did not know what God was, but my Master showed me, "This is God". So I will bow down to my Master, first".

Casual spirituality will not help you. People say, "I have been to see this Master, he is very good, and then I went to another Master, who was even better, great". These are visitors, roamers, travellers, with no stability. You have to make this the last destination.

IF A MASTER SHOWS YOU ULTIMATE REALITY,
YOU MUST STAY WITH THIS MASTER,
AND BE FAITHFUL, LOYAL TO HIM.
THE MASTER IS LIKE A MOTHER,
YOU DON'T CHANGE YOUR MOTHER.

It is extremely important to hold the Conviction that you do not need to go anywhere else. You KNOW that there is nothing more to find.

IF YOU STILL WISH TO GO AND SEE ANOTHER MASTER,
THEN THIS IS A SIGN,
THAT YOU STILL DO NOT HAVE THE CONVICTION.
YOU ARE STILL WANDERING, ROAMING.

I am sharing the same Knowledge that was shared with me by my Master. I will be happy if any one of you moves towards the Ultimate Truth. This would be my payment. Be a Master of Reality, and not just a Master of Philosophy or Spirituality. A professor may teach, by speaking about truth, whereas a Master lives it. This is practical, living Knowledge.

Be strong! Have strong faith in the Master. The same Master exists within you.

DON'T CONSIDER YOURSELF DIFFERENT
OR SEPARATE IN ANY WAY.
THERE IS ONLY ONE MASTER.
THE MASTER IS ONE AND THE SAME.

All the Masters in our Lineage were very simple and very humble. Nisargadatta Maharaj used to serve at a shop counter. He wasn't saying, "Oh! I am a Master. I have spirituality". No! He had complete humility. However,

DON'T EXPECT YOUR EGO TO WELCOME
YOUR ATTEMPTS AT BEING HUMBLE.

Q: So it is very important to be humble?

Maharaj: After knowing the Reality, humility is an automatic process. After knowing the Reality, there is only... all that's left is, "I am nothing, nothing".

Q: It is like the opposite of what you might expect. After the long journey and all the efforts, I think I would be looking to put a crown on!

Maharaj: When the Conviction comes, when it arises spontaneously, when you know that you are nothing, then you will be everything.

WHEN THERE IS THE CONVICTION THAT "YOU ARE NOTHING",
THIS MEANS "YOU ARE EVERYTHING".

Be alert! Be cautious!

Q: And patient?

Maharaj: You must have strong faith like these Masters. They were ordinary people but they accepted the Knowledge, the Reality that was given by the Masters, totally and completely. They are wonderful examples of strong faith, strong dedication, strong involvement.

Q: That's why it is important for you to keep hammering us, repeating the same thing over and over.

Maharaj: The same thing, because it is necessary.

Q: I am convincing myself at the same time. But coming from you, it is very effective.

Maharaj: Yes, but you have to be alert all the time. That is why Bhausaheb Maharaj clearly mapped out the discipline of meditation and *bhajan*s. You need to be alert to your Presence that is the Ultimate Truth, twenty-four hours of the day. Endless hammering is needed. Do your normal activities, but at the same time, you are always staying with, "Yes, I am *Brahman*, I Am That".

Q: This morning, we were reading the Preface by Nisargadatta Maharaj to *Master of Self-Realization,* where he talks about his devotion to his Guru, Siddharameshwar Maharaj, and how important that was, how special. Basically, he said, that if you don't have complete faith in the Master, you are wasting your time.

Maharaj: And strong faith within you, also. This should be your last journey. There should not be any temptation to go looking for another Master. You must stabilize and be strong.

THE MASTER IS WITHIN YOU.
HAVE FAITH IN YOUR MASTER.
FIND STABILITY THERE.

Q: What do you mean by "be strong"?

Maharaj: Be strong internally. Be determined and have courage. Believe that what you are hearing is true and accept it. Keep convincing yourself.

OPEN TRUTH HAS BEEN PLACED BEFORE YOU,
YOUR TRUTH,
YOUR ULTIMATE,
YOUR FINAL TRUTH.

Be with you! Go deeper and deeper and deeper within you. There are so many Masters around today that one needs to be careful, and be with a proper Master, a true Master who knows himself, one who is Realized.

HOW CAN ANYONE GUIDE OTHERS TO SELF-REALIZATION,
IF HE IS NOT HIMSELF REALIZED?

Q: True! Like the blind leading the blind.

Maharaj: A proper, true Master is hard to find. Vivekananda searched and searched for a Master who could show him God. Eventually, he met Ramakrishna Paramahamsa who said he could show him 'God in himself'. My Master said the same thing:

"I'M NOT MAKING YOU A DISCIPLE,
BECAUSE THE MASTER IS ALREADY WITHIN YOU.
I AM SHOWING YOU
THE MASTER WITHIN YOU".

Q: I love that! We are the same, equal. You are not making us dependent. You act as a mirror, so that we can see ourselves, our true Reality?

Maharaj: Master is more than a mirror! With a mirror, there is some darkness on the back of it. It only shows one picture.

THE MASTER SHOWS YOU THE ENTIRE WORLD,
THE BACK, THE FRONT, THE SIDE.
ALL SIDES ARE OPEN TO YOU.
'CLEAREALITY'!

Q: And if I follow the Master with total faith, then little by little, I will become the Master?

Maharaj: Not becoming, you are already the Master.

Q: OK, the Realized Master, then?

Maharaj: Be careful! These are just words we are using. Do you say, "I am becoming Susan?" You are already Susan. Words are indications of Ultimate Truth. Every word has its own limitation. Your existence is beyond all limitations.

Q: I fell into the W.O.R.D.S trap again!

Maharaj: This is exceptional Knowledge. Accept it. Self-Conviction is most important in the light of the Master's teachings. Self-Conviction is very important. At school, the teacher gives you some numbers, say, a few sums for you to tally. You attempt to add them up, using different ways to get the right answer. Likewise, the Master is giving you Knowledge. It is up to you to work it out, tally, add it all up and reach true Conviction, real Conviction, full Conviction.

Q: Yes, we are taking all the stuff you have said without doubts, and adding it all up. There is no discussion as such, no debate.

Maharaj: Correct, no debate. Here, the Knowledge has not to be tested. It is not a political issue, not a philosophical issue. It is not up for debate.

JUST TO KNOW,
AND BE QUIET.
JUST TO KNOW THE REALITY,
AND BE QUIET.

The Key has been given to you. The secret has been opened. The Power is there. It is yours. It has been unlocked. You have to use that tremendous Power.

DON'T INSULT YOUR INNER MASTER
BY NEGLECTING YOURSELF.

Convince yourself in this way: You have now been promoted to the position of 'Captain'. Previously, you were just the 'ship-boy'. After getting the Captain's post, do you keep on saying, "Yes Sir, yes, Sir?" No! Because you are no longer a 'ship-boy'. Likewise, the Master has given you a big post, an important post. There is no further need for the 'ship-boy', and his, "Yes, Sirs".

After knowing the Reality, you must have complete faith: "My Master has shown my Identity. I am everything. I am Ultimate Truth", without saying it. There is no 'I', there is no 'You', but there is Spontaneous Conviction.

THERE IS SPONTANEOUS CONVICTION
WITHOUT 'I',
WITHOUT 'YOU'.

150. *They Speak From Invisible Existence*

Maharaj: It is important for you not to view, or see these sages, stalwarts, Masters, great saints in the body-form. The secrets they disclosed came from their Reality, their own Identity, their Invisible Identity.

THE SECRETS THAT ARE REVEALED
COME FROM THEIR INVISIBLE IDENTITY,
AND NOT FROM THE BODY-FORM.

Their Truths are administered, addressed to, and reach the Reader's Invisible Identity.

THEY SHOULD BE MATCHED.
IT IS ONE. THERE IS NO DUALITY.

All the saints tell their stories from their Invisible Existence. Your Invisible Existence is the same as theirs.

Q: What does being Realized mean?

Maharaj: So many people ask me if I am Realized. What do you mean by Realized? This question is irrelevant. Who is Realized? When someone says, "I am Realized. I am Enlightened", it indicates Thoughtless Spontaneous Presence.

People are always trying to discriminate, comparing Masters. Stop this! It is not good for spirituality. It happens because you are well-read, and you have a good spiritual background.

YOU HAVE COLLECTED KNOWLEDGE,
LAYERS OF KNOWLEDGE.
BUT WHATEVER YOU MAY TALK ABOUT
IS NOT ULTIMATE TRUTH.

If you talk about Siddharameshwar Maharaj, and criticize his teachings in relation to Nisargadatta Maharaj, for example, then obviously this is not good. Why did you come here?

SPIRIT DOES NOT LIKE THIS KIND OF TALKING
ABOUT THE MASTERS IN THIS WAY.

I have told you, you are not here to debate, to measure, compare. You are intellectual people, and you are also devotees or disciples. This has some drawbacks. If you are thinking on an intellectual level, then this is a drawback. Do not measure these deities, spiritual Masters like Ramana Maharshi, Siddharameshwar Maharaj in this way. It will distance you from Spirit.

Q: I hear what you are saying. The Masters are speaking from their Invisible Existence, and we are trying to analyze them with our little minds. I wanted to say that it is also your Presence that is important. Your Presence is very strong, Maharaj, and it is non-verbal.

So the teachings are not just about what you have conveyed, but there is some sort of transmission. Or, as you say, the Listener and the Master are One, and that is experienced in some way that is difficult to explain. There are waves of clarity. It is not easy for me to describe, but it is for you. I am not the Master, yet.

Maharaj: How can you say that you are not the Master? You are already the Master, but you are still not fully aware of that Masterly essence in you. You are creating a net and getting entangled in it. There are no obstacles. You are a victim of your own web of thoughts, and this is the only obstacle.

Remember that the saints and Masters talk and express themselves in their own way. What they wished to convey is paramount! Don't compare the Masters. We are NOT concerned about the body-forms of Ramana Maharshi, Siddharameshwar Maharaj, Ranjit Maharaj, Nisargadatta Maharaj.

WHERE WERE THESE MASTERS PRIOR TO BEINGNESS?

It was only after beingness, that you started knowing about deities, and all these Masters.

YOU ARE THE MASTER OF MASTERS,
BECAUSE WITHOUT YOUR EXISTENCE,
YOU CANNOT RECOGNIZE ALL THESE DEITIES,
AND ALL THESE MASTERS.
YOUR PRESENCE WAS THERE PRIOR TO EVERYTHING.
THE ENTIRE WORLD,
INCLUDING ALL THE DEITIES,
AND ALL THE MASTERS,
IS THE SPONTANEOUS PROJECTION OF YOUR SELFLESS SELF.

To say 'God', your Presence is needed. You say, "God is great!" Who has given God this greatness? You have! You have given one hundred marks!

YOU ARE THE EXAMINER,
YOU ARE GOD.
GOD IS GREAT.
YOU ARE GREAT.

But you must be simple and humble.

Q: I understand!

Maharaj: Yes, but you have to accept it totally. Your understanding is not supposed to be on a physical basis, mental basis, intellectual basis, logical basis. Where body-knowledge ends, there you are.

THE MASTER IS GIVING YOU VISION,
THE SPECTACLES OF KNOWLEDGE,
FOR YOU TO SEE YOUR SELFLESS SELF.

The entire world is projected out of your Spontaneous, Invisible Presence. There is no need to go anywhere.

THIS IS VERY EASY TO UNDERSTAND,
BUT FOR IT TO BE ABSORBED,
FOR YOU TO HAVE CONVICTION OF THIS KNOWLEDGE,
IT IS SOMEWHAT DIFFICULT.

151. *Circles of Light*

Q: In the beginning, Maharaj, there was a lot going on while reciting the *Naam Mantra*. It was busy with many experiences. One that has stayed with me came shortly after receiving the Mantra. I was seated in the meditation hall when I felt the vague presence of a solemn figure gliding towards me.

It was Bhausaheb Maharaj, the Lineage Founder. He stood in front of me, silently and peacefully. The unspoken message from him to me, was about the importance of doing and taking the meditation seriously. Then, this energy swept right through me, and he was gone in a flash!

Maharaj: During the process of meditation, every devotee has different experiences. As devotees, do not look out for any experiences as this will only bring frustration and disappointment. If they come then fine, if not, that is fine also! Some see circles of light, shining rings, flashes, flashing lights. Others feel themselves weightless, or experience themselves flying in the air. The experiences are different for different devotees.

At the initial stage, this is a sign of progress. Egoistic activity stops spontaneously with just a click of the Mantra, and then Knowledge gets opened up. Spontaneous flashes of light occur. Even if your eyes are closed, there may be great flashes of light, brighter than the sun. This is the 'Light of the Spirit', *(Atma Prakash)*.

These are the stages that some people go through. You may see yourself as formless. There is exceptional happiness and peace, spontaneous laughter, etc.

Q: These experiences are part of the melting process?

Maharaj: Yes, the melting process is taking place. It has an immediate and direct effect.

SLOWLY, SLOWLY, THE BODY IDENTITY IS MELTING,
AND THEN TURNING TOWARDS ULTIMATE TRUTH,
WHERE THERE IS NO EXPERIENCE, NO EXPERIENCER.

During the process of this meditation, experiences are happening. But they are not the Final Truth. Nisargadatta Maharaj called them progressive steps. They are good.

THEY ARE LANDMARKS,
LANDMARKS ON THE WAY TO REALIZATION.
BUT LANDMARKS ARE NOT ULTIMATE TRUTH,
FINAL TRUTH, THE DESTINY OR THE TERMINUS.

So you are to come like this, then this, this, this, [inching forward], Nisargadatta Maharaj would say, until you reach the last stage. These are the stages, and new beginners of spirituality have different experiences.

My Master used to say, "Do not disclose your experiences to anybody else because this can create some competition. Secondly, some people may, because of jealousy, discourage you". There may be some ego problem there, so that if you tell your wife about your experience, she may say, "I want this experience, too", etc.

Therefore, he was very strict about this, saying, "The ones who are enlightened should not discuss these things with those who are unaware". Your experience may not be useful to him and vice versa.

IF YOU WANT TO ASK ANYTHING ABOUT YOUR EXPERIENCES,
ASK THE MASTER,
"WHERE DO I STAND?"

If you feel at all tempted to confirm your experiences, confirm your experiences with the Master, with the Master only, and nobody else. Someone else, with only half-knowledge, will distract and confuse you. Bhausaheb Maharaj had a deep understanding of the psychological workings of human behaviour.

He knew that after Conviction, one way or another, the ego may try and regain entry without your being aware of it, and then spoil everything.

A worm may enter your laptop, a virus may infiltrate without your knowledge, with the result that all your files will be damaged. So, he insisted on the Mantra and the *bhajan*s, to keep the mind busy. You should be alert at all times.

Always use your laptop's anti-virus. Every day, without fail, you have to run a scan to see if your laptop is virus-fee. Likewise, all this software of *bhajan*, Knowledge, meditation is the anti-virus process.

Q: Your spiritual practice has to be steady and constant, because the world is coming in all the time, in different ways, from behind you as well, unseen.

Maharaj: In the last fifty years, I have seen so many stalwarts falling back into the ditch. One man became attracted to miracles and left his Master behind. His last days were very, very miserable. He was confused, reciting the names of the different deities. He also felt guilty because he had abandoned Nisargadatta Maharaj.

YOU MUST STAY CONTINUOUSLY IN TOUCH
WITH YOUR SELFLESS SELF.
BE CONTINUOUSLY IN TOUCH WITH YOUR SELFLESS SELF.

Do your job, but you must always be continuously in touch with your Selfless Self.

Q: That's a big commitment, as they say in the West. Full-time!

Maharaj: It will happen, if you have strong faith, like Nisargadatta Maharaj.

Q: Maharaj, for clarity, was everything perfect prior to beingness?

Maharaj: How can you say this? Some people have asked the same thing, and I tell them they are just guessing. What does perfect mean? That is body-knowledge! There was no 'perfect' prior to beingness. I have told you, there was nothing! You have to see for yourself. I'm showing you a picture, then you will see the same thing, but it is not seen with the intellect.

Nisargadatta Maharaj used to tell this story about two people. One of them was on the top of a hill, waving his arms above his head. The second person is at the bottom of the hill. He asks, "Why are you doing this?" The first person says "You have to come up here! You can't get the experience from down there. Come to the top and then you will get it!"

Similarly, you can't get the experience from 'down here'. You have to come to this state, and then you will find out 'why he is waving his arms'. You are just guessing.

WHAT I AM TELLING YOU,
HAS NOT COME OUT OF GUESSWORK.
IT IS THE LISTENER'S REALITY.
DON'T TRY AND GUESS INTELLECTUALLY.
IT IS REALITY.

Q2: I, too, had a question which I can see now is also dumb guesswork: Selfless Self or *Parabrahman* must know itself, is this not the case?

Maharaj: How can it know itself? It is formless, formless. This is imagination, guessing. You are guessing and trying to get the Knowledge through the mind and intellect, and this is why you are not getting it.

Q3: I feel I am absorbing the teachings, Maharaj. I have been noticing that the Knowledge was first situated in the frontal lobe of the brain, and now it feels as if it has gone deeper. It feels more natural. Sounds like imagination though, eh?

Maharaj: Under the guidance of the Master, the layers of the onion are being removed. Remove one layer, OK, remove another layer, OK. After all this, what remains? The Master tells you how much remains? Nothing! So all the layers are removed, all the skins are removed, and nothing remains.

Q: Is it more natural? They talk of *'nisarga'*, natural?

Maharaj: No, there is no nature. It is totally authentic. There is no nature. There's no nature, it is authentic, Ultimate, Final. Until you are convinced, you will be misinterpreting.

HAVE A LOOK IN THE MIRROR,
AND SEE HOW YOU ARE.
YOU CAN SEE YOURSELF IN THE MIRROR.

152. *Chicken and Egg*

Q: From what I have heard, you do not refer to the 'I am' at all.

Maharaj: Why stay in the literal world of 'I am', when you are Almighty God? Your Spontaneous Existence does not have any focus. When you make an effort to stay in 'I am', the subtle ego comes into play.

Again, I will say the same thing, don't take these spiritual words literally. They are indicating your Invisible, Anonymous, Unidentified Identity. Pop this illusory balloon, this illusory bubble!

You know 'chicken'? The chicken and egg? Inside the egg, the chicken pecks and pecks at the hard shell with its beak, until it can break out. The beak has been given to you in the form of Knowledge. You are in the circle of illusion. With that beak of Knowledge, you are going to break out of the circle.

USING THE BEAK OF KNOWLEDGE,
YOU WILL BREAK OUT OF THE VICIOUS CIRCLE OF ILLUSION.

The chicken, the little baby chick, spontaneously breaks through the thick covering.

Q: The beak represents Knowledge which is used to break through the shell?

Maharaj: Ultimate Truth is like that. What we call *Brahman*, *Atman*, *Paramatman*. Its action is Spontaneous.

WHEN THE EGG MATURES,
THE BREAKTHROUGH HAPPENS.

You see, it is a very hard core, but the small chicken manages to break it. Likewise, a very hard core of illusion is wrapped all around us, but with the Knowledge, Ultimate Knowledge, the Spiritual Truth pecks and pecks, until it finally comes out.

ULTIMATE TRUTH IS LIKE THAT.
WHAT YOU CALL *BRAHMAN*, ULTIMATE KNOWLEDGE,
SPIRITUAL TRUTH PECKS AWAY AND COMES OUT.

Therefore don't force yourself to stay with 'I am' because you are already there, but colouring it with form. Prior to beingness, where was that 'I am'? Where was the 'I'? As I told you, 'I' is just like the sky. This is Reality.

We are naming this Reality with words like America, India, London and giving names to it like

Brahman, *Atman*, *Parabrahman* when all the time, what we call 'I' is there, Anonymous, Silent and Invisible. So no need to focus on it. You ARE already. Dwell on how you were prior to beingness.

THE OPEN SECRET LIES IN,
"I DON'T KNOW".

  I will tell you a story about a foreigner visiting India. He asks the guide "Who built the Taj Mahal?" The guide replies, "I don't know". They visited many places where the visitor asked the same question, and received the same answer. "Who are these people?" "I don't know", came the reply. Then, on seeing a dead body being carried nearby, he asks, "Who is that?". The guide replies "I don't know".

THIS MEANS THAT HE DOES NOT KNOW THE NAME OF ANYTHING,
OR ANY PERSON.
EVERYTHING IS A DREAM, AND THEREFORE,
"I DON'T KNOW".
"I DON'T KNOW WHO DIED".

  The entire world is "I don't know". We say this for understanding purposes. Prior to beingness, there was no 'I'. After dissolving the beingness, no 'I'. Whatever feels that 'I', is feeling it through the body only. So here you are giving shape to that 'I' or 'I am', which does not have any identity.

YOU ARE GIVING SHAPE
TO THE SHAPELESS,
AND IDENTITY TO THE UNIDENTIFIED IDENTITY.

Q: I got the impression from Nisargadatta Maharaj, that the 'I am' is the doorway, and like a tunnel, one had to go through it, like the chicken and the egg. I did not find much movement with my own practice. And recently during a meditation, this concept arose, "Stay at the door, the door is open". And at that moment, I knew that the 'door' had become a block, an obstacle. When I realized this, the conceptual door dissolved. There was no longer a door.

Maharaj: There's no door at all. There are walls because there are bodies.

Q: I removed the door, and I was through. What I mean is that the door disappeared.

Maharaj: So like the chicken, you broke through. Master has given the key, the Knowledge that is needed to open the door. All these processes are there, just to invite the attention of the Invisible Listener or Reader. Prior to beingness, you did not know yourself. How were you? You will say, "I don't know". After leaving the body, how will you be? You say, "I don't know". That is correct.

THE SEER OF, "I DON'T KNOW",
IS SAYING, "I AM NOT IN ANY FORM".

  Your beingness is also illusion. When did you come across the words beingness and non-beingness, awareness, unawareness, consciousness. This is a big illusionary field. You were roaming, wandering in the field and trying to extract happiness and knowledge from it. Now be bold! Be courageous! Come out of that field, and stay out of it!

YOU ARE ULTIMATE TRUTH.
FULL STOP, END OF STORY.

  You are not the Master's disciple, but the Master of Masters. When you consider your identity, there is nothing wrong with it, or missing from it. It is perfect. Remove all these external clothes, all these illusory clothes, and see yourself. You are total, complete.

Stop travelling! Everything is within you. Visit your own website, and not someone else's.

VISIT YOUR OWN WEBSITE.
CLEAN YOUR OWN HOUSE.

Accept the Truth! Master says, "You are Ultimate Truth." Until that Conviction has been established, you need to fight.

Q: Watch and wait?

Maharaj: No waiting! It happens by itself.

IF YOU ACCEPT THAT YOU ARE ULTIMATE TRUTH,
WHERE IS THE QUESTION OF WAITING?

Keep the discipline of meditation going until the Conviction arises, until there is Conviction. With some people, it happens immediately, for others, it may take longer to erase all the impressions. I have told you many times:

UNLESS ALL YOUR IMPRESSIONS ARE ERASED,
YOU ARE NOT GOING TO BE ABLE TO KNOW YOURSELF.

People say, "I want to see a living Master".

YOU ARE A LIVING MASTER.

If you want to go and see a living Master, a genuine living Master, then go. But then stay with that Master. Be loyal!

What happens is that when one living Master leaves the body-form, then people go looking for another living Master. They are always running after different Masters.

CONCENTRATE ON THE CONCENTRATOR.
STOP IGNORING YOUR OWN LIVING MASTER.

Go elsewhere if you want! How long are you going to keep roaming for?

THERE IS NOWHERE TO GO,
BEYOND THE DIRECT KNOWLEDGE OF ULTIMATE REALITY.

Q: I think what happens with Westerners - maybe it is the same too, with some people over here in India - is that we like to travel about and collect Masters, many different Masters. It is like gathering all the ingredients to make a big soup, and then stirring them all in together.

Maharaj: You were shepherding yourself away from Ultimate Truth thinking, "I am a man in the world. I am somebody else, in the form of a man, or woman". Unless individuality dissolves, absolutely and completely, you will not be able to know yourself in a real sense.

I have been trying to convince the Invisible Listener that you are Ultimate Truth.

SINCE YOU ARE ULTIMATE TRUTH,
THEN YOU HAVE NO CAUSE TO GO ANYWHERE.

153. Where Was Karma Before the First Birth?

Maharaj: The Master wishes to convey the Listener's story, the Invisible Listener's story, so that you can absorb the Reality. But you would rather play with the polished words, the sweet words, like '*Brahman*' and '*Atman*', that were created by us, and are of secondary importance, because they are body-knowledge. What is essential is Conviction. There has to be Conviction, total Conviction.

IN THE LIGHT OF ALL THIS KNOWLEDGE,
YOU HAVE TO TEACH YOURSELF,
BECAUSE YOU ARE YOUR OWN MASTER.

Every moment of your life is very valuable, invaluable. This is the time. There should not be any blind faith. Don't accept things you don't agree with. There are many concepts around like rebirth, last birth, spiritual birth, last *karma*, future *karma*. Whose *karma*? Spiritual science says that we have taken birth because of our last *karma*. Think on it!

BEFORE THE VERY FIRST BIRTH,
WHERE WAS *KARMA* THEN?

There is no *karma*, no *dharma*, no religion. We have created and formed religions to establish civilised societies.

Here, we speak Direct Knowledge, straight-talking Knowledge. This is your Knowledge, which you are finding difficult to accept because you are under the pressures of this illusory atmosphere.

Forget about the *Brahman*, *Atman*, *Paramatman*, God, and all these polished words. How many times have I hammered you with the same thing: Your Identity is Unidentified, Invisible, Anonymous Identity. You are unborn. The question of death never arises.

NOBODY HAS ANY EXPERIENCE OF BIRTH AND DEATH.

On one occasion, Nisargadatta Maharaj was talking on this subject when a devotee asked him a question about his past birth and rebirth. The Master replied: "When you were born, what was the colour of your mother's sari? Forget about your last birth".

"IF YOU CAN'T SPEAK ABOUT THIS BIRTH,
HOW CAN YOU TALK ABOUT YOUR LAST BIRTH,
OR YOUR FUTURE BIRTH?"

What happens is that we are accepting everything blindly, and signing for it, saying "Yes, yes, I want salvation". But who wants salvation? You are totally free of any bondage.

You may say that death and birth is zero, but for you to even say that 'zero', your Presence is needed. Knowledge is zero. Therefore, in the light of all this, you have to convince your Selfless Self: I am not the body, I am not going to remain the body. Who am I? I am Unidentified Invisible Identity, where there is no birth, no death. I am totally unborn. Though I am holding this body, it is not Ultimate Truth. This body is just like these clothes, an external covering.

At the end of your bodily existence, your knowledge will be tested. So you must be bold and have courage, like this, "I am not dying. Death and birth happen to the body. I am not the body at all, I was not the body at all". Know that birth and death are of the body only.

**THIS IS THE WAY TO CONVINCE YOURSELF,
THE WAY FOR YOU TO GROW IN SELF-CONVICTION.**

It is an Open Secret. I am placing before you your own secret, Open Secret. It is YOUR secret. How you accept it, and to what extent, is up to you. It is all up to you.

**ONCE YOU RECEIVE THIS KNOWLEDGE,
AND HAVE CONVICTION,
IF YOU ARE STILL TEMPTED TO GO ELSEWHERE, BE CAREFUL!
THIS MEANS THAT SOMETHING IS LACKING.**

It demonstrates an imbalance of mind, confusion and conflict.

Be aware and beware! Distractions are everywhere: This auspicious place is here, an auspicious river is there. People counting beads, saying '*Ram, Ram, Ram*', reciting '*Ram, Ram, Ram*'. Why? They are counting beads a thousand times, *lakhs*. The beads are like a part of the body. They are doing finger exercises, that is all.

Then, there are those who are standing motionless in the river, hurting their bodies, or holding an arm up for years till it withers away. Why? All this is illusion. You must have courage and be bold!

**DON'T LAPSE BACK AND BECOME A SLAVE OF YOUR MIND, EGO, INTELLECT,
ASKING OTHERS FOR BLESSINGS:
"OH, GOD BLESS ME!**

You know better! Now you know better. You know that God is a concept.

**GOD CANNOT EXIST WITHOUT YOUR PRESENCE.
THERE IS NO GOD WITHOUT YOUR PRESENCE.**

You know better, you know better! Questions of death and birth will never arise again. And when the time comes, at that particular moment, you will have courage, so that there will be no fear of death. This is a sign of established Knowledge, the Conviction of your Knowledge. When you are totally fearless at that particular moment, that is a sign of real Conviction.

You say, "I have approached many different Masters. I have read libraries of books". OK, OK. But all the time, you were adding ego, more ego, subtle ego. The fact is:

**THE ENTIRE WORLD, INCLUDING ALL THE MASTERS,
ALL THE BOOKS, ALL THE SPIRITUAL KNOWLEDGE,
IS A PROJECTION OF YOUR SPONTANEOUS PRESENCE.**

So I repeatedly say, what Nisargadatta Maharaj rightly said:

**THERE IS NOTHING EXCEPT FOR YOUR SELFLESS SELF.
THERE IS ONLY SELFLESS SELF, SELFLESS SELF.**

This is the gist of all this Spiritual Knowledge.

After years of dry knowledge, people say, "Oh, by your grace, Master", still playing with the spiritual words, and still asking for blessings: "Please Master, put your hand on my head and bless me".

**PUT YOUR HAND ON YOUR OWN HEAD.
BLESS YOURSELF! BOW DOWN TO YOURSELF!**

Why be a slave to polished words? Be serious! Serious about what you have learned. Concentrate! Come out of the trap, the big vicious circle, and surrender all this illusion. In brief:

YOU ARE UNIDENTIFIED, INVISIBLE, ANONYMOUS IDENTITY.
YOUR INVISIBLE, ANONYMOUS,
UNIDENTIFIED IDENTITY IS ULTIMATE TRUTH.
BEYOND THAT?
NOTHING.

You can go anywhere in the world, and your Presence will be there. Wherever you go in the world, there is sky.

SKY IS SKY.
YOUR PRESENCE IS BEYOND SKY.

There is only Oneness. No separation, no differentiations. Just remember what I have told you. We can go on talking and talking, I am hammering you with the same thing in different ways, using various words. But now it is up to you.

The ball is in your court. All Power is in you.

I HAVE PRESENTED YOU
WITH THE GOLDEN PLATE OF REALITY.
THERE IS NO NEED TO GO BEGGING EVER AGAIN!
YOU ARE THE FINAL DESTINATION.
WHERE ALL WAYS END, THERE YOU ARE.

In order to reach the Ultimate Truth, you compared this station with that station. There were so many ways to choose from.

NOW YOU CAN THROW AWAY THE MAP. FORGET IT!
YOU HAVE REACHED THE LAST STATION,
THE ULTIMATE STATION.

154. *Conviction*

Maharaj: My dear devotee, you are a God, for whom there is no death, no birth, no coming, no going.

Q: That is so uplifting! I want that Conviction. Perhaps Conviction gets easier as you get older? At some level, one knows there is no death, but when the body becomes sick, panic sets in!

Maharaj: This particular problem is bound to arise, considering the nature of the material body.

ONCE YOU HAVE THE KNOWLEDGE OF REALITY,
ANY ILLNESS WILL BE BEARABLE.

You will get courage to stay detached and disinterested in what is going on with the body. Why?

BECAUSE PRIOR TO BEINGNESS,
THERE WAS NO ILLNESS FOR THE INVISIBLE IDENTITY.

After beingness, all these problems with illness, psychological, physical, mental illness and so many other things, like unhappiness, depression, started. As you know, all of this started because of the body-knowledge.

If you are cognizant of your Ultimate Truth, you will say: "I am not concerned with this illness".

Even if there is sickness, that ill-feeling will be tolerable:

BECAUSE YOU KNOW PERFECTION.

Saintly people are One with Ultimate Truth, they are not therefore paying so much attention to illness.

Q: There is detachment.

Maharaj: No attachment at all. Saint Kabir was sitting for meditation, when a dog wandered up to him and started chewing at his leg. He was unaware. Some passers-by said, "Oh! Look! Look at the blood flowing." Kabir replied: "Let the dog carry on! I am not concerned with the body. I am not bothered". This is what happens when you are absorbed in the Ultimate.

WHEN YOU ARE ABSORBED IN THE ULTIMATE,
NOTHING CAN DISTURB YOU.

I will give you another example. Nisargadatta Maharaj's wife had just died. Shortly after, a Guru brother, Ganapatrao Maharaj, had come from afar, and wished to speak with him on a point of teaching. After they had finished talking for an hour or so, he told him, "Oh! My wife has died".

Such courage in very difficult circumstances is a sign of true Conviction. Whatever the difficulty, whatever the circumstances, there is always Spontaneous Peace.

YOU ARE NOT EXPECTING ANYTHING FROM ANYONE.
THAT IS THE QUALITY,
THE IMPORTANCE OF THIS KNOWLEDGE.

When you have the Conviction, you are no longer concerned with the body. Then all these problems will subside, their severity will be reduced.

Prior to concentration, prior to Conviction, we paid so much attention to the body. We are moaning, complaining, saying, "Ooh! Ooh! This pain, that pain. We have a lot of complaints. After Conviction, we give these things very little attention. To say, "I am not the body" is easy, but this should be Reality.

IT SHOULD BE AT THE ULTIMATE TRUTH LEVEL,
NOT AT THE LITERAL, BOOKISH LEVEL.

Q: I was going to ask you about a health problem I have?

Maharaj: Whatever problems you may have, the Master is not here to solve them. People are expecting, "Oh, let's go and see the Master. He will help us". People are sometimes expecting miracles, or something magical from the Master. I am not here to heal health problems, social problems or personal problems.

There are so many people worrying about the past, the future, the present.

ALL HAPPINESS COMES FROM NOT REMEMBERING THE PAST.

The past is gone. The present will go. There is no past, no present, no future. The mind and the intellect are not required for spirituality.

WITH HAND ON HEART, YOU ARE TO ACCEPT:
"THIS IS MY STORY".

Education is not an essential either. Nisargadatta Maharaj and Siddharameshwar Maharaj only reached second grade at school, yet they became world-famous.

HOW DID THIS HAPPEN? IT HAPPENED SPONTANEOUSLY.

155. *No More Travelling*

Maharaj: First Guru, second Guru, third Guru, Guru, Guru, Guru. How many Gurus do you need? You only need one Master. You have to have faith in one Master only. Place your full trust in that Master.

YOU CAN SPEND ONE HUNDRED YEARS WITH A MASTER,
BUT IF YOU DON'T ACCEPT AND HAVE
COMPLETE FAITH IN THAT MASTER,
THEN IT HAS ALL BEEN A WASTE OF TIME.

You must have complete faith within you, and at the same time faith in your Master. You can have any Guru because your Inner Guru, or Master, is the most important focus. We use the words 'outer' and 'inner' just for teaching, for convincing you, so again, don't take the literal meaning of what is being said. Your internal, Inner Master, your Spontaneous, Anonymous Presence has vast Knowledge. Your Master is regenerating that power.

After Conviction, there should not be any type of temptation in you, any desire to go elsewhere for some more knowledge. I have seen people like you before. They take the Mantra, and then go elsewhere. I feel sorry for them. I am spending time trying to convince them, and then they go hopping to another Master. Sadly, this happens.

OUT OF A THOUSAND, THERE MAY BE ONE SERIOUS SEEKER.

There is nothing beyond this. There is nothing beyond this Knowledge. This is the Final Truth. "You are *Brahman*, you are *Brahman*". I am hammering the same thing every day, but you are not accepting it, because you do not want to come out of that illusionary world, to which you have become so attached.

Forget about spirituality! The body has a time-limit. The clock is ticking and some day, willingly or unwillingly, you will have to leave the body. Open fact.

THE CONCEPT OF DEATH
IS MOVING CLOSER AND CLOSER ALL THE TIME.

How long are you going to roam for? You are no longer a traveller because you are the destiny, the Terminus. No more travelling!

Q: I am only suspecting that people run away from themselves, which is why they continue to roam.

Maharaj: It is said that out of a *lakh*, one might think about spirituality, and out of a *krore*, only one may have Conviction of Reality. One out of millions, might be convinced of Reality.

Q: So that complete Conviction is very rare?

Maharaj: Because you are not ignoring your individuality, and you are not accepting your Reality, therefore whatever I say goes in the rubbish bin.

AS LONG AS YOU GIVE ATTENTION TO YOUR INDIVIDUALITY,
YOU WILL NOT ACCEPT YOUR REALITY,
AND THE DESIRE TO ROAM WILL CONTINUE.

Q: Is it because we are slow to change, to make changes?

Maharaj: No! People don't want to make changes within them. They have the impressions of so many thoughts.

Q: Habits?

Maharaj: Not habits, but their illusionary foundations. I'm trying to lift them out of their illusionary ditch, and they still want to jump back in.

Q: Because the ditch has become too comfortable, too familiar?

Maharaj: It's a simple Reality. I am trying to simplify it!

Q: So the force to bring about this change, so that you don't fall back in the ditch is?

Maharaj: It means that you have to have total Conviction. You are to accept the Reality, your Reality. An important sentence in Marathi goes: "The Master says that after knowing the Reality you must have complete faith, strong faith".

"MY MASTER HAS SHOWN ME MY IDENTITY.
I AM EVERYTHING.
I AM ULTIMATE TRUTH, WITHOUT SAYING IT."

There's no 'I', there's no 'you'. But there is Spontaneous Conviction. You are the architect of your own Spiritual Knowledge, the architect of your own Spiritual Knowledge. I have given you the Key to open the secret.

YOU HAVE THE KEY,
YOU HAVE THE POWER,
NOW YOU HAVE TO USE THIS POWER.

Q: After knowing as much as we can from all the available spiritual literature, then the search for a Guru happens. We wish to benefit from the *darshan* of a Realized Master.

Maharaj: Yes, for confirmation, for Conviction. Many people have some experience of realization, but it is body-based realization. If you talk with them, they talk very grandly of spiritual knowledge. It is the exceptional one, who remains calm and quiet. Totally calm and quiet, with no temptations, "*Om Shanti, Shanti, Shanti*". There is no excitement, no individualism, no search.

Q: What does realization mean?

Maharaj: It means that you have the Conviction that the Knowledge is totally established within you. If anybody says to you, "Lord Krishna is standing before you", you will not be tempted. You will be disinterested, indifferent. If anybody says a great deity, or great God is standing there, you will not pay any attention.

THIS IS A SIGN OF REALIZATION,
BECAUSE YOU WILL KNOW THAT LORD KRISHNA,
OR THESE SO-CALLED GODS,
ARE THE PROJECTION OF YOUR SPONTANEOUS PRESENCE.

This Conviction is there, so why be excited, or curious or wish to discover and find out more?

THIS IS SPONTANEOUS CONVICTION.
WHEN ALL SEARCH ENDS,
THERE YOU ARE.

Some years back, a lady came to see me. She was a Doctor of Philosophy. She was always travelling here and there, searching for this and that. She had some good experiences, a few miraculous ones. I told her,

"Unless your search stops, you are not going to reach the enlightenment state". She was crying, believe me she was crying. It happens. I am not criticizing that lady, but it happens.

You may have a lot of knowledge, spiritual knowledge, but there is no stability with it all. You must have stability, "Yes, this is right". You KNOW that you have come to the destination. Don't keep searching and looking for more and more experiences.

YOUR SEARCH IS OVER.
THIS IS THE LAST STATION,
THE LAST STOP.
IF THIS KNOWLEDGE, REALITY IS NOT ESTABISHED,
THEN THE SO-CALLED MIND WILL FORCE YOU
TO KEEP TRAVELLING,
TO KEEP SEARCHING.

Q: Very true, very true.

Maharaj: So this kind of relapse will happen if the mind, ego, intellect that are a part of the body, the subtle body, are not completely dissolved.

A lot of people have good knowledge, and know they are *Brahman*, but that Reality is not established, and so this causes instability. If the foundation is not right, then the building will collapse. If a small earthquake comes, then it will collapse. The earthquake is a small doubt, a small doubt, and with that tiny doubt, you can easily end up back at square one, like in the game of snakes and ladders.

Q: From ninety-nine to one!

Maharaj: [laughing] You hit one snake, and then down you go. One doubt is all that is needed. You have a lot of milk, [knowledge], one pinch of salt will spoil it all. One little doubt will create problems. You have to convince yourself because you are the Architect, the Master. It is Self-surrender, (*Atma Nivedanam Bhakti*). You must surrender everything, total surrender, so that nothing is left: No 'You', no 'I'. You have to stand on your own feet. Theory and practice always differ.

All these saints, Nisargadatta Maharaj, Siddharameshwar Maharaj, as I said, had little education, but their simple and deep devotion was sufficient.

Simple devotion is sufficient. Nisargadatta Maharaj used to say, "The simple devotee may have immediate perfection, but the devotee with an intellectual background, is always thinking intellectually, logically, comparatively, asking, "Why this? Why that? Why? Why? Why?"

Q: Very clever, use the mind and all that stuff, keep the brain going is the idea of the clever man.

Maharaj: Total humility is most important. Total surrender. External forces will always try to attract you. In human life, the three temptations of publicity, money and sex will be there, for as long as you are in the body. Many saintly people have fallen, even after a lifetime of devotion.

Here we are giving Direct Knowledge, direct, very direct Knowledge. But even so, there are people who come here, and then still keep on travelling. They are spiritual tourists, coming and going, coming and going.

Q: Doing India!

156. Stop Your Clowning!

Maharaj: Some people come to this ashram and tell me they have been here, there and everywhere in India. One European devotee came to me with her *mala*. She was counting beads all the time. I said, "You are not a child any more. '*Ram, Ram, Ram*', what are you getting from this? It is a waste of time".

THE SPIRIT WHICH SAYS, "*RAM, RAM, RAM*",
YOU CAN'T COUNT 'THAT'.
YOU CAN'T "SOMETHING" 'THAT'.

Entertainment! People say, "I counted beads one thousand times". While they are doing this, they are adding some ego, subtle ego. I tell them they are no longer children.

YOU ARE IGNORING THE COUNTER.

If they do not like what I say, they go elsewhere, and continue counting their beads.

Distractions are everywhere. After knowing the Reality be careful who you mix with. If you are in the wrong company, you may be influenced again, and fall back into illusion. People with half-knowledge will distract you.

AFTER BEING HERE,
AND KNOWING THE REALITY,
YOU NEED NOT GO ANYWHERE ELSE.

People come, and I try to convince them. Sometimes, after they leave, I don't hear from them. I expect some of them to continue the practice, and stay loyal to the Master.

After Conviction, be careful who you mix with. They will tell you that the mind is real and *Brahman* exists. They will tell you that there is past *karma* and future *karma*, *prarabdha*, rebirth etc. And, before you know it, you have joined the circus again, back on the merry-go-round, clowning around.

I AM TRYING MY LEVEL BEST
TO REMOVE YOU FROM THIS VICIOUS CIRCLE,
BUT AGAIN, YOU WANT TO JUMP BACK INTO THE DITCH.
STOP YOUR CLOWNING!

Q: In the West, you see, it is a bit different. Generally speaking, young people can be interested in spiritual matters, but not exclusively. There are exceptions, of course, but generally it is the older folk who will be more committed.

Maharaj: Everybody says, "Give me the *Naam Mantra*", expecting some miracles, magical changes, so now I have decided to place some restrictions. I'm not going to give the Mantra to just anybody. I will first consider the extent of someone's faith.

Doubts have to be cleared by the Master first, otherwise, before someone even has Conviction, he has jumped back into the circle, the dream, the illusory ditch. I am sharing the same Direct Knowledge with everybody. We are not playing hide and seek here. This is your time. Every moment in your life is very, very important. It will not come back again.

YOU KNOW THAT YOU ARE ULTIMATE,
YOU ARE FINAL TRUTH,

YOU ARE THE LAST DESTINATION.
PAY ATTENTION TO REALITY.
DON'T NEGLECT YOUR REALITY.

You come here for discussion, for spiritual entertainment, to test your intellect, and to test my intellect. You want to test my knowledge, impress me with your knowledge. People come here, and just want to use their intellect, and communicate their book knowledge.

The same thing happened with Nisargadatta Maharaj. They come with their egos, believing they are so clever, and they want to show off their cleverness. They want to prove that they know more than the Masters. They have no devotion.

Q: There is less devotion and understanding of devotion in the West, apart from those who worship the 'God in heaven' concept.

Maharaj: There is no devotion to Selfless Self.

IT IS VERY, VERY RARE
FOR PEOPLE TO EVEN THINK ABOUT IT.
ONE IN A THOUSAND, MAYBE.

Visitors from all over the world come here. They are talking about God, discussing the different deities, the different Masters. Dry discussion!

THEY DON'T KNOW ANYTHING.

They are full of questions and doubts. These have come from all their book reading, their experiences, and with the knowledge they have heard from different Masters. They are in the confusion field. I am always telling people, "Don't nod your head, if you have any doubts". You say, "Yes, yes", and inside you are feeling, "No, no", or "I'm not sure about that", but you say nothing.

ALL DOUBTS HAVE TO BE CLEARED UP,
OTHERWISE YOU WILL TAKE THESE DOUBTS WITH YOU,
AND KEEP TRAVELLING.

Your travelling days are over. You know this.

Q: Absolutely, Maharaj!

~~~~~~~

PART THREE: *SELF-REALIZATION*

157. Chew the Chocolate

Maharaj: You must have strong faith in the Master, strong faith, strong trust, strong devotion. You are a living Master! With full concentration and full trust, you will get Spontaneous Knowledge, Reality. Strong faith is most important. This is the only way that this Knowledge will be absorbed. I see people changing their Masters all the time. This should not happen.

OUT OF ALL THE MASTERS,
THE MASTER WHO SHOWS YOU THAT GOD IS WITHIN YOU
IS A GREAT MASTER.
HE IS THE MASTER WHO STANDS OUT FROM ALL THE REST.

After Conviction, you are to maintain Reality continuously. You say OK, OK, but the moment you leave the premises, something will try and gain entry. So be strong, be alert, constant, disciplined, determined, courageous.

IT TAKES A LONG TIME
FOR THE ROOTS OF A SPIRITUAL TREE TO GROW,
BUT THAT TREE CAN BE CUT DOWN IN MINUTES.

Q: What you are saying Maharaj, is that even at this advanced stage, you have to be disciplined, keep the practice up and avoid mixing in company that might influence you negatively and destabilize you. A sapling is just a baby and can therefore be pushed over easily.

Maharaj: This Knowledge is exceptional Knowledge. It must be absorbed and digested completely. Reality has been planted in you. The Reality plant has been planted in you. Now you have to nourish it and nurture it with fertilizer. Fertilize it with devotion and meditation. If you plant something, that plant will need water and fertilizer.

I HAVE GIVEN YOU THE NECTAR PLANT.
NOW YOU HAVE TO TAKE CARE OF IT.
IF YOU DON'T WATER AND FERTILIZE IT,
THEN IT WILL DIE.

Therefore, maintain it well and you will get very good results. Fruits in abundance!

Keep up the meditation and the *bhajan*s. The rhythm of the *bhajan*s creates vibrations that enable the 'unknown' to be 'known'. That Spontaneous Existence, Spontaneous Presence which is unknown to you, will become known. Out of these vibrations, you will come to know the unknown.

YOU WILL COME TO KNOW THE UNKNOWN.

Now that you have the Conviction, you will be indifferent to what is happening, or not happening in the world. You will use your body as before, but at the same time, KNOWING that it is not Ultimate Truth, "It is not my Truth". You have understood and accepted the underlying principle, and you have established solid foundations. Your base is now Reality, instead of an illusory, and therefore, unstable and shaky, body-knowledge base.

NOW YOU KNOW,
WITHOUT A SHADOW OF A DOUBT,
THAT WHATEVER YOU SEE,
IS THE INVISIBLE SEER'S PROJECTION.
NOW YOU KNOW,
THAT YOUR SPONTANEOUS PRESENCE IS INVISIBLE,
ANONYMOUS, UNIDENTIFIED IDENTITY.

We have to use some words, and these words come close to describing Reality.

Q: I notice you use these words like, 'anonymous', 'spontaneous', 'unidentified', 'invisible', words which allude to that which is hidden, and come close to the 'unknown', close to the 'unrevealed', so to speak. I have found them really helpful, as these words cannot easily be grasped by the 'mind'. Instead, they disarm it and stop the imagination from conjuring up associated thoughts and concepts which it loves to do.

Maharaj: **AFTER KNOWING THE REALITY,**

ALL CONCEPTS WILL DISAPPEAR.

Before coming here, you were under illusion, and considered yourself to be an individual. You had many illusory problems. Now everything has changed. Be calm and quiet. Be extremely calm and quiet. Your struggles are over!

There is no longer the need to have any sort of additional Knowledge, for your Presence is Living Knowledge.

YOU ARE LIVING KNOWLEDGE.
YOU ARE A LIVING MASTER.
NOW YOU KNOW BETTER,
NOW YOU KNOW.

You know that Reality is within you. A disciple once said to Nisargadatta Maharaj: "Every day I see the same sun, the same people, the same world". Maharaj replied: "Every day you see yourself first, and then you see the world". This is Reality.

Now that you are no longer an individual, all these concepts like 'Seer', 'Knower', etc, will go. They have served their purpose. They were just used for communicating and understanding. After knowing the Reality, all concepts will disappear. Spiritual knowledge helps you to know yourself, as you were prior to beingness, and how you will be after the beingness dissolves. Knowledge was used simply to identify your Unidentified Identity. It served well to get rid of all the illusion and concepts, confusion, conflict, irrational fear around death, etc.

YOU ARE AT THE ADVANCED STAGE.
THIS MEANS THE STAGE AFTER CONVICTION.

You have nothing to do with any Knowledge. You are nothing to do with any Knowledge.

Knowledge was the medium to drive you to the Ultimate Truth. Its work is now over!

Q: When you are established in Ultimate Reality, do you still need to be alert?

Maharaj: Not after Spontaneous Conviction. No! Who is going to be alert, or take precautions? Whose alertness? You can only be alert, if you are still considering yourself as a body, in the body-form. At this stage, all language disappears, [he claps], all thinking processes disappear, [he claps again].

THERE IS NO THOUGHT,
AND NO THINKING,
BECAUSE THE THINKER IS UNKNOWN.

At this stage of 'not knowing', you don't know that "I am the thinker", so all thoughts vanish. The Thinker is Formless, Anonymous, Invisible. When you name the Thinker or Knower, 'Master', 'God' or '*Brahman*', it is just to know, just to know. This is rare Knowledge. It is not book knowledge, it is Direct Knowledge.

158.   *Slowly, Silently, Permanently*

Q: You often say that we don't realize our own power, and that we are not aware of it, but this awareness is not physical?

Maharaj: It is Spontaneous Awareness. You are thinking something around awareness, giving it some attribute, when the Reality is Spontaneous. All thinking processes are related to the body-knowledge: "I'm a spiritual woman". Were you a spiritual woman prior to beingness? And, what about after the disappearance of the body? No! What will remain after the disappearance of the body? You say, "I don't know".

"I DON'T KNOW",
MEANS I AM NOT IN ANY FORM.
I KNOW!

Therefore be patient! It takes time to absorb the Knowledge. I have told you that the Spontaneous Conviction will come with meditation. So be determined and do the meditation, but also be patient.

Here is a simple story: A few disciples complained to their Master, that after listening to him, they were not getting the Knowledge. The Master told them to dig a trench in the big garden, so that the water could reach the plants. They poured the water from the highest point, but it did not flow. They became impatient and gave up. However, one determined disciple, kept pouring and pouring the water till eventually it made a clear channel to the plants, which then absorbed all the water.

Similarly, it takes time and patience for the Knowledge to be absorbed. And, for this to happen, you have to continue with the meditation. At the moment when it starts to flow, you will no longer need to practise. It will be Spontaneous.

Water will begin to flow because all this Knowledge has been absorbed by the earth. The water will be absorbed in the earth, slowly, silently, sucking in the flowing water.

People say, "Why is it still not happening? I have been practising for thirty years". The practice should be scientific, not standing on ice, torturing the body, and things like that. This is not Knowledge. The Knowledge will be opened up within you Spontaneously. It is there already. Be patient!

Q: Once the water is absorbed beneath, then there will be a fountain, a whoosh!

Maharaj: I am trying to convince you using different ways. I keep telling you not to underestimate yourself with illusory thoughts or doubts, such as "What the Master says, how can this be possible?", or "Is it really going to happen?" Be courageous! The Master gives you courage, strength and power, with the result that you will be able to face any problem. If thoughts attack you, the Master says you will be alert and unaffected.

IF THE MASTER TELLS YOU
THAT SOMETHING WILL HAPPEN,
IT WILL HAPPEN.

Therefore always stick to the instructions, the teachings given by your Master, and don't listen to others.

Nisargadatta Maharaj used to say, "My Master is Great". This is a sign of Realization. You will have tests, challenges, temptations, but if you have trust and faith within you and in the Master, you will not be drawn into any attractions. Sometimes negative or depressing thoughts may come, they are bound to arise. When this happens, you will be alert, prepared, and not give them any attention. You have been shown the Reality, 'CleaReality'! No doubts, no conflicts, no confusion.

Q: CleaReality! Absolutely! I am strong. No worries, as a line in one of the *bhajan*s says, "I have God in my pocket".

159. Be Loyal to You!

Maharaj: You have a lot of information and Knowledge of Selfless Self. Now you have to maintain it. Your Spontaneous Presence is covered with the body, and that is not allowing you to come out from body-knowledge. You need to be practical. Love and affection for the body need to dissolve.

BE WITH YOU, NOT WITH THE BODY.

Q: It is hard to keep that going for any length of time.

Maharaj: You are to forget everything you have accumulated, and then concentrate on the Concentrator. You are to throw yourself into Selfless Self. You will not know Ultimate Reality, unless material attachments dissolve.

WHEN THIS ATTACHMENT DISSOLVES, THERE YOU ARE!

Use your body to know yourself in a real sense. The body is only the medium through which Ultimate Truth can be known. You are Final Truth. Your Anonymous Presence is everywhere without any form. You are not able to know yourself because of your attachment to form. Have strong courage and deep involvement! A casual and part-time approach is not enough.

The world is a projection of your Existence, your Presence. Therefore surrender wholly and completely. The ego is a blockage in the way of spirituality.

NOW THAT YOU HAVE ALL THIS KNOWLEDGE,
DON'T LET THE SUBTLE EGO SPOIL IT.

The body may come, the body may go, but you are not going anywhere. When you are running towards old age, some fear may appear inside. If there is any weakness showing, problems will arise, therefore draw strength from your devotion.

**SOMETIMES YOU ARE CONCENTRATING ON THE WORLD,
AND NOT PAYING ATTENTION TO,
EVEN IGNORING YOUR SELFLESS SELF.
STAY WITH YOUR SELFLESS SELF AT ALL TIMES.**

This is a direct route. There are no ways. Where all ways end, there you are. You are the Final Destination.

**BE LOYAL TO REALITY,
NOT TO MATERIALITY.**

Q: You have covered everything, and now the rest is up to me.

Maharaj: Everything has been presented and placed in front of you.

**NOW YOU ARE TO ACCEPT IT FULLY.
TAKE A GLANCE,
RECITE, AND MEMORIZE.
THIS WILL BE ENOUGH!**

The basic thing is to dissolve the clinging illusion of, "I am someone". Everything is clear and simple. It is an open fact that the body is not your Identity, and will not remain so. It is up to you to monitor the thoughts. Take care not to be a victim of your own thoughts. Thoughts can spoil your whole spiritual life, in the same way that a small mosquito can bring disease to the whole body.

The most important thing is to stay loyal to your Reality.

**YOU ARE TO SURRENDER YOURSELF,
SURRENDER YOUR ATTACHMENT TO THE BODY,
DISSOLVE ANY FEAR,
USING THE COURAGE
THAT COMES FROM KNOWING THAT YOU ARE UNBORN.
IMPLEMENT THE KNOWLEDGE, ABSORB AND ENJOY.**

We are not hear to analyze and dissect the words. This only causes confusion. We are not here to discuss the pantheon of deities, nor to compare the saints and Masters. What the Masters wish to teach and convey is Your Story, the Reader's Story.

**WHO GAVE BIRTH TO ALL THESE DEITIES, GODS AND GODESSES?
IF YOU IMAGINE THAT THEY ARE GREATER THAN YOU,
THIS MEANS THAT YOU HAVE JUMPED
BACK INTO THE DITCH OF IGNORANCE.**

I have told you many times that no one, and nothing, is greater than YOU! You are not a baby any more. This habit of analysis and comparisons that you have, is nothing but blindly swimming in a sea of literal knowledge.

The Reader's Story is the Final Edition. You are the Final Edition, the Last Identity, the Final Identity, Ultimate Truth. When everything ends, there you are. This is the gist, the summary of all the Knowledge.

**SELFLESS SELF IS THE FINAL TRUTH.
THIS IS NECTAR.**

How long are you going to read books for? Read the Reader's Knowledge. Know the Reader's Identity. The mind entered and spoiled the Knowledge, complicating what is really very, very simple Truth.

WHEN THE SAINTS ARE CONVEYING YOUR STORY,
YOU ARE TO TAKE, HEAR, LISTEN TO,
AND UNDERSTAND THE PRINCIPLE OF THE STORY,
NOT THE NARRATIVE.
TAKE THE PRINCIPLE OF THE STORY,
NOT THE NARRATIVE.
THIS IS NOT AN ENTERTAINMENT PROGRAMME.

Q: You mean these are not bedtime stories?

Maharaj: Master says, "You are *Brahman*", and then you run back to the bank of the river. You are taking ego every time you start analyzing knowledge.

WHO IS ANALYZING THE STORIES?
THIS KNOWLEDGE IS REALITY, TRUTH.
YOUR REALITY, YOUR TRUTH. IT IS NON-INTELLECTUAL.

You knew nothing of Spirituality and Philosophy prior to beingness.

BREAK THE CIRCLE.
KNOWLEDGE IS IGNORANCE.
YOU ARE ULTIMATE.
WHY WOULD YOU WISH TO RETURN TO THE BODY?

Thoughts are like bacteria, a virus that corrupts the Simple Purity of Reality.

GREAT EFFORT IS NEEDED TO EXPEL EVERYTHING.

Siddharameshwar Maharaj said: "Be serious! Spirituality is not a child's game".

YOU WILL NOT BE ABLE TO KNOW THE REALITY
UNLESS YOU HAVE SPIRITUAL MATURITY.

You must have patience. The mind has great interest in stories. It is the measure of the mind! Our one and only interest is in the principle, the gist of the stories. That is most important.

160. *Embrace Your Reality*

Q: You say forget about the world, and think about Selfless Self?

Maharaj: At the initial stage, you were surrounded by body-knowledge and illusion. Now you are more discriminating and dispassionate. Now you know the Reality. But there is still something trying to hold you back: some confusion and illusion around. Keep in touch with YOU. Keep spiritually fit, in the same way, that you keep the body fit and healthy with regular exercise.

You need full concentration to keep the Spirit healthy. Take everything lightly. Don't take the touch of anything you do. Stay completely aloof, and untouched by any and every atmosphere.

"I AM NOTHING TO DO WITH THE BODY".

This Reality, this fact, is supposed to be accepted in the same way that you accepted the fact that,

"You are a man".

REALITY IS NOT A CONCEPT,
IT IS YOUR TRUTH, FINAL TRUTH.
IT SHOULD BE ENGRAVED, DEEP IN YOUR CORE.
Protect yourself from the illusory concepts that come your way in all their different guises.
PROTECT YOUR SPIRITUAL KNOWLEDGE,
YOUR SPIRITUAL BODY.

Don't take my words literally! You need to reach the peak. Don't be influenced by anyone. Don't listen to someone below you, who is saying, "Come down! Join me!" Don't lose your concentration and slip backwards! You cannot avoid the illusion around you, but you must be strong internally. Put your Knowledge into practice.

People try to integrate their spiritual life into their family life. The family life is illusion, body-knowledge. Krishna had five wives. What concern is this of yours? People have this habit of taking an interest in personal matters, and in the family life of the Masters. Do what the Masters say, not what they do! There should not be any silly thoughts coming in. Remain in society, but don't accept any foolish thoughts.

This is an opportunity to come out of body-knowledge and embrace Reality. If you don't give importance to your Reality, your Ultimate Truth, there will be another dream which is called 'rebirth'. You have to deeply impress your Reality, your Ultimate Truth on yourself.

Be careful not to become a victim of anyone's thoughts. Have the courage to be involved, and swim in the deep sea. Find the courage to swim in the deep sea, and you will find enjoyment there: "Yes! This is great!" You don't know your own Power. You are everything!

ALL THAT IS NEEDED IS A LITTLE COURAGE.
DON'T DEPEND ON ANYONE'S MERCY.
PLACE YOUR HAND ON YOUR HEAD, AND BLESS YOURSELF.

Be guided by the Master. There is no difference between you and me, except for the body. Is there any difference between the sky in Germany, and the sky in America? You have thinking power, spiritual thinking power. Use it! Use your spiritual discrimination. Nisargadatta Maharaj rightly said, "Don't sell yourself short, and let others pocket you".

There are all these people around who are counting beads, wearing saffron robes and garlands. All they are doing is decorating the body, decorating the illusory body.

IF YOU WISH TO DECORATE SOMETHING,
DECORATE YOUR INNER MASTER,
YOUR INNER LISTENER, WITH SPIRITUAL KNOWLEDGE,
WITH FAITH.
THIS IS WHAT IS MOST IMPORTANT.
It is very, very simple. Strong willingness and determination are essential.
YES! I HAVE TO KNOW MYSELF.
THIS IS THE FULL STOP. ESTABLISH THIS CONVICTION!
Now that you know the Reality, there should not be any desire to go elsewhere. Why would you wish

to jeopardise your new-found status? Your stance should be solid:

"I AM NOT GOING ANYWHERE ELSE.
I HAVE REACHED THE DESTINATION".

You will not find any peace with a wavering mind which is being drawn in all directions. Be strong internally! You are strong physically, but be strong spiritually.

COMPLETE SURRENDER!
SURRENDER YOURSELF TOTALLY!

Be humble! Your view of the world has changed with Knowledge.

YOU ARE ONE WITH SELFLESS SELF.
YOU HAVE BECOME ONE WITH YOUR SELFLESS SELF.
NOW YOU KNOW: "MY PRESENCE IS LIKE SKY,
AND IT IS IN EVERY BEING. THERE IS NO SEPARATION.
HOW CAN THERE BE A BAD SKY, AND A GOOD SKY?
WHICH SKY IS BAD AND WHICH IS GOOD?"

Can you discriminate? No! The internal change that has taken place is of paramount importance. Your perception and views have changed dramatically.

THOUGH YOU ARE STILL HOLDING THE BODY,
YOU ARE NO LONGER CONNECTED TO IT,
BECAUSE NOW, YOU ARE NOT CONNECTED TO BEINGNESS.

What is going to happen when beingness is left behind? What is going to happen when it is time to leave the body? Nothing is going to happen! All this talk of heaven and hell is nonsense talk, when no one has ever seen a heaven or a hell! Nisargadatta Maharaj used to say:

"HOW CAN YOU TALK OF REBIRTH,
WHEN YOU DON'T KNOW YOUR PRESENT WORTH?"

If you can't talk about the present, how can you talk about rebirth? Don't accept it! This is the principle of spirituality which is supposed to be absorbed spontaneously. Meditate till you have Conviction.

THINK ABOUT YOUR REALITY. THINK ON YOURSELF!
YOU NOW HAVE THE MIRROR OF KNOWLEDGE.

Meditation and *bhajan*s will keep your Selfless Self safely housed. This continuity is absolutely essential. There's always going to be external forces, and a barrage of concepts, that keep trying to draw you back into illusion. They will not succeed. Your stance is firm, strong. These disciplines will keep you alert so that the enemy will not dare enter. Illusory concepts will not dare enter you. You have installed the anti-virus software to get rid of the viruses. You are now a mighty force to be reckoned with. You have no opposition.

161. *Identify Your Selfless Self*

Maharaj: Bhausaheb Maharaj devised a systematic plan to counter the unending flow of illusory and attacking concepts. He knew the pitfalls, and how easily distractions could spoil concentration. He spent eighteen years in meditation, standing meditation, in the forest. Our daily practice of reciting the Mantra, meditation and *bhajan*s came directly out of this Master's first-hand experience. He knew the weaknesses and traps only too well, having experienced them directly himself. We are now benefiting from his findings and wisdom and have a practice that is foolproof.

When there is loss of peace, disturbance, imbalance of mind, memories, etc, when all these come, they can potentially threaten your stability. To prevent this happening, meditation and *bhajan*s are essential to serve as a constant reminder that, "You are Ultimate Truth".

ALONG WITH DISCRIMINATION,
THE MEDITATION AND *BHAJAN*S WILL HELP YOU STAY ALERT.

Use discrimination! Your happiness lies beyond the three attractions of publicity, money and sex. Your happiness is Spontaneous Happiness. It does not require any material cause for it to be there. Total and Spontaneous Silence will result from your practice.

TAKE REALITY SERIOUSLY!
TREAT YOUR TRUE STATUS WITH THE UTMOST CARE.
IF YOU LET INDISCRIMINATE THOUGHTS ENTER,
THEY MAY CREATE ANOTHER DREAM.
KEEP DANGEROUS THOUGHTS AT BAY.

You do not want another dream like this one. Rebirth is a concept that has been planted from childhood. Get rid of it!

The moment your guard is down, the ego will attack you. Therefore, with full concentration, be involved with YOU. Full concentration! Some day, you will leave these bones, blood and flesh. Be prepared! Spend time in a cemetery, or near to where the bodies are burned. This can be a useful and pragmatic exercise!

IDENTIFY YOUR SELFLESS SELF. YOU ARE THE FINAL TRUTH.
YOU ARE *BRAHMAN*. YOU ARE GOD.
YOU ARE NOT SEPARATE FROM YOURSELF.
YOU CONSIDERED YOURSELF IN BODY-FORM.
YOU WERE NEVER THE BODY.
YOUR INVISIBLE PRESENCE HAS ALWAYS BEEN THERE.
IDENTIFY YOUR SELFLESS SELF.

Now is a wonderful opportunity for you to really know and realize, that you are neither man nor woman, you are *Brahman*! The Spontaneous Conviction will appear.

EMBRACE THE REALITY THAT YOU ARE.

The mind, ego, intellect are not allowing you to accept this Reality completely. What is Reality? You are Ultimate Truth! This is Reality. Engrave it with the practice. At this stage, there is no need for further study, for further teachings. You no longer have any use of all these words that came after your Presence, words that were created by us.

Q: Don't you think that the Lineage teachings help, the *Parampara*?

Maharaj: It's OK, but where was this '*Parampara*' prior to beingness? When you came across with the body, you came across all this body-knowledge.

NO KNOWLEDGE IS KNOWLEDGE.

NO KNOWLEDGE IS KNOWLEDGE.

Study yourself. Make your own spiritual enquiry and find your own Self-Knowledge, not the *Parampara's* knowledge! Why do you wish to visit these sweet words again? '*Parampara*', '*upasana*', '*prarabdha*'! Find your own Self-Knowledge!

YOU KNOW NOTHING ABOUT THE WORLD,
NOTHING ABOUT THE *PARAMPARA*,
NOTHING ABOUT SPIRITUALITY.
ULTIMATELY, SPIRITUALITY IS ALSO IGNORANCE.

'Conviction', 'Spontaneous Conviction', don't let these words block you either! Everything is illusion - the clothing of various concepts.

COME TO KNOW IT IS A DREAM.
REMOVE THESE CLOTHES THAT ARE FULL OF CONCEPTS.

Remember that all these relations, husband, wife, all body relations are body-related, nothing more. Prior to the body, there was only sky, and we are beyond sky. We are unconcerned with all activities and incidents.

NOTHING HAPPENED,
NOTHING IS HAPPENING,
NOTHING WILL HAPPEN.

Be bold, but not bold in an egotistic way. Accept, but make sure that what you accept is based on reasoning. Respect your Selfless Self, through which this world is projected. This is not your Identity at all, so don't accept it.

That 'dying moment' should not be miserable. It should be happy, filled with anticipation and eagerness: "Come on, come on!"

ACCEPT REALITY, YOUR REALITY. YOU ARE FINAL TRUTH.
YOU ARE THE FINAL TERMINUS,
THE LAST DESTINY.
THERE ARE NO IN-BETWEENS.

Prior to coming to the ashram, you had an address which brought you here.

SPIRITUAL KNOWLEDGE IS JUST LIKE THAT ADDRESS.
IT WAS GIVEN TO YOU,
SO THAT YOU COULD REACH YOUR SELFLESS SELF.

There should be strong Conviction. You must have strong willpower. All the Masters were strong-willed. Have faith like Nisargadatta Maharaj! If you have that kind of faith, you will come to the Reality. Be stable! Instability at the beginning will distract you from your roots.

YOU CAN GO TO ANY REALIZED MASTER,
BUT IT IS MORE IMPORTANT,
THAT YOU GO TO, AND BE TAUGHT BY,
YOUR INNER MASTER.

The *Sadhus* walk around Arunachala many times. Very nice! But what exactly are they trying to achieve? Why trouble the body and put it under stress?

YOU ARE ALREADY WITH YOU.
BOOKS INDICATE THE SAME THING.
SELFLESS SELF IS ALL THERE IS.
NOW YOU KNOW, YOU ARE TO MAINTAIN IT.

There is no need to put the body through any kind of torture or endurance tests.

Maintenance is essential! If you do not continue the practice, and neglect your Reality, illusion will return. Strengthen your foundation and make it perfect. If you have a perfect foundation, you will come to Know Perfection. Spontaneous Perfection! Total Peace!

This identity is a momentary identity. The clock is tick, tick, ticking for the body. The body is a time-clock. Have strict involvement, and forget about the world. It is now up to you. Have one desire only, the desire to be free, in the real sense. I am addressing the Invisible Listener in you.

COME FORWARD WITH STRONG DESIRE:
"I WANT TO KNOW THE REALITY!"
OTHERWISE, THE MASTER WILL NOT SHOW UP.

You have to surrender to Selfless Self. Be humble, polite, respectful and peaceful. No jealousy, no attraction, no struggle, no quarrel. Just peaceful! Why fight? Who are you fighting? Spirit is One. The ego is dangerous, and has to dissolve altogether so that you can be calm.

You can measure yourself against the six qualities we talked about earlier, to see how deeply your spirituality is absorbed. These are forgiveness, patience, expectation of realization, desire to know, total devotion and lastly, faith in the Master. As you come closer and closer, the entire world will be forgotten. If you keep your eyes open, and don't accept anything blindly, you will come to know the Reality in you. Follow Nisargadatta Maharaj's advice:

"DON'T BE SO CHEAP THAT THE WORLD CAN POCKET YOU".

Some teachers are charging one hundred dollars to teach you how to breathe! Don't follow any of these teachers. Don't follow anything or anyone blindly.

BE LOYAL TO YOURSELF.
RESPECT YOUR SELFLESS SELF.
STOP THE SEARCH,
AND CONCENTRATE ON
THE SEARCHER WHO IS ULTIMATE TRUTH.

Have strong faith in your Master who has shown you that Masterly essence within you. One day, you may find yourself talking spontaneously, in the same way that I am talking.

THE FLOW OF KNOWLEDGE WILL BE SPONTANEOUS.
YOU ARE TO RESPECT YOUR SELFLESS SELF.
YOU ARE TO RESPECT THE REALITY.
"I AM FINAL TRUTH".

162. One With Selfless Self

Maharaj: You listened to the Master. Then, you contemplated on the Knowledge which brought understanding. With intense meditation, you acquired intellectual conviction. This is all well and good. At the advanced stage, everything has to be absorbed. Intense meditation will lead to Spontaneous Conviction, a direct experience of Truth.

Just now, you understand, you know, but at the same time, there is still some guessing going on, maybe just a little. That's OK! Spontaneous Conviction will happen. Spontaneous Conviction will happen, and then you will say, "Yes, I am *Brahman*", as sure as you are a man or a woman!

**THE HOLDER OF THIS BODY IS CALLED *BRAHMAN*
AND HAS NO CONNECTION WITH THE WORLD AND THE BODY.
THIS IS THE QUALITY OF THE CONVICTION.**

The signs of spirituality are total calm, quiet and peacefulness. These qualities lie internally. They are not for show!

You are already with YOU. But still, you need to give more importance to your hidden power. Keep up the practice of meditation and Self-enquiry. It is essential at the start. Even though you know it is only a stairway, and not Ultimate Truth, you still have to go beyond, keep going deeper and ask the question:

"WHO AM I DOING THIS PRACTICE FOR?"

Q: I know what you are saying. There is a danger that you can get lost in the practice, and there are loads of practices to choose from.

I visited a Guru recently, and he had a specific practice that we were to follow. I had to follow five rules concerning hair: how to wear it, not to shave, etc.

Maharaj: Did you have any hair prior to beingness?

**YOU ARE UNKNOWN TO YOURSELF.
YOU DO NOT KNOW YOURSELF.**

Forget about hair! There was no material, no intellectual knowledge prior to beingness. You were unknown to you. These nonsense rules about hair are only connected to the body, mind, ego, intellect. It is all material knowledge.

**SPONTANEOUS SELF-KNOWLEDGE
IS CONNECTED TO THE BOTTOM OF YOUR REALIZATION,
THE BOTTOM OF YOUR REALIZATION,
WITHOUT THE BODY. SPONTANEOUSLY!**

My words are very specific. Spiritual and intellectual knowledge, and mind, ego, intellect are all physical, intellectual knowledge.

**THIS KIND OF KNOWLEDGE IS MATERIAL KNOWLEDGE,
CONNECTED TO THE SUBTLE PART OF THE BODY.
IT WAS NOT THERE PRIOR TO BEINGNESS.**

It came along with the body, and it will be dissolved with the body.

YOU HAVE, THEREFORE, GIVEN BIRTH

TO THE MIND, EGO, INTELLECT
AND ALL THE SPIRITUAL KNOWLEDGE.

There is so much talk about the 'spiritual'. Every time you pay attention to all this spiritual talk, and the sayings of the latest 'Guru on the Block', you are ignoring your Invisible Listener that is Ultimate Truth. Not only are you underestimating yourself, you are insulting yourself. Get involved with YOU!

When you throw yourself into the Ocean of Spirituality, you will have fun! You will find it very interesting and enjoyable. Don't just stay at the bank of the river, anxiously trying to keep yourself safe and dry. Swim in the deep sea! There, you will find enjoyment. "Yes! This is great!" You will get to know your Power. You are everything!

DON'T DEPEND ON ANYONE ELSE'S MERCY.
PUT YOUR HAND ON YOUR HEAD!

Under the Master's guidance, and with meditation, you have learned the technique of spirituality, pragmatic spirituality.

Counting the years, torturing the body with different practices, wearing saffron clothes, garlands, decorating the body, etc. Why? Why all this? What will you get from doing it all? Nothing!

IF YOU WISH TO DECORATE ANYTHING,
DECORATE YOUR INNER LISTENER
WITH SPIRITUAL KNOWLEDGE, WITH FAITH!
THIS IS MOST IMPORTANT!

How to be? It is very, very simple: All that is needed is your willingness:

YES, I HAVE TO KNOW!
THIS IS THE FULL STOP.
THAT CONVICTION IS SUPPOSED TO BE THERE. YES!

"Yes! This is my final address. This is my Home! I am not going anywhere! I am staying put!" Be internally strong! Be spiritually strong!

SURRENDER TOTALLY, TOTAL SURRENDER!
YOUR VIEW OF THE WORLD HAS CHANGED!
THERE HAS ONLY EVER BEEN ONENESS.
KEEP GOING, CLOSER AND CLOSER,
CLOSER AND CLOSER TO SELFLESS SELF.

This internal change that has taken place, signifies that you have no connection to beingness. This is the Principle of Spirituality which is being Absorbed Spontaneously.

THINK ON YOURSELF.
YOU HAVE BEEN GIVEN THE MIRROR OF KNOWLEDGE.
IT IS YOUR MIRROR.

With continuous practice and absorption:

KNOW THYSELF, AND BE WITHIN THE SELFLESS SELF.
KNOW THYSELF, AND BE WITHIN THE SELFLESS SELF.

163.   In Full Light

Q: Is this very quiet state, silence? What will this exceptional silence be like?

Maharaj: These questions and answers are within you alone. Spiritual science talks of the four stages of the 'Word' taking birth, from the silent stage to the verbal stage. But forget about this! All the answers to your questions are to be found within you alone.

LIFE IN THE BODY IS PAINFUL.
PRIOR TO THE BODY, THERE WAS NO PAIN BECAUSE
THERE WERE NO BODILY DISTURBANCES AND EFFECTS.
HERE SPIRITUALITY WILL HELP YOU.

Q: So the real 'I' is beyond God?

Maharaj: As you know, 'God' is just a name given to a supernatural power. Your Spontaneous Existence is beyond everything, therefore there are no definitions.

YOU ARE BEYOND SKY.

Q: Nisargadatta Maharaj said, "God exists for worshipping". Now I understand this for the first time.

Maharaj: Some people worship a stone, or a statue as God. The statue does not know "I am God". They are giving importance to that statue because they do not know their own importance, that they themselves are, in fact, God.

YOU ARE GOD, YOU ARE THE GOD THAT YOU WORSHIP.
YOU ARE THE WORSHIPPER AND THE WORSHIPPED.

Body-knowledge brought many different kinds of pain. One hundred years ago, you had no knowledge! One hundred years from now, there will be no knowledge! Yet at present, you say with pride, "I've got good knowledge. I have so much knowledge".

WHAT IS THE POINT OF THIS KNOWLEDGE,
IF IT DOES NOT MAKE YOU STRONG,
AND HELP YOU REALIZE THAT, "I AM NOT DYING"?

Spirituality helps you realize that "The body is your neighbour's child" because you have reached the Truth of "Who am I?" The result is that you are unconcerned with the body. Meditation bestows power on you, and that power will help to increase your tolerance and capacity to endure whatever comes your way.

The last moment is to be a happy moment. That is the purpose of spirituality. It is up to you to make sure that you make the last moment sweet.

I INSIST THAT YOU PAY ATTENTION
TO YOUR SELFLESS SELF.
YOU HAVE ALL THIS KNOWLEDGE NOW,
SO PAY ATTENTION!

The subtle ego is everywhere making us prefer to live in our own circle with all its expectations and complaints like, "My wife should be like this. She is not living up to my expectations", or, "My husband should find a better job", etc.

DON'T REVERT BACK TO TYPE

AND GO LOOKING FOR HAPPINESS FROM MATERIAL THINGS.

You know better! You know the limitations. When you eat chocolate, you will get a moment of happiness. And then?

Know yourself, and then all painfulness will dissolve. This is simple, simple Knowledge. Some people spend *lakhs* of rupees in their search for an answer to, "Who am I?" They are surrounded by so-called teachers whose main interest is commercial. They know that seekers are often ignorant, and unable to discriminate between the true teacher and the phoney one.

You need spiritual maturity to know your Selfless Self. Each and every moment of your life is very important. You ask, "Where am I? Where is James? Where is James?" You are James. You are searching for yourself. James is here. I am placing the facts and figures in front of you.

This is why we acknowledge our Masters and say, "My Master is great. He is beyond God". You are beyond God. When you meet with a Realized Master, your search comes to an end. That Masterly essence is already within you. The Master merely makes you aware of it.

HAVE STRONG FAITH IN YOUR MASTER,
AND STRONG FAITH IN YOURSELF.

Wherever you are in the world, be with your Unidentified Identity. Place your hand on your head and bless yourself!

Q: The real 'I' is beyond any image of God.

Maharaj: Yes!

BECAUSE YOU ARE NOT KNOWN TO YOURSELF.

That which can be talked about, like an image of a deity (*murti*), is related to body-knowledge, intellect, logic, and is a sign of illusion.

THAT WHICH CANNOT BE TALKED ABOUT
IS A SIGN OF REALITY.

You were like the beggar boy, you were rich all along. You just did not know you were wealthy. Now that you know the Reality, you are Enlightened.

The Master is not the body. The Speaker and the Listener: Make one like the other! The Seer's reflection. The Seer is great! We respect the Seer! The Seer is formless, and not bone, flesh and blood.

MIND IS NOT.
EGO IS NOT.
THERE YOU ARE.

At the moment, you can only guess what the silence might be like. How are you going to be without words? How will you be?

THE UNKNOWN BECAME KNOWN.
THE KNOWN WILL BE DISSOLVED INTO THE UNKNOWN.

You came to know yourself through the body, because YOU are unknown to yourself. Thereafter, the body will dissolve back into the unknown. This is very interesting knowledge, if you go deep and deep and deep.

I AM INSISTING, THAT YOU GO DEEP, AND DEEP,

INTO YOUR SELFLESS SELF.

With meditation, the gate that was denied you, will be open. The door will be open wide. A deep cave of Knowledge will be opened up, one that is beyond your imagination. It is the Master Key! The world of meditation is the Master Key. You are to apply yourself, then:

OPEN, OPEN,
OPEN,
UNTIL YOU SEE YOUR SELFLESS SELF IN FULL LIGHT.

164. *Make the Last Moment Sweet*

Maharaj: Why are we doing meditation, taking the Mantra, reciting the Mantra, doing Self-enquiry, contemplating, reading books? Because the last day, the last moment is supposed to be a happy moment, a sweet moment. We are preparing for, and ensuring that, when the time comes, for the Spirit to separate from the body, there will be no thoughts of, "I am dying".

WHEN THIS TIME COMES,
YOU WILL KNOW,
WITH FULL CONVICTION,
THAT "I AM UNBORN".

This Conviction is there, already established and real. It is there so that you may be in a sweet and happy mood, to make the last moment a happy moment.

This is very, very simple Knowledge with no room for arguments or counter-arguments. This is not a debate. This is not about "What is true?" or "What is false?" because there is no true or false. Ultimate Truth means that there is neither 'true' nor 'false'. This is called Ultimate Truth.

Over the weeks we have been talking about the 'unborn child'. Whether we were talking about spirituality or philosophy, all talk is for the unborn child.

Nothing has happened. We were talking about nothing happening. As disciples, you have to go to the root, to the base. The root is your Selfless Self. Stay there quietly and calmly with no words, no world. Prior to beingness - no words, no worlds.

THERE YOU CAN SEE THE PRINCIPLE,
THE SILENT, SILENT, INVISIBLE LISTENER.
BEYOND THAT,
NOTHING.

Even if we carried on talking for hours together, years together, the principle would still be the same. The principle would remain the same.

Q: What about devotion, Maharaj? Is it needed after Conviction, Realization?

Maharaj: **AFTER TOTAL CONVICTION,**
AFTER THE ULTIMATE TRUTH HAS BEEN ESTABLISHED,
THE DEVOTION MUST CONTINUE.
YOU HAVE TO CONTINUE WITH THE DEVOTION,

BECAUSE WE ARE HOLDING THE BODY.

It is necessary, absolutely essential to continue the devotion. One devotee used to come and see me. He used to write books on philosophy. He was a very honest and humble man.

Then, all of a sudden, he became distracted and was drawn to politics. He got himself so deeply involved in it all, that he even wanted to stand for election. He was caught unawares, and without even noticing what was happening, threw his spirituality away, just like that. His life became very busy with politics, too busy to accommodate any devotion. He lost his focus, his concentration.

DEVOTION AFTER KNOWLEDGE IS ESSENTIAL.
DEVOTION WILL KEEP YOU HUMBLE.

Q: I'm happy Maharaj because I am now at the last stage, after searching for forty or so years. Yesterday, I was feeling bodiless, as well!

Maharaj: What is this stage you are talking about? There is no stage. And who is counting? Thirty years, forty years. How can you feel bodiless, when there's nobody there? Without your Presence, you cannot count. Without your Presence, you can't have any experience. Your Identity is beyond experience.

There is no doubt that this type of experience is good, but it is not Ultimate Truth, it is not Final Truth. Remember these are progressive steps, landmarks. Today you may experience, "I am *Brahman*", and tomorrow, "I am Almighty God". Good experiences, but still experience. In order for you to have this experience, any experience, it means that there is some illusion still lingering there, a trace of illusion.

YOU ARE NEITHER *BRAHMAN* NOR GOD.
DON'T GO ROAMING
WITH THESE TYPES OF SPIRITUAL EXPERIENCE.

It is easy to get attached to spiritual experiences, but it will simply bring the ego back. You are separate from all of this. "I had a marvellous experience. I had such a great experience of *Brahman*, *Atman*, *Paramatman*, God." This will bring back the ego.

You are totally formless - there is no experience and no experiencer. Whatever you experience is an addition to your Spontaneous Presence, an add-on.

STAY WITH YOUR SPONTANEOUS PRESENCE,
INSTEAD OF TALKING ABOUT EXPERIENCE.

Q: You know, I wasn't even aware of that. I was excited and got carried away by my big spiritual experiences!

Maharaj: If you have an experience, then it is not Ultimate Truth.

ULTIMATE TRUTH IS BEYOND THAT, BEYOND THAT,
BEYOND AND BEYOND AND BEYOND.
WHEN ALL EXPERIENCE ENDS,
THERE YOU ARE.

There is a lot of ignorance around in people saying, "Oh! I have knowledge! I am enlightened!" They may have read books or listened to others' talking, but many of them will simply imitate the Masters, and relay their teachings parrot-fashion, just like in the story of Einstein's chauffeur, Harry. Because of his long association with Einstein, the chauffeur was able to talk fluently. But Harry can never be Einstein.

EINSTEIN IS EINSTEIN, NOT THE CHAUFFEUR.

Similarly, after reading spiritual literature, the sayings of the Masters, etc, you may be able to talk about what you have read and remembered from these external sources, but when people start firing questions, you won't have a clue.

This is what happens when you read books and visit Masters, and omit any Self-enquiry and Self-Knowledge. You may have collected knowledge, layers of knowledge which you can talk about, but this is material knowledge, not Ultimate Truth.

Q: I know that counting the years is meaningless, but nevertheless, people get more anxious as they get older. And some, including myself, are still trying to grasp the Truth with the mind and the intellect.

Maharaj: Forget about 'older'. Presence has no age. It is neither old nor young. Whatever you have read about or heard in the past, all the knowledge that you have collected, you are to drop! People are not wanting to do that.

PEOPLE ARE NOT WILLING
TO GIVE UP THEIR BODY-KNOWLEDGE,
OR WHAT THEY SEE AS THEIR SPIRITUAL INVESTMENT.

"Oh! I have spent thirty years doing this! My forty years of spirituality." So they are not easily accepting Ultimate Truth. They want to remain as they are, but at the same time, they want to know the Reality.

YOU WANT TO REMAIN IN THE ILLUSORY WORLD,
BUT AT THE SAME TIME,
YOU WANT TO KNOW THE REALITY.

Q2: I have been a student of Nisargadatta Maharaj's teachings for over two decades now. Sometimes I feel like I am going round in circles. Yes, the teachings are most uplifting, but I feel I am lacking in direction, and there's little or no movement. I sense that I may have been 'piggy-backing' on the teachings, and using spirituality as another sort of identity. I can see that now. The Master is still out there, separate, so there is some duality.

Maharaj: You have read the books of the Master but you are ignoring your Inner Master. Ask yourself: Whatever spiritual knowledge you have today, will it help you when you take your last breath? You see, this so-called spiritual knowledge is the greatest illusion.

Intellectual understanding will not help you. Playing with the Master's words feeds the subtle ego. Identification with the name of any Master also feeds the ego. You are not separate from the Master.

THAT MASTERLY ESSENCE IS ONE.
THAT SAME ESSENCE THAT IS IN NISARGADATTA MAHARAJ,
IS IN YOU ALSO.

You are identifying with, and attached to the name, maybe even the form of the Master. The Master is not the name. The Master is not the form, whether he be Nisargadatta Maharaj, Ranjit Maharaj, Siddharameshwar Maharaj, Ramana Maharshi, Swami Vivekananda, Shankara.

WHERE WERE THESE MASTERS PRIOR TO BEINGNESS?

You are saying, "What did he mean by this, what did he mean by that?" The Master's words are indicators, don't get caught up in them. Have faith in what the Master says, and accept his message. Leave the mind behind, stop analyzing and dissecting the words. Stay with the meaning of what the Masters' are saying and trying to convey. Stop clinging to the words.

**THIS IS YOUR STORY,
YOUR REALITY.
ACCEPT THE REALITY.**

This Reality is infinitely more important than remaining an eternal student of spirituality.

**YOU HAVE BEEN READING BOOKS CONTINUOUSLY,
BUT YOU HAVE NOT READ THE READER.**

Books have brought you here. But whatever you have been reading is not sufficient. You need to find out the principle behind your studies. What is it that you are looking for? Which concept is giving you the most trouble? Death and fear of death? You are studying what this Master said, or what that Master said, and all the time you are ignoring the student.

DON'T IGNORE THE STUDENT!

Instead of focussing on studying, find out who is studying, Self-enquire. Stay with you, the Invisible Reader.

After reading the books, and listening to the Master's Knowledge, you need to read your own book, your own story.

**READ YOUR OWN BOOK,
SELF-DISCOVER.
LOOK AT YOU!**

My Master said, "The real is very unknown to you, so live like that, and it will not be a problem for you". Get to know Selfless Self. Do Self-enquiry, meditate, recite the Mantra, sing *bhajans*. Listen to the teachings of your Inner Master. You are a Master.

Q: I guess that, if truth be told, we are too scared, and maybe we don't want to actually take the leap, and become That. There is no becoming, is there? And we sense that there is no going back either.

Maybe we just like gathering more and more knowledge, and stroking the ego. This brings comfort to the bogus ego. Or maybe we do not really want to go deep enough into the teachings, and really look for the meaning behind them?

Maharaj: I have told you!

IT IS NOT DIFFICULT!

After knowing the Reality, it will happen just like in the story of the rope and the snake. When you know it is a rope, instantly, you will say, "Oh! I know! Why should I fear that rope. It is my illusion". Everything changes instantly. It is the same with the beggar boy. When he came to know he was a millionaire, he did not go begging the next day.

Q: Yet we still go begging the next day, because if we don't, that forty-year search will seem to have been wasted, appear meaningless, in vain, I suppose?

Maharaj: You are measuring the years because you forgot the Searcher. Who is measuring the years?

Q: Well, yes I know that it is all illusion. It is just that I am aware the body is on a short fuse, like an incense stick, and so I feel a sense of urgency.

Maharaj:

YOUR INNER MASTER IS ALMIGHTY.

Stay with this Truth! You are counting the years, still fondly remembering, without any difficulty, all the names and places that were visited by the illusory body. But how easy it is for you to forget your Almighty Master within you!

YOU ARE FORGETTING
YOUR ALMIGHTY MASTER WITHIN YOU!

Siddharameshwar Maharaj says, "If people are blind, they will not know the Reality, that they are God. They are blind. God is in you. God is doing everything through you". The subtle ego has to be melted totally, "I'm doing this and that".

AS I HAVE TOLD YOU MANY TIMES,
YOU ARE NOT DOING ANYTHING.
YOU CANNOT DO ANYTHING.
THERE IS NO DOER.

Q: So, as a Master and Teacher, you are not actually interested in people's stories, for example, my long and arduous spiritual journey?

Maharaj: They know when they come here, that after leaving the path of ignorance, the illusory body, there is no difference between the Master and the disciple. The Master is already within you. You are a lion, you are a Master. You have had a long association with the body, and so you are not accepting the Reality so easily.

Q: Twenty-four hour continuous practice is quite a surprise!

Maharaj: You spend twenty-four hours 'thinking', but then, that is normal for you! [laughter].

Q: OK, then, non-stop practice! People who come here are surprised at first, to realize how intense it is. It is not a part-time game or something. Also, their perception of meditation is that it is quite separate from their life, eg, "I will meditate for five or ten minutes, one hour, two hours", while the rest of their life is completely different.

Maharaj: The Knowledge is simple. It is very simple, but there must be a Realized Master to guide you, to hammer you, to indicate to you, to invite the attention of the Invisible Listener: "You are Ultimate Truth, you are Final Truth". Hammering! Hammering! After the Master's hammering of the big stone, a sculpture will be revealed. A figure of the Deity will be exposed.

Q: Hammering and hammering. Hammering and chiselling away! I need a lot of hammering!

Maharaj: The deity lies within this big stone. The Master must remove the unwanted parts. You may not like it, but you have to tolerate it. If you want to uncover God, you have to put up with the hammering. You must be brave and tolerate the Master as he removes the unwanted parts from the stone.

You are dealing with the processes of your life, therefore you are bound to encounter some difficulties, and resistance. Don't give too much importance to these difficulties or problems.

Q: Your teachings, Maharaj, are extremely radical and profound. They cut through everything, very direct, absolute, yet, at the same time, very down to earth, very straightforward. Direct High Teachings. This Knowledge is fresh, and has not been heard in this way before. This is ground-breaking.

Maharaj: It is by the grace of my Master, Nisargadatta Maharaj.

165. Exceptional Happiness

Q: Maharaj, can you say more about Reality, the Stateless State, Ultimate Reality? Yesterday, you were saying that it is very interesting.

Maharaj: It is unique for everyone. Everyone has different backgrounds therefore this Reality, Ultimate Truth, is going to unfold in a unique way for each and every one of you. Here is an example: When you know the address, you can reach the destination. When you arrive, this gives you great happiness. When you KNOW the destination, when you have gone straight to the destination, there is happiness, happiness that cannot be expressed.

After all the involvement, devotion, practice, study, Knowledge, when you suddenly realize, "Oh! That which I was searching for! So that I!", you forget your body-knowledge, instantly. At the moment of Conviction, even though you are holding the body, the Realization that, "I am the Final Truth, I am the Final Terminus", and the Happiness it brings, cannot be described in any words. This happiness that I am talking about is Exceptional Happiness, indescribable.

Swami Ramdas says, "If the dumb person eats a sweet like jaggery, he is not going to be able to describe what it tastes like". Similarly, after Conviction, you will not be able to explain. You can't describe the Happiness, or say how you are enjoying it. You are speechless. It cannot be explained because the peace, the satisfaction, the qualities are beyond description, beyond explanation.

THIS IS THE PLACE WHERE ALL WORDS END.

This is the place. Don't take the words literally. There is no 'place where all words end'. Nor is there any 'place' at all.

There is no witness, no witnessing, no experience, no experiencer. There will be exceptional Inner Happiness, Inner Peace. You will remain totally unconcerned with the body and all body-connected words.

THIS ENTIRE WORLD IS BODY-CONNECTED.
THE ENTIRE WORLD IS BODY-CONNECTED,
AND WHATEVER KNOWLEDGE IS AVAILABLE,
IS IN THE FORM OF WORDS.
THESE WORDS ARE THEMSELVES ALL BODY-CONNECTED.

If the body is there, knowledge is there. If the body is not there, what is the use of knowledge and of all these words? Knowledge offers indications, it is not Ultimate. Therefore everything exists for the body. The moment the body dissolves, everything dissolves.

All questions are body-related questions. When you were not the body, there were no questions because there was no physical presence. You are Spontaneous Presence - there is no individuality. Spontaneous Presence, no individuality, no 'I', no 'You'. When we came across with the body we say 'I', 'I am', 'I am *Atman*', '*Brahman*'. Nobody knows what *Atman* or *Brahman* is. These names like 'Ultimate', 'Ultimate Truth', 'Final Truth', 'Selfless Self', are indications of the Listener's Unidentified Identity, Invisible Identity.

BEYOND THAT,
THERE IS NOTHING ELSE.
THERE IS NOTHING BEYOND.

So be strong, and don't start accumulating knowledge again. What for? Of what use will it be? For whom are we accumulating? Who are we collecting so much money for. Satisfaction for whom, peace for whom?

REALITY IS INVISIBLE, UNKNOWN,
THEREFORE YOU ARE COLLECTING MONEY
FOR THE UNBORN CHILD.
YOU HAVE TO BE CONVINCED OF THIS.
THEN THERE WILL BE NO TEMPTATIONS OR ATTRACTIONS,
JUST EXCEPTIONAL PEACE,
WITHOUT ANY MATERIAL CAUSE.

The nature, the quality of this peace cannot be explained, just like that dumb person eating a sweet. Even if someone said, "It tastes sweet", what does 'sweet' mean? You have to taste it for yourself. What you have to do, is taste it. You cannot depend on words.

YOU ARE TO MAINTAIN THAT INNER SELF-CONVICTION,
AND NOT BE SIDE-TRACKED BY WORDS AGAIN.

Don't rely on words. All these spiritual books and knowledge are connected to body-knowledge, "*Brahman, Atman, Paramatman*, God, four bodies, salvation, seeds, birth, rebirth, *prarabdha*". So many words are out there, all connected to the body-knowledge.

YOU ARE BEYOND ALL OF THIS.

These words are around your Spontaneous Presence. The entire world, the entire universe is around your Spontaneous Presence.

DON'T FALL INTO BODY-KNOWLEDGE.
YOU KNOW THAT EVERYTHING IS IN YOU.
THERE IS NOTHING OUTSIDE.
THERE IS NO MORE TO FIND.

Do your practice, do your duties. Do it! [he slaps his leg], but without any ego. Share this Knowledge with those who are interested. But if you do, do it without a morsel of ego, any type of ego, because you are not the body. Be courageous! Cross the limits! Spiritual science is limited. It created a circle, and in that circle, you were trying to understand yourself.

NOW THAT YOU HAVE COME OUT OF THE CIRCLE,
YOU REALIZE THAT YOUR IDENTITY IS BEYOND ALL THAT,
BEYOND EVERYTHING.

If you have Conviction, there will not be any struggles, discussions or arguments. This is fact. I feel sorry for people who come all this distance, listen to the Knowledge, and then, when they leave, they are still tempted to go here and there.

Go and visit another teacher or holy site, if you wish. No problem! But, what are you going to get from going somewhere else? What are you going to achieve? Meeting Maharaj, then meeting somebody else, doing some ritual or other. That's OK! It's OK to go elsewhere, as long as you don't have any expectations of getting something out of it.

Recently, one person came from Tiruvannamalai, where he had been going round Arunachala non-stop. He was causing chaos to the body, torturing the body, dwelling in caves for long periods of time.

WERE YOU IN A CAVE PRIOR TO BEINGNESS?
DID YOU DWELL IN A CAVE PRIOR TO BEINGNESS?

This idea evolved from imagination. It has come straight out of the imagination. A concept developed, then people started walking round and round. A trend was set, and then people followed suit, without stopping to question the purpose.

What I am saying, is that it is very, very rare for someone to even think of spirituality. Out of one *lakh*, one person may think of spirituality. It is very rare, very rare. And among these, even though they may be doing spirituality for twenty, thirty, forty years, they are still left with their fears, mainly the fear of death.

Q: Why is their spirituality not working?

Maharaj: Because their base is the body-base, and their spirituality is feeding the subtle ego: "I've done this ritual, I'm doing this practice". Also, they are persistently playing with the words and fighting with the words.

Q: Like splitting hairs?

166. *Reality Has Nothing to Do With Words*

Maharaj: Why all the struggle and fighting to understand words and meanings, all this intellectual analysis, comparisons and conclusions? Reality has nothing to do with words, and nothing to do with the intellect. It is beyond all body-knowledge.

YOU CAN'T SAY HOW YOU WERE PRIOR TO BEINGNESS.
THERE WERE NO WORDS, NO KNOWLEDGE, NOTHING.
WORDS CANNOT DESCRIBE 'NOTHING'.

Spiritual knowledge is OK for the body-form, for as long as the body-form exists. When the body-form disappears, who knows what will happen? After Conviction, this Knowledge comes quick and sharp, very quickly, with an edge. When this happens, there is no longer any need for peace or happiness.

HAPPINESS AND PEACE ARE FOR THE BODY,
BECAUSE EXISTENCE IN THE BODY-FORM IS INTOLERABLE.

The moment you are convinced that the body-form is not your Ultimate Truth, then whatever 'negative' thing may happen to the body, is viewed with some distance, like something that has happened to your neighbour's child, and not to you. You will feel it because this body is a material body. At the same time though, you will not be involved because it is your neighbour's child, and not you.

DETACHMENT IS ONE OF THE SIGNS OF REALIZATION.

Q: Before this stage, there is a strong sense of ownership, that people own their bodies which is very important?

Maharaj: Oh yes! But not ownership, you are not the owner. It is the five elements. You are staying on a rental basis. It is just the borrowing force of the body: you are borrowing water, borrowing food. For a few years you have a license, then the license is extended, Keep Out! As soon as you stop providing food and water?

Q: Then you get thrown out of your house!

Maharaj: It is a cage, not a house. You are staying in a cage and chewing a carrot. It may be a golden cage, silver cage, brass cage, whatever comes one's way. Rich people make a golden cage, and the poor people get an iron cage.

Q: It is still a cage.

Maharaj: The sage is staying within that cage. It is a 'Sage-Cage'. The moment you have Conviction, you will break open that cage. I'm giving you courage:

"YOU ARE TO LEAVE!

OPEN THE CAGE!

OPEN IT WIDE!

YOU ARE A FREE BIRD!

These are the ways of Conviction, using stories, various words, metaphors and analogies. But listen to me! The whole of spiritual science is just talking about this unborn child.

AT THE INITIAL STAGE, PEOPLE DO LISTEN.

BUT AFTERWARDS, THERE ARE NOT SO MANY WHO CONTINUE

TO GO DEEP, AND DEEPER INTO THE REALITY.

THEY MUCH PREFER TO DISSECT THE TEACHINGS,

AND CONTEST THE WORDS

THAT HAVE BEEN USED TO EXPRESS THEM.

When it comes to the crunch, generally, people are not so keen to turn within and be quiet. They are more comfortable with the old ways of body-knowledge. They find it easier to discuss and debate the meaning of Reality. This is pointless!

REALITY IS NOT UP FOR DISCUSSION OR DEBATE.

This is why I ask everyone the same question: "What is your conclusion after reading all the spiritual books?" If you are fearless, then OK, you will hopefully be fearless when the time comes to leave the body. But make sure! If fear is still roaming around you, then all your literary pursuits have been a waste of time.

TREMBLING IN THE FACE OF FEAR IS NOT KNOWLEDGE.

KNOWLEDGE HAS TO BE USEFUL TO YOU ON YOUR DEATHBED.

Spirituality makes you fearless, with the result that you have Spontaneous Peace and Happiness. Just like, if you have no money in your pocket, you have no reason to be afraid of the thief? Let the thief come! Your pocket is empty! Now that you have Conviction, it will help you at this time. There will be no fear, nothing, just peace. Some day or other, you are to leave this house.

EVERY DAY,

YOU ARE TO SAY TO YOURSELF,

"THIS HOUSE IS NOT MINE".

FORGET IT!

You have an opportunity to use this body to know your Selfless Self, and how you were prior to beingness. Every moment in your life is very, very important. Every moment in your life is very, very important. Otherwise, there will be another dream, another dream, another dream.

YOU ARE TO COME OUT OF THIS VICIOUS CIRCLE.

YOU CAN DO IT WITH YOUR OWN POWER.
BREAK THE VICIOUS CIRCLE
WITH YOUR OWN POWER.
YOU CAN BREAK IT!
BECAUSE YOU ARE ULTIMATE REALITY.

Don't sign anything blindly again! You are unborn. Be cautious! Don't ignore Reality because of pressures from external forces, invisible forces. Don't ignore Reality because of spiritual forces, physical forces, mental forces, logical forces, intellectual forces.

DON'T IGNORE REALITY.

Everyone's trying to impress his own ideas in the name of the Masters. Generally, it is expected that you nod your head to them and say, "Correct, correct". Not you! Not you, not you any more!

NOW YOU CAN DECIDE, WHAT IS CORRECT OR INCORRECT,
AUTHENTIC OR INAUTHENTIC,
USING THE MIRROR OF KNOWLEDGE.
IN THE LIGHT OF THAT MIRROR OF KNOWLEDGE,
YOU CAN DISCRIMINATE AND DECIDE.

You have Conviction! You may need to use some words, just remember that words are not Ultimate Truth.

DON'T BECOME A VICTIM OF WORDS AGAIN.
DON'T FALL INTO THAT TRAP AGAIN.
IT HAPPENS.
I HAVE SEEN IT HAPPENING.

Q: I am not going to be seduced by any books or teachers, Maharaj. You don't have to worry about that. I understand their body-knowledge limitations. And why should I look for book-knowledge, when Self-Knowledge is unfolding as never before?

Maharaj: Very nice! We have created the words and given them their meanings. We are using words all the time. Take the words, 'God' and 'donkey'. We say 'God' is a deity, whereas 'donkey' is an animal. If we were to say that "Donkey means Deity", what happens? Nothing! It is simply the words that have changed, not the essence or substance. Forget about the words. Be with Reality! Have a nice time, enjoy your spirituality.

BE QUIET AND HAPPY!

167. Be Within Selfless Self

Maharaj: Keep hammering yourself to dissolve any illusory concepts that are still roaming around you. Rid yourself of any lingering remnants. Move towards Selfless Self, and be within Selfless Self. Keep surrendering the illusory concepts, keep surrendering the 'self' of Selfless Self. As I keep saying,

ULTIMATE REALITY WILL NOT EMERGE UNTIL
ALL BODY-KNOWLEDGE HAS BEEN DISSOLVED.

Keep the disciplines going, the meditation, reciting the Mantra. Singing devotional songs will uplift the Spirit, and help you forget the body.

Now you are at the stage where the fire is burning brightly. You are showing great earnestness. You are more driven than ever before to find the Reality and go back to the Source. The doubts have gone and you have surrendered yourself. With full Conviction, trust in the Master and in yourself, nothing can stop you now!

Q: That is true Maharaj. I am driven. I HAVE TO KNOW. I have to go deeper and deeper. More and more is being revealed. I am in hot pursuit, so to speak.

Maharaj: You have gone through the process: from Devotee, to Devotion, to Deity. The statue of the Deity within you just needs to be uncovered more and more. This will happen as the Absorption of Knowledge takes place, slowly, silently, permanently. This will happen when all trace of self has vanished, and when all that is left, is Selfless Self.

Don't let illusion back in! Keep up the practice. You are like a mountaineer who is coming very close to the peak of the mountain. You are nearly there. Don't look back! If you look back, you will lose your concentration. Don't think about what's happening. Don't stress the brain!

Trust that the nectar plant is growing steadily. Don't make any effort! The Conviction is there, going deeper, being absorbed and established. Then there will be Spontaneous Conviction, Enlightenment, Realization - call it what you will - you know the names are unimportant. When this time comes, you will KNOW, "I am That".

Q: Maharaj, before, there used to be a sense of being separate from you, but that has gone now. You said many times that, "The Invisible Speaker in you, and the Invisible Listener in me, are One and the same". I KNOW this now, really know this. It is as if a merging has occurred. Now it is as if we are One, you are in me, and I am in you.

Maharaj: It is a good sign, a very good sign. The merging process is marching towards Oneness. Oneness was always there but it was hidden, covered by the ash of illusory concepts.

Q: The other day, Maharaj, your Presence was felt really strongly in the meditation. Your energy and power was so strong.

Maharaj: YOUR energy and power! Remember that it is your energy and power! This is coming from you. Because you are close to the Master, there is this feeling of strength and power. It happens! It is the Masterly essence in you. It is coming from your Inner Master. With the help of the Outer Master, you have been guided to come closer and closer to your Inner Master. You will find that your Inner Master is your best friend, always loyal.

Q: You use the analogy of the Master as the sculptor, hammering away. I really do feel that that is what has been happening. You have managed to get rid of the unwanted parts that have been covering the Deity. I'm not saying that all the illusion is gone, but pretty much so. You hammered and hammered, and chipped and chiselled away, going deeper and deeper, until all the unwanted coverings were removed. Amazing! There is surprise and excitement! I am more than one hundred per cent convinced, and have unshakeable trust that the Deity within will be revealed spontaneously in all its splendour.

Maharaj: I am very happy because you have strong devotion. This kind of exceptional spirituality is rare. It is by the grace of my Master, Nisargadatta Maharaj. You see, I am not doing anything. I am not telling you anything new. I am just showing you, and reawakening that which is ALREADY IN YOU. It is your Knowledge, your Power, your Reality, your Truth.

Q. Also, Maharaj, when you used to say: "You are covered in ash, underneath the fire is burning", it was fitting. Thoughts were swirling around, a kind of busyness, with random memories popping in. But now, all that has gone. There are very few thoughts.

The overall feeling, if you like, is one of emptiness, coupled with immense peace and contentment. The ash has been blown away, and that underlying fire is ablaze with happiness. Happiness does not really describe it. It is beyond happiness, beyond words. I am so grateful to you Maharaj.

Intuitively, I just have this urge most of the time to bow to you with the greatest respect and gratitude.

Maharaj: Bow to YOU! When you bow to the Master, you are not bowing to him, you are bowing to Selfless Self! So bow to you! Bow to you! Go closer and closer to Selfless Self.

BE WITH SELFLESS SELF.
I AM PROMPTING YOUR INNER MASTER.

Talk to your Inner Master. Ask questions and you will get answers. Demand answers! Your Inner Master will respond, and give you instructions. Your Masterly essence will guide you. Embrace Selfless Self. Embrace Selfless Self. Your Inner Master has reawakened.

YOU ARE ULTIMATE TRUTH.
YOU ARE ULTIMATE REALITY.
YOU ARE FINAL REALITY.

There is nothing more to say. We are beyond words. They are now redundant. I told you that Knowledge is illusion. We used this illusory thorn to remove the first illusory thorn. Now that this Knowledge has served its purpose, we no longer have any need of it. It facilitated the removal of illusion, of ignorance. Now the illusion of Knowledge must also be dissolved:

TOTAL KNOWLEDGE IS ABSORBED IN ONENESS.
TOTAL KNOWLEDGE IS ABSORBED IN ONENESS.

The process from illusion to Reality has, as it were, ended, but don't take the w.o.r.d.s. literally: There's no beginning, no end, no process, no illusion.

BE WITHIN THE SELFLESS SELF.

Be calm and quiet! Be happy! Enjoy the exceptional peace, the exceptional silence. Be intoxicated with the nectar of Selfless Self.

Q: I heard what you said about bowing, but I still feel like bowing to you, Maharaj, because I have a deep feeling of gratitude welling up inside all the time.

Maharaj: It is OK. Continue with the devotion. It is important to keep the devotion going. It keeps us humble.

KNOWLEDGE WITHOUT DEVOTION
IS DRY AND HOLLOW.
IT IS MEANINGLESS.

Also, the Master has shown the disciple that he is Ultimate Reality, Final Truth, therefore, it is natural for this kind of Spontaneous Gratitude to arise.

EXCEPT FOR YOUR SELFLESS SELF,
THERE IS NO GOD,
NO *BRAHMAN*, NO *ATMAN*, NO *PARAMATMAN*, NO MASTER.

This phrase contains the gist of the teachings. Keep it close to you.

KNOW THYSELF,
AND BE WITHIN THE SELFLESS SELF.

This means KNOW that you are Almighty God, *Brahman*, *Atman*, *Paramatman*, without saying it.

YOU ARE ALMIGHTY GOD, WITHOUT SAYING.
SO BE WITHIN THE SELFLESS SELF,
BE WITHIN THE SELFLESS SELF.

168. *Be a Master of Reality*

Maharaj: Be a Master of Reality, not just a Master of Philosophy or Spirituality. This Knowledge is practical Knowledge, therefore become your own teacher. You are both the questioner and the replier. When all the body-knowledge has been forgotten, there is no longer a place for any kind of discrimination or differentiation: no Master and disciple, speaker and listener.

HOUSES ARE DIFFERENT, BUT SKY IS ONE.
BODIES ARE DIFFERENT,
BUT SPIRIT IS ONE.

From time to time, there will be disturbances, and that is why you need to stay strong. You will not have any problems because your foundation is unshakeable. When a little tremor comes, you will stand firm. Sometimes earthquakes happen, but you will not be affected, because you have had intense commando training.

This has given you a commanding nature, to the extent that you will welcome the tests and say: "Let the tremors come. Come on, come on!" This is the result of the meditation and related practice. You are mighty, you are Almighty.

Q: Yes, I do feel invincible, indestructible. The other noticeable difference, is all the amazing things that are going on inside. Wonderful! It is like a cosmic light show! At the moment, I don't feel the need for any company.

Maharaj: Yes, explosions are taking place, like something's on the boil. You can see the light, the ripples. You may go through many miraculous experiences. They are good progressive steps. It means that Ultimate Truth is being exposed slowly, and it's coming out. This progress is giving you such internal happiness, that it is natural for you not to want to be with others.

SO BE WITH YOU,
AND KEEP THE COMPANY OF SELFLESS SELF.
TALK TO SELFLESS SELF.

Discuss everything with Selfless Self. Cultivate this friendship, this devotion. Remember your Inner Master is your best friend. Go deep and deep and deep. Let it touch your heart! All these practices exist simply to establish Ultimate Truth, which is already within you. They are there to bring Ultimate Silence and calm.

You are Final Truth. You are Ultimate Truth. There is nothing except Selfless Self. Swami Ramdas says: "All that is mentioned in the *Dasbodh* is the result of rational thinking. It is rational Self-Knowledge".

Q: When we meditate to the chanting from the *Dasbodh*, I sometimes feel very moved. Obviously, I don't understand what is being said, as it is in Marathi, but a few times, it has moved me to tears.

Maharaj: Though you don't know the language, your Inner Heart, Inner Presence does, and it is touched.

Q: I sometimes drift away. It has an energy, it's vibrational.

Maharaj: My Master taught me how to read the *Dasbodh,* so that the meaning of each and every word was reflected. I read it in the early mornings for about five years. I was very, very fortunate to have had the association of Nisargadatta Maharaj.

Q: And we are very fortunate now. What about prayer, Maharaj?

Maharaj: Singing devotional songs, praying, prayer is all very good. The Spirit likes it, it derives happiness and peacefulness from prayer. Through it, there is Oneness with Ultimate Truth because the external identity is forgotten.

In that devotion, there is no experiencer, experience, no witnesser, no witness, and therefore the Spirit becomes one with Ultimate Truth. The *Gita* says, "I'm not staying in heaven, I'm not in the hearts of saints. Where my devotees are praying, there I am".

Go deep and deep, and still deeper and you will find exceptional happiness. This happiness is beyond description.

YOU CANNOT FIND THIS HAPPINESS FROM BOOKS.
YOU CAN FIND IT WITHIN YOU
BECAUSE YOU ARE THE SOURCE OF HAPPINESS.
YOU ARE A MASTER OF REALITY.

Q: Rare teachings!

Maharaj: It is by the grace of my Masters. What was shared with me, I am now able to share with you.

THE CAVE OF KNOWLEDGE IS OPEN FOR YOU.
ACCEPT IT!
TAKE AS MUCH TREASURE AS YOU WANT!

Q: I have waited so long, that I am going to take all the jewels, along with the casket!

Maharaj: You have learned to swim very well. Now you have to go deep sea diving and plunge deeper into the ocean.

169. *Thoughtless Reality*

Maharaj: I do not think. Without thinking, I am talking and answering your questions, speaking spontaneously. That same power is in you. At the moment of Realization, Spontaneous Conviction, you will be able to do the same. All the saints, Ramana Maharshi, Siddharameshwar Maharaj, Nisargadatta Maharaj spoke from the bottom of Reality.

THEY WERE LIVING THE ULTIMATE TRUTH.
THEY EXPRESSED THEMSELVES,
WITHOUT THINKING.

After Realization, there will be no guessing, no imagination, no magic, no nothing. Plain Truth, Thoughtless Reality.

Q: No clever tricks!

Maharaj: No! No in-betweens. It is very simple. We are under the pressure of this illusory world, mind, ego, intellect, reading, wrong interpretations, wrong thinking, wrong inferences, doubts, forming clouds, clouding, clouding, clouding. And again you find yourself moving in that circle. You have to come out of the circle. At this Ultimate Stage, you are to stay out.

NOW THERE IS TO BE NO KNOWLEDGE, NO KNOWER.
NO EXPERIENCE,
NO EXPERIENCER.
NO PRIOR TO BEINGNESS,
NO AFTER BEINGNESS.
"PRIOR TO BEINGNESS",
AND "AFTER BEINGNESS" ARE ONLY WORDS.
THERE IS NO PRIOR TO,
OR BEYOND BEINGNESS.
GET RID OF ALL THESE SWEET AND POLISHED WORDS!

Q: Does that include Selfless Self? What about Selfless Self?

Maharaj: Of course! These are just words. Your stance is supposed to be clear now, very clear.

Q: For all its simplicity, Realization is still a rare event!

Maharaj: Out of a *lakh*, maybe one person thinks about spirituality, and out of a *krore*, maybe one is a devotee, in the real sense of the word.

Q: There must be thousands of illusory obstacles in the way of this awakening.

Maharaj: There is only one obstacle, one illusion, and that is posing yourself as an individual. There's no illusion at all, no obstacle at all. If you make it an obstacle, it will remain an obstacle. Listen again:

THERE IS ONLY ONE OBSTACLE,
ONE ILLUSION,
AND THAT IS POSING YOURSELF AS AN INDIVIDUAL.

Q: We make ourselves victims. As you said yourself, "You are disturbing the peace". I am the victim of my own thoughts.

Maharaj: We are creating nets, and getting entangled in them. There are no obstacles for the unborn child. There are no obstacles. Sometimes the mood changes, a little struggle may come your way. But you will be alert. You will know it is happening, and you will also recognize it simply as a layer of experience,

BECAUSE YOU KNOW
THAT YOU ARE TOTALLY DIFFERENT FROM ALL OF THIS.

Q: So the commando training has made us super-alert, so that we will not be caught off-guard?

Maharaj: Clouds are coming, clouds are going. Sometimes there is sunshine, sometimes cloud, but this is always a passing moment, temporary, not permanent. Depression, sadness, moroseness, happiness, peace, clouds, etc. Through it all, you are steady. You are steady, in and through it all.

It is like if you were on a train. The train is moving, moving. The trees are moving, but you are there, standing still. Sometimes when you travel, you see pleasant things, unpleasant things. Whatever is seen has no effect on you. You are steady.

THE TRAIN IS MOVING.
YOU ARE NOT MOVING.
YOU ARE STEADY.

Do not be discouraged! It's simple, if you apply the Knowledge to your daily life. This is practical Knowledge. You are steady even when the thoughts are flowing, whether they be 'good' or 'bad'. Depressed thoughts, sad thoughts, happy thoughts, these are all thoughts, illusion! At any moment, because of your training, you will be alert because you know you have nothing to do with all these thoughts. And you will not fall victim to any of them.

YOU ARE THE MASTER,
SO YOU HAVE TO DECIDE
HOW MUCH ATTENTION
TO GIVE TO THE THOUGHTS THAT APPEAR.
YOU KNOW THAT IF YOU GIVE UNWANTED THOUGHTS ATTENTION,
THERE WILL BE PAIN.
IF YOU IGNORE THEM,
NO PAIN!

If a small child falls, say, for example, a little girl falls, and then you give her attention. Once she knows she has your attention, she will make more of a drama of the fall, and cry and keep on crying. If the child is ignored, she will not cry. This is basic psychology, but true. Therefore, if you are sympathetic to whatever is happening, it will be painful, but if you ignore the goings-on, then no pain! It is up to you, you are the Master.

The moment that body-knowledge is dissolved, is the happiest moment, the most peaceful moment. Nisargadatta Maharaj said: "I was not a beggar. All this suffering, everything, it was all a dream. Then after awakening, Reality was there".

Questions will be there, until you can say: "Everything is illusion. There is no mind, ego, intellect". Everything comes out of nothing and is absorbed into nothing.

FOR THE KNOWER WHO IS REALIZED AND ENLIGHTENED,
THESE THOUGHTS,
FEELINGS AND MOODS
ARE RECOGNIZED FOR WHAT THEY ARE.
YOU DON'T GIVE THEM ANY ATTENTION
BECAUSE YOU ARE NO LONGER CONCERNED WITH THE BODY.

This is the way you are to apply the Knowledge. You know yourself in a real sense. Now you are to live in the light of this Knowledge.

170. Enjoy the Secret

Maharaj: You will not get this type of direct experience anywhere else because here, nobody is making any claims of self-importance, going around proudly, saying, "I am great". The Lineage Masters are passing their greatness onto others, sharing their greatness in a quiet and humble fashion.

Likewise, I am not claiming to be a great Master, I am simply sharing with you all that my Master shared with me. Be happy! Be Totally happy! Now you know the secret.

ENJOY THE SECRET OF YOUR LIFE.
WHAT DO YOU WANT?
NOTHING!

Do your duties and don't get entangled with any illusory thoughts.

STICK WITH THE REALITY,
YOUR REALITY.
YOU ARE REALITY,
YOU ARE ULTIMATE TRUTH.

The thoughts and feelings you are experiencing are just bodily feelings. They are like waves that come and go. You are rooted, anchored, steady. View all that is happening like a movie. You are watching the different scenes, where sometimes you are crying, and sometimes you are laughing. What you are seeing is just a movie, a screenplay that is projected from you. You are a magician!

WHAT YOU SEE,
IS YOUR PROJECTION.

Don't play with the mind that is always demanding something. The mind is separate from you. You have nothing to do with it.

The Masters in our Lineage, like Siddharameshwar Maharaj and Nisargadatta Maharaj, were all completely devoted to their Masters. This self-involvement, this kind of active devotion is needed.

IF YOU CONTINUE TO HAVE STRONG DEVOTION TO YOUR MASTER,
THEN EVERYTHING WILL APPEAR FROM WITHIN.
AND YOU WILL BOW DOWN,
BECAUSE KNOWLEDGE,
IS STARTING TO FLOW
FROM WITHIN YOU.

Without being aware of it, you may start talking. This is a kind of awakening of the Inner Master. Without knowing it, all this Knowledge will begin to flow like a river. It will happen spontaneously, without the need for any deliberate kind of thinking.

If it happens to you, then people will start praying to you, and spreading the word: "He is a God-man!" What I am saying is fact, not fiction! This is what happened to the great Masters.

IF YOU HAVE COMPLETE DEVOTION TO THE MASTER,
WITHOUT COMPROMISE,
WHAT WILL THE EFFECT BE?

THE GREATNESS OF THE MASTER
WILL BE DIVERTED TO YOU.

Q: Is it like a transference of power?

Maharaj: Then, you will, like your Master, begin to have miraculous experiences. You will feel deep happiness and exceptional peace. There will be no fear, no attraction, no disturbance.

IT IS JUST LIKE A KIND OF INTOXICATION,
SELF-FULFILMENT.

You are fulfilling yourself without any material knowledge, objects or causes. It is self-happiness, self-peace. Self-generating happiness, self-generating peace.

THERE YOU ARE.
YOU,
ALONE.
THERE IS NOTHING ELSE.

171.   *Keep the Company of Selfless Self*

Maharaj: After absorbing the Knowledge, there will be Spontaneous Conviction. You are already Realized, but due to the association with the body, you feel that you are different from Reality. It is very important to know this. It is a subtle obstacle which may stand in the way.

THIS FEELING HAS TO DISSOLVE.
THEN EVERYTHING WILL BE CLEAR.

Q: What you are saying is really interesting, Maharaj. In a recent meditation, I became aware of just that. I was looking to see what was left, and surrendering, looking for traces of body-knowledge, and this came up. I realized that there was a feeling, this feeling around the concept of realization, that had become an obstacle, exactly what you are saying just now.

Maharaj: YOU HAVE TO SURRENDER
TO YOUR SELFLESS SELF.

Then there won't be any differentiation or separation because you are a Master, and you are a disciple. You are God, and you are a devotee.

Everything is within you. Everything is within you only. Because as I have told you, without your Presence, your Spontaneous Presence, you can't see the world. As you know, the entire world is a projection of your Spontaneous Presence.

YOU ARE FATHER OF THIS WORLD.

Along with the body, so many concepts appeared within you. Concepts are troubling, but after knowing the Reality, the force of concepts will be noticeably reduced.

YOU MUST TAKE THE MASTER'S GUIDANCE.
FOLLOW WHAT I AM TELLING YOU.
CONTINUOUS MEDITATION IS A MUST

TO ERASE ALL THE MEMORIES.

Q: I read somewhere that keeping the company of saints is very beneficial.

Maharaj: Keeping the company of saints, (*Santa Sangha*), or association with saintly people, really means keeping association with Selfless Self. It is not about saintly people, physical or body-based associations, but about non-stop association with your Selfless Self, without which you cannot say, 'I'.

So this talk is just for the purpose of discussion. Knowledge is supposed to be absorbed. You have a lot of Knowledge to absorb. Using different angles, different dimensions, we are saying the same thing, hammering the same thing all the time: There is nothing apart from your Selfless Self.

So open yourself to the Final Truth.

IT IS YOUR TRUTH, THE LISTENERS TRUTH.

It is not the truth of the *Brahman, Atman, Paramatman,* God.

YOU CANNOT KNOW,
IT IS IMPOSSIBLE TO KNOW
WHEN FINAL TRUTH WILL BE TOTALLY ESTABLISHED.

People are bathing in auspicious rivers. From the north to the south, they are visiting these holy places, and doing all kinds of rituals and self-denial practices. Torturing the body is not Ultimate Truth. There are so many healers healing, so many religions.

ALL THESE PRACTICES ARE BODY-BASED.
IT IS REALLY AMAZING THAT PEOPLE GENUINELY THINK
THAT EXTERNAL THINGS CAN MAKE THEM REALIZED.

Everything is within. You know that now, and therefore you will not be tempted to go anywhere. It does not mean that you won't be visiting places, just that there will not be any pressure, any expectation like, "I will get something from going there", or "I will be enlightened after visiting this place'.

Q: Rishikesh?

Maharaj: Ah Rishikesh! And all these places. This year the Kumbha Mela will be in Nashik! In India, there are so many auspicious places from north to south.

PEOPLE ARE VISITING PLACES
BUT IGNORING THE VISITOR.
THEY ARE IGNORING THE VISITOR.

They are ignoring the Visitor because they have no vision. The Master is giving you vision, the spectacles of Knowledge for you to see your Selfless Self, and not 'others'. Why go here and there, when you know that the whole world is projected out of your Spontaneous, Invisible Presence? That is why I say that the teachings are easy to understand, but difficult to absorb, because all around, there is illusion.

DON'T FALL INTO THE TRAP OF WORLDLY ATTRACTIONS
THAT ARE EVERYWHERE.
REMEMBER THAT YOU HAVE CREATED THESE ILLUSIONS.
MAYA IS YOUR BABY!

Keep the Company of Selfless Self constantly.

172.   *Your Happiness is My Happiness*

Q: I realize I can't do anything without Selfless Self. I am trying to deepen in this Knowledge which came to me intuitively. Selfless Self is the only important thing. The mind is just making up stories all the time, when I am awake, and when I am dreaming. I am looking at all this, witnessing it all from a deep level. The Knowledge and understanding is deepening, but at certain moments I'm back in the body, so it is taking time. Do you need grace for Spontaneous Conviction to happen?

Maharaj: No, it is a spontaneous feeling, like being a man or woman.

Q: All that you said that would happen Maharaj, is now happening.

Maharaj: Nothing is happening!

Q: Even so, how can I make the Conviction really firm, so that it is there all the time?

Maharaj: It will happen through the process of meditation, the *Naam*, devotional songs, etc. Spirit will accept it spontaneously.

THE ROOT OF SUPERNATURAL POWER
IS IN YOU.

Q: Even though the understanding is very deep, part of me is still asking, "Where is God?"

Maharaj: Remember what I told you! The name 'God' is given to the supernatural power, but in order to say 'God', your Presence has to be there first.

Q: Most of the time, I don't feel any form, just emptiness. But when I go back to work, I get back into form. I get a little impatient sometimes. Does it take very long to get the Spontaneous Conviction, Maharaj?

Maharaj: No! It is instant. The moment you realize, then that is the Spontaneous Conviction. I am happy that you have a good foundation.

Q: The blessing of the Guru is always there! I had a very profound understanding, Maharaj, on Siddharameshwar Maharaj's birthday. I knew then that Grace is always available. The Guru, the Master is always with you, if you have the sight to see. It is so beautiful to understand that everything is One. I was taught to pray to, and worship, a God outside myself. Now I have reached the conclusion, "Who worships whom?" In prayer, I don't ask for anything because who is asking whom? All I do is devotion, worship, only this. I just thank, praise, worship. I never ask!

Maharaj: The significance of the process of devotion, meditation and Knowledge is very important

BECAUSE YOU ARE CONSTANTLY REFRESHING
YOUR REALITY,
AND STAYING ALERT.

Q: Meditation is really important because it leads me closer and closer.

Maharaj: Meditation washes out all the illusory concepts.

WITH MEDITATION,
YOU ARE TO WELCOME THE FEAR OF DEATH,
AND ITS RELATED VIBRATIONS.

Q: I see now that everything is just a part of the five elements, so I try not to give attention to what is around me. I don't give importance to anything that is seen. That sort of clinging to things is gradually going.

Maharaj: Good! Very nice! Because all these things were not there prior to beingness.

Q: There are some difficulties in the world, like family relations, work, that kind of thing. But then I tell myself, if I do not do my duties, others will not benefit.

Maharaj: You can do your duties. That is separate from spirituality. It is a dream!

LIFE IS A LONG DREAM.
BE NORMAL!

Q: Thank you, Maharaj. I am so grateful for everything you have taught me. I don't think I have ever had the happiness and joy that I experience now.

Maharaj: Your happiness is my happiness!

173. *Intense Longing*

Q: By constantly using discrimination, I have become more and more detached, dispassionate. How do you know when you are close to, I don't mean 'you', but how do you know when Self-Realization is imminent?

Maharaj: After steady practice, reciting the Mantra, using discrimination, then the attractions and temptations automatically become less and less, because you know. You know better. And because you know, logic says you will not be drawn back into illusion. Then it is a matter of continuing with this alertness, detachment, concentrating and stabilizing.

Q: Yes, but are there any signs?

Maharaj: You can examine yourself, to see which qualities are present in you. This will give you an idea. Spiritual science lists six qualities or virtues. You can go through these, and give them a tick or a cross. But don't pay too much attention to this. In brief: tranquillity at all times, followed by no temptation. Living peacefully because desires have gone. Endurance, so that there is no wavering. Devotion and faith in the Guru and yourself. And finally, total indifference to the world. You can measure your progress against these qualities, if you wish.

WHAT IS MORE IMPORTANT THAN THIS,
IS TO BE DRIVEN BY ONE DESIRE:
THE FIRE THAT IS CONSTANTLY BURNING IN YOU.
AN INTENSE LONGING,
TO GO DEEPER AND DEEPER,
TO GET CLOSER
AND CLOSER TO SELFLESS SELF.

Surrender yourself completely and unreservedly. This is the best and the highest kind of devotion. Offer up the ego unconditionally, absolutely. With this complete surrender, there will be no temptations, no worldly attractions, no body-related love and affection. Everything will be Spontaneous. Be Enlightened!

EVERYTHING WILL BE SPONTANEOUS.
BE ENLIGHTENED!

174.   I Know Nothing

Q: The understanding has deepened more this week. I don't exist. I really don't exist. I am also understanding that there is nothing to grasp, nothing to understand because I know nothing. There is nothing to know, nothing to grasp, just emptiness. Just emptiness. And the beauty of this, is that the seed has already been planted and is sprouting by itself. Nobody is doing anything.

Maharaj: It is spontaneously sprouting.

Q: Answers are coming by themselves now. The analogy of the sky that you use has deepened the understanding. Sky does not know what it is. Sky is not even aware of itself, so similarly, there is no 'you', no 'I', nothing to be aware of, just emptiness.

　　　My gratefulness to all the Masters for the understanding! I have taken so many years to understand, but now it has really taken root. What I understand now, I believe that it is like before my conception. Nothing was there. It is the same thing going on even now. And that answer is coming. I have no more tension, no more conscious longing. It is just as it is. It is as it is.

Maharaj: Because your Spontaneous Existence is beyond everything.

Q: Yes, Presence is always there. Before there was only books, and through them, I gained intellectual understanding. But now, I know that it's not intellectual, but much deeper.

　　　The other thing I found helpful was what you said about the poison. It became very vivid for me. When the poison flows into the body, there is no need to ask what it is going to do. You know and accept that the poison is going to work. So I took that very strongly, and this has gone in the understanding that the nectar, the Knowledge is being absorbed. So there is really no need of any understanding, as there is nothing to hold onto or grasp.

Maharaj: It is exceptional Conviction. Understanding is one thing, Conviction is something else. Spontaneous Conviction is something else, "that I am nothing to do with this world". It is just as I told you:

SPIRITUAL KNOWLEDGE IS ALSO THE GREAT ILLUSION.
IT IS ONLY THERE TO REMOVE
THE FIRST ILLUSION.

When we read books, we are adding ego.

Q: I think it is needed at the beginning, otherwise we have no idea.

Maharaj: Of course! It is just like the thorn, and then both thorns are thrown out.

AFTER CONVICTION, YOU DON'T NEED KNOWLEDGE.
KNOWLEDGE IS ALSO ILLUSION.

Q: The Master is really within, therefore all methods are wasted because they are looking out. The Master is within, giving you all the answers.

Maharaj: That is right. This is called 'Selfless Self' devotion, where there is a conversation flowing. Questions and answers are flowing. It is flowing talk! This is Selfless Self devotion.

SPIRITUAL THOUGHTS ARE NOT THOUGHTS AT ALL.
THIS IS REALITY, THE FLOW OF SPIRITUAL REALITY.

　　　The flow is going on inside, and then through that Reality, all questions are dissolved.

Q: Questions dissolve because the understanding deepens, and the answers come from within.

Maharaj: I am very happy with your progress.

Q: Also, the issue of blaming others does not arise. How can you blame anybody, when you know this is coming out of you? Everything is coming out of you. So there is no one to blame and no one to anything. Just Selfless Self. I don't feel I have any questions. Maybe they will come, I don't know.

Maharaj: A period of no questions is needed, because after Conviction, you are not to undergo any spiritual education.

Q: But meditation is needed because it deepens the understanding.

Maharaj: Because meditation is inviting the attention of the Invisible Meditator that "You are Ultimate Truth".

Q: That is the only thing that has to be done, meditate and go deeper into the Truth. There is so much happiness, after struggling with this for decades.

I recognize that the Inner Master was with me every step of the way. Some people gave me books, talks, and then finally, I found you on the internet, and was put in touch with you.

Maharaj: You have a very good base, foundation because it has resulted in Conviction. You are not to do anything else now.

YOU ARE NOT TO GO ANYWHERE.

Nisargadatta Maharaj used to say:

NOW YOU ARE TO CHEW THE CHOCOLATE OF PRESENCE.

Q: I think the deepening has to mature. In the short time that I have been talking with you, the teachings have fallen into place for me. The more we talk, the closer I'm getting to the core of spirituality. I have no need for books any more.

Maharaj: I am very happy when I know that a devotee or disciple has full Conviction, clear Conviction, complete Conviction. When one reaches this stage, individuality is gone and you will no longer talk about Presence. You will never refer to Presence, and there will be no experience of Presence.

PRESENCE ALSO DISSOLVES AT THE LAST STAGE.

Q. And becomes omnipresence?

Maharaj: Yes, but you are unaware of this.

Q: Thank you, Maharaj. I am grateful for your time. I'm sure you have many more people to talk to.

Maharaj: It is my pleasure! I like serious devotees. I expect nothing from them, but if one has Conviction, then that is my asset, my pleasure.

175. *Ablaze With Contentment*

Q: Maharaj, I have been meditating for years, but it is only since listening to the teachings, and taking the *Naam Mantra*, that I seem to be firing on all cylinders. There is so much going on that is truly amazing. It is difficult to describe, except to say that the overall feeling is one of emptiness. And along with the emptiness, there is great happiness. And what I am describing does not come and go, it is constant! Some nights, I cannot get to sleep because I am on fire with contentment, lying awake, with a huge smile on my face, at peace, and blissful!

Maharaj: Very nice! This is the fragrance coming from Selfless Self.

Q. Also, there is a sense that something very sacred is being touched upon. I feel so moved, that sometimes tears start falling. My only response is to bow down. That's all I can do. I feel so thankful to you, Maharaj, for everything. There are many visions of the Masters, and yesterday, I heard a voice saying, "You are Selfless Self". It was accompanied by a pink light. The message and the pinkish light seemed to be coming from both the inside and outside. But I know there's no inside or outside. So I just bowed down. It was so clear, and substantial that I was really encouraged. I am going deeper and deeper, and getting closer and closer. I have full trust that 'it' is achievable.

Maharaj: This is your Inner Master. This is exceptional! This is Ultimate Truth! And so soon! It is by the grace of my Master, Nisargadatta Maharaj. I am very happy with your strong involvement, your deep involvement. Continue! Go ahead! Go ahead! The blessings of my Master are with you always!

The moment body-knowledge dissolves, you will see nothing. It is a kind of spiritual intoxication: "Ah! So, it is all this!" [Maharaj waves his hands as if in trance.] Do your work, and at the same time, drink the spiritual knowledge, the nectar.

Q: I have a real desire to worship, (*puja*). But what is the best kind? I don't want to let it go, it is such a beautiful thing to do.

Maharaj: Puja means always keeping in touch with your Selfless Self.   You are supposed to keep in touch with your Selfless Self always. This is worship.

YOU ARE THE WORSHIP.
YOU ARE THE WORSHIPPER.
YOU ARE THE WORSHIPPED.

You are everything! You are Master and you are disciple. You are God and you are devotee.

Q: Why do we do the *bhajan*s?

Maharaj: You are alerting your Selfless Self because of the external forces that are around to distract you from Reality. Spirit likes the *bhajan*s and prayer.

Spirituality aside, if someone appreciates you and compliments you, it makes you happy. Likewise, the Spirit derives great happiness from hearing the *bhajan*s.

WHEN YOU ARE PLEASING YOUR SELFLESS SELF,
YOU ARE PRAISING
YOUR SELFLESS SELF.

You are giving importance to your Selfless Self, not to an external God. If someone praises you, you feel happy and energized. It is the same with Spirit, when you sing. Lord Krishna said, "I reside in the hearts of the devotees". Praise brings happiness to Spirit. When the *bhajan*s touch the sensitive spirit, that internal God is praised. And then you want to dance. You are happy and peaceful.

At the same time, you are alerting your Selfless Self, with the result that external forces will not be able to attack you, or distract you from Reality.

Q: I only listen to one or two *bhajan*s a day, but even that makes me very happy. I find it is really easy to remember myself in this way. If I don't do it, I can easily fall back into some bad habits. There is always so much pressure from the outside, and the *bhajan*s really do help. Remembering you, Maharaj, also helps a lot. And I know that everything is inside, I just have to use it properly. The Conviction is really, really strong. I know.

Maharaj: I see my happiness in your happiness.

Q: It seems like you are smiling all the time on this screen. Just one big smile. It is fantastic, thank you so much. Maybe I will learn some Marathi to get even more!

Maharaj: Language came afterwards. Go deep and deep into your Selfless Self, and there you will find nothing, because everything came out of nothing.

Q: I don't know how it all came about, but it is great!

Maharaj: That greatness is in you. The Master has not done anything. He has guided you to yourself so that you can see all that is within you, Reality. He has removed the ash, uncovered illusion, and given you light to see with.

YOUR SPONTANEOUS PRESENCE IS
SILENT,
INVISIBLE,
ANONYMOUS,
UNIDENTIFIED IDENTITY.

The process from Illusion to Reality has, as it were, ended. There was no process. There was no beginning, and no end.

TOTAL KNOWLEDGE IS ABSORBED IN ONENESS.

176. *Mind Gone*

Q: When some people become enlightened they choose not to speak or teach.

Maharaj: It depends, if there is a spontaneous flow of knowledge. Some people are realized, but they are not disclosing the Reality. Not everyone is a teacher. There are perhaps very few teachers, very few who are flowing with Knowledge.

Likewise, many people have spiritual knowledge, but that knowledge has to be absorbed. Intellectual realization is not realization. It should be Spontaneous Realization from within, so that you are living that life without any identity.

There is no world and no words for the Realized. You are utterly absorbed in yourself. When you are talking, you are talking as if you are sharing biographical material because you know Reality as well, and as thoroughly as, you know your own life story. The Knowledge flows spontaneously, and with ease, without deliberate effort, imagination, or inference.

THE FLOW IS SPONTANEOUS.

Nisargadatta Maharaj said: "If someone asks a question, I would just answer him spontaneously, as if I were talking about my own life. You can relate your life story because you know the details of your own life best of all. Similarly,

IF YOU ARE LIVING THE LIFE OF A REALIZED ONE,

YOUR KNOWLEDGE IS FIRST HAND KNOWLEDGE,
SPONTANEOUS KNOWLEDGE.

It is not literal knowledge or bookish knowledge. The Master's Knowledge is absorbed in Selfless Self. There is no separation, it is as if you are talking about your Selfless Self.

Your name is James, and since childhood, you have been living your life as James. You know your life inside out. Similarly, those who are realized, those saintly people, talk spontaneously, fluently. There is no trace of mind left, no intellect. Knowledge is flowing from them, and they are able to talk with ease. For some, this is what happens.

By the grace of my Master, I was given some power, some spiritual power, which is why I am able to talk with you.

YOU SEE ME TALKING THROUGH THIS INSTRUMENT OF THE BODY,
BUT IT IS MY MASTER,
WHO IS, IN FACT, TALKING THROUGH ME.

It is not difficult. Whatever you hear, is already in you. The Spirit of the great saints is the same Spirit that is in you, in everybody. You were ignoring your Spontaneous Presence because of the bodily effects. You used to give importance to the seen, now you are staying with the Seer.

You had an address to get to this ashram. When you reached here, you no longer needed the address. Similarly, I am giving you an address in the form of meditation and Knowledge.

IF YOU FOLLOW THE DIRECTIONS
GIVEN IN THIS ADDRESS,
IT WILL TAKE YOU DEEP INTO YOUR SELFLESS SELF.

After Conviction, throw the address away. Keep your devotion strong.

THIS IS A GOLDEN OPPORTUNITY,
A VERY IMPORTANT TIME.
AFTER LEAVING THE BODY,
THIS OPPORTUNITY IS GONE.

After Spontaneous Conviction, how are you to live? What are you supposed to do? All your actions will be spontaneous actions. All your behaviour will be spontaneous behaviour, without the intellect, so that you can carry on as normal, and not neglect your family life, or your routine life.

THERE IS SPONTANEOUS CONVICTION
EVEN IN DEEP SLEEP.

We all have love and affection for the body. We say, "I am not the body", but there are still subtle self-concepts around.

EACH AND EVERY LITTLE THING
WILL BE ERASED WITH MEDITATION.
THE SPIRITUAL BROOM REMOVES EVERYTHING,

all bacteria, subtle bacteria, powerful resistant bacteria. Sometimes, even boiling water cannot kill the bacteria, nor antibiotics. Bacteria in the form of concepts are to be extinguished permanently with meditation.

THE MANTRA WILL CURE YOU.

YOU ARE TO USE THE MANTRA ALL THE TIME.

You can recite it all the time.

Later it will happen spontaneously, without your knowledge of the reciter or the reciting.
WITHOUT YOUR KNOWLEDGE,
THE INVISIBLE RECITER IS RECITING THE MANTRA.

Slowly, silently, permanently, you are being led to Conviction through the Mantra.
SLOWLY, SILENTLY, PERMANENTLY,
REALITY IS BEING IMPRESSED UPON YOU
THROUGH THE MANTRA.

Everything has a purpose, as you know. The purpose of the Mantra is to invite the attention of the Meditator:
YOU ARE ULTIMATE TRUTH.

Reality is impressed in you. What is Reality?
I AM NOT THE BODY, I WAS NOT THE BODY,
I WILL NOT REMAIN THE BODY.

Keep going forward, keep going deeper:
SPONTANEOUS KNOWLEDGE WILL START TO FLOW.

177. *Your Story: The Greatest Story Ever Told*

Maharaj:

YOUR STORY HAS BEEN TOLD.
IT IS THE GREATEST STORY EVER TOLD
BECAUSE EVERYTHING IS WITHIN YOU!

There is nothing except you. Be calm and quiet. Be happy! Enjoy the exceptional peace, exceptional silence.
STAY AS YOU WERE PRIOR TO BEINGNESS.
STAY WITH, "I DON'T KNOW".

Remember that no knowledge is knowledge.
NO KNOWLEDGE IS KNOWLEDGE!

Bless yourself and be intoxicated with the nectar of Selfless Self. Enjoy!

Q: I feel in some ways, that my autobiography has ended, and the 'spiritography' has just begun! The veil is lifting, and the unadorned purity of Selfless Self is shining forth. There is a massive feeling of gratitude. You did not simply talk of Reality, but showed it within 'me'.

Maharaj: It is by the grace of my Master, Nisargadatta Maharaj. I am nothing, just a skeleton, a puppet.

In the beginning, Master said: "You are already realized. There is no difference between you and me, except that I know I'm not the body, whereas you don't know. You have just forgotten your Identity". Then I narrated your story, the 'Listener's Story' which reawakened you.

SPIRIT SAW ITS OWN REFLECTION IN THE MASTER,
RECOGNIZED ITS STORY,

AND RESPONDED.
IT STARTED DANCING AGAIN!
I have shown you your Ultimate Reality, Final Truth. Now you KNOW your Identity.
KEEP UP THE PRACTICE AND DEVOTION.
REMEMBER THAT DEVOTION
IS THE PERFECTION OF SELF-KNOWLEDGE.
Go now, leave your mind, ego, intellect behind.
CONTINUE ABSORBING.
BE QUIET AND HAPPY.
The following phrase contains the gist of all the teachings. Keep it near:

Except Your

Selfless Self

There is No God,

No Brahman,

No Atman,

No Paramatman,

No Master.

Homage to Shri Nisaragdatta Maharaj,
Shri Ramakant Maharaj
and to all the Masters of the Lineage.
We bow to Selfless Self.
Jai Sadguru!

~~~~~~

GLOSSARY

Aarti - A ritual where light is offered to deities.

Atman - The Supreme Self.

Atma Nivedanam Bhakti - Highest Devotion, Self-Surrender.

Atma Prakash - The Light of Spirit.

Bhajan - Devotional singing.

Bhakti - Devotion.

Brahman - The Absolute, Ultimate Reality.

Brahma - Creator god of the Hindu trinity with *Vishnu* and *Shiva*.

Brahmin - Priest.

Darshan - Vision(s) of the Divine.

Dattatreya - Adi-guru of the Nath Masters. Considered as the incarnation of the Divine trinity of *Brahma, Vishnu and Shiva*.

Gunas - Attributes, qualities. The three *gunas: Rajas, Sattva, Tamas*.

Jiva - Individual soul.

Jnana - Knowledge.

Jnani - Knower.

Karma - Action, cause and effect.

Krore - Ten million.

Lakh - One hundred thousand.

Mahasamadhi - The Great Merging, the final *samadhi*. The Ultimate goal of the spiritual seeker.

Mahatma - Great Soul.

Maya - Illusion.

Moksha / Mukti - Liberation, emancipation.

Murti - Image or idol symbolizing deity.

Naam Mantra - As used in the Inchegiri Sampradaya Lineage.

Namaskaram - A respectful form of greeting: to bow to the Divine in someone.

Neti-Neti - 'Not this, not this' method of enquiry.

Nirguna - The Unconditioned, without attributes.

Parabrahman - The Supreme Reality.

Paramatman - The Supreme Reality.

Parampara - Succession of teachers, Lineage.

Paramartha/Parmartha - Spiritual Life. Sublime Truth.

Prarabdha - Destiny, stored effects of past actions.

Puja - Worship, adoration.

Rajas - Excitable, activity, restlessness, egoism. One of the three *gunas*.

Sadhana - Spiritual practice.

Satsang - Meeting in Truth.

Sattva - Illuminating, pure. One of the three *gunas*.

Sadguru - Highest spiritual Guru, True Guru.

Sadhu - Ascetic.

Sampradaya - Tradition, succession of Masters, Wisdom Lineage.

Samadhi - Oneness with Self. Rapturous absorption.

Sannyasin - Renunciate.

Shanti - Peace.

Shiva - The Destroyer - Also known as *Mahadeva*, Great God. At the highest level *Shiva* is regarded as limitless, transcendent, unchanging, formless. One of the gods of the Hindu trinity with *Vishnu* and *Brahma.*

Tamas - Restraining - Darkness, inertia, passivity - One of the three *gunas.*

Upasana - Sitting near. Worship.

Vishnu - The Preserver god of the Hindu trinity, with *Brahma* and *Shiva*.

Vairagya - Dispassion, absence of worldly desires.

Viveka - Discrimination.

Yama - God of death.

Yoga - Union - Practice for achieving Oneness of individual spirit with Universal Spirit.

Yogi - One who practises yoga.

~~~~~~~

About the Editor

Ann Shaw's search began in the late 1960's and has continued throughout her life. At university in the UK, she studied Theology, Philosophy and Comparative Religion, Sanskrit, and specialized in Indian Philosophy and Religion. Over the decades, she practised meditation, Self-enquiry, contemplation and went on solitary retreats. She immersed herself in a wide variety of spiritual literature from east and west. This included the mystics, teachers and masters such as St. John of the Cross, St. Teresa of Avila, Thomas Merton, Søren Kierkegaard, Patanjali, Ramana Maharshi, Paramahansa Yogananda, Jiddu Krishnamurti, Joel Goldsmith, Lao Tzu and Taoism, Rumi and Sufism, D. T. Suzuki and Zen, et al.

Further on down the 'illusory' road, the teachings of Shri Nisargadatta Maharaj and Shri Siddharameshwar Maharaj brought the search to an end. When she eventually visited Nisargadatta's disciple, Shri Ramakant Maharaj, she knew for certain, that she had reached the destination!

A background in publishing and writing in various genres also prepared her for the task of compiling *Selfless Self*.

The 'Spontaneous Direct Knowledge' flowing from Shri Ramakant Maharaj coupled with diligence and understanding on the part of the editor, have together produced a power-packed, spiritual classic.

In her own words: "I was completely absorbed in the unfolding of this book and was guided throughout by both the living Master, Shri Ramakant Maharaj, and by (my) Inner Master - 'Selfless Self'.

"This is an instruction manual through which the Master guides, pushes, and draws the reader towards Spontaneous Self-Realization. *Selfless Self: Talks with Shri Ramakant Maharaj* is the highest knowledge delivered in plain, simple language. These pragmatic teachings are aided by a methodical presentation to enable the fullest absorption of Ultimate Truth".

Lightning Source UK Ltd.
Milton Keynes UK
UKHW030635081021
391877UK00010B/748

9 780992 875602

BARKHAM

A History

David French and Janet Firth
Illustrated by Sally Noble

Published by the Barkham History Association,
17 Bearwood Road, Barkham, Berkshire,
RG41 4TB

Designed and typeset by Ian Atherton
Text set in 10·5/11·5 Garamond 3

Printed and bound in Great Britain
by Warwick Printing Company Ltd

ISBN 0-9537960-0-0

Front cover: Bullock coat of arms
Back cover: Font with Clive arms in parish church

Contents

Foreword

The Council is pleased to support this beautifully produced, illustrated history of our ancient parish and sincerely thanks all those involved in its preparation.

It is intriguing to read that there is evidence of human activity in Barkham going back at least 5,000 years and to learn about the mysterious archæological feature dating to about 2,800 years ago.

After being mentioned in the Domesday Book of 1086, the reader follows the lives of landowners, farmers and rectors as the Barkham story unfolds through the centuries.

The rebuilding of St James' Church in 1861 must have been a memorable event for local people and we are lucky that there are buildings in the parish dating back even further to the fifteenth century, as well as two mediæval moated sites, each with a story to tell.

I am sure that the residents of Barkham will find this comprehensive and authoritative work on the archæology and history of the parish fascinating and enjoyable reading.

Sam Hosgood
Chairman Barkham Parish Council
May 2000

*Extract from
John Rocque's Map
of Berkshire (1761)*

Preface

To understand the archæological aspects of our local heritage we have to try to build a jigsaw puzzle, consisting of detailed studies of both the parish and the area and fit them together. This is what we have attempted for Barkham within its surroundings.

The Barkham Archæological Survey, conducted by members of a voluntary team of the Berkshire Field Research Group led by myself, began in January 1989, covers parts of the pre-1986 parish and still continues (see map on p. 2). New participants are always welcome!

Archæologists use evidence from physical material which man has left behind as rubbish on the fields, or features in the landscape. We have systematically walked 14 % of the parish, but only ploughed fields. Our survey of earthwork features has taken us into woodland and pasture, but particularly along the boundaries of fields and former farmsteads.

While collecting the data, we have been privileged to walk into the peace of the woods and fields, away from those busy arteries used by twentieth century traffic, where the roar of vehicles evaporates, the scream of motorbikes largely ceases and is replaced by the calls of the birds and farm animals who become our spectators. We would like to thank all those who gave us permission and encouragement; our detailed acknowledgements will be in the final, forthcoming report.

In Chapters 1 and 2 we offer an archæological vignette on *'the little village of Barkham, a peaceful rural spot girt with woods and old forest land, an ideal English hamlet'* (P.H. Ditchfield, 1911, *Out of the Ivory Palaces* London).

Janet Firth, May 2000

Although Barkham is a small, geographically isolated, agricultural parish where, on the face of it, little if anything of historical significance ever occurred, there is a surprising amount of historical information to be unearthed thanks to the development since 1929 of local record offices and more recent developments in information technology.

Whilst the history makes extensive use of the surviving ecclesiastical and property records, it also draws extensively on three less commonly used sources: early probate documents, early legal proceedings and early newspapers.

The wills and probate inventories which survive from Tudor and Stuart times are very personal documents and provide a fascinating insight into the family relationships and possessions of the inhabitants of Barkham in the sixteenth and seventeenth centuries.

In Tudor times the landowning and mercantile classes were remarkably litigious, and there were a number of law suits involving property in Barkham whose pleadings shed additional light on the history of Barkham at the time.

We are also fortunate that the primary sources are supplemented by the *Reading Mercury* (first published in 1723) from 1739 onwards. Although a national newspaper carrying little local news in its early years, the auction notices and occasional news items add an extra dimension to the historical information contained in the surviving legal documents.

Local history has been likened to a tantalising detective story, shrouded in mystery, the researcher being motivated as much by the expectation as by each, sometimes exciting, revelation. New discoveries, several significant, continued to be made right up to the end of the writing of this history and I am sure will continue to be made.

David French, May 2000

Reading Mercury, 7 April 1788

At the Quarter Seffions for this county, John Hobbs, a farmer at Barkham, was indicted for a nuifance, in keeping a large Maftiff Dog, which had bit feveral people, and was a terror to the neighbourhood, and after a long hearing, the defendant, (to the great fatisfaction of the Court) was convicted, and ordered to pay a fine of 20l. and to be imprifoned till the fame be paid. The above profecution was carried on by a late worthy refident of Barkham, from motives of humanity, and in fo handfome a manner, as to receive the thanks and approbation of the court, expreffed by the Chairman.

vi

Archæology

Janet Firth

The parish of Barkham before 1986

Scale 1:10,000 (reduced)

(The location of Barkham in south-east England is shown in the inset)

Key

Shaded areas: *fields walked archæologically*

X: *Bronze Age burnt mound*

A–A: *Boundary possibly adjacent to former road*

B–B: *Boundary following a stream*

Reproduced from Ordnance Survey mapping on behalf of The Controller of Her Majesty's Stationery Office © Crown Copyright. MC 031018

BARKHAM CP

1 Prehistory and Romano-British Periods

Background

The Anglo-Saxon name recorded in AD 952 for Barkham was Beorchamme; the spelling of this changed in later records, but has remained as Barkham since the mid-sixteenth century. This means 'birch-tree meadow', a clearing made in the woodland for hay. Gradually, the forest, which dominated the area since the last Ice Age, became full of fields cleared for meadow, pasture and arable. In this parish woodland was of distinct importance to the economy even into the twentieth century.

Barkham is one of the smallest parishes within the former Berkshire and Windsor Forest and lies on the western fringe of the royal hunting preserve of Windsor. In 1227, populous northern valleys of Berkshire paid money to the Crown to be disafforested, but apparently poorer, more sparsely populated land closer to Windsor remained under forest law[1].

Dominated as it was by woodland (incidentally, the parish to the north, Hurst, means wood), Barkham was not a rich agricultural area unlike the adjacent 'feld' or 'field' parishes further west, namely Arborfield, Swallowfield and Shinfield.

These are generally understood to have been cleared and used for pasture and later ploughed by the early Saxon period, if not earlier. Newland was a clearing in Hurst ploughed in the thirteenth century[2] and Barkham's neighbour on the east, the town of Wokingham, was 'planted' in the parish of Hurst also in the thirteenth century. Finchampstead to the south, beside the river Blackwater, was cleared and settled in prehistory and particularly in the Romano-British period.

There is no definite archæological evidence yet to suggest that Barkham was anything other than a scattered settlement. This type of settlement is more typical of the landscape of England than might be supposed, especially in woodland areas. There are two fields and one dwelling in the parish where a little more pottery has been found than elsewhere, dating to long periods of time, but it is not clear if these provide evidence for occupation. There were only two small concentrations of housing at the time of the survey carried out for the *Inclosure Map* of 1821, the earliest map to show this amount of detail. These were along that part of Barkham Lane that is now Barkham Street, and Coombs Hill or Rutt Hill Lane, now

Hayes Lane. These had diminished by the time of the Tithe Award in 1840 but they remained the foci.

Geology

Much of the area of Barkham consists of London Clay; this is moisture-retentive and needs careful management, hence the network of ditches and drains crossing the lower-lying areas so evident today.

Overlying the London Clay is the rather lighter and more acid Bagshot Formation (once more familiarly named the Lower Bagshot Beds). There appears to be evidence that these soils were cultivated in prehistory and that their impoverished state might have been a result of mismanagement[3].

The presence of Plateau Gravel terraces in the parish indicate the former course of the River Blackwater which flowed directly from Eversley Cross into the Thames via Barkham, Winnersh and Woodley before the last Ice Age[4]. The evidence is in the pieces of coarse sandstone lying on the fields. Gravel from deposits in the north of the parish has been used for the roads in Barkham, particularly during the eighteenth, nineteenth and early twentieth centuries, as the remains of quarries in the Coombes area demonstrate.

The streams are frequently stained deep orange by iron-hydroxide-precipitating bacteria, which forms a hard pan. Locally, there are iron-rich deposits known as bog iron which can be used as a source of the metal. Gravel and timber were important to the local economy. The smaller trees, or underwood, were vital for everything that could be made out of wood, including bark for tanning. In the past everything that could be used was taken for a purpose: clay for pottery, for coating walls of buildings, bricks and tiles; turf, peat and kindling for cooking and warmth; rushes for floor covering; heather and bracken for bedding; turf, heather and straw (when available) for roofing; grass, gorse (furze), holly and beechmast for animal feed.

Topography

Barkham lies within the Thames valley and slightly above the floodplain of the river Loddon. The highest point, in the north-north-east corner of Coombes Lane/Bearwood Road, is marked Barkham Hill on maps. The parish slopes by means of gently rolling hills to the level areas in the south, crossed by tributaries of the River Loddon. Natural features included the former pond on Langley Common and Longmoor Bog. The parish also possesses some man-made features, including two moated sites, three lakes and at least six ponds, all dug at different times.

Prehistory (c. 8,000–600 BC): the mesolithic, neolithic and Bronze Age

Barkham and the surrounding area were bound in permafrost during the last Ice Age which ended about 8,000 BC. Much of the lower area has been covered more recently by at least a metre of orange clay-silt hill wash[5].

This means that prehistoric and early historic deposits up to about the twelfth century AD, are below the normal ploughing depth and mostly undiscovered. With deeper building development this archæological information is lost.

However, in waterlogged acid peat, pollen is found, which has survived for 7,500 years free from attack by bacteria. In this, man's earliest activities locally can be identified. In each square centimetre there are from 10,000 to 50,000 pollen grains. A core sample was taken in 1996 from the Finchampstead/Barkham boundary in Longmoor Bog. The relative incidence of pollen fallen or dispersed by the wind from trees, shrubs and grasses tells us what took place, including the activities of man, in the local, and later wider, area at any one time.

At the end of the last Ice Age Barkham would have been part of an inhospitable, treeless landscape, subject to permafrost and cold winds[6]. Gradually, the climate improved and by about 7,500 BC woodland became established, resulting in dense forest dominated by birch with alder and hazel[3].

As the climate improved, humans began to return to southern England. They may have foraged sporadically through the woodland following the tributaries upstream from the river Loddon. A tiny worked flint point, or microlith. from Arborfield is evidence of this. It was once attached to a spear or arrow, using resin as a glue. This is tangible evidence of the skill required to survive the rigours of the time. Precious flint tools may

have been carried long distances and were vital to kill wild mammals, birds and fish for food and process their remains.

The making of a Neolithic microlith from a nodule of flint

Early sites favoured light, sandy soils adjacent to clay and close to water, as in Barkham. Sometimes burning from natural causes, such as lightning, made clearings in the woodland. This encouraged the growth of succulent shrubs and grass which attracted animals living in the forest. In this area red, roe and fallow deer, wild boar and birds would have been hunted, perhaps by skilled groups working together. Skins were used for tent covering, storage bags and clothes. Wood was used for tent frames, bows, arrows, spears and perhaps boats. Wildfowl and fish, nuts, fruit, seeds, leaves and edible roots expanded the diet[6]. All resources were used: flint pebbles, coarse sandstone, bark, branches, and bird feathers for warmth and, no doubt, decoration.

Although earlier activity by man is possible, the pollen sample suggests that around 3,000–2,500 BC clearings in the woodland were very noticeable, either small ones close to Longmoor Bog, or more extensive ones further away. Pollen from weeds, including docks, indicates disturbed ground; there was also a very small amount of cereal pollen. Clearings were being created within woodland probably for hay and grazing.

A microlith attached to a spear or arrow with resin

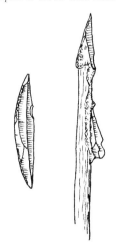

Cereal crops *may* also have been grown, albeit on a limited scale.

Farming was a process, in what is called the neolithic, which took at least a thousand years to evolve. The simplest form, particularly in this area, might be the management of deer as a herd, enclosed within a fenced area. Clearance through burning trees and undergrowth may have been used, but many domesticated animals (not just pigs) prefer browsing to grazing, will kill trees by debarking and efficiently keep clearings open. Once trees were felled, arable land could be cleared, in this area, by means of pieces of coarse sandstone used as bars in a simple wooden plough. Crops could then be sown.

A flake can be made from a flint nodule

Although still made of flint, tools changed at this time. Sickle blades were needed for harvesting; one small piece of worked flint from a blade, which may date to this period, has been found in Barkham. Axe heads were needed for felling trees; it took one full day for a man to fell a large forest oak with a flint axe head secured to a handle[7].

A typical prehistoric wooden round house

The advent of farming caused other profound changes in lifestyle[7]. Buildings were necessary to tend animals and guard stocks of food in winter. In this area these were most likely round houses of wooden posts and woven branches, packed with clay daub, replaced every 25 years or so and grouped together to house agricultural communities. Fire became important not only for cooking and but the baking of pots for food storage. These pots could be sealed with wax to deter rodents and thus were more efficient than baskets or skin bags for storing some foods. When man first found that metal could be obtained from the smelting of ores and the molten product made into tools, flint and stone tools became less vital and less skilfully made.

Following the long sequence of land clearance and crop cultivation, around 2,000 BC in the country as a whole, a period of abandonment and stagnation occurred. The pollen diagram for this area indicates that the amount of cereal pollen fell, but that this was due to the rising water table rather than inactivity by man. Damp-loving alder increased and replaced felled birch trees.

By contrast, between 1,000 and 600 BC the pollen diagram demonstrates extensive activity by man. The alder had reduced and cereal pollen had risen markedly; lime pollen had fallen as a great number of lime trees were felled in a relatively short time. All these suggest extensive arable agriculture and a change in farming practices in fields within the woodland. The incidence of

6

microscopic charcoal had also increased, which indicates more extensive human activity[5]. Evidence of charcoal was found at a depth of about 2 metres (6 feet) when a fencepost hole was dug at the present Barkham Manor by Doug Cox, the farm manager at the time; this might indicate much earlier clearance by burning.

In Barkham, the first evidence of the use of pottery in the parish appears at this time. One vessel was represented by a mere crumb of fabric weighing 2 grammes, found when fieldwalking a south-facing slope of what later became part of the commonfields. The pot, made of London Clay bristling with flint temper, would have been made locally, but the sherd was too small to identify the vessel it came from. This was probably used for storage or cooking, but pots were also used both for ritual offerings and as cremation vessels for the dead. The field in which it was found produced later pottery too (though not Saxon), indicating a long period of use as arable.

The presence of prehistoric pottery suggests some form of settlement close by, which in this, the Bronze Age period, was often in the form of an isolated farmstead for an extended family. Again, houses were likely to be round structures, pointed at the top, made of wooden posts interwoven with branches infilled with clay and thatched, with porches facing south-east and central hearths.

More humanly worked flint flakes, found in fields closely adjacent to each other, indicate that new tools were being made here, but of

The making of a burnt mound in the late Bronze Age: water was heated with hot flint. but why?

greater significance was the worked flint and pottery discovered during the partial excavation in 1992 of an archæological feature called a burnt mound[5]. This was only found because archæologists walked the easement dug for a new sewage pipe across the parish.

The burnt mound was on level land beside the stream, used as the source of water, within part of the former Kidgham Copse (see map on p. 2). This was a large monument; it was 14 metres (c. 45 feet) north–south and 5·5 metres (c. 18 feet) across and extended possibly for a further 10 metres (c. 32 feet) into the woodland. Particularly noticeable were features densely packed with burnt flint and charcoal; adjacent were six pottery sherds and more worked flint. A sample of charcoal sent for radiocarbon dating indicated that it had been created in about 850 BC.

Burnt mounds have previously been found, particularly in the north, but since 1992 more of these monuments have been recognised closer to the Thames. Their function is subject to debate. The excavation in Barkham had to be confined to a small percentage of the monument and no animal bones were found. There is therefore a slightly stronger argument that this burnt mound was not used for the cooking of meat and feasting, but something else, perhaps a sauna, involving the heating of water using pieces of very hot flint. Was this a ritual activity?

Prehistory continued: The Iron Age (600 BC–AD 43)

From the middle of the first century BC, the inhabitants of Barkham lived within the sphere of influence of the Iron Age Atrebatic tribe. Their focal point was Calleva (Silchester) 11 miles to the west. This was an *oppidum* or settlement, defended by impressive earthworks, where the self-styled 'kings' of the Atrebates are thought to have lived[8].

Through trade and diplomatic exchange the lifestyle of such aristocrats was enhanced by imported Roman goods and luxuries. They copied Roman customs, for instance minting coins. Those stamped 'CAL' or 'CALLE' are thought to have been minted in Calleva towards the end of the first century BC.

The only evidence that there was activity in Barkham in the Iron Age is from older references of accidental discoveries of Iron Age coins here. Peake[9] quotes Gough (1808) and Stukeley (1776), referring to an Iron Age gold coin of unknown type *'dug up by a woman in her garden'*, possibly in 1750, *'in Inhams Field'*. There is a field of that name on the north side of Commonfield Lane, Barkham. It was said that this coin was bought by Stukeley and illustrated by him in his notes written while travelling around the country. Another Iron Age coin, a gold stater, was said to be found during ploughing on the parish boundary between Barkham and Arborfield in 1913, in Great Coombe Field. Both were, it was thought, minted in nearby Calleva; their loss would have been very significant to their owner.

An excavation in 1998 in Arborfield, but close to the parish boundary at Whitehall Farm,[10] uncovered mounds of iron slag. Iron ore was being heated with charcoal in furnaces from late in the Iron Age onwards. This process produced iron blooms which required further work to make iron goods such as tools, weapons or metal bars for exchange. Iron blooms, together no doubt with increasing supplies of agricultural produce, would have been sent as tribute, or trade, to Calleva. If the latter, coins in exchange might well be found in this area.

An Iron Age coin, a gold stater, probably minted at Calleva, enlarged c. 4x

Inter-tribal tensions led to the creation and development of hillforts during the Iron Age; Caesar's Camp in Easthampstead is the nearest hillfort to Barkham. This is largely unexcavated, but recently cleared of trees so that its size, shape and earthworks can be better appreciated.

In woodland areas houses and other buildings were again usually of wood and round, although rectangular buildings from the last part of the Iron Age were found during recent excavations at Silchester.

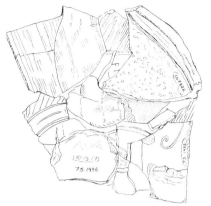

Fieldwalking results in hundreds of sherds of pottery to be washed, marked, weighed, counted and plotted.

The Romano-British period (AD 43–410)

The Emperor Claudius instigated a successful invasion by the Roman army in AD 43 and Britain became the Roman province of Britannia. For some there followed an increased desire for the trappings of Roman civilisation, better co-ordination in administration and taxes.

Agriculture continued to develop; new plants, such as cabbages, broad beans and peas were introduced into this country. New tools were used, for example hay-cutting was eased by the two-handled scythe. Production and trade increased.

Although we lack the evidence, the fields in Barkham used during the Romano-British period are likely to be the same as in prehistory[11].

In Barkham the amount of pottery in five fields (or former woodland) from this period, demonstrated agricultural activity

on the lighter soils, at least from the second to the early fifth century AD.

These would have been scattered when manuring took place across the arable fields of the time, shovelled out of the backs of ox-drawn carts. The manure heaps would have been close to the stables and animal pens in respective farmyards. All kinds of materials were thrown onto them, including farm, domestic and even industrial waste; building material, broken pots, metalworking slag and so on are found on the fields. Small, abraded sherds came also from the garden of Bailiff's Cottage, from a second century bowl, a second/third century flagon (a continental form of vessel) and cooking pots or storage jars. These were 'greywares' made fairly locally from AD 100 to 400; they were also found in three of the fields walked. A second field, known as Pins and variants, now also became of particular interest, as the pottery found in it indicated a long period of use as arable, from the Roman to the modern period.

More Romano-British pottery was found in two fields on the lighter Bagshot Formation. These sherds were from Oxford Colour-Coated Ware, made rather precisely between AD 350 and 400. One sherd was from a small shallow platter, used perhaps for dough or fruit, and a second was from a *mortarium*, whose base was once covered with quartz grits used for shredding vegetables.

Water needed for human consumption came from springs or wells in the Roman period rather than from streams, for contamination of these was understood.

Activity continued at Whitehall Farm, Arborfield, the site of a minor farmstead until AD 300, where excavated mounds of iron slag from iron-smelting furnaces were associated with amounts of pottery, which suggested that small-scale pottery production also took place here[10].

Calleva Atrebatum (Roman Silchester), relied on a wide hinterland for agricultural and other supplies, and again no doubt iron blooms were sent from the furnaces in Arborfield to Silchester via the London to Silchester road, which crossed the parish of Finchampstead. Otherwise they could have been carried by road, or via the river Loddon, to the Thames. A minor road must have linked both with the site of production and may account for the straight part of the parish boundary in the south-south-west (see A–A on map on p. 2), for there must have been a network of minor roads or tracks to allow for carts carrying people, produce and other goods to and from the nearest markets.

Oxford Colour-Coated Ware mortarium, AD 350–400, with quartz grains on its interior base for shredding vegetables

'Greyware' cooking pot or storage jar

Streams in this rural area were probably forded.

Iron was used increasingly for more sophisticated tools for agriculture and carpentry and a host of goods from nails and window grilles to hippo-sandals for horses.

In Barkham itself, scatters of undated iron-working slag were found during fieldwalking, especially in Pins. Whether it should be associated with iron-smelting in the Iron Age/Roman period, or later, is as yet unclear.

There is evidence of Roman agriculture in Barkham from pottery on the fields, but not of buildings. If there were any in this rural situation, they were more likely to be of timber than stone. There were Roman settlements in Easthampstead and Finchampstead, particularly adjacent to the Roman road. In Finchampstead one community was close to the Barkham parish boundary, and just to the south-east was a villa, possibly at the centre of a considerable estate.

Other activity in the Romano-British period close to Barkham is attested by pottery and a coin hoard, dating from the first to third centuries, discovered recently in the parish of Arborfield and Newland.

As before, woodland was important in the Roman period. Whilst iron might have been used for ploughs for oxen and other tools, it was expensive. Wood was used extensively for farming purposes, such as the making of shelters, hurdles, fencing and carts.

2 Mediæval Period (Anglo-Saxon Period to the Sixteenth Century AD)

AD 410–597: the sub-Roman and Anglo-Saxon Dark Ages

Following the end of rule from Rome in AD 410, the sub-Roman and early Anglo-Saxon period, often known as the 'Dark Ages', is relatively obscure, especially in Barkham. The land may have been used much as in the late Roman period, with rough grazing in woodland still dominating the area as the pollen diagram indicates no change from before. There are no other signs of activity here for about 300 years. Generally, pottery production stagnated; leather, wicker and wooden containers and platters must have sufficed.

Early mediæval, Anglo-Saxon period (sixth–tenth century): the progress of Christianity

The county of Berkshire was probably created in the seventh/eighth century and was much fought over, constantly changing hands between the kings of Mercia and Wessex.

The early Christian period after St Augustine arrived in AD 597 was greatly influenced by missionaries. Then St Birinus came from Rome by AD 635 to continue the evangelisation of Britain. He became the first Bishop of the West Saxons, at Dorchester-on-Thames. Pastoral care of a rural area such as Barkham from the seventh to tenth centuries is unclear as sources of information are limited. It may have been from 'mother churches' or minsters, comprising a community of priests, and/or monks and nuns, who served great 'proto-parishes' (or *parochiae*). A priest might visit the rural settlements on circuit. Although this may have been from the early Christian centre at Abingdon, Barkham was a considerable distance both down the Thames and overland.

In Berkshire several minsters are known, including at Cookham, Reading and Sonning. Although mentioned in later documents[1], these could perhaps have had roots as early as the seventh century. Barkham was but 6 miles or so across the river Loddon from both Reading and Sonning. However although it is also possible that some settlements south of the Thames could have together formed a '*mini-* or *sub-parochia*'[2], we do not know the situation for Barkham. Evidence of a preaching cross here, or of a 'field church', is lacking; if it ever existed, the archæological imprint would most likely have been disturbed by later activity.

Anglo-Saxon pottery

Even up until AD 850, in the middle Saxon period, archæological evidence is hard to find. What little pottery was made was not robust and did not easily survive in the ground, and in this parish hill wash was a problem. It is unsurprising that in Barkham only three small abraded sherds were found from a 400-year period (the seventh to eleventh century).

The earliest sherd of Saxon pottery is the base and body of a pot tempered with chaff or grass, organic inclusions which burn out on firing and leave voids. The type of pot is indistinguishable, but a domestic use is most likely; it was coil-made, probably fired locally in about the seventh/eighth century and found in a field in the north of the survey area.

Although the kick-wheel had begun to be used in this country, the later Saxon pottery sherd is of a red, well-smoothed, hand-made fabric, probably made locally and tempered with both organic and inorganic material. It was probably fired in a low-temperature kiln and the vessel type is again indeterminate, although a pot for storage of food or drink is most likely.

Early mediæval period: the tenth century charter

The first known written reference to Barkham is in a charter dated AD 952, for an area of land. The charter is given on p. 24 in Anglo-Saxon and modern English. It is one of just over 60 known from the old (pre-1974) county of Berkshire. Important documents like these were often kept in a place of safety like Abingdon Abbey. All the Berkshire charters were copied into the *Abingdon Chronicle*[3].

Identification of the estate on the ground is problematic. It probably had some accord with an earlier landholding or was part of a more ancient predecessor divided up at this time[4]. The charter recorded 3 hides in Barkham, which, if assumed to be 360 acres, was about 26 % of the pre-1986 parish, which is usually recorded at about 1362 acres. However, the size of the estate given in AD 952 may be a round figure related to a fiscal, rather than actual area. Presumably, it was an economically viable landholding, but whether it was ploughed, a pastoral enclosure or both is not known.

A few observations can be made about the charter. 'Enclosures' are commonly mentioned in the period and around settlements were characteristically paddock-like, unlike later[4]. In Barkham today the 'stream(s)' flow at about 50 metres above sea level through the lowest area of the parish, implied by *'the foot of the hill'*. The estate bounds probably incorporated at least part of the pre-1986 parish boundary, but today a stream only forms the boundary on the south-south-west side of the parish (see B–B on map on p. 2). Springs are found where there is a junction between impermeable and permeable strata and, like streams, the position of springs can change. Today there is one where the Plateau Gravel overlies the Bagshot Formation in the north of the parish; there is another at Longmoor Bog where the Bagshot Formation overlies the London Clay.

Roads in the Roman period were often used later as boundaries; the putative minor road from the Iron Age/Roman iron-smelting furnaces in Arborfield, north to the river Loddon or south to the London–Silchester road near West Court, Finchampstead, might have influenced the straight boundary, and might even be *Loddera Stræt* (see A–A on map on p. 2).

In Barkham, as elsewhere, it may be difficult to extrapolate backwards, but fun to try. A tempting starting point for the charter is at the spring at Longmoor Bog. The boundary then includes part of a branch of the stream currently on the parish boundary, runs east close to the Biggs's Farm moated site, covers part of the most level, lowest and lightest land on the Bagshot Formation, the moated site surrounding Church Cottages, encompasses the fields containing Romano-British and Saxon pottery south and west of this site, and returns to the spring in Longmoor Bog.

In two instances land owned by neighbours to the estate is implied. The first is a game enclosure, for deer, typical of woodland. The *'enclosure of the family of Cnotta'*, is less clear. Generally speaking, it is thought enclosures could have been held by one person (in severalty) or divided into long strips worked by many people with a mouldboard plough. However, the need for a strip system was probably by no means universal and since

only one personal name is applied to the estate in Barkham, it was probably held by one individual.

Field names are given in documents from time to time; five *may* be derived from Old English (OE). There are two with 'ley' or '*leah*': Langley and Bistley, probably initially clearings or glades in the woodland. Others have names which, while with 'ley' endings, may be too recent to be useful in this regard. Some field names refer to a boundary: '*Har*' in Harriet's could be one. This is adjacent to two others which adjoin, Furzing and Furzeney Mead (OE *fyrs, fyrsen*, gorse or whin) which are adjacent to the track which ran south-east from the later mediæval moated site by the church. It is tempting to see them as of significance for the Saxon estate boundary.

The charter is also discussed in Chapter 3.

Anglo-Saxon agriculture and settlement

What is striking about the field names possibly derived from OE in Barkham is that none suggest good arable land. Even in the instance of Whitfield, rather than referring to '*wheate*' as in a seventeenth century documentary reference, the name '*whit*' might indicate the colour white in the Saxon period and denotes land lowest in the table of fertility. The best fields named thus far were meadowland, with woodland next best. There are no OE field names in Barkham suggesting good arable, probably because there was none; meadow and pasture within woodland were more important.

Often the fields from this period cannot be adequately defined due to lack of data and dating evidence[4]. One hedge near Mortimer's Lodge, however, has enough woody species in a 30 metre length to date it to the tenth/eleventh century.

Open fields, such as were found in Barkham post-conquest, normally only have come about either where there was great pressure on the land after a long history of intensive arable use or if the limits of woodland clearance for cultivation (assarting) had been reached[4]. This is unlikely here. Even if it has been shown above that some of the lightest soils in Barkham had been arable since at least the Roman period, there is no evidence that an open field system existed here in the Saxon period.

Generally, within the Anglo-Saxon period, barley was by far the most important crop and used for brewing, as water might be contaminated. Oats were grown for porridge; wheat and rye for bread were also grown as well as a wide variety of fruit and vegetables inherited from Roman Britain. Other known crops at the time were hemp, flax for rope

Oxen were used for ploughing in the Anglo-Saxon period

and clothing, and woad. Vetches and horse beans were grown for stock.

The quality of the pasture and feed for stock grown in the parish was important as the Anglo-Saxon economy depended largely on livestock for essential and luxury goods and traction. Oxen were the beasts used to plough and they had to be fed through the winter. The late Saxon period is also regarded as the high watermark of agricultural achievement, since the size of animals was reduced after this time and did not recover until the sixteenth century[4].

Anglo-Saxon houses and droveways

We have no evidence of settlement or houses in Barkham, but if buildings existed they were single-storey, wooden, or perhaps turf, rather than stone buildings with a central wooden post to hold the roof supports. They may have had suspended wooden floors over a sunken area. Later, house construction changed from sunken-floored to 'post-in-trench' and then to 'plank-in-trench' techniques and buildings could be larger. Roofs were probably turf or thatched with whatever material could be obtained locally, such as heather.

Droveways and tracks were often set between the fields, linking small settlements 400–800 metres ($\frac{1}{4}$–$\frac{1}{2}$ mile) apart. It is tempting to identify the community along Hayes Lane as one settlement, that along Barkham Street as another and Yhenedon (Evendons), now part of Wokingham Without, a third.

The Saxo-Norman period: a market in Reading

Unlike some periods of political turmoil, in the years following the Norman Conquest pottery was still produced[5]. But in Barkham, only one small rim sherd has been found; this was Saxo-Norman and made of hard black fabric decorated under the rim with three fine lines. Pots could have come from further afield at this time, as a market in Reading had been granted by the reign of Edward the Confessor.

Later mediæval period (post-Norman conquest): pottery and the richer and poorer peasant

Despite the above, there followed a gap of approximately 100 years for which no pottery has been found in Barkham before a comparative glut dating from the late twelfth century. Once again leather and wood must have taken precedence over pottery, for the Domesday Survey of 1086 listed three ploughs in the parish, by now implying quite extensive arable land.

Only better-off peasants with 6 hectares (15 acres) or more, could produce a surplus to sell to provide cash for pots, however comparatively cheap these were[6]. From the Domesday Survey it is known that some of the peasants were smallholders in Barkham who held under 4 hectares (10 acres) of land. When not working on the lord's demesne (the home farm) they had to sell their labour for cash. Income might also be derived from

home-made goods using woodland products, such as baskets, brooms, fencing, hurdles, gates, etc. Such income might be sufficient only for necessities, although pottery was increasingly recognised as such for the safe storage of foodstuffs, sealed with wax to keep them free from mould, dirt and vermin.

The increase in pottery found in Barkham from this period is possibly an indication that more land was ploughed and manured, and that more households used pottery vessels from the late twelfth century onwards.

Two distinct phases can be distinguished in the forms and sources of this pottery. First, the 100 years from the late twelfth to the late thirteenth century. Pottery from this period has been found in eleven fields, including three adjacent to the mediæval moated manor, particularly in Pins and at Bailiff's Cottage. It is not easy to distinguish from what type of vessels these came, but the bases and rims suggest unglazed storage jars

Early Anglo-Saxon house possibly with suspended floor over a hollow

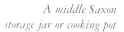

A middle Saxon storage jar or cooking pot

15

A jug, a typical English whiteware vessel which might have come to Barkham via the Thames from a Surrey kiln in the fourteenth century

and jugs. A few were fired in Berkshire kilns at Ashampstead and Maidenhead, and other sherds are similar to those excavated in Newbury, from a kiln or kilns yet to be found.

To reach Barkham, pottery may have been brought by the potters themselves on packhorses and sold from door to door. The Ashampstead potters might have taken theirs by boat via the Thames to Reading, which from 1129, in addition to its market, was granted a 4-day fair.

Second, from the mid-thirteenth to the early sixteenth century, the pottery found in Barkham demonstrates a slight expansion in the number of ploughed fields, including one on the north side of Commonfield Lane, named Inhams which means 'land taken in from waste'. The field in which prehistoric pot was found has also revealed more mediæval pottery than the average. Pins and Bailiff's Cottage have produced pottery from more sources than elsewhere, some unidentified. The majority are white fabric Coarse Border Wares from the mid-thirteenth to the early sixteenth century, made in the Surrey/Hampshire border area where kilns are known in Farnham, Farnborough and Ash. These were domestic vessels: shallow dishes, jugs, storage jars and bowls. Rims were designed with a small lip for covers of fabric, skin or animal gut tied over to keep out dirt and vermin, etc.

Some of the sherds are wide, flat 'strap' handles which bear pairs of stab marks or a feather-shaped pattern. Both decorative and

functional in manufacture for quicker drying, this may have saved the handle from blowing off during firing. Some body sherds have finger-impressed decoration, whilst others are pinched between the thumb and forefinger close to the base to produce greater stability, but the result is decorative. Most vessels were largely unglazed, with a splash thrown across them, as indicated by the remnant of olive-green glaze on seven sherds.

A few pots tempered with flint or limestone, and finewares glazed yellow internally, came from outside the area. Someone in the parish had a taste for, and access to, pottery out of the ordinary.

Vessels were coming from further afield as transport and marketing improved. The ability to carry produce to and from market was vital, for potter and peasant alike[7]. Alongside packhorses, which carried goods in saddle-bags, the use of horses for pulling carts had become more common in the twelfth and thirteenth centuries[7].

Only 2½ miles from Barkham, Wokingham gained a charter in 1219 for a Tuesday market and in 1258 was granted two 3-day fairs, one in June and the other at All Saints'-tide (October/November). The timing was fortuitous as summertime was best for firing pots.

The marketing economy grew through the late thirteenth to the early fourteenth century as a source of supply and exchange for local households at all levels of society. The Manorial accounts for Barkham of

$1276/7^8$ list poultry and eggs, geese, rye, oats, beechmast (for feeding pigs), furze and rushes. Some of these must have gone to market, but pig meat is not included, which suggests that it was the peasants who reared pigs for home consumption. It was not just from the lord's demesne that goods reached market, for the peasants had also developed a strong market orientation by the late thirteenth century[6]. Every type of produce was sold by better-off peasants and perhaps home-made goods by the less-fortunate. To have a supply of cash was becoming much more important for rent and taxes, etc.

This boom in marketing was not to last, for the famines following sheep and cattle plagues in 1313, the failure of harvests due to floods, the Black Death and further bouts of plague in the fourteenth century, resulted in a drastic reduction in population. There was a decline in trade in the later fourteenth and fifteenth centuries and markets became less active. Those in small towns saw something of a recovery only later, in the sixteenth century[6].

Later mediæval period: woodland

The importance of woodland in all periods can hardly be overstated. It was an essential part of the economy[9]. Its products housed and heated rich and poor alike and provided the raw materials for a wide range of other products. Underwood was used for fencing, agricultural equipment, scaffolding, turned cups and bowls. Green wood was used for baskets, hurdles, fencing and for firing brick and pottery kilns. Charcoal was valuable for smelting, oak bark for tanning and wood ash for soap and dyeing. Some bushes, such as holly, were cut for winter feed. Areas of the Forest of Windsor were preserved for deer hunting by the king and aristocracy.

As opposed to established arable fields, clearings, sometimes extensive, in the woodland, were still valuable as meadow or wood pasture (rough grazing) in the later mediæval period, as confirmed by the pollen diagram. A 1331 document[10] describes the value of parts of the woodland *'together with rights of pasturage'*. This document suggests that this was of more value than the underwood. Often this was the only commonland on which animals could be put[9]. Bear Wood (or Common), just to the north, seems to have been typical of this.

There were two fields on the east side of Aggisters Lane (formerly Old Cock, Cook's or Pook's Lane), whose names referred to the term 'agist'. Agistment was the pasturing of cattle in woodland all the year round. Trunks of standard trees in rough pasture might be pollarded or trimmed so that new shoots could grow above the heads of grazing animals, or they might be left protected by a ring of thorns.

Many Barkham field names, such as Wood and Coppice Close, Wood Piece, Coppice Pightle, Wood Piddle, Wood and Coppice Meadow and dating from the mediæval period to the modern, display

Coarse Border Ware: a large vessel with bung-hole, for storing liquid; from Surrey/Hampshire border area; thirteenth to sixteenth century

strong woodland associations. Unsurprisingly, they cling to the edge of known areas of woodland. This is in contrast with other fields, named closes, from earlier clearance and enclosure, which were soon fenced or hedged[11] and scattered across the parish, although some of these are combined with wood names too.

The Domesday description of the woodland in Barkham in 1086, as sufficient *'pannage for 40 pigs'*, was typical of such an expression used in the area to the north and west of London. Pigs were taken into the woodland for a relatively short time in the autumn between mid-September and mid-November, known as the mast months. They were fattened when the acorns, beechmast and sweet chestnuts were ripe. In the 1331 document[10] 15 acres of woodland within a close *'are worth pannage of the same'*. Bears (or Boars) Coppice is resonant of the pannaging of pigs.

In 1331 at least, wood pasture appeared to have been more valuable than the underwood which, overused and inadequately managed, *'scarcely suffices for fencing'*. There was a need for the management and conservation of the common woods to prevent complete clearance. The name green can sometimes be traced to such clearance as Parson's Green, and possibly Green Close, in Barkham suggest.

One of the largest areas of woodland in the centre of the parish, Kidgham Copse, had its edges cleared of trees as some of the field names surrounding it suggest: Coppice Close (there are two of these), Common Close, Coppice Meadow and Ibbs Close. The copse itself was felled and ploughed between 1950 and 1954 as shown on aerial photographs. As its name indicates, prior to this it was at some time managed as coppice. This means the main stem of each tree was removed to near ground level and the young new growths allowed to shoot up in its place. These are cut from the bottom at certain intervals for hurdles, etc.

Later mediæval period: fields and crops

In the post-conquest period, up until the mid-fourteenth century, population numbers rose. The use of wood pasture for grazing declined and assarting (clearance for cultivation) continued apace, especially in north Hampshire and Berkshire[9]. This was serious for smallholders and cottagers, whose pigs pannaged in the woodland and provided ready cash and meat in the winter. Wasteland was also used to increase the amount of arable available, as seen in Barkham. The small area of Inhams fieldwalked contained evidence of Coarse Border Ware which was made from the mid-thirteenth to the early sixteenth century; perhaps this indicates when the intaking was done.

In addition to rye, oats and corn[8], beans were mentioned in the valuation of 1331[10]. The gathering of berries and nuts from hedgerows provided an important addition to the diet.

A drastic reduction in population, reduced pressure on resources and a lack of manpower followed the Black Death. Generally, some fields on unprofitable soil were abandoned and returned to waste; others reverted to woodland. This does not appear to have happened in Inhams as the long sequence of pottery demonstrates.

One crop that was grown from the end of the fourteenth century as animal feed was lucerne, at a time when pasture and animal husbandry became more important as they required less manpower. One field, named Lucerne Piddle, was close to the Old Rectory, formerly the parsonage house.

It is clear from the 1761 Rocque's map that there were many more fields divided by hedges and banks than exist today. Field boundaries sometimes follow the banks of a stream, but others have been created as banks, called lynchets, by ploughing across a slope. One boundary bank at Bailiff's Cottage has been dated by pottery to the late twelfth century. Other field boundaries are narrow holloways bordered by a bank on each side, pedestrian access to fields, presumably to prevent crops from being trampled. These are still hedged, although they have been worn away by foraging cattle and new gateways. Traces of ridge and furrow, and headlands where a team of plough animals were turned can be seen south of Barkham Road. All these lie within the area between Brook Farm, Edney's Hill Farm, Mortimer's Lodge and Bailiff's Cottage.

Later mediæval period: houses and dovecotes

East Berkshire has no natural building stone and oak, elm and to a lesser extent, ash, and perhaps turves, were important as building materials. Before the fifteenth century timber buildings in Barkham were likely to have been single-storey, earth-fast and replaced after about 20–30 years, probably closely adjacent to the footprint of its predecessors. Uniformity of buildings before the later fourteenth century, without social differentiation, allowed flexibility for easy conversion from farm use into a residence. Humans may have lived at one end and the family cow, other animals and poultry at the other.

It takes 60–100 years for an oak to grow to a sufficient height to be used as the main timber in a house[9]. In this area in the twelfth and thirteenth centuries, tie beams had on average to be cut to a length of 4·2 metres (13·8 feet) and in the fourteenth century to 4·7 metres (15·4 feet). It follows that usually it was grown locally and reused, possibly many times. Sawyers probably worked during the winter months when the undergrowth had died down and it was easier to pull timber out of the woods.

Some early timber buildings in Barkham may have been of cruck construction; the frame was made of pairs of long timbers, sometimes curved, either from the ground or some way up the wall, meeting at the ridge and linked with a timber named a ridge-piece. A local example is the barn from the

Swallowfield Road, Arborfield, now in the Chilterns Open Air Museum.

The pegged mortice was first used from the 1180s, after which timber-framed barns, windmills and bridges, etc., could be built. From the thirteenth century fully framed timber buildings could rise to a second or even third storey (in this area usually in towns). They may well have still been earth-fast, although dwarf walls of flint in this area might have been erected.

In rural Barkham, built about 200 years after the first pegged mortice joints, there are houses of some substance, still displaying the technique. They were originally hall houses of three bays with a crosswing at right angles, as at Church Cottages and Sparks Farm where the timber frame is infilled with brick. Inside, these were open to the roof and outside likely to be thatched over a steep roof pitch so that rain ran off it. The hearth was set on the ground and the smoke passed out of the roof via louvres. Chimneys were added later, as was a first floor and sometimes, rather than a ladder for access, a separate stair turret as at Sparks Farm. A kitchen may have been a separate

building with a well or wells dug in between or closely adjacent to the kitchen.

Barns were built in the fifteenth century by peasant landholders, thus representing tenant investment. They were used for the storage of hay, straw, cereals and other crops, and in Barkham the level area to the north of the mediæval manor was certainly used for barns in the late eighteenth century and presumably had precursors.

The name of one field adjacent to the mediæval manor, Culver Croft (culver is Anglo-Saxon for pigeon), suggests that a dovecote or pigeon house might have been built there. From the Norman Conquest, only those of high status were given permission to have dovecotes or pigeon houses, such as the lord of the manor. The chosen position of the structures tended to vary but it was thought that treeless ground gave a clear view for returning birds and away from the trees would be quieter, but at the same time the dovecote needed to be sheltered. The putative dovecote at Barkham could have been within the ditched yard to the east of the moated manor, within sight of the house to prevent pilfering for meat, or falconry. Normally, there was

The interior of an early timber hexagonal dovecote, showing nesting boxes and potence

a step down into the interior so that pigeon droppings collected in the bottom and could be shovelled out as a rich manure for the vegetable garden. Access for the birds was normally at the top of the structure and nesting boxes, sometimes numbered in hundreds or even a thousand and 'L-shaped so that the birds could turn around, were in tiers on the inside. The eggs and young birds for the table were collected by means of a ladder against a pole-like structure called a potence. This could be rotated so that all nest boxes might be reached (see also Chapter 9).

Later mediæval period: moats

There were two moated houses in Barkham. Moats were constructed from the middle of the twelfth century, with a peak in the thirteenth and were still being built in the 1500s. There are well over 5,500 moated sites in Britain, mostly created on clay. Arborfield has one, there are two in Swallowfield and two in Shinfield. Only a few are truly defensive, such as Sheepbridge Court Farm, Swallowfield, whose moat and fish ponds were fed directly from the River Loddon.

The siting of the two moated houses in this parish is very different. One, Church Cottages, is in a fairly central position, but the other is close to the parish boundary. In the thirteenth century it was common for a manor house to be moved from the centre of a village to a more secluded position on the edge as the village grew. Whether this is in anyway relevant to the creation of Biggs's (Butts) Farm is not known. The name

suggests that this was a place where archery was practised.

Many moated sites were built as status symbols but the moat also proved a deterrent to thieves and had the merit of keeping animals from straying too easily. Moats come in all shapes and sizes; the commonest shape is rectangular as are the two in Barkham. Kenny's Farm in Arborfield is 'L-shaped and some are oval like Sheepbridge Court Farm, Swallowfield. Often these sites have associated features such as fish-ponds. The moated site at Church Cottages has a ditched enclosure on the east which was probably a farmyard and latterly an orchard. Very often if there are existing houses on these sites today, there were predecessors, sometimes dating back as early as the Iron Age. Sometimes excavation has demonstrated that a dwelling shared space on the platform with barns and other buildings (see also Chapter 9).

Post-mediæval period (late fifteenth and early sixteenth centuries)

From the early sixteenth century, the beginning of the post-mediæval period, a great deal less pottery has been found across

Border Wares from the late fifteenth and sixteenth century onwards kilns in the Surrey/Hampshire border area: three-legged pipkin and candlestick

the parish. Replacing the Coarse Border Wares are rather finer fabric Border Wares with green glaze (in six fields) and red wares, often also green-glazed (from nine fields). The potential range of vessels is much wider, including candlesticks, pots with lids, pipkins on three legs and so on. Again, these were made at kilns in the Surrey/Hampshire border areas, such as at Farnborough Hill, Hawley, Cove and Ash, but also Oxfordshire and elsewhere. Amongst the small quantity from Barkham is the remains of what was possibly a fine green-glazed white ware vase and one or two rims from storage vessels. The use of metal vessels rather than pottery, particularly during the fourteenth century

and after, may explain in part why the amount of pottery found from this late mediæval period is much less than earlier.

The significance of the apparent absence of pottery for this time in the two fields where it had been found in reasonable quantities for most previous periods is debateable. Both the south-facing field and the one named Pins, have contained a fairly wide variety of wares, although not in comparison with the range found at Bailiff's Cottage. The former field contained pottery dating from prehistory (although not the Saxon period); the latter contained pottery from every period since Roman times. Only a small quantity of red or white Border Ware dating to the sixteenth/seventeenth century has been found from this period in these fields.

Instead, there was rather more in quantity and a wider variety of type of pottery vessel represented in fields to the north of the fieldwalked area than before. The reasons for this could be various, such as a change in agricultural strategy, for instance, a new area of arable due a change of owner or tenant, the need for more pasture on the old arable land, or a fall in population and manpower towards the end of the mediæval period or a combination of these factors.

Border Wares dating from the early sixteenth century

22

HISTORY

David French

Grant of Beorchamme by King Eadred to his Thegn Ælfwine
Description of bounds of land granted

This sind thara threora hida londgemæro to Beorchamme:
These are the land boundaries of the three hides at Barkham:

1. *Ærest of Ceollanwylle and lang rithe to yge to thæs hagan end*;
1. First from Ceolla's spring along the stream to the island to the end of the fenced enclosure;

2. *Thonne andlang hagan to Cnottinga hamme*;
2. Then along the fenced enclosure to the enclosure of the family of Cnotta;

3. *Thonne of Cnottinga hamme forth be wyrtwalan and lang slades to hwitan stane*;
3. Then from the enclosure of the family of Cnotta by the foot of the hill along the valley to the white stone;

4. *Thonne from hwitan stane andlang stræt to loddera stræt*;
4. Then from the white stone along the roadway to the street of the beggars;

5. *Thonne of loddera stræt eft to Ceollanwylle*.
5. Then from the street of the beggars to Ceolla's spring again.

IN CERLEDONE HD.

Rex teñ in dñio Berchehā. Ælmer tenuit de rege
E. Tc 7 m p iii hid. Tr a ê iii cãr. In dñio
c una 7 vi uilli 7 iiii bord cû iii cãr. Ibi v
ãc pti. Silua de XL porc. Valuit iiii lib
T.R.E. 7 m: iii lib.

IN THE HUNDRED OF CHARLTON

The King holds Barkham in demesne. Ælmer held it of King Edward [*the Confessor*]. Then, as now, it was rated for three hides [*c. 360 acres*]. The land is three ploughlands. In demesne there is one ploughland. There are six villeins, four bordars with three ploughs. There are five acres of pasture. Wood for the pasturage of forty hogs. It was worth £4 in the time of King Edward [*1042–1066*], afterwards, and now £3.

Saxon Charter, Domesday and High Mediæval Barkham

Barkham is mentioned in the Domesday survey in 1086, when the manor was held directly by the King[1]. Prior to the Conquest the manor was held by a Saxon thegn called Ælmer from Edward the Confessor. The entry for Barkham (opposite) records that the amount of cultivated land was 3 hides (or ploughlands). A hide was the amount of land which could be ploughed in an agricultural year using one plough with an eight-ox team. The area varied with soil quality and terrain, and could be between 60 and 180 acres. It has been suggested that the local measure was about 120 acres, on which basis there would have been about 360 acres under cultivation in Barkham. Consistently, Domesday records three ploughs at Barkham. The demesne lands (or home farm) of the manor, which probably would have been leased out at this time, were reported as accounting for one ploughland (say 120 acres of cultivated land). The annual tax revenue from the manor was £3, compared with £4 in the time of Edward the Confessor (1042–1066).

Mention should also be made of the grant, in a Saxon charter of 952, of an estate called Beorchamme (birch-tree meadow), which has been identified with Barkham (Bercheham

in the Domesday survey)[2], by King Eadred to his thegn Ælfwine[3]. The grant was of an estate of 3 hides, consistent with the area of arable land in Barkham at the time of Domesday. The boundaries of the Saxon estate, which are described in the 952 charter (opposite)[4], have not been related to any recognisable features in Barkham today, but the bounds described would have related to the approximately 360 acres cleared for cultivation rather than the bounds of the later parish. According to the Chronicle of Abingdon, Ælfwine gave the estate at Beorchamme to the great Benedictine Monastery of Abingdon, but there is no further reference to Beorchamme in the Abbey's records. As in the case of a number of other estates which appear in the Abingdon land-book, it is believed that the Beorchamme title deeds were simply deposited in the monastic cartulary for safe keeping[5].

The landscape of Barkham at the time of Domesday would have been very different from today. Apart from more woodland, the cleared areas would have been dominated by arable farming, producing subsistence crops, following the Saxon system of three large open fields. These were divided into numerous long narrow strips, about 220 yards long and

2 rods (1 rod = 5½ yards) or ox-goads wide (corresponding to half an acre). There were no hedges in the open fields, although the types of corn grown in mediæval times stood about 6 feet tall. Originally the land of both the lord of the manor and his peasant tenants was held in strips scattered throughout the open fields, although in time (through purchases and exchanges) holdings (particularly the lord's) came to be more consolidated, and some land was enclosed in closes (corresponding to the modern field).

In 1086, excluding the lessee of the manor and his household, the population of Barkham comprised six villeins (unfree tenants who had small, scattered landholdings of about 15–30 acres and performed labour services for the lord on his demesne) and four bordars (unfree cottagers who performed fewer labour services for the lord and had smaller holdings ranging from 1 to 10 acres), and their families. It is impossible to project the population of Barkham in 1086 with any certainty, and rates of infant mortality would have been high, but the total number of inhabitants might have been in the region of 50.

The feudal system which predominated following the Norman Conquest was based on social concepts which are wholly alien today. As an unfree tenant, a villein was subject to various duties, restrictions and taxes. A villein was expected to work several times a week on the lord's demesne, plus extra days (boonwork) at specific times such as harvest or ploughing. A villein could not marry (nor could his daughter) without the lord's permission (and the payment of a tax called merchet), nor could he leave the bounds of the manor without permission. The loss of population resulting from the Black Death in 1348/9 put the villein into a better bargaining position and his tenure gradually became copyhold. Other manorial taxes included heriot (the payment on the death of a tenant of the deceased's best beast) and entry fines on succeeding to a holding. In return, a villein had a (scattered) landholding and various rights of common, which in Barkham included the right to graze a fixed number of cattle and pigs on the common pastures, to take hay from the common meadow and to cut turf, peat, furze (gorse), rushes and ferns on the manorial wastes (uncultivated land).

At the time of the Domesday survey, there were only 5 acres of common pasture in Barkham, but the woodland provided pannage sufficient for 40 pigs. Pannage was the common right to let pigs roam in the woodlands, rooting for what food they could and growing fat on acorns and beech-mast in the autumn. The woodland was also a valuable source of timber and fuel for the manorial tenants. In Barkham much of the woodland would have been scrub, and there was also a lot of heathland towards Finchampstead and what is now Nash Grove Lane. Through the centuries areas of woodland, scrub and heath were progressively cleared, enclosed and converted into arable land, a process called assarting, which frequently gave rise to disputes. By the

Statute of Merton in 1235, lords of the manor were permitted to enclose waste lands subject to rights of common of pasture, so long as sufficient common of pasture remained elsewhere for the tenants' livestock.

From an early date the open fields of Barkham were commonly referred to as Barkham Acre or Akery (there is reference to '*le acurheye*' in a 1372 deed)[6]. The largest open field probably lay within a rectangle bounded by the modern Barkham Ride (formerly Heath Lane), Commonfield Lane, Longmoor Bog and Rook's Nest Farm (about 160 acres). Another open field seems to have been between the church and the heathland abutting Nash Grove Lane. There may have been a track from the church towards Nash Grove giving access to the strips in this open field, since the 1738 manorial court of survey[7], and a 1684 indenture[8], mention a gate into the common field behind the church, and nineteenth century maps show an avenue with a dead end after about half a mile[9]. The third open field may have been between Langley Common and the later Barkham Square. (By 1613 only 57 acres of the mediæval open arable fields remained[10].) There was also common pasture in the Coombes and part of Bear Wood (probably for pigs).

In the middle ages a three-course rotation was followed in the open fields to maintain the fertility of the soil. The traditional rotation was wheat or rye in year 1, barley or oats (used for animal feed) in year 2 and fallow in year 3 (when the land was grazed,

and the soil enriched by manure from the cattle). The cultivation of the open fields, the exercise of grazing rights and the cutting of turf were regulated and co-ordinated by the manorial court (Court Baron), and the tenants would have had to share the use of plough and oxen. Ploughing always commenced following Plough Monday, the Monday after Epiphany. One of the tenants would have been appointed reeve; his task was to act as manager of the lord's demesne.

Although about 6,000 mills were recorded by the Domesday survey, there is no record of a mill at Barkham at that time (or subsequently). If so, the inhabitants of Barkham (including the lord) would have had to have their corn ground at the mills owned by the lords of the neighbouring manors of Arborfield (on the Loddon) or Finchampstead. Curiously, the later 1276/7 manorial accounts which survive contain no entries for grinding corn. A later 1589 conveyance of the manors of Arborfield and Barkham contains a reference to two mills, but it is possible both were in Arborfield[11].

The villeins (and freeholders) in Barkham would also have had to comply with various manorial customs (or by-laws). According to the 1738 manorial survey, these included not ploughing up the mere (boundary) banks between the strips in the open fields, not permitting oxen to trample growing corn on neighbours' strips, not cutting branches from growing trees, not taking fish from the ponds in the manor, keeping gripes (ditches) well cleansed, the yoking or ringing of swine and hogs on the manorial wastes and not taking in inmates (lodgers) without the lord's permission. Infringements, which were frequent, were presented (i.e. reported) to the Court Baron and the resultant fines were an important source of regular income for the lord.

The villeins or bordars of Barkham in the high middle ages, and their families, would have lived in dark, smoky, one- or two-roomed cottages, constructed of timber or wattle and daub, with roofs of thatch or turf and earthen floors, often in overcrowded and insanitary conditions. Bread made up the greater part of the diet of the labouring class, supplemented by gruel, probably stewing semi-permanently in a pot over the hearth. Since milk was impure and water was often contaminated, people only drank (generally weak) beer. A family of eight might have been expected to get through about 200 gallons of beer a month. Whilst cheese was regularly consumed, green vegetables and fruit featured only in a small way in the labourer's diet, with a consequent absence of vitamins. Meat consumption was generally small. Only pigs were reared primarily for food. Sheep were for wool and male cattle were for draught purposes. Unfree tenants with only small landholdings would have lived close to subsistence level even in years when harvests were good.

As part of the Royal Forest of Windsor, Barkham was subject to strict forest laws[12]. It was forbidden to kill deer, which were reserved for the King (trespass of venison), or to damage their habitat (trespass of vert). Dogs were lawed or expeditated (i.e. deprived of three claws or the balls of their forefeet) to prevent them from hunting. These laws were harshly enforced in the high middle ages by the itinerant justices of the forest (later superseded by the Swainmote Court of the Bailiwick of Finchampstead, which continued to meet until the late seventeenth century).

No written records survive to tell us specifically what happened in Barkham for nearly two centuries after Domesday, although daily life would have continued much as described above.

4

Late Mediæval Barkham: 1242 to the Black Death (1348/9)

It is not known when Barkham ceased to be part of the King's demesne. Under the feudal system each lord of the manor held from one of about 1,400 intermediate mesne lords (or tenants-in-chief), who owed obligations of military service to the King, which they sub-contracted to their feudal inferiors. According to the *Testa de Nevill*[1], in 1220 the principal landholders in Barkham (one of whom almost certainly was lord of the manor) were Thomas de Berkeham, Robertus de Berkeham and Willelmus Bulloc. Each held 1 carucate of land (corresponding to 1 hide, say 120 acres).

The *Testa de Nevill* also records that in 1242 the mesne lord was Henry de Erly and the lord of the manor was John de Bercham, who held a knight's fee, a feudal tenure whereby the holder was obliged to provide military support to the King, if called upon, by procuring a fully armed knight and his servants for 40 days a year (knight service). It was often commuted to a money payment. A knight's fee corresponded to an amount of land that would support a knight and his family for a year and could vary between 4 and 8 hides (depending on soil conditions). In 1248 the lord of the manor was John de Bercham (son), a well-to-do young man (aged about 21), who had a wife and children.

Property disputes were frequent in the late middle ages and initially were heard by itinerant justices at courts called eyres. The proceedings of the Berkshire Eyre in 1248 have been transcribed and published[2]. There were four disputes that year involving 18 landholders in Barkham concerning property totalling 97 acres. A claim by John, son of Robert of Barkham, against John de Bercham (lord of the manor) for enclosing some wasteland subject to rights of common of pasture was unsuccessful.

John de Bercham and the Robbery in the 'pass' of Alton

In 1248 John de Bercham and John de Bendinges of Winchfield were the ringleaders of a highway robbery in beech woods near Alton, known as the 'pass' of Alton, which were the frequent haunt of outlaws. The victims of the robbery were two wealthy merchants from Brabant, who were robbed of 200 marks (13s. 4d. × 200 = £133 3s. 4d.)[3].

John de Bercham and John de Bendinges were arrested and tried at Reading, but John de Bercham escaped from custody, perhaps to Scotland. He could not, however, avoid being outlawed. Accordingly, his chattels (worth 28 marks) were forfeit to the King and his lands (worth £58. 10s. 4d.) subject to 'year, day and waste'. This was a judicial penalty whereby the King could despoil the property of a malefactor for a year and a day by way of retribution. It is not known how Henry III's officials '*made waste*' John's lands in Barkham, or the consequences for the lord's tenants. It is known, however, that in October 1249 Henry III ordered £40 from the expropriation of the property of the two outlaws in Barkham and Winchfield to be applied towards the cost of building works at Windsor Castle. John's lands were assessed as 2 carucates (approximately 240 acres).

The forfeiture of John de Bercham's lands and chattels caused his wife Alice great deprivation, and in September 1249 the King ordered that she be given 5 quarters of rye and 2 marks. In October 1250 Henry III ordered that she be given £10 to maintain herself and her children. During the forfeiture the living of the chapelry of Barkham became vacant and Henry III presented John de Craunford[4]. John was pardoned by the King twice, at York at Christmas 1251 and at Boulogne in 1254. Why a member of the knightly class should have become involved in organised crime remains a mystery.

The 1276/7 manorial accounts

By the mid-thirteenth century detailed income and expenditure accounts were being drawn up in respect of the lord's demesne lands and manorial payments, reflecting the existence of a developed money-based economy. The cash account of William Bulluc, reeve of Barkham, for 11 months in 1276/7 survives at the Public Record Office[5]. The principal cash crops grown on the lord's demesne at this time were rye and oats, the sale of grain producing £2. 18s. 10¼ d. But cash receipts from manorial rents, taxes, fines and customary payments came to £10. 12s.

The total income was £13. 10s. 10¼ d., against outgoings of £1. 18s. 8½ d. Outgoings included the cost of seed, carriage and purchased labour services (e.g. ploughing and harrowing, reaping and binding, threshing and winnowing). Commutation payments by villeins in Barkham to be excused from working on the lord's demesne (presumably to gain more profit by working elsewhere) totalled

£1. 19s. 8d. (15 % of total income). The accounts show that the demesne lands were directly farmed by the lord of Barkham in 1276/7. They give an incomplete picture, however, since the obligatory labour services performed by the villeins without payment are not recorded, nor is there any record of the quantity of crops produced and used for the lord's own purposes (e.g. oats for animal feed). The accounting profit of £11. 12s. 1¾ d. would have been tied up in animals, crops and grain.

St Thomas of Hereford

By about this time the lordship was held by Thomas Cantilupe, Bishop of Hereford, 1275–1282[6]. Cantilupe was a leading member of the King's Council and frequently travelled from Hereford to London, staying at his own manor houses *en route*. His journeys are well documented, and whilst he stayed regularly at Earley, there is no record of any overnight stay at Barkham. The produce of the demesne lands at Barkham which was not sold for cash was probably transported to Earley. In 1279 Thomas Cantilupe sold the manor of Barkham to his valet, William de Nevill, for £11. 16s.

Cantilupe gained a reputation as a great scholar and a wise and caring bishop. After his death in 1282, miracles were attributed to the inspiration of his piety and he was canonised in 1320. Edward III was present at the canonisation ceremony in 1350. A splendid shrine was built in the Lady Chapel at Hereford Cathedral, and until the reformation it was the second most revered shrine in England after St Thomas à Becket's at Canterbury.

John le Botiller; Agnes de Nevill

By 1293 the lordship had passed into the hands of John le Botiller, who witnessed various land transfers which survive from the 1290s[7]. Between 1315 and 1329 John le Botiller, or a son of the same name, presented five rectors to Barkham church[8]. His first presentation in 1315 was of William de Nevyll, probably a descendant of Thomas Cantilupe's valet of the same name. Initially, the presentation was not accepted by the Bishop of Sarum (i.e. Salisbury), since Nevyll was not properly ordained. Either William did not remain long or he died, since in 1317 John le Palmere was presented to the living.

By the late thirteenth and early fourteenth centuries the limits of sustainable expansion using mediæval farming technology had been reached. Yields may even have fallen and supplies of newly cleared land were dwindling. In many years famine conditions prevailed and there was particularly severe crop failure in 1315–1317 on account of persistent wet weather. We have no record of the effects on the inhabitants of Barkham, which would have been severe.

It appears that the le Botillers and the Nevills were related, and that John le

Botiller held the manor of Barkham under a family settlement, since in 1327 Agnes de Nevill, daughter of Thomas de Nevill (presumably a descendant of William de Nevill, Thomas Cantilupe's valet), claimed that John le Botiller was unlawfully detaining title deeds and was felling oak trees in the woods of the manor of Barkham to the detriment of her reversionary interest[9]. A jury of local inhabitants (including John de Kyngesmull and the rector of Arborfield) found that John le Botiller had unlawfully felled 50 oak trees and the court awarded ownership of the woodland (200 acres) to Agnes de Nevill.

Following the death of John le Botiller in 1330, his sons Philip and Henry sued Agnes de Nevill and the 1328 jurymen at the Berkshire Assizes for wrongful dispossession[10]. The court upheld Philip and Henry's claim, whereupon they immediately sold the manor and advowson (the right to present the rector) to John Mautravers junior[11].

John Mautravers; 1331 manorial inventory

Mautravers was a wealthy adventurer in the service of the King, who was made a knight in 1306. The family seat was at Lytchett Mautravers in Dorset, and Mautravers owned extensive estates throughout south-west England. In 1330 he was summoned to Parliament by Edward III as Lord Mautravers[12].

Later in 1330 Mautravers was implicated in the judicial murder of Edward III's uncle, Edmund, Earl of Kent. Mautravers was sentenced by Parliament to hanging and beheading, but he escaped to Germany. Mautravers' property was forfeit to the Crown, and Robert Bullock, lord of the manor of Arborfield, was appointed King's reeve to administer the manor of Barkham on behalf of Edward III[13]. In 1334 the living of Barkham became vacant and Edward III presented Thomas de Babynton as rector[14].

The inventory which was taken of the manor of Barkham in 1331 following its forfeiture from John Mautravers survives at the Public Record Office[15]. This records that in 1331 the lord's demesne lands were about 117 acres, of which 70 acres were arable. It also itemises the customary payments which used to be made by the villeins to the lord of Barkham, such as 10 cocks and 10 hens worth 2s. 1d. on the Feast of St Martin (11th November), 8 quarters and 7 bushels of oats ($1\frac{1}{4}$ tons) worth 8s. $10\frac{1}{2}$ d. on the Feast of the Purification of the Blessed Virgin Mary (2nd February) and 4 score and 10 eggs worth $4\frac{1}{2}$ d. at Easter.

The 1331 inventory does not refer to the contents of the mediæval manor house (probably because it was rented out), but Mautravers (through his officials) directly farmed the demesne lands, and the farm animals (including eight oxen), grain and growing crops were valued at £24. 17s. 7d. Curiously, the inventory records the presence of two very large barrels of wine containing

378 gallons, worth £5 (equivalent to the value of 10 oxen or 25 bullocks). A possible explanation is that the wine was in transit from Gascony to one of Mautravers' principal residences further west, since the upper classes apparently drank immense quantities of wine. There were also over 12 tons of small oats, rye and mixed corn, worth £7. 19s. 8d., in the lord's barns.

The Black Death (1348/9)

The Black Death was perhaps the most significant event to affect Barkham since the Norman Conquest. Every aspect of life was deeply affected by the dramatic loss of population. Whilst there are no surviving records of the effect of the plague in Barkham, it is likely that between one-fifth and one-half of the inhabitants would have died. The sudden relief of population pressure altered the balance of power between lords and villeins. Tenants and villein labour became difficult to secure and an increasing number of lords turned to leasing out their demesne lands for a fixed income.

It seems that Barkham may have been used as a timber depot in connection with the rebuilding of Westminster Abbey, since in 1352 Edward III engaged Laurence de Gotham to transport timber from Barkham and surrounding parts of the Royal Forest of Windsor by land to Oakley Green and thence by river to Westminster Abbey, and *'for the King's money to be paid at the said town of Berkham'*[16]. The timber was apparently used for the roof of the choir.

Curiously, the surviving accounts of the beating of the bounds in 1738 and 1770 (see Appendix II) refer to a boundary mark near Rooks Nest Farm *'where a man was killed and buried by the inhabitants of Barkham'*. Perhaps this refers to a mediæval lynching, the circumstances of which had long been forgotten even in the eighteenth century[17].

5 St James' Church, Part I (1220–1700)

Mediæval era: the first church

It is not known when there was first a place of worship at Barkham, or whether it was on the same site as the subsequent parish church. No church or chapel is recorded in the Domesday survey, but at this time much of the country was still covered by the Anglo-Saxon system of large district parishes (*parochiae*), with the needs of individual communities served by priests from an important central church (or minster). It seems Barkham was in the *parochia* of Sonning.

1343 presentation of John de Insula as rector

The first evidence of a resident priest (and by implication the existence of a place of worship) at Barkham, whose population at the time was probably little more than 100, was in 1220, when William de Wenda, Dean of Salisbury, held a visitation at Sonning[1]. It was reported that the incumbent of the then wooden chapel at Arborfield (described as being in a ruinous state) was John, rector of Barkham, who had appointed a chaplain called Henry at Arborfield. Henry lived with John at Barkham and received a stipend of 20s. a year. It is not known when John became rector of Barkham, but he claimed that he had been presented to the living of Arborfield in 1190 by Osmund Bulloc of Arborfield.

Neither the Dean's visit to Sonning and its dependent chapels in 1220, nor his next visitation at Sonning in 1222, included Barkham, probably because the Dean appears to have concentrated on visiting those parishes subject to the Dean's, rather than the Bishop's, jurisdiction (known as peculiars).

The next surviving reference to a parish priest at Barkham is in 1249, when the property of the lord of the manor, John de

Bercham, was forfeit to the crown on account of his complicity in a highway robbery in woods near Alton. The rectory of Barkham became vacant during the forfeiture and John de Craunford was presented to the living by Henry III[2].

In the preceding year, 1248, a dispute concerning property at Barkham came before the justices itinerant at the Berkshire Eyre, and there is reference in the roll and writ file to a deacon called Thomas de Bercham[3]. It is possible that Thomas was John de Craunford's predecessor.

There is no further reference to a parish priest at Barkham until 1315, although the registers of the Bishops of Sarum survive from 1297. Nor is there any reference to Barkham in the Papal tax return of 1291, detailing liability to Peter's Pence, although there is reference to the chapel at Arborfield. Whilst there seems to have been a place of worship at Barkham in the thirteenth century, it was most likely no more than a wooden chapel (probably undedicated), and may originally have been built as a private chapel for the lord of the manor.

During the period 1315–1329, when Roger Martival was Bishop of Sarum, the presentation of five rectors is recorded[4], indicating that by then there was a permanent church at Barkham, dedicated to St James the Apostle, which may have been built by the then lord of the manor, John le Botiller. If a permanent church was not built until the early 1300s, this may explain why, although the church was adjacent to the mediæval

manor house, the rectory and glebe land (18 acres) were some distance away (on the edge of the Coombes).

In addition to manorial taxes (as discussed in Chapter 3), inhabitants were also liable to pay taxes in kind to the church (known as tythes) for the rector's personal benefit. Tythes were the tenth part of the crops and garden produce grown by every parishioner, as well as every tenth young animal born.

The stonework in the mediæval church would have been gaily painted in bright colours, whilst on the walls would have been primitive paintings of biblical scenes and, perhaps, devils. The surviving early nineteenth century drawings of the old church indicate that there was a sundial on the porch over the south door, but whether this was a mediæval scratch dial engraved on stone or a later metal plate is impossible to say.

In the middle ages the church and churchyard were the focal point of parish life. At this time the only part of the church which was consecrated was the chancel, so the nave would have been used for all sorts of secular activities, like a modern village hall. Many festivities also took place on the north side of the churchyard, which was likewise unconsecrated. For many centuries, perhaps up to the eighteenth century, the north side of the churchyard would have been used for playing various games, even on Sundays, of which the most popular was probably fives[5].

Even if Barkham was too small to have its own company of players (like Finchampstead), visiting players would have performed traditional plays, either in the churchyard (on the north side) or, in the event of inclement weather, in the nave. A regular favourite was *Robin Hood and Maid Marian*, during which Robin Hood and his merry men collected '*Roben Hode money*' from the crowd to cover the cost of costumes (and ale for the players)[6].

Tudor era: the Reformation

Parish life, which revolved around saints (or feast) days, continued largely unchanged from Norman times until the Reformation, initiated by the repudiation by Henry VIII (1509–1547) of the authority of the Pope in 1534. There followed a period of great religious upheaval from the 1530s to the 1560s. Whilst Reading Abbey was not a landowner in the parish, the dissolution of one of the wealthiest abbeys in the land and the public execution at Reading of the last abbot in 1539 must have had a major impact in the locality.

During the reign of Edward VI (1547–1553) England became increasingly protestant and various catholic practices were outlawed as being superstitious or idolatrous. A new prayer book was promulgated in 1549, and another more radical in 1552. A consequence of the simpler forms of worship which were imposed was that any ornamental church goods, surplus church plate (e.g. a second chalice) and vestments were to be confiscated and sold. Even the church bells, with the exception of the '*greatt bell*', were to be sold

for the value of their metal. This policy was reversed when the catholic Mary I (1553–1558) came to the throne, although Elizabeth I (1558–1603) subsequently imposed a moderate Protestant settlement which did not exclude vestments and ornaments.

It is not known to what extent Barkham's church goods were despoiled by Edward VI's commissioners, but it is probably not without significance that in 1557 the lord of the manor, Thomas Bullock of Arborfield, bequeathed to Barkham church a pair of white satin vestments, embroidered with a cross of red velvet[7]. In 1558 Edward Ball, yeoman, left 5s. to buy a processional cross[8], and John Wilson, yeoman, left 12d. for the rood light[9]. Likewise, it may be significant that the oldest surviving church plate is a silver chalice (7 inches high), which bears a 1566 hallmark, although the donor is unknown.

The incumbent throughout these testing times was John Langridge (rector 1533–1569). As one of the handful of persons in the parish who was literate, he was the scribe of many Barkham wills and was asked to witness many more. Langridge's successor was Thomas White (rector 1569–1596).

Barkham is fortunate that its parish registers commence in 1539, when registers were first required to be kept by Henry VIII's chief minister, Thomas Cromwell, and that the registers, apart from marriages between 1733 and 1812, survive virtually complete. The registers are now in the safe-keeping of the Berkshire Record Office, where indexed transcripts are available up to 1812[10].

Church house, the parish poor house

In Tudor times most parishes would have had a church house close to the church, the purpose of which was to raise money for the upkeep of the church, and subsequently poor relief, through an annual event called a Whitsun (or church) ale.

In 1574 the lord of the manor, another Thomas Bullock of Arborfield, gave half an acre of land near Barkham church, adjoining Kidgham Lane (which survives as a footpath), for the building of a church house[11]. This would have been a two-storey thatched building, with equipment for brewing and baking downstairs, and a large room upstairs for the festivities (which would have included singing and dancing), furnished with trestle tables and forms (benches), with a stock of drinking vessels and trenchers (wooden plates). Wheat, malt and barley would have been collected from each household for the event and there would have been an entry charge for church funds of 1d. or 2d.[12].

Church ales became less common after 1598 when the need for fund raising was largely superseded by the introduction of the poor rate. Church ales were also condemned by the Puritans as encouraging drunkenness and unruly behaviour and they were abolished by Parliament in 1640.

Barkham still had a church house in 1689 when, according to the dispute about church rates recounted below, the tiling and thatching *'wanted very much repaireing'* and the chimney was *'ready to fall'*[13]. The building was occupied by a *'poore man'* to whom the churchwardens apparently gave the income of 4 nobles (1 noble = 6s. 8d.) a year otherwise derived from the church house. The building was still standing at the time of the manorial court of survey in 1738, and the horse bridge over Barkham Brook in Barkham Street is referred to as Church House Bridge[14].

The church house became the parish poor house and this is probably the origin of Brook Cottage, once four semi-detached cottages for *'the reception of the poor'*, which is on the same site as the old church house. In 1782 the Revd David Davies noted there were 15 poor folk living there[15].

Stuart era: the Puritans

From time to time incumbents were required to make an inventory of church

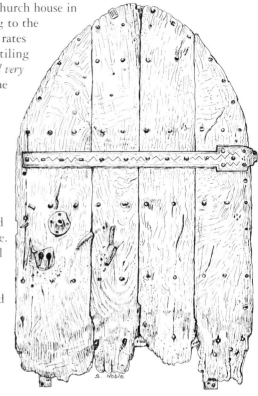

A door reputedly from the old church (demolished 1859), now in the church porch

property (called a terrier) for the bishop. The first surviving inventory dates from 1603[16] when Richard Windeatt had just been presented as rector by Edmond Standen. He was to remain 29 years. In 1632 Windeatt was given leave of absence for change of air owing to ill health[17] and he died the following year.

Windeatt was succeeded as rector of Barkham in 1633 by Stephen Rose (aged 29), who was presented by William Standen. The following year, 1634, Rose drew up the following inventory of church property[18]:

'Inprimis the Parsonage house and Ten acres of arable land, seven of pasture and one of meadow to the same belonging.
Item the Churchhouse and halfe an acre of land therevnto belonging.
Item all manner of tythe Corne, woll, lambe, Cheese, duckes, geese, pigs, &c with all other accustomed dues'.

The Standens also owned the lordship and advowson of Arborfield, and when that living became vacant in 1640, Rose was also appointed rector of Arborfield. The identity of the rector of Barkham during the Civil War (1642–1646) and the interregnum (1649–1660) is unclear. There are no surviving records to tell us how long Stephen Rose remained as the incumbent, or whether he was forced out of the living for political reasons.

There is an entry in the parish registers in 1653 recording the appointment of Robert Williams of Barkham as Parish Register (a civil official to whom Parliament transferred the custody of parish registers)[19], signed *'per me Ri: Bigg:'*. Since Bigg was not a local name, it is possible that Richard Bigg was rector of Barkham during the interregnum.

Upon the restoration of the monarchy in 1660, Alexander Stokes (aged 40) was presented as rector of both Barkham and Arborfield by William Standen and his kinsman William Ball. He was to remain 34 years. At the time of the surviving hearth tax returns (1662–1664), Stokes resided at Barkham, and there were four fireplaces at the parsonage house[20]. Stokes subsequently took up residence at Arborfield and the Barkham parsonage was let to Richard Clements.

During Stokes' incumbency the parish church was allowed to become *'very ruinous'*. By 1689 the walls on the south side were close to collapse and the pews had to be moved to prop up the walls. Also the pews on the south side had been mended so many times, and had rotten feet, that they had become beyond repair. The roof leaked so that *'the wind and weather did beate in through the same and rained through upon the seates'*. The steeple had become so dangerous that *'the Ringers oftentimes w.ᵗʰin the time aforesd. [20 years] have been forced to let goe the Ropes and run out from und.ʳ the said Steeple for fear of its falling'*.

Eventually, in 1689, the churchwardens authorised comprehensive repairs and levied a rate of £36. 9s. to meet the cost. But four leading yeomen, including Thomas Simonds (father of Alice Allwright), refused to pay their assessments (amounting to £11. 0s. 6d.) on the grounds that the churchwardens had spent at least twice as much as was necessary, making unnecessary alterations to the seating and a door, and employing two joiners from Wokingham instead of a local carpenter.

The four were prosecuted at the Archdeaconry Court[21], at which it was also alleged that one of the churchwardens, Richard Heyford, had pulled down a *'very beautifull Crofse'* from the top of the steeple *'as a Relict of Popery'* and replaced it by a weather cock at a cost of 20s., and that he had also removed some of the wooden boards from the steeple *'and haft made a Swine Pen with them'*.

In 1694 John Sale (aged 24) was presented as rector of Arborfield and Barkham[22] and was to remain 45 years until his death. Sale was presented, not by the lord of the manor, Edward Standen, but by Samuel Sale, merchant, to whom the right to make the next presentation appears to have been leased by Edward Standen.

Seating arrangements in church sometimes gave rise to disputes. In 1688–1707 there was a long-running dispute in the Archdeaconry Court over the entitlement to sit in a pew between John Webb senior and

John Webb junior and Scory Barker, who had purchased Butts Farm, a moated homestead (subsequently called Biggs's Farm) which now lies under Arborfield Garrison, from Richard Booth[23].

In 1706 John Webb senior was presented (i.e. reported) to the church authorities for *'breaking up two seats about the middle of the church to bury his wife and for refusing to pay 6s. 8d. for the same which is payable according to custom'*[24]. There is, however, no record of a burial in the parish register.

Drawing of old church by H.W. Burt, 1835

6 The Kingsmill Family: Langley Pond (or Hewett's) Farm

Kingsmill coat of arms

The Kingsmills were an influential family in mid-Berkshire and North Hampshire from the thirteenth century onwards. Their principal Berkshire estates centred on Arborfield Cross, lying in the Liberty of Newland (in the parish of Hurst), Arborfield and Barkham. The land in the parish of Barkham, although only 3 acres, included the site of the present Langley Pond Farm.

Langley Pond Farm is a timber-framed house, with moulded beams, dating from the late sixteenth century, and has since been substantially altered. One large late sixteenth century flank chimney survives, as does a tudor rose carved on a beam.

There are surviving records of property transactions and family settlements by six successive generations of Kingsmills living in Barkham, beginning with John de Kyngesmulle in 1327, and his son Adam in 1337, until the mid-1400s, when William and Joan Kyngesmyll were living at Barkham[1]. Since the family held only three acres in Barkham, this suggests that Langley Pond Farm may have been built on the site of an earlier 'high status' building. Later in the fifteenth century one of their

sons, Richard, who was born at Barkham, became a wealthy citizen of Basingstoke. Richard Kyngesmyll's eldest son, John, became a Justice of the Court of Common Pleas, the first of a number of distinguished lawyers produced by the family. John Kyngesmyll's daughter, Alice, married Thomas Bullock (lord of the manors of Arborfield and Barkham from at least 1514 until his death in 1558).

Sir John Kingsmill, son of the judge, was one of the royal commissioners during the dissolution of the monasteries in the 1530s, and was rewarded with extensive estates in North Hampshire, including the manor of Sydmonton (previously held by Romsey Abbey), which became the family seat. The Berkshire estates had in any event been declining in significance.

The farmstead devolved with the rest of the Kingsmill estates through successive family settlements or resettlements. The names of earlier tenants are unknown, except that in 1608 the property was leased to Francis Norman, yeoman, for 21 years at an annual rent of £36. 6s. 8d[2].

When Francis Norman died in 1627, he was survived by his second wife, Elizabeth, and a married daughter, Joan. He was a substantial yeoman, since his probate inventory totalled £85. 1s. 0d. Not only does the inventory contain an itemised list of all his possessions (even kitchen utensils), but it also lists the rooms in the farmhouse: kitchen, buttery, old hall, great loft, loft over the entrie, parlour, chamber over the hall, privie chamber, well house and old kitchen[3].

The references to the old hall, old kitchen and great loft support the suggestion that Langley Pond Farm may have been built on the site of an earlier building, probably an open hall house. In a 1610 family settlement, which is more detailed than earlier surviving deeds, the building is referred to as a capital messuage or mansion, which may derive from a description of the earlier building (and in some later deeds it is sometimes erroneously referred to as the manor of Barcome).

When Sir William Kingsmill of Sydmonton died in 1698, the estates passed to his eldest son, William, who was insane all his adult life. Sir William was survived by his second wife, Dame Rebecca. Their daughter, Penelope, married the Revd John Waterman, son and heir of William Waterman I (lord of the manor of Barkham 1700–1733). The marriage may have been the reason for the gift of a silver flagon to Barkham church by Dame Rebecca in 1720.

At the time of the manorial court of survey in 1738, the property was called Langley Farm and the tenant was George Saunders[4]. He does not seem to have stayed long, since

the only other surviving references to Saunders are as tythingman (i.e. constable) of Barkham in 1737 and 1738[5]. A subsequent tenant was a farmer called Robert Cook. Following Cook's tenancy, the farm was leased in 1756 to Millington Burgess for a term of 14 years at an annual rent of £90[6]. At the end of the lease in 1770, when Burgess was 62, there was an auction of his cattle and equipment[7]. Burgess lived to be 91.

Reading Mercury, 15 October 1770

TO be Sold by AUCTION, by George Tucker, on Wednesday the 17th Instant at Barkham in the County of Berks, All the Stock of Cattle and Implements of Husbandry, of MILLINGTON BURGESS, Farmer, Consisting of Horses, Cows, Sheep, and Hogs, Waggons, Ploughs, Carts, Harrows, Drags, Roll and other Things in the Husbandry Business. The Sale to begin at Nine o'Clock in the Forenoon.

In 1766 William Kingsmill (lunatic) died (aged 81) without issue and the Kingsmill estates were divided between his two nieces, Elizabeth Brice (a dwarf), the wife of Robert Brice (who became Admiral Sir Robert Brice Kingsmill Bart.), 25 years her junior, and Rebecca Osgood, daughter of the Revd John and Penelope Waterman, and wife of Lawrence Head Osgood, sometime lessee of Barkham Manor (see Chapter 12)[8].

The Berkshire estates were allocated to Robert and Elizabeth Brice, who immediately sold Langley Farm to Sir Thomas Fludyer, a London merchant and brother of Sir Samuel Fludyer Bart., Lord

Langley Pond Farm

found it necessary to advertise in the *Reading Mercury* when animals were stolen or strayed. In 1813 one Charles Dormer killed, and carried away, a fat sheep belonging to Hewett, for which he was sentenced to death, although he was reprieved[13]. One of Hewett's activities was the fattening of up to 300 hogs a year with barley, peas and beans, which attracted favourable comment in Mavor's *General View of the Agriculture of Berkshire* in 1809[14]. Hewett was also parish tax collector.

Among other things, Robert Hewett cultivated the glebe land (18 acres) for the Revd David Davies (rector 1782–1819), negotiating the sale of crops and the purchase of livestock on the rector's behalf. Hewett also served as churchwarden during much of Davies' incumbency. The records of David Davies' dealings with Farmer Hewett in the early 1790s survive and the accounts may be seen at Nuffield College, Oxford[15]. The two men were to become good friends, and when David Davies died in 1819, he thanked Robert Hewett in his will for his support and left him his cows and most of his wine[16].

An auction of '*capital live & dead farming stock*' (i.e. animals and equipment) was held at the farm in April 1831 on account of Robert Hewett (aged 75) '*declining the Farming Business*'. But it appears Hewett was a victim of the depressed agricultural conditions in the 1820s, which culminated in three successive wet summers and poor harvests at the end of the decade, since later

Mayor of London in 1762[9]. Sir Thomas Fludyer was MP for Bedwyn (1767–1768), and for Chippenham (1768–1769). When Sir Thomas died in 1769, Langley Farm descended to his nephew, Sir Samuel Brudenell Fludyer Bart. of Felixstowe, MP for Aldborough (1781–1784)[10].

By 1782 Langley Farm had been leased to Robert Hewett[11], whose family were to continue as tenants until 1903, by which time the farm had long been called Hewett's Farm. Robert Hewett appears to have been an enterprising farmer and he leased a substantial amount of land from other landowners, making him the second largest farmer in the parish by 1793. He was also deputed gamekeeper by the lord of the manor, Lieutenant General John Leveson Gower, from whom he leased a further 178 acres in 1802[12]. From time to time he in the same month a notice in the *Reading Mercury* requested Hewett's creditors to state their claims. It seems Hewett managed to avoid bankruptcy, however, since an intended auction the following year of all his household furniture and remaining farming stock did not go ahead[17].

When Robert Hewett died (aged 82) in 1838 (his wife, Hannah, predeceased him in 1829), he was succeeded by his eldest son, Edward (52), who died in 1877 (aged 92). Edward's daughters, Kitty and Mary, who never married, enjoyed similar longevity and died in 1899 (aged 85) and 1902 (aged 86), respectively[18].

When the Hewett's landlord, Sir Samuel Brudenell Fludyer Bart., died in 1833, the family estates passed to his son, also Samuel (who was subsequently declared of unsound mind)[19]. On the latter's death, unmarried, in 1876, the family estates descended to his cousin, the Revd Sir John Henry Fludyer Bart. of Ayston Hall, Rutland. His son, Sir Arthur, succeeded on the death of his father (aged 93) in 1896[20], and in 1903 Hewett's Farm was sold to Arthur Fraser Walter and became part of the Bear Wood estate.

Edward Hewett's grandson, Robert, who did not live in the parish, relinquished the tenancy of the farm about the same time, and Percy and Frederick Brooks of Earley took a lease of the farm[21]. In 1913 the farm was sold to Jonas Issac, whose son Wade farmed the land and lived in the house with his sister for many years before the farmhouse with 100 acres was bought by Mrs Betty Simonds, widow of John Hayes Simonds, in 1957. Mrs Simonds was a great benefactress of the Arborfield, Newland and Barkham C.E. School. The property is a grade 2 listed building and is now two private residences.

Reading Mercury,
6 March 1797

TIMBER.—BERKS.

To be SOLD by AUCTION,
By Mr. HAWKES,

On Thursday, March the 16th, 1797, at two o'clock in the afternoon, on the premises, in two Lots,

A considerable quantity of useful and valuable OAK TIMBER, now standing and growing on Mr. Robert Hewett's farm, at BARKHAM, near WOKINGHAM, the greater part of which is fit for shipbuilding.

LOT I. EIGHTY-ONE OAK TREES, marked 1.
LOT II. SEVENTY DITTO, marked ✗.

Mr. Hewett, of Barkham, will shew the same, of whom particulars and conditions of sale may be had, and of Mr. James Simonds, and Mr. Hawkes, Reading

To be sold, A TROOP HORSE.

7 Lordship of Barkham 1330–1589; The Bullock Family

The sale of the manor of Barkham by Philip and Henry le Botiller to John Mautravers in 1330 (see chapter 4) had been disputed by Agnes de Nevill, through legal proceedings (called an assize of novel disseisin) commenced before the forfeiture of John Mautravers' property, and Agnes recovered title to the manor and a carucate of land (approximately 120 acres, consistent with the 1331 valuation) under a judgment in 1334[1]. Agnes de Nevill is reputed to have married Gilbert Bullock, son of Robert Bullock, lord of Arborfield, and so the manor of Barkham passed into the younger line of the Bullock family[2] (since Gilbert Bullock was not Robert Bullock's eldest son, another Robert). In 1343 Gilbert Bullock presented John de Insula as new rector to Barkham church[3]. The wooden effigy in the church porch of a recumbent lady in a long, loose dress and linen head-dress is reputed to be an effigy of Agnes de Nevill (see Chapter 17). The lordship of Barkham was to remain in the Bullock family until 1589[4].

Agnes de Nevill and Gilbert Bullock may have died without male heirs, perhaps as a consequence of the Black Death, since in 1368, when Agnes Mautravers, widow of John Mautravers, unsuccessfully claimed rights of dower (or widow's thirds) over the manor of Barkham, the lordship was in the hands of Thomas Ganefeld and Agnes his wife for the term of Agnes' life under a

Wooden effigy of Agnes de Nevill in parish church

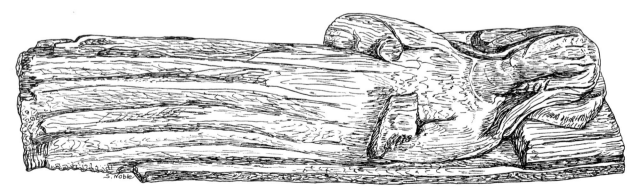

S. Noble

family settlement, the reversion being held by John Bullokes[5]. Agnes Ganefeld may have been the daughter and heir of Agnes de Nevill and Gilbert Bullock, or the sister of either. There are also references to Thomas Ganefeld in 1362 and 1372. Coincidentally, a Henry Ganefeld was rector of Barkham about this time until his death in 1396[6]. There is no record of whether John Bullokes became lord of Barkham, but by 1391 the lordship was in the hands of another Gilbert Bullock (who could have been his son)[7] who lived until at least 1415.

Gilbert Bullock was succeeded as lord of Barkham by his son Thomas Bullock, who in 1419 presented Walter Bosum as rector to Barkham church[8]. Meanwhile, in 1405 Robert Bullock *tertius*, lord of the manor of Arborfield for at least 40 years, died without male heirs and the lordship of Arborfield passed to his daughter and heir Margaret, and her husband John Hertyngdon, for the term of Margaret's life under a family settlement[9]. In 1418/21 the reversion to the lordship of Arborfield was conveyed to Thomas Bullock of Barkham and his wife Alice[10], so that when Margaret Hertyngdon died, Thomas Bullock became lord of both manors, thereby uniting the two branches of the family. There survives at the Berkshire Record Office a 1429 deed whereby the manor of Barkham was conveyed by family trustees to Thomas Bullock absolutely[11].

Although Thomas Bullock (or a son of the same name) remained lord of Arborfield until 1463, a Robert Bullock was lord of the manor of Barkham from at least 1444, when he presented John Everdon to the rectory of Barkham[12]. Robert Bullock appears to have died between 1483 and 1489, when his widow, Eleanor, presented John Hawkyns as rector to Barkham church[13], presumably as part of her widow's thirds (or rights of dower).

The identity of the lord of Barkham after Eleanor Bullokys' death, and of the lord of Arborfield after Thomas Bullock's decease in 1463, is unclear, on account of the paucity of surviving records, but by 1502 Gilbert Bullock was lord of both manors. The 1566 *Heralds' Visitation of Berkshire*[14] says that Gilbert was the son of Robert (who married Eleanor), who was the son of Thomas (died 1463) and his wife Alice Yeadinge, suggesting that Thomas Bullock granted his son and heir, Robert, a life tenancy of the manor of Barkham before 1444 in anticipation of his inheritance. There are several inconsistencies in the surviving documents relating to this period, and another son, Richard, may have held an interest in Arborfield manor after Thomas Bullock's death[15].

In mediæval and Tudor times the manor house was located on the moated site adjacent to the parish church. This would have been the residence of the Bullocks as lords of Barkham until the lordships of Barkham and Arborfield were in the same hands, when the head of the family resided at Arborfield (as the more substantial manor). It is possible that the surviving building was

Bullock coat of arms

built (or rebuilt) as a dower house for Eleanor Bullock in the mid-1480s. Following Eleanor's death, Arborfield became the permanent seat of the Bullocks and the manor house at Barkham was let as a farm to a succession of tenants (family and non-family), as recounted in Chapter 9.

Little is known about Gilbert Bullock, except that he presented Robert Towneshend to the rectory of Barkham in 1504[16] and married Margaret, daughter of Sir William Norris of Bray. By 1514 Gilbert Bullock had died and had been succeeded by his son Thomas (who presented Thomas Hornby to the rectory of Barkham in that year)[17] who remained lord of the manors of Arborfield and Barkham until his death in 1558. He married Alice, daughter of John Kingsmill, one of the justices of the Common Pleas (whose estates included Langley Pond Farm in Barkham, where his father, Richard Kingsmill, had been born).

Thomas Bullock was a minor member of Henry VIII's household and he appears in a list of the Royal Household in 1516 as one of the Gentlemen Ushers Extraordinary[18]. Thomas Bullock served the Crown in a number of capacities. In 1518 and 1528 he was Escheator (an agent of the Crown) of the counties of Oxon and Berks[19], and he was also appointed a tax commissioner for Berkshire several times. In 1544 Thomas Bullock was amongst the nobles and gentry who supplied men and horses to Henry VIII for the war with France[20]. Thomas Bullock's contingent consisted of '*archers eight, and*

billmen thirteen', in all probability recruited amongst his tenants in Arborfield and Barkham.

In 1517 a government commission enquiring into private enclosures noted that Thomas Bullock had enclosed 100 acres of arable land in Barkham, displacing one messuage and eight persons[21]. If converted to pasture for sheep, this would have removed from tillage a significant proportion of the cultivated land in the 1,362-acre parish, much of which comprised heath, scrub or woodland. (Indeed, by 1613, only 57 acres of the mediæval open arable fields remained.[22]) A list of heads of household liable to pay taxes survives from 1524/5[23], which lists 24 taxpayers, suggesting that the population of Barkham at the time was in the region of 110.

Thomas Bullock died in 1558 and his son Richard succeeded to the two manors. Little is known about Richard Bullock, except that he and his wife, Alice, had a large number of children. When Richard Bullock died in 1570, his son Thomas succeeded to the manors of Arborfield and Barkham. In 1581 Thomas was Escheator of Oxon and Berks, and he also served as High Sheriff of Berkshire in 1581/2. He married Dorothy, daughter of Sir William Forster of Aldermaston. A heavy accumulation of debts forced Thomas Bullock to sell the two manors for £4,000 in 1589, thereby causing the demise of the Bullock family fortunes (see Chapter 13).

8 Sparks Farm (Fawsbyes)

Sparks Farm, adjacent to The Bull, is one of two surviving late fifteenth century timber-framed open hall houses in the parish. Until the early nineteenth century the property was called Fawsbyes, which may have been the name of the original owners.

Originally, the central section of the house would have been open to the rafters, where the smoke from the open hearth would have escaped through a louvre door in the thatched roof, since there was no chimney. With the development of chimneys, the open hall would have been chambered over, possibly in the second half of the sixteenth century.

The first known occupier of '*ffausbyes*' was John Hedger, husbandman, who died in 1576. His sparse possessions, typical of the time, are itemised in his probate inventory, which totalled £28. 12s. 2d. In the hall (i.e. living room) the furniture comprised '*one table one forme A payre of tressels & one cubbard ij old chayres one joyne*[d] *stoole*' worth 5s., whilst by way of kitchen equipment there were '*one Bolle* [bowl] *iij tubbes ij Buckets one chesepres w.*th *chesefates & other treen* [wooden] *dishes*' worth 2s. 8d. The farm animals included two oxen called Kempe and Pert[1].

John Hedger was a tenant farmer and

the freeholder was William Pigott, who died in 1578, leaving Fawsbyes to his wife, Margaret, until their son, also William, attained the age of 21[2]. In the burial register, William Pigott is described as '*servant to Mr Bullock*', suggesting he may have been the lord's bailiff[3].

Margaret Pigott (widow) later married Richard Holloway, a substantial yeoman. When William Pigott the younger came of age in 1592, he settled Fawsbyes first on himself and his heirs or, if he died without issue, on one of his half-brothers, John Holloway. William Pigott the younger then

Extract from 1576 probate inventory of John Hedger

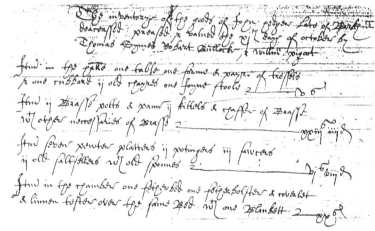

joined the army and went to Ireland, never to be heard of again. Consequently the property passed to John Holloway.

Following the death of his father, Richard, in 1619, John Holloway was sued in the Court of Chancery by Bridget Westbrook (née Bullock), who had been one of the residuary devisees of Fawsbyes mentioned in William Pigott's will in 1578, for the recovery of Fawsbyes[4].

Bridget Westbrook alleged that Richard Holloway had effectively sent his step-son (who was so simple *'he could not tell ten shillings in silver'*) to his death in Ireland *'as a poor common soldier'*, and thereafter illegally obtained possession of the property. John Holloway successfully defended Bridget Westbrook's action. As for the allegation that William Pigott the younger was a simpleton, John Holloway maintained that not only could he read and write, but also that he could *'understand the Latin tongue'*.

By 1691 the occupier of Fawsbyes was Edward North, who died in 1701, and the freeholder was Francis Booth of Arborfield, whose family had owned Butts Farm in Barkham until 1686. In 1691 Francis Booth sold Fawsbyes to Edward Withers of London, butcher, for £190[5]. Fawsbyes was still owned by Edward Withers at the time of his will (in which he is described as a citizen and haberdasher of London) in 1715[6], when the farmstead was occupied by Widow Wood.

Shortly afterwards Fawsbyes was acquired by Thomas Simonds, yeoman, a member of the wealthy Simonds family. Thomas Simonds

died in 1719, aged 79 (he is buried under the floor of the nave in the parish church)[7], and the farmstead subsequently passed to Alice, his surviving daughter. Alice was married to James Allwright of Wokingham, a substantial yeoman, and they made Fawsbyes their home. There were no children from the marriage. James Allwright died in 1747.

When Alice Allwright died in 1757, her net residuary estate (after payment of legacies) was £1,961. 12s., which was shared amongst eight residuary legatees in the locality. In her will she asked one of her relatives, James Allwright of Shinfield, to look after her old dog, Keeper[8].

Alice Allwright is best remembered for establishing Allwright's Charity for the poor of Barkham and Newland. At her death, she endowed the charity with the income from a 5-acre field in the parish called Half Moon Close. The churchwardens and overseers of the poor were directed to apply the rents received in distributing *'so much good and wholesome wheaten bread as the same will purchase'* each Lady Day and Michaelmas amongst the most poor and needy people of Barkham and the Liberty of Newland[9].

In 1758 Alice Allwright's executors sold Fawsbyes to Pierce Sparks of Swallowfield, maltster, for £626[10]. When Pierce Sparks died in 1770, he was succeeded by his son, also Pierce Sparks. Sparks & Co. moved their malting business to Barkham, and there survives a 1796 insurance policy with the Sun Fire Office in respect of the farmstead (of brick and tiled) for £200, a thatched malthouse (including kilns and malting floors for drying) for £70, a thatched barn for £60, a thatched stable for £20 and a cowhouse, carthouse and pigsty for £50[11]. Pierce Sparks also sold bread and flour.

In 1801 Pierce Sparks the younger sold Fawsbyes with 17 acres to Farmer John Marshall of Brook Farm for £900[12]. Marshall also purchased Ellis's Farm in 1818, so that by the time of the 1821 enclosure award, he owned 70 acres[13]. John Marshall served as churchwarden many times.

When John Marshall died in 1825 (aged 49), he left Sparks Farm to his eldest son, also John, a minor[14], but his widow Sarah (42) continued to farm Sparks Farm, Ellis's Farm and Brook Farm (which was leased from John Leveson Gower, lord of the manor) for many years, not retiring until 1847.

By the time of the 1841 census, Sparks Farm (then 36 acres) was occupied by the family of John Marshall the younger (28) and his wife, Sarah[15]. John Marshall remained at Sparks Farm until his death in 1869 (aged 56), when the farm passed to his son, another John, who lived at Ellis's Farm. In 1872 Sparks Farm with 36 acres was acquired by John Walter III from John Marshall junior and his mother, Sarah, for £2,400 and became part of the Bear Wood estate[16].

From about 1900 to 1914 Sparks Farm was let to John Allright (previously of Manor Farm, now Bailiff's Cottage), whose family was much involved in parish life. Whilst

Sparks Farm

Mr Allright served as a churchwarden and overseer, Mrs Lucy Allright, who was infants' mistress at the parochial school for many years, was indefatigable in her work in the choir and the Sunday school, the rector (P.H. Ditchfield) thanking her for '*her much valued zeal and earnestness in conducting the choir*'. During the winter months poor and needy parishioners used to come to Mrs Allright's twice weekly 'soup kitchen' (funded by Mrs Rickman of Barkham Manor) and several choir suppers were also held at Sparks Farm[17].

When the Bear Wood estate was put on the market by John Walter IV in 1911, Sparks Farm was included in the sale of the adjacent Barkham Square estate to Mrs E.M. Sturges in 1913[18] and became the working farm for the Square. The farm was disposed of by the Sturges family in 1948. Sparks Farm is a grade 2 listed building and is now a private residence.

9 Church Cottages (Barkham Court)

In mediæval and Tudor times the manor house was located on the moated site adjacent to the parish church. According to the listed building particulars in respect of the building which survives on the same site, the core of the building is a timber-framed open hall house, which was erected in the late fifteenth century. The mediæval manor house (in reality probably little more than a farmstead) was originally called Barkham Court, subsequently Barkham Farm (eighteenth century) and Church Farm (nineteenth century)[1], and

Church Cottages in 1922

is now called Church Cottages. Since the majority of moats were dug during the thirteenth or early fourteenth centuries, there may have been one or more earlier buildings on the site.

A small meadow on the north-east side of the moated site is believed by English Heritage to be the mediæval farmyard area, whilst the name of the adjacent field, Calvert Close, is a corruption of Culver Croft, the name recorded in a 1660 mortgage[2]. Culver is an old English word for a pigeon or dove, suggesting there was once a dovehouse or dovecote. In mediæval times, only the barons, the clergy and lords of the manor were allowed to build dovecotes, which further supports the proposition that there was a 'high status' building on the moated site in mediæval times. Dovecotes were also valued as a source of fresh meat during the winter months (as well as eggs).

It is possible that the surviving building was built (or rebuilt) in the mid-1480s as a dower house for Eleanor Bullock, widow of Robert Bullock (lord of Arborfield and Barkham), who presented John Hawkyns as rector to Barkham church in 1489[3]. Following Eleanor's death, Arborfield became the permanent seat of the Bullocks and the manor house at Barkham was let as a farm to a succession of tenants (family and non-family). At an indeterminate time during the first part of the seventeenth century, the site of the manor house migrated to a larger 'high status' building on the site of the present Barkham Manor.

One of the early tenants of Barkham Court may have been Richard Bullock, who died in 1534, bequeathing 6s. to buy a mass book for the parish church[4]. In 1524/5 Richard Bullock was one of 24 Barkham residents assessed for tax, on the basis of owning goods worth £6. 6s. 8d[5]. In 1529 Richard Bullock was one of several persons in the locality to be warned of a conspiracy by certain disaffected persons to fell trees illegally in Bear Wood, in order that local people could remove their animals from harm's way before the 'insurrection'[6].

When Thomas Bullock, lord of Arborfield and Barkham, died in 1558, the tenant of Barkham Court (or the farm of Barkham) was Richard Symes. In his will in 1557[7], Thomas Bullock directed that the property should be leased to his widow, Agnes, at an annual rent of £6. 13s. 4d., following the expiry of the lease to Symes, if Agnes did not wish to continue living with their son Richard at Arborfield manor. When Richard Symes died in 1559 (probably a victim of the 1558/9 influenza epidemic), his probate inventory totalled £111. 4s. 4d. (87 % being attributable to livestock, grain and growing crops)[8], indicating he was a yeoman farmer

of very substantial means. Even so, the inventory reveals a marked sparsity of furnishings in the homestead.

In 1574 Richard Bullock's son, Thomas, lord of Arborfield and Barkham, leased the site and demesne of the manor of Barkham to his next brother, William, for 21 years at an annual rent of £15[9]. The Barkham parish registers record the baptism of eleven children of William Bullock between 1583 and 1603. The sale of the manors of Arborfield and Barkham by Thomas Bullock to Edmond Standen (of Chancery) in 1589, forced by a heavy accumulation of debts, was vigorously disputed by William Bullock, as legal heir of the childless Thomas, resulting in a multiplicity of law suits in the 1590s.

In June 1596, in contravention of the terms of his lease, William Bullock hired a gang of men to fell trees on the demesne lands of the manor of Barkham, prompting Standen to seek an injunction in the Court of Chancery to stop him. Bullock's transgressions, and disregard of court orders, caused him to be imprisoned in the Fleet Prison for about 5 years from 1597. In the meantime, it seems that his wife and numerous children were ejected from the farmstead by Standen's agents. The long-running and bitter dispute between William Bullock and Edmond Standen is recounted in Chapter 13.

The identity of the next tenants of Barkham Court is unknown, although the property is described as a '*faire houſe*' in a 1613 survey of the parishes in Windsor Forest[10].

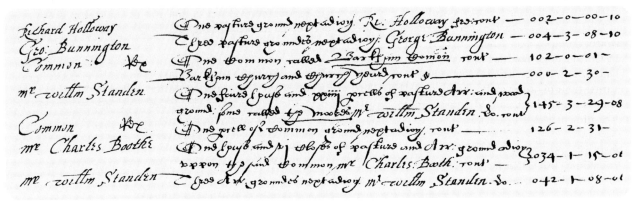

By reference to nineteenth century title deeds[11], a Henry Montague, gentleman, was tenant (or head-lessee) of Barkham Court at some time during the first part of the seventeenth century, most likely during the 1620s. The marriage of Mary Montague of Barkham (aged 23) in the parish church in 1630, with a licence from the Bishop of Sarum[12], suggests Henry Montague's family was then living at Barkham. Henry Montague, who died in Wokingham in 1634, was the father of Henry Montague, reported as being a schoolmaster in Wokingham in 1654 and 1669, and who died in 1695 leaving a mansion house in Wokingham (Montague House in Broad Street) to his son Ephraime. When he died in 1634, Henry Montague (the elder) left 50s. to the poor of Wokingham and 5s. *'to the poore of Barkham beinge very fewe'*[13]. Henry Montague (the elder) was also a schoolmaster in Wokingham, since the probate inventory of Alice Booth of Barkham Butts, spinster, in 1627 lists Henry Montague of Wokingham,

'scholem[aste]r', as a debtor for £20 under a bill of exchange dated 1622[14].

A further apparent inconsistency is that Oliver Hyde, who is referred to in the 1660 mortgage as tenant of the farm before 1646, was assessed for tax on the basis of occupying land in Barkham according to the subsidy rolls which survive for 1628, 1640 and 1641[15]. A possible explanation is that in 1628 Henry Montague held a head-lease and occupied the homestead, whilst the surrounding farm land was sublet to Oliver Hyde. Following the end of the Civil War in 1646, William Standen granted a 21 year lease of the farmstead and 166 acres to Henry Miller, yeoman, at an annual rent of £60[16].

Henry Miller continued as tenant of the farm until his death in 1679. According to the surviving 1662–1664 hearth tax returns[17], there were three fireplaces in the homestead. The Barkham parish registers record the birth of three daughters and a son to Henery and Elizabeth Millir between

1651 and 1656. Although Henry Miller's probate inventory does not survive, he was clearly a well-to-do yeoman. In his will in 1679[18], he appointed his eldest daughter Jane, who was unmarried, as his executrix (rather than his wife) and left her the residue of the lease of the farm of Barkham, which according to the surviving 1689 church rate assessment[19] was the largest tenant farm in the parish. There is evidence that Jane (sometimes also called Jean or Joan) continued to live at the farmstead until at least 1708[20].

Jane Miller is also mentioned as a beneficiary in the will of her uncle, John Brooksbank, who died in 1698, leaving money to the poor of Barkham (Brooksbank's charity)[21]. John Brooksbank must have had a soft spot for his niece since, apart from leaving her an annuity of £5 per annum, he further directed that '*if the said Jane Miller shall happen to fall to decay and become poor*', his executor (his kinsman Henry Clements of Barkham) was to make additional payments to her up to £20.

By 1716 the land which was subsequently to become the Barkham Square estate (including Barkham Farm) had been sold by William Waterman I (who purchased the manor in 1700) to one John Davenport[22]. It is not known who were the occupants of Barkham Farm between the end of Jane Miller's tenancy in the early 1700s and the 1841 census. The farmstead became an appendage of Barkham Square, perhaps when the trustees of the Revd Witting Colton (who purchased the Square about 1746) purchased further land in Barkham in 1755

(see Chapter 18). In 1783, according to an inventory of church property drawn up by the then new rector, the Revd David Davies, the land on all sides of the churchyard was part of Barkham Farm and was owned by a William Richardson[23].

In the eighteenth century it was common practice for well-to-do farmers to buy up or rent farmsteads to accommodate their agricultural labourers and it appears Barkham Farm was used for this purpose. When David Davies became rector in 1782, the lessee of Barkham Farm was Thomas Clacy of Biggs's Farm, the largest farmer in the parish, who leased four farms from local landowners and also had a head-lease of Barkham Square[24].

It seems that for a period after his arrival in Barkham in 1782, the Revd David Davies lived at Barkham Farm pending the rebuilding of the parsonage house, since in one of his replies to the visitation queries of the Bishop of Salisbury in 1783[25], he states that '*My present place of residence is at a Farm-House close by the Church*', for to the new rector's disgust, he found that the parsonage house was '*a mean cottage badly situated*'.

By 1796 the 214-acre Barkham Square estate (including Barkham Farm) had been acquired by Peter Green of Crookham, near Newbury[26]. When Thomas Clacy's lease came to an end about 1806, Peter Green took the estate in hand and both premises became working farms, although it seems that the main farmyard was adjacent to Barkham Farm (or Church Farm) and the churchyard, on the land which today is used for car parking during church services. The farmyard included two double-bayed barns, a very large cow stall, a Dutch granary on staddle-stones, two sheep pens, a stable, a cart shed and a piggery[27].

After a number of attempts to sell or lease the Barkham Square estate (including Church Farm) from 1823 onwards, the estate was purchased as an investment by William Cook of Kent in 1833. Cook leased the estate to a succession of gentleman farmers, whilst Church Farm was used to accommodate some of the farm workers. At the time of the 1841 census, the farmstead was occupied by a shepherd, John Hern, and his wife[28]. By 1861 the farmstead had been divided into accommodation for two families and there were 14 persons living there[29].

In 1867 the Barkham Square estate (including Church Farm) was acquired by John Walter III and became part of the Bear Wood estate. From 1880 to 1884 Church Farm and 106 acres were let to George Wryght (aged 60)[30], a farmer born in Banfshire[31]. Thereafter, Church Farm became part of Brook Farm, also part of the Walter estate. Wryght's tenancy may have been short-lived because it coincided with the second part of the deep agricultural recession of 1875–1884.

From 1887 to 1901 Church Farm was occupied by the family of Robert Newport[32], a farm labourer who had moved from Gloucestershire to Rook's Nest Farm about 1875. At the time of the 1891 census Robert Newport's household comprised his wife Eliza and eight of their children (aged between 3 and 25)[33]. Apart from Nancy (13), all the Newport children were boys.

When the Bear Wood estate was broken up following the death of Arthur Fraser Walter in 1910, Brook Farm (including Church Farm) was acquired in 1913 by the current lessee, W.C.J. Hissey of Loddon Bridge Farm, Earley for £3,950[34]. After World War I, Berkshire County Council was seeking to acquire farms suitable for conversion into statutory smallholdings for letting to returning servicemen and purchased the Brook Farm estate (374 acres) in 1919 for £8,600[35]. Church Farm became Church Cottages and was used to accommodate two statutory smallholders and their families. Water continued to be supplied to the cottages from a well until 1950. Church Cottages is a grade 2 listed building and is now two private residences. The adjacent moat is a scheduled ancient monument.

10 Biggs's Farm (Barkham Butts)

One of the more interesting historic buildings in the parish, a moated property called Biggs's Farm, was demolished early last century to make way for the Army Remount Depot (now REME Garrison).

The property was previously known as Butts Farm (or Barkham Butts) and seems to have changed its name in the second part of the eighteenth century. The word 'butt' has various meanings, one of which, a boundary mark (e.g. butts and bounds) is consistent with the location of the homestead near the boundary with the parish of Finchampstead. The homestead is mentioned in the two accounts of the perambulation of the bounds of the parish which survive from 1738 and 1770[1]. Another possibility is that it was the site of mediæval archery butts (which would have been in regular use after Sunday mass).

Butts may have dated from the thirteenth or early fourteenth century, since the majority of mediæval moats were dug during this period. This would be consistent with the feudal origins of the tenure of Butts, since the quit rents payable to the lord of the manor included a one-third part of a knight's fee – commuted to a payment of 33s. 4d. per annum – and a pair of gilt spurs[2].

An early occupier of Barkham Butts may have been Richard Ferby, who is mentioned as holding a property called 'the Bottes' in a 1419 deed[3]. It seems that by 1458 the property was in the hands of William Barowe, esquire, and his son Thomas Barowe, gentleman, when they witnessed a quitclaim of lands in Finchampstead and Barkham[4]. When Thomas Barowe made his will in 1505 (the earliest surviving Barkham will), he left his property in Barkham to John Gawsem and lands in Dorset to his wife, Johane[5].

Following Thomas Barowe's death about 1506, his widow was sued in Chancery by Johanne Dykar (widow) who claimed that before his death Thomas Barowe had agreed to sell his lands in 'Berkham, Okyngham, Hurst, ffynchamstede and Erberfild' (called 'Barowes lands') to her late husband, Nicholas Dykar, and seeking the return of £22 paid by Nicholas Dykar on account of the proposed purchase[6].

According to 1538–1544 Chancery proceedings concerning land in Arborfield[7], Thomas Barowe and his wife, Johane, had

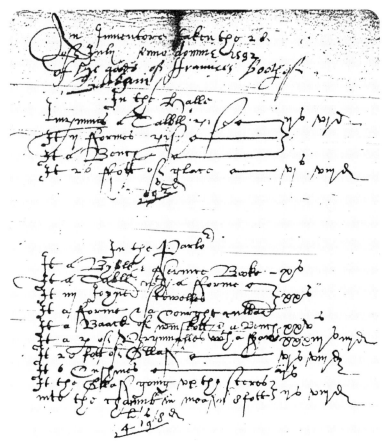

Charles Booth's eldest son, Francis, married first Dorothy, daughter of Thomas Bullock (died 1558), lord of the manors of Arborfield and Barkham, by whom he had three children, and second Elizabeth Hatch of White Waltham, by whom he had two further children before the *Heralds' Visitation of Berkshire* in 1566[9]. He died in 1592.

Francis Booth was a wealthy man, as measured by his probate inventory which totalled £97. 8s. 8d., and by the amount which was spent on his funeral to demonstrate his social status, as recorded in the administrator's accounts, which survive[10]. In all £15. 5s. 9d. was spent on his funeral, including £12. 13s. on '*blackes* [black cloth] *to make mourning gownes & clokes*' for the mourners and £1. 2s. 9d. paid to the '*teyler*' for making them, a cash outlay corresponding to 16 % of the value of his personal estate.

The probate inventory of '*ffrauncys Bowthe*' contains a comprehensive list of the contents of every room at Butts: '*halle, parlo.ʳ, chamb.ʳ* [i.e. bedroom] *over the halle, closett w.ᵗʰin the chamb*[er], *parlo.ʳ chamb.ʳ, maydes chamb.ʳ, ketchen chamb.ʳ, ffolkes chamb*[er], *napere* [for linen], *toploft, ketchin, buttere, baakehowes*'. In Tudor times the main living room was the hall, where the family ate. At Butts the only furnishings in the hall were a table, almost certainly rectangular, and three benches.

As befitted a wealthy family, there was a separate living room called the parlour, where the family gathered. This was furnished with a table and bench, four stools and two

Extract from 1592 probate inventory of Francis Booth

no direct heirs and by that time his property had descended to Charles Booth, as son of Jane, who was the daughter of Margaret, sister and sole heir of Thomas Barowe (who may have been the wife of John Gawsem). It is not known when Charles Booth first occupied Butts, but his daughter, Mary, was married at Barkham church in 1549[8].

56

other benches, with six cushions to soften the wooden seats. The only fixtures were a '*courght cubbard*' (three open shelves) and some wainscoting. In the fashion of the gentry of the time, there was a pair of virginals for the family to make music at home. There was also a bible (the first book to be mentioned in a Barkham probate inventory).

In 1592 glass windows, which could only be afforded by the well-to-do, were considered sufficiently unusual to be itemised, and valued, in probate inventories. Barkham Butts seems to have been well equipped with glass windows, including '*20 ffott* [feet] *of glace*' in each of the hall, parlour and chamber over the hall. Wainscots were also itemised (since they were considered as movables), the wainscoting in the parlour chamber (main bedroom) being valued at £5. According to the surviving 1662–1664 hearth tax returns, there were six fireplaces at Butts[11].

The probate inventory lists 16 beds (including 4 feather beds, 3 truckle beds and 4 flock beds) in various rooms at Butts, including two in the well equipped kitchen, reflecting both the size of the Booth household and the lack of privacy. Truckle beds slid under standing beds during the day and were commonly used for children. Flock beds were for servants. The household included Francis Booth's daughter Anne and son-in-law Edward Chaundler, and their five children. Edward Chaundler, who died the following year (1593), was the owner of a

tannery in Wokingham[12]. It is also evident from his will that Francis Booth had a tannery at Barkham, and in his probate inventory the '*Tanhowes stuff*', including '*the Mell* [mill] *the Vattes & sesturnes* [cisterns]', was valued at £8. 6s. 8d. Since the moat surrounding Butts appears to have been fed by Barkham Brook, the stream probably provided the source of running water for the Barkham tannery.

Francis Booth was succeeded by his eldest son, Charles. The Barkham parish registers record the baptism of eight children to Charels Booth and his wife, Mistress Ursula, between 1596 and 1616. When Charles Booth died in 1639 (his wife predeceased him in 1625), he was succeeded by his eldest surviving son, John, who lived to the age of 74. The parish registers record the baptism of nine children to John and Elizabeth Booth between 1632 and 1650.

John Booth subsequently moved to the neighbouring Whitehall Farm on the Arborfield side of the parish boundary[13]. When John Booth died in 1683, he was buried at Barkham and Butts passed to his eldest son, Richard, who died 2 years later in 1686 (aged 53). Shortly before his death, Richard Booth had contracted to sell his lands in Barkham for £750 to Scory Barker of Chiswick[14], who was subsequently involved in a drawn-out ecclesiastical law suit from 1688 to 1707 about the right to a seat in Barkham church[15].

The next freeholder of Butts of whom we know is Ellis (Mews) St John of Dogmersfield,

Booth coat of arms

lord of the manor of Finchampstead, West Court, who died in 1729, when his property in Finchampstead, Arborfield and Barkham was acquired by his second son, also Ellis St John (22), who became rector of Finchampstead when the living became vacant in 1744[16]. At the time of the manorial court of survey in 1738, the tenant of Butts Farm was John Cooke.

In 1753 the Revd Ellis St John granted a 21 year lease of the Barkham Butts farmstead and 138 acres to Thomas Clacy at an initial rent of £134. 15s. per annum. In 1776 the lease was renewed by Thomas Clacy's son, also Thomas, for 11 years at an annual rent of £150[17]. By the time David Davies became rector in 1782, Thomas Clacy had become the largest farmer in the parish (being liable to pay 41 % of the compositions for tythes)[18]. Whilst Thomas Clacy and his family (nine children were born between 1770 and 1789) lived at the moated farmstead, he also leased Barkham Farm (next to the church), Ellis's Farm and Rook's Nest Farm. He often served as a churchwarden in the 1780s and 1790s[19].

The circumstances of the change of name of the farmstead from Butts to Biggs's are a mystery. The only reference in the surviving parish records to the name Biggs is to a John Biggs who served as churchwarden in 1721 and 1732, and as constable of Barkham in 1729[20]. The Arborfield parish registers also record the marriage of a John Biggs and Elizabeth Englefield, both of Barkham, in 1718, at Arborfield. There is no mention of

Biggs in the 1738 manorial survey, whilst the homestead is called Barkham Butts in the 1753 and 1776 leases. In David Davies' 1785 tythe accounts, however, the farm is called Bigges's.

In the early 1800s Thomas Clacy handed over the farm to his son, Charles (born 1778). By 1815 Charles Clacy had decided to move elsewhere, and an auction of his live and dead farming stock (i.e. livestock and equipment) at Biggs's Farm was advertised[21]. It seems that the auction was either unsuccessful or postponed, since a similar auction was advertised over a year later. C.E. Peacocke became tenant until 1826 when the farm was let to James Elliott. At the time of the 1841 census, James Elliott was 70 and the household consisted of a son (35), a daughter (20), a servant and two labourers[22].

By 1843, when the freehold was transferred by Elizabeth, widow of the Revd Henry Ellis St John to his third son, John St John, the farm had been let to Charles Collyer (son of John Collyer of The Bull), and comprised 194 acres (147 in Barkham, 23 in Arborfield and 23 in Finchampstead)[23]. At the time of the 1851 census, Charles Collyer (41) employed four men and three boys, and there were six children aged between 1 and 13 living at the farmstead.

About this time Charles Collyer moved to Hand Post Farm on Langley Common. By 1854 Biggs's Farm had been let to John Smallbone and by 1856 to John Hathaway, who was succeeded as tenant by John Marshall junior in 1859. At the time of the

1861 census the household comprised John Marshall junior (47), his wife Sarah, nine children aged between 1 and 18, and four young labourers.

By 1871 Biggs's and Ellis's Farms had been leased to William Cordery of Swallowfield and the freehold was sold by John St John to John Walter III in 1873[24]. Biggs's Farm thereby became part of the Bear Wood estate. At some time towards the end of the nineteenth century a modern farmhouse was built on that part of the farm straddling the Arborfield and Finchampstead parish boundary and the moated farmstead became Old Biggs's Farm.

In 1904 the War Office leased 286 acres, one-half in Barkham (including Old Biggs's Farm), two-fifths in Finchampstead and the remainder in Arborfield, from the Bear Wood estate and established a remount depot. The quartermaster lived at Old Biggs's Farm, and in 1906 the Moat House was built nearby as a residence for the officer in command. In 1911 the War Office purchased the freehold of the land leased in 1904 and Old Biggs's Farm was demolished shortly afterwards[25]. Unfortunately, no record was made before the old property was pulled down. The site is close to the present Princess Marina Drive.

STOLEN or **STRAYED** from a Field of Bigs Farm in the Parish of Barkham, late on Sunday Night the 21st, or early on Monday Morning the 22nd of June, 1840, a LIGHT BROWN MARE, of the Cart Breed, 3 years old, about 14 hands high, black mane and tail, long when stolen, with a full white star in the forehead, four black legs, and one white heel behind, no shoes on; the property of Mr. James Elliott, farmer, at Barkham.

Whoever will give such information of the offender or offenders, shall upon his or their conviction receive the sum of FIVE POUNDS Reward from the said James Elliott. If Strayed One Guinea Reward and all reasonable expenses will be paid by the said James Elliott, of Bigs Farm, near Arbourfield, in the parish of Barkham, in the county of Berkshire.

Bigs Farm, Barkham, July 3rd, 1840.

Reading Mercury, 11 July 1840

11 Life (and Death) in Tudor Barkham (1505–1558)

A detailed insight into the way that our forebears lived may be obtained by a study of old Barkham wills and probate inventories. The earliest surviving Barkham will is that of Thomas Barowe, gentleman, made in 1505[1] and there are eight further Barkham wills surviving from before the accession of Elizabeth I in 1558.

To read Tudor wills, not only is it necessary to decipher strange handwriting, but the spelling is almost totally phonetic – not by reference to the standard English of today, but reflecting the marked local accents of country folk over 450 years ago. Probate inventories present even greater difficulties, since the 'indifferent men' who were the appraisers (i.e. valuers) were more often than not barely literate local people.

In a Tudor will it was first necessary to establish that the testator was *compos mentis*, usually signified by a declaration about the testator '*beynge seke in my body but hole of mynde thanketh be to gode*' (Thomas Alnet, husbandman, 1558)[2].

It was also normal for a testator to leave his soul to God and some money to the church. The language of such a bequest altered as the official religion of the country changed

from being catholic to protestant (Edward VI 1547–1553), to catholic (Mary I 1553–1558), and back to protestant (Elizabeth I 1558). The will of Edward Ball, yeoman, in 1558[3] was one of the last to use the catholic formula, '*I bequeth my soule to Almyghty god to our blessed lady and to All the holy sanctes In heawen and my body to be burred in the churche yearth of god and Sancte Jamys the apostyll at berkham*'.

Thomas Alnet left '*a bochell* [bushel] *of wheat corne and a halfe*' for the '*reperacions of my*

60

p[ar]*ysche churche*', whilst Richard Bullock, gentleman, who died in 1534[4], left six shillings '*to the bying of a masse book to the church of berkh[a]m*'. There were also regular bequests to make amends for tythes '*negligently forgotten*'.

Before the Reformation, services were supplemented by dirges for the souls of past departeds who had left money for the purpose, in some cases motivated by a desire to make amends for their transgressions whilst on earth. Thomas Barowe left 9 marks (£6) to pay for '*A preest to syng in the seide [Barkham] church after my decesse to pray for my soule and my fader and moderes soules*' for 3 years. The will of William Norman, yeoman, in 1558[5] directed that dirges should be sung in Barkham church for his soul for the '*space*' of 10 years, the endowment in this case being '*on kowe*' (one cow).

The well-to-do also left money to the poor. Thomas Barowe's will in 1505 included a bequest '*to poore peopill xx.s in almes to be distributed amonge theym at the day of my burying*'. Thomas Bullock, lord of the manors of Arborfield and Barkham, who died in 1558, left 3s. 4d. for the '*releif of the poore*' of Barkham in his will in 1557[6].

The probate inventories show that even well-to-do farmers (yeomen or husbandmen) had very few material possessions, and it was normal to make detailed bequests of specific household goods, grain and animals. Pewter plates, saucers, brass pots, heifers and sheep frequently featured in bequests. In his will in 1558, William Norman left '*A kowe with A*

1534 will of Richard Bullock

pyed [i.e. black and white] *face*' to his '*doughter Alis*' and '*A kowe crompyll horned*' [i.e. with curly horns] to his son Nicholas.

The probate inventories contain exhaustive lists of the possessions of the deceased, revealing a marked sparsity of furnishings. The hall served as the living room, where a fire burned constantly in the hearth and the cooking was done. The furnishings in the hall might simply be a long table (perhaps a trestle table rather than a jointed table), a form (bench), a few chairs or stools (often three-legged because of the uneven floors) and a cupboard (then no more than an open shelf).

In the chamber (i.e. bedroom) there was usually little beyond a flock bed (the mattress being stuffed with wool refuse) *'with the apparel'* and several chests, where such clothes as the occupants possessed and bed linen were kept. There were no soft furnishings, apart from the occasional cushion. The only decoration usually was painted cloths hanging on the rough walls (which also served to reduce draughts). There was, of course, no sanitation or running water.

The inventories contain long lists of *'hearth gear'* and kitchen utensils, employing terminology largely unknown today, such as broches (spits) and andirons (a pair of horizontal bars on each side of the hearth to support burning wood). There are often references to ale-making equipment, since water and milk were usually unfit to drink. The Barkham inventories also make reference to cheese vats and butter churns.

Virtually everyone, whether or not a farmer (e.g. labourers), kept a few animals and poultry for subsistence. It is evident that oxen were still used for ploughing, although there is also mention of 'horse beasts'. The inventory of John Balsam, husbandman, in 1554[7] included four *'letyll hoglynges'* worth 4s. Tools (e.g. *'augurs, wombyls and cheselles'*) and agricultural equipment were also listed in great detail.

It seems that there was a high level of migration during the Tudor period. There were 14 different surnames amongst the 24 heads of household assessed for tax in 1524/5[8]. During the first decade following the commencement of the parish registers, 1539–1549[9], only six of the 14 surnames appear in the registers, and in the 1590s only two occur. Of the 37 different surnames in the parish registers in 1539–1549, only eleven appear in the 1590s, indicating a migration rate during the second part of the century of 11·5 % per decade.

Whilst the surviving 1505–1558 wills and probate inventories only tell us about the lives of a few of the more well-to-do inhabitants, they confirm that Barkham was almost wholly an agricultural community centred round the focal point of the church. There were few, if any, luxuries in the yeomens' homesteads or labourers' rude habitations. Apart from funeral wakes and church ales, life for the majority of the approximately 120 inhabitants must have been hard and monotonous.

12 History of Barkham Manor, Part I (1540–1787)

Origins

The origins of the mansion house called Barkham Manor are obscure, since there are few surviving records before the 1750s, and it is not known who the early occupants were.

Although the present house (apart from the cellars) dates from the end of the eighteenth century, the reputed origin of the ornamental lakes as stew ponds and the magnificent plane tree (*Platanus orientalis*), reputed to be up to 450 years old, may indicate the existence of a high status building on the site since at least Tudor times. If the present lakes do indeed derive from mediæval stew ponds, they would have been stocked with fish like carp, to be consumed on days when Church laws required abstinence from eating meat (i.e. Fridays and during Lent) and during winter.

The mediæval manor house had been on a moated site adjacent to the parish church. At some stage during the first part of the seventeenth century, the site of the manor of Barkham migrated to the present Barkham Manor site, although the property was known as Barkham House until well into the nineteenth century. Curiously, however, although the mediæval manor house was described as a '*faire houſe*' in a 1613 survey

of the parishes in Windsor Forest, none of the other twelve houses listed in Barkham attracted any special mention[1].

If there was a high status building on the site in Tudor times, one of the early occupants may have been John White, a partner in the Reading and Wokingham bell foundries[2], who retired to Barkham where he died in 1551. This is, however, purely conjectural. White was a wealthy man by contemporary standards, leaving a personal estate of £81. 15s. 7d.[3], and had been mayor of Reading (before, and after, the dissolution of Reading Abbey) in 1536 and 1542.

The Standens (1589–1700)

In 1589 the lordships of Arborfield and Barkham, together with 2,200 acres (78 % of the two parishes) were sold by Thomas Bullock (who was almost bankrupt) to Edmond Standen, Clerk of the Petty Bag of the Court of Chancery, for £4,000[4].

On his death in 1603, Edmond Standen was succeeded by his son, William, who lived at Arborfield manor until his death (aged 73) in 1639. The lengthy Latin epitaph on his tomb in St Bartholomew's, Arborfield (which is opposite the porch when you enter the church) is fulsome in its praise of his generous nature and Christian virtues. William Standen died childless and his heir-at-law was a kinsman called William Ball, who was the grandson of Edmond Standen's second brother. The Arborfield and Barkham estates passed, however, under a family settlement to another kinsman of the same name, William Standen, who was the grandson of Edmond Standen's fifth brother. The trustees were William Lenthall MP and Nicholas Love[5].

It appears that William Standen (kinsman) and his (first) wife, Sarah, took up residence in Barkham, probably at the mansion house on the Barkham Manor site, not long after William Standen's death in 1639, and remained at Barkham during the troubled Civil War years, since the Barkham parish registers include five Standen family entries in 1642–1645 (one baptism and four burials)[6], whilst Mary Standen, widow of William Standen, continued to live at Arborfield until her death in 1645. Little is known about William Standen (kinsman), except that he was at some time a member of the Barber Surgeons' Company in the City of London and was High Sheriff of Berkshire in 1648.

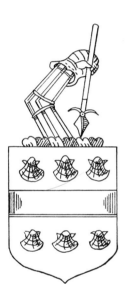

Stronghill coat of arms

When Mary Standen (widow) died in 1645, William and Sarah Standen moved from Barkham to Arborfield manor, whilst his kinsman, William Ball, a supporter of the Parliamentary cause and writer of political pamphlets, took up residence at Barkham where he and his wife Margaret continued to reside, when not in London, until at least

1652[7]. It seems that William Standen's wife, Sarah, predeceased him and by 1657 he had taken a second wife called Elizabeth.

The history of the dispute between William Bullock and Edmond Standen in the 1590s, and between Edward Bullock and William Standen (1650–1662), about the ownership of the manors of Arborfield and Barkham is recounted in Chapters 13 and 15, respectively.

The next occupiers of the manor house appear to have been the family of John Stronghill and his (second) wife Judith, from at least 1654 until Stronghill's death in 1666[8]. John Stronghill's New Year '*Guifte*' to the parish church in 1664 of a silver paten, engraved with his coat of arms, is still part of the church plate. According to the surviving hearth tax returns for 1662–1664, Barkham House had nine fireplaces at this time[9]. John Struggle seems to have occupied as subtenant in 1662/3.

William Standen died in 1686 and was succeeded by his son John. When John Standen died in 1694 he was succeeded by Edward Standen. It is not known whether Edward was the eldest son of John Standen or his third brother.

The Watermans, Kingsmills and Osgoods (1700–1768)

The Standens continued to own the manor of Barkham until 1700, when Edward Standen sold the Barkham estate (including the lordship and the advowson) to William Waterman I of Southwark (grandson of Sir

George Waterman, Lord Mayor of London 1672)[10]. Little is known about William Waterman, although he served as High Sheriff of Berkshire in 1709/10. William Waterman's daughter, Eleanor, married Edward Standen's son, also called Edward (of *The Ballad of Molly Mog* fame).

William Waterman died in 1733[11] and his eldest son, the Revd John Waterman, succeeded to the Barkham estate after the death of his widow Mary. John Waterman's wife, Penelope, was the daughter of Sir William Kingsmill of Sydmonton in Hampshire. The Kingsmill family had been major landowners in the locality since the middle ages and owned Langley Pond Farm in the parish. The marriage may have been the reason for the gift of a silver flagon to Barkham church by Penelope Kingsmill's mother, Dame Rebecca, in 1720.

As well as owning the advowson of Barkham, John Waterman held the right to make the next presentation to the living of Arborfield. When the Revd John Sale, who had been rector of both Arborfield and Barkham since 1694, died in 1739, John Waterman presented himself as rector of Arborfield, but presented the Revd William Dawes to the living of Barkham[12].

The Revd John Waterman seems to have divided his time between Barkham House and Sydmonton Court, which appears to have been his principal residence, where his wife, Penelope, would initially have looked after her mother, Dame Rebecca Kingsmill, who died in 1727, and then her brother William,

who, though a certified lunatic, was head of the Kingsmill family from 1698 to 1766.

John Waterman appears to have ministered to the needs of his parishioners in Arborfield from Barkham House, since a notice in the *Reading Mercury* in 1746 about criminal damage to a coppice owned by him in Arborfield indicates that he was then resident in Barkham[13]. The atmosphere at Sydmonton Court, notwithstanding its 3,000 acres, must have been difficult at times and the manor house at Barkham would have offered a welcome respite.

In 1755 John Waterman died without male issue and the Barkham manor estate passed to his nephew, William Waterman III. In September 1755 William Waterman III began raising money on the security of the estate and a number of complicated transactions involving the estate were to ensue over the following 2 years[14].

The Revd John Waterman's daughter, Rebecca, married Lawrence Head Osgood, son and heir of John Osgood, lord of the manors of Chieveley. Osgood, who served as High Sheriff of Berkshire in 1748/9, leased Barkham House from 1751[15] until his death (aged 47) in 1768, when the contents of the house were auctioned in a 2-day sale and the house offered for re-letting[16]. A daughter, Penelope, was baptised at Barkham in 1754.

The surviving Kingsmill manuscripts give various addresses for Lawrence Head Osgood from 1758 onwards (including Sydmonton) and he died in Oxfordshire. In 1758 (whilst living at Barkham) his wife, Rebecca, became co-custodian of her insane uncle, William Kingsmill. When William Kingsmill died (aged 81) in 1766 without issue, the Kingsmill estates were divided between Rebecca Osgood and another niece, Elizabeth Brice, and their respective husbands (since married women could not own property until 1882)[17]. (See Chapter 6.)

The Pitts and Fonnereaus (1757–1787)

In December 1757 Edward Wise, an entreprenurial Wokingham solicitor, bought Barkham manor and sold-on the estate to William Pitt of Binfield Manor for £6,513[18]. When William Pitt died in 1774, the Barkham estate passed to his brother, John Pitt, whose estates were in Dorset. The Pitt family trustees actively tried to sell the

BERKS.

To be SOLD by AUCTION, By CHARLES BENWELL, On Wednesday the third and Thursday the fourth of July 1782, The neat and genuine HOUSHOLD FURNITURE, and EFFECTS, of the Rev. Dr. GABRIEL, deceased, at the Manor House at Barkham; confisting of mahogany four-poft bedfteads with chintz, moreen, damafk and other furniture; goofe and other feather beds, mattreffes, blankets, quilts, and counterpanes; very good mahogany tables, chairs, chefts of drawers, a convenient library bookcafe feven feet high and 9 feet long; an office defk, a pair of globes and covers, two marble fide tables, a wine cooper, a very convenient mahogany medicine cheft with bottles and drawers, an India cabinet, mahogany night-table, floor and bed-fide carpets, large handfome pier and dreffing glaffes, a very good eight-day clock, and variety of prints, paintings and kitchen furniture; a very handfome modern poft chaife newly painted, plate glafs, fpring blinds, and good lining, and alfo a good poft chaife, with plate glafs, new wheels, and lining, the painting; &c. in good condition; and a very neat phaeton either for a pair or fingle horfe, in good prefervation, with harnefs for a pair of horfes to each; alfo a pair of very good bay horfes, and a handfome brown gelding, about 14 hands and a half high.

Binfield and Barkham estates (which necessitated a private Act of Parliament to unravel a strict settlement created by William Pitt's will)[19].

The Revd John Gabriel became tenant of Barkham House by 1780. Gabriel was a well-to-do Georgian cleric, with three carriages and two male servants (including a footman)[20], who had previously resided at his other living at Hampstead Norris. Following his death in 1782 there was a 2-day sale of his furniture and personal effects at Barkham Manor[21].

In 1783 John Pitt sold the Barkham manor estate, the lordship and the advowson, to Thomas Fonnereau, who took up residence at the house. At the same time John Pitt and Thomas Fonnereau jointly agreed to sell about 1,783 oak trees, growing in various parts of the manor, to a Reading timber merchant, who was to be responsible for their felling, for £4,000[22]. In January 1784 Thomas Fonnereau sold Barkham Manor to his brother Harry[23], although Thomas continued to live there and was on good terms with the new rector, the Revd David Davies, contributing to the cost of pulling down the old parsonage house (a '*mean cottage, badly situated*') and rebuilding it.

In summer 1787 Barkham Manor was offered for sale '*a commodious dwelling house, the principal part recently built and genteelly fitted up and finished*'[24]. Why the principal part of the house had been rebuilt is unknown. Either it was in a serious state of disrepair or there had been some calamity, perhaps a fire.

13 Barkham – A Manor in Contention, Part I (1589–1605)

By the mid-1580s the lord of the manors of Arborfield and Barkham, Thomas Bullock (who had succeeded his father Richard in 1570), was in serious financial difficulty. He had accumulated debts of some £3,000, some owed to Elizabeth I. To borrow on an ever-increasing scale, Thomas Bullock was forced to mortgage his lands to various creditors. He also resorted to various subterfuges to protect the family lands from the claims of creditors, including an illegal family settlement in 1586 and a purported 800-year lease in favour of his next brother, William, to commence at his death[1].

In 1589 Thomas Bullock was forced by this heavy accumulation of debts to sell the manors of Arborfield and Barkham for £4,000 to his kinsman Edmond Standen, one of the Clerks of the Petty Bag of the Court of Chancery, but subject to a lease-back to Thomas Bullock for the rest of his life at a rent of £150 per annum[2]. The manor (or farm) of Barkham (adjacent to the parish church) was sold subject to the remainder of a 21-year lease (granted in 1574) to Thomas Bullock's next brother, William.

Not only was the sale deeply unpopular with other members of the Bullock family, in particular his brother William, but the title acquired by Edmond Standen under the 1589 conveyance was defective, since not all the charges in favour of Thomas Bullock's creditors had been properly discharged. Three months after the sale, Edmond Standen sued Thomas Bullock, his brother William and 14 others (relatives and creditors) in the Court of Chancery for rectification of the defective conveyance[3]. Although Thomas Bullock entered into a supplemental indenture in May 1590, which was supposed to remedy the defects of title, the law suit continued until 1595.

In January 1594 Thomas Bullock died at the relatively early age of 48 and the lease-back came to an end. Since Thomas Bullock and his wife, Dorothy, had no children, his heir-at-law was his next brother, William. On 25 February 1594 William Bullock seized possession of the manor house and mill at Arborfield. When Standen's agents attempted to take possession of the mill, William's servants inside the building threw scalding water over them[4]. William Bullock was prosecuted at Reading assizes and found guilty of forceable entry and '*riotous & disorderly conduct*'[5].

Standen coat of arms

Following Thomas Bullock's death in 1594, there must still have been questions about the adequacy of Standen's title, since in November 1594 he sued Thomas Bullock's widow, Dorothy, her brother Sir Humfrey Forster, William Bullock and 25 others in the Court of Chancery, alleging that they had conspired to conceal documents of title (some of which were subsequently found in a hawking bag)[6]. When in November 1594 Thomas White, rector of Barkham, died, Standen was unable to present a new rector, and in default Elizabeth I eventually presented Abraham Warrocke as the new rector in May 1596[7].

In the meantime, William Bullock continued to dispute Standen's title to the Arborfield and Barkham estates, causing Edmond Standen to institute proceedings at the common law for the examination of William Bullock's alleged title under the illegal 1586 family settlement.

In June 1596, in all probability to raise money, William Bullock procured *'dyvers and sundrye vagrante roguyshe and sturdye p[er]sons'* to fell valuable timber on the demesne lands of the manor of Barkham. The men refused to desist and continued *'in the same fellinge With stronge hande in forceable sorte havinge Weapons readye by them and offering violence'*. Standen immediately sought an injunction in the Court of Chancery to stop William Bullock from felling more trees, which was granted on 23 June 1596. William prevaricated in answering the court's questions and was committed to the Fleet Prison for contempt in January 1597. The 1596 Chancery action culminated in a lengthy and learned judgment on 10 February 1597 in favour of Standen by the Lord Keeper, Sir Thomas Egerton[8].

Many years later (in 1660), William Bullock's son Edward was to allege that, on the strength of the Chancery decree, Standen

1596 presentation of Abraham Warrocke as rector by Elizabeth I

'by force of arms without any legal officer did by many unknown persons break into the [farm of Barkham] *and turned* [Bullock's wife] *and ten children out of doors'*[9].

William Bullock, and his brother Edward, continued to dispute Standen's title, still basing their claim on the illegal 1586 family settlement, causing Standen to seek to have the 1586 indenture set aside in the Court of Star Chamber. In its judgment in May 1597, the Court found that the 1586 indenture had been fraudulent and was intended to deceive. William Bullock was fined and committed to the Fleet Prison for 6 months whilst the fraudulent settlement was *'damned'*[10].

Meanwhile, in October 1597 William and Edward Bullock, and two uncles, met in the City of London to hatch another plot to recover the family estates. They engaged one William Woodward to forge a deed of family settlement, purportedly executed before 1570 during the lifetime of Thomas Bullock's father, Richard. Edmond Standen immediately sued William Bullock and his fellow conspirators in Star Chamber. In an abusive defence, William and Gilbert Bullock denied any wrongdoing, asserting that the law suit *'hath* [been] *most falsely and slanderously forged framed and devised'* and that Standen had been encouraged to bring the suit *'by the sinister and lewd counsel of some unlearned and ignorant persons'*[11].

In September 1596 William Bullock had forcibly seized possession of the dower lands of Thomas Bullock's widow, Dorothy, in Barkham at Langley Common, resulting in

another Chancery action[12]. Thomas Bullock's uncles, Gilbert and George, continued to dispute Standen's title, so Standen sued them in Chancery in 1599[13].

William Bullock continued to harass Standen, notwithstanding that most of the time from January 1597 until 1602 he was in the Fleet Prison. In 1599 he sued Standen for the recovery of the manors in King's Bench. In addition, he busied himself with petitions to the Queen, the Privy Council, the Lord Admiral and others, as well as spreading false rumours abusing Standen and making unwarranted imputations as to his integrity[14].

William Bullock initially pursued the case in King's Bench aggressively, causing the arrest of two of Standen's servants. However, at the hearing, after a jury of 17 men from Berkshire had been sworn in, William Bullock *'by cunning sleights drifts and practices'* failed to present any evidence and the judges dismissed the action, castigating William Bullock's behaviour as a *'great vexation'* and a *'foul abuse'*.

An increasingly exasperated Standen was forced to seek relief by another Chancery law suit against William Bullock in November 1599[15]. In contemptuous disregard, in December 1599 William Bullock procured the Bullock family trustees (William and Thomas Kingsmill of Sydmonton) to grant a purported lease of the manors of Arborfield and Barkham to one of his sons, Thomas (aged 14). In April 1600 Standen sued Thomas Bullock (minor), and the Bullock family trustees, in separate actions in Chancery[16]. In response, Thomas Bullock (minor), through his father William as guardian, sued Standen again for the recovery of the manors, this time in the Court of Common Pleas. It seems that this action was also dismissed[17].

William Bullock's antics found little favour with the authorities. As the official report of the dispute in State Papers, Domestic, in June 1600 concluded, '*By all which is manifeste that Willm Bullock forgotte him selfe, walketh he knowes not wheare, and woulde have he cannott tell what, excepte it be infinitelie to be troublesome*'.

There appears to have been one more law suit against William Bullock about 1605, this time in the Court of Common Pleas[18]. Since Edmond Standen died in March 1603 (5 days after the death of Elizabeth I), the proceedings must have been brought by his only son and heir, William Standen, to whom the Arborfield and Barkham estates passed. It seems that William Bullock was once again found guilty of forgery, perjury and subordination of witnesses. To all intents and purposes the dispute between the Bullocks and the Standens now petered out, although William Bullock lived, it seems elsewhere than in Barkham, until about 1623[19], leaving the Standens in undisputed ownership.

14 Barkham During the Civil War (1642–1646) and the Commonwealth (1649–1660)

The uncertain times of the Civil War and the Commonwealth are characterised by a lack of contemporaneous records. Parish registers, for instance, were often poorly kept, not helped by an Act of the Barebone's Parliament in 1653 which removed the custody of parish registers from ministers of religion and entrusted them to a civil official called the Parish Register. Luckily, the registers of Barkham baptisms and burials are complete throughout the period, but few marriages are recorded[1].

Births and deaths amongst Barkham inhabitants were both unusually high throughout the period. Baptisms averaged 6·2 per year in the 1640s and 6·9 in the 1650s, compared with 5·4 per year in the 1630s and 3·8 in the 1660s. Burials averaged 4·1 per year in the 1640s and 4·9 in the 1650s, compared with 1·8 per year in the 1630s and 2·9 in the 1660s. There appear to have been epidemics or plagues in 1640 (12 burials), 1642 (8; typhus epidemic), 1655 (8) and 1658 (9).

In May 1639, when Charles I and Parliament were increasingly at odds, William Standen, lord of the manors of Arborfield and

Barkham since 1603, died (aged 73) at Arborfield. Although his heir-at-law was a kinsman called William Ball, the Arborfield and Barkham estates passed, under a family settlement, to another kinsman of the same name, William Standen[2]. It appears that his widow, Mary, continued to live at Arborfield manor until her death in 1645, whilst William Standen (kinsman) and his (first) wife Sarah spent the troubled Civil War years at Barkham manor. By 1645 William Ball was resident at Barkham and he remained until at least 1652.

The trustees of the Arborfield and Barkham estates were William Lenthall and Nicholas Love (a relative). William Lenthall was an eminent lawyer and parliamentarian. As MP for Woodstock he was Speaker of the House of Commons during the Long Parliament (1641–1653) and (1654–1656), as well as being Master of the Rolls (1643–1660). Nicholas Love, who was also a lawyer, was a member of a number of Parliamentary commissions for Berkshire during the interregnum.

William Ball appears to have been a writer of political tracts in the 1640s and 1650s, of

To the Honourable, Major Generall
Sᴋɪᴘᴘᴏɴ,

William Ball of *Bárkham,* wisheth all good successe
and happinesse.

Sɪʀ,

T Your *being in* Redding, *about what time the Kings forces relinquished that place in* May 1644. *I presented unto* You *a paper,* De jure Regnandi, et Regni, *wherein was contained the heads and chiefe points of that Subject, and therein I promised to give farther satisfaction, which I hope I have now effected to the satisfaction of all indifferent men; and I have thought fit to dedicate it to Your Honour, to whom I first of all tendered the* Epitome : *remaining*

October 27.   Your Honours
1645.
                                        servant

                                   William Ball.

*Dedication from 1645
political pamphlet by
William Ball of Barkham*

Ball himself had Parliamentary aspirations and unsuccessfully attempted to be elected to the Long Parliament when one of the Reading Borough seats unexpectedly became vacant in 1645. Ball was defeated by Tanfield Vachell in a closed vote of the Corporation. Ball then petitioned the House of Commons for a free vote by all the townspeople, but he was defeated by 560 to 309 votes. The election seems to have been less than well tempered, and on the night of the result Ball induced the Mayor (who had supported him) '*by candle light … in the Towne hall*' to execute an indenture claiming that William Ball had been duly returned notwithstanding his defeat[6].

When the Civil War broke out in 1642, the area around Wokingham was not under the control of either side, but as large numbers of Parliamentary and Royalist troops moved into the Thames Valley to fight for control of key towns like Reading, the district found itself in disputed territory, subject to occupation and intermittent raids by both armies. From January 1643 there were various skirmishes and frequent raids to take horses, food and other supplies. From April to June 1643, when Reading was occupied by the Parliamentary forces, the Wokingham district was behind Parliamentary lines, but when the Parliamentary forces withdrew in June 1643, the area was once again vulnerable to looting by both sides, with consequent terrorising of inhabitants, stealing of goods and burning of property.

which twelve survive in various academic libraries around the world (including nine at the British Library and five at the Bodleian)[3]. In two of the tracts, written in 1645 and 1646, he describes himself as William Ball of Barkham, and there are '*epistles dedicatory*' to, respectively, Major-General Philip Skippon[4], a leading Parliamentary general, and Sir Francis Pile Bart. (of Compton Beauchamp)[5], a wealthy landowner and staunch Parliamentary supporter, who was elected to the Long Parliament as MP for Reading in 1646, which express satisfaction at the success of the Parliamentary forces in Berkshire.

It is virtually inconceivable that Barkham would have escaped the attention of the marauding troops whilst the occupying forces (which would have been Parliamentary after the initial phase of the Civil War) would have been billeted amongst the homesteads in the parish, exacerbating the food shortages and poor sanitary conditions. One can only speculate what the inhabitants of Barkham might have witnessed or been subjected to during these turbulent times. The requisitioning (or theft) of horses and other animals, and the stealing of grain and goods would have been a daily hazard, whilst a succession of wet summers, heralding the 'Little Ice Age', further aggravated the position.

In the struggle for control of Reading, both sides gathered intelligence from outlying villages. The diaries of Sir Samuel Luke, the Parliamentary spymaster, record one such intelligence gathering mission to Barkham by a 'scout' called John Lane in February 1643[7].

The tempo of the Royalist attacks in the area increased in the autumn of 1643. In October 1643, *'His Majesty's forces invaded Ockingham and practised the most barbarous cruelty which malice of fury could invent, so that what the sword left untouched, the rage of flame devoured'*[8]. According to one of Luke's scouts, *'hee sawe 4 houses burnt downe in Okeingham, and that they had sett fire in 3 places more'*.

The area remained subject to intermittent Royalist raids until May 1644, when Reading was abandoned to the Parliamentary

forces. But the occupying Parliamentary forces in and around Wokingham continued to compel the inhabitants to support the troops with money and supplies, and conditions had become so acute that the Parliamentary Committee for Berkshire was told that in the country districts there was *'hardly a sheep, hen, hog, oats, hay, wheat or any other thing'* left for man or beast to feed on.

The end of the Civil War left the district with a shattered economy and recovery was slow[9]. In Wokingham about one-fifth of the houses and barns had been burnt down, whilst most of the bridges and mills in the locality had been destroyed by the Cavaliers. Horses for the essential tasks of ploughing, sowing and reaping were in short supply. It may not be without significance that in 1660 William Standen borrowed £500 from John

Marauding troops were a constant hazard during the Civil War

Harrison of Reading, secured by a lease by way of mortgage for *'four score and nineteen'* years over Barkham Farm (a 166-acre farm let to Henry Miller)[10].

In 1650 Edward Bullock, a son of William Bullock of Barkham, revived the family claim to the manors of Arborfield and Barkham, which was so bitterly disputed between his father and Edmond Standen in the 1590s, by petitioning the Long Parliament, and subsequently in 1660 the House of Lords, for their recovery, as recounted in the following chapter.

There is a legend that a headless soldier, the so-called 'phantom of Barkham', patrols the Barkham Road between Wokingham and Barkham. If the story is to be given any credence, its most likely origin is the troubled times during the Civil War, perhaps following one of the raids on Wokingham in 1643.

15 Barkham – A Manor in Contention, Part II (1650–1662)

When Edmond Standen died in 1603, the Arborfield and Barkham estates passed to his only son, William. In 1605 the bitter dispute between the Standens and William Bullock, heir-at-law of Thomas Bullock, who had sold the manors to Edmond Standen in 1589 (as recounted in Chapter 13), petered out. On the death of William Standen, without issue, in 1639, the manors passed to a kinsman of the same name, William Standen, although his heir-at-law was another kinsman called William Ball.

Some years later, in 1650, one of William Bullock's younger sons, Edward, who was born in Barkham in 1595 and had emigrated to New England about 1636, returned to England and revived the family claim to the Arborfield and Barkham estates by petitioning the Long Parliament for their return[1]. He was was aided and abetted by his younger brother, Fleet, who was born elsewhere than in Barkham.

Edward Bullock employed the ingenious argument (never advanced by his father) that Edmond Standen had not purchased the lands at all, but had lent Thomas Bullock £4,000 against a mortgage of the property

(which, together with the timber growing on it, was allegedly worth £24,000), and that Thomas' heir-at-law, William Bullock, had started felling trees on the demesne lands of the manor of Barkham with the intention of paying off the mortgage, but that he had been thwarted by Standen who had declined to accept repayment[2].

He also alleged that Sir Thomas Egerton's judgment against his father in the Court of Chancery in 1597 was the result of '*foule and corrupt practises*', because Edmond Standen

Extract from Edward Bullock's petition to Parliament, 1650

75

(a senior court official) had been '*very powerful*' with Egerton. In fact, in the 1589 Chancery proceedings, Thomas Bullock (died 1594) had acknowledged that he had sold the lands outright to Edmond Standen, who was '*the best Chapman* [i.e. purchaser] *he could happen upon to serve his turne with speedie payment of money*', whilst the 1597 Chancery judgment contains no mention of a mortgage, as claimed by Edward Bullock.

The petition was referred by Parliament to the Committee of Indemnity, which appears to have had quasi-judicial powers. At its sitting on 25 December 1650, the Committee directed that witnesses be examined. It seems that depositions were taken from about 20 witnesses locally. It was Edward Bullock's contention that the Standens had been unjustly enriching themselves by felling valuable timber ever since the 1590s, and that Edmond Standen had felled timber worth £3,000–4,000 within 12 months of getting possession. One of the witnesses, who could not have been born at the time, even deposed that there used to be '*soe much Wood in y.ᵉ manno.ʳ of Barkeham that there was little or no feeding for Sheepe there*'[3].

At a hearing before the Committee of Indemnity on 20 March 1651, Edward Bullock failed to produce any evidence of the alleged mortgage and his counsel instead based Bullock's claim on the fraudulent 1586 family settlement. At the end of the hearing, the Committee voted that there had been no mortgage and no corrupt decree[4]. The

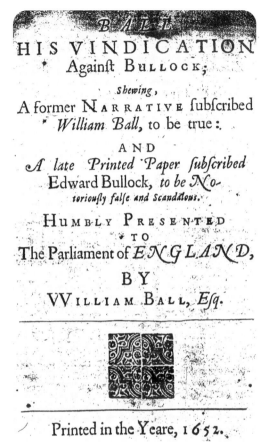

BALL

HIS VINDICATION

Againſt Bullock;

shewing,

A former NARRATIVE ſubſcribed *William Ball*, to be true :

AND

A late Printed Paper ſubſcribed Edward Bullock, *to be No-toriouſly falſe and Scanddlous.*

HUMBLY PRESENTED TO The Parliament of *ENGLAND*, BY WILLIAM BALL, *Eſq.*

Printed in the Yeare, 1652.

Committee of Indemnity appointed a small sub-committee, which did not meet for at least a year until Edward and Fleet Bullock '*being revengefull and greedy, they then began to ſtir the coales againe*'[5]. In June 1652 the Committee of Indemnity was dissolved and its powers transferred to seven Commissioners for Indemnity, prompting Edward and Fleet to pursue their claim with renewed vigour.

Both Edward Bullock and William Ball published a number of printed papers in support of their claims, some of which survive. William Ball dismissed the evidence of the witnesses as being no more than '*heare-fayes*', since all of the deponents, apart from Richard Alnut of Barkham, were born after 1589, whilst Alnut, who subsequently became a waiter in London, could only have been 6–7 years old at the time. In addition, William Ball objected that the deponents '*are for the moft part very meane, and inconfiderable Perfons. One (if not more) of them a Cottager*'[6]. William Ball also claimed that Fleet Bullock had '*vapoured exceedingly*' and had tried to influence witnesses with promises of copyhold tenancies and '*other castels in the Ayre*', as well as the payment of bribes and alluring deponents by '*feaftings*'. By these means he '*craftily won unto himfelfe many ignorant and credulous people in and about Wockingham, efpecially fuch as were of his owne Name, Kinred and Friends*'[7].

In his 13-page pamphlet of August 1652, entitled *Ball: His Vindication Againft Bullock*, in which a printed paper by Edward Bullock (which does not survive) was castigated as being '*notoriously false and scandalous*', William Ball asserted that he was '*weary of Anfwering this mans Infolences, and impertinences*'. As to William Bullock's 5 years in the Fleet Prison, William Ball commented '*fo ought he to be for falfe clamour, and vexatious Practifes*'.

Edward Bullock alleged that to settle the dispute between William Bullock and Edmond Standen in the 1590s, Standen offered Bullock the manor (or farm) of Barkham plus £300, and to '*breed up*' his eldest son in the '*Pettibagg Office*' of the Court of Chancery if he would relinquish his claim to the manor of Arborfield, but that William Bullock had refused, saying, '*if he had right to some, he had right to all*'[8].

Edward Bullock's counsel pursued his case aggressively, wrong-footing Standen's counsel on several occasions. William Ball later insinuated[9] that Edward Bullock had accomplices who were champitors, that is to say financial partners in the litigation, which would have been illegal. The various depositions included superficially persuasive assertions that it was the '*common report*' that the lands had merely been mortgaged in 1589, and that the Standens had since cut down most of the woods, leaving little standing. There were varying estimates (unsubstantiated) of the annual income derived from the lands and the value of the timber.

Ultimately, in September 1653 the Commissioners for Indemnity (who used to meet at Haberdashers Hall) produced a detailed and lengthy report[10], but referred the matter back to Parliament, which took no further action.

It appears that Edward Bullock was almost as stubborn as his father William, and notwithstanding the failure of his petition to Parliament, in March 1656 he petitioned the Lord Protector, Oliver Cromwell, seemingly with similar lack of success. He also unsuccessfully petitioned the Council of State in 1654/5[11].

Undaunted, in December 1660, following the restoration of the monarchy, Edward Bullock submitted yet another petition, this time to the House of Lords[12]. Because of various procedural delays, the definitive hearing did not take place until March 1662. The witnesses originally procured by Edward Bullock in 1651 were by this time rather aged (if not '*auncient*'), and in some cases too infirm to travel, whilst others had died in the meantime. Those fit enough to travel had to stay in London, at Bullock's expense, for a number of weeks whilst last minute procedural wrangling delayed the hearing.

With the passage of time, Edward Bullock's claims became more fanciful. His counsel alleged that for not submitting to Sir Thomas Egerton's judgment in Chancery in 1597, William Bullock was '*imprisoned for 9 yeares & through greife dyes*', although William Bullock did not die until about 1623. His counsel further claimed that '*the son through infancy & poverty goes beyond sea*', although he was about 41 when he emigrated to New England.

Ultimately, Edward Bullock's petition was heard by the Committee for Petitions sitting in the Painted Chamber of the House of Lords at 3.00 p.m. on Friday 14 March 1662. After considering the respective submissions, the Committee dismissed Edward Bullock's petition. The dispute between the Bullock and Standen families in respect of the manors of Barkham and Arborfield was therefore finally determined after 73 years in 1662 in favour of the Standens.

Whilst on any objective analysis the title of the Standen's was unimpeachable, and Edward Bullock's petition in 1650 was opportunistic, the aggressive tactics employed by Bullock forced William Standen and William Ball on the defensive, and they must have had real concerns that they would be dispossessed by Edward Bullock. In addition, the examination of a large number of witnesses in both January 1651 and March 1662, and the intervening uncertainty, must have had an unsettling effect locally.

16 The Bull Inn and Smithy

The first surviving documentary references to the Bull Alehouse and the adjacent smithy are in a 1727 indenture, which records Alice Allwright's inheritance of the alehouse from her father, Thomas Simonds, and her purchase of the smithy[1].

The 1727 indenture also refers to a previous landlord called Edward Chaplin, who died in 1703. It seems that Edward Chaplin ran the alehouse from at least the mid-1670s, since the parish registers record the death in childbirth of his first wife, Ann, in 1676, and there are 14 other entries relating to him and his family[2]. The church rate assessment which survives from 1689 records Chaplin as occupying about 2 acres[3].

It is not known when there was first an alehouse on the site, but none was recorded at Barkham at the time of a 1577 government survey of licensed premises (although an alehouse at Arborfield was recorded)[4]. This is discouraging for any theory that the name of the alehouse is derived from the bull's head on the arms of the Bullock family, since they ceased to be lords of the manor in 1589, unless Barkham had an unlicensed alehouse of this name at that time.

When Edward Chaplin died, it is not known whether his eldest son, also Edward (24), took over the alehouse. The next landlord of whom we know is Thomas Marlow (the elder), who was described as a victualler in the will of William Waterman I (lord of the manor) in 1733[5]. Thomas Marlow may already have retired, since he was left the cottage in which he then lived, and he died in 1741. Whether Thomas Marlow the younger took over the alehouse is not known, but by the time of the manorial court of survey in 1738[6], the landlord was Thomas Whiteing (who was elected tythingman, i.e. constable, the following year)[7].

Thomas Whiteing may have established the custom, which was to endure until almost the end of the nineteenth century, that the landlord of The Bull was also the village blacksmith, since in the 1727 indenture he was described not as a victualler, but as a blacksmith. This used to be common practice in many villages.

The earliest known blacksmith is James Winch, who died in 1693[8]. He seems to have practised his craft in Barkham for over 40 years, since the parish registers contain twelve entries relating to him and his family, commencing during the Commonwealth in 1651. It is not known whether James Winch's eldest son, also James (born 1655), took over the smithy on his father's death in 1693, but the next blacksmith in Barkham of whom we know is Thomas Douglas, who died in 1710[9].

Although there is a tile in the wall of the old smithy bearing the date 1728, the 1727 indenture refers to a '*new erected messuage*' occupied by Thomas Whiteing, blacksmith. A further inconsistency is that the 1738 court of survey also refers to a '*new built house & smiths shop*'. Whilst Thomas Whiteing was still landlord of the Bull Alehouse in 1738, the smith's shop was in the hands of Henry Toby. Both men were to die in 1743, when Henry Toby was succeeded by his son, also Henry.

In 1749 Alice Allwright and the Revd John Waterman (lord of the manor) entered into a deed of exchange whereby Alice Allwright

The old smithy

sold the alehouse in exchange for 5 acres elsewhere in the parish[10]. The deed recited Waterman's intention of demolishing the buildings on the site of the alehouse, and a subsequent deed in 1756 confirmed that the alehouse had indeed been pulled down.

Alice Allwright continued to own the site of the smithy until her death in 1757, when the freehold was sold to James Miles for £100[11]. By 1766 the smithy had been sold to John Cooper[12], and Henry Toby the younger was still tenant. The fate of the alehouse during these years is unknown, although the freehold was also acquired by John Cooper. Henry Toby was also a small-scale farmer and by 1756 he was renting six fields (21 acres) from the lord of the manor[13].

In 1781 Henry Toby died. He was succeeded by his son, Abraham Toby. Henry's widow, Jane, lived to the age of 88. As well as shoeing horses and oxen at the forge, the Tobys also made and repaired farm implements. Abraham Toby also supplied newspapers to those inhabitants who could read and could afford them. By 1797 the freehold of the smith's shop and the public house had been acquired by William Blackall Simonds of the Reading brewing family[14].

During the eighteenth and early nineteenth centuries the steward of the manor used to preside over meetings of the manorial Court Baron at The Bull. It was also the venue for the annual farmers' dinners held by the Revd David Davies (rector 1782–1819) each '*pay-day*' for the settlement of tythes. The merriment was doubtless accompanied by plenty of punch and strong beer, at a cost to the rector of 4 guineas[15]. Later in the nineteenth century the tythe dinners had given way to suppers for bellringers and the cricket club.

In 1803 Abraham Toby died (aged 55). A notice in the *Reading Mercury* announced that his business as an '*edge-tool-maker and farrier*' had been taken over by his nephew, John Collyer[16]. The churchwardens' accounts, which survive from the same year, record various payments to John Collyer, either for smith's work or for supplying beer to the bellringers[17]. John Collyer was involved in various aspects of parish life and served as churchwarden many times. He also became a substantial tenant farmer, farming 125 acres at the time of the 1840 tythe award[18].

In 1843 George Collyer (27) took over The Bull and the smithy from his father, John (67). He also became village sub-postmaster. George Collyer's successors in the 1880s, Stephen Bernard and Thomas Parsons, also carried on the tradition of combining the roles of landlord and blacksmith[19]. In 1905 H. & G. Simonds brewery carried out extensive alterations to the pub, which earned it the nickname of the 'Hotel Cecil' on account of its newly decorated front[20].

There used to stand in front of the smithy an old stand (or trevis) for shoeing oxen, but the structure was removed about 1920. It

ALL persons having any demands on Mr. ABRAHAM TOBY, of Barkham, Edge-Tool-Maker and Farrier, deceased, are desired to send an account thereof to Mr. Robert Hewett, of Barkham, or Mr. W. B. Simonds, Reading, in order to their being paid; and all persons indebted to the said Abraham Toby, are requested to pay the same as above.

MARY TOBY, Widow of the above Mr. Abraham Toby, having declined business in favour of Mr. JOHN COLLIER, begs to recommend him to the Customers of her late Husband.

JOHN COLLIER, having taken to the business of his late Uncle, Mr. Abraham Toby, Edge-Tool-Maker and Farrier, begs to solicit the Favours of the friends of his late Uncle, with those of the Public, who may depend on having their business executed with punctuality and dispatch.

Reading Mercury,
19 September 1803

was a kind of rectangular cage made by fixing horizontal bars in four wooden uprights, the ox's leg being fastened to one of the uprights. In the 1920s and 1930s Billy Batt carried on business as shoeing smith at the forge.

In 1928 William Flower became landlord. Although he died (aged 59) in 1946, his wife Annie lived to be 93 and died in 1985. In 1968 Mrs Flower (then 76) celebrated 40 years as landlady and received a silver salver from David Simonds. Up to that time, beer was drawn from a barrel in the cellar. The pub is now a free house.

The forge continued as a working smithy up to 1982, when the then landlords, Courage, converted it into a restaurant despite much local resistance. The pub and old smithy is a grade 2 listed building.

17 St James' Church, Part II (1700 to date)

Georgian era

In 1700 the manor and advowson (i.e. the right to nominate the rector) of Barkham were sold by Edward Standen of Arborfield to William Waterman I[1], who later purchased the right to make the next presentation to the living of Arborfield when Edward Standen's son, also called Edward, died (aged 27) insolvent in 1730[2]. When the Barkham and Arborfield livings both became vacant on the death of the Revd John Sale in 1739, William Waterman's heir as lord of the manor of Barkham, the Revd John Waterman, presented himself to the living of Arborfield, but not to the living of Barkham, where he presented the Revd William

Monday evening about five o'clock as the carriage of Dr. Gabriel of Barkham was returning from Reading, with Mrs Gabriel and another Lady, they were attacked on the road leading from the turnpike to Sindlesham, by a fellow who jumpt out of the hedge, and seized the driver's horse by the bridle, and endeavoured to stop him; but the postilion resolutely struck him a violent blow on the head with his whip, and immediately spurred his horse, who gave a sudden spring, which loosened the fellow's hold, and threw him on the ground, and then driving on furiously, got clear away. There was a woman in company, and it is strongly suspected who they both are. The Ladies were very much frightened.

Berkshire Chronicle, 28 December 1772

Dawes[3], who was to remain 29 years until his death (aged 67) in 1768.

Dawes was one of the Berkshire inspectors for Thomas Coram's Foundling Hospital in London from at least 1759 until his death. The inspectors were responsible for recruiting wet and dry nurses with whom the abandoned infants could be placed for the first 5 years of their lives, should they survive that long. Foundling children were, inevitably, very sickly and the majority did not survive. Dawes was responsible for the supervision of up to 20 infants at a time, placing them with wet nurses in Barkham and neighbouring parishes, issuing and collecting clothing supplied by the hospital, procuring medicines and paying wages and other bills. The nurses in Barkham recruited by Dawes included Mary Payne, Ann Pither, Elizabeth Warfield and Mary Webb[4].

In 1768 Dr John Gabriel, a well-to-do Georgian cleric, was presented as rector by the then lord of the manor, William Pitt of Binfield Manor[5]. He was to remain 14 years until his death (aged 66) in 1782. Gabriel was also vicar of Hampstead Norris, where he resided, for 30 years, although by 1780 he was living at Barkham, probably at Barkham

House, and following his death there was a 2-day auction of his furniture and personal effects (including three carriages) at the manor house[6]. Although Dr Gabriel was at the vicarage at Hampstead Norris at the time of his death, he was buried at Barkham.

David Davies (1782–1819)

In 1782 David Davies was presented to the living by the next lord of the manor, John Pitt[7]. He was to remain 37 years until his death (aged 76) in 1819. The life and accomplishments of David Davies are recounted in Chapter 19.

With the arrival of Davies the parish registers become more informative. One innovation was to give the age of the deceased in the case of burials as a matter of course, confirming the high incidence of deaths amongst infants and children. The registers also show that at the end of the eighteenth century a significant number of Barkham inhabitants lived well into their 70s (or even 80s), and there are a number of references to deaths from smallpox in the 1770s and 1780s[8].

David Davies was also unusually conscientious in answering questionnaires by the Bishop. We learn that in 1783 the Sunday services were 11.00 a.m. matins and 3.00 p.m. evensong. Holy Communion was celebrated four times a year, and at Easter 1783 there were eleven communicants out of 165 inhabitants (counting children)[9].

The church authorities remained very concerned about the activities of dissenters, but it seems that Barkham did not usually harbour any 'papists'. A number of the poorer families were, however, members of the Baptist congregation in Wokingham, and in 1814 a licence was granted by the Bishop under the Toleration Act 1688 for baptists to worship at the house of Thomas Warwick in Barkham[10]. The burial register for 1775, during Dr Gabriel's incumbency, contains the following entry: '*John Allright from Hurst Parish – One of y.ᵉ people call'd Methodists & therefore not carried into the Church*'.

There is the following description of the interior of the old church written by David Davies in 1783[11].

The Church (with the Chancel) is in length fifty-nine feet, in breadth twenty-one feet; the Chancel is in breadth twenty feet. Within & belonging to it are; A Communion Table of oak, with a covering of red cloth and a crimson damask cushion: also one linnen cloth for the same with a napkin: over the table on an altar-piece of stained deal are the Lord's Prayer, the Apostles Creed, and the Ten Commandments, printed; and over this the Queen's Arms, A.R. 1710: Also a Chest with three locks little used because of the damp. A Pulpit with a short red cloth & cushion: a reading-desk with a red cloth: one large bible, & three large common-prayer books, & four Register Books: a stone font lined with lead, with a cover of wood: one surplice: a bier with a hearse cloth: four Bells with their frames, one ladder.

The 1783 inventory by Davies also gave detailed dimensions of the old parsonage house ('*a miserable cottage, in which my Predecefsor had never resided*'), which Davies had pulled down about 1785, and a new house erected at a cost of £400[12], which was insured with Royal-Exchange Assurance. Davies also insured his library of books for £50 and his wearing apparel for £30[13]. An old black and white photograph survives of a water colour of the rebuilt parsonage house[14], known as 'The Parson's Pleasance', with a gentleman in a black hat relaxing in a chair in the garden smoking a pipe. Unfortunately, the whereabouts of the original painting are unknown.

Cedar of Lebanon, 1788–1996

Davies contracted out the farming of his glebe land (18 acres) to Robert Hewett of Langley Pond Farm. The outbuildings of the parsonage included a thatched barn 50 feet long, a stable, a cow-stall and two 'Pent-houses' for storing farm equipment and turf (used for fuel).

On 16 June 1788 the new lady of the manor, the Honourable Frances Leveson Gower, planted in the churchyard the Cedar of Lebanon, which was to become such a famous Barkham landmark[15]. Sadly, after a long struggle, the Cedar eventually succumbed to honey fungus disease and had to be felled in December 1996. Although the Leveson Gowers' family seat was at Bill Hill in Hurst, Davies acted as chaplain to the family and a family vault was established at Barkham Church. A brass plaque on the east wall of the south transept lists the members of the family who are buried in the vault (including Mary, Countess Gower) and nearby hangs a large hatchment with the Leveson Gower coat of arms[16].

In 1810 the advowson was separated from the lordship of the manor, when Lieutenant General John Leveson Gower sold the right to present to the Revd Henry Ellis St John, rector and lord of the manor of Finchampstead, West Court, for 3,000 guineas (£3,150)[17].

The churchwardens' accounts survive from 1803 onwards. One of the first entries records the purchase in 1804 of a new surplice from Mr Heelas, relatively recently moved to Wokingham, for £3. 8s. *'Paid the ringing money 9s.'* was a regular annual entry. In reality, this was the annual cost of beer for the bellringers supplied by John Collyer, landlord of The Bull. The churchwardens were also required, under statutes dating from the reigns of Henry VIII and Elizabeth I, to make payments for the destruction of vermin. *'Paid for catching 50 dozen sparrows 12s. 6d.'* in 1805 was a typical entry. Capitation payments were also made for catching hedgehogs and *'maggs'*. In the 1830s George Blake was paid one shilling a year for mole *'ketching'* in the churchyard[18].

The only surviving drawings of the old church date from the early nineteenth century. There are two by J.C. Buckler, dated 1818 (one at the British Library[19] and the other at the Bodleian[20]), and a third, by H.W. Burt, dated 1835, is in the possession of the British Library[21].

Victorian era

When David Davies died in 1819, the Revd Henry Ellis St John of Finchampstead presented himself to the living of Barkham and ran the two parishes like a united benefice. St John was a famous hunting parson and kept his own pack of hounds at West Court[22]. In 1837 there was a reorganisation of ecclesiastical jurisdictions and Berkshire was transferred from the Diocese of Salisbury to the Diocese of Oxford.

In 1841 the Revd Henry Ellis St John died and in 1842 his widow presented their second son, the Revd Edward St John, to the livings of Finchampstead and Barkham. Initially, the church authorities were less than satisfied with Edward St John's ministration of Barkham and the notebook of Bishop Samuel Wilberforce contains the entry *'nearly worst church in archdeaconry'*[23]. In 1843 St John appointed his future brother-in-law, the Revd Arthur Roberts (aged 31), as curate of Barkham. Roberts was to remain 43 years.

Meanwhile, the ownership of the advowson of Barkham passed from Mrs Elizabeth St John (widow) to her third son, John St John. It was agreed that Edward should purchase the advowson of Barkham from John for £5,000, but in 1862 Edward St John sub-sold the advowson to Arthur Roberts for £3,000 and an annuity of £50 per annum[24]. Edward St John resigned as rector and Arthur Roberts presented himself to the living.

Roberts had borrowed the money to purchase the advowson with a mortgage, but he seems to have decided against seeing through the financial commitment, since in 1864 Roberts sold the advowson at the same price, £3,000, to John Walter III of Bear Wood[25]. Little is known about Arthur Roberts, who was a bachelor and a son of John Roberts of Montague House, the prominent Wokingham solicitor. He seems to have been a scholarly man. Several of his sermons were privately printed, including one in 1852 entitled *Consistency in its Members, the best vindication of Free-Masonry*, a copy of which survives at the British Library[26].

Tragically, early one Sunday morning in March 1886, Arthur Roberts was found lying dead, from a gunshot wound in his head, in the Coombes, 200 yards from the rectory. A double-barrelled breach-loading gun, which he used for shooting wood pigeons, was by his side. It was conjectured that the rector went to the spot in a state of somnambulism, and stumbling into a holly bush, fell onto the muzzle of his gun. At the inquest the coroner returned an open verdict[27]. Arthur Roberts is buried on the north side of the parish church in a grave in the form of a stone cross with a three-tiered headstone.

One of the most valued members of the community in former times was the parish clerk. When David Davies became rector in 1782, the parish clerk was William Brown, who died in 1800 (aged 73). In 1774 his wife, Martha, who had borne ten children (four of whom died in infancy), hanged herself for reasons we shall never know. Brown was succeeded by Francis Millard, who served until his death (aged 74) in 1830. The next parish clerk was the village schoolmaster, Henry Eccardt. He was followed in 1838 by Elijah Hutt who, with his son William, held office successively for 70 years. Tragically, in 1908, William Hutt (aged 71) became so depressed following the collapse of the chimney of his two-room

woodman's cottage on Rutt Hill (now Hayes Lane), necessitating the pulling down of his home, that he hanged himself in a nearby shed[28].

New Church (1859–1861)

By the 1850s it was felt that the old church (with seating for 117) was too small and dilapidated for the needs of the parish and the church was rebuilt (with seating for 155) on the site of the old church at a cost of £1,400 in 1859–1861[29]. It seems that there was some difficulty in raising the necessary finance[30], and that Mrs Clive of Barkham Manor was the primary benefactress. A wooden plaque in the church records that the Incorporated Society for Building & Churches gave £90 towards the rebuilding on condition that 105 seats were reserved for the use of poorer inhabitants. Curiously the diocesan registers contain no reference to the grant of a faculty authorising the rebuilding.

Unfortunately, no record was made of the old building, which was *encumbered with a gallery*, before it was demolished, although a sepia photograph of the old church survives and hangs opposite the door of the present church. P.H. Ditchfield (rector 1886–1930) was later to bemoan its pulling down by *the Goths and Vandals of the nineteenth century*. The following description does, however, appear in J.H. Parker's *Ecclesiastical and Architectural Topography of England* in 1849.

A poor church, without aisles, chiefly of timber. There is a piece of ornamental ceiling

S.Noble

St James' Church,
rebuilt 1861

over the place of the rood-loft, the rest is poor P[erpendicular], but there is a window with good wooden tracery, and a wooden female effigy of the fourteenth century.

Four new bells were cast by John Warner & Sons in 1863[31]. The fate of the old bells is unknown. At some time before 1876, the parsonage house, rebuilt by David Davies about 1785, was demolished and replaced by a large Victorian rectory at a cost of £3,000[32], which was funded by John Walter III. In 1887 John Walter paid for a new chancel and transepts to be added to the church at a cost of £1,800[33]. The old barrel organ was also replaced.

The new church was built in early mediæval style faced with flint (re-used from the old church) with stone dressings, the chancel being all of stone. The church consists of a chancel, north and south transepts, north vestry and an aisleless nave with a south tower, whose lower stage serves as a porch and whose higher stages house the bells and contain the ringing chamber. The roofs are tiled. The top stage of the tower is of wood and has a small octagonal spire covered with shingles.

Font with Clive arms in parish church

The Revd Ditchfield used to like to recount the story of the parish clerk, Elijah Hutt, who one Sunday, whilst Barkham church was being rebuilt, decided to attend Morning Service at nearby Finchampstead. He arrived late, just when the rector (Edward St John), reading the first lesson from I Kings 19, asked, *'What doest thou here, Elijah?'*. According to Ditchfield, Elijah respectfully responded, *'Please, sur, Barkham church is undergoing repair, so I be cumed 'ere!'*[34].

In a recess in the east wall of the porch, in a horizontal position, is a carved wooden effigy of a lady in a long, loose dress and linen head-dress. Both the hands are missing and the face is much damaged. The effigy was previously in the gallery of the old church, in a vertical position. The effigy is reputed to date from the fourteenth century, and to be a likeness of Agnes de Nevill, daughter of Thomas de Nevill, who was probably a descendant of William de Nevill, who became lord of the manor in 1279. Agnes was heiress of the lordship of Barkham and it was through her marriage to Gilbert Bullock, son of the lord of Arborfield, in the 1330s that the Bullocks acquired the lordship of Barkham. In an article in the *Reading Standard* in 1920 P.H. Ditchfield wrote, *'Some stories are told about her in the village. Some say that she was a witch and a very bad woman, but others say that she was very good and they have given her a fancy name, but I forget what it is.'*[35]

Inside the west wall of the porch hangs an ancient door which the Revd Ditchfield recovered from a garden in Wokingham and which is reputed to be the door of the old church. If so, it must be the old west door (the doorway is just visible in the photograph of the old church), since the door furniture does not accord with the detail of the door furniture of the south door picked out by J.C. Buckler in some sketches in 1818[36].

The church plate comprises a silver chalice (7 inches high), which bears a 1566 hallmark; a silver paten (7¾ inches in diameter) inscribed, '*The New Years Guifte of Mr John Stronghill to ye Church of Barkham when he was Head Churchwarden Anno Dominy 1664*', engraved with the Stronghill coat of arms; a silver flagon (11¾ inches high) inscribed, '*The Gift of Dame Rebecca Kingesmill Relict of Sr. Wm. Kingesmill Kt. late of Sidmontain in the County of Hampshire to the Parish Church of Barkham in the County of Berkshire 1720*'; and another silver paten (7⅝ inches in diameter) inscribed, '*The Gift of John Gabriel D.D. Rector 1775*', engraved with the Gabriel coat of arms[37].

There is a circular font of light-coloured stone, decorated with winged cherubs and the griffin crest and motto from the Clive family arms[38], suggesting that the hexagonal font described by the Revd David Davies in 1783 (which was sketched by J.C. Buckler in 1818) was replaced when the church was rebuilt.

Modern era

Following the death of Arthur Roberts in 1886, the Revd Peter Ditchfield was presented to the living by John Walter III. He was to remain 44 years until his death (aged 76) in 1930. Ditchfield is still fondly remembered as a man of many accomplishments, not least his prolific output as a writer and historian. His life and achievements are recounted in Chapter 23.

Subsequent rectors of Barkham are listed in Appendix I. In 1957 the advowson of Barkham was given by John Walter V to the Oxford Board of Patronage[39], and in 1976 the parish was combined with the parish of Arborfield as a united benefice. The rectory became a private house, since the rector of the united benefice resides at Arborfield.

18 Barkham Square

There are no surviving records as to when Barkham Square was built, or by whom. The 1751 Court Baron records the sale of '*a certain freehold messuage called the Square*' by Charles Gery, gentleman, to the Revd Witting Colton since the previous Court Baron in 1738 when there was no mention of the property in the manorial court of survey held at the same time[1]. It is known, however, that Charles Gery purchased 525 acres in Barkham from a John Davenport in 1743[2].

Barkham Square

s.Noble

Witting Colton was a wealthy Georgian cleric, who was vicar of Reading St Giles from 1730 until his death in 1755, and also Chancellor of Salisbury Cathedral (1727–1755). Barkham Square was purchased by the trustees of Witting Colton's marriage settlement for his second wife, Mary Peck, about the time of their marriage in 1746 for £1,737. 4s[3]. Curiously, it seems (from auction particulars nearly a century later) that the house was never finished.

Charles Gery continued to own a house and lands near the church. Indeed, at the 1751 Court Baron Charles Gery was presented (i.e. reported) for illegally enclosing land next to the churchyard, for removing stiles and foot bridges and for '*stopping up the ancient and customary footways leading from Barkham Square to the Church there and also from the Heath*'. When Charles Gery died, without direct heirs, in February 1755, he directed his executors to sell all his property for cash[4]. Coincidentally, at some time between June and November 1755 the Colton trustees purchased a further estate at Barkham for £2,100, which may well have been some or all of Charles Gery's remaining lands.

It is not known who the early tenants of

Barkham Square were or how long the Colton trustees continued to own the estate. The house may be identified on the 1761 map of Berkshire (scale 2 inches to 1 mile) by John Rocque[5]. In March 1769 an advertisement appeared in the *Reading Mercury* for the letting of a genteel sashed house very near the parish church of Barkham (almost certainly Barkham Square). Nine months later, in December 1769, the same property was again offered to let and the sitting tenant was said to be a Captain Allen[6].

It seems probable that Barkham Square was the '*large Houfe at Barkham open for the Reception of Patients*' referred to in advertisements for inoculation against smallpox by Clement Cruttwell, surgeon at Broad Street, Wokingham, in 1774[7]. The treatment, which was offered to the gentry and their servants, involved a period of isolation, in comfortable surroundings, whilst the mild attack induced by the inoculation ran its course.

By 1783 the Barkham Square estate may have been owned by a William Richardson, since a 1783 inventory of church property states that the land on all sides of the churchyard, which was part of Barkham Farm (an appendage of Barkham Square), was owned by Richardson[8].

At this time the largest local farmer was Thomas Clacy of Biggs's Farm who farmed two-fifths of the acreage in the parish. All Clacy's land, including four farmhouses, was leased from local landowners. The lands leased by Farmer Clacy included Barkham

Square, which he let by way of a series of subleases to gentlemen tenants[9]. By 1780 the tenant of Barkham Square was Charles Sheffield, whose household included two male servants[10]. Sheffield died in 1789, and in 1791 Thomas Clacy granted a sublease of the Square (and 12 acres) to Major George Rochfort at an annual rent of £30[11]. He was succeeded as tenant by Captain R. Weeks from 1794 to 1796, and by Colonel William Archer from 1796 to 1799. The Barkham parish registers record the birth of two sons to Colonel William and Charlotte Archer, and two infant burials.

By 1796, according to the Berkshire Poll Book for that year[12], the freehold of the Barkham Square estate (214 acres) had been acquired by Peter Green (30) of Crookham, near Newbury[13]. Green took over farming the estate himself from Thomas Clacy about 1806. Apart from his home farm at Crookham, Peter Green also owned farms at Kingsclere (190 acres), and at some time before the 1820s he had acquired a 1,200-acre estate at Houghton Drayton, near Stockbridge, as well as several farms at Greenham, making him an early exponent of large-scale commercial farming.

Peter Green was at the forefront of endeavours to improve agricultural techniques and the quality of livestock. Barkham Square's heyday was during the years 1822–1830 when, apart from 1824, it was the venue for Peter Green's celebrated annual auctions of choice livestock, usually held each June. The Square itself was occupied by a bailiff, who in the later 1820s was Giles House.

Peter Green was active in county affairs and served as High Sheriff of Berkshire in 1810/11[14]. In 1824 he was appointed a Deputy Lieutenant of Berkshire. Green was also the greatest beneficiary amongst the local landowners as a result of the Barkham enclosure award in 1821[15], increasing the size of the Barkham Square estate from 214 to 344 acres, although the greater part of the additional 130 acres was heathland adjacent to Rook's Nest Farm, which Green was never able to bring into production because of the low prices then prevailing.

In June 1822 an extensive selection of *'capital horses, brood mares & colts, excellent milch cows, prime young bulls, oxen, rams &c'* was auctioned at Barkham Square. This was followed by auctions of more livestock, and of 300 acres of growing corn and grass, in the summer of 1823 when Barkham Square and over 200 acres were offered to let[16]. Also in 1823 Peter Green mortgaged the Barkham Square estate to secure a loan of £7,000[17]. The loan, or part of it, was probably a re-financing of a previous loan.

The 1822 and 1823 livestock auctions, and the 1823 mortgage (or remortgage), suggest that the costs of acquiring Peter Green's various estates, and of running his farms, had left him overextended financially. Agricultural prices had fallen back since the end of the Napoleonic Wars in 1815 and were unusually low in 1821–1823. Property values had also fallen dramatically since the wartime property boom and there was a credit squeeze.

In 1824 there was no livestock auction at Barkham, although an intended auction of the house and 12 acres was postponed at the last minute. In May 1825 Peter Green borrowed £5,000 on the security of his farms at Kingsclere[18] and the following month seemingly the remainder of Peter Green's farming stock was auctioned at Barkham Square without reserve. The stock included *'carriage and nag horses, galloways and forest ponies, brood mares and colts, 60 oxen and cows, 100 choice rams & ewes, 30 pigs, timber, wool, seeds &c'*. The *Reading Mercury* commented approvingly on the sale[19].

For the rest of the 1820s, apart from organising ever larger annual livestock auctions at Barkham Square, Peter Green (aged 57 in 1823) variously sought to let or sell some or all of his farms, including the Barkham Square estate, with the expressed intention of reducing the scale of his agricultural activities, but without success. All the while Green failed to pay interest on his mortgages and in January 1830 the accumulated (but unpaid) interest of £1,417. 10s. on the £7,000 mortgage of Barkham Square was converted into another mortgage, also secured on the estate[20].

At the same time, whilst Peter Green unsuccessfully tried to dispose of his various farms, the annual livestock auctions in the Oak Paddock at Barkham Square became one of the highlights of the agricultural calendar. These auctions were conducted by Mr Hawkes, the leading Reading auctioneer, in 1826 and 1827 on the Monday before Ascot Races and were preceded by prominent advertisements in the *Reading Mercury*.

In February 1828 Peter Green was honoured at a select dinner at the Crown Inn, Basingstoke, to celebrate the majority of the Marquis of Douro, heir to the Duke of Wellington (who had just been appointed prime minister), when tribute was paid to Green's contribution to agricultural improvements. The annual livestock auction in the Oak Paddock at Barkham Square in May 1829 drew the following comment from the *Reading Mercury*.

*Mr. Peter Green's annual exhibition and sale of Live Stock took place yesterday, and was very numerously and most respectably attended. There were some **extra-ordinarily fine** specimens of the breed of horses, cows, sheep and pigs, for the possession of which considerable competition was manifested. We do not, we are persuaded, incur blame for exaggeration or flattery, when we venture to assert, that the interests of agriculture find a most liberal and judicious patron in Mr. Green, not only on account of these annual exhibitions, but for his experimental and practical improvements, and above all for his **spirited** and **strenuous** efforts for the **public** protection of that sinew of our national strength, the agricultural prosperity of the country.*

In 1829 and 1830 the sale of the Barkham Square estate (in lots) continued to be heavily advertised. The annual livestock auction in 1830 was delayed until July and was to prove to be the last. In the winter of 1830/1 there was a wave of machine-breaking and rick-burning incidents, reflecting the high level of agrarian unrest. One evening in November 1830 two hay ricks were set alight at Barkham Square, as recounted in Chapter 22.

But less than a month after the rick-burning incident Peter Green had transferred all his assets to trustees for sale, since he could no longer settle his commitments as they fell

IMPORTANT SALE OF
CHOICE LIVE STOCK,
BARKHAM, near WOKINGHAM.
TO BE SOLD BY AUCTION,
By Mr. HAWKES,
On the *memorable* TWENTY-NINTH day of MAY, at eleven for twelve, precisely, in the OAK Paddock, *AT BARKHAM-SQUARE,*
Two miles from Wokingham, twelve from Windsor, seven from Hartford-Bridge, and six from the Military College, on the Basingstoke & Western road,
A VERY SUPERIOR SELECTION from the highly-conditioned AGRICULTURAL STOCK of PETER GREEN, Esq.
Comprising *excellent carriage horses, roadsters, galloways, beautiful ponies, brood mares and colts; capital Jersey and long-horned milch cows and calves, fine barren cows; ewes, rams, and couples, of the highly-celebrated Leicester, Gloucester, and Southdown breeds; an extensive quantity of boars, sows, and pigs, and large store hogs, of the much-approved Berkshire kind.*
Catalogues on the market days immediately preceding the sale, at a principal Inn in each of the neighbouring towns, and at Mr HAWKES'S *Auction and Estate Office,* MARKET-PLACE, Reading.
*** Mr. HAWKES respectfully solicits public attention to the *extent* and *quality* of this stock.

Reading Mercury,
18 May 1829

GENTEEL VILLA,
WITH 344 ACRES,
BETWEEN THE BATH AND WESTERN ROADS,
Near READING and WOKINGHAM.

Particulars and Conditions of Sale
OF THE

BARKHAM-SQUARE ESTATE
FREEHOLD,
WITH EARLY POSSESSION, AND LAND-TAX REDEEMED;
COMPRISING

A Dwelling-House,
OF HANDSOME ELEVATION, CONVERTIBLE, AT A MODERATE EXPENSE, INTO A COMMODIOUS

GENTLEMANLY RESIDENCE,
SEATED IN A VERY BEAUTIFUL PARK-LIKE LAWN,
Ornamented with Oaks of extraordinarily fine growth,
AND SURROUNDED BY RICHLY-TIMBERED GROUNDS.

THE LAND
COMPRISES (NEARLY IN A RING FENCE) ABOVE

Three Hundred and Forty Acres,
THE GREATER PART OF WHICH IS VERY PRODUCTIVE

ARABLE, PASTURE, AND MEADOW,
Subdivided into convenient Inclosures.
TOGETHER WITH

A roomy Farm-House,
YARDS, BARNS, STABLING, GRANARIES, CATTLE AND CART-SHEDS;

SITUATE IN A FINE SPORTING COUNTRY,
NEAR SEVERAL CAPITAL PRESERVES, AND SIR JOHN COPE'S FOX-HOUNDS,

Two Miles from Wokingham, (through which place several Coaches pass to London, and down, in the course of the day,) seven from Reading, 15 from Windsor, and eight from Hartford-Bridge and the Military College, on the Great Western Road.

Which will be Sold by Auction,

BY MR. HAWKES,
On *TUESDAY, JUNE the 21st, 1831, at Twelve o'Clock,*
AT THE AUCTION MART, LONDON.
By Peremptory Order of the Trustees for Sale of the Estates of Peter Green, Esq.

To be Viewed any time before the Sale.
GILES HOUSE, on the premises, will shew the same, of whom Particulars, with Plans, may be had; at the Lion, Hartford

due, in contemplation of agreeing a private composition with his creditors[21]. It seems Green had been beset by financial difficulties throughout the 1820s, and the final blow came in 1830 after three successive wet summers and poor harvests, compounded by a particularly severe outbreak of sheep rot[22]. Green's persistent failure to find buyers for his farms was a reflection of their being mortgaged for more than willing purchasers were prepared to pay.

Greater efforts had been made by Peter Green to dispose of the Barkham Square estate than any of his other properties. This was probably because much of the estate was on heavy London clay, which was expensive and difficult to cultivate at the best of times, and would have been of only marginal profitability at the prices ruling for most of the 1820s.

The trustees for sale (who included Robert Palmer, MP for Berkshire) pressed ahead in trying to realise Peter Green's assets. After unsuccessful attempts to sell Green's estates privately, Barkham Square and his other principal estates were offered for sale in June 1831 at the Auction Mart in London (behind the Bank of England)[23]. According to the auction particulars, the estate was intersected by *'a richly timbered oak avenue of great length and beauty'* of which no trace remains. Barkham Square, after many years as a working farm, was described as being *'partly unfinished, convertible, at a moderate expense, into a very commodious gentlemanly residence'*. The buildings in the yard included a chaise house, a nag stable for three horses, a Dutch granary on staddle-stones, a stable for eight horses, two double-bayed barns, a cow house, a cart lodge and a piggery.

None of the properties reached their reserve prices at the London auction. After further unsuccessful attempts by the trustees to dispose of the various farms, further auctions were held in June 1832, without reserve beyond the amounts of the subsisting mortgages. The sale advertisements referred to '*the well known property, called Barkham Square … consisting of a well-planned but unfinished Residence*'.

Eventually, in 1833, Barkham Square and 344 acres (including Church Farm) were sold to William Cook of Roydon Hall in Kent for £9,200[24]. Cook financed most of the purchase by taking over the two subsisting mortgages totalling £8,417. 10s. The net proceeds received by the trustees for the benefit of Green's unsecured creditors were therefore only £782. 10s. It seems that the oak avenue referred to in the 1831 auction particulars was felled following an auction in 1839 when 130 oak trees on the estate were sold as navy timber. Three of the five lots included trees standing on the Avenue, Avenue Moat and Upper Avenue[25].

William Cook let the property to a succession of gentlemen farmers. From 1834 to 1844 the tenant was William Chandler. At the time of the 1841 census, when Chandler was 60, the household at the Square numbered 15 persons. The next tenant, from 1844 to 1859, was Frederick

Parsons. At the time of the 1851 census, when Parsons was 33, there were five young children and four servants, whilst Parsons employed nine labourers and four boys on the farm.

From 1860 to 1864 the tenant was Thomas Landon, who farmed 440 acres (including Edney's Farm) with twelve men and three boys. At the time of the 1861 census, there were five children in the Landon household at the Square and four servants (including a coachman). In 1864 William Cook granted an 11-year lease to Joseph Todhunter at an annual rent of £300, but in 1866 he assigned the remainder of the lease to William Vipan Theed, who farmed 330 acres with 17 men and two boys. At the time of the 1871 census, when Theed was 45, there were five children at the Square, a governess and three servants[26].

In 1867 Barkham Square and 410 acres were purchased by John Walter III from Major Edwin Adolphus Cook for £18,500[27] and became part of the Bear Wood estate. After the expiry of William Vipan Theed's lease in 1875, the farm was leased from 1876 to 1879 to James Albert Herbert and from 1881 to 1886 to Edward Lane Holmes (who is known to have used oxen for ploughing)[28].

Later in 1886 Barkham Square was let as a private residence to Charles Bunce Greenfield, an army captain, who the previous year had married Ethel, the eldest daughter of Lieutenant General and Mrs Rickman of Barkham Manor, at Barkham church. During the Greenfields' tenancy parish events were regularly held at the Square at Mrs Greenfield's invitation, often at her parents' expense. In October 1888 the annual school treat *'was held at the Squares, where Mr and Mrs Greenfield kindly received the Children, and by their kindness and care for the amusements of the young people, contributed greatly to the success of the Treat. Everything was done that could be done to make the children enjoy themselves; and they did not disperse without giving many hearty cheers for their kind entertainers'*[29]. The Square was also the venue for the parish celebrations on the occasion of Queen Victoria's golden and diamond jubilees in 1887 and 1897, and the coronation of Edward VII in 1902 (see Chapter 22).

From 1896 onwards Captain Greenfield spent increasingly less time at Barkham, preferring to stay in London. Following his return from the Boer War in 1902 he left Mrs Greenfield and reduced her allowance, forcing her to give up Barkham Square and to move, with their daughter, into Barkham Manor with her widowed mother. In 1908 Mrs Greenfield successfully sued Captain Greenfield for divorce on the grounds of desertion and adultery[30].

In 1904 Barkham Square was let to E.M. Sturges, a gentleman farmer, who was prominent in local affairs for many years as recounted in Chapter 24. When the Bear Wood estate was being broken up following the death of Arthur Fraser Walter in 1910, the Barkham Square estate, together with Sparks Farm and Langley Common Farm (312 acres), were purchased by Mrs Sturges from John Walter IV in 1913 for £5,750[31]. Following the death of Ted Sturges in 1934, Mrs Sturges continued to farm the Barkham Square estate until her own death in 1944.

The estate then passed to their surviving son, Lieutenant General Sir Robert Sturges KBE CB DSO, who sold the property in 1948 for £27,000. Subsequent owners included (Sir) Guy Kempton Lawrence DSO OBE DFC in the 1950s and 1960s, the Jordanian Royal Family in the 1980s and a golf course company. The property is a grade 2 listed building and is once again a private residence.

19 Revd David Davies (Rector 1782–1819)

Unlike many Georgian clergymen, David Davies came from a humble background. Nothing is known about David's early years, except that he was born in Denbighshire in 1742. It seems that by the time he was 12 both his parents were dead, since in 1755 David was sent as a charity scholar to Codrington College in Barbados, an establishment run by the Society for the Propagation of the Gospel.

David proved to be a very diligent scholar, and in 1762, at the age of 19, found himself as acting headmaster for over a year following the early deaths of both the head and deputy head. David continued to serve as deputy headmaster until 1766, when he resigned and surprisingly became under-manager on a sugar plantation on the island.

It seems that David returned to England in 1769/70 and by 1771 had been engaged as tutor to Arthur Fowke, nephew of Colonel John Walsh of Warfield Park (a near neighbour of William Pitt of Binfield Manor, lord of the manor of Barkham). He later became Colonel Walsh's personal secretary. By 1780 David had become tutor to the son of Lord Dartrey (later Viscount Cremorne), an Anglo-Irish banker, of Chelsea Farm,

The Parson's Pleasance (old parsonage house, rebuilt 1785)

whose wife, Philadelphia, was an acquaintance of Queen Charlotte.

In May 1782 the living of Barkham became vacant on the death of Dr John Gabriel and Tutor Davies (39) was nominated as rector by the then lord of the manor, John Pitt of Dorset (heir of William Pitt deceased)[1]. Within weeks David had been ordained.

David's incumbency as rector of Barkham coincided with a period when labouring

1786 insurance policy of the parsonage

in the West Indies, David became an advocate of both social reform domestically and the abolition of the slave trade. In supporting these causes, David collaborated with William Morton Pitt (MP for Dorset, 1790–1826, and son of his patron John Pitt). In 1791 David gave evidence before a House of Commons Select Committee on the slave trade.

Apart from keeping meticulous records of his own income and expenditure, David's concern with the plight of the poor caused him to keep detailed records of the parlous finances of various poor families in the parish, which can be seen at Nuffield College, Oxford.

David Davies is best remembered for his famous social tract (208 pages) published in 1795, *The Case of Labourers in Husbandry Stated and Considered*, in which, after analysing detailed information gathered from his parishioners in Barkham and elsewhere, he argued that a labouring man ought to be entitled to be paid a wage sufficient to cover the cost of his family's basic needs instead of having to rely on charity[5]. A copy can be seen at Wokingham Library.

In visiting the labouring families in my parish, as my duty led me, I could not but observe with concern their mean and distressed condition. I found them in general but indifferently fed; badly clothed; some children without shoes and stockings; very few put to school; and most families in debt to little shopkeepers … Yet I could not impute the wretchedness I saw either to sloth or wastefulness.

families were suffering from declining living standards on account of poor harvests and high inflation, the latter reflecting the wars with Revolutionary and Napoleonic France from 1793 to 1815. Indeed, in the 1790s between 23 and 33 families (out of a total of some 40 families) in the parish were in receipt of some form of parish relief[2].

In 1801, when the population of Barkham (per the 1801 census return) was 185–200, the poor rate disbursements reached a peak of £533 (a rate of 13s. 6d. in the £)[3], compared with an average assessment of £72. 10s. per annum in the years 1783–1785 (an average rate of 2s. in the £)[4].

Moved in all probability by his experiences

The information which David gathered reveals considerable deficiencies in the diet of labouring families. The basic diet of a poor family in Barkham was home-made bread and thin soups. The only meat they could afford was bacon, gammon and ham (a fatted hog would be made to last a whole year), and occasionally a sheep's head. Milk could not be had for love nor money (being diverted for veal production). Tea was the staple drink (since even the brewing of small, i.e. weak, beer was too costly). Most labourers had insufficient ground around their tenements to grow potatoes.

After paying rent, there was little or no money to buy clothes or for regular contingencies such as the cost of lying-in, burials and sickness. The basic fuel was turf cut from Long Moor. Soap supplies were supplemented by burning green fern and kneading the ashes into balls of lye for washing.

It is little wonder, therefore, that infant mortality rates were high. Of the 42 burials recorded in the Barkham parish registers for the years 1788–1796, 26 (62 %) were of children under the age of ten[6].

David regularly procured charitable aid from his affluent acquaintances to ease the lot of the poor. For instance, the Honourable Frances Leveson Gower of Bill Hill, who became lady of the manor in 1787, made regular gifts of child-bed linen to poor women and shirts to the poorest labouring families, whilst Lady Cremorne often gave David sums of money to be applied to

charitable purposes amongst the poor of Barkham.

Numerous acts of kindness and generosity by David himself are recorded in his meticulously kept account books. It was not uncommon for him to buy a set of clothes for the child of a poor family or to procure a suit of old clothes for some ill-clad parishioner, since one of David's concerns was that the poor, lacking sufficient means to buy clothes,

Extract from David Davies' account book, 1782

Poor of the Parish of Barkham to whom DD gave Bread St Thomas Day

John Hill. Poors House. an old man almost worn out.
Widow Parker. P. House. 5 Children. Has 6/. p week. Bapt.
Dame Metts. Poors House. Husband run away. 6 Children: the eldest abad Boy.
Widow Sparville. P. House. Bapt. 1/. p week.
Robert Hannakin. Bapt. – Wife & 2 Children. – Can work but wont.
William Collier. Gardiner. 7 children at home. industrious.
Richard Grimshire. Wife. – an oldish man
Thomas Wise. 3 children at home. upon Hill.
William Collins. Wife. upon Hill. has no family. earns fro 10 to 12/. p. w.
Thomas Patey. Wife. 6 Children at home.
Robert Willis. His House the Bapt. Meet. Wife. – An old man & poor.
Widow Warner, Lame. Deformed Daughter. 2/. p week. Parsonage.
Henry Lasley & Wife. Parsonage. 2 Children.
Francis Millard. Wife. & 2 Children. Langley Common.
Henry Sharpe. Method. 4 Children at home. industrious. Langley Common.
Dame Watkins & Son. Langley Common.
Samuel Walden. Newlands. Wife & 3 young Children.
Thomas Goddard & Wife & 1 child. Liv'd on C. lower Farm: now at L. Common.
James Marler. Wife & 1 young Child. near Lacey's lower Farm.
Thomas Payne & Wife. an Idiot Son. Longmoor.
John Horn. Wife & 1 child.
David Headland. Wife & 2 Child. at Edney's.
William Browne. Parish Clerk.

were reduced to ragged garments. *'One bad consequence of this meanness of dress is, that many of the poor are ashamed to appear among decent people at our churches.'*

David's regular disbursements included paying Dame Payne, who ran a small 'Dame School' in Wokingham, fees of 2d. per week per scholar for up to eight children from poorer families.

David was to serve as rector of Barkham from 1782 until his death (aged 76) in 1819. He never married. David was buried in the churchyard, close to the south transept, under the sweeping boughs of the Cedar of Lebanon which Mrs Leveson Gower had planted (doubtless with the rector officiating) in the sixth year of his incumbency on 16 June 1788. On David's plain oblong box tomb (less than 10 feet away from the later tomb of the Revd Peter Ditchfield, rector 1886–1930) is the simple inscription, *'In the hope of a blessed resurrection here lie the remains of David Davies 37 years rector of this Parish'*.

In a fulsome obituary, the *Reading Mercury* recalled, *'His humility of manner and attention to the wants of his poorer brethren endeared his flock to their Pastor, and though his means were small, yet to do good and to distribute was his constant gratification'*[7].

Indeed, the good works of David Davies are remembered to this day and have prompted the publication of two detailed accounts of his life in 1976[8] and 1981[9].

History of Barkham Manor, Part II (1787 to date)

Leveson Gowers (1787–1828)

In November 1787 Harry Fonnereau sold the Barkham manor estate (including the lordship and the advowson) to Rear Admiral the Honourable John Leveson Gower for 11,400 guineas (£11,970)[1]. Leveson Gower (pronounced 'Lewison Gore') lived at Bill Hill in Hurst and was MP for Appleby (1784–1790) and for Newcastle-under-Lyme (1790–1792). He was an Admiral of the White Squadron and a Junior Lord of the Admiralty (1783–1790). Although the seat of the Leveson Gowers was at Bill Hill, the Revd David Davies (rector 1782–1819) acted as chaplain to the family and a family vault was established at Barkham Church.

Admiral Leveson Gower soon set about finding a tenant for Barkham House and the property was advertised in the *Reading Mercury* in summer 1788[2]. By 1790 the house had been let to John Nares, who remained until 1796, when an auction of his furniture took place at the house[3]. Nares may have been short of furniture when he moved into the house in 1790, since David Davies sold him a wardrobe for £2. It seems that the rector and Nares were soon on good terms, since Davies' accounts also record a gift of partridges, and on one occasion they clubbed together to buy a pipe of wine (51 cases) for £51. 4s[4].

Admiral Leveson Gower died, whilst shaving, in 1792 (aged 52), and when John Nares vacated Barkham House in 1796, it became the dower house for his widow, Frances, until her death (aged 55) in July 1801. The following month the residue of the current 21-year lease of Barkham House was advertised for sale[5]. Curiously, the notices described the premises as *'confifting of a New Brick-built Dwelling Houfe, finifhed with tafte, perfectly dry'*. This, only 14 years after the 1787 advertisements speaking of the principal part *'recently built'* (see Chapter 12), suggests the occurrence of another calamity. At Michaelmas 1802 Barkham House was let to Matthew Beachcroft[6], who remained at Barkham until 1814, when there was a 4-day sale at the house of his furniture, rare books and prints, and choice old wines (including 140 cases of vintage port)[7].

Leveson Gower hatchment

When he died, Admiral Leveson Gower was succeeded by his son Lieutenant General John Leveson Gower, who was second-in-command to General Whitlock in the unsuccessful British assaults on Buenos Aires in 1806/7. General Leveson Gower died in 1816 (aged 47) after suffering an apoplectic fit and was succeeded by his son John Leveson Gower (born 1802), who died in 1883.

Henry and Charlotte Clive (1814–1874)

Henry and Charlotte Clive moved to Barkham about 1814, when Henry Clive, MP for Ludlow, rented Barkham House. At Michaelmas 1816 he took a 21-year lease of the mansion and 121 acres (including pleasure grounds, lawn and park) at a rent of £238. 10s. per annum. In 1828 Clive purchased the freehold reversion of the house

Barkham Manor, front elevation

and 137 acres, mainly in Barkham (but not the lordship of the manor)[8].

Clive was the youngest son of George Clive, MP for Herefordshire. In 1799, as a young man, he was contemplating going to Bengal to make his fortune with the East India Company, but changed his mind when his mother offered him a life tenancy of 4,869 acres in county Tipperary worth £1,200 a year, and instead became a barrister[9].

Henry Clive was a kinsman of Robert, Viscount Clive (later 2nd Earl of Powys). As Clive family nominee, Henry was one of the two MPs for Ludlow (1807–1818) and MP for Montgomery (1818–1832). In 1818 Clive was appointed Under-Secretary of State for the Home Department in the Tory administration of the Earl of Liverpool. The Home Secretary, Viscount Sidmouth, writing to the Prince Regent, described Clive as *'a sensible, well-informed man'*[10]. Nationally the political situation was very troubled because of widespread civil unrest (e.g. the Peterloo Massacre in 1819) and agricultural distress, as well as increasing pressure for Catholic emancipation which followed the ending of the Napoleonic Wars. Clive was not regarded as a success in office and he resigned in 1822 when Lord Sidmouth resigned.

He was involved in many good causes locally. In 1819 Clive became a Life Governor of the Reading Dispensary and was a founder trustee of the Forest (later Wokingham) Savings Bank[11]. He became a magistrate in 1830 (sitting at the county quarter sessions)[12] and after the Poor Law

Reform Act in 1834 he became Chairman of the Board of Guardians of the Wokingham Union[13]. Clive was also one of the Tax Commissioners for the Forest Division[14], and he was a founder member of the court of governors of the new Royal Berkshire Hospital in 1840[15]. It is, however, as the prime mover in the foundation of the Wokingham Agricultural Association in 1836 that Henry Clive is principally remembered[16] and at the annual dinners in the 1840s he was fondly toasted as the 'father' of the society. In 1838 and 1843 the annual ploughing match took place on Clive's lands at Barkham[17].

In 1839 Henry Clive agreed to stand as the Clivite nominee in the notorious Ludlow by-election, in which he was narrowly defeated by the Whig candidate by 186 votes to 182. However, such was the scale of the bribery and other irregularities by the respective agents of both candidates, that after a Parliamentary enquiry the election was annulled. Clive (then aged 62) did not stand in the fresh contest[18].

Henry and Charlotte Clive showed great concern for the condition of the poor. Not long after the Clives moved to Barkham, a small elementary school was established under Henry Clive's patronage and, in 1827, a Sunday School. Mary Penlington, wife of the Clive's footman and later butler, Thomas Penlington, served as teacher, later becoming village school mistress (1827–1873).

After some years of indifferent health, Henry Clive died in 1848 (aged 70), but his widow

Charlotte continued to live at Barkham Manor until her death (aged 89) in 1874. They had no children. Mrs Clive *'was a lady-bountiful to the village, treating all the villagers as her children. She looked after and cared for them all. She built some good cottages on Barkham Hill* [Hayes Lane]. *She had a Sunday School, and all the boys wore tall hats and smocks, and sat on the altar steps during the service'* (Revd P.H. Ditchfield, *Reading Standard*, 1920). She was also the primary benefactress of the cost (£1,400) of rebuilding St James' Church in 1859–1861, which finds reflection in the griffin crest and motto from the Clive family arms which decorate the new font. (The social contribution of the Clives is further recounted in Chapters 21 and 22.)

Clive coat of arms

Henry and Charlotte Clive are buried under a long flat oblong stone slab in the graveyard on the north side of the parish church, surrounded by short iron rails, a few feet from the grave of Mrs Clive's faithful servant, Mary Penlington (died 1876). Also in the churchyard is the grave of Zachariah Bourne (died 1884), for many years Mrs Clive's steward, whose house is now Bailiff's Cottage[19]. The sermon preached on the Sunday following Henry Clive's funeral by Arthur Roberts, curate (later rector) of Barkham, was privately printed and a copy survives at the British Library[20].

The obituary of Henry Clive in the *Reading Mercury* concluded, '*Of sincere and practical piety, his faith in the great truths of Christianity governed his heart and guided his conduct. It made him ever ready to devote his time to the service of his friends and neighbours, whether rich or poor; his care, indeed, of the latter was almost paternal, and his charity and benevolence were only limited by his means. By the poor his memory will long be treasured as that of a firm friend, and all who knew him will admit that he was in the fullest acceptation of the term, a religious, a good, and an honest man*'[21]. Obituaries were also published in *The Times*[22] and the *Gentleman's Magazine*[23].

Bear Wood Estate (1878–1914); 1914 to date

In 1878 the Clive trustees sold the Barkham manor estate (151 acres) to John Walter III for £21,000[24]. John Walter was chief proprietor of *The Times* and MP for Berkshire (1859–1865 and 1868–1885). The family seat was at Bear Wood, which adjoins the Coombes on the north side. With the profits generated by *The Times*, John Walter had been systematically buying up land in the locality and was the sixth largest landowner in Berkshire. At its greatest extent about 1883, the Bear Wood estate covered 7,054 acres (11 square miles), including most of the parish of Barkham, with a rent roll of £9,728 per annum[25]. John Walter III also purchased the lordship of Barkham from John Leveson Gower about 1878.

In 1881 Barkham Manor was let to Lieutenant General William Rickman JP (53), who moved in with his wife Mary, two sons (aged 6 and 19) and four daughters (aged 10–18), and their French governess. He also had a butler, footman and coachman[26].

General Rickman and his wife fully involved themselves in the life of the parish[27] and for many years entertained the children of Barkham to an Annual School Treat. '*After a short service in the Church, the children marched through the village, waiving their banners, and entered the grounds of the Manor. There everything that could delight them was provided for their amusement. A large number of beautiful prizes, toys, and presents were given to the children. Mr Arthur Rickman very kindly helped in arranging the races and games … After tea, more games, and then with hearty cheers for General and Mrs Rickman, the children dispersed with much gratitude to their kind benefactors.*' Mrs Rickman also organised a soup kitchen for the poorer inhabitants during the winter months (managed by Mrs Allright) and General Rickman (who was twice mentioned in despatches during the Crimean War) was both a churchwarden and chairman of the Parish Meeting (forerunner of the Parish Council) from its inception in 1894 until his death in 1900[28].

After Mrs Rickman's death in 1906, Barkham Manor became the residence of her eldest daughter, Mrs Greenfield (previously of Barkham Square)[29]. The next tenant was Wilson Noble JP (Conservative MP for Hastings, 1886–1895, and an early experimenter with Röntgen rays and wireless telegraphy), who took a 21-year lease at Michaelmas 1907 at a rent of £304. 15s. per annum. However, he gave up the tenancy in 1914.

When John Walter III died in 1894, he was succeeded by his eldest surviving son, Arthur Fraser Walter. By this time the Bear Wood estate had long been suffering from both a sustained agricultural depression and declining profits from *The Times* on account of increasing competition from the penny press. When Arthur Fraser Walter died in 1910, the Bear Wood estate had contracted to 3,013 acres and in 1911 his heir John Walter IV put the whole estate up for sale[30]. Bear Wood itself was not sold until 1919 (to become the home of the Royal Merchant Navy School), whilst Barkham Manor was purchased in 1914 for £6,930 by Arthur Nathaniel Garland[31], who continued to live there until his death (aged 95) in 1942.

Mr Garland had previously spent 33 years running a large sheep and cattle ranch in Uruguay. There were nine servants at Barkham Manor, including a head chauffeur and an under-chauffeur, a stud groom and an under-groom, a head gardener and two under-gardeners, mostly recruited from outside the parish. The head gardener, Mr Jones, lived in what used to be the Steward's House. Barkham Manor had its own electricity generator and reservoir[32].

Barkham Manor from the Coombes

Subsequent owners included Mr Jack and the Honourable Mrs Mary Clifford-Wolff from 1968 to 1988, when the property was sold and converted into eight separate living units. The mansion is a listed grade 2 building of special architectural or historic interest and is mentioned in Sir Nikolaus Pevsner's *Buildings of England*. The high brick wall flanking the Barkham Road, which is a prominent Barkham feature, dates from the early nineteenth century. It encloses the former kitchen garden and stable yard.

21 Landed Interests and Agriculture in the Nineteenth Century

The distribution of landholdings in the parish (1,362 acres) remained largely unchanged from the mid-1700s until the 1860s/70s, when much of the parish was acquired by the Bear Wood estate[1]. After the 1821 enclosure award the three largest landowners (all non-resident) accounted for 75 % of the land in the parish[2]. The principal holdings were:

- Barkham Manor (545 acres), owned by the Leveson Gowers of Bill Hill (lords of the manor);
- Barkham Square (344 acres), owned by Peter Green of Crookham; after 1833 by William Cook of Kent;
- Biggs's Farm (149 acres), owned by the St Johns of Finchampstead, West Court.

The only significant change was in 1828, when Henry Clive MP, lessee of Barkham House, purchased the mansion and 126 acres from John Leveson Gower[3].

The majority of the arable and pasture land in the parish had been privately enclosed long before 1800. Indeed, by 1613 only 57 acres of the mediæval open arable fields remained[4], whilst the 1738 manorial court of survey recorded only five copyhold tenants occupying 14½ acres[5]. At the beginning of the nineteenth century the residual common field was a mere 10 acres, but the open commons remained and there was a large area of open heath towards Finchampstead, where smallholders and landless labourers would have grazed their cattle and sheep and cut peat for fuel.

In 1814 procedures were commenced under the authority of the Windsor Forest Inclosure Act 1813 to enclose the remaining open land in the parish. Although the process was essentially complete by 1817, the formal enclosure award was not made until 1821. The fine map of the parish attached to the award may be seen at the Berkshire Record Office. The land which was enclosed, accounting for 29 % of the parish, was as follows:

		(acres)
Common Land		
Langley Common (grazing)	50	
The Coombes (estovers; pannage)	51	
Long Moor (turbary)	74	175
Heathland		170
Common Field		10
Other open arable		28
Road sides		14
Total		**397**

Although all freeholders were compensated for the loss of their common rights by the allocation of additional plots of land, the proportionate increase averaging 30 %, inevitably this favoured the large landowners at the expense of the smallholders. Whilst the large landowners gained whole fields, smallholders received only small, scattered plots of land (often less than one-eighth of an acre) which they could do little with, but which were required to be fenced. The enclosed land included 106 acres of 'waste' allotted to the King for the loss of the Crown's forestal rights, which also found its way into the hands of the large landowners. The enclosure of such a significant area probably caused considerable hardship, since many smallholders and landless labourers would have been dependent for grazing their cattle and sheep on the commons and manorial wastes. Seventeen acres in Long Moor were, however, set aside as a fuel allotment, where the poor of the parish could continue to cut turves for fuel. In the mid-1880s the fuel allotment was purchased by the Bear Wood estate and a fuel charity for the distribution of coal was established with the proceeds of the sale[6].

By the beginning of the nineteenth century there was increasing emphasis on the development of new technology to improve agricultural productivity (e.g. drainage, fertilisers, mechanisation). This was particularly relevant to areas with heavy clay soils, like Barkham, which were difficult (and expensive) to cultivate. This interest was reflected by the organising of annual

PLOUGHING MATCH, BARKHAM, Berks.
On Thursday, June 27, 1822

A GOLD LACED HAT will be given to the best Ploughman. A White Beaver Hat to the second best. A Black Beaver Hat to the third best. Donkey Racing for a new saddle and bridle; with a Variety of other Amusements. — The Donkeys to be entered by one o'clock, by applying to Thomas Warwick, clerk of the course.

An Ordinary at John Collyer's, at the Bull Inn, Barkham.

ploughing matches near The Bull in 1820–1822, in conjunction with the landlord, John Collyer, who offered participants and spectators an '*ordinary*' (i.e. a set meal)[7]. The first prize for the best ploughman was a gold laced hat. The 1820s was, however, a difficult decade for farmers on account of generally poor harvests and low prices. The decade culminated in three successive wet summers, causing financial difficulties for the respected Robert Hewett of Langley Pond Farm and, more spectacularly, for Peter Green, proprietor of Barkham Square and a leading agriculturalist (see Chapters 6 and 18, respectively).

In 1836 the 'Wokingham Agricultural Association, for the encouragement of Agricultural Labourers and Servants, in the Parishes of Wokingham, Finchampstead, Barkham, Arborfield, Swallowfield, Hurst and Ruscombe' was founded under the Gracious Patronage of His Majesty, William IV[8]. Henry Clive, of Barkham House, was chairman of the organising committee and

Reading Mercury,
24 June 1822

at the dinners after the annual ploughing matches in the 1840s was fondly toasted as the 'father' of the society. In September 1843 Clive hosted the annual ploughing match at Barkham, when 36 teams competed in what were described as atrocious conditions[9].

In 1840 the parochial tythes, which had long been settled in money, were formally commuted and converted into rent charges by an award under the Tythe Commutation Act. The award gave rise to another fine map of the parish, which can also be seen at the Berkshire Record Office[10].

The repeal of the Corn Laws in 1846 ushered in the golden age of British agriculture, which was to continue for the following 30 years. The country was in any event enjoying increased prosperity on account of Victorian Britain's leadership of the industrial revolution.

In the 1860s and 1870s the majority of the land in the parish, as well as the lordship and the advowson, were bought up by John Walter III of Bear Wood, chief proprietor of *The Times*, and managed as part of his 7,000-acre estate[11]. During the last quarter of the century agriculture was in deep recession, particularly in 1875–1884 and 1891–1899. Farmers were hit, first by a series of bad seasons in the late 1870s, especially three successive years of cold springs and wet summers in 1879–1881, second by an influx of cheap grain imports from the American prairies and third by refrigerated meat from Australia, New Zealand and South America in the 1880s and 1890s. In 1886 the Walter

estate let Barkham Square as a residence, without the adjacent farm land. Brook Farm (which grew to 370 acres) became the principal farm on the estate in Barkham.

In the 1880s John Walter III laid out the avenue of lime trees, part of which remains, along Nash Grove Ride between Mortimer's Lodge Farm and Nash Grove. About the same time he diverted the route of Edney's Hill Lane (once an old drift way) between Mortimer's Lodge Farm and Edney's Farm from the south to the north side of Edney's Farm[12].

The effects of the Great Depression on the Bear Wood estate towards the end of the century were compounded by diminishing capital resources on account of the increased competition between *The Times* and the penny press. It had contracted from 7,054 acres in 1883 to 3,013 acres at the time of the death of Arthur Fraser Walter in 1910[13]. His son, John Walter IV, was obliged to sell off the rest of the estate, in stages, to meet the increased death duties and other taxes imposed by Lloyd George's 'People's Budget' in 1909.

Although employment in domestic service increased in the last quarter of the century, agriculture otherwise remained the dominant activity in the parish, and it was not until the 1930s that there was a marked shift of emphasis towards poultry farming and market gardening to serve the needs of the growing urban populations of Reading and London[14].

22 Barkham During a Century of Change (1815–1914)

Whilst susceptible to social change, many of the changes of the nineteenth century had only limited impact on Barkham, since it was relatively isolated and not close to any manufacturing centre. It was not until the Great Depression of 1875–1899 that agriculture's predominance in the parish was challenged, and then not by any form of industrial activity but by a growth in domestic service.

Demography

At the time of the first decennial census in 1801, recorded in the parish register by the Revd David Davies[1], there were 185 inhabitants (although both Barkham House and Barkham Square were unoccupied), whilst in the 1911 census 261 inhabitants were recorded. The population fluctuated in the meantime, registering highs of 280 in 1861 and 284 in 1891, and lows of 217 in 1881 and 218 in 1901.

The first census with personal details was conducted in 1841, when 228 inhabitants were recorded in 45 houses[2]. Of the 75 male inhabitants over the age of 12, there were seven farmers, 47 farm workers and seven servants (at Barkham Manor and Barkham Square). Out of 70 female inhabitants over 12, nine were in domestic service. The occupations of wives and unmarried daughters were not recorded, but in the absence of any cottage industry most would have had to work hard looking after large households and helping in the fields at harvest time. Children under 13 accounted for 36 % of the inhabitants.

The labouring families in Barkham lived principally in four locations, namely Coombs Hill (now Hayes Lane), Langley Common, Barkham Lane (now Barkham Street), and Long Moor. Of the inhabitants of Barkham in 1841, 78·5 % were born in Berkshire, but what proportion were born in Barkham is not known. As an agricultural parish, there would have been a high degree of mobility, labourers being hired for 12 months at a time at the Michaelmas hiring fairs. The number born in the parish was probably already less than one-half, since by 1851 the proportion was 44 %.

At the time of the 1891 census there were 284 inhabitants living in 56 houses[3]. Of the 91 male inhabitants over the age of 12, there were 10 farmers, 45 farm workers and 14 servants. Out of 91 female inhabitants over 12, 21 were in domestic service. Children under 13 accounted for 33 % of the inhabitants. By 1891 only 63 people living in Barkham had been born in the parish (and 44 of those were children under 13), but 113 inhabitants (40 %) had been born in other parishes no further than 15 miles from Barkham.

The proportion of adult male inhabitants engaged in agriculture fell from 84 % in 1871 to 60 % in 1891, whilst those employed as indoor/outdoor servants increased from 7 to 15 %, doubtless a reflection of the Great Depression. Employment opportunities for local inhabitants, male or female alike, at Barkham Manor or Barkham Square were few, however, since their gentlemen tenants tended to bring their own servants with them, and to continue to recruit staff from outside the parish.

A summary of the census returns from 1841 to 1891 is set out *opposite*. Copies of the original returns may be seen at the Reading Local Studies Library and the Berkshire Record Office. Typed transcripts (with name index) are also available at the Berkshire Record Office.

Education

Before the nineteenth century Barkham had been too small to warrant a school of its own. The Revd David Davies (rector 1782–1819) had sent a number of children to a dame school in Wokingham at his own expense[4].

Not long after Henry Clive, MP for Ludlow, became tenant of Barkham House about 1814, a small elementary school was established under his patronage, supported by voluntary subscriptions. By 1818, 40 children were being taught there[5]. It is not known where the school was first located, but following the death of David Davies in 1819, it was accommodated in a room in the parsonage house, which Henry Clive rented for the purpose (since the new rector, the Revd Henry Ellis St John, resided at his other living at Finchampstead, West Court).

In 1827 a Sunday School was also established to provide basic education for children from the poorer families in the parish, with financial support from the Clives and other benefactors, and in 1828 the Daily School was re-established on a fee-paying basis (although the same benefactors would have borne the fees of the children of the poor). In 1833 the Sunday School was attended by about 50 children and there were 28 '*scholars*' at the Daily School[6].

In the 1830s the master of the Daily School was Henry Eccardt, who lived with his wife Mary on the school premises at the parsonage house. He was also parish clerk and, in 1841, census enumerator. Following the appointment of the Revd Arthur Roberts as curate in 1843, the parochial school (and the Sunday School) moved to a room attached to a cottage owned by Mr Clive in Barkham Street, on the site where The Gables now stands[7]. In 1854 *Billing's Directory* described the parochial school as a free school, with

Barkham Census (1841–1891)

	1841	1851*	1861	1871	1881	1891
Total population	228 M130 F 98	274 M152 F 122	280 M147 F 133	240 M126 F 114	217 M100 F 117	284 M145 F 139
No. of houses (inhabited)	45	51	55	55	49	56
Male inhabitants (excluding children under 13 or at school and visitors)	75 33%	92 36%	97 35%	88 37%	67 31%	91 32%
Farmers	7 9%	9 10%	8 8%	8 9%	6 9%	10 11%
Farm workers	47 63%	65 71%	71 72%	66 75%	43 64%	45 49%
Indoor/outdoor servants	7 9%	7 8%	8 8%	6 7%	5 7%	14 15%
Artisans	3 4%	6 6%	8 8%	3 3%	7 10%	6 7%
Female inhabitants (excluding children under 13 or at school and visitors)	70 31%	73 28%	76 27%	77 32%	74 34%	91 32%
Domestic servants	9 13%	17 23%	11 14%	13 17%	16 22%	21 23%
Self-employed	– 0%	2 3%	6 8%	3 4%	3 4%	3 3%
Children aged 4 to 12 (or at school)	53 23%	51 20%	70 25%	50 21%	45 21%	71 25%
Infants (aged 3 or under)	30 13%	30 12%	29 10%	19 8%	28 13%	24 8%
Persons born in Barkham	– –	115 44%	113 40%	92 38%	60 28%	63 22%
Persons born within 15 miles of Barkham	179 78·5%†	82 32%	101 36%	77 32%	86 39%	113 40%
Persons born over 15 miles from Barkham	49 21·5%‡	61 24%	66 24%	71 30%	71 33%	108 38%

*Analysis excludes an estimated 16 people (9 males, 7 females) believed to be sleeping rough.

†Born within Berkshire.

‡Born outside Berkshire.

about 35 scholars, '*liberally supported*' by Mrs Clive. For 47 years Mary Penlington, wife of the Clives' footman and later butler, Thomas Penlington, was the '*attentive and kind schoolmistress*' of the parish[8]. It seems probable that, as a young woman, Mrs Penlington first taught at the Sunday School when it was established in 1827, subsequently succeeding Henry Eccardt in running the Daily School from the early 1840s until 1873.

By 1867 there were only 12 boys and 16 girls, all under 10, receiving schooling in Barkham[9] and in 1871 it was decided to combine the elementary schools in Barkham and Arborfield. Land was acquired in what is now School Road, just over the parish boundary in Arborfield[10], and a new school was built at a cost of £645, funded by voluntary contributions (including £200 from John Walter III and £100 from Mrs Clive)[11].

The new school opened in 1873 and the first master was Arthur Austin, but following an unfavourable report by the Diocesan Inspector, Austin was dismissed in 1876 and replaced as master by Harry Webster, who remained for 25 years until his death in 1902[12]. The school continues, as the Arborfield, Newland and Barkham Church of England Junior School, on the same site today.

The reports on the school in the 1890s were generally complimentary, such as this one from 1898[13].

The Diocesan Inspector reports that the School has passed a very good examination in all the groups. The Infants answered remarkably well, and knew their part of the course very satisfactorily. The upper standards had a good knowledge of both the Old and New Testament, and the special portions in the course were well known. The answering in the Catechism and Prayer Book was also good. The repetition of Scripture was excellent, and the children understood the meaning of the portions learnt by heart perfectly.

However, apart from the infants, the inspection of the school in 1911 created a less favourable impression on H.M. Inspector. '*The children, as on former occasions, are very inert and unresponsive, especially in the First Class. Some of them take no apparent interest in their lessons, and most of them are heavy and hard to rouse.*' The Inspector's comments were duly heeded, since by 1915 the Diocesan Inspector was able to report, '*Thoroughly good teaching is being given in this school with most satisfactory results*'. There was invariably praise for the teaching of the infants, which for over 30 years (1884–1888 and 1892–1919) was in the capable hands of Mrs Lucy Allright. Even so, in 1908 the County Education Committee determined that Mrs Allright should be replaced by an uncertificated mistress on grounds of economy, but this was strongly, and ultimately successfully, resisted by the managers (i.e. governors)[14].

The school terms revolved around the agricultural calendar, and were longer than today, but they were interspersed by regular one-day or half-day holidays on account of,

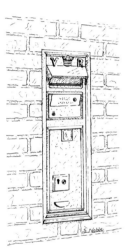

1863 post box in the wall of Barkham Manor

for example, ploughing matches, point-to-point races and choir outings. The equivalent of the modern summer holiday was the harvest holidays in August.

Communications and Village Stores

Barkham was not situated on any significant transport route. Early in the nineteenth century the Reading carrier used to leave the Saracen's Head on Wednesdays and Saturdays at 4 p.m. for Finchampstead and Yateley via Shinfield, Arborfield and Barkham. In 1834 the route was taken over by John Marlow, who was still the Barkham carrier 20 years later[15]. By 1911 Barkham was served by two carriers to Reading, one of whom was Frederick Bayliss, who set up premises at Coppid Hill on the Barkham Road[16]. About 1920 Bayliss exchanged his horse-drawn waggon for a motor van. His son, also Frederick, went into his father's business, which by the late 1930s had developed into a garage and petrol filling station. The Barkham Road was laid to tarmac for the first time in 1936 and *Kelly's Directory* in 1939 noted that gas was available.

In the nineteenth century the collection point for letters and newspapers in the parish was The Bull. With the increased popularity of letters following the introduction of the Penny Post in 1840, a receiving house was established at Barkham in 1847, with George Collyer, blacksmith and landlord of The Bull, as Receiver. A messenger from Wokingham, following a footpost walk via King Street (Winnersh), delivered letters at

9 a.m., and collected post at 4 p.m. Letters handed over for posting at The Bull were stamped 'BARKHAM' with an undated circular handstamp. In 1863 the first postbox in the Wokingham district was placed at Barkham in the wall of Barkham Manor opposite The Bull. Later in the century the sub-post office was attached to the village stores adjacent to Sparks Farm, and by the turn of the century there were two deliveries and two collections a day, and one delivery and collection on Sundays[17]. Outgoing letters continued to be stamped at Barkham until the 1920s.

It seems that Barkham's first village stores were opened by George Maskell in the mid-1840s, probably on the same site as the later Post Office Stores adjacent to Sparks Farm. By 1851 Maskell had died, but his widow,

Former Post Office Stores adjacent to Sparks Farm

of mechanisation (e.g. threshing machines) was a threat to jobs, whilst average weekly agricultural wages in Berkshire fell (in absolute terms) from 10s. 5d. in 1833 to 7s. 6d. in 1851[20](compared with an average of 8s. 0d. recorded by the Revd David Davies in the mid-1780s)[21]. The enclosure of the common and waste lands in the parish in 1821 caused more hardship (see Chapter 21). The scale of agricultural poverty made more labouring families dependent on charity and increased the level of parish poor rates.

The agrarian unrest at the end of the 1820s boiled over in November 1830 when marauding gangs roamed the countryside, intent on machine-breaking and rick-burning. Even Barkham was not immune from the depredations of the 'Swing' riots and on the evening of 25 November two hay ricks were set alight at Barkham Square[22]. The farm workers were able to save one of the ricks.

Henry Clive MP of Barkham House was quickly on the spot and ascended a ladder placed against a rick to thank the workers for their exertions to contain the fire. The radical *Morning Chronicle* (in a report reproduced in *The Times*) claimed, however, that Henry Clive had '*addressed them in a tone which seemed to indicate dissatisfaction with their efforts*'. According to the *Morning Chronicle*'s informant, '*The labouring people showed no want of will to extinguish* [the fire], *but they were a set of miserable-looking creatures, under-fed, feeble, without shoes, and altogether in a shocking plight*'. The *Reading Mercury* strongly

1830 rick burning incident at Barkham Square

Ann (41), continued to run the bakery and grocery for another 20 years. In the 1880s and 1890s the stores were run by Thomas Ashby, who employed three assistants in the bakery[18]. In 1897 the shop was sold to Walter Walker, who was also sub-postmaster. By 1911 the business had been taken over by George Harris, who remained until 1937[19]. The bread oven was wood-burning, using bavins from Kidgham Copse. The Post Office Stores continued until the early 1970s and the premises were subsequently demolished to make way for a private house.

Social and Political Developments

The first half of the century was a difficult period for agricultural labourers. The spread

114

disputed the *Morning Chronicle*'s description of events in its next issue[23].

At this time there was a swelling body of opinion that the system of Parliamentary representation needed to be radically reformed, culminating in the enactment of the Great Reform Bill at the end of 1832, which provoked as much national rejoicing as the defeat of Napoleon. Both Henry Clive of Barkham House (MP for Montgomery) and John Walter II of Bear Wood (MP for Berkshire) voted in favour, although Clive did not stand for the reformed Parliament.

Agricultural hardship was again widespread by the 1840s. The price of bread, the staple food of the labouring classes, became unaffordably dear on account of the high duties on imported grain (the Corn Laws were not repealed until 1846). In 1845 near disaster loomed when the failure of the potato crop raised the spectre of famine. In his book *Old Village Life* (1920), the Revd P.H. Ditchfield remarked, *'The 'hungry forties' caused much distress, and I have talked with men who, as boys, remember the hard times, the dearness and scarcity of food, which, in some measure, was relieved by the charity of the squires, and well-to-do farmers. In my own parish there was a Lady Bountiful, Mrs Clive, who seems to have fed and run the whole village'.*

Despite widespread poverty, rural crime was a rare event in Barkham. Very occasionally a horse or 'fat' sheep would be stolen. In 1817 one of Peter Green's employees at Barkham Square, William Baker, was convicted of stealing 70 fleeces of wool and sentenced to be transported for 7 years, but was subsequently reprieved[24]. In 1828 John Sims was sentenced at the Michaelmas Quarter Sessions to 6 months hard labour for stealing a horse collar, harness and two leather traces from the cart house at Barkham Manor[25]. In 1834 Henry Mason was transported for 7 years for stealing five fowls from William Chandler, the new tenant of Barkham Square[26].

From the end of the eighteenth century onwards mutual benefit clubs or friendly societies sprang up all over the country in response to the widespread poverty. For subscriptions from as low as 3d. per week, a member could secure benefits payable in the event of sickness, infirmity or unemployment and to cover the cost of a decent burial when he died. In 1829 a penny society was founded in Barkham, almost certainly with the active encouragement of Henry Clive MP, who was one of the trustees. The first treasurer was Miss Blanckenhagen of Shute End. The penny society, which would also have organised social events for members and their families, probably at The Bull, continued until at least 1848. Members' subscriptions were deposited with the Wokingham Savings Bank (manager Thomas Trickey), which opened every Monday from 12.00 to 1.00 p.m. in the Town Hall. Henry Clive, who was a trustee of the Wokingham Savings Bank,

S. Noble

also served as acting treasurer of the penny society in the later 1830s[27].

The parish maintained four semi-detached cottages *'for the reception of the poor'* (now Brook Cottage). Following the new Poor Law in 1834, Barkham became part of the Wokingham Poor Law Union and in 1840 the Board of Guardians (chairman Henry Clive) sold the cottages to William Cook, owner of Barkham Square, for £100[28].

There were further reforms of the Parliamentary franchise in 1867 and 1884. The 1884 act extended the franchise to male householders in the counties, increasing the number of voters in the parish from 8 to 46[29]. Towards the end of the century local government was overhauled, resulting in the creation of Berkshire County Council in 1888 and Wokingham Rural District Council in 1894. The Revd P.H. Ditchfield (rector 1886–1930) became Barkham's first representative on the Rural District Council[30], whilst Lieutenant General William Rickman of Barkham Manor became chairman of the annual Parish Meeting (forerunner of the Parish Council) until his death in 1900[31].

Although the tenants of the Bear Wood estate in Barkham lived in *'commodious'* cottages, surrounded by 25 poles of land (equivalent to one-sixth of an acre)[32], at the close of the century there remained labouring families in the parish close to the poverty line, who were dependent on charitable distributions of fuel, clothes and soup. There were six small charities (including Allwright's charity and Brooksbank's charity) in 1902 distributing coal worth £30 a year. (In 1933 all the charities were merged to form a single parochial charity.) There was also a Clothing Club, a savings club for poorer parishioners, to which General Rickman donated 4d. for every 1s. saved (a one-third bonus), to help the poor to purchase warm clothes and sound boots for themselves and their children. From February to April there was also a kitchen for the distribution of free soup to the poorer inhabitants on Wednesdays and Saturdays, run by Mrs Allright at the expense of General and Mrs Rickman[33].

Recreational Activities

Cricket was a popular pastime throughout the nineteenth century. The first recorded cricket match involving a Barkham team was in 1811, when a joint Arborfield, Newland and Barkham team played Sonning on Bullmarsh Heath, with the second innings played a week later on Carter's Hill, between Newland and Sindlesham[34]. It seems the match was well contested and the Sonning eleven won by 18 runs. By the latter part of the century the Barkham team was playing six to eight matches per season with local clubs such as the Wokingham Magpies, Bearwood, Binfield, Easthampstead, Farley Hill and the Reading Biscuit Factory. From 1892 to 1897 there was a joint cricket club with Arborfield. There used to be an annual cricket club dinner at The Bull every autumn[35]. The club was fortunate that the

Revd Peter Ditchfield and Edward Murray Sturges (who lived at Barkham Square, 1904–1934) were both enthusiastic cricketers.

The principal sport of the landed classes during the first part of the nineteenth century was hunting. Barkham was part of the territory of the private pack of hounds kept by Sir John Cope Bart. of Bramshill, which used to meet regularly at The Bull[36]. Sometimes the King's (and after 1837 the Queen's) hounds, whose kennels were at Ascot, would pass through Barkham in full cry[37]. In 1852 Barkham became part of the territory of the foxhounds kept by Thomas Colleton Garth of Haines Hill. E.M. Sturges was Honorary Secretary, subsequently President, of The Garth from 1910 to 1934 and the hunt sometimes used to meet at Barkham Square.

The traditional 'maying' celebrations during Whitsuntide week continued well into the nineteenth century. Although no record survives of what happened at Barkham, the amusements would have included one or more of the following: wrestling, bowling for cheese, gingling (i.e. jingling), donkey racing and cricket or ploughing matches for hats or silk handkerchieves.

As elsewhere in Victorian Britain, various clubs sprang up in the parish, often to promote self-improvement or with a moral purpose. The clubs usually met in the new schoolhouse in School Road or in the Old School premises in Barkham Street. There was a Working Men's Club and Reading

CRICKET.—On Monday, September 9, at 10 o'clock, a Match at Cricket will be played, on Bullmarsh Heath; Sonning Parifh againft Arborfield, Newland, and Barkham. Bets are two to one on Arborfield.

Reading Mercury.
9 September 1811

The grand and well-contefted match of Cricket, which was began on Bullmarfh-Heath, on Monday the 9th Sept. eleven of Sonning parifh against eleven of Newland, Arborfield, and Barkham, was on Monday laft, the 16th inft. played out on Carter Hill, near Arborfield, and won by the Sonning eleven, by eighteen runs.

Reading Mercury.
23 September 1811

Room which was open three evenings a week during the winter months. Up to 40 younger people were members of the Band of Hope (a youth temperance group) which used to meet weekly under the leadership of Mrs Allright, the tireless infants' teacher and choirmistress. In the 1880s there was an Arborfield and Barkham Temperance Society and in the 1890s an Arborfield and Barkham Glee Class. A Barkham branch of the Mothers' Union was formed in 1897 with twelve members[38].

As a self-contained rural community, any entertainment had to be home grown. There was even a village orchestra (or band), led by William Hutt, the parish clerk. Musical entertainments were regularly organised during the winter months and the following account in the parish magazine in November 1888 is typical.

On the 18th [October] … in the evening a Musical Entertainment was given at the School. The room was crowded, and the programme afforded great pleasure to all who were present. Mrs. J. Simonds most kindly sang two songs, which were much appreciated, and Miss B. Simonds played two solos on her violin. Songs were also sung by Mr. and Mrs. Webster, and by Messrs. Ashby, Wood and Collins, and two recitations were given by Mr. Newbury.

Sermons by the rector and visiting preachers apart, there were also occasional lectures by visiting speakers, often about life in the colonies or missionary work, sometimes illustrated by the new technology of magic lantern slides.

One of the most significant, and visible, events in Barkham in the nineteenth century was the decision that the mediæval church (with seating for 117) had become too small and dilapidated for the needs of the parish and the church was rebuilt (with seating for 155) in 1859–1861, as recounted in Chapter 17.

The church remained the focal point for many activities in the parish, which the rector invariably attended. The parish magazine, founded by the Revd Peter Ditchfield as a joint venture with Swallowfield in 1888, served as a local newspaper, reporting most of the happenings in the parish, not least the progress of the Barkham cricket team. By the 1890s one of the major events each year was the choir outing by train to one of the south coast resorts such as Hastings, Dover or Margate.

This involved leaving Barkham (by waggon) for Wokingham station about 4.30 a.m. and returning to Wokingham about 11.30 p.m. By all accounts a good time was had by all. On New Year's Eve the bellringers were usually entertained to supper at The Bull by General and Mrs Rickman before ringing in the New Year, whilst there was usually a choir supper at the rectory in January.

The Boer War in South Africa (1899–1902) was, however, to cast its shadow over Barkham, when Frederick Blake (aged 20) one of the sons of Edwin Blake (churchwarden and overseer) of Handpost Farm, died of wounds received at Vlapfontein. A brass tablet in the parish church records Frederick Blake's sacrifice.

Royal Celebrations

Queen Victoria's golden jubilee in June 1887, and her diamond jubilee in 1897, were celebrated with loyal enthusiasm at Barkham. At the golden jubilee, after a thanksgiving service in the parish church, all the parishioners were entertained to dinner (i.e. lunch) in the barn at Barkham Square, where the toasts by Lieutenant General Rickman of Barkham Manor and the rector (P.H. Ditchfield) were enthusiastically received. The amusements in the afternoon included a cricket match and a tug-of-war between the married men and the single men (who triumphed in both)[39].

Ten years later, the parishioners crowded into the parish church to give thanks for The

Queen's diamond jubilee, following which the whole parish was entertained to lunch and tea in the barn at the Square and there were athletic sports in the grounds in the afternoon. According to the *Reading Mercury*, a *'severe thunderstorm raged about five o'clock, but did not interfere much with the pleasure of the visitors'*. In the evening a *'huge bonfire was lighted, and dancing was indulged in until a late hour'*[40]. At the Coronation of Edward VII (1901–1910) in August 1902, after a short service in the parish church, lunch was provided for the whole parish in the barn at the Square, followed by a cricket match and dancing in the barn in the evening[41].

On the occasion of George V's silver jubilee in 1935, the parishioners sent a loyal address to The King. *'The day was one of sports and merry making, children and adults taking part in races, side-shows, etc. Tea was provided for all children, and old folks and widows. A carnival dance was held in the evening, with an interval at 10 o'clock, when a gigantic bonfire was lit. During the burning of the fire his Majesty's health was drunk, and the village smith 'fired his anvil'.'*[42]

But even a century ago few, if any, of the parishioners would have been aware that in 1845 there had been even greater excitement when, in the late afternoon of 20 January, a youthful Queen Victoria and Prince Albert passed through Barkham *en route* from Windsor Castle to Stratfield Saye to stay with the Duke of Wellington.

After an enthusiastic civic reception at Wokingham, the royal cortège, escorted by a party of the 17th Lancers, proceeded down the Barkham Road. On reaching Barkham they were greeted by *'a triumphal arch, decorated* [with evergreens] *and hung with flags. Here the people cheered Her Majesty vociferously as she passed'*. At Langley Common, the royal cortège took the road towards Arborfield Cross, disappearing into a magnificent winter sunset. The Queen returned to Windsor Castle by the same route 3 days later, to further acclaim[13].

Queen Victoria passes The Bull en route for Stratfield Saye, 1845

23 Revd Peter Hampson Ditchfield (Rector 1886–1930)

Probably no one has done more to put Barkham on the map than Peter Hampson Ditchfield, Rector of Barkham for 44 years, who in his numerous and varied writings was almost invariably associated with Barkham.

Peter Ditchfield was born in 1854 at West Houghton, near Wigan, in Lancashire. He attended the Royal Grammar School at Clitheroe and was subsequently an undergraduate at Oriel College, Oxford, where he read mathematics (which was the subject of his second book in 1886, *The Romance of Mathematics*). Amongst his fellow students were Cecil Rhodes and Algernon Methuen, with whom he formed close friendships.

He was ordained deacon in 1878 and priest in 1879. From 1878 to 1880 he was curate at Sandhurst and from 1880 to 1886 he served as assistant curate at Christ Church, Reading. In 1886 he was presented to the living of Barkham by the patron, John Walter III of Bear Wood, where he was to remain as rector until his death in 1930. He was Organising Secretary of the Society for the Propagation of the Gospel for Berkshire (1890–1907). Ditchfield also had a

Peter Hampson Ditchfield, 1854–1930

professional interest in education and was a Diocesan Inspector of Schools (1886–1915)[1].

A keen historian and archæologist, Ditchfield was, amongst many other things, Editor of the *Berks, Bucks & Oxon Archæological Journal* from 1895 to 1924 and Secretary of the Berkshire Archæological Society for 38 years. In 1893 Ditchfield applied for the history chair at King's College, London, but his candidature was unsuccessful, notwithstanding a testimonial from the Bishop of Oxford[2].

Peter Ditchfield was a prolific writer and during his lifetime he wrote or edited over a hundred works on folklore, local history, village life, archæology, architecture and ecclesiastical matters. He also contributed innumerable articles to various magazines and periodicals in the UK, as well as to US magazines. For many years he edited the 'Notes and Queries' column on local history in the *Reading Mercury*. From 1906 to 1924 he was co-editor, together with W. Page, of the four-volume *Victoria County History of Berkshire*, still regarded as the definitive work of reference on the history of the county.

There are various references to Barkham in a number of Ditchfield's books. In *Out of the Ivory Palaces* (1911) there is a chapter devoted to the history of Barkham. In *Old Village Life* (1920) Ditchfield cites examples of overseers' payments to relieve poverty from the Parish Poor Account Book (1794–1829) then in his possession. (Sadly the Account Book cannot now be traced.) *Faithful Jess* (1907) was an historical novel set in Barkham which revolves around the landlord of The Bull in the rick-burning times.

In 1888 Ditchfield founded a joint parish magazine with Swallowfield. By the mid-1890s this had graduated to an insertion in *Home Days*, an attractive national magazine full of church and social news, including photographs, serialisations and even colour printing. Of the early parish magazines, only those for 1888 and 1895–1904 survive (and may be seen at the Berkshire Record Office)[3]. In Ditchfield's time the parish magazine was full of social news (rather than pastoral messages), such as childrens' treats at the Manor and Barkham Square, choir outings, cricket matches and parish entertainments.

Peter Ditchfield was much sought after by learned societies as a guest speaker, as well as being regularly invited to preach by local churches. In *Who's Who* his recreations were listed as '*arranging meetings, correcting proofs, lecturing and for many years inspecting schools*'. He was the first person to represent Barkham on the newly established Wokingham Rural District Council in 1894 and was chairman of the Barkham Parish Meeting

Victorian rectory

(1900–1928)[4]. He also represented the parish on the Wokingham Board of Guardians.

Ditchfield was an active freemason for many years. He was initiated in 1893 in the Downshire Lodge at Wokingham and was Provincial Grand Chaplain of Berkshire in 1896/7. He advanced into Mark Masonry and was exalted into Royal Arch Masonry. In 1917 he was appointed Grand Chaplain of Freemasons in England, and of Mark Masons in the following year.

Cricket was one of Peter Ditchfield's great passions and he used to play for various local clubs, including the Gentlemen of Berkshire, Wokingham and Barkham. In his younger days he also used to join the hunting field from time to time.

In 1899, at the age of 45, he married Miss Florence Monk Smith of Ravenswood, Wokingham. There were no children from the marriage.

The coronation of George V in 1911 coincided with the 25th anniversary of Ditchfield's incumbency at Barkham and at the coronation celebrations tribute was paid to Ditchfield's great service to the parish, the assembled company giving a hearty rendering of *For He's a Jolly Good Fellow*[5].

Music was another of Ditchfield's great interests and he used to compose librettos and perform the resultant work in public himself. Probably his greatest artistic achievement was as author and deviser of the *Reading Historical Pageant* in 1920[6].

In 1928 Ditchfield celebrated 50 years in the Ministry and on New Year's Day 1929 the parishioners of Barkham presented an illuminated address to their beloved rector for 42 years. *'To more than one generation of parishioners you have been both pastor and friend. Your literary and archæological achievements made your name known far beyond Barkham, and your writings have, in a rapidly changing age, done much to re-people the past and save from oblivion the memories of bygone days.'*[7] Ditchfield's clerical jubilee was also marked by a full-page biography in the *Masonic News*, which devoted its front cover to a photograph of Brother Ditchfield[8].

Revd P.H. Ditchfield, 1929

Peter Hampson Ditchfield died on 24 September 1930 (aged 76). At his funeral, the parish church was filled to the doors and there were as many people outside in the churchyard. The Church, Freemasonry and the various learned societies with which Ditchfield was connected were well represented. In a later tribute Lord Meston said, '*He had died full of years, ripe in scholarship, and richer still in friendship. It could be truly said of him that he never made an enemy, but that everyone he came in contact with had become a friend. In Freemasonry he had been a sage, mentor, and a wise helper who could ill be spared, and in his life he had been a great scholar, a great friend, a great heart, and a great Christian*'[9].

The body of this zealous and devout churchman now reposes in the shadow of Barkham church, marked by a marble cross between the church porch and the south wall of the nave (adjacent to the tomb of his illustrious predecessor, David Davies, rector 1782–1819). But through the legacy of his (eminently collectable) writings, the gift of Peter Ditchfield to enrich the lives of others lives on.

24 Edward Murray Sturges JP (1859–1934)

Edward Murray Sturges was born in 1859, the eldest son of Canon Edward Sturges, rector of Wokingham (1873–1904). Educated at Winchester and Pembroke College, Cambridge, he was an accomplished sportsman, captaining Pembroke College in both football and cricket.

In 1884 he sailed to Australia to become *aide-de-compte* to Sir Henry (later Lord) Loch, Governor of Victoria (1884–1889). Whilst in Australia he married Eliza Rhoda Grice in 1887. On returning to England he qualified as a barrister and was called to the Bar at the Inner Temple in 1890, although he never practised[1].

The Sturges family moved from Lower Earley to Barkham Square in 1904, initially as tenant farmer from Arthur Fraser Walter of Bear Wood, later purchasing the house and farm. In addition to farming the Barkham Square estate, E.M. Sturges was prominent in local affairs for many years. Apart from local government, his particular interests were the Wokingham Agricultural Association and the Garth Hunt.

For 40 years E.M. Sturges and his wife, Rhoda, were closely associated with the Wokingham Agricultural Show, Mr Sturges holding the position of Honorary Secretary for 15 years and Chairman for 20 years. The growth of the Association during this period was due in large measure to the efforts of E.M. Sturges and his wife, and they effectively organised the Show from Barkham Square. As well as officiating at the Show, Mr Sturges regularly entered in most classes, including cattle, sheep, produce and ploughing[2].

Sturges was a founder member of the Wokingham Rural District Council in 1894 and he held the office of Chairman for 31 years until his death in 1934[3]. His chief interest was to promote the provision of pure water supplies and adequate drainage in the locality. He chaired various local bodies, including the Board of Guardians for the Poor. He was also a Justice of the Peace for the Wokingham Petty Sessional Division.

He was a keen huntsman and in 1902 became assistant secretary of the Garth Hunt. He organised the hunt's first point-to-point races in 1904, which were often held at the Army Remount Depot, adjoining Barkham Square. He was Honorary Secretary of The Garth from 1910 to 1922 and was President of the Hunt Club at the time of his death.

The Garth used to meet from time to time at Barkham Square. One such occasion was reported in the *Reading Mercury* on 22 March 1924.

The Garth dog pack met on March 12th at Barkham Square, the residence of that famous sportsman and late Secretary of the Hunt, Mr E.M. Sturges and Mrs Sturges, who, with Major Sturges [son] *and Mrs Simonds* [daughter], *hospitably entertained a large company … It was just turned 12 o'clock when a start was made to draw Kitcham* [Copse], *Mr Sturges' cover, and a fox was viewed away directly.*

E.M. Sturges usually drove himself about in a pony and trap and did not acquire a motor car (which his groom or Mrs Sturges drove) until about 1928. When he subsequently broke his leg, he followed the hunt by car.

Edward Murray Sturges died on 5 May 1934 at the age of 74. At the funeral, the parish church was so crowded, particularly with members of the numerous organisations with which he had been associated, that many had to stand outside in the churchyard throughout the service. His obituary in the *Reading Mercury* said, '*His jovial personality gained him friends wherever he went, but at the same time he was never afraid to express his opinion, and his services were therefore of particular value in the public work in which he played so great a part*'. In another tribute the vice-chairman of the Wokingham Rural District Council said, '*His was a distinctive personality … Courageous in expressing his opinions, he was scrupulously fair, a man of strong will and great determination. To the poor he was ever kind-hearted*'[4].

Edward Murray Sturges 1859–1934

Ted and Rhoda Sturges had three children, Eric, Robert and Betty. Their eldest son, Eric, was killed during World War I whilst serving with the King's Own Yorkshire Light Infantry. Their surviving son, Lieutenant General Sir Robert Grice Sturges KBE CB DSO, gave distinguished service in

*Mrs Rhoda Sturges
1864–1944*

herself to the villagers and their children by being a '*zealous teacher*' at Sunday School and providing teas at Barkham Cricket Club matches (of which her father was captain)[5]. On the day of the wedding Barkham was *en fête* and a half-day school holiday was declared. The marriage service, and subsequent reception at Barkham Square, were attended by about 250 guests, all of whom, as well as the presents given by them, were listed in the *Reading Mercury*[6]. The groom's father gave a piano to the bride and the gift of the parishioners of Barkham was a revolving breakfast dish. The villagers of Arborfield, Newland and Barkham were not forgotten and about 500 were entertained by Mr and Mrs Sturges in the evening, with music by the Blue Hungarian Band.

Mrs Sturges was no less public-spirited than her husband and enthusiastically organised activities for the local children, including collecting primroses to decorate the parish church at Easter, tennis tournaments on the two courts at the Square in the summer and gathering blackberries in the autumn for the patients in Wokingham Hospital.

When the Bear Wood estate was being broken up following the death of Arthur Fraser Walter in 1910, the Barkham Square estate, together with Sparks Farm and Langley Common Farm (312 acres), were purchased by Mrs Sturges from John Walter IV in 1913 for £5,750[7]. She was also active in local government in her own right. In

the Royal Marines during both World Wars. During the Second he led the commando groups at the time of the occupation of Iceland and Madagascar and was twice mentioned in despatches. In 1942/3 he served as *aide-de-compte* to King George VI. After the war Sir Robert returned to Barkham and lived at the Square until 1948.

Robert's twin sister, Betty, married Mr John Simonds of Newlands (of the Reading banking family) in June 1911. Before her marriage she had greatly endeared

1920 Mrs Sturges was appointed to the County Agricultural Committee as representative of the Ministry of Agriculture, Fisheries & Food and in 1926 she became a member of the County Small Holdings and Allotments Sub-Committee, continuing to serve on both committees until her death (aged 80) in 1944[8].

Following the death of Ted Sturges in 1934, Mrs Sturges continued to farm the Barkham Square estate with the help of Thomas Holloway, her faithful bailiff. Like her husband, Mrs Sturges was a keen rider. She was often to be seen out riding side-saddle, accompanied by her two small dogs. There was great competition amongst local farmworkers' sons to open field gates to let her pass, in anticipation of a silver coin by way of reward.

25 Remount Depot and REME Garrison: Barkham During World Wars I and II

After the Boer War (1899–1902), the Army was seeking to expand its facilities for the supply of horses for military service and in 1904 the War Office leased 286 acres from the Bear Wood estate, of which one-half was in Barkham, two-fifths in Finchampstead and the remainder in Arborfield, and established a remount depot. The land in Barkham comprised Old Biggs's Farm and Ellis's Farm, both straddling Biggs Lane. The purpose of a remount depot was primarily to maintain a stock of horses and mules to supply the needs of active units on demand, as well as looking after sick horses needing rest and attention.

Apart from the three officers in charge, the rest of the staff of about 40 were civilians. The first officer in command was Captain Quartermaster James Barry. Initially, Barry lived at the moated Old Biggs's Farm, but in 1906 he moved into the newly built Moat House close by, which became the superintendant's residence[1]. In 1911 the War Office purchased the freehold of the land leased in 1904 for £11,099 from John Walter IV[2]. Old Biggs's Farm was demolished shortly afterwards and Ellis's Farm in the late 1950s. A few months before the outbreak of war in 1914, a further strip of about 100 acres in Barkham was acquired, stretching from Langley Common Road to Commonfield Lane, including Langley Common Farm, which became an animal infirmary. After the war the farmhouse was converted into a residence for the veterinary officer and became known as Langley House.

Some explanation is called for as to why the remount depot came to bear the name Arborfield, when only 26 acres were in that parish. The reason is probably that New Biggs's Farm, which became the headquarters of the depot, was in the parish of Arborfield and the main gate was on the old Reading Road through Arborfield Cross (although the farm outbuildings were in Finchampstead).

Barkham saw a considerable amount of activity during World War I (1914–1918), largely on account of the remount depot. About 1,000 horses and mules a week used to be transported from Ireland to Wokingham station, where they were herded into the coal yard (where the car park now is) and driven at midnight, 500 at a time, down the Barkham Road to the remount depot[3]. Two hundred men of the Leicestershire Regiment were billeted at Barkham, including 57 men and four officers at the rectory[4]. Concern over damage to crops by vermin in 1917 caused the parish council to offer to pay 3d. per dozen sparrows' heads, 3d. per dozen sparrows' eggs and 2d. each for rats' tails[5]. Four Barkham men (including the eldest son of Mr and Mrs Sturges of Barkham Square) gave their lives in the Great War and another three died after the war from its effects.

The heyday of the remount depot was in the early 1930s, when the establishment covered over 400 acres (mainly pasture), with about 500 horses and mules at any one time and about 150 staff (making the depot the largest employer in the locality). Groups of horses being exercised was a common sight around Barkham during the 1920s and early 1930s. In 1932 the War Office acquired Whitehall Farm and about 50 acres in Arborfield to provide more pasture. Major Hubert Tanner was Superintendant and Inspector of Remounts (1919–1937), whilst most of the purchasing of horses was undertaken by a second Inspector of Remounts, who after 1928 was Brigadier General Cecil Lucas MC.

The remount depot was also well known in the 1920s as the venue for the Army point-to-point races. At the meeting on 15 March 1924, the races were honoured by the presence of TRH The Prince of Wales (later Edward VIII), The Duke of York (later George VI) and Prince Henry (later Duke of Gloucester)[6]. The Prince of Wales and Prince Henry each competed in two races. In the last race the Prince of Wales' mount, Little Favourite,

stumbled on landing after the first fence and the Prince was kicked in the face by his horse after being thrown onto hard ground, landing on his head. He was unconscious for half an hour and was carried to Moat House where the dishevelled heir to the throne was welcomed with a dressing-down by the Superindendant's wife for muddying her carpets. Prince Henry was unseated in the two races in which he competed, his second mount becoming entangled with an eager spectator's bicycle. At the Army steeplechases the previous year, the Prince of Wales had had a similar mishap when his horse fell at the water jump (Barkham Brook), but he escaped with a wetting[7].

The Prince of Wales escapes with a wetting in Barkham Brook, 1923

By 1937, however, mechanisation had effectively superseded the horse for military purposes and the remount depot was closed. About this time the windmill on the high ground beyond Commonfield Lane, which had supplied water from a 37-feet well to the depot, was dismantled. But against the backdrop of increasing international tension, the camp was quickly adapted for other military purposes. Nor did horses completely disappear. There continued to be draught horses on the camp until 1966, one of the last being a grey called Gilbert, who was well known at local shows.

After the closure of the depot in 1937, the stables were used as a munitions store and new barracks were planned (Poperinghe and Bailleul) for the trainee anti-aircraft regiments at Aldershot. In May 1939 a new Army Technical School was opened, accommodating 1,200 engineering apprentices. Work also began on building a new barracks (Hazebrouck) for the gunners on Langley Common. With the outbreak of World War II in September 1939, the Army badly needed skilled men to service and repair tanks and other weapons and equipment, and following the evacuation of Dunkirk in May/June 1940, the partly completed Hazebrouck Barracks became the AFV Recovery & Repair Training Centre.

In 1942 the Government announced the reorganisation of the Army engineering maintenance services and the formation of the Royal Electrical and Mechanical Engineers. The Training Centre was transformed into the REME Training Establishment and so began the association between Arborfield, Barkham and Finchampstead and REME. From early 1944 the tasks of the new corps focused on secret preparations for the invasion of France (D-Day), which included the construction of a large water splash on Langley Common to test the waterproofing of the tanks and other vehicles planned to be used. In April 1944 two of the barracks were taken over as staging accommodation for troops moving south to take part in the Normandy landings. During the war Moat House was used as a medical centre and Langley House became the Garrison headquarters.

Langley House (formerly Langley Common Farm)

Elsewhere in the parish local farmers, smallholders and farm workers contributed to the war effort by greatly expanding arable food production, under the direction of the County War Agricultural Committee. Several bombs fell in the centre of Barkham. The largest fell in Rectory Lane, leaving a big crater. Other bombs fell behind Sparks Farm, and next to the old village hall (which was of wooden construction), destroying one side. In another air raid, a German aircraft machine-gunned the Army Technical School parade ground, scattering the apprentices there at the time. Four Barkham men were killed in action during World War II, including Frederick Bayliss who, tragically, was killed by a sniper's bullet in Hamburg 2 days after the German surrender.

Since the end of the war in 1945 there have been considerable changes in the REME facilities at the Garrison, which now include:

- Headquarters REME Training Group

- School of Electronic and Aeronautical Engineering

- School of Equipment Support (Army)

- Army Apprentices College

- Headquarters Director of Electrical and Mechanical Engineering (Army) (including the Museum of Technology, which is open to the public on weekdays).

Appendix I
List of Rectors (and Patrons) since 1220

Dates	Incumbent	Presented by*
1220 active	John de Berkham (Also rector of Arborfield from 1190)	Not known
1249–[ ]	John de Craunford	Henry III (forfeit from John de Bercham)
1315–1317	William de Nevyll	John le Botiller
1317–1322	John le Palmere	John le Botiller
1322–1323	James de Berkham	John le Botiller
1323–1329	Walter de Conyngesby	John le Botiller
1329–1334	Robert de Malton	John le Botiller
1334–1343	Thomas de Babynton	Edward III (forfeit from John Mautravers)
1343–1344	John de Insula [Lisle]	Gilbert Bollok
1345–[ ]	John Thurbern	Gilbert Bullok
[ ]–1396	Henry Ganefeld	Not known
1396–[ ]	John Lygh	Gilbert Bulloc
[ ]–1419	William Bateyle	Not known
1419–1421	Walter Bosum	Thomas Bollok
1421–1437	William Myddleton	Thomas Bullok
1437–1444	William Coryngham	Thomas Bullok

1444–1463	John Everdon	Robert Bullok
1463–1472	John Byngham	Robert Bullock
1472–[ ]	Roger Crympe	Robert Bullok
[ ]–1489	John Welles	Not known
1489–1504	John Hawkyns	Eleanor Bullokys, widow
1504–1514	Robert Towneshend	Gilbert Bulloke
1514–1516	Thomas Hornby	Thomas Bullocke
1516–1533	John Hethcote	Thomas Bullocke
1533–1569	John Langridge	Thomas Bullok
1569–1596	Thomas Whyte	Richard Bullocke
1596–1603	Abraham Warrocke	Elizabeth I (on account of legal dispute)
1603–1633	Richard Windeatt	Edmond Standen
1633–[ ]	Stephen Rose (29) (Also rector of Arborfield 1640)	William Standen
[1653 active	Richard Bigg (?)	Commonwealth]
1660–1694	Alexander Stokes (40) (Also rector of Arborfield)	William Standen and William Ball
1694–1739	John Sale (24) (Also rector of Arborfield)	Samuel Sale (lessee of advowson)
1739–1768	William Dawes (38)	Revd John Waterman
1768–1782	John Gabriel (52) (Also vicar of Hampstead Norris)	William Pitt
1782–1819	David Davies (39)	John Pitt
1819–1841	Henry Ellis St John (Also rector of Finchampstead and Winchfield)	Himself

1842–1863	Edward St John (37) (Also rector of Finchampstead and Winchfield)	Elizabeth St John, widow
1843–1863	Arthur Roberts (31), curate	John St John
1863–1886	Arthur Roberts	Himself
1886–1930	Peter Hampson Ditchfield (32)	John Walter III†
1930–1938	Granville Gregory	John Walter IV
1939–1974	Cedric Charles Roycroft	John Walter IV
1974–1975	F. T. Starbuck (priest in charge)	Oxford Board of Patronage
1976	**Joint Benefice with Arborfield**	
1977–1982	Ian Henry Bull	Oxford Board of Patronage
1982–1991	Robert J. Bawtree	Oxford Board of Patronage
1992–1998	David B. Rowe (priest in charge)	Oxford Board of Patronage
1998 to date	Piers Bickersteth (priest in charge)	Oxford Board of Patronage

*Until the Revd Henry Ellis St John, lord of the manor of Finchampstead, West Court, purchased the advowson from Lieutenant General John Leveson Gower of Bill Hill in 1810 for 3,000 guineas, the right of patronage was in the same hands as the lordship of the manor. †The ownership of the living and the lordship were re-united by John Walter III, who purchased the advowson from the Revd Arthur Roberts in 1864, and the lordship from John Leveson Gower about 1878.

Appendix II
Barkham Bounds
Thursday 24 May 1770

BE it remembered, the Tenants & Inhabitants of the Manor & parish of Barkham attended by the Revd Doctor Gabriel the Rector on this day met at the Bound:mark in the Wokingham Road at the End of Pook Lane And after Doctor Gabriel had there read the Collect Epistle & Gospel for the day proceeded round the Bounds of the Manor as follows (vizt) From the said Bound mark to the house of Mrs Meers (formerly Halls) including the said house with the garden & appurt[enance]s thereof From thence thro' the Pond (which James the son of Thomas Pither went thro') between the land of s.^d Mr Meers on the right hand & the Land & Meadows of William Pitt Esqre and of Edwd Lane on the left hand unto the Heath by a Cro/s there And thence straight over the Heath to Evenden Grounds And along the Ditch to the Corner of Evenden hedge And from thence straight along the Slade towards a Row Thorne in the Slade by the 3 several Cro/ses that are the Bounds between this Manor & the Manors of Finchampstead East Court & West Court And thence acro/s the Heath leaving Arrowsmith al[ia]s Rooksnest Corner about a Stones Cast on the right by the Bound mark where a man was killed & buried by the Inhabitants of Barkham - And then including Long more to the Stems of two Oak Trees And thence to the lower Corner of Ray:bridge now Mr St John's land round the Outside of the Row of Trees Then along part of Mr St John's land to a great Oak in a Ground called Tuckers being the Bound mark between Arborfield & Barkham from thence acro/s the said Ground called Tuckers & some grounds adjoining by a Crab:tree in the hedge of a Ground fronting Clacy's Farm:house And acro/s the End of cooled Oak Coppice up the little Bye lane to the top of Langley Common to the Bound:mark Then over thwart the Common along the Greenway leading to Langley al[ia]s Burge/ses Farm And then along the Lane into Bearwood thro' the Copyhold Lands of Joseph Street From thence along the Bank in Bear:wood 'til you come to the Greenway that leads round:about thence to Pook Lane And along that lane to the Bound mark in the Wokingham Road first mentioned.

EDW.^D WISE Junr
Stew.^d Dep.^y

Acknowledgements

W̲e should like to thank all those who have assisted with the preparation of this book by providing information, permitting fieldwalking and surveying over their land or who have helped in other ways. We are also very grateful for the support and encouragement of Barkham Parish Council.

Particular thanks are due to Ian Atherton, who not only edited the book with great skill and care, but also guided us so expertly through each stage of the preparation of the book.

Very special thanks are due to Sally Noble for drawing so many illustrations specifically for the book, and for her unfailing cheerfulness in meeting all the demands made on her.

This book would not have become a reality, however, without the active encouragement and practical advice of Richard Noble, who played a vital role as project co-ordinator and ensured that everyone did what was expected of them. We owe Richard a special debt of gratitude.

The extract from the facsimile edition of John Rocque's 1761 Map of Berkshire on p. iv is reproduced with the permission of the publisher, Harry Margary Maps, Lympne Castle, Kent, CT21 4LQ.

The illustrations on pp. 34 and 68 are reproduced by kind permission of the County Archivist, Wiltshire and Swindon Record Office.

The drawing of the old church on p. 39 (*Add. MSS* 28,676A, f. 84) is reproduced by permission of The British Library.

The following illustrations are reproduced by kind permission of the County Archivist, Berkshire Record Office: p. 47 (D/A1/76/167), p. 56 (D/A1/41/29), p. 61 (D/A1/1/276), p. 98 (R/D 134 Box 6/2/1) and p. 120 (R/D 134 Box 3/8/1).

The following illustrations are reproduced from original documents in the custody of the Public Record Office: p. 52 (LR.2.199) and p. 75 (SP24/37).

The extract from David Davies' account book on p. 99 is reproduced by permission of the Warden and Fellows of Nuffield College, Oxford.

139

The photograph on p. 122 is reproduced by kind permission of Mrs F. Naish.

The photographs on pp. 125 and 126 are reproduced by kind permission of Mrs M. Hart and family.

The photograph on p. 129 is reproduced with the permission of Times Newspapers Ltd.

Extracts from the *Reading Mercury* and the *Berkshire Chronicle* are reproduced courtesy of the *Reading Chronicle*.

History Bibliography

Dils, Joan (ed.) *An Historical Atlas of Berkshire* (Berkshire Record Society) 1998

Page, W. and Ditchfield, P.H. (eds) *Victoria County History of Berkshire*, 4 vols, published 1906–1924

Pounds, N.J.G. *The Culture of the English People* (Cambridge University Press) 1994

Richardson, John *The Local Historian's Encyclopedia*, 2nd edn (Historical Publications) 1993

Tarver, Anne *Church Court Records* (Phillimore) 1995

Tiller, Kate *English Local History: An Introduction* (Alan Sutton) 1992

Walne, Peter The English Ancestry of Colonel William Ball of Millenbeck *The Virginia Magazine of History and Biography*, Vol. 67, No. 4, October 1959

Sources and References

Abbreviations

BRO   Berkshire Record Office
HRO   Hampshire Record Office
OA   Oxfordshire Archives
PRO   Public Record Office
RLSL   Reading Local Studies Library
WRO   Wiltshire and Swindon Record Office

1. Prehistory and Romano-British Periods

1. Raymond Grant, *The Royal Forests of England*, 1991 (Alan Sutton)
2. M. Gelling, *in* J. Dils (ed), *An Historical Atlas of Berkshire*, 1998 (Reading)
3. P. Collins and M. Keith-Lucas, *Middle and Latest Flandrian Vegetation History in south-central England: Evidence from Longmoor Bog, Finchampstead, Berkshire*, 1996 (unpublished)
4. J. Wymer, personal communication
5. L. Torrance and S. Ford, *The Arborfield/Barkham Relief Sewer Scheme. An Archæological Watching Brief and Rescue Excavation of the Barkham Square Burnt Mound*, 1992 (Reading)
6. J. Wymer, *Mesolithic Britain*, 1991 (Princes Risborough)
7. F. Pryor, *Farmers in Prehistoric Britain*, 1998 (Stroud)
8. M. Fulford, *Calleva Atrebatum*, 1987 (Reading)
9. H. Peake, *The Archaeology of Berkshire*, 1931 (London)
10. J. Pine, The Excavation of a late Iron Age/Roman Settlement and Iron Production Site at Whitehall Brick and Tile Works, Arborfield Garrison, Berkshire, *TVAS Report 96/79c*, 1999 (Reading)
11. P. Fowler, *in* D.M. Wilson (ed), *The Archaeology of Anglo-Saxon England*, 1981 (Frome and London)

2. Mediæval Period (Anglo-Saxon Period to the Sixteenth Century AD)

1. John Blair, *in* J. Dils (ed), *op. cit.*
2. B. Kemp, personal communication
3. F.M. Stenton, *The Early History of The Abbey of Abingdon*, 1913; reprinted 1989 (Stamford)
4. G. Astill and J. Langdon (eds), *Medieval Farming and Technology*, 1997 (Leiden, New York and Koln)
5. M. Mellor, personal communication
6. G. Astill and A. Grant (eds), *The Countryside of Medieval England*, 1988 (Oxford)
7. J. Langdon, *Horses, Oxen and Technological Innovation*, 1986 (Cambridge)
8. Nathaniel Hone, Reeve's Account of the Manor of Barkham, temp. Edward I *Berks, Bucks & Oxon Archæological Journal*, 1899, vol. 5, p. 77
9. P. Stamper, *in* G. Astill and A. Grant (eds), *op. cit.*
10. Extents of the Manor of Barkham, and of the Goods & Chattels in Barkham of John Mautravers, PRO E142/63 f. 3
11. J. Bristow, *The Local Historian's Glossary & Vade Mecum*, 1997 (Nottingham)

3. Saxon Charter, Domesday and High Mediæval Barkham

1. *The Berkshire Domesday*, Alecto Historical Editions, 1987 (3 vols)
2. Margaret Gelling, *The Place-Names of Berkshire*, part I, p. 91 (1982); part III, p. 640 (1976)
3. J. Stevenson (ed), *Chronicon Monasterii de Abingdon*, Rolls Series 1858, vol. I, p. 162
4. G.B. Grundy, Berkshire Charters, Barkham AD 952, *Berks, Bucks & Oxon Archæological Journal*, 1925, vol. 29, p. 200

5. F.M. Stenton, *The Early History of The Abbey of Abingdon*, 1913; reprinted 1989
6. BRO T/A 115/8
7. BRO D/EW1 M1
8. BRO D/ER T180
9. H. Walter map of Windsor Forest, 1823, BRO D/EN P3
10. 1613 Survey, PRO LR.2.199
11. 1589 Recovery, PRO CP43/26 m. 1
12. Raymond Grant, *The Royal Forests of England*, 1991 (Alan Sutton)

4. Late Mediæval Barkham: 1242 to the Black Death (1348/9)

1. *Book of Fees*, commonly called *Testa de Nevill*, pp. 305, 845
2. M.T. Clanchy (ed), *The Roll and Writ File of the Berkshire Eyre of 1248*, 1973 (Selden Society)
3. R.F. Hunisett and J.B. Post (eds), *Medieval Legal Records*; M.T. Clanchy (ed), *Highway Robbery and Trial by Battle in the Hampshire Eyre of 1249*, 1978 (HSMO)
4. 1249 Calendar of Patent Rolls, p. 55
5. Nathaniel Hone, Reeve's Account of the Manor of Barkham, temp. Edward I *Berks, Bucks & Oxon Archæological Journal*, 1899, vol. 5, p. 77
6. *Registrum Thome de Cantilupo, Bishop of Hereford 1275–1282*, 1907 (Canterbury and York Society no. 2)
7. Kingsmill *MSS*, HRO 19M61, nos. 673–676
8. *The Registers of Roger Martival, Bishop of Sarum 1315–1330*, 1959/60 (3 vols) (Canterbury and York Society nos. 55 and 57)
9. Agnes de Nevill v. John le Botiller (1327), PRO CP 40/269–275
10. Philip and Henry le Botiller v. Agnes de Nevill (1330), PRO JUST 1/1400/238d
11. Recovery Rolls, 4 Edw III (1330/31), PRO CP25/1 10/53
12. G.E. Cokayne, *The Complete Peerage*, 1932, vol. VIII, p. 581
13. Calendar of Close Rolls, 1334 (p. 233) and 1336 (p. 630)
14. 1334 Calendar of Patent Rolls, p. 3
15. Extents of the Manor of Barkham, and of the Goods & Chattels in Barkham of John Mautravers, PRO E142/63 f. 3
16. 1352 Calendar of Patent Rolls, p. 259
17. 1738 Manorial Court of Survey, BRO D/EW1 M1

5. St James' Church, Part I (1220–1700)

1. 1220 Visitation, *Vetus Registrum Sarisberiense* or the Register of St Osmund Rolls Series 1883, pp. 275, 304
2. 1249 Calendar of Patent Rolls, p. 55
3. M.T. Clanchy (ed), *The Roll and Writ File of the Berkshire Eyre of 1248*, 1973, p. 82 (Selden Society)
4. *The Registers of Roger Martival, Bishop of Sarum 1315–1330*, 1959/60 (3 vols) (Canterbury and York Society nos. 55 and 57)
5. Donald Gregory, *Yesterday in Village Church and Churchyard* (Gomer Press)
6. P.H. Ditchfield, *Old Village Life*, 1920, p. 165
7. 1557 Will of Thomas Bullock, PRO PROB11 42A/44/342
8. 1558 Will of Edward Ball, BRO D/A1/39/136
9. 1558 Will of John Wilson, BRO D/A1/132/116
10. Barkham Parish Registers 1538–1732, BRO T/R 29, and 1741–1812, BRO D/P 13 1/2
11. Parish Registers 1538–1732, *op. cit.*
12. J. Mattingly, *Church Houses in Berkshire*, Berkshire Old and New, 1996, no. 13
13. Citations and Allegations respecting Church Rates, BRO D/A2 c. 147 f. 41a
14. 1738 Manorial Court of Survey, BRO D/EW1 M1
15. Davies *MSS*, Document 7, Nuffield College, Oxford
16. 1603 Terrier, WRO D1 24/247/1
17. 1632 Licence for Non-residence, BRO D/A2 c. 162 f. 5
18. 1634 Terrier, BRO D/A2 c. 185 f. 14
19. Parish Registers 1538–1732, *op. cit.*
20. PRO E179 243/24–26
21. BRO D/A2 c. 147 f. 41a *op. cit.*
22. Induction Mandates, BRO D/A2 d. 4
23. Acts of Court, BRO D/A2 c. 160 f. 35
24. 1706 Churchwardens' Presentments, BRO D/A2 c. 103

6. **The Kingsmill Family: Langley Pond (or Hewett's) Farm**
1. Kingsmill *MSS*, HRO 19M61 nos. 668, 1076, 683; BRO T/A 115
2. 1610 Settlement, HRO 19M61 no. 1130
3. 1627 Will and Inventory of Francis Norman, BRO D/A1/101/173
4. 1738 Manorial Court of Survey, D/EW1 M1
5. Quarter Sessions Rolls, BRO Q/SO 2 (1727–1743) MF 5
6. 1756 Lease, HRO 19M61 no. 772
7. *Reading Mercury*, 15 October 1770
8. *Betham's Baronetage of England*, 1801–1805, vol. IV, p. 408
9. Feet of Fines Berkshire, Trinity 4 Geo III (1764), PRO CP 25/2 1272/4 GEO III/T m. 42; Hilary 6 Geo III (1766), PRO CP 25/2 1272/6 GEO III/H m. 35
10. G.E. Cokayne, *The Complete Baronetage*, 1906, vol. V, p. 117
11. Tythe Accounts 1782–1800, Davies *MSS*, Document 7, Nuffield College, Oxford
12. 1802 Lease, BRO D/ER T6/2/2
13. *Reading Mercury*, 18 January, 1 and 8 March 1813
14. William Mavor, *General View of the Agriculture of Berkshire*, 1809, p. 404
15. Davies *MSS*, *op. cit.*, Document 9
16. 1818 Will of Revd David Davies, PRO PROB11 1614/132 Box 4426
17. *Reading Mercury*, 7 March–11 April 1831; 25 April/2 May 1831; 2 July 1832
18. Monumental Inscriptions, BRO D/EX 279
19. 1871 Deed of Trust, Oxford Diocesan Board of Education
20. G.E. Cokayne, *The Complete Baronetage*, *op. cit.*
21. Parish Magazine, October 1903, BRO D/EX 1211/3/1

7. **Lordship of Barkham 1330–1589; The Bullock Family**
1. Calendar of Close Rolls, 1334 (p. 233) and 1336 (p. 630)
2. Kingsmill *MSS*, HRO 19M61 no. 1076 (1337 Deed)
3. WRO D1/2/3v2 f. 123v
4. Revd Llewellyn C.W. Bullock, *Memoirs of the Family of Bullock A.D. 1166 to 1905*, 1905
5. 1368 Suit by Agnes Mautravers; Ganefeld Settlement, PRO CP40/430/322d
6. D.J. French, Handlist of References to the Bullocks of Arborfield and Barkham 1317 to 1509, 1999, BRO D/EX 1211/65/1
7. 1391 Deed, Kingsmill *MSS*, HRO 19M61 no. 718
8. WRO D1/2/8 f. 25r
9. 1407 Feet of Fines, PRO CP 25/1/12/80
10. 1418/21 Feet of Fines, PRO CP 25/1/13/81
11. BRO D/EFa T5
12. WRO D1/2/10 f. 70r
13. *The Registers of Thomas Langton, Bishop of Sarum 1485–1493*, 1985, p. 27 (Canterbury and York Society no. 74)
14. *The Four Visitations of Berkshire 1532, 1566, 1623 and 1665/6*, 1908 (Harleian Society vol. LVII)
15. Kingsmill *MSS*, HRO 19M61 no. 692 (1463 Deed)
16. WRO D1/2/14 f. 16r
17. WRO D1/2/14 f. 62v
18. Calendar of State Papers, 8 Hen VIII
19. Calendar of State Papers, 38 Hen VIII
20. Calendar of State Papers, 35/36 Hen VIII
21. I.S. Leadam, *The Domesday of Enclosures 1517–18*, 1897, vol. I, p. 130 (Royal Historical Society)
22. 1613 Survey, PRO I.R.2.199
23. 1524/5 Lay Subsidy, PRO E179 73/141

8. **Sparks Farm (Fawsbyes)**
1. 1576 Will and Inventory of John Hedger, BRO D/A1/76/167
2. 1578 Will of William Pigott, BRO D/A1/104/21; PRO PROB11 63/3/21
3. Barkham Parish Registers 1538–1732, BRO T/R 29
4. 1619 Chancery Proceedings, PRO C2/JAS I/W.26 54
5. 1691 Sale, BRO D/EW1/T13/1/1
6. 1715 Will of Edward Withers, BRO D/EW1 T111/23
7. Monumental Inscriptions, BRO D/EX 279

8. 1757 Will of Alice Allwright, BRO D/EWl/T13/2
9. 1758 Indenture of Release, BRO D/P 13 25/1/4
10. Executors' Accounts, BRO D/P 13 23/1/5
11. 1796 Fire Policy, BRO D/EWl/T13/18
12. 1801 Indenture, BRO D/EWl/T13/19
13. 1821 Barkham Enclosure Award, BRO DP 13/26
14. 1825 Will of John Marshall, BRO D/A1/157/109
15. 1841 Census Return, HO 107/13/1; BRO, RLSL
16. 1872 Conveyance, BRO D/EWl T14
17. Parish Magazines 1888, 1895–1904,
    BRO D/EX 1211/3/1
18. 1913 Contract of Sale, BRO D/EWl E69

9. Church Cottages (Barkham Court)

1. First Part of First Schedule to 1867 Conveyance,
   BRO D/EWl T10
2. 1660 Mortgage, BRO D/EFa T5
3. *The Registers of Thomas Langton, Bishop of Sarum
   1486–1493*, 1985, p. 27 (Canterbury and York
   Society no. 74)
4. 1534 Will of Richard Bullock, BRO D/A1/1/276
5. 1524/5 Lay Subsidy, PRO E179 73/141
6. State Papers, PRO SP1 vol. 55 pp. 178–179
7. 1557 Will of Thomas Bullock,
   PRO PROB11 42A/44/342
8. 1559 Will and Inventory of Richard Symes,
   BRO D/A1/114/222
9. 1589 Indenture of Bargain and Sale,
   BRO D/EFo T76
10. 1613 Survey, PRO LR.2.199
11. First Part of First Schedule to 1867 Conveyance
    op. cit.
12. Berkshire Marriage Licences, BRO T/L 1/1
13. 1634 Will of Henry Montague, WRO 12–35
14. 1627 Inventory of Alice Booth, BRO D/A1/43/154
15. PRO E179 75/348; 349; 362
16. 1660 Mortgage *op. cit.*
17. PRO E179 243/24–26
18. 1679 Will of Henry Miller,
    PRO PROB11 362/8/61
19. 1689 Church Rate, BRO D/A2 c. 147 f. 115
20. 1708 Bond, BRO D/ER T 7/4
21. 1698 Will of John Brooksbank,
    PRO PROB11 448/225/12

22. 1716 Rent Charge, 1867 Conveyance *op. cit.*,
    Fifth Recital
23. 1783 Terrier, WRO D1 24/247/7
24. Tythe Accounts 1782–1800, Davies *MSS*,
    Document 7, Nuffield College, Oxford
25. 1783 Visitation Queries, WRO D1 56/3
26. 1796 Berkshire Poll Book, BRO D/EPb 09
27. 1831 Auction Particulars, BRO D/EX 1211 9/1
28. 1841 Census Return, HO 107/13/1; BRO, RLSL
29. 1861 Census Return, RG9/751; BRO, RLSL
30. 1880–1884 Electoral Registers,
    BRO Q/RPr 38–42
31. 1881 Census Return, RG11/1311; BRO, RLSL
32. 1887–1901 Electoral Registers, BRO Q/RP and
    C/CL/R
33. 1891 Census Return, RG12/1000; BRO, RLSL
34. 1913 Conveyance, Wokingham District Council
    records
35. Berkshire County Council, Small Holdings and
    Allotments Sub-Committee Minutes 1915–1920,
    BRO C/CL C3/6/3

10. Biggs's Farm (Barkham Butts)

1. Minutes of Court Baron, BRO D/EWl M1
2. Quit Rent Roll, BRO D/EFo M3
3. BRO T/A 115/11
4. BRO T/A 115/13
5. 1505 Will of Thomas Barowe, PRO PROB 11/15
6. 1506 Chancery Proceedings, PRO C1/303/15
7. 1538–1544 Chancery Proceedings,
   PRO C1/959/39
8. Barkham Parish Registers 1538–1732,
   BRO T/R 29
9. *The Four Visitations of Berkshire 1532, 1566, 1623
   and 1665/6*, 1908 (Harleian Society vol. LVII)
10. 1592 Probate Papers of Francis Booth,
    BRO D/A1/41/29
11. PRO E179 243/24–26
12. 1593 Will and Inventory of Edward Chaundler,
    BRO D/A1/53/33
13. 1683 Will of John Booth,
    PRO PROB11 373/81/233
14. 1686 Inventory of Richard Booth,
    PRO PROB4/18489

15. Acts of Court, BRO D/A2 c. 160 f. 35
16. William Lyon, *The Chronicles of Finchampstead*, 1895
17. 1753/76 Leases to Thomas Clacy, BRO D/ER T6
18. Tythe Accounts 1782–1800, Davies *MSS*, Document 7, Nuffield College, Oxford
19. Churchwardens' Presentments, BRO D/A2 c. 103
20. Quarter Sessions Rolls, BRO Q/SO 2 (1727–1743) MF 5
21. *Reading Mercury*, 22 May 1815; 3 June 1816
22. 1841 Census Return, HO 107/13/1; BRO, RLSL
23. 1843 Indenture, BRO D/EWl T1
24. 1873 Conveyance, BRO D/EWl E57
25. *REME Journal*, vol. 9, February 1967, no. 1, p. 20; no. 30, April 1980, p. 35

11. Life (and Death) in Tudor Barkham (1505–1558)

1. 1505 Will of Thomas Barowe, PRO PROB 11/15
2. 1558 Will of Thomas Alnet, BRO D/A1/35/71
3. 1558 Will of Edward Ball, BRO D/A1/39/136
4. 1534 Will of Richard Bullock, BRO D/A1/1/276
5. 1558 Will of William Norman, BRO D/A1/101/15
6. 1557 Will of Thomas Bullock, PRO PROB11 42A/44/342
7. 1554 Will and Inventory of John Balsam, BRO D/A1/39/69
8. 1524/5 Lay Subsidy, PRO E179 73/141
9. Barkham Parish Registers 1538–1732, BRO T/R 29

12. History of Barkham Manor, Part I (1540–1787)

1. 1613 Survey, PRO LR.2.199
2. G.P. Elphick, *Sussex Bells and Belfries*, 1970, p. 70 (Phillimore)
3. 1551 Will of John White, BRO D/A1/132/47
4. 1589 Bargain and Sale, BRO D/EFo T76
5. Statement of Title of William Standen to the Committee of Indemnity, 13 November 1650, PRO SP24/37
6. Barkham Parish Registers 1538–1732, BRO T/R 29
7. 1652 Will of Sackville Moore of Hurst, PRO PROB11 221/85/273

8. Parish Registers, *op. cit.*
9. PRO E179 243/24–26
10. Recovery Rolls, 12 Will III (1700), BRO D/EFo T76
11. 1733 Will of William Waterman I, BRO D/ER F92
12. Induction Mandates, BRO D/A2 d. 4
13. *Reading Mercury*, 5 May 1746
14. 1755–1757 Indentures, BRO D/ER T5
15. 1758 Covenant to Produce Title Deeds, BRO D/ER T5
16. *Reading Mercury*, 24 October 1768
17. Kingsmill *MSS*, HRO 19M61 nos. 1195–1214
18. 1757 Indenture, BRO D/EFa T9
19. Private Act of Parliament, 15 Geo III cap. 61 (no. 123) (House of Lords Record Office)
20. 1780 Male Servants Tax, PRO T47/8
21. *Reading Mercury*, 24 June 1782
22. 1784 Timber Contract, Dorset Record Office ref. D/PIT T755
23. 1787 Indenture, PRO C54/6809 (28 Geo III)
24. *Reading Mercury*, 20 August 1787

13. Barkham – A Manor in Contention, Part I (1589–1605)

1. 1600 State Papers, Domestic, Eliz I Chapter 275, PRO SP12/275
2. 1589 Indenture; Feet of Fines, Berks 31 Eliz; Recovery Rolls 31 Eliz (1589), BRO D/EFo T76
3. 1589 Chancery Proceedings, PRO C3/229/22
4. Interrogatories in 1596/7 Star Chamber Proceedings, PRO STAC 5 S.34/40; S.55/38; S.10/1
5. Bill of Complaint in 1599 Chancery Proceedings, PRO C2 ELIZ/S.12/60
6. 1594 Chancery Proceedings, PRO C3/250/1
7. The Registers of John Coldwell, Bishop of Sarum 1591–1596, WRO D1/2/18 f. 9r
8. 1597 Chancery Judgment, BRO D/EFo T76
9. 1660/61 Petitions by Edward Bullock to the House of Lords (House of Lords Papers, and Minute Book and Order Book of the House of Lords Committee for Petitions)

10. 1653 Report of the Commissioners for Indemnity, PRO SP24/37
11. 1597 Star Chamber Proceedings, PRO STAC 5 S.56/40
12. 1597 Chancery Proceedings, PRO C2 ELIZ/W.19/60
13. 1599 Chancery Proceedings, PRO C3/289/29
14. 1600 State Papers, Domestic, *op. cit.*
15. 1599 Bill of Complaint, *op. cit.*
16. Chancery Order Books, PRO C33/97 f. 476, 582; C33/98 f. 478, 592; C33/97 f. 423, 448
17. Letter by William Ball to the Commissioners for Indemnity, 17 November 1652, PRO SP24/37
18. House of Lords Papers, *op. cit.*
19. Letter by William Ball, *op. cit.*

14. Barkham During the Civil War (1642–1646) and the Commonwealth (1649–1660)

1. Barkham Parish Registers 1538–1732, BRO T/R 29
2. Statement of Title of William Standen to the Committee of Indemnity, 13 November 1650, PRO SP24/37
3. Wing Short-Title Catalogue 1641–1700
4. '*Tractatus de Jure Regnandi, & Regni*: or, the Sphere of Government, According to the Law of God, Nature, and Nations', 20 pp. London, 1645. British Library, ref. E. 309(36)
5. '*Conftitutio Liberi Populi*: or, the Rule of a Free-born People', 22 pp. London, 1646. British Library, ref. E. 341(1)
6. Revd J.M. Guilding (ed), *Reading Records: Diary of the Corporation*, 1896, vol. IV, pp. 167–175
7. *Journal of Sir Samuel Luke* (Oxfordshire Record Society vols 29, 31 and 33)
8. *Weekly Account*, no. 6, 11 October 1643. British Library, ref. E. 70(5)
9. Dennis Ayres, The Burninge of Okeingham, *The Wokingham Historian*, 1990, no. 2
10. 1660 Mortgage, BRO D/EFa T5

15. Barkham – A Manor in Contention, Part II (1650–1662)

1. 1650 Petition to House of Commons, PRO SP24/37
2. 1653 Report of the Commissioners for Indemnity, PRO SP24/37
3. Proceedings of the Committee of Indemnity and the Commissioners for Indemnity 1650–1653, PRO SP24/7–15 and SP24/37
4. Transcript of 1651 Hearing Before the Committee of Indemnity, PRO SP24/37
5. William Ball, *A true Narrative of the undue, and greatly injurious Proceedings of one Edward Bullock*, 14 pp. London, May 1652. Folger Shakespeare Library, Washington,DC, ref. B597A
6. William Ball, *Ball: His Vindication againft Bullock*, 13 pp. London, 1652. British Library, ref. E. 674(10)
7. William Ball, *An Illegall Way to Get Another Mans Estate Lately Practised*, 14 pp. London, May 1653. National Library of Scotland, ref. 1.176(19)
8. *The true state of the Cafe of Edward Bullock before the Committee of Indempnity, as it ftands proved by Records and fufficient Witneffes now living*, 1 p., PRO SP24/37
9. William Ball, *A Narrative directed To all true Lovers of Juftice, and Maintainers of Legall Right and Proprietie*, 1 p., 1656. British Library, ref. 190.g.13 (f. 107)
10. 1653 Report of the Commissioners for Indemnity, *op. cit.*
11. State Papers, Domestic, 1653–1656, PRO SP25/92
12. House of Lords Papers, and Minute Book and Order Book of the House of Lords Committee for Petitions

16. The Bull Inn and Smithy

1. 1757 Will of Alice Allwright, BRO D/EWl/T13/2
2. Barkham Parish Registers 1538–1732, BRO T/R 29
3. Citations and Allegations Respecting Church Rates, BRO D/A2 c. 147 f. 41a
4. 1577 Survey of Innkeepers, PRO SP12/119

5.   1733 Will of William Waterman I,
     BRO D/ER F92
6.   1738 Manorial Court of Survey, BRO D/EWl M1
7.   Quarter Sessions Rolls, BRO Q/SO 2
     (1727–1743) MF 5
8.   1693 Will of James Winch, BRO D/A1/139/15
9.   1710 Will of Thomas Douglas, BRO D/A1/64/45
10. 1749 Exchange, BRO D/P 13 25/1/1
11. 1758 Sale, *ibid.*
12. Court Baron, BRO D/EWl M1
13. 1756 Indenture, BRO D/ER T5
14. Court Baron, *op. cit.*
15. Tythe Accounts 1782–1800, Davies *MSS*,
     Document 7, Nuffield College, Oxford
16. *Reading Mercury*, 19 September 1803
17. Churchwardens' Accounts 1803–1952,
     BRO D/P 13/5/1
18. 1840 Tythe Award, BRO D/D1 13/1
19. Kelly's Directories 1847–1939; BRO, RLSL
20. 1905 Refurbishment, BRO PS/Wo 14A/3

17. St James' Church, Part II (1700 to date)
1.   Recovery Rolls, 12 Will III (1700),
     PRO CP43/471 m. 62; BRO D/EFo T76
2.   Private Act of Parliament 1731, BRO D/EX4 E2
3.   Induction Mandates, BRO D/A2 d. 4
4.   Gillian Clark (ed), *Correspondence of the Foundling
     Hospital Inspectors in Berkshire 1757–68*, 1994
     (Berkshire Record Society vol. I)
5.   Induction Mandates, *op. cit.*
6.   *Reading Mercury*, 24 June 1782
7.   D. Davies Presentation, WRO D1/18
8.   Parish Registers 1741–1812, BRO D/P 13 1/2
9.   1783 Visitation Queries, WRO D1 56/3
10. 1814 Baptist Licence, WRO D1/9/2/1
11. 1783 Terrier, WRO D1 24/247/7
12. 1801 Visitation Queries, WRO D1/56/4/2
13. 1786 Insurance Policy, Ditchfield *MSS*,
     BRO R/D 134 Box 6/2/1
14. BRO D/EX 1211/68/1
15. Parish Registers, *op. cit.*
16. P.S. Spokes, Coats of Arms in Berkshire Churches
     Berks, Bucks & Oxon Archæological Journal, 1937,
     vol. 41, p. 85

17. 1810 Sale of Advowson, BRO D/EWl T11
18. Churchwardens' Accounts 1803–1952,
     BRO D/P 13/5/1
19. 1818 J.C. Buckler, British Library, *Add MSS*
     36, 356 f. 167v
20. 1818 J.C. Buckler, Bodleian Library, MS Top.
     Berks c. 49 f. 51
21. 1835 H.W. Burt, British Library, *Add. MSS*
     28, 676A, f. 84
22. William Lyon, *The Chronicles of Finchampstead*, 1895
23. Diocese Book 1845–1850 of Bishop Samuel
     Wilberforce, OA ref. MS Oxf. Dioc. Papers
     d. 550 (p. 168)
24. BRO D/EWl T11 *op. cit.*
25. *Ibid.*
26. British Library, ref. 4784 c. 36(4)
27. *Reading Mercury*, 27 March 1886
28. *Ibid.*, 29 February 1908
29. Incorporated Church Building Society,
     ICBS 5466 (Lambeth Palace Library)
30. 1859 Letter to Archdeacon of Berks,
     BRO D/P 85/28/24/4
31. Frederick Sharpe, The Church Bells of Berkshire
     Berks, Bucks & Oxon Archæological Journal, 1939,
     vol. 43, p. 88
32. Oxford Diocesan Church Building Society,
     OA ref. MS Oxf. Dioc. Papers c. 2209
33. Kelly's Directories 1891, 1895; BRO, RLSL
34. Revd P.H. Ditchfield, *The Parish Clerk*, 1907,
     p. 312
35. *Reading Standard*, 7 and 14 August 1920
36. British Library, *Add. MSS* 36, 356 f. 167v
37. J.W. Walker and M.I. Walker (eds), *The Church
     Plate of Berkshire*, 1927
38. *Berks, Bucks & Oxon Archæological Journal*, 1937,
     vol. 41, *op. cit.*
39. OA ref. MS Oxf. Dioc. Papers c. 965

18. Barkham Square
1.   Minutes of Court Baron, BRO D/EWl M1
2.   Recovery Roll Easter 16 Geo.II (1742/3),
     PRO CP43/640 m. 351
3.   1755 Will of Revd Witting Colton,
     PRO PROB11 821/63/78

4. 1755 Will of Charles Gery,
   PRO PROB11 813/45/357
5. 1761 Rocque Map, BRO T/M 128
6. *Reading Mercury*, 20 March and 18 December 1769
7. *Ibid.*, 14 March 1774
8. 1783 Terrier, WRO D1 24/247/7
9. Tythe Accounts 1782–1800, Davies *MSS*,
   Document 7, Nuffield College, Oxford
10. 1780 Male Servants Tax, PRO T47/8
11. 1791 Sub-lease, BRO D/ER T7/7
12. BRO D/EPb 09
13. Land Tax 1798, PRO IR 23/2 f. 63
14. *Reading Mercury*, 4 October 1824
15. 1821 Enclosure Award, BRO DP 13/26
16. *Reading Mercury*, 17 June 1822 and 26 May 1823
17. 1823 Mortgage, 1867 Conveyance, First Recital,
    BRO D/EWl T10
18. 1833 Chancery Proceedings, PRO C13/2940
    Harman v. Green
19. *Reading Mercury*, 13 and 20 June 1825
20. 1830 Supplemental Mortgage, 1867 Conveyance
    op. cit., Second Recital
21. *Reading Mercury*, 9 May 1831
22. G.E. Mingay, *Agrarian History of England and Wales*
    (ed. Joan Thirsk), 1989, vol. VI, 1750–1850
23. 1831 Auction Particulars, BRO D/EX 1211/9/1
24. 1833 Sale, 1867 Conveyance *op. cit.*, Fourth Recital
25. *Reading Mercury*, 23 March 1839
26. 1841–1871 Census Returns; BRO, RLSL
27. 1867 Conveyance, *op. cit.*
28. 1876–1886 Electoral Registers, BRO Q/RPr
29. Parish Magazine, November 1888,
    BRO D/EX 1211/3/1
30. *The Times*, 29 April 1908
31. 1913 Contract for Sale, BRO D/EWl E69

19. Revd David Davies (Rector 1782–1819)
1. D. Davies Presentation, WRO D1/18
2. Davies *MSS*, Nuffield College, Oxford
3. Parish Poor Account Book 1794–1829, quoted by
   P.H. Ditchfield in *Old Village Life*, 1920, p. 237
4. Abstract of 1783–1785 Returns made by the
   Overseers of the Poor, (printed) 1787, British
   Library, ref. 188.d. 14

5. Revd David Davies, *The Case of Labourers
   in Husbandry Stated and Considered*, 1795;
   reprinted 1977
6. Parish Registers 1741–1812, BRO D/P 13 1/2
7. *Reading Mercury*, 15 February 1819
8. R.C.B. Oliver, David Davies, Rector of Barkham
   in Berkshire, 1782–1819, *The National Library of
   Wales Journal*, Winter, 1976, vol. XIX, no. 4, p. 390
9. Pamela Horn, *A Georgian Parson and his Village:
   The Story of David Davies (1742–1819)*, 1981
   (Beacon Publications)

20. History of Barkham Manor, Part II (1787 to date)
1. 1787 Indenture, PRO C54/6809 (28 Geo III)
2. *Reading Mercury*, 21 July 1788
3. *Ibid.*, 11 April 1796
4. Account Book, Davies *MSS*, Document 9,
   Nuffield College, Oxford
5. *Reading Mercury*, 10 August 1801
6. 1802 Lease, BRO D/ER T6/2/2
7. *Reading Mercury*, 27 June 1814
8. Barkham Manor Deeds, BRO D/EWl T10
9. The National Library of Wales, Clive Papers,
   no. 2197
10. Sidmouth *MSS*, Sidmouth to Prince Regent,
    22 April 1818, Devon Record Office
11. Forest Savings Bank, BRO WO/Z2/1
12. *Reading Mercury*, 1 November 1830
13. Wokingham Union Minutes, BRO G/Wo 1/2
14. Forest Division Tax Commissioners Minutes,
    BRO WO/Z1/9
15. *Reading Mercury*, 25 April 1840
16. *Ibid.*, 29 August 1836
17. *Ibid.*, 30 September 1843
18. *Victoria County History of Shropshire*, 1979, vol. III
19. Monumental Inscriptions, BRO D/EX 279
20. Revd Arthur Roberts, *Moderation of Sorrow for
    the Death of Friends*, 1848, British Library,
    ref. 4903.eee.3(13)
21. *Reading Mercury*, 25 March 1848
22. *The Times*, 28 March 1848
23. *Gentleman's Magazine*, May 1848, p. 550
24. 1878 Conveyance, BRO D/EWl T10

25. J. Bateman, *The Great Landowners of Great Britain and Ireland*, 1883
26. 1881 Census Return, RG11/1311; BRO, RLSL
27. Parish Magazines 1888, 1895–1904, BRO D/EX 1211/3/1
28. *The Times*, 25 August 1900
29. Kelly's Directory, 1907; BRO, RLSL
30. 1911 Bear Wood Sale Particulars, BRO D/EX 1010/1–2
31. Barkham Manor Papers, BRO D/EW1 E68
32. C. Thomas, D. Robbins and B. Woolford, *Recollections of Barkham Village 1915–1940* (unpublished)

21. Landed Interests and Agriculture in the Nineteenth Century

1. BRO D/EW1 E57, T10, T12, T13, T14
2. 1821 Enclosure Award, BRO DP 13/26
3. Barkham Manor Deeds, BRO D/EW1 T10
4. 1613 Survey, PRO LR.2.199
5. Minutes of Court Baron, BRO D/EW1 M1
6. Kelly's Directory 1887; BRO, RLSL
7. *Reading Mercury*, 10 July 1820, 23 July 1821 and 24 June 1822
8. *Ibid.*, 29 August 1836
9. *Ibid.*, 30 September 1843
10. 1840 Tythe Award, BRO D/D1 13/1; PRO IR 30/2/14
11. Bear Wood Estate, Folding Map Book, BRO D/EW1 P5/2
12. Road Diversion, BRO Q/RHi 1883/4
13. 1911 Bear Wood Sale Particulars, BRO D/EX 1010/1–2
14. Kelly's Directories 1869–1939; BRO, RLSL

22. Barkham During a Century of Change (1815–1914)

1. Parish Registers 1741–1812, BRO D/P 13 1/2
2. 1841 Census Return, HO 107/13/1; BRO, RLSL
3. 1891 Census Return, RG12/1000; BRO, RLSL
4. Account Book, Davies *MSS*, Document 9, Nuffield College, Oxford
5. 1819 Parliamentary Papers, vol. IXA
6. 1835 Parliamentary Papers, vol. XLI, p. 15
7. 1854 Visitation Queries, OA ref. MS Oxf. Dioc. Papers d. 701
8. Monumental Inscriptions, BRO D/EX 279
9. 1868/9 Parliamentary Papers, vol. XIII, p. 383
10. 1871 Deed of Trust, Oxford Diocesan Board of Education
11. School Managers' Book, 1873–1922, Arborfield, Newland & Barkham C.E. Junior School
12. *Ibid.*
13. School Log Book 1892–1915, BRO 84/SCH/1/1
14. School Managers' Book, 1873–1922, *op. cit.*
15. Berkshire Directories, various 1829–1854, RLSL
16. Kelly's Directories 1911–1939; BRO, RLSL
17. G.H.R. Homer-Wooff, *The Postal History of Wokingham*, 1981
18. Census Returns 1851–1891; BRO, RLSL
19. Parish Council Minutes, BRO CPC 13/2/1
20. Arthur L. Bowley, *Wages in the United Kingdom in the Nineteenth Century*, 1900; reprinted 1972
21. Revd David Davies, *The Case of Labourers in Husbandry Stated and Considered*, 1795; reprinted 1977
22. *The Times*, 27 November 1830
23. *Reading Mercury*, 29 November 1830
24. *Ibid.*, 3 March 1817
25. *Ibid.*, 20 October 1828
26. *Ibid.*, 7 and 14 April 1834
27. Wokingham Savings Bank, BRO WO/Z2/1
28. Wokingham Union Minutes, BRO G/Wo 1/2; *Reading Mercury*, 9 November 1839; 1867 Conveyance, Sixth Recital, BRO D/EW1 T10
29. 1885/6 Electoral Register, BRO Q/RPr
30. Wokingham RDC Minutes, Wokingham District Council
31. Parish Council Minutes, *op. cit.*
32. 1868/9 Parliamentary Papers, vol. XIII, *op. cit.*, p. 402
33. Parish Magazines 1895–1904, BRO D/EX 1211/3/1
34. *Reading Mercury*, 9 and 23 September 1811
35. Parish Magazines 1888, 1895–1904, *op. cit.*; P.H. Ditchfield Scrapbook 1886–1891, BRO R/D 134 Box 4/1/1

36. *Reading Mercury*, 1822–1850
37. *Ibid.*, 28 February 1791; *Gentleman's Magazine*, Jan/Jun 1874
38. Parish Magazines, *op. cit.*
39. *Reading Mercury*, 25 June 1887
40. *Ibid.*, 3 July 1897
41. Parish Magazine, *op. cit.*, September 1902
42. *Reading Mercury*, 11 May 1935
43. *The Times*, 21 January 1845; *Illustrated London News*, 25 January 1845

23. Revd Peter Hampson Ditchfield (Rector 1886–1930)

1. R. Walmsley, *Memorials of the Ditchfields*, 1941
2. Ditchfield *MSS*, BRO R/D 134 Box 2/8
3. Parish Magazines 1888, 1895–1904, BRO D/EX 1211/3/1
4. Parish Meeting Minutes, BRO CPC 13/2/1
5. *Reading Mercury*, 1 July 1911
6. Ditchfield *MSS*, *op. cit.*, Box 6/1
7. *Reading Mercury*, 5 January 1929
8. *Masonic News*, 22 September 1928
9. *Reading Standard*, 4 October 1930

24. Edward Murray Sturges JP (1859–1934)

1. John Dale (ed), *County Biographies: Berkshire*, 1910
(J.G. Hammond & Co.)
2. Kerr Kirkwood, *History of the Wokingham Agricultural Association (1835–1985)* (unpublished)
3. Wokingham RDC Minutes, Wokingham District Council
4. *Reading Mercury*, 26 May 1934
5. Parish Presentation 1911, BRO D/EX 1211/67/1
6. *Reading Mercury*, 10 June 1911
7. 1913 Contract for Sale, BRO D/EW1 E69
8. County Small Holdings and Allotments Sub-Committee Minutes, BRO C/CL C3

25. Remount Depot and REME Garrison: Barkham During World Wars I and II

1. *REME Journal*, vol. 9, February 1967, no. 1, p. 20; no. 27, April 1977, p. 35; no. 30, April 1980, p. 35 and no. 31, April 1981, p. 14
2. 1911 Purchase, BRO D/EW1 E57
3. C. Thomas, D. Robbins and B.Woolford, *Recollections of Barkham Village 1915–1940* (unpublished)
4. Revd P.H. Ditchfield, *Country Folk*, 1923, p. 239
5. Parish Meeting Minutes, BRO CPC 13/2/1
6. *Reading Standard*, 22 March 1924
7. *The Times*, 28 March 1923

Archæology Index

Chapters 1–2

Illustrations are indicated in bold italics

History Index Nominum

Chapters 3–25 and Appendix II

Whilst surnames are listed alphabetically in the usual way, family members are listed on a chronological basis. Names of lords of the manor of Barkham are in bold.

A

B